JOHN WILLIS

Screen World

1991

Volume 42

CROWN PUBLISHERS, INC.
201 East 50th Street
New York, New York 10022
Member of the Crown Publishing Group

TO

FRANK SINATRA

one of the great artists of the Twentieth Century, whose triumphant recording career has often overshadowed his exceptional abilities as an actor.

FILMS: Las Vegas Nights (1941), Ship Ahoy (1942), Reveille with Beverly, Higher and Higher (1943), Step Lively (1944), Anchors Aweigh (1945), Till the Clouds Roll By (1946), It Happened in Brooklyn (1947), The Miracle of the Bells, The Kissing Bandit (1948), Take Me Out to the Ball Game, On the Town (1949), Double Dynamite, Meet Danny Wilson (1951), From Here to Eternity (Academy Award for Best Supporting Actor 1953), Suddenly (1954), Young at Heart, Not as a Stranger, The Tender Trap, Guys and Dolls, The Man with the Golden Arm (Academy Award nomination 1955), Meet Me in Las Vegas (cameo), Johnny Concho, High Society, Around the World in 80 Days (cameo, 1956), The Pride and the Passion, The Joker is Wild, Pal Joey (1957), Kings Go Forth, Some Came Running (1958), A Hole in the Head, Never So Few (1959), Can-Can, Ocean's 11, Pepe (cameo 1960), The Devil at 4 O'Clock (1961), Sergeants 3 (also producer), The Road to Hong Kong (cameo), The Manchurian Candidate (1962), Come Blow Your Horn, The List of Adrian Messenger (cameo 1963), Four for Texas, Robin and the 7 Hoods (also producer 1964), None But the Brave (also director and producer), Von Ryan's Express, Marriage on the Rocks (1965), Cast a Giant Shadow, The Oscar (cameo), Assault on a Queen (1966), The Naked Runner, Tony Rome (1967), The Detective, Lady in Cement (1968), Dirty Dingus Magee (1970), That's Entertainment (1974), The First Deadly Sin (also executive producer 1980), Cannonball Run II (cameo 1984).

**Glenn Close and Jeremy Irons
in "Reversal of Fortune"
© Warner Bros.**

CONTENTS

EDITOR: JOHN WILLIS
Associate Editor: Barry Monush

Staff: Marco Starr Boyajian, William Camp, Mark Cohen, Mark Gladstone,
Miles Kreuger, Tom Lynch, Stanley Reeves,
John Sala, Van Williams
Designer: Peggy Goddard

Acknowledgments: Bob Aaronson, Michelle Abbrecht, Barry Abrams, Marina Bailey, Nina Barron, Brian Caldwell, Diane Clinton, Willa Clinton, Richard D'Attile, Gerard Dapena, Steven Early, Mike Elliott, Renee Furst, Jamie Geller, Stan Hayes, Peter Herzog, Jeff Hill, Doris Hirsch, Susan Jacobs, Robert Kershner, Lori Koonin, Zbigniew Kozlowski, Don Krim, Sabrina Laufer, Wendy Lidell, Bruce Lynn, Audrey Mahler, Jonathan Marder, Lisa Martin, Rikki Matthews, Kevin O'Grady, Elizabeth Petit, Heather Probert, Velvet Probert, Jeffrey Sakson, Steven Soba, Mark Urman, Lynn Vanderwater

1. Arnold Schwarzenegger

2. Julia Roberts

3. Bruce Willis

4. Tom Cruise

5. Mel Gibson

6. Kevin Costner

7. Patrick Swayze

8. Sean Connery

9. Harrison Ford

10. Richard Gere

11. Michael J. Fox

12. Demi Moore

13. Macaulay Culkin

14. Robin Williams

15. Tom Hanks

16. Michelle Pfeiffer

17. Steven Seagal

18. Sylvester Stallone

19. Bette Midler

20. Michael Douglas

1990 RELEASES

January 1 through December 31, 1990

TOP BOX OFFICE STARS OF 1990

(Tabulated by Quigley Publications)

21. Al Pacino

22. Eddie Murphy

23. Winona Ryder

24. Robert De Niro

25. Meryl Streep

Kirstie Alley

Steve Martin

Cher

7

INTERNAL AFFAIRS

(PARAMOUNT) Producer, Frank Mancuso, Jr.; Executive Producers, Pierre David, René Malo; Co-Executive Producer, David Streit; Director, Mike Figgis; Screenplay, Henry Bean; Photography, John A. Alonzo; Designer, Waldemar Kalinowski; Editor, Robert Estrin; Music, Mike Figgis, Anthony Marinelli, Brian Banks; Costumes, Rudy Dillon; Casting, Carrie Frazier, Shani Ginsberg; Stunts, Gary Hymes; Assistant Director, J. Stephen Buck; Dolby Stereo; Technicolor; Rated R; 115 minutes; January release

CAST

Dennis Peck	Richard Gere
Raymond Avilla	Andy Garcia
Kathleen Avilla	Nancy Travis
Amy Wallace	Laurie Metcalf
Grieb	Richard Bradford
Van Stretch	William Baldwin
Dorian Fletcher	Michael Beach
Tova Arrocas	Katherine Borowitz
Penny	Faye Grant
Steven Arrocas	John Kapelos
Rudy Mohr	Xander Berkeley
Chief Healy	John Capodice
Kee	Victoria Dillard
Cheryl	Pamella D'Pella
Lolly	Susan Forristal
Judson	Allan Havey
Buster	Lew Hopson
Sgt. Trafficante	Tyde Kierney
Newscaster	Dinah Lenney
Freddy	Scott Lincoln
Cousin Gregory	Julio Oscar Mechoso
Surgeon	Harry Murphy
Dorian's Wife	Billie Neal
Megan	Heather Lauren Olson
Demetrio	Marco Rodriguez
Heather	Annabella Sciorra
Capt. Riordan	Arlen Dean Snyder
Jaeger	Ron Vawter
T.V. Reporter	Deryn Warren
May	Valerie Wildman
Sean	Elijah Wood

and Domingo Adkins (Party Guest), Hamlet Arman (Carlos), Camilla Bergstrom (Surfer Chick), Mitchell Claman (Kevin), Mark A. Cuttin (Honor Guard Sgt.), Justin DeRosa (Latino Driver), Mike Figgis (Hollander), Geoffrey Grider (Dinner Guest), Father Andrew Herman (Priest), Brian Johnson (Busboy), Waldemar Kalinowski (Surgeon #2), Helen Lin (Dina), Frank Mancuso, Jr. (Radio Cop), Christopher Raymond Mullane (Guard), Hank McGill (Medic), Jimmy Ortega (Oscar), S. Grant Sawyer (Surfer Dude), Richard B. Whitaker (Marksman)

Top: Richard Gere, Andy Garcia Below: Nancy Travis, Garcia
© *Paramount Pictures*

Laurie Metcalf, Andy Garcia Above: Nancy Travis,
Richard Gere

Richard Gere, William Baldwin

8

Nick Nolte, Frank Military, Debra Winger Top Right: Winger, Nolte (also top left) © *Orion Pictures*

EVERYBODY WINS

(ORION) Producer, Jeremy Thomas; Co-Producer, Ezra Swerdlow; Director, Karel Reisz; Screenplay, Arthur Miller; Executive Producers, Terry Glinwood, Linda Yellen; Music, Mark Isham, Leon Redbone; Editor, John Bloom; Photography, Ian Blake; Designer, Peter Larkin; Costumes, Ann Roth; Casting, Ellen Chenoweth; Assistant Director, Timothy M. Bourne; Dolby Stereo; Duart color; Rated R; 97 minutes; January release

CAST

Angela Crispini	Debra Winger
Tom O'Toole	Nick Nolte
Jerry	Will Patton
Connie	Judith Ivey
Amy	Kathleen Wilhoite
Judge Harry Murdoch	Jack Warden
Charlie Haggerty	Frank Converse
Felix	Frank Military
Father Mancini	Steven Skybell
Jean	Mary Louise Wilson
Bellanca	Mert Hatfield
Sonny	Peter Appel
Montana	Sean Weil
Defense Attorney	Timothy D. Wright
Judges	Elizabeth Ann Klein, T. M. Nelson George
Reporter	James Parisi
Driver	R. M. Haley

Debra Winger, Nick Nolte Above: Will Patton, Nolte

THE PLOT AGAINST HARRY

(NEW YORKER) Producers, Michael Roemer, Robert Young; Director/Screenplay, Michael Roemer; Photography, Robert Young; Editors, Terry Lewis, Georges Klotz; Music, Frank Lewin; Associate Producers, Michael Hausman, Martin Priest; Costumes, Lily Partridge; a King Screen Production; 1969; Black and white; Not rated; 81 minutes; January release

CAST

Harry Plotnick	Martin Priest
Leo Perlmutter	Ben Lang
Kay Plotnick	Maxine Woods
Max	Henry Nemo
Jack Pomerance	Jacques Taylor
Irene Pomerance	Jean Leslie
Mae Klepper	Ellen Herbert
Margie Skolnik	Sandra Kazan
Mel Skolnik	Ronald Coralian
Linda Skolnik	Ruth Roemer
Sidney	Max Ulman
Millie Plotnick	Margo Solin
Stevie Pomerance	Paul Guskin
Hattie	Zviah Ralbag
Tillie	Sarah Christie
Dr. Feinstein	Jack Hirsch
Cheryl Perlmutter	Jeanette Wilkins
Tony Natale	Nicholas Ponzini
Jesus	Jose Ocasio
Fernando	Paul Zayas
Jimmy Hong	Stephen Cheng
Carlos	Ernesto Gonzalez
Miss Pike	Sylvia Glickman
Salvator Natale	Angelo Deluca

Top: Ben Lang, Martin Priest Left: Sandra Kazan, Maxine Woods, Lang © New Yorker Films

Above: Michael Rooker

HENRY:
Portrait of a Serial Killer

(GREYCAT FILMS) Producers, John McNaughton, Lisa Dedmond, Steven A. Jones; Director, John McNaughton; Executive Producers, Waleed B. Ali, Malik B. Ali; Screenplay, Richard Fire, John McNaughton; Photography, Charlie Lieberman; Music, John McNaughton, Ken Hale, Steven A. Jones; Editor, Elena Maganini; a Maljack Productions presentation; Color; Not rated; 83 minutes; January release

CAST

Henry	Michael Rooker
Otis	Tom Towles
Becky	Tracy Arnold
TV Salesman	Ray Atherton

© Maljack Productions

Michael Rooker, Tom Towles, Ray Atherton Above: Tracy Arnold, Rooker

Kevin Bacon Top Right: Fred Ward, Finn Carter
Top Left: Bacon, Ward
© *Universal City Studios*

TREMORS

(UNIVERSAL) Producers/Screenplay, Brent Maddock, S. S. Wilson; Director, Ron Underwood; Story, S. S. Wilson, Brent Maddock, Ron Underwood; Executive Producer, Gale Anne Hurd; Line Producer, Ginny Nugent; Photography, Alexander Gruszynski; Designer, Ivo Cristante; Editor, O. Nicholas Brown; Music, Ernest Troost; Assistant Director, Mike Topoozian; Creature Effects, Tom Woodruff, Jr., Alec Gillis; Visual and Miniature Effects, 4-Ward Productions, Inc.; Visual Effects Director, Robert Skotak; a No Frills/Wilson-Maddock Production; Dolby Stereo; Deluxe color; Rated PG-13; 98 minutes; January release

CAST

Valentine McKee	Kevin Bacon
Earl Basset	Fred Ward
Rhonda LeBeck	Finn Carter
Burt Gummer	Michael Gross
Heather Gummer	Reba McEntire
Melvin Plug	Bobby Jacoby
Nancy	Charlotte Stewart
Miguel	Tony Genaro
Mindy	Ariana Richards
Nestor	Richard Marcus
Walter Chang	Victor Wong
Edgar	Sunshine Parker
Old Fred	Michael Dan Wagner
Jim, the doctor	Conrad Bachmann
Megan, doctor's wife	Bibi Besch
Howard (Road Worker)	John Goodwin
Carmine (Road Worker)	John Pappas

Finn Carter Above: Reba McIntire, Michael Gross

Jessica Lange, Joan Cusack Top Left: Chris O'Donnell, Lange,
Charlie Korsmo Left: Cusack, Lange
© Geffen Film Co.

MEN DON'T LEAVE

(WARNER BROS.) Producer, Jon Avnet; Director/Executive Producer, Paul Brickman; Screenplay, Barbara Benedek, Paul Brickman; Story, Barbara Benedek; Photography, Bruce Surtees; Designer, Barbara Ling; Costumes, J. Allen Highfill; Music, Thomas Newman; Casting, David Rubin; Editor, Richard Chew; Assistant Director, Dan Kolsrud; a Geffen Company release; Dolby Stereo; CFI color; Rated PG-13; 115 minutes; February release

CAST

Beth Macauley	Jessica Lange
Chris Macauley	Chris O'Donnell
Matt Macauley	Charlie Korsmo
Charles Simon	Arliss Howard
John Macauley	Tom Mason
Jody	Joan Cusack
Lisa Coleman	Kathy Bates
Winston Buckley	Corey Carrier
Mr. Buckley	Jim Haynie
Mrs. Buckley	Belita Moreno
Dale Buckley	Shannon Moffett
Mike	Kevin Corrigan
Fred	David Cale
Carly	Constance Shulman
Ian	Mark Hardwick
1st Officer	Ernesto D. Borges Jr.
Nina Simon	Lora Zane
Craig	Rick Rubin
Evan Taylor	Tom Towles
Nick	Richard Wharton
Nurse	Rosemary Knower
Laura	Jane Morris
Susan	Annabel Armour
Fay	Deanna Dunagan
Gary	Tom Irwin
Julia	Stacey Guastaferro
Blues Artist	Jesse James
Sam Burrows	Richard Burton Brown
Real Estate Agent	Mary Seibel

and Robert D. North (Moving Man), Stesha Merle (Girl Student), William DeAcutis (Mark), Ann McDonough (Female Customer), Theresa Wozniak (Polka Dancer), Sandra V. Watters (Bureaucrat), Zaid Farid (Store Clerk), Wandachristine (School Teacher), Richard DeAngelis (Tailor), Peter Miller (Chris' Friend), Gerry Becker (Uncle Hugh), Dick Sasso (Lottery Winner), Chuck McLennan (Lottery Announcer), Eddie Korosa (Polka Band Leader), Antonio M. Calderon (Joey)

Joan Cusack, Chris O'Donnell Above: Jessica Lange,
Arliss Howard

STELLA

(TOUCHSTONE/SAMUEL GOLDWYN) Producer, Samuel Goldwyn, Jr.; Director, John Erman; Screenplay, Robert Getchell; Based on the novel *"Stella Dallas"* by Olive Higgins Prouty; Executive Producer, David V. Picker; Co-Producer, Bonnie Bruckheimer-Martell; Editor, Jerrold L. Ludwig; Designer, James Hulsey; Costumes, Theadora Van Runkle; Music, John Morris; Song: "One More Cheer" by Jay Gruska and Paul Gordon/performed by Bette Midler; Casting, Howard Feuer; Unit Production Manager/Associate Producer, David Coatsworth; Assistant Directors, Brian Cook, Michael Steele; Distributed by Buena Vista Pictures; Dolby Stereo; Technicolor; Rated PG-13; 106 minutes; February release

CAST

Stella Claire	Bette Midler
Ed Munn	John Goodman
Jenny Claire	Trini Alvarado
Stephen Dallas	Stephen Collins
Janice Morrison	Marsha Mason
Mrs. Wilkerson	Eileen Brennan
Debbie Whitman	Linda Hart
Jim Uptegrove	Ben Stiller
Pat Robbins	William McNamara
Bob Morrison	John Bell
Jenny (age 3)	Ashley Peldon
Jenny (age 8)	Alisan Porter
Security Guard	Kenneth Kimmins
Bartender	Bob Gerchen
Dancing Waiter	Willie Rosario
Minister	Rex Robbins
Tony De Banza	Ron White
Sid	Matthew Cowles
Cocaine Dealer	Justin Louis
Bobby	Peter MacNeill
Billy	Michael Hogan
George	George Buza
Wendell	Eric Keenleyside
Leider Singer	Catherine Robbin
Stephen's Friend	Rob McClure
Man in theatre	Sam Malkin
Nurse	Jayne Eastwood
Parent at PTA	Charles Gray
Mr. Wilkerson	Jon Kozak
Bingo Announcer	Terrence Langevin
Mrs. Hough	Elva Mai Hoover
Mrs. Douglas	Glynis Davies

and Philip Akin (Police Officer), Jayne Rager, Megan Gallivan, Todd Louiso, Jeff Nichols (Preppies), Christian Hoover, Philip Astor (Bar Customers), Eve Crawford (Janice's Secretary), Elizabeth Lennie (Airline Reservation Clerk), Dwayne McLean (Tom), Tedd Dillon (Freddie), Jane Dingle (Bingo Winner), Jamie Shannon (Teenage Heckler)

Top: Trini Alvarado, Bette Midler Below: Stephen Collins, Midler Left: Alvarado, Midler
© *Touchstone Pictures/Samuel Goldwyn Co.*

John Goodman, Bette Midler

Bette Midler, Trini Alvarado

MACK THE KNIFE

(21st CENTURY FILM CORP.) Producer, Stanley Chase; Executive Producers, Menahem Golan, Yoram Globus; Director/Screenplay, Menahem Golan; Photography, Elemer Ragalyi; Editor, Alain Jakubowicz; Music, Kurt Weill; Lyrics, Bertolt Brecht; Lyrics written and adapted by Marc Blitzstein, Menahem Golan, Dov Seltzer; Musical Director, Dov Seltzer; Costumes, John Bloomfield; Associate Producers, Zoli Ben Chorin, Michael Kagan; Designer, Tivadar Bertalan; Choreographer, David Toguri; Assistant Directors, Avner Orshalimy, Gabor Varadi; Dolby Stereo; Rank color; Rated PG-13; 123 minutes; February release

CAST

MacHeath	Raul Julia
Mr. Peachum	Richard Harris
Jenny	Julia Migenes
Street Singer	Roger Daltrey
Mrs. Peachum	Julie Walters
Polly Peachum	Rachel Robertson
Money Matthew	Clive Revill
Tiger Brown	Bill Nighy
Lucy	Erin Donovan
Coaxer	Julie T. Wallace
Dolly	Louise Plowright
Molly	Elizabeth Seal
Betty	Chrissie Kendall
Esmerelda	Miranda Garrison
Jimmy Jewels	Mark Northover
Wally the Weeper	Roy Holder
Johnny Ladder	Clive Mantle
Hookfinger Jake	Russel Gold
Reverend Kimball	John Woodnut
Warden	Peter Rutherford
Filch	Iain Rogerson
Sergeant Smith	Steven Law
Sukey Tawdry	Dong Ji Hong
Organ Grinder	Sandor Kaposi

Top Left: Raul Julia, Julia Migenes
Below: Roger Daltrey Top Right: Julia
© *21st Century Film Corp.*

Julia Migenes, Richard Harris, Julie Walters, Bill Nighly
Above: Raul Julia, Rachel Robertson

HARD TO KILL

(WARNER BROS.) Producers, Gary Adelson, Joel Simon, Bill Todman, Jr.; Executive Producers, Lee Rich, Michael Rachmil; Director, Bruce Malmuth; Associate Producer/Screenplay, Steven McKay; Photography, Matthew F. Leonetti; Designer, Robb Wilson King; Music, David Michael Frank; Editor, John F. Link; Co-Producer, Jon Sheinberg; Casting, Glenn Daniels; Assistant Director, Douglas Wise; Stunts, Buddy Joe Hooker; Adelson/Todman/Simon Production; Dolby Stereo; Technicolor; Rated R; 96 minutes; February release

CAST

Mason Storm	Steven Seagal
Andy Stewart	Kelly Le Brock
Vernon Trent	Bill Sadler
Kevin O'Malley	Frederick Coffin
Felicia Storm	Bonnie Burroughs
Capt. Dan Hulland	Andrew Bloch
Max Quentero	Branscombe Richmond
Jack Axel	Charles Boswell
Sonny Storm	Zachary Rosencrantz
Carl Becker	Lou Beatty, Jr.
Calabrese	Nick DeMauro
James Valero	Nick Corello
Mikey	Justin DeRosa
Counterman	Stanley Brock
Danny	Evan James
Shotgun Punk	Tomas Trujillo
Punks	Robert LaSardo, Haruo Matsuoka, Craig E. Dunn
Detective #1	Tony Perez
E.R. Doctor	Steve Jones
Martha Coe	Francesca P. Roberts
Nolan	James DiStefano
Det. Sgt. Goodhart	Dean Norris
Team Leader Doctor	Michael Fosberg
Russ/Security	Buddy Joe Hooker
Newscasters	Jerry Dunphy, Janet Zappala
Henrietta Wade	Barbara Townsend
Neighbor	Carlos Gomez
Joe Bear	Christian Duffy
Housewife	Andrea Stein
Youth	Eddie Frias
Desk Clerk	Michael Adler
Sonny (age 5)	Geoffrey Bara
Hans	Kent Turnipseed
Commander	Ernie Lively
Van Driver	Frank H. Conn
Doctor Weyland	Philip Weyland
Sheri	Sheri Hueffmeir
Nurse	Linda Klein
Shotgun Man	Gary McLarty
Bad Guy #2	Jim Thompson
Muzila	Tom Muzila
Amtrak Lady	Catherine Quinn
Man #2	Richard Kwong
Parking Attendant	Osama Joseph Sabbagh
Asian Driver	Richard Wakasa
Chinese Clever Man	Al Goto
Taxi Driver	Bernie Bielawski
Girl in hot tub	Julia Stormson
Cops	Jack Eiseman, Michael McMeel
Swat Cop	Jim Kindelon

Top: Steven Seagal Below: Seagal, Kelly LeBrock
© *Warner Bros.*

Branscombe Richmond, Steven Seagal Above: Seagal

STANLEY & IRIS

(MGM) Producers, Arlene Sellers, Alex Winitsky; Director, Martin Ritt; Screenplay, Harriet Frank, Jr., Irving Ravetch; Based on the novel *"Union Street"* by Pat Barker; Executive Producer, Patrick Palmer; Photography, Donald McAlpine; Designer, Joel Schiller; Editor, Sidney Levin; Music, John Williams; Costumes, Theoni Aldredge; Casting, Dianne Crittenden; Associate Producer, Jim Van Wyck; from MGM/UA Distribution Co., a Latana production; Dolby Stereo; Panavision; Duart color; Rated PG-13; 102 minutes; February release

CAST

Iris King	Jane Fonda
Stanley Cox	Robert De Niro
Sharon Fuller	Swoosie Kurtz
Kelly	Martha Plimpton
Richard	Harley Cross
Joe	Jamey Sheridan
Leonides Cox	Feodor Chaliapin
Elaine	Zohra Lampert
Bertha	Loretta Devine
Belinda	Julie Garfield
Melissa	Karen Ludwig
Bernice	Kathy Kinney
Muriel	Laurel Lyle
Joanne	Mary Testa
Jan	Katherine Cortez
Mr. Hentley	Stephen Root
Mr. Hagen	Eddie Jones
Mr. Delancey	Fred J. Scollay
Librarian	Dortha Duckworth
The Pursesnatcher	Jack Gill
Bakery Foreman	Bob Aarron
Oscar Roebuck	Gordon Masten
Park Ranger	Richard Blackburn
Nurse	B. J. Reed
Apple Picker Foreman	Conrad Bergschneider
Man in car	Guy Sanvido
Kids	Michael Blackburn, Paul Horruzey
Bellhop	Gerry Quigley

**Top: Jane Fonda, Robert De Niro
Below: Fonda Right: Fonda, De Niro
© *Metro-Goldwyn-Mayer***

Jane Fonda, Robert De Niro

Robert De Niro, Jane Fonda

16

FLASHBACK

(PARAMOUNT) Producer, Marvin Worth; Director, Franco Amurri; Co-Producer/Screenplay, David Loughery; Executive Producer, Richard Stenta; Photography, Stefan Czapsky; Designer, Vincent Cresciman; Editor, C. Timothy O'Meara; Costumes, Eileen Kennedy; Music, Barry Goldberg; Casting, Nancy Foy; Assistant Director, Frank Bueno; Technicolor; Dolby Stereo; Rated R; 108 minutes; February release

CAST

Huey Walker	Dennis Hopper
John Buckner	Kiefer Sutherland
Maggie	Carol Kane
Stark	Paul Dooley
Sheriff Hightower	Cliff DeYoung
Barry	Richard Masur
Hal	Michael McKean
Sparkle	Kathleen York
Phil Prager	Tom O'Brien
Prison Guards	Eric Lorentz, Jan Van Sickle
Man in dining car	Jack Casperson
Waiter in dining car	Dwayne Carrington
Barmaid	Liz Jury
Girl in bar	Kelli Van Londersele
Studie	Allan Graf
Buckner's Father	Kenneth Jensen Bryan
Buckner's Mother	Donna McMullen
Young Buckner	Adam Seils
Hal's Son	Alan August
Barry's Son	Jason Iselin
Conductor	Norm Silver
Loomis	Delbert Highlands

and David Underwood, Bobby Price, Timothy G. Riley (Deputies), Jason Campbell (Kid on train), Wendelin Harston (Woman on train), Steve Spencer (Man on train)

Top Right: Kiefer Sutherland, Carol Kane, Dennis Hopper
Below: Hopper, Richard Masur, Michael McKean
© *Paramount Pictures*

Kirstie Alley, John Larroquette, Dennis Miller Above: Alley, Larroquette, Jessica Lundy

MADHOUSE

(ORION) Producer, Leslie Dixon; Co-Producer, Donald C. Klune; Director/Screenplay, Tom Ropelewski; Photography, Denis Lewiston; Designer, Dan Leigh; Editor, Michael Jablow; Costumes, Jim Lapidus; Music, David Newman; Assistant Director, Jerram A. Swartz; a Boy of the Year Production; Dolby Stereo; Foto-Kem color; Rated PG-13; 90 minutes; February release

CAST

Mark Bannister	John Larroquette
Jessie Bannister	Kirstie Alley
Claudia	Alison La Placa
Fred	John Diehl
Bernice	Jessica Lundy
Jonathan	Bradley Gregg
Wes	Dennis Miller
Dale	Robert Ginty
Grindle	Wayne Tippit
Stark	Paul Eiding
C.K.	Aeryk Egan
Katy	Deborah Otto
Prick Automaton Cop	Mark Bringelson
Female Cop	Karen Kronwell
Karen Kelly	Heather McNair
Russell Fenn	Mark Manning
Field Reporter	Bob Sorenson
Shady Character Outside Strip Joint	Rob Camilletti
Mark's Secretary	Elizabeth Lang
Receptionist	Peppi Sanders
Kaminsky	Jay Bernard
Mailroom Employees	Frank Dworsky, Rene L. Moreno

and Deborah Swartz, Lisa Rubin, Hart Throb, Aaron Berger, Elaine Moe, Loy Burns, Jack Edward, Pat Willoughby, Dick Alexander, Francis Brooks, Marlon Darton, Freida Smith, Jon Proudstar, Mel Coleman, Kimberly Steuter, Elizabeth Kneeland, Ed Peterson, Grant Moran, Michael Waltman, Darwin Hall, Karen Deconcini, Earl Smith, Kevin Wadowski, Ethan Aronson (Jessie's Interviewees)

© *Orion Pictures Corp.*

REVENGE

(COLUMBIA) Producers, Hunt Lowry, Stanley Rubin; Executive Producer, Kevin Costner; Director, Tony Scott; Screenplay, Jim Harrison, Jeffrey Fiskin; Based on the novella by Jim Harrison; Photography, Jeffrey Kimball; Designers, Michael Seymour, Benjamin Fernandez; Editor, Chris Lebenzon; Music, Jack Nitzsche; Casting, Bonnie Timmerman; Assistant Director, Hunt Lowry; a Rastar Production presented in association with New World Entertainment; Dolby Stereo; Panavision; Deluxe color; Rated R; 124 minutes; February release

CAST

Jay Cochran	Kevin Costner
Tiburon	Anthony Quinn
Miryea	Madeleine Stowe
Cesar	Tomas Milian
Mauro	Joaquin Martinez
Texan	James Gammon
Madero	Jesse Corti
Rock Star	Sally Kirkland
Ramon	Luis De Icaza
Elefante	Gerardo Zepeda
Amador	Miguel Ferrer
Ignacio	John Leguizamo
Ibarra	Joe Santos
Diaz	Christofer De Oni
Vaquero	Daniel Rojo
Roxanne	Edna Bolkan
Rochelle	Pia Karina
Neli	Monica Hernandez
Quinones	Julian Pastor
Barone	Claudio Brook
La Vieja	Trini Rodriguez
Resabio	Mauricio Ruby
Roberto	Gilberto Compan
Madam	Karmin Murcelo
Antonio	Alfredo Cienfuegos
Doctor	Salvador Garcini
Mother Superior	Kathleen Hughes
Nuns	Rosa Radjune, Julieta Egurrola
Mendoza	Jorge Pascual Rubio

Top: Kevin Costner, Madeleine Stowe, Anthony Quinn
Below: Stowe, Costner
© *Columbia Pictures*

Kevin Costner Above: Anthony Quinn, Madeleine Stowe

Kevin Costner, Anthony Quinn Above: Sally Kirkland

Anjelica Huston Top Left: Jasen Fisher, Mai Zetterling
Left: Huston
© *Warner Bros.*

THE WITCHES

(WARNER BROS.) Producer, Mark Shivas; Executive Producer, Jim Henson; Director, Nicolas Roeg; Screenplay, Allan Scott; Based on the book by Roald Dahl; Photography, Harvey Harrison; Music, Stanley Myers; Designer, Andrew Sanders; Costumes, Marit Allen; Editor, Tony Lawson; Line Producer, Dusty Symonds; Photography (Model Unit), Paul Wilson; Assistant Director, Barry Wasserman; Animatronics Designer, John Stephenson; Makeup for Grand High Witch, Steve Norrington; Mice Designs, Pauline Fowler; Animatronics, Jim Henson's Creature Shop; a Lorimar Film Entertainment presentation from Jim Henson Productions; Dolby Stereo; Color; Rated PG; 92 minutes; February release

CAST

Miss Ernst/Grand High Witch	Anjelica Huston
Helga	Mai Zetterling
Luke	Jasen Fisher
Mr. Stringer	Rowan Atkinson
Mr. Jenkins	Bill Paterson
Mrs. Jenkins	Brenda Blethyn
Bruno Jenkins	Charlie Potter
Woman in black	Anne Lambton
Miss Irvine	Jane Horrocks
Marlene	Sukie Smith
Dora	Rose English
Elsie	Jenny Runacre
Nicola	Annabel Brooks
Millie	Emma Relph
Beatrice	Nora Connolly
Janice	Rosamund Greenwood
Henrietta	Anjelique Rockas
Ladies	Ann Tirard, Leila Hoffman
Head Chef	Jim Carter
Witch Chef	Roberta Taylor
Elderly Waiter	Brian Hawksley
Waitress	Debra Gillett
Luke's Mother	Darcy Flynn
Luke's Father	Vincent Marzello
Doctor	Serena Harragin
Norwegian Witch	Greta Nordra
Erica	Elsie Eide
Child Helga	Kirstin Steinsland
Erica's Mother	Merete Armand
Erica's Father	Ola Otnes
Policemen	Johan Sverre, Arvid Ones, Sverre Rossummoen

Anjelica Huston, Charlie Potter Above: Huston

Bheki Tonto Ngema, Patrick Bergin Top Left: Iain Glen, Bergin
Left: Glen, Richard E. Grant
© *Tri-Star Pictures*

MOUNTAINS OF THE MOON

(TRI-STAR) Producer, Daniel Melnick; Executive Producers, Mario
Kassar, Andrew Vajna; Director, Bob Rafelson; Screenplay, William
Harrison, Bob Rafelson; Based on the biographical novel "*Burton and
Speke*" by William Harrison, and on original journals by Richard
Burton, John Hanning Speke; Photography, Roger Deakins; Designer,
Norman Reynolds; Editor, Thom Noble; Sound, Simon Kaye; Cos-
tumes, Jenny Beavan, John Bright; Associate Producer, Chris Curling;
Music, Michael Small; Casting, Celestia Fox; Assistant Director, Pat
Clayton; a Carolco International N.V. release; a Daniel Melnick/
Indieprod production; Dolby Stereo; Rank color/Technicolor; Rated R;
135 minutes; February release

CAST

Richard Burton	Patrick Bergin
John Hanning Speke	Iain Glen
Oliphant	Richard E. Grant
Isabel	Fiona Shaw
Lord Murchison	John Savident
Lord Oliphant	James Villiers
Edward	Adrian Rawlins
Lord Houghton	Peter Vaughan
Mabruki	Delroy Lindo
Dr. Livingstone	Bernard Hill
William	Matthew Marsh
Lord Russell	Richard Caldicot
Herne	Christopher Fulford
Stroyan	Garry Cooper
Ben Amir	Roshan Seth
Jarvis	Jimmy Gardner
Mrs. Speke	Doreen Mantle
Mrs. Arundell	Anna Massey
Norton Shaw	Peter Eyre
Mr. Arundell	Leslie Phillips
Lady Houghton	France Cuka
Lord Cowley	Roger Ashton-Griffiths
Swinburne	Craig Crosbie
Sidi Bombay	Paul Onsongo
Jemadar	Leonard Juma
Ngola	Bheki Tonto Ngema
Veldu	Martin Okello
Colonel Rigby	Philip Voss
Lt. Hesketh	Pip Torrens
Lema	Esther Njiru
Papworth	Roger Rees
Sheik	Omar Sharif

and Alison Limerick (Sorceress), Asiba Asiba (Nubian Servant), Ian
Vincent (Lt. Allen), Ralph Nossek (Doctor), George Malpas (Lead
Actor), Robert Whelan, Bill Croasdale, Renny Krupinski (Reporters),
Rod Woodruff (Fencer)

Leonard Juma, Iain Glen Above: Patrick Bergin, Fiona Shaw

Suzy Amis, David Hewlett, Uma Thurman, Dabney Coleman,
Christopher Plummer, Joanna Cassidy, Sheila Kelley Top Left:
Thurman, Hewlett, Amis Left: Amis, Thurman
© *Buena Vista Pictures*

WHERE THE HEART IS

(TOUCHSTONE) Producer/Director, John Boorman; Screenplay,
Telsche Boorman, John Boorman; Executive Producer, Edgar F.
Gross; Music, Peter Martin; Photography, Peter Suschitzky; Designer,
Carol Spier; Costumes, Linda Matheson; Editor, Ian Crafford; Casting,
Bonnie Finnegan; Sound, Ron Davis; Production Manager/Associate
Producer, Sean Ryerson; Assistant Director, Tony Lucibello; Chloe's
Paintings & Body Make-up, Timna Woollard; Presented in association
with Silver Screen Partners IV; Distributed by Buena Vista Pictures;
Dolby Stereo; Technicolor; Rated R; 94 minutes; February release

CAST

Stewart McBain	Dabney Coleman
Daphne McBain	Uma Thurman
Jean McBain	Joanna Cassidy
Lionel	Crispin Glover
Chloe McBain	Suzy Amis
The Shit	Christopher Plummer
Jimmy McBain	David Hewlett
Harry	Maury Chaykin
Tom	Dylan Walsh
Hamilton	Ken Pogue
Sheryl	Sheila Kelley
Lionel's Father	Michael Kirby
Marvin X	Dennis Strong
Marcus	Timothy D. Stickney
Olivia	Emma Woollard
Secretary	Paulina Gillis
Presidential Aide	Gary Krawford
Edgar	Albert Schultz
Woman Speaking in Tongues	Sandi Ross
Preacher	George Seremba
Eviction Man	Ralph Small

and Ann-Marie MacDonald, Frances Flanagan (TV Reporters), Najma
Uddin (Porna), Prabha Gandhi (Mya), Juan Sanchez (Jose), Ida Carne-
vali (Mrs. Jose), Philip Williams (Man with writ), Howard Lende (Wall
Street Man), Maurice Godin, David Bronstein (Stock Exchange Dealers), Eric Moreau (Cop), Sean Ryerson (Man at dump)

Suzy Amis, Joanna Cassidy, David Hewlett, Christopher
Plummer, Dabney Coleman Above: Plummer

21

THE HUNT FOR RED OCTOBER

(PARAMOUNT) Producer, Mace Neufeld; Director, John McTiernan; Screenplay, Larry Ferguson, Donald Stewart; Based on the novel by Tom Clancy; Executive Producers, Larry De Waay, Jerry Sherlock; Photography, Jan De Bont; Designer, Terence Marsh; Editors, Dennis Virkler, John Wright; Music, Basil Poledouris; Casting, Amanda Mackey; Assistant Director, Jerry L. Ballew; Visual Effects Consultant, Michael Fink; Stunts, Charles Picerni, Jr.; Dolby Stereo; Panavision; Technicolor; Rated PG; 137 minutes; March release

CAST

Marko Ramius	Sean Connery
Jack Ryan	Alec Baldwin
Bart Mancuso	Scott Glenn
Captain Borodin	Sam Neill
Admiral Greer	James Earl Jones
Andrei Lysenko	Joss Ackland
Jeffrey Pelt	Richard Jordan
Ivan Putin	Peter Firth
Dr. Petrov	Tim Curry
Seaman Jones	Courtney B. Vance
Captain Tupolev	Stellan Skarsgard
Skip Tyler	Jeffrey Jones
Bill Steiner	Timothy Carhart
Chief of the Boat	Larry Ferguson
Admiral Painter	Fred Dalton Thompson
Captain Davenport	Daniel Davis
Seaman Beaumont	Ned Vaughn
Lt. Comm. Thompson	Anthony Peck
Lt. Melekhin	Ronald Guttman
Loginov (Cook)	Tomas Arana
Ivan	Michael George Benko
Red October Officers	Anatoly Davydov, Ivan G'Vera
Diving Officer	Artur Cybulski
Russian COB	Sven-Ole Thorsen
Kamarov	Michael Welden
Slavin	Boris Krutonog
Andrei Bonovia	Christopher Janczar
Helicopter Pilot	Don Oscar Smith
Navigator C-2A	Rick Ducommun
DSRV Officer	George H. Billy
Lt. Jim Curry	LCDR Reed Popovich
Andrei Amalric	Andrew Divoff
Admiral Padorin	Peter Zinner
Padorin's Orderly	Tony Veneto
Admirals at Briefing	Ben Hartigan, Robert Buckingham
Judge Moore	Ray Reinhardt
General at Briefing	F. J. O'Neil
Advisors	A. C. Lyles, John McTiernan, Sr.
Sunglasses	David Sederholm
Foxtrot Pilot	John Shepherd
Lt. Comd. Mike Hewitt	William Bell Sullivan
Caroline Ryan	Gates McFadden
Sally Ryan	Louise Borras
Stewardess	Denise E. James

and Mark Draxton, Tom Fisher, Pete Antico (Dallas Seamen), Kenton Kovell, Radu Gavor, Ivan Ivanov, Ping Wu, Herman Sinitzyn (Red October Seamen), Vlado Benden, George Winston (Konovalov Seamen)

Top: Sean Connery Below: Ned Vaughn, Anthony Peck, Courtney B. Vance, Scott Glenn
© *Paramount Pictures*
1990 Academy Award for Best Sound Effects Editing

Alec Baldwin, Sean Connery Above: Jeffrey Jones, James Earl Jones

Daniel Davis, Alec Baldwin

Sean Connery, Alec Baldwin, Scott Glenn Top Left: Baldwin, James Earl Jones
Above Left: Richard Jordan Top Right: Michael Welden, Boris Krutonog, Sam Neill,
Sean Connery Above Right: Baldwin

Robert Duvall, Faye Dunaway Top Left: Blanche Baker,
Natasha Richardson Left: Elizabeth McGovern, Richardson
© *Cinecom*

THE HANDMAID'S TALE

(CINECOM) Producer, Daniel Wilson; Director, Volker Schlondorff;
Screenplay, Harold Pinter, based on the novel by Margaret Atwood;
Executive Producer, Wolfgang Glattes; Photography, Igor Luther;
Music, Ryuichi Sakamoto; Editor, David Ray; Designer, Tom Walsh;
Costumes, Colleen Atwood; Associate Producers, Gale Goldberg,
Alex Gartner; Casting, Pat Golden; Assistant Director, Anthony Git-
telson; Presented with Master Partners, in association with Cinetude
Film Productions and Odyssey/Cinecom International; Dolby Stereo;
Technicolor; Rated R; 109 minutes; March release

CAST

Kate	Natasha Richardson
Serena Joy	Faye Dunaway
Nick	Aidan Quinn
Moira	Elizabeth McGovern
Aunt Lydia	Victoria Tennant
Commander	Robert Duvall
Ofglen	Blanche Baker
Ofwarren/Janine	Traci Lind
Doctor	David Dukes
Aunt Helena	Zoey Wilson
Aunt Elizabeth	Kathryn Doby
Luke	Reiner Schoene
Cora	Lucia Hartpeng
Aunt Sara	Karma Ibsen Riley
Rita	Lucile McIntyre
Officer on bus	Gary Bullock
June	Allison Holmes
Preacher	J. Michael Hunter
Dick	Robert Raiford
Alma	Mirjam Bohnet
T.V. Announcer	Julian E. Bell
Guard	David Barnes
Angel at desk	James A. Carleo III

and Jim Grimshaw (Eye in van), Ivan Migel (Eye), Doris Boggs (Aunt),
Annemarie Fenske (Aunt Christina), Linda Pierce (Another Wife),
Nina Lynn Blanton (Third Wife), Rhesa Reagan Stone (Mrs. Warren),
Sara Seidman (Handmaid), Muse Watson (Guardian), Janell McLeod
(Martha), Elke Ritschel (Hostess), Jane Learned (Nun), Randall
Haynes (Condemned Man), Rhonda Bond (Black Woman), Mil
Nicholson (Wardress), Robert Penz, Tom McGovern (Guards), Danny
Simpkins (Walter), James G. Martin, Jr. (Steve), Stefanie J. Chen
(Ofglen #2), Ed L. Grady (Old Man), Molly Sandick (Baby), Blair
Nicole Struble (Jill), Bill Owen (T.V. Announcer #2)

Natasha Richardson, Aidan Quinn Above: Victoria Tennant,
Traci Lind

HOUSE PARTY

(NEW LINE CINEMA) Producer, Warrington Hudlin; Director/Screenplay, Reginald Hudlin; Executive Producer, Gerald Olson; Photography, Peter Deming; Editor, Earl Watson; Designer, Bryan Jones; Music, Marcus Miller; Assistant Director, Kelly St. Rode; Costumes, Harold Evans; a Hudlin Bros. presentation; Dolby Stereo; Metro Color; Rated R; 105 minutes; March release

CAST

Kid	Christopher Reid
Pop	Robin Harris
Play	Christopher Martin
Bilal	Martin Lawrence
Sidney	Tisha Campbell
Sharane	A. J. Johnson
Stab	Paul Anthony
Pee-Wee	Bowlegged Lou
Zilla	B. Fine
Principal	Edith Fields
La Donna	Kelly Jo Minter
Older Brother	Clifton Powell
Sharane's Sister	Verda Bridges
Peanut	Desi Arnez Hines, II
Uncle Otis	Lou D. Washington
Sunni	Kimi-Sung
Cops	Barry Diamond, Michael Pniewski
Lovers	Diana Mendoza, Randy Harris
Waiter	Barry Wiggins
D.J.	George Clinton
Sidney's Mom	Ellaraino
Sidney's Dad	J. Jay Saunders
Guest	Myra J.
Mildred	Norma Donaldson
Groove	Eugene Allen
Chill	Darryl Mitchell
Herman	Belal Miller
Clint	Shaun Baker
Benita	Leah Aldridge
La Shay	Val Gamble
Mr. Strickland	John Witherspoon
Mrs. Strickland	Bebe Drake-Massey
Evrette	Richard McGregor
E. Z. E.	Anthony Johnson
Guy	Ronn Riser
Girl #1	D-Zire
Tall Teen	Bentley Evans
Crooks	Reginald Hudlin, Warrington Hudlin
Pimp	George Logan
Albert	Rodney Hill
Brutus	Cliff Frazier
Rock	Cederick Hardman
Hatchett	Stan Haze
Fats	Chino Williams
Tattoo	Jaime Cardriche
Guard	Alexander Folk

Top: Christopher Reid, Christopher Martin
Below: Reid,
Tisha Campbell
© *New Line Cinema*

Christopher Reid, A. J. Johnson Above: Robin Harris

Paul Anthony, Bowlegged Lou, B. Fine

Ossie Davis, Tom Hanks Top Left: Hanks, Meg Ryan (also left)
© *Warner Bros.*

Tom Hanks, Abe Vigoda, Meg Ryan Above: Lloyd Bridges;
Robert Stack

JOE VERSUS THE VOLCANO

(WARNER BROS.) Producer, Teri Schwartz; Executive Producers, Steven Spielberg, Kathleen Kennedy, Frank Marshall; Director/Screenplay, John Patrick Shanley; Photography, Stephen Goldblatt; Designer, Bo Welch; Editor, Richard Halsey; Music, Georges Delerue; Song: *"The Cowboy Song"* by John Patrick Shanley/performed by Tom Hanks; Costumes, Colleen Atwood; Casting, Marion Dougherty; Assistant Director, William M. Elvin; Visual Effects, Industrial Light & Magic; Visual Effects Supervisor, David L. Carson; an Amblin Entertainment Production; Dolby Stereo; Panavision; Technicolor; Rated PG; 102 minutes; March release

CAST

Joe Banks	Tom Hanks
DeDe/Angelica/Patricia	Meg Ryan
Graynamore	Lloyd Bridges
Dr. Ellison	Robert Stack
Chief of the Waponis	Abe Vigoda
Mr. Waturi	Dan Hedaya
Luggage Salesman	Barry McGovern
Dagmar	Amanda Plummer
Marshall	Ossie Davis
Nurse	Jayne Haynes
Mike	David Burton
Tony	Jon Pochran
Fred (Guard)	Jim Hudson
Italian Tailor	Antoni Gatti
Underwear Salesman	Darrell Zwerling
Bellman	Jim Ryan
Ralph	Karl Rumberg
Emo, Waponi Lookout	Brian Esteban
Baw, the Waponi Advance Man	Nathan Lane
Spanish Singers	Wally Ruiz, Guilermo Guzman, Tommy Franco
Clerk	Tony Salome
Saleswoman	Courtney Gibbs
Waitress	Lala
Statue of Liberty	Jennifer Stewart
Salesman—Hammacher Schlemmer	William Ward
Hairdresser	Lisa LeBlanc
God Woo	Paul Michael Thorpe

COUPE DE VILLE

(UNIVERSAL) Producers, Larry Brezner, Paul Schiff; Executive Producers, James G. Robinson, Joe Roth; Screenplay/Co-Producer, Mike Binder; Photography, Reynaldo Villalobos; Designer, Angelo Graham; Editor, Paul Hirsch; Music, James Newton Howard; Costumes, Deborah Scott; Casting, Marci Liroff; Associate Producer/Unit Production Manager, Jerry Baerwitz; Assistant Director, Dennis Maguire; Song: "Louie Louie" by Richard Berry; a Morgan Creek Prods. Presentation of a Rollins, Morra, Brezner Production; Dolby Stereo; Panavision; Deluxe color; Rated PG-13; 99 minutes; March release

CAST

Bobby Libner	Patrick Dempsey
Buddy Libner	Arye Gross
Marvin Libner	Daniel Stern
Tammy	Annabeth Gish
Betty Libner	Rita Taggart
Uncle Phil	Joseph Bologna
Fred Libner	Alan Arkin
Doc Sturgeon	James Gammon
Rick	Ray Lykins
Raymond	Chris Lombardi
Billy	Josh Segal
Kloppner	John Considine
Cops	Steve Boles, Don Tilley
Gas Station Attendants	Terry Loughlin, Reid "Pete" Shook
Finkelstein	Rod Swift
Barney	Fred Ornstein
Fishing Buddy	Don Sheldon
Waitress	Boots Crowder
Young Bobby	Edan Gross
Young Buddy	Michael Weiner
Young Marvin	Dean Jacobson

Top: Patrick Dempsey, Arye Gross, Daniel Stern
Left: Rita Taggart, Alan Arkin
© *Universal City Studios*

Daniel Stern, Patrick Dempsey, Arye Gross Above: James Gammon, Dempsey, Gross, Stern

Alan Arkin, Daniel Stern, Patrick Dempsey, Arye Gross Above: Gross, Annabeth Gish

27

BAD INFLUENCE

(TRIUMPH RELEASING) Producer, Steve Tisch; Director, Curtis Hanson; Screenplay, David Koepp; Executive Producers, Richard Morrie, Becker Eisenman; Photography, Robert Elswit; Designer, Ron Foreman; Co-Producer, Bernie Goldmann; Line Producer, Iya Labunka; Editor/Associate Producer, Bonnie Koehler; Music, Trevor Jones; Costumes, Malissa Daniel; Casting, Lisa Beach; an Epic Productions and Sarlui/Diamant presentation of a Steve Tisch/Producer Representatives Organization Production; Dolby Stereo; Color; Rated R; 99 minutes; March release

CAST

Alex	Rob Lowe
Michael Boll	James Spader
Claire	Lisa Zane
Pismo Boll	Christian Clemenson
Leslie	Kathleen Wilhoite
Patterson	Tony Maggio
Howard	John de Lancie
Club Bartender	Grand L. Bush
Ruth Fielding	Marcia Cross
Dr. Fielding	John Mahon
Mrs. Fielding	Joyce Meadows
Claire's Friend	Perri Lister
Britt	Rosalyn Landor
Bouncer	Michael Kristick
Hamburger Clerk	Said Faraj
Bumped Woman	Bianca Rossini
Banker	Warren Stanhope
Stylish Eurasian Woman	Charisse Glenn
Blonde	Adrienne Leigh
Woman in bar	Susan Lee Hoffman
Man in bar	Jeff Kaake

Arguing Couple .... Brendan Hughes, Tilghmann Branner and Palmer Lee Todd (Naked Woman), Sunny Smith (Waitress), Jay Della (Chez Jay Bartender), David Duchovny (Club Goer), Lilyan Chauvin, Eddy Armani (Art Gallery Patrons), Leslie Bernard Joseph (Stylish Woman's Husband), Belle Avery (Gallery Bartender), Wanda Norman (French Woman), John Verea (Rito), Kelly Miller (Receptionist), Christina Cocek (Female Executive), Joey Miyashima (Man at tar pit), Dominique Jennings (Woman at tar pit)

Top: Rob Lowe, James Spader Below: Spader, Lisa Zane
Left: Lowe
© *Epic Productions*

Christian Clemenson, James Spader

Lisa Zane, Rob Lowe

Tom Berenger, Elizabeth Perkins Top Right: Kate Capshaw,
Berenger Right: Anne Archer, Berenger © *Orion Pictures*

LOVE AT LARGE

(ORION) Producer, David Blocker; Director/Screenplay, Alan
Rudolph; Photography, Elliot Davis; Designer, Steven Legler; Editor,
Lisa Churgin; Music, Mark Isham; Costumes, Ingrid Ferrin; Associate
Producer, Stuart Besser; Casting, Pam Dixon; Assistant Director, Jerry
Ziesmer; Dolby Stereo; Deluxe color; Rated R; 97 minutes; March
release

CAST

Harry Dobbs	Tom Berenger
Stella Wynkowski	Elizabeth Perkins
Miss Dolan	Anne Archer
Ellen McGraw	Kate Capshaw
Mrs. King	Annette O'Toole
Frederick King/James McGraw	Ted Levine
Doris	Ann Magnuson
Art	Kevin J. O'Connor
Corrine Dart	Ruby Dee
Marty	Barry Miller
Rick	Neil Young
Bellhop	Meegan Lee Ochs
Taxi Driver	Gailard Sartain
Tavern Bartender	Robert Gould
Hiram Culver	Dirk Blocker
Harley	Bob Terhune
Missy McGraw	Ariana Lamon-Anderson
Maitre D'Blue Danube	Michael Wilson
Blue Danube Waitress	Debra Dusay
Ranch Foreman	Sunshine Parker
Motel Manager	Billy Silva
Nanny	Pamela Abas-Ross
Tavern Waitress	Laura Kenny
Rick's Girlfriend	Leticia Keith
King Children	Andrew Barr, Jessica Boegel
Counterperson	Stan Asis
Stewardess	Holly Morrison

and Ileane Meltzer (Angry Neighbor), Jeffrey Calvin (Mario), William
Lee (Chinese Man), Evelyn Ching (Chinese Woman), Susan Medak,
Kate Suzanne Medak (Neighbors), Greg Murphy, Shawnee Rad (Valets), Paul Till (McGraw Taxi Driver), Stephen Kimberley (Man on
train)

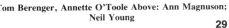

Tom Berenger, Annette O'Toole Above: Ann Magnuson;
Neil Young

29

LORD OF THE FLIES

(COLUMBIA) Producer, Ross Milloy; Executive Producers, Lewis Allen, Peter Newman; Director/Editor, Harry Hook; Screenplay, Sara Schiff, based on the novel by Sir William Golding; Co-Producer, David V. Lester; Photography, Martin Fuhrer; Supervising Editor, Tom Priestley; Designer, Jamie Leonard; Costumes, Doreen Watkinson; Make-up, Sarah Monzani; Music, Philippe Sarde; Casting, Janet Hirshenson, Jane Jenkins, Michael Hirshenson; Assistant Director, Matt Hinkley; Associate Producer, Walker Stuart; from Castle Rock Entertainment in association with Nelson Entertainment; a Jack's Camp/Signal Hill Ltd. production; Dolby Stereo; Deluxe color; Rated R; 90 minutes; March release

CAST

Ralph	Balthazar Getty
Jack	Chris Furrh
Piggy	Danuel Pipoly
Simon	Badgett Dale
The Twins (Eric & Sam)	Edward Taft, Andrew Taft
Roger	Gary Rule
Andy	Terry Wells
Larry	Braden MacDonald
Greg	Angus Burgin
Sheraton	Martin Zentz
Peter	Brian Jacobs
Patterson	Vincent Amábile
Mikey	David Weinstein
Steve	Chuck Bell
Pablo	Everado Elizondo
John	James Hamm
Will	Charles Newmark
Tony	Brian Matthews
Rapper	Shawn Skie
Luke	Judson McCune
Tex	Zane Rockenbaugh
Billy	Robert Shea
Rusty	Gordon Elder
Marine Officer	Bob Peck
Marine Petty Officer	Bill Schoppert
The Pilot	Michael Greene

Top: Balthazar Getty Below: Chris Furrh, Getty, Danuel Pipoly
© Castle Rock Entertainment

Chris Furrh

Balthazar Getty, Danuel Pipoly Above: Brian Jacobs, Chris Furrh

Jamie Lee Curtis (also right) Top Right: Clancy Brown, Curtis
© *Vestron Pictures*

BLUE STEEL

(MGM) Producers, Edward R. Pressman, Oliver Stone; Executive Producer, Lawrence Kasanoff; Director, Kathryn Bigelow; Screenplay, Kathryn Bigelow, Eric Red; Co-Producer, Michael Rauch; Photography, Amir Mokri; Editor, Lee Percy; Designer, Toby Corbett; Music, Brad Fiedel; Associate Producers, Michael Flynn, Diane Schneier; Costumes, Richard Shissler; Casting, Risa Bramon, Billy Hopkins; Assistant Director, Herb Gains; from MGM/UA Distribution Co., in association with Lightning Pictures, Precision Films and Mack-Taylor Prods.; Dolby Stereo; CFI Color; Rated R; 102 minutes; March release

CAST

Megan Turner	Jamie Lee Curtis
Eugene Hunt	Ron Silver
Nick Mann	Clancy Brown
Tracy Perez	Elizabeth Peña
Shirley Turner	Louise Fletcher
Frank Turner	Philip Bosco
Asst. Chief Stanley Hoyt	Kevin Dunn
Attorney Mel Dawson	Richard Jenkins
Husband	Markus Flannagan
Wife	Mary Mara
Instructor	Skipp Lynch
Police Commissioner	Mike Hodge
Superintendent	Mike Starr
Officer Jeff Travers	Chris Walker
Wool Cap	Tom Sizemore
Counterman	David Ilku
Cashier	Andrew Hubatsek
Doorman	Joe Jamrog
Howard	Matt Craven
TV Announcers	Reginald Wells, Heidi Kempf
Prostitute	Toni Darling
Hood	William J. Marshall
Maitre D'Hotel	James Shannon
Businessman-Victim	Thomas Dorff
Internal Affairs Man	William Wise

and Lauren Tom, Doug Barron, Carol Schneider, L. Peter Callender (Reporters), Faith Geer (Bum), Becky Gelke (Nurse), Frank Girardeau (Uniform Cop), Larry Silvestri (Precinct Cop), John Capodice (Trial Commissioner), Sam Coppola (PBA Rep), Bellina Logan (Rookie), Ralph Nieves (Homicide Detective), Al Cerullo (Helicopter Pilot), Michael Philip Del Rio (John Perez), Harley Flannagan, James Drescher (Punks)

Jamie Lee Curtis Above: Ron Silver

31

PRETTY WOMAN

(TOUCHSTONE) Producers, Arnon Milchan, Steven Reuther; Executive Producer, Laura Ziskin; Director, Garry Marshall; Screenplay, J. F. Lawton; Photography, Charles Minsky; Designer, Albert Brenner; Editor, Priscilla Nedd; Costumes, Marilyn Vance-Straker; Co-Producer, Gary W. Goldstein; Music, James Newton Howard; Casting, Dianne Crittenden; Assistant Director, Ellen H. Schwartz; Presented in association with Silver Screen Partners IV; Distributed by Buena Vista Pictures; Dolby Stereo; Technicolor; Rated R; 117 minutes; March release

CAST

Edward Lewis	Richard Gere
Vivian Ward	Julia Roberts
James Morse	Ralph Bellamy
Philip Stuckey	Jason Alexander
Kit De Luca	Laura San Giacomo
David Morse	Alex Hyde-White
Elizabeth Stuckey	Amy Yasbeck
Bridget	Elinor Donahue
Hotel Manager	Hector Elizondo
Susan	Judith Baldwin
Magician	Jason Randal
Howard	Bill Applebaum
Party Guests	Tracy Bjork, Gary Greene
Carlos	William Gallo
Happy Man	Abdul Salaam El Razzac
Detective	Hank Azaria
Landlord	Larry Hankin
Rachel	Julie Paris
Bermuda	Rhonda Hansome
Man in car	Harvey Keenan
Tourists	Marty Nadler, Lynda Goodfriend
Cruiser	Reed Anthony
Pops	Frank Campanella
Artist	Jacqueline Woolsey
Angel	Cheri Caspari
Skateboard Kid	Scott A. Marshall
Night Elevator Operator (Dennis)	Patrick Richwood
Desk Clerks	Kathi Marshall, Laurelle Brooks, Don Feldstein
Room Service Waiter	Marvin Braverman
Doormen	Alex Statler, Jeff Michalski
Bellhops	Patrick D. Stuart, Lloyd T. Williams
Darryl (Limo Driver)	R. Darrell Hunter
Lounge Pianist	James Patrick Dunne
Woman in hotel lobby	Valorie Armstrong
Italian Businessman	Steve Restivo
Japanese Businessman	Rodney Kageyama
American Businessman	Douglas Stitzel
Mr. Hollister	Larry Miller
Snobby Saleswoman	Dey Young
Saleswomen	Carol Williard, Minda Burr, Robyn Peterson, Mariann Aalda
Tie Salesman	RC Everbeck
Maître d'	Michael French
Beverly Hills Waiter	Allan Kent
Senator Adams	Stacy Keach Sr.
Olsen Sisters	Lucinda Sue Crosby, Nancy Locke
Sod Stomping Announcer	Calvin Remsberg
Polo Game Announcer	Lloyd Nelson
Polite Husband	Norman Large
Woman at car (polo game)	Tracy Reiner
Vance	Tom Nolan
Mark	John David Carson
Jake	Daniel Bardol
"Violetta"	Karin Calabro
"Alfredo"	Bruce Eckstut
Matron	Amzie Strickland
Opera Usher	Mychael Bates

Top: Richard Gere, Julia Roberts (also below)
© *Touchstone Pictures*

Hector Elizondo, Laura San Giacomo

Richard Gere, Julia Roberts Top Right: Roberts, Gere (also top left and above left)

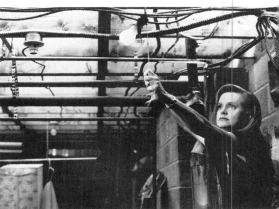

Elizabeth McGovern, Michael Caine Top Right: Swoosie Kurtz
Right: Will Patton, McGovern
© *Corsair Pictures*

A SHOCK TO THE SYSTEM

(CORSAIR PICTURES) Producer, Patrick McCormick; Director, Jan Egleson; Executive Producer, Leslie Morgan; Screenplay, Andrew Klavan, based on novel by Simon Brett; Associate Producer, Alice Arlen; Photography, Paul Goldsmith; Editors, Peter C. Frank, William A. Anderson; Designer, Howard Cummings; Music, Gary Chang; Costumes, John Dunn; Casting, Mary Colquhoun; Assistant Director, Amy Sayres; Dolby Stereo; Color; Rated R; 91 minutes; March release

CAST

Graham Marshall	Michael Caine
Stella Anderson	Elizabeth McGovern
Robert Benham	Peter Riegert
Leslie Marshall	Swoosie Kurtz
Lieutenant Laker	Will Patton
Melanie O'Connor	Jenny Wright
George Brewster	John McMartin
Lillian	Barbara Baxley
Tara Liston	Haviland Morris
Henry Park	Philip Moon
Executives	Kent Broadhurst, Zach Grenier, David Schramm
David Jones	Sam Schacht
Convention Speaker	Christopher Durang
Graham's Secretary	Mia Dillon
Benham's Secretary	Alice Haining
Wanda Maas	Patience Moore
Mailroom Boy	Darrell Wilks
Secretaries	Scotty Bloch, Kim Staunton, Alicia Hoge
Beggar (Subway)	Mike Cicchetti
Beggar #2	Rick Petrucelli
Bums	Victor Truro, Rik Colitti, Mike Starr
Transit Cop	Michael Perez
Motorman	John Finn
Messenger	Tyrone Jackson
Waitress/Dazzles	Marie Sylvia
Ulysses	Samuel L. Jackson
Decorator	Jonathan Freeman
Partygoer	Elizabeth Morin
Hot Dog Vendor	Joe Zaloom
Rental Car Attendant	Socorro Santiago
Kennel Driver	Welker White
Cab Driver	Frank Ferrara
News Anchor Woman	Sheila Stainback

John McMartin, Michael Caine Above: Caine

TEENAGE MUTANT NINJA TURTLES

(NEW LINE CINEMA) Producers, Kim Dawson, Simon Fields, David Chan; Executive Producer, Raymond Chow; Director, Steve Barron; Co-Producer, Graham Cottle; Screenplay, Todd W. Langen, Bobby Herbeck; Story, Bobby Herbeck; Based on characters created by Kevin Eastman, Peter Laird; Executive in Charge of Production, Thomas K. Gray; Photography, John Fenner; Designer, Roy Forge Smith; Music, John Du Prez; Costumes, John M. Hay; Stunts/Martial Arts Choreographer, Pat Johnson; Special Effects Supervisor, Joey Di Gaetano; Creatures Designed by Jim Henson's Creature Shop; a Golden Harvest presentation of a Limelight Production, in association with Gary Propper; Dolby Stereo; Deluxe color; Rated PG; 93 minutes; March release

CAST

April O'Neil	Judith Hoag
Casey Jones	Elias Koteas
Raphael/Passenger in cab	Josh Pais
Michaelangelo/Pizza Man	Michelan Sisti
Donatello/Foot Messenger	Leif Tilden
Leonardo/Gang Member	David Forman
Danny Pennington	Michael Turney
Charles Pennington	Jay Patterson
Chief Sterns	Raymond Serra
The Shredder	James Saito
Tatsu	Toshishiro Obata
Head Thug	Sam Rockwell
June	Kitty Fitzgibbon
Cab Driver	Louis Cantarini
Movie Hoodlums	Joseph D'Onofrio, John D. Ward
Shinsho	Ju Yu
Charles' Secretary	Cassandra Ward-Freeman
Technician	Mark Jeffrey Miller
New Recruit	John Rogers
Talkative Foot #1	Tae Pak
Talkative Foot #2	Kenn Troum
Tall Teen	Robert Haskell
Beaten Teen	Joshua Bo Lozoff
Police Officers	Winston Hemingway, Joe Inscoe

and the voices of: Josh Pais (Raphael), Robbie Rist (Michaelangelo), Kevin Clash (Splinter), Brian Tochi (Leonardo), David McCharen (The Shredder), Michael McConnohie (Tatsu), Corey Feldman (Donatello)

Top: Josh Pais, Splinter, David Forman, Michelan Sisti, Leif Tilden Below: Judith Hoag, Pais Right: Elias Koteas, Splinter, Michael Turney
© Northshore Investments Ltd.

Judith Hoag, David Forman, Leif Tilden

Toshishiro Obata (Center)

I LOVE YOU TO DEATH

(TRI-STAR) Producers, Jeffrey Lurie, Ron Moler; Executive Producers, Charles Okun, Michael Grillo; Director, Lawrence Kasdan; Screenplay, John Kostmayer; Photography, Owen Roizman; Designer, Lilly Kilvert; Editor, Anne V. Coates; Costumes, Aggie Guerard Rodgers; Music, James Horner; Co-Producers, Lauren Weissman, Patrick Wells; Casting, Wallis Nicita; Assistant Director, Michael Grillo; Associate Producers, John Marsh, Lori Cristina Weiss, Lynn Isenberg, John Kostmayer; Chestnut Hill production; Dolby Stereo; Technicolor; Rated R; 96 minutes; April release

CAST

Joey Boca	Kevin Kline
Rosalie Boca	Tracey Ullman
Nadja	Joan Plowright
Devo Nod	River Phoenix
Harlan James	William Hurt
Marlon James	Keanu Reeves
Lt. Schooner	James Gammon
Wiley	Jack Kehler
Lacey	Victoria Jackson
Joey's Mother	Miriam Margolyes
Carla	Alisan Porter
Dominic	Jon Kasdan
Bridget	Heather Graham
Donna Joy	Michelle Joyner
Benny	John Kostmayer
Dewey Brown	Kathleen York
Girl at disco	Phoebe Cates
Lawyer	Lawrence Kasdan
Jailhouse Informant	John Billingsley
Waitress	Samantha Kostmayer
Blue Light Bartender	Michael Chieffo
Java Jive Bartender	Robert Radonich
Young Man with bat	Jeff Klein
Cabbie	G. Valmont Thomas
Priest	Art Cahn
Librarian	Audrey Rapoport
Millie	Shiri Appleby
Sammy	Luke Rossi
Wendel Carter	Henry Beckman
Reporters	Susan Chin, Tony Romano, Johnny Willis
Pizza Guy	Joe Lando
Biker	William R. Breyette

Top: Kevin Kline, Tracey Ullman Below: William Hurt, Keanu Reeves Left: Reeves, River Phoenix, Hurt, Ullman, Joan Plowright, Kline
© Tri-Star Pictures

Kevin Kline, Jack Kehler, James Gammon, Jon Kasdan, Alisan Porter

Tracey Ullman, Kevin Kline, Joan Plowright

THE FIRST POWER

(ORION) Producer, David Madden; Executive Producers, Ted Field,
Robert W. Cort, Melinda Jason; Director/Screenplay, Robert Resni-
koff; Photography, Theo Van Sande; Designer, Joseph T. Garritz;
Editor, Michael Bloecher; Music, Stewart Copeland; Casting, Mindy
Marin; Assistant Director, Matt Hinkley; Stunts, John Moio; a Nelson
Entertainment presentation of an Interscope Communications Pro-
duction; Dolby Stereo; Deluxe color; Rated R; 105 minutes; April
release

CAST

Russell Logan	Lou Diamond Phillips
Tess Seaton	Tracy Griffiths
Patrick Channing	Jeff Kober
Det. Oliver Franklin	Mykel T. Williamson
Sister Marguerite	Elizabeth Arlen
Commander Perkins	Dennis Lipscomb
Lt. Grimes	Carmen Argenziano
Grandmother	Julianna McCarthy
Bag Lady	Nada Despotovich
Carmen	Sue Giosa
Mazza	Clayton Landey
Father Brian	Hansford Rowe
Cardinal	Philip Abbott
Monsignor	David Gale
Priest	J. Patrick McNamara
Anchorwoman	Lisa Specht
Driver in alley	Mark Bringelson
Detectives	William Fair, David Partington
Bum/Detective	Brian Libby
Uniform	Michael McNab
Cop at arrest	Dan Tullis, Jr.
Cop at tenement	Michael Wise
Reporters	Andrew Amador, Paula McClure
	Tiiu Leek
Uniform Cops	Mitch Carter, Jeff Mooring
Cop	Todd Jeffries
Reservoir Worker	Grand L. Bush
Street Vendor	Gokul

and David Katims (Man in parking structure), Lynn Marta (Nun),
Charles Raymond, Scott Lawrence (Gang Members), Bill Moseley
(Bartender), Melanie Shatner (Shopgirl), R. David Stephens (Desk
Clerk), Oz Tortoa (Antonio), Robert Volaizzi (Driver), Ron J. Good-
man (Bum in hotel)

Jeff Kober, Lou Diamond Phillips
Above: Phillips, Tracy Griffith

CRY-BABY

(UNIVERSAL) Producer, Rachel Talalay; Executive Producers, Jim Abrahams, Brian Grazer; Director/Screenplay, John Waters; Editor, Janice Hampton; Photography, David Insley; Designer, Vincent Peranio; Assistant Director, Mary Ellen Woods; Music, Patrick Williams; Song: *"King Cry Baby"* by Doc Pomus & Dave Alvin/performed by James Intveld; Choreographer, Lori Eastside; Casting, Paula Herold, Pat Moran; Imagine Entertainment presentation; Dolby Stereo; Deluxe color; Rated PG-13; 85 minutes; April release

CAST

Wade "Cry-Baby" Walker	Johnny Depp
Allison Vernon-Williams	Amy Locane
Ramona Rickettes	Susan Tyrrell
Mrs. Vernon-Williams	Polly Bergen
Belvedere	Iggy Pop
Pepper Walker	Ricki Lake
Wanda Woodward	Traci Lords
Mona "Hatchet Face" Malnorowski	Kim McGuire
Milton Hackett	Darren E. Burrows
Baldwin	Stephen Mailer
Lenora	Kim Webb
Toe-Joe	Alan J. Wendl
Jo-Jo Malnorowski	Troy Donahue
Gertie Malnorowski	Mink Stole
Reverend Hackett	Joe Dallesandro
Mrs. Hackett	Joey Heatherton
Mr. Woodward	David Nelson
Mrs. Woodward	Patricia Hearst
Hateful Guard	Willem Dafoe
Snare-Drum	Jonathan Benya
Susie-Q	Jessica Raskin
Dupree	Robert Tyree
Dupree's Girlfriend	Angie Levroney
Whiffles	Drew Ebersole, Kenny Curtis, Scott Neilson
Judge	Robert Walsh
Inga	Jeni Blong
Mrs. Tadlock	Vivienne Shub
Angelic Boyfriend	Robert Marbury

and Craig Wallace, Phillip Broussard, Reggie Davis, Nick Fleming, Robbie Jones (Conks), Skip Spencer (Strip Poker #1), Holter Graham (Strip Poker #2), Susan Lowe (Night Court Parent), Dan Griffiths (Snake-Eyes Hood), Kirk McEwen, Eric Lucas, Frank Maldonado, Patrick Mitchell (Convicts), Mary Vivian Pearce (Picnic Mother), Steve Aronson (Mean Guard), Kelly Goldberg (Pepper's Baby)

Top: Willem Dafoe; Polly Bergen Below: Amy Locane, Johnny Depp Right: Susan Tyrrell; Mink Stole, Troy Donahue
© *Universal City Studios*

Patricia Hearst, David Nelson; Joey Heatherton, Joe Dallesandro

Kim McGuire, Darren E. Burrows, Johnny Depp, Ricki Lake, Traci Lords

IN THE SPIRIT

(CASTLE HILL) Producers, Julian Schlossberg, Beverly Irby; Director, Sandra Seacat; Screenplay, Jeannie Berlin, Laurie Jones; Associate Producer, Phillip Schopper; Photography, Dick Quinlan; Music, Patrick Williams; Editor, Brad Fuller; Costumes, Carrie Robbins; Designer, Michael Smith; Assistant Director, Lisa Zimble; Running River production; TVC Color; Rated R; 93 minutes; April release

CAST

Crystal	Jeannie Berlin
Sue	Olympia Dukakis
Roger Flan	Peter Falk
Lureen	Melanie Griffith
Marianne Flan	Elaine May
Reva Prosky	Marlo Thomas
Pamela	Laurie Jones
Lt. Kelly	Chad Burton
Det. Pete Weber	Thurn Hoffman
Yolanda	Agda Antonio
New Age Lecturer	Hope Cameron
Abu Bashanti	Michael Emil
Tomaso	Emidio La Vella
Attacker in hall	Brian Hickey
Homeless Executive	Phil Harper
Handymen	David Eigenberg, David Baer
Bartender	Rockets Redglare
Ambulance Attendant	Christopher Durang
Sheriff	Danny Davin

and Phillip Schopper (The Voice), Matt Carlson, Angelo Florio, Mark Boone Jr. (Policemen), Gary Swanson (Detective), Candy Trabucco, Nora York, Roy Nathanson (Accident Bystanders)

Top: Marlo Thomas, Peter Falk, Elaine May Left: Melanie Griffith Below Left: May, Olympia Dukakis Below Right: Jeannie Berlin
© *Castle Hill Prods.*

TORN APART

(CASTLE HILL) Producers, Danny Fisher, Jerry Menkin; Director, Jack Fisher; Screenplay, Marc Kristal; Based on novel "A Forbidden Love" by Chayym Zeldis; Co-Producer, Doron Eran; Music/Executive Producer, Peter Arnow; Photography, Barry Markowitz; Editor, Michael Garvey; Associate Producer, Tobi Wilson; Dolby Stereo; Precision Color; Rated R; 95 minutes; April release

CAST

Ben Arnon	Adrian Pasdar
Laila Malek	Cecilia Peck
Mahmoud Malek	Machram Huri
Prof. Ibrahim Mansour	Arnon Zadok
Ilana Arnon	Margrit Polak
Moustapha	Michael Morim
Fawzi	Amos Lavi
Jamilah	Hanna Azulai
Arie Arnon	Barry Primus

© *Castle Hill Prods.*

Cecilia Peck, Adrian Pasdar

J. T. Walsh, Doug Yasuda, Paul Reiser, Dudley Moore,
Bill Smitrovich Top Right: Moore, Daryl Hannah
Right: Moore, Reiser
© *Paramount Pictures*

CRAZY PEOPLE

(PARAMOUNT) Producer, Thomas Barad; Director, Tony Bill;
Screenplay/Associate Producer, Mitch Markowitz; Executive Producer, Robert K. Weiss; Photography, Victor J. Kemper; Designer,
John J. Lloyd; Editor, Mia Goldman; Costumes, Mary E. Vogt; Music,
Cliff Eidelman; Casting, Lynn Stalmaster; Assistant Director, Allan
Wertheim; Song: *"The Hello Song"* by Cal DeVoll; Dolby Stereo;
Technicolor; Rated R; 90 minutes; April release

CAST

Emory Leeson	Dudley Moore
Kathy Burgess	Daryl Hannah
Stephen Bachman	Paul Reiser
Charles F. Drucker	J. T. Walsh
Bruce Concannon	Bill Smitrovich
Judge	Alan North
George Cartelli	David Paymer
Saabs	Danton Stone
Manuel Robles	Paul Bates
Mort Powell	Dick Cusack
Hsu	Doug Yasuda
Eddie Avis	Floyd Vivino
Dr. Liz Baylor	Mercedes Ruehl
Dr. Horace Koch	Ben Hammer
Mark Olander	David Packer
Young Executive Anderson	Joyce L. Bowden
Powell	Randell Haynes
Taxi Driver	James V. Albanese
Draftsman	Scott Kitts
Stephen's Secretary	Lorri Lindberg
William Holden	Ann Pierce
Naked Man	Faris Herbert Harton
Very Large Man	Kim Clark
Ficus Tree Man	Don Hupp
Heavy Woman	Pam La Testa
Heavy Man	Bob Martana
Heavy Daughter	Jill Pierce
Operators	Christine Larson, Doris Dworsky, Elaine Bays
Pharmacist	John Bennes
TV Anchor	Julian Bell
Connie Vega-Margolis	Maggie Han

and Robert K. Weiss (Outraged Movie Patron), Farryl Lovett (Girl in
booth), Sharon Frazier (Exercise Therapist), Lynda Clark, Mark Joy
(Executives), Pamela D. Reid (Bahamas Receptionist), J. Michael
Hunter (Eric the Orderly), Alex Barad (Boy in T.V. dept.), David Muir
(Continental Express Driver), Alan Haufrect (Hit and Run Victim), Ed
Lillard (Senior Exec. Matthews), Steve Bradford (Nervous Exec. Harris), Margaret Poole Griffin (Art Therapist), Mitch Markowitz (Utility
Nut), Mick McGovern (Rig Driver), Raf Nazario (Taxi Driver), Lloyd
Kino (Mr. Yamashita), Robert Ito (Yamashita's Aide), John Terlesky
(Adam Burgess), Larry King (Himself)

David Paymer, Dick Cusack, Paul Bates, Dudley Moore,
Danton Stone, Bill Smitrovich, Alan North, Floyd Vivino
Above: Moore, Mercedes Ruehl, Ben Hammer

CHATTAHOOCHEE

(HEMDALE) Producers, Aaron Schwab, Faye Schwab; Director, Mick Jackson; Executive Producers, John Daly, Derek Gibson; Screenplay, James Hicks; Co-Producer, Sue Baden-Powell; Casting, Mindy Marin; Designer, Joseph T. Garrity; Editor, Don Fairservice; Photography, Andrew Dunn; Music, John Keane; Assistant Director, J. Stephen Buck; Costumes, Karen Patch; Dolby Stereo; TVC Color; Rated R; 99 minutes; April release

CAST

Emmett Foley	Gary Oldman
Walker Benson	Dennis Hopper
Mae Foley	Frances McDormand
Earlene	Pamela Reed
Dr. Harwood	Ned Beatty
Morris	M. Emmet Walsh
Missy	William De Acutis
Vernon	Lee Wilkof
Lonny	Matt Craven
Clarence	Gary Klar
Harley	Timothy Scott
Dr. Debner	Richard Portnow
Jonathan	William Newman
Mr. Johnson	Whitey Hughes
Duane	Wilbur Fitzgerald
Ella	Yvonne Denise Mason
Leonard	Ralph Pace
Cops	Wesley Mann, Tim Monich
Pa Foley	Laurens Moore
Ma Foley	Mary Moore
Mae's Mother	Peggy Beasley
Women on street	F. Drucilla Brookshire, Dorothy L. Grissom Hardin
Ambulance Driver	David Fitzsimmons
Sadistic Attendant	Gary Bullock
Goading Attendant	David Dwyer
Lucas	Robert Gravel
Theo	Marc Clement
Dr. Towney	John Brasington
Dr. Everly	Jim E. Quick
Baker	C. K. Bibby
Earl	Bob Hannah
Patient without shoes	George Nannerello
Stream of Conciousness Man	Ed Grady
Upside Down Inmate	Kevin Barber
Hymn Singing Patient	James "Fred" Culclasure
Ozell	Shane Baily
Inmate in cesspool	Kevin Campbell
Inmate in movie theatre	E. Pat Hall
Inmate in tunnel	Jerry Campbell
Inmate	Roger Jackson
Harwood's Secretary	Suzi Bass
Governor's Secretary	Jill Rankin
Jimbob	F. Douglas McDaniel

and Chris Robertson, Bill Collins, Bud Davis, Michael Easler (Attendants), Randy Randolph (Miami Guard), Kathryn Cobb (Miami Nurse), Jim Gloster (Miami Attendant), Charles Lawler, Traber Burns (Miami Cops), Kristi Frankenheimer (Weather Girl), Perry Simpson, Joe Loy (Quincy Cops), Wallace Merck (Patrolman), Don Wayne Bass (First Guard), Mykel Mariette (Male Nurse), Raul Apartella (1st Man at investigation), BJ Koonce (Woman at investigation)

Top: Dennis Hopper, Gary Oldman Below: Pamela Reed, Oldman © *Hemdale Releasing Corp.*

Gary Oldman (C)

Gary Oldman, M. Emmet Walsh, Dennis Hopper Above: Oldman

MIAMI BLUES

(ORION) Producers, Jonathan Demme, Gary Goetzman; Co-Producers, Kenneth Utt, Ron Bozman; Director/Screenplay, George Armitage; Based on novel by Charles Willeford; Executive Producers, Edward Saxon, Fred Ward; Photography, Tak Fujimoto; Designer, Maher Ahmad; Music, Gary Chang; Editor, Craig McKay; Costumes, Eugenie Bafaloukos; Casting, Howard Feuer; Associate Producer, William Horberg; Assistant Director, Ron Bozman; a Tristes Tropiques Production; Dolby Stereo; Deluxe color; Rated R; 97 minutes; April release

CAST

Frederick J. Frenger, Jr.	Alec Baldwin
Stewardess	Cecilia Perez-Cervera
Little Boy	Georgie Cranford
Krishna Ravindra	Edward Saxon
Pablo	Jose Perez
Blink Willie	Obba Babatunde
Sergeant Hoke Moseley	Fred Ward
Susie Waggoner	Jennifer Jason Leigh
Sergeant Bill Henderson	Charles Napier
Mourning Hare Krishna	Matt Ingersoll
Pickpocket Victim	Jack G. Spirtos
Pickpocket	Raphael Rey Gomez
Pickpocket's Accomplice	Tony Paris
Toy Store Cashier	Wendy Thorlakson
Crack Dealer	William Taylor Anderson, Jr.
Hotel Desk Clerk	Gary Goetzman
Noira	Martine Beswicke
Krishna Ramba	Kenneth Utt
Hooker	Kerrie Clark
Ellita Sanchez	Nora Dunn
Big Fish Waitress	Maureen Fitzgibbon
Big Fish Robber	Steve Geng
Edna Damrosch	Bobo Lewis
Musclehead	Tony Tracy
Shorty	Buddy Joe Hooker
Julio	Roy Datz
Purse Snatch Victim	Catlin Brown
Purse Snatcher	Mark Mercury
Eddie Cohen	Herb Goldstein
Sergeant Frank Lackley	Paul Gleason
Bookie	Vic Hunter
Head Bookie	Gary Klar
Convenience Store Clerk	Lou Garr
Convenience Store Robber	Patrick Cherry
Newswoman	Nancy Duerr
Sausage Girl	Lisa Bell
Supermarket Stud	Edward Knott, III
Edie Wulgemuth	Shirley Stoler
Pedro	Joe Hess
Woman in sports car	Carmen Lopez

Top: Alec Baldwin, Jennifer Jason Leigh
Below: Fred Ward, Leigh Left: Tony Perez, Baldwin
© *Orion Pictures Corp.*

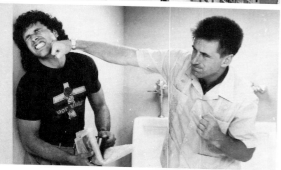

Charles Napier, Fred Ward

Jennifer Jason Leigh, Alec Baldwin

**Armand Assante, Jenny Lumet Top Left: Timothy Hutton,
Nick Nolte Left: Charles Dutton, Hutton, Luis Guzman,
Tommy A. Ford**
© *Tri-Star Pictures*

Q & A

(TRI-STAR) Producers, Arnon Milchan, Burtt Harris; Director/
Screenplay, Sidney Lumet; Based on book by Edwin Torres; Photogra-
phy, Andrzej Bartkowiak; Designer, Philip Rosenberg; Executive Pro-
ducer, Patrick Wachsberger; Costumes, Ann Roth, Neil Spisak; Editor,
Richard Cirincione; Music, Rubén Blades; Assistant Director, Burtt
Harris; Casting, Joy Todd; Associate Producer, Lilith A. Jacobs; a
Regency International Pictures/Odyssey Distributors Ltd. presentation;
Dolby Stereo; Technicolor; Rated R; 134 minutes; April release

CAST

Mike Brennan	Nick Nolte
Al Reilly	Timothy Hutton
Bobby Texador	Armand Assante
Kevin Quinn	Patrick O'Neal
Leo Bloomenfeld	Lee Richardson
Luis Valentin	Luis Guzman
Sam Chapman	Charles Dutton
Nancy Bosch	Jenny Lumet
Roger Montalvo	Paul Calderon
Jose Malpica	International Chrysis
Larry Pesch	Dominick Chianese
Nick Petrone	Leonard Cimino
Preston Pearlstein	Fyvush Finkel
Alfonse Segal	Gustavo Brens
Armand Segal	Martin E. Brens
Detective Zucker	Maurice Schell
Lubin	Tommy A. Ford
Hank Mastroangelo	John Capodice
District Attorney	Frederick Rolf
Altshul	Hal Lehrman
Mrs. Bosch	Gloria Irizarry
Sylvester/Sophia	Brian Neill
Flo	Susan Mitchell
Magnus	Drew Eliot
Seabury	Frank Raiter
Tony Vasquez	Harry Madsen
Bruno Valli	Jerry Ciauri
Inspector Flynn	George Kodisch

and Burtt Harris (Phil), Michael A. Joseph (Pimp), Cynthia O'Neal
(Agnes Quinn), Victor Colicchio ("After Hours" Alvarado), Anibal
Lleras, Jose Rafel Arango ("After Hours" Patrons), David Dill (Bar-
tender), Alex Ruiz (Danny), Richard Solchik (Phillie), Edward Rogers
III (Jose's Apt. Detective), Junior Perez ("Nancy" Captain), Javier Rios
(Boat Lover), June Stein (A.D.A.), Rod Rodriguez (Carlo), Sonny
Vito (Gino), Olga Merediz (Mrs. Valentin), Peter Gumeny (Guard),
Edward Rowan (Ed), Danny Darrow (Phone Investigator), Jose Col-
lazo (Fisherman)

**Timothy Hutton, Nick Nolte Above: Luis Guzman,
Armand Assante**

SPACED INVADERS

(TOUCHSTONE) Producer, Luigi Cingolani; Executive Producer, George Zecevic; Director, Patrick Read Johnson; Screenplay, Patrick Read Johnson, Scott Lawrence Alexander; Line Producer, John S. Curran; Photography, James L. Carter; Music, David Russo; Editors, Seth Gaven, Daniel Gross; Makeup Effects and Animatronics, Criswell and Johnson Effects; Casting, Barbara Remsen, Anne Remsen Manners; Associate Producers, Caroline Pham Johnson; Production Manager/First Assistant Director, Kelly Van Horn; Designer, Tony Tremblay; Special Effects Supervisor, Frank Ceglia; Presented in association with Silver Screen Partners IV; Smart Egg Pictures-Luigi Cingolani production; Distributed by Buena Vista Pictures; Ultra-Stereo; CFI color; Rated PG; 102 minutes; April release

CAST

Earthling Cast:

Sam Hoxly	Douglas Barr
Wrenchmuller	Royal Dano
Kathy Hoxly	Ariana Richards
Brian (Duck)	J. J. Anderson
Steve W. Klembecker	Gregg Berger
Vern/Verndroid	Wayne Alexander
Russell Pillsbury	Fred Applegate
Mrs. Vanderspool	Patrika Darbo
Ernestine	Tonya Lee Williams
Sid Ghost	Ryan Todd
Clown Kid	Barry O'Neill
Pig Kid	Adam Hansley
Radio Announcer	Casey Sander
Old Wife	Rose Parenti
Old Guys	Glen Vernon, Hal Riddle
Dumb Guys	William Holmes, Kent Minault
Clown	Jim Eusterman
Dody	Justine L. Henry

Martian Cast:

Blaznee	Kevin Thompson
Captain Bipto	Jimmy Briscoe
Pez	Toni Cox
Dr. Ziplock	Debbie Lee Carrington
Giggywig	Tommy Madden

and *Martian Voices:* Kevin Thompson (Blaznee), Jeff Winklis (Captain Bipto), Bruce Lanoil (Pez), Joe Alaskey (Dr. Ziplock), Tony Pope (Giggywig), Patrick Johnson (Commander/Enforcer Drone), Kirk Thatcher (Spiff)

Top Right: Kevin Thompson, Jimmy Briscoe, Tony Cox, Debbie Lee Carrington, Tommy Madden © *Buena Vista Pictures*

Matt Frewer, Dabney Coleman

SHORT TIME

(20th CENTURY FOX) Producer, Todd Black; Executive Producers, Joe Wizan, Mickey Borofsky; Supervising Producer, Malcolm R. Harding; Director, Gregg Champion; Screenplay, John Blumenthal, Michael Berry; Photography, John Connor; Designer, Michael Bolton; Editor, Frank Morriss; Music, Ira Newborn; Co-Producer/Assistant Director, Rob Cowan; Casting, Lynne Carrow; Stunts, Conrad Palmisano; a Gladden Entertainment presentation; Dolby Stereo; Deluxe Color; Rated PG-13; 97 minutes; May release

CAST

Burt Simpson	Dabney Coleman
Ernie Dills	Matt Frewer
Carolyn Simpson	Teri Garr
Captain	Barry Corbin
Scalese	Joe Pantoliano
Stark	Xander Berkeley
Dan Miller	Rob Roy
Dougie Simpson	Kaj-Erik Eriksen
Vito	Tony Pantages
Hostage Man	Sam Malkin
Coffin Salesman	Wes Tritter
Michael Lutz	Kim Kondrashoff
Jonas Lutz	Paul Jarrett
Spivak	Deejay Jackson
Dr. Goldman	Paul Batten
Dr. Drexler	Kevin McNulty
Older Dougie	Shawn Clements
Clerk	Betty Phillips
Elderly Man	Jack Ammon
Elderly Woman	Enid Saunders
Car Salesman	Dwight Koss
Waiter	Russell J. Roberts
Psychiatrist	Meredith Bain Woodward
Nurses	Brenda Crichlow, Gillian Barber
Priest	J. McRee Elrod
Stark's Cohorts	Tony Morelli, Gene Heck
Sidewalk Preacher	Jack Bastow
Soap Opera Policewoman	Beverley Henry
Soap Opera Man	Peter Yunker
Soap Opera Woman	Kimelly Anne Warren
Hospital Cop	Jack Little
Helicopter Pilot	Steven J. Wright

© *Gladden Entertainment*

TALES FROM THE DARKSIDE
The Movie

(PARAMOUNT) Producers, Richard P. Rubinstein, Mitchell Galin; Director, John Harrison; Co-Producer, David R. Kappes; Photography, Robert Draper; *Lot 249* Screenplay, Michael McDowell, inspired by a story by Sir Arthur Conan Doyle; *Cat From Hell* Screenplay, George A. Romero, based on a story by Stephen King; *Lover's Vow* Screenplay, Michael McDowell; Designer, Ruth Ammon; Editor, Harry B. Miller III; Special Make-up Effects, K.N.B. EFX Group; Make-up Effects Consultant, Dick Smith; Casting, Julie Mossberg, Brian Chavanne; Music: Donald A. Rubinstein *(Wraparound Story)*, Jim Manzie, Pat Regan *(Lot 249)*, Chaz Jankel *(Cat From Hell)*, John Harrison *(Lover's Vow);* Costumes, Ida Gearson; Special Effects, Drew Jiritano; Dolby Stereo; Technicolor; Rated R; 93 minutes; May release

CAST

The Wraparound Story

Betty	Deborah Harry
Priest	David Forrester
Timmy	Matthew Lawrence

Lot 249

Andy	Christian Slater
Lee	Robert Sedgwick
Bellingham	Steve Buscemi
Moving Man	Donald Van Horn
Mummy	Michael Deak
Susan	Julianne Moore
Museum Director	George Guidall
Dean	Kathleen Chalfant
Cabbie	Ralph Marrero

Cat From Hell

Halston	David Johansen
Cabbie	Paul Greeno
Drogan	William Hickey
Carolyn	Alice Drummond
Amanda	Delores Sutton
Gage	Mark Margolis

Lover's Vow

Preston	James Remar
Jer	Ashton Wise
Maddox	Philip Lenkowsky
Wyatt	Robert Klein
Carola	Rae Dawn Chong
Cops	Joe Dabenigno, Larry Silvestri
Gallery Patron	Donna Davidge
Margaret	Nicole Leach
John	Daniel Harrison

Michael Deak, Christian Slater Above: David Johansen

LONGTIME COMPANION

(SAMUEL GOLDWYN CO.) Producer, Stan Wlodkowski; Executive Producer, Lindsay Law; Director, Norman René; Screenplay, Craig Lucas; Co-Producer, Lydia Dean Pilcher; Photography, Tony Jannelli; Music, Greg DeBelles; Song: *Post-Mortem Bar* written and performed by Zane Campbell; Designer, Andrew Jackness; Editor, Katherine Wenning; Costumes, Walker Hicklin; Casting, Jason Lapadura, Natalie Hart; Assistant Director, Howard McMaster; American Playhouse Theatrical Films presentation; DuArt Color; Rated R; 100 minutes; May release

CAST

Willy	Campbell Scott
Fuzzy	Stephen Caffrey
Sean	Mark Lamos
David	Bruce Davison
Paul	John Dossett
Howard	Patrick Cassidy
Lisa	Mary-Louise Parker
Michael	Michael Schoeffling
Bob	Brian Cousins
John	Dermot Mulroney
Waiter	Brad O'Hare
Henry	Pi Douglass
Martin	Keith Charles
Walter	Dan Butler
Soap Actress	Alexandra Neil
Soap Actor	Brent Barrett
Man with soap script	Kelly Connell
Triage Nurse	Hazel J. Medina
Dr. Seth	Bajika Puri
Office Manager	Tanya Berezin
Rochelle	Welker White
Office Workers	Michael Pointek, Joyce Reehling
Heroin Addict	Annie Golden
Nurse with addict	Freda Foh Shen
Disco Bartender	Eric Gutierrez
Restaurant Bartender	Phillip Moon
Soap Opera Reader	Marceline Hugot
Casting Director	Margo Skinner
Transvestite	Robi Martin
Ron	Robert Joy
Paul's Doctor	Tony Shalhoub
Gym Instructor	Sam Silver
GMHC Volunteer	David Drake
Alberto	Michael Carmine
Finger Lakes Trio	Melora Creager, Jesse Hultberg, Lee Kimble

Top: Bruce Davison, Campbell Scott Below: Patrick Cassidy Left: Mark Lamos, Dermot Mulroney, Davison
© *Samuel Goldwyn Co.*

Campbell Scott, Stephen Caffrey

Stephen Caffrey, Michael Schoeffling, Mary-Louise Parker, Campbell Scott

A SHOW OF FORCE

(PARAMOUNT) Producer, John Strong; Executive Producer, Raymond Chow; Co-Producer, Fred Weintraub; Director, Bruno Barreto; Screenplay, Evan Jones, John Strong; Based on the book "*Murder under Two Flags*" by Anne Nelson; Executive in Charge of Production, Thomas K. Gray; Photography, James Glennon; Designer, William J. Cassidy; Music, Georges Delerue; Editor, Henry Richardson; Costumes, Kathryn Morrison-Pahoa; Casting, Pamela Rack; Assistant Director, John O'Connor; Presented in association with Golden Harvest; Dolby Stereo; Technicolor; Rated R; 93 minutes; May release

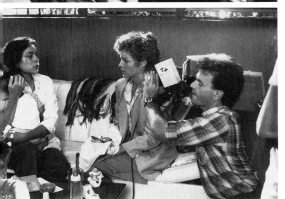

CAST

Kate Ryan de Melendez	Amy Irving
Luis Angel Mora	Andy Garcia
Jesus Fuentes	Lou Diamond Phillips
Howard Baslin	Robert Duvall
Frank Curtin	Kevin Spacey
Machado	Erik Estrada
Captain Correa	Juan Fernandez
Pepita	Lupe Ontiveros
Julio Dominquez	Leon Singer
Alice Ryan	Priscilla Pointer
Foster	Hattie Winston
Walker Ryan	Joe Campanella
Asencio	Jorge Luis Ramos
Fernando Quinones	Fernando Quinones
Carla De Ruiz	Claribel Medina
Felicia	Marilyn Sanabria
Jorge Rey	Michel Corbiere
Alfredo Ruiz	Tony Chiroldes Carbia
Senators	Roger Pretto, Jaime Montilla, Luis Llanos
Senate President	Daniel Fern
Governor Villanueva	Luis G. Oquendo
Juanito	Kidany Lugo
Sophie	Alexa Jacobs
Reporter	Ramon Saldana
Crazy Lady	Cira Hernandez
Jorge Alberta Rey	James M. Maloy
Boy/Kid Fuentes	Josue Rodriguez
Domingo	John Garcia
Martin	Javier O Del Valle

and Luigi Rivera (Opposition Senator), Luz Minerva Rodriguez (Head Nurse), Jorge Castillo (Nestor Chavez), Victor Arrillaga (Jaime), Mery C. Gray (Lila Torres), Walter Rodriguez (Espano), Tinno Acosta (Prison Guard), Robert Shuman (Dr. Martin), Samuel Molina (Dr. Pablo Salazar), Esther Mari (Woman in cemetery), Robert Vigorequx (Newsman), Gil Raldiris Aguayo (Police Photographer), Jose Maldonado (Priest), Joe Fitos, Carlos Miranda (Thugs)

Erik Estrada, Andy Garcia Above: Claribel Medina,
Amy Irving

BIRD ON A WIRE

(UNIVERSAL) Producer, Rob Cohen; Director, John Badham; Executive Producers, Ted Field, Robert W. Cort; Screenplay, David Seltzer, Louis Venosta, Eric Lerner; Story, Louis Venosta, Eric Lerner; Photography, Robert Primes; Designer, Philip Harrison; Editors, Frank Morriss, Dallas Puett; Co-Producers, Fitch Cady, Louis Venosta, Eric Lerner; Music, Hans Zimmer; Costumes, Wayne Finkelman, Eduardo Castro; Casting, Mike Fenton, Judy Taylor, Lynda Gordon, Lynne Carrow; Associate Producers, Dana Satler, Keith Rubinstein; Assistant Director, Peter Marshall; Stunts, Mic Rodgers, Betty Thomas; a Badham/Cohen-Interscope Communications production; Dolby Stereo; System 35 Widescreen; Deluxe color; Rated PG-13; 113 minutes; May release

CAST

Rick Jarmin	Mel Gibson
Marianne Graves	Goldie Hawn
Eugene Sorenson	David Carradine
Albert Diggs	Bill Duke
Joe Weyburn	Stephen Tobolowsky
Rachel Varney	Joan Severance
Marvin	Harry Caesar
Lou Baird	Jeff Corey
Raun	Alex Bruhanski
Jamie	John Pyper-Ferguson
Mr. Takawaki	Clyde Kusatsu
Paul Bernard	Jackson Davies
Molly Baird	Florence Paterson
Paul	Tim Healy
Scottie	Wes Tritter
Lossen	Lossen Chambers
Neff	Ken Camroux
Secretary	Wendy Van Riesen
Night Receptionist	Lesley Ewen
Dex	Robert Metcalfe
Brad	Kevin McNulty
Bank Teller	Robert Thurston
Bank Vice-President	Brian Torpe
Bank Guard	Oscar Goncalves
Beggar	Tim Price
Cop at fire	Oscar Ramos
Fireman	Dan Zale
Plainclothesman	Blu Mankuma
Cop at cafe	Doug Judge
Nikita Knatz	Jon Garber
Carl Laemmle	Paul Jarrett
Underworld Boss	James Kidnie
Guard at gate	Kim Kondrashoff
Maitre d'	Michel Barbe
Sales Clerk	Maria Leone
Cement Worker	Danny Wattley

**Top: Mel Gibson, Goldie Hawn Below: Blu Mankuma, Gibson
Right: David Carradine; Bill Duke**
© *Universal City Studios*

Mel Gibson, Goldie Hawn

Mel Gibson, Joan Severance

48

Robin Williams, Pamela Reed Top Right: Williams, Tim
Robbins Right: Williams, Fran Drescher, Zack Norman
© Orion Pictures Corp.

CADILLAC MAN

(ORION) Producers, Charles Roven, Roger Donaldson; Director,
Roger Donaldson; Screenplay, Ken Friedman; Photography, David
Gribble; Designer, Gene Rudolf; Editor, Richard Francis-Bruce; Cos-
tumes, Deborah La Gorce Kramer; Music, J. Peter Robinson; Associate
Producer, Ted Kurdyla; Casting, David Rubin; Assistant Director,
Lewis Gould; Donaldson/Roven-Cavallo Production; Dolby Stereo;
Deluxe Color; Rated R; 95 minutes; May release

CAST

Joey O'Brien	Robin Williams
Larry	Tim Robbins
Tina O'Brien	Pamela Reed
Joy Munchack	Fran Drescher
Harry Munchack	Zack Norman
Donna	Annabella Sciorra
Lila	Lori Petty
Little Jack Turgeon	Paul Guilfoyle
Big Jack Turgeon	Bill Nelson
Benny	Eddie Jones
Ma	Mimi Cecchini
Lisa	Tristine Skyler
Molly	Judith Hoag
Helen—Dim Sum Girl	Lauren Tom
Captain Mason	Anthony Powers
Tony Dipino	Paul Herman
Henry	Paul J. Q. Lee
Funeral Director	Jim Bulleit
Davey	Erik King
Frankie Dipino	Richard Panebianco
Detective Walters	Gary H. Klar
Soviet Husband	Boris Leskin
Soviet Wife	Elzbieta Czyzewska
Korean Customer	Benjamin B. Lin
Korean Wife	Wai Ching Ho
Hearse Driver	William Hugh Collins
Grave Digger	Bill Nunn
Louie	Vinnie Capone
Antique Salesman	Bill Moor
Dim Sum Cook	Kim Chan
Widow	Elaine Stritch

and Mario Todisco, Max, Kenneth Simmons (Steel Jaws), Bunny
Levine (Woman Customer), Carmen A. Mathis (Police Woman), Har-
lan Cary Poe (Mason's Aid), Jordan Derwin (Paramedic), Philip Moon
(Nightclub Selector), Sal Lioni (Nightclub Customer), Brian Sanet
(Paparazzi), Merwin Goldsmith (Showroom Buyer), Richard Mark
Arnold (Porsche Buyer), Marilyn Dobrin (Porsche Buyer's Wife),
David Stepkin (Maroni), Matt Nikko, Keenan Shimizu, Tony Masa,
Ken Kensei, Toshio Sato (Japanese Buyers), Chester Drescher (Ches-
ter)

Pamela Reed, Lori Petty, Fran Drescher Above: Tim Robbins,
Robin Williams, Drescher, Zack Norman

49

Christopher Lloyd, Michael J. Fox Top Right: Mary
Steenburgen, Lloyd Below: Lloyd
© *Universal City Studios*

BACK TO THE FUTURE PART III

(UNIVERSAL) Producers, Bob Gale, Neil Canton; Executive Produc-
ers, Steven Spielberg, Frank Marshall, Kathleen Kennedy; Director,
Robert Zemeckis; Screenplay, Bob Gale; Story, Robert Zemeckis, Bob
Gale; Photography, Dean Cundey; Designer, Rick Carter; Editors,
Arthur Schmidt, Harry Keramidas; Music, Alan Silvestri; Song:
"Doubleback" written and performed by ZZ Top; Costumes, Joanna
Johnston; Associate Producer, Steve Starkey; Casting, Mike Fenton,
Judy Taylor, Valorie Massalas; Assistant Director, David McGiffert;
Visual Effects Supervisors, Ken Ralston, Scott Farrar; Stunts, Walter
Scott; Special Effects, Industrial Light & Magic; Amblin Entertainment
production; Dolby Stereo; Deluxe Color; Rated PG; 118 minutes; May
release

CAST

Marty McFly/Seamus McFly	Michael J. Fox
Dr. Emmett Brown	Christopher Lloyd
Clara Clayton	Mary Steenburgen
Buford "Mad Dog" Tannen/Biff Tannen	Thomas F. Wilson
Maggie McFly/Lorraine McFly	Lea Thompson
Jennifer	Elisabeth Shue
Bartender	Matt Clark
Barbwire Salesman	Richard Dysart
Saloon Old Timers	Pat Buttram, Harry Carey, Jr., Dub Taylor
Marshal Strickland	James Tolkan
Dave McFly	Marc McClure
Linda McFly	Wendie Jo Sperber
George McFly	Jeffrey Weissman
Buford Tannen's Gang	Christopher Wynne, Sean Gregory Sullivan, Mike Watson
Mayor	Hugh Gillin
Colt Gun Salesman	Burton Gilliam
Engineer	Bill McKinney
Deputy	Donovan Scott
Needles	Flea
Needles' Gang	J. J. Cohen, Ricky Dean Logan
Mortician	Marvin J. McIntyre
Strickland's Son	Kaleb Henley
Jules	Todd Cameron Brown
Verne	Dannel Evans
Celebration Man	Leslie A. Prickett
Photographer	Dean Cundey
Pie Lady	Jo B. Cummings
Festival Men	Steve McArthur, John Ickes
Festival Dance Caller	James A. Rammel
Townsmen	Michael Klastorin, Michael John Mills, Kenny Myers
Eyepatch	Brad McPeters
Toothless	Phinnaes D.
Ticket Agent	Rod Kuehne
Conductor	Leno Fletcher
Joey	Joey Newington
Train Fireman	Larry Ingold
Barbwire Salesman's Companion	Tim Konrad
Boy with gun	Glenn Fox
Copernicus	Foster
Einstein	Freddie
Musicians	ZZ Top

Lea Thompson, Michael J. Fox Above: Thomas F. Wilson, Fox

ANOTHER 48 HRS.

(PARAMOUNT) Producers, Lawrence Gordon, Robert D. Wachs; Director, Walter Hill; Screenplay, John Fasano, Jeb Stuart, Larry Gross; Story, Fred Braughton; Executive Producers, Mark Lipsky, Ralph S. Singleton; Photography, Matthew F. Leonetti; Designer, Joseph C. Nemec III; Editors, Freeman Davies, Carmel Davies, Donn Aron; Costumes, Dan Moore; Co-Producer, D. Constantine Conte; Music, James Horner; Associate Producers, Raymond L. Murphy, Jr., Kenneth H. Frith, Jr.; Casting, Jackie Burch; Assistant Director, James R. Dyer; presented in association with Eddie Murphy productions; Dolby Stereo; Technicolor; Rated R; 98 minutes; June release

CAST

Reggie Hammond	Eddie Murphy
Jack Cates	Nick Nolte
Ben Kehoe	Brion James
Blake Wilson	Kevin Tighe
Frank Cruise	Ed O'Ross
Willie Hickok	David Anthony Marshall
Cherry Ganz	Andrew Divoff
Kirkland Smith	Bernie Casey
Tyrone Burroughs	Brent Jennings
Malcolm Price	Ted Markland
Amy Kirkland	Tisha Campbell
Warden	Felice Orlandi
Detective Joe Stevens	Edward Walsh
Angel Lee	Page Leong
Girl Bartender	Cathy Haase
Barroom Tough	Dennis Hayden
Diner Waitress	Kelly Goodman
Desert Bartender	Hoke Howell
CHP Officers	Yana Nirvana, Ken Medlock
Mechanic	John Del Regno
Pit Man	Joel Weiss
Lawyer	Oz Tortora
Review Board Chairman	John Bluto
Prison Guard Ronard	Jason Ronard
Prison Guard Morgan	Stafford Morgan
Prison Guard Dunnam	Bill Dunnam
Prison Clerk	Thornton Simmons
Doctors	Nancy Everhard, Mark Phelan
County Sheriffs	Biff Yeager, John H. Evans
Traffic Cop	Rick Cicetti
Pickpocket	Laurie Morrison
Pickpocket Victim	Steve Monroe
Barroom Fighters	Dave Efron, Rex Pierson
Second Bartender	Judy Lea
Restroom Girls	Dawn Tshombe, Cigi, Nanci Rogers, Deborah Atkinson
King Mei Clerks	Karen Huie, Benjamin Lum
Hotel Guest	George Cheung
Arguing Men	Dana Lee, Richard Lee-Sung
Girl in movie	Kitten Natividad
Morgue Attendant	Jerome Holmes
District Attorney	Victor E. Brandt
Judge	Edgar Small
Doorman	Russ McCubbin
Elevator Operator	Linda Cox
Birdcage Showgirl	Alisa Christensen

and Michael Williams, Rodney Shelton, Jake Hunter, Ray Fuller, Del Atkins, David McLaurin (Bar Band), Deirdre Fitzpatrick, Lauren Grey, Nicole Cummins (Birdcage Waitresses)

Top: Nick Nolte, Eddie Murphy
Below: David Anthony Marshall
© *Paramount Pictures*

Nick Nolte Above: Nolte, Eddie Murphy

TOTAL RECALL

(TRI-STAR) Producers, Buzz Feitshans, Ronald Shusett; Director, Paul Verhoeven; Screenplay, Ronald Shusett, Dan O'Bannon, Gary Goldman; Story, Ronald Shusett, Dan O'Bannon, Jon Povill; Inspired by the short story *"We Can Remember It for You Wholesale"* by Phillip K. Dick; Executive Producers, Mario Kassar, Andrew Vajna; Photography, Jost Vacano; Special Makeup Effects Designer and Creator, Rob Bottin; Designer, William Sandell; Editor, Frank J. Urioste; Costumes, Erica Edell Phillips; Music, Jerry Goldsmith; Associate Producers, Elliot Schick, Robert Fentress; Casting, Mike Fenton, Judy Taylor, Valorie Masslas; Special Visual Effects, Dream Quest Images; Visual Effects Supervisor, Eric Brevig; Miniatures, Stetson Visual Services, Inc.; Optical Effects, Industrial Light & Magic; Stunts, Vic Armstrong, Joel Kramer; a Carolco/Ronald Shusett Production; Dolby Stereo; Technicolor; Rated R; 109 minutes; June release

CAST

Doug Quaid	Arnold Schwarzenegger
Melina	Rachel Ticotin
Lori	Sharon Stone
Cohaagen	Ronny Cox
Richter	Michael Ironside
George/Kuato	Marshall Bell
Benny	Mel Johnson, Jr.
Helm	Michael Champion
Dr. Edgemar	Roy Brocksmith
McClane	Ray Baker
Dr. Lull	Rosemary Dunsmore
Ernie	David Knell
Tiffany	Alexia Robinson
Tony	Dean Norris
Bartender	Mark Carlton
Thumbelina	Debbie Lee Carrington
Mary	Lycia Naff
Harry	Bobby Costanzo
Stevens	Michael LaGuardia
Fat Lady	Priscilla Allen
Immigration Officer	Ken Strausbaugh
Everett	Marc Alaimo
Rebel Lieutenant	Michael Gregory
Hotel Clerk	Ken Gilden
Burly Miner	Mickey Jones
Martian Husband	Parker Whitman
Martian Wife	Ellen Gollas
Woman in phone booth	Gloria Dorson
Miss Lonelyhearts	Erika Carlson
Punk Cabbie	Benny Corral
Doctor	Bob Tzudiker
Lab Assistant	Erik Cord
Technician	Frank Kopyc
Scientists	Chuck Sloan, Dave Nicolson
Newscaster	Paula McClure
Reporter	Rebecca Ruth
Commercial Announcer	Milt Tarver
Agent	Roger Cudney
Mutant Mother	Monica Steuer
Mutant Child	Sasha Rionda
Tennis Pro	Linda Howell
Voice of Johnnycab	Robert Picardo

© *Tri-Star Pictures*
Top: Arnold Schwarzenegger Below: Ronny Cox, Schwarzenegger
1990 Academy Award for Best Special Visual Effects

Rachel Ticotin, Arnold Schwarzenegger Above: Schwarzenegger, Ray Baker, Rosemary Dunsmore

Arnold Schwarzenegger (also above)

Arnold Schwarzenegger

Michael Ironside, Dean Norris, Debbie Lee Carrington Above
Left: Arnold Schwarzenegger, Sharon Stone

Arnold Schwarzenegger, Rachel Ticotin Above Right:
Schwarzenegger, Mel Johnson

DICK TRACY

(TOUCHSTONE) Producer/Director, Warren Beatty; Executive Producers, Barrie M. Osborne, Art Linson, Floyd Mutrux; Screenplay, Jim Cash, Jack Epps, Jr.; Based on characters created by Chester Gould for the Dick Tracy Comic Strip distributed by Tribune Media Services, Inc.; Photography, Vittorio Storaro; Designer, Richard Sylbert; Co-Producer, Jon Landau; Editor, Richard Marks; Costumes, Milena Canonero; Casting, Jackie Burch; Original Songs, Stephen Sondheim; Music, Danny Elfman; Musical Numbers Staged by Jeffrey Hornaday; Visual Effects, Michael Lloyd, Harrison Ellenshaw; Associate Producer/Assistant Director, Jim Van Wyck; Special Character Makeup, John Caglione, Jr., Doug Drexler; Produced in association with Silver Screen Partners IV; Distributed by Buena Vista Pictures; Dolby Stereo; Technicolor; Rated PG; 110 minutes; June release

CAST

Dick Tracy	Warren Beatty
Kid	Charlie Korsmo
McGillicuddy	Michael Donovan O'Donnell
Stooge	Jim Wilkey
Shoulders	Stig Eldred
The Rodent	Neil Summers
The Brow	Chuck Hicks
Little Face	Lawrence Steven Meyers
Flattop	William Forsythe
Itchy	Ed O'Ross
Tess Trueheart	Glenne Headly
Soprano	Marvelee Cariaga
Baritone	Michael Gallup
Sam Catchem	Seymour Cassel
Pat Patton	James Keane
Chief Brandon	Charles Durning
Reporters	Allen Garfield, John Schuck, Charles Fleischer
Breathless Mahoney	Madonna
88 Keys	Mandy Patinkin
Lips Manlis	Paul Sorvino
Lips' Bodyguard	Robert Costanzo
Customer at raid	Jack Kehoe
Lips' Cop	Marshall Bell
Doorman	Michael G. Hagerty
Lefty Moriarty	Lew Horn
Diner Patron	Arthur Malet
Mike	Tom Signorelli
Steve the Tramp	Tony Epper
Big Boy Caprice	Al Pacino
Numbers	James Tolkan
Pruneface	R. G. Armstrong
Mumbles	Dustin Hoffman
Mrs. Green	Kathy Bates
Lab Technicians	Jack Goode, Jr., Ray Stoddard
D. A. Fletcher	Dick Van Dyke
Store Clerk	Hamilton Camp
Cops at Tess'	Ed McCready, Colm Meaney
Texie Garcia	Catherine O'Hara
Influence	Henry Silva
Ribs Mocca	Robert Beecher
Spaldoni	James Caan
Bartender	Bert Remsen
Judge Harper	Frank Campanella
Club Ritz Patrons	Sharmagne Leland-St. John, Bing Russell
Bug Bailey	Michael J. Pollard
Uniform Cop at Ritz	Tom Finnegan
Newspaper Vendor	Billy Clevenger
Radio Announcers	Ned Claflin, John Moschitta, Jr., Neil Ross, Walker Edmiston
Mrs. Trueheart	Estelle Parsons
Forger	Ian Wolfe
Welfare Person	Mary Woronov
Night Clerk	Henry Jones
Old Man at hotel	Mike Mazurki

and Rita Bland, Lada Boder, Dee Hengstler, Liz Imperio, Michelle Johnston, Karyne Ortega, Karen Russell (Dancers)

© *Touchstone Pictures*
Top: Charlie Korsmo, Warren Beatty
Below: Madonna, Al Pacino

1990 Academy Awards for Best Art Direction, Make-Up, and Original Song ("Sooner or Later")

James Tolkan, William Forsythe, Warren Beatty, Al Pacino, Ed O'Ross Above: Beatty

Warren Beatty

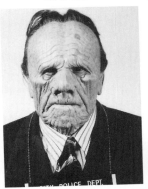

Ed O'Ross Above: Mandy Patinkin, Madonna

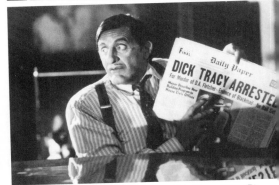

William Forsythe Above Left: Glenne Headly, Warren Beatty

Al Pacino Above: R. G. Armstrong (L); Henry Silva (R)

55

GREMLINS 2
The New Batch

(WARNER BROS.) Producer, Michael Finnell; Executive Producers, Steven Spielberg, Kathleen Kennedy, Frank Marshall; Director, Joe Dante; Screenplay, Charlie Haas; Co-Producer/Gremlins and Mogwai Effects Supervisor, Rick Baker; Photography, John Hora; Music, Jerry Goldsmith; Designer, James Spencer; Editor, Kent Beyda; Costumes, Rosanna Norton; Casting, Marion Dougherty, Glenn Daniels; Assistant Director, Victor Hsu; Sound Effects, Mark Mangini, David Stone; Visual Effects Supervisor, Dennis Michelson; an Amblin Entertainment Picture; Dolby Stereo; Technicolor; Rated PG-13; 106 minutes; June release

CAST

Billy Peltzer	Zach Galligan
Kate Beringer	Phoebe Cates
Daniel Clamp	John Glover
Grandpa Fred	Robert Prosky
Forster	Robert Picardo
Dr. Catheter	Christopher Lee
Marla Bloodstone	Haviland Morris
Murray Futterman	Dick Miller
Sheila Futterman	Jackie Joseph
Katsuji	Gedde Watanabe
Mr. Wing	Keye Luke
Microwave Marge	Kathleen Freeman
Martin	Don Stanton
Lewis	Dan Stanton
Wally	Shawn Nelson
Forster's Technicians	Archie Hahn, Leslie Neale, Ron Fassler, Time Winters
Yogurt Jerks	Heather Haase, Jason Presson
Yogurt Customers	Lisa Menda, Patrika Darbo, Jerry Goldsmith
Security Guard	Rick Ducommun
Fire Chief	John Capodice
Movie Theatre Mom	Belinda Balaski
Movie Theatre Kid	Nicky Rose
Theatre Manager	Paul Bartel
Projectionist	Kenneth Tobey
TV Reporters	Heidi Kemp, Eric Shawn, Michael Salort
Cop	Frank P. Ryan
TV Reporter at Wing's	Diane Sainte-Marie
TV Anchor in bar	Kristi Witker
Reporter in lobby	Sarah Lilly
Taxi Driver	Vladimir Bibic
Tour Guides	Page Hannah, Liz Pryor
Janitor	John Astin
Fired Employee	Henry Gibson
Messenger	Raymond Cruz
Lab Receptionist	Julia Sweeney
Forster's Assistant	Jeff Swanson
Casper	Charlie Haas

and Dale Swann (Surveillance Supervisor), Gray Daniels (TV Cameraman), Stephanie Menuez (Clamp's Secretary), Jacque Lynn Colton (Lady at elevator), May Quigley, Anthony Winters (Hallway Employees), Isiah Whitlock, Jr. (Fireman), Dean Norris (Swat Team Leader), Saachiko (Newsstand Lady), Hulk Hogan, Dick Butkus, Bubba Smith (Themselves); Voices: Howie Mandel (Gizmo), Tony Randall ("Brain" Gremlin), Frank Welker (Mohawk), Kirk Thatcher, Mark Dodson (Gremlins), Neil Ross (Announcer), Jeff Bergman (Bugs Bunny and Daffy Duck)

Top: Zach Galligan, Gizmo Below: Robert Prosky
© *Warner Bros.*

Daffy, Kathleen Freeman Above: John Glover

ROBOCOP 2

(ORION) Producer, Jon Davison; Director, Irvin Kershner; Story,
Frank Miller; Screenplay, Frank Miller, Walon Green; Based on
characters created by Edward Neumeier, Michael Miner; Executive
Producer, Patrick Crowley; Photography, Mark Irwin; Designer, Peter
Jamison; Music, Leonard Rosenman; Supervising Editor, William An-
derson; Casting, Sally Dennison, Julie Selzer, Justine Jacoby; Assistant
Director, Tom Davies; Robocop 2 Animation Sequences, Phil Tippett;
Robocop Designer/Creator, Rob Bottin; Costumes, Rosanna Norton;
Associate Producers, Jane Bartelme, Phil Tippett; Stunts, Conrad E.
Palmisano; Special Effects Supervisors, Dale Martin, William Greg
Curtis; a Tobor Picture; Dolby Stereo; Deluxe color; Rated R; 118
minutes; June release

CAST

Robocop	Peter Weller
Anne Lewis	Nancy Allen
Donald Johnson	Felton Perry
Sgt. Reed	Robert DoQui
Cain	Tom Noonan
Dr. Juliette Faxx	Belinda Bauer
Mayor Kuzak	Willard Pugh
Hob	Gabriel Damon
Angie	Galyn Gorg
Old Man	Daniel O'Herlihy
Duffy	Stephen Lee
Whittaker	Roger Aaron Brown
Lab Technician Garcia	Patricia Charbonneau
Holzgang	Jeff McCarthy
Estevez	Wanda De Jesus
Schenk	John Doolittle
Delaney	Ken Lerner
Tak Akita	Tzi Ma
Sunblock Woman	Fabiana Udenio
Magnavolt Salesman	John Glover
Casey Wong	Mario Machado
Gillette	George Cheung
Catzo	Michael Medeiros

and Leeza Gibbons (Jess Perkins), John Ingle (Surgeon General), Mark
Rolston (Stef), Phil Rubenstein (Poulos), Lila Finn (Old Woman), John
Hateley (Purse Snatcher), Gage Tarrant (Hooker), Tommy Rosales
(Chet), Brandon Smith (Flint), Wallace Merck (Gun Shop Owner),
Dick Hancock (Checkers), Linda Thompson (Mother with baby), Lily
Chen (Desperate Woman), Clinton Austin Shirley (Jimmy Murphy),
Jimmy Pickens (Mesnick), Eric Glenn (Injured Cop), Richard Reyes,
Charles Bailey, Jo Perkins, Erik Cord (Angry Citizens), Martin Casella
(Yuppie), Gary Bullock (Hack Doctor), Bill Bolender (Cabbie), Wayne
De Hart (Vendor), Yogi Baird (Contortionist), Jerry Nelson (Darren
Thomas), Michael Weller, Woody Watson (OCP Security), Rutherford
Cravens, Christopher Quinten (Reporters), Ed Geldhart (Electronics
Store Owner), David Dwyer (Little League Coach), Adam Faraizl
(Little League Kid), James McQueens (Dr. Weltman), Cynthia Mackey
(Surgeon), Justin Seidner (Brat)

Ally Sheedy, Alan Alda, Molly Ringwald, Dylan Walsh,
Madeline Kahn Top Left: Ringwald, Alda
Left: Catherine O'Hara; Joey Bishop
© *Buena Vista*

BETSY'S WEDDING

(TOUCHSTONE) Producers, Martin Bregman, Louis A. Stroller; Director/Screenplay, Alan Alda; Photography, Kelvin Pike; Designer, John Jay Moore; Editor, Michael Polakow; Costumes, Mary Malin; Music, Bruce Broughton; Casting, Mary Colquhoun; Assistant Director, Yudi Bennett; Associate Producer, Michael Scott Bregman; Presented in association with Silver Screen Partners IV; Distributed by Buena Vista Pictures; Dolby Stereo; Technicolor; Rated R; 94 minutes; June release

CAST

Eddie Hopper	Alan Alda
Eddie's Father	Joey Bishop
Lola Hopper	Madeline Kahn
Stevie Dee	Anthony LaPaglia
Gloria Henner	Catherine O'Hara
Oscar Henner	Joe Pesci
Betsy Hopper	Molly Ringwald
Connie Hopper	Ally Sheedy
Georgie	Burt Young
Grandma	Julie Bovasso
Henry Lovell	Nicolas Coster
Nancy Lovell	Bibi Besch
Jake Lovell	Dylan Walsh
Angelica	Camille Saviola
Nate Tobias	Allan Rich
Morris (Lola's Dad)	Sully Boyar
Joy	Monica Carr
Zack Monroe	Frankie R. Faison
Dave Delahaas	Tom Mardirosian
Barber	Larry Block
Fitter	Helen Hanft
Bandleader (Video)	J. K. Loftin
Anselmo (Bodyguard)	Mario Todisco
Plumber	Paul B. Mixon
Caterer	William Duff-Griffin
Man at wedding	Thomas John Caligiuri
Taxi Dispatcher (Mickey)	Samuel L. Jackson
Georgie's Companion	Janet Pasquale

Burt Young; Anthony LaPaglia Above: Molly Ringwald,
Dylan Walsh

58

DAYS OF THUNDER

(PARAMOUNT) Producers, Don Simpson, Jerry Bruckheimer; Director, Tony Scott; Screenplay, Robert Towne; Story, Robert Towne, Tom Cruise; Unit Production Manager/Executive Producer, Gerald R. Molen; Photography, Ward Russell; Art Directors, Benjamin Fernandez, Thomas E. Sanders; Editors, Billy Weber, Chris Lebezon; Music, Hans Zimmer; Costumes, Susan Becker; Casting, David Rubin; Assistant Director, James W. Skotchdopole; Racing Consultant, Dan Greenwood; Stunts, Gary McCarty; Dolby Stereo; Technicolor; Panavision; Rated PG-13; 105 minutes; June release

CAST

Cole Trickle	Tom Cruise
Harry Hogge	Robert Duvall
Dr. Claire Lewicki	Nicole Kidman
Tim Daland	Randy Quaid
Russ Wheeler	Cary Elwes
Rowdy Burns	Michael Rooker
Big John	Fred Dalton Thompson
Buck Bretherton	John C. Reilly
Waddell	J. C. Quinn
Aldo Bennedetti	Don Simpson
Jennie Burns	Caroline Williams
Darlene	Donna Wilson
Harlan Hoogerhyde	Chris Ellis
Cole's Crew	Peter Appel, Stephen Michael Ayers, Mike Slattery
Len Dortort	John Griesemer
Lauren Daland	Barbara Garrick
Dr. Wilhaire	Jerry Molen
Russ Wheeler's Girlfriend	Tania Coleridge
Autograph Fan	Alexandra Balahoutis
NASCAR Official	Steve Boyd
ESPN Announcer	Daniel D. Greenwood
Hardee's Pit Crew Chief	Jim Grimshaw
Field Doctor	James Martin, Jr.
Donna	Margo Martindale
Young Doctor	Michael Burgess
Dr. Crowther	Jim Crowther
Doctor	James D. Henson, M.D.
Nurses	Cyndi Vicino, Shari Ellis
Highway Patrol Officers	Leilani Sarelle, Nick Searcy
Orderly	Xavier Coronel
Aldo's Girlfriend	Jamie Johnson
Themselves	Dr. Jerry Punch, Neil Bonnett, Harry P. Grant, Rusty Wallace

Top: Tom Cruise, Robert Duvall Below: Michael Rooker,
Cruise Left: Nicole Kidman, Cruise
© Paramount Pictures

Donna Wilson, Robert Duvall, Chris Ellis, John C. Reilly

Cary Elwes, Robert Duvall, Tom Cruise

DIE HARD 2

(20th CENTURY FOX) Producers, Lawrence Gordon, Joel Silver, Charles Gordon; Director, Renny Harlin; Screenplay, Steven E. de Souza, Doug Richardson; Based on the novel "58 Minutes" by Walter Wager, and certain original characters created by Roderick Thorpe; Co-Producer, Steve Perry; Photography, Oliver Wood; Designer, John Vallone; Supervising Editor, Stuart Baird; Executive Producers, Lloyd Levin, Michael Levy; Music, Michael Kamen; Costumes, Marilyn Vance-Straker; Casting, Jackie Burch; Assistant Director, Terry Miller; Stunts/2nd Unit Director, Charles Picerni; Associate Producer, Suzanne Todd; Special Effects Supervisor, Michael J. McAlister; Visual Effects, Industrial Light & Magic; a Gordon Company/Silver Pictures production; Dolby Stereo; Panavision; Deluxe color; Rated R; 124 minutes; July release

CAST

John McClane	Bruce Willis
Holly McClane	Bonnie Bedelia
Dick Thornberg	William Atherton
Sgt. Al Powell	Reginald VelJohnson
Esperanza	Franco Nero
Col. Stuart	William Sadler
Capt. Grant	John Amos
Carmine Lorenzo	Dennis Franz
Barnes	Art Evans
Trudeau	Fred Dalton Thompson
Marvin	Tom Bower
Samantha Copeland	Sheila McCarthy
Garber	Don Harvey
Baker	Tony Ganios
Thompson	Peter Nelson
O'Reilly	Robert Patrick
Sheldon	Michael Cunningham
Burke	John Leguizamo
Kahn	Tom Verica
Cochrane	John Castelloe
Miller	Vondi Curtis Hall
Shockley	Mark Boone Junior
Mulkey	Ken Baldwin

and Danny Weselis, Gregg Kovan, Don Charles McGovern, Vincent Joseph Mazzella, Jr., Jeff Langton, Danial Donai, Bob "Rocky" Cheli, Dale Jacoby (Blue Light Team), Pat O'Neal (Corp. Telford), Ben Lemon, Jason Ross-Azikiwe (Sergeants), Anthony Droz (Soldier); Northeast Plane: Michael Francis Clarke (Pilot), Steve Pershing (Co-Pilot), Tom Everett (Navigator), Sherry Bilsing, Karla Tamburrelli (Stewardesses), Jeanne Bates (Older Woman); Windsor Plane: Colm Meany (Pilot), Steffen Gregory Foster (Co-Pilot), James Lancaster (Navigator), Amanda Hillwood, Felicity Waterman (Stewardesses), Alan Berger (Passenger), Jessica Gardner (Little Girl); Foreign Military Plane: Vance Valencia (Pilot), Gilbert Garcia (Co-Pilot), Julian Reyes (Young Corporal); WNTW: Richard Domeier (Cameraman), David Katz (Soundman), Robert Lipton (Chopper Pilot); WZDC: Robert Steinberg (Victor), Paul Abascal (Director), John Rubinow (Producer), Bob Braun, Dominique Jennings, Carl Barbee (Newscasters); Jerry E. Parrott, Robert Sacchi, Edward Gero, Robert J. Bennett, Jim Hudson, Thomas Tofel, Wynn Irwin, Ken Smolka, Martin Lowery, Dick McGarvin, Stafford Morgan, Nick Angotti, Tom Finnegan, Earl Bullock, Rande Scott (Engineers), Robert Costanzo (Vito Lorenzo), Lauren Letherer (Rent-a-Car Girl), Connie Lillo-Thieman (Information Booth Girl), Ed DeFusco (Morgue Worker), Charles Lanyer (Justice Man), Bill Smillie (Custodian), Dwayne Hargray (Luggage Worker), John Cade (Lobby Cop), Paul Bollen, Joseph Roth (Airport Cops), David Willis, Sr. (Tow Truck Driver)

Top: Bruce Willis, Bonnie Bedelia
Below: William Atherton, Robert Steinberg
© 20th Century Fox

Bruce Willis, Dennis Franz, Fred Dalton Thompson
Above: Willis

Bob Elliott, Bill Murray Top Left: Murray, Geena Davis,
Randy Quaid Left: Jason Robards, Richard Joseph Paul
© *Warner Bros.*

QUICK CHANGE

(WARNER BROS.) Producers, Robert Greenhut, Bill Murray; Directors, Howard Franklin, Bill Murray; Executive Producer, Frederic Golchan; Screenplay, Howard Franklin; Based on the book by Jay Cronley; Photography, Michael Chapman; Music, Randy Edelman; Editor, Alan Heim; Assistant Director, Thomas Reilly; Clown Makeup Designer, Peter Montagna; a Devoted Production; Dolby Stereo; Technicolor; Rated R; 87 minutes; July release

CAST

Grimm	Bill Murray
Phyllis	Geena Davis
Loomis	Randy Quaid
Chief Rotzinger	Jason Robards
Lt. Jameson	Richard Joseph Paul
Cab Driver	Tony Shalhoub
Bank Guard	Bob Elliott
Mr. Edison	Phil Hartman
Mrs. Edison	Kathryn Grody
Johnny	Stanley Tucci
Skelton	Victor Argo
Bus Driver	Philip Bosco
Mario	Gary Klar
Interrogating Policeman	Paul Herman
Russ Crane/Lombino	Kurtwood Smith
Mrs. Russ Crane/Lombino	Susannah Bianchi
Yuppie Hostage	Jack Gilpin
Bank Manager	Brian McConnachie
Mugger	Jamey Sheridan
Street Sign Workers	Anthony Bishop, Larry Joshua
Bus Rider with guitar	Stuart Rudin
Shut-up Lady	Michelle Lucien
Flower Lady	Teodorina Bello
T.V. Reporter	Randle Mell
Businessman in Mens Room	Ira Wheeler
Bicycle Jousters	Elliot Santiago, Manny Siverio
Grocery Cashier	Steve Park
Customer	Alfa-Betty Olsen
Police Artist	Jim Ward

and Dale Grand (Street Barker), Kimberleigh Aarn (Bank Teller), Ron Ryan (Bank Customer), Jordan Cael, Rhe DeVille, Marya Dornya, Barbara Flynn, Elizabeth A. Griffin, Connie Ivie, Skipp Lynch, J. D. Montalbo, Suzen Murakoshi, Anthony T. Paige, Jane Simms, Wendell Sweda, Angel Vargas (Hostages), Reg E. Cathey (Sound Analyst), William Sturgis (Forensic Detective), Sam Ayers (Esu Commander), Joe Pentangelo, Bill Raymond (Policemen), Tim Halligan, Deborah Lee Johnson, Lucia Vincent (Reporters), Bobby Harrigan (Fat Person), Gary Goodrow (Radio D.J.), Frank Maldonado, Ryan Mitchell (Kids at grocery), Davenia McFadden (Policewoman), Barton Heyman (Airport Security Guard), Justin Ross (Airline Clerk), Margo Skinner (Flight Attendant)

Geena Davis, Bill Murray, Randy Quaid Above: Murray, Davis

GHOST

(PARAMOUNT) Producer, Lisa Weinstein; Director, Jerry Zucker; Screenplay, Bruce Joel Rubin; Executive Producer, Steven-Charles Jaffe; Photography, Adam Greenberg; Designer, Jane Musky; Music, Maurice Jarre; Editor, Walter Murch; Costumes, Ruth Morley; Casting, Jane Jenkins, Janet Hirshenson; Associate Producer, Bruce Joel Rubin; Assistant Directors, Mark Radcliffe, John Hockridge; Pass-Through Visual Effects, Industrial Light & Magic; ILM Visual Effects Supervisor, Bruce Nicholson; Good Spirits and Dark Spirits Visual Effects Supervisors, John Van Vliet, Kathy Kean; a Howard W. Koch Production; Dolby Stereo; Technicolor; Rated PG-13; 127 minutes; July release

CAST

Sam Wheat	Patrick Swayze
Molly Jensen	Demi Moore
Carl Bruner	Tony Goldwyn
Elevator Men	Stanley Lawrence, Christopher J. Keene
Susan	Susan Breslau
Rose	Martina Degnan
Movers	Richard Kleber, Macka Foley
Willie Lopez	Rick Aviles
Emergency Room Ghost	Phil Leeds
Surgeon	John Hugh
Minister	Sam Tsoutsouvas
Cemetery Ghost	Sharon Breslau Cornell
Subway Ghost	Vincent Schiavelli
Rosa Santiago	Angelina Estrada
Clara Brown	Armelia McQueen
Louise Brown	Gail Boggs
Oda Mae Brown	Whoopi Goldberg
Workman in loft	Thom Curley
Police Sergeant	Stephen Root
Policewoman	Laura Drake
Orlando	Augie Blunt
Ghosts	Alma Beltran, J. Christopher Sullivan
Ortisha	Vivian Bonnell
Ortisha's Friend	Derek Thompson
Bank Officer	Charlotte Zucker
Bank Guard	Tom Finnegan
Lyle Furgeson	Bruce Jarchow
Nuns	Sondra Rubin, Faye Brenner
Bank Co-Worker	William Cort
Apartment Women	Minnie Lindsey, Mabel Lockridge
Cab Driver	Said Faraj

© *Paramount Pictures*
Top: Demi Moore, Patrick Swayze
Below: Whoopi Goldberg, Moore

1990 Academy Awards for Best Supporting Actress
(Whoopi Goldberg) and Original Screenplay

Demi Moore, Patrick Swayze

Demi Moore, Patrick Swayze

Armelia McQueen, Whoopi Goldberg, Patrick Swayze, Augie Blunt, Vivian Bonnell
Top Left: Demi Moore, Swayze Above Left: Swayze, Moore, Tony Goldwyn
Top Right: Swayze, Moore

John Goodman, Brian McNamara, Jeff Daniels Top Right:
Julian Sands Right: Harley Jane Kozak, Goodman
© *Hollywood Pictures/Amblin Entertainment*

ARACHNOPHOBIA

(HOLLYWOOD PICTURES/AMBLIN ENTERTAINMENT) Producers, Kathleen Kennedy, Richard Vane; Director, Frank Marshall; Executive Producers, Steven Spielberg, Frank Marshall; Screenplay, Don Jakoby, Wesley Strick; Story, Don Jakoby, Al Williams; Photography, Mikael Salomon; Designer, James Bissell; Music, Trevor Jones; Editor, Michael Kahn; Co-Executive Producers, Ted Field, Robert W. Cort; Stunts, Chuck Waters; Casting, Mike Fenton, Judy Taylor, Valorie Massalas; Co-Producer, Don Jakoby; Assistant Director, Bruce Cohen; Costumes, Jennifer L. Parsons; Supervising Entomologist, Steven Kutcher; Spider Creator and Designer/Creature Effects Supervisor, Chris Walas; Distributed by Buena Vista Pictures; Dolby Stereo; Deluxe color; Rated PG-13; 103 minutes; July release

CAST

Ross Jennings	Jeff Daniels
Molly Jennings	Harley Jane Kozak
Delbert McClintock	John Goodman
Dr. James Atherton	Julian Sands
Sheriff Parsons	Stuart Pankin
Chris Collins	Brian McNamara
Jerry Manley	Mark L. Taylor
Dr. Sam Metcalf	Henry Jones
Henry Beechwood	Peter Jason
Milton Briggs	James Handy
Irv Kendall	Roy Brocksmith
Blaire Kendall	Kathy Kinney
Margaret Hollins	Mary Carver
Tommy Jennings	Garette Patrick Ratliff
Shelley Jennings	Marlene Katz
Edna Beechwood	Jane Marla Robbins
Bunny Beechwood	Theo Schwartz
Becky Beechwood	Cori Wellins
Bobby Beechwood	Chance Boyer
Brandy Beechwood	Brandy
Evelyn Metcalf	Frances Bay
Henrietta Manley	Lois de Banzie
Dick Manley	Warren Rice
Mayor Bob	Robert Frank Telfer
Irv's Assistant	Michael Steve Jones
Little Girl	Fiona Walsh
Mom	Terese Del Piero
Todd Miller	Nathaniel Spitzley
Mover	Jay Scorpio
Girlfriend	Mai-Lis Kuniholm
Helicopter	Robert "Bobby Z" Zajonc

Brian McNamara, Roy Brocksmith, James Handy, Jeff Daniels
Above: Daniels

Matthew Broderick, Bruno Kirby, Marlon Brando Top Right:
Frank Whaley, Broderick Right: Brando, Maximilian Schell
© *Tri-Star Pictures*

THE FRESHMAN

(TRI-STAR) Producer, Mike Lobell; Director/Screenplay, Andrew Bergman; Photography, William A. Fraker; Designer, Ken Adam; Music, David Newman; Editor, Barry Malkin; Costumes, Julie Weiss; Casting, Mike Fenton, Judy Taylor, Lynda Gordon; Assistant Director, Louis D'Esposito; *"Maggie's Farm"* by Bob Dylan/performed by Bert Parks; a Lobell/Bergman production; Dolby Stereo; Technicolor; Rated PG; 102 minutes; July release

CAST

Carmine Sabatini	Marlon Brando
Clark Kellogg	Matthew Broderick
Victor Ray	Bruno Kirby
Tina Sabatini	Penelope Ann Miller
Steve Bushak	Frank Whaley
Chuck Greenwald	Jon Polito
Arthur Fleeber	Paul Benedict
Lloyd Simpson	Richard Gant
Dwight Armstrong	Kenneth Welsh
Liz Armstrong	Pamela Payton-Wright
Edward	B. D. Wong
Larry London	Maximilian Schell
Himself	Bert Parks
Leo	Tex Konig
Lorenzo	Leo Cimino
Maitre D' Gourmet Club	Gianni Russo
Father Frank	Warren Davis
Aunt Angelina	Vera Lockwood
Hunter	Jefferson Mappin
Gas Attendant	Daniel Dion
Mall Mother	Marnie Edwards
Mr. Glassman	Doug Silberstein
FBI Man	J. H. Millington
Waiter in restaurant	Joe Ingoldsby

and Drake Arden, David Stratton, Geraldine Quinn, Derek Mitchell (Students in Fleeber classroom), Adrienne Howe, Patricia Andrews, Edward Roy, Amanda Smith, Andrew Airlie, Daniel DeSanto, Wendy Dickson, Christina Trivett (Mall Patrons), Fifi Donahue (Grand Central Information Booth Lady)

Marlon Brando, Penelope Ann Miller, Bruno Kirby, Matthew
Broderick Above: Bert Parks

NAVY SEALS

(ORION) Producers, Brenda Feigen, Bernard Williams; Director, Lewis Teague; Screenplay, Chuck Pfarrer, Gary Goldman; Photography, John A. Alonzo; Designers, Guy J. Comtois, Veronica Hadfield; Music, Sylvester Levay; Editor, Don Zimmerman; Costumes, Brad Loman; Casting, Sally Dennison, Julie Selzer; Assistant Director, Jose Kuki Lopez Rodero; Special Effects Supervisor, John Stears; Dolby Stereo; Deluxe color; Rated R; 113 minutes; July release

CAST

Lt. (jg) Dale Hawkins	Charlie Sheen
Lt. James Curran	Michael Biehn
Claire Verens	Joanne Whalley-Kilmer
Leary	Rick Rossovich
Rexer	Cyril O'Reilly
Dane	Bill Paxton
Graham	Dennis Haysbert
Ramos	Paul Sanchez
Ben Shaheed	Nicholas Kadi
Captain Dunne	Ron Joseph
Jolena	S. Epatha Merkerson
U.S. Helicopter Pilot	Greg McKinney
U.S. Helicopter Co-Pilot	Rob Moran
Admiral Colker	Richard Venture
Jim Elmore	Mark Carlton
Warren Stinson	Ira Wheeler
General Mateen	Ron Faber
Elliott West	Bill Cort
Navy Seal #8	Randy Hall
EOD Officer	Duncan Smith
Submarine Captain	William Knight
Ali	Nehme Fadlallah
Villa Hostage	Marc Zuber
Terrorist	Vic Tablian
Latanya Captain	Adam Hussein
Druze Fighter	George Jackos
Shepherd	Ian Tyler
Israeli Intelligence	Michael Halphie, Ezra Abraham
Local TV Announcer	John Pruitt
Crewman C130	Tom Sean Foley
Aircraft Carrier Officers	William Roberts, Michael Fitzpatrick
Bartender	Cathryn De Prume
Redneck in bar	Titus Welliver

**Top: Michael Biehn, Charlie Sheen Below: Sheen, Biehn
Right: Biehn, Joanne Whalley-Kilmer, Sheen**
© *Orion Pictures*

Dennis Haysbert, Cyril O'Reilly, Paul Sanchez, Michael Biehn,
Bill Paxton, Charlie Sheen, Rick Rossovich

Rick Rossovich, Michael Biehn, Charlie Sheen

THE UNBELIEVABLE TRUTH

(MIRAMAX) Producers, Bruce Weiss, Hal Hartley; Director/Screenplay/Editor, Hal Hartley; Executive Producer, Jerome Brownstein; Photography, Michael Spiller; Music, Jim Coleman; Designer, Carla Gerona; Assistant Director, Ted Hope; an Action Features Inc. production; Color; Rated R; 90 minutes; July release

CAST

Audry Hugo	Adrienne Shelly
Josh Hutton	Robert Burke
Vic Hugo	Christopher Cooke
Pearl	Julia McNeal
Mike	Mark Bailey
Emmet	Gary Sauer
Liz Hugo	Katherine Mayfield
Todd Whitbread	David Healy
Otis (Driver/Bum)	Matt Malloy
Jane, the Waitress	Edie Falco
Irate Driver	Jeff Howard
His Wife	Kelly Reichardt
Their Son	Ross Turner
Bill	Paul Schultze
Bob	Mike Brady
Gus	Bill Sage
News Vendor	Tom Thon
Girl at counter	Mary Sue Flynn

Top: Adrienne Shelly, Robert Burke Left: Julia McNeal, Shelly
© Miramax Films

PROBLEM CHILD

(UNIVERSAL) Producer, Robert Simonds; Director, Dennis Dugan; Screenplay, Scott Alexander, Larry Karaszewski; Executive Producer, James D. Brubaker; Photography, Peter Lyons Collister; Editors, Daniel Hanley, Michael Hill; Designer, George Costello; Costumes, Eileen Kennedy; Music, Miles Goodman; Title song by Terry Melcher/performed by The Beach Boys; an Imagine Entertainment production; Dolby Stereo; Deluxe color; Rated PG; 85 minutes; July release

CAST

Ben Healy	John Ritter
Big Ben Healy	Jack Warden
Junior	Michael Oliver
Igor Peabody	Gilbert Gottfried
Flo Healy	Amy Yasbeck
Martin Beck	Michael Richards
Roy	Peter Jurasik
Lorraine	Charlotte Akin
Catcher	Adam Anderly
2nd Baseman	Cody Beard
All American Dad	Dennis Dugan
All American Boy	Eric Elterman
Freddy	Justin Elledge
Mr. Henderson	Ward Emling
Warden	John William Galt
Sister Mary	Corki Grazer
Mother Superior	Helena Humann
Sister Abigail	Melody Jones
Lucy	Colby Kline
Mrs. Henderson	Kristen Lowman
Harriet	Julie Mayfield
Sister Samantha	Norma Moore
Psychiatrist	John O'Connell
Dr. Strauss	Eric Poppick

and Anna Marie Allred, Jordan Burton, Joseph Kolb, Kristy Lynne Patrick, Josh Stoppelwerth (Kids), Melissa Martin, Abby Newman, Symone Redwine (Friends), John Rainone (Circus Clown), Judy James (Anchorperson), Ellen Locy (Nun), Joshua Martin (Shortstop), S. "Monty" Moncibais (Prisoner), Florence Shauffler (Mrs. Perkins)

© Universal City Studios

Michael Richards, Michael Oliver Above: Jack Warden, John Ritter

Harrison Ford Top Left: Ford, Raul Julia
Left: Ford, Greta Scacchi
© *Warner Bros.*

PRESUMED INNOCENT

(WARNER BROS.) Producers, Sydney Pollack, Mark Rosenberg; Director, Alan J. Pakula; Screenplay, Frank Pierson, Alan J. Pakula; Based on the novel by Scott Turow; Executive Producer, Susan Solt; Photography, Gordon Willis; Designer, George Jenkins; Music, John Williams; Editor, Evan Lottman; Costumes, John Boxer; Casting, Alixe Gordin; Assistant Director, Alex Hapsas; a Mirage production; Dolby Stereo; Technicolor; Rated R; 127 minutes; July release

CAST

Rusty Sabich	Harrison Ford
Raymond Horgan	Brian Dennehy
Sandy Stern	Raul Julia
Barbara Sabich	Bonnie Bedelia
Judge Larren Lyttle	Paul Winfield
Carolyn Polhemus	Greta Scacchi
Detective Lipranzer	John Spencer
Tommy Molto	Joe Grifasi
Nico Della Guardia	Tom Mardirosian
Eugenia	Anna Maria Horsford
"Painless" Kumagai	Sab Shimono
Jamie Kemp	Bradley Whitford
Lydia "Mac" MacDougall	Christine Estabrook
Mr. Polhemus	Michael Tolan
Sgt. Lionel Kenneally	Madison Arnold
Stew Dubinsky	Ron Frazier
Nat Sabich	Jesse Bradford
Wendell McGaffney	Joseph Mazzello
Detective Harold Greer	Tucker Smallwood
Leon Wells	Leland Gantt
Ernestine	Teodorina Bello
Morrie Dickerman	David Wohl
Guerasch	John Michael Bennett
Mike Duke	Bo Rucker
Glendenning	Peter Appel
Chet	John Ottavino
Cody	Robert Katims
Mr. McGaffney	Joseph Carberry
Balestrieri	John Seitz
Tom	Bill Winkler
Judge Mumphrey	John Vennema
Court Clerk	Michael Genet
Undercover Cop	Richard L. Newcomb
Jim, Arresting Detective	Ed Wheeler
Arresting Detective	Miles Watson
Loretta	DeAnn Mears
Moderator	Julia Meade
Camp Counselor	Thom Cagle
Camper	Ricky Rosa

and Allison Field, Janis Corsair, Bill Corsair, Carla Goff (Reporters), Rick De Furia, Victor Truro, Elizabeth Williams, Jeffrey Wright, Ted Neustadt, Kimberleigh Aarn (Prosecuting Attorneys)

Harrison Ford, Bonnie Bedelia Above: Brian Dennehy, Ford

Raul Julia, Bonnie Bedelia, Harrison Ford Top Left: Harrison Ford (also top right)
Above Left: Jesse Bradford, Bedelia, Ford Above Right: Ford, Greta Scacchi

Balthazar Getty, Alan Ruck, Emilio Estevez, Kiefer Sutherland, Lou Diamond Phillips, Christian Slater Top Left: William Petersen, Estevez Left: James Coburn; Ruck
© *Morgan Creek Film Partners*

YOUNG GUNS II

(20th CENTURY FOX) Producers, Irby Smith, Paul Schiff; Executive Producers, James G. Robinson, Joe Roth, John Fusco; Director, Geoff Murphy; Screenplay, John Fusco; Co-Executive Producers, Gary Barber, David Nicksay; Photography, Dean Semler; Designer, Gene Rudolf; Music, Alan Silvestri; Songs written and performed by Jon Bon Jovi; Editor, Bruce Green; Costumes, Judy Ruskin; Associate Producer, Dixie J. Capp; a Morgan Creek Production; Dolby Stereo; Deluxe color; Rated PG-13; 105 minutes; August release

CAST

William H. Bonney	Emilio Estevez
Doc Scurlock	Kiefer Sutherland
Chavez Y Chavez	Lou Diamond Phillips
Arkansas Dave Rudabaugh	Christian Slater
Pat Garrett	William Petersen
Hendry French	Alan Ruck
D. A. Ryerson	R. D. Call
John Chisum	James Coburn
Tom O'Folliard	Balthazar Getty
Ashmun Upson	Jack Kehoe
Deputy Carlyle	Robert Knepper
J. W. Bell	Tom Kurlander
John W. Poe	Viggo Mortensen
Bob Ollinger	Leon Rippy
Beever Smith	Tracey Walter
Charles Phalen	Brad Whitford
Governor Lew Wallace	Scott Wilson
Jane Greathouse	Jenny Wright
Pendleton	John Hammil
Second Aide	William Fisher
Deluvina Maxwell	Carlotta Garcia
Juanita	Joy Bouton
Jesus Silva	Albert Trujillo
Sonia	Alina Arenal
Guano Miner	John Alderson

and Lee Debroux, Sixto Joost, Rudy Sena, Adam Taylor (Bounty Hunters), Redmond Gleeson (Murphy Man), David Paul Needles (Cutter), Jerry Gardiner (Sheriff Kimbel), Domingo Ambriz, Sonny Skyhawk (Vaqueros), Richard Schiff (Rat Bag), Stephan Kraus (Pietro), Nicholas Sean Gomez (Fernando), Mark Bustamante (Ignio), Airen Balen (Student), Don Simpson (Pinkerton Man), Holt Parker (Sumner Priest), Tony Frank (Judge Bristol), Frank Fierro, Jr., Rene L. Moreno (Villagers), Chief Buddy Redbow (Chief Victorio), Danielle Blanchard (Tom's Dove), Joey Joe Hamlin (Chivato's Pal), Alexis Alexander, Ginger Lynn Allen (Doves), Iris Pappas (Barmaid), Ed Adams, Mark Silverstein, Boots Southerland, Bud Stout, Howie Young (Poe Posse), John Fusco (Branded Man), Walter Feldbusch, Bo Gray, Tom Byrd, Donald Guideau (Pit Inmates), Robert Harvey (Townsman), Ted Kairys (Town Dweller), William Upchurch (Drunken Idiot), Michael Eiland (Shop Keeper), Jon Bon Jovi

Balthazar Getty Above: Christian Slater

FLATLINERS

(COLUMBIA) Producers, Michael Douglas, Rick Bieber; Director, Joel Schumacher; Screenplay, Peter Filardi; Executive Producers, Scott Rudin, Michael Rachmil, Peter Filardi; Photography, Jan De Bont; Designer, Eugenio Zanetti; Music, James Newton Howard; Editor, Robert Brown; Costumes, Susan Becker; Casting, Mali Finn; Assistant Directors, Jeff Rafner, John Kretchmer; Visual Effects Supervisor, Peter Donen; a Stonebridge Entertainment production; Dolby Stereo; Panavision; Technicolor; Rated R; 111 minutes; August release

CAST

Nelson Wright	Kiefer Sutherland
Rachel Mannus	Julia Roberts
David Labraccio	Kevin Bacon
Joe Hurley	William Baldwin
Randy Steckle	Oliver Platt
Winnie Hicks	Kimberly Scott
Billy Mahoney	Joshua Rudoy
Rachel's Father	Benjamin Mouton
Young Nelson	Aeryk Egan
Young Winnie	Kesha Reed
Anne	Hope Davis
Uncle Dave	Jim Ortlieb
Young Labraccio	John Joseph Duda
Playground Kids	Megan Stewart, Tressa Thomas, Gonzo Gonzalez
Ben Hicks	Afram Bill Williams
Terry	Deborah Thompson
Rachel's Mother	Elinore O'Connell
Bag Lady	Marilyn Dodds Frank
Bridget	Sanna Vraa
Edna—Ward Nurse	Patricia Belcher
Terminal Woman	Susan French
Housewife	Beth Grant
Near Death Patient	Cage S. Johnson
Young Nelson's Friends	Jared Milmeister, Patrick Gleeson
Man on crack	John Benjamin Martin
Nurse	Lynda Odums
Doctors	John Fink, Angela Paton

and Nicole Niblack, Cynthia Bassham, Sarabeth Tucek, Ilona Margolis, Julie Warner, Iilana B'Tiste, Deborah Torchio, Deborah Goomas, Michelle McKee, Nancy Moran, Dede Latinopoulos (Joe's Women), Evelina Fernandez (Latin Woman), Miguel Delgado (Latin Husband), Ingrid Oliu (Latin Wife), Raymond Hanis (Latin Orderly), Zoaunne LeRoy (Waitress), Tom Kurlander (Medical Student), Nili Levi (Little Girl), Anne James (Beth), K. K. Dodds (Jill), Natsuko Ohama (Professor)

Top: Oliver Platt, Kevin Bacon, Julia Roberts
Below: Kiefer Sutherland Left: Sutherland, Bacon
© *Columbia Pictures*

Kevin Bacon, Oliver Platt, William Baldwin, Julia Roberts, Kiefer Sutherland

Kiefer Sutherland, Kevin Bacon, William Baldwin, Julia Roberts, Oliver Platt

Denzel Washington, Cynda Williams Top Right: Giancarlo
Esposito, Spike Lee, Washington Right: Washington, Lee
© *Universal City Studios*

MO' BETTER BLUES

(UNIVERSAL) Producer/Director/Screenplay, Spike Lee; Co-
Producer, Monty Ross; Line Producer, Jon Kilik; Photography, Ernest
Dickerson; Music, Bill Lee; Song: *"Harlem Blues"* by W. C. Handy/
performed by Cynda Williams, with the Brandford Marsalis Quartet; *"A
Love Supreme (Part 1—Acknowledgment)"* composed and performed
by John Coltrane; Designer, Wynn Thomas; Editor, Sam Pollard;
Casting, Robi Reed; Costumes, Ruth E. Carter; Assistant Director,
Randy Fletcher; a 40 Acres and a Mule Filmworks production; Dolby
Stereo; Deluxe color; Rated R; 127 minutes; August release

CAST

Bleek Gilliam	Denzel Washington
Giant	Spike Lee
Shadow Henderson	Wesley Snipes
Left Hand Lacey	Giancarlo Esposito
Butterbean Jones	Robin Harris
Indigo Downes	Joie Lee
Bottom Hammer	Bill Nunn
Moe Flatbush	John Turturro
Big Stop Gilliam	Dick Anthony Williams
Clarke Bentancourt	Cynda Williams
Josh Flatbush	Nicholas Turturro
Rhythm Jones	Jeff "Tain" Watts
Madlock	Samuel L. Jackson
Rod	Leonard Thomas
Eggy	Charles Q. Murphy
Born Knowledge	Steve White
Petey	Ruben Blades
Lillian Gilliam	Abbey Lincoln
Jeanne	Linda Hawkins
Rita	Raye Dowell
Cora	Angela Hall
Roberto	Coati Mundi
Young Bleek/Miles	Zakee L. Howze
Tyrone	Deon Richmond
Shanika	Anaysha Figueroa
Joe	Raymond Thomas
Benny	Sheldon Turnipseed
Louis	Christopher Skeffrey
Sam	Terrence Williams

and Darryl M. Wonge, Jr. (Miles at birth), Jelani Asar Snipes (Miles at
1 yr.), Glenn Williams, III (Miles at 3 yrs.), Arnold Cromer (Miles at 5
yrs.), Leon Addison Brown (Smith), Scot Anthony Robinson (Cooley),
Rev. Herbert Daughtry (Minister), Bill Lee (Father of the Bride),
Brandford Marsalis (Party Guest), Douglas Bourne (Jimmy the Bus-
boy), Tracy Camilla Johns, John Canada Terrell, Monty Ross, Isabella,
Mamie Louis Anderson (Club Patrons), Joe Seneca (Big Stop's
Friend), John Sobestanovich (Taxi Driver)

Spike Lee, Ruben Blades Above: Joie Lee, Denzel Washington

DUCKTALES: THE MOVIE
Treasure of the Lost Lamp

(BUENA VISTA/WALT DISNEY) Producer/Director, Bob Hathcock; Co-Producers, Jean-Pierre Quenet, Robert Taylor; Animation Screenplay, Alan Burnett; Sequence Directors, Paul Brizzi, Gaetan Brizzi, Clive Pallant, Mattias Marcos Rodric, Vincent Woodcock; Associate Producer, Liza-Ann Warren; Music, David Newman; "Duck-Tales" Theme composed by Mark Mueller/performed by Jeff Pescetto; Designer, Skip Morgan; Editor, Charles King; a Disney Movietoons presentation of a Walt Disney Animation (France) S.A. Production; Dolby Stereo; Technicolor; Rated G; 74 minutes; August release

VOICE CAST

Scrooge McDuck .... Alan Young
Launchpad .... Terence McGovern
Huey, Dewey, Louie and Webby .... Russi Taylor
Dijon .... Richard Libertini
Merlock .... Christopher Lloyd
Mrs. Featherby .... June Foray
Duckworth .... Chuck McCann
Mrs. Beakley .... Joan Gerber
Genie .... Rip Taylor
Additional Voices: Charlie Adler, Jack Angel, Steve Bulen, Sherry Lynn, Mickie T. McGowan, Patrick Pinney, Frank Welker

Top: Webby, Scrooge McDuck Right: Scrooge, Huey, Dewey, Launchpad McQuack
© *Walt Disney Animation*

Huey, Dewey, Elephant, Genie, Webby, Louie Above: Merlock, Genie

Genie, Huey, Dewey, Webby, Louie Above: Scrooge McDuck, Webby

Mel Gibson, Robert Downey, Jr. Top Left: Gibson
Left: Gibson, Downey
© Tri-Star Pictures

AIR AMERICA

(TRI-STAR) Producer, Daniel Melnick; Director, Roger Spottis-
woode; Screenplay, John Eskow, Richard Rush; Based on the book by
Christopher Robbins; Executive Producers, Mario Kassar, Andrew
Vajna; Line Producer, Michael J. Kagan; Co-Producers, Allen Shapiro,
John Eskow; Photography, Roger Deakins; Designer, Allan Cameron;
Music, Charles Gross; Editors, John Bloom, Lois Freeman-Fox; Cos-
tumes, John Mollo; Casting, Janet Hirshenson, Jane Jenkins; Assistant
Director, Albert Shapiro; Aerial Unit Director, Marc Wolff; Stunts, Vic
Armstrong; Special Effects Supervisor, George Gibbs; a Daniel Mel-
nick/Indieprod production from Carolco Pictures; Dolby Stereo; Wide-
screen; Deluxe color; Rated R; 112 minutes; August release

CAST

Gene Ryack	Mel Gibson
Billy Covington	Robert Downey, Jr.
Corinne Landreaux	Nancy Travis
Major Donald Lemond	Ken Jenkins
Rob Diehl	David Marshall Grant
Senator Davenport	Lane Smith
Jack Neely	Art La Fleur
Pirelli	Ned Eisenberg
O.V.	Marshall Bell
Saunders	David Bowe
General Lu Soong	Burt Kwouk
Babo	Tim Thomerson
Nino	Harvey Jason
Gene's Wife	Sinjai Hongthai
Gene's Daughter	Natta Nantatanti
Gene's Son	Purin Panichpan
Gene's Brother-in-Law	Yani Tramod
Kwahn	Chanarong Suwanapa
Tribal Warrior	Chet Vimol
Nightclub Singers	Wasan Uttamayodhin, Meesak Naakkarat
Truck Driver	Ernie Lively
Recruiter	Burke Byrnes
D.J.	Greg Kean
Ambassador	Roger Welty

Mel Gibson, David Bowe, Marshall Bell, Art La Fleur, Tim
Thomerson, Robert Downey Jr., Ned Eisenberg Above: Nancy
Travis; David Marshall Grant

THE TWO JAKES

(PARAMOUNT) Producers, Robert Evans, Harold Schneider; Director, Jack Nicholson; Screenplay, Robert Towne; Photography, Vilmos Zsigmond; Designers, Jeremy Railton, Richard Sawyer; Editor, Anne Goursaud; Associate Producer, Alan Finkelstein; Music, Van Dyke Parks; Costumes, Wayne A. Finkelman; Casting, Terry Liebling; Assistant Director, Michael Daves; Dolby Stereo; Technicolor; Rated R; 138 minutes; August release

CAST

Jake Gittes	Jack Nicholson
Jake Berman	Harvey Keitel
Kitty Berman	Meg Tilly
Lillian Bodine	Madeleine Stowe
Cotton Weinberger	Eli Wallach
Mickey Nice	Rubén Blades
Chuck Newty	Frederic Forrest
Loach Jr.	David Keith
Earl Rawley	Richard Farnsworth
Tyrone Otley	Tracey Walter
Lawrence Walsh	Joe Mantell
Khan	James Hong
Capt. Lou Escobar	Perry Lopez
Ralph Tilton	Jeff Morris
Gladys	Rebecca Broussard
Liberty Levine	Paul A. DiCocco, Jr.
Mark Bodine	John Hackett
Linda	Rosie Vela
Rippey	Allan Warnick
Dolores	Susan Forristal
Judge Detmer	Will Tynan
Francis Hannah	Van Dyke Parks
Desk Sergeant	William Duffy
Mattie Rawley	Sue Carlton
Bartender	Don McGovern
Colorist	Luana Anders
Cop with parrot	Dean Hill
Dr. Elsa Brandhauer	Pia Gronning
Saul	John Herman Shaner
Benny	Michael Shaner

and Lee Weaver, Malek Abdul-Mansour (Caddies), Ken Cervi (Prowler), Annie Marshall (Client with dog), Ian Thorpe (Errol Flynn lookalike), Collette Northrop (Cigarette-Hat Check Girl), Patricia Durham (Clarissa), Randi Ingerman (Lana), Joy Wayman (Lady asleep), Bob George (Bar Maitre d'), Suzanne Mitchell (The Redhead), Alan Chaffin (Bar Manager), Wyn Costello (Black Eye Woman), Lisa Regina Croisette (Actress at Max Factor), Jessica Z. Diamond (Receptionist), Faye Dunaway (Voice of Evelyn Mulwray), Tom Waits

Top: Richard Farnsworth, Frederic Forrest, Jack Nicholson
Below: Madeleine Stowe, Meg Tilly
Left: James Hong, Nicholson
© *Paramount Pictures*

Eli Wallach, Harvey Keitel

Tom Waits, Jack Nicholson, David Keith

METROPOLITAN

(NEW LINE CINEMA) Producer/Director/Screenplay, Whit Stillman; Co-Producer, Peter Wentworth; Line Producer, Brian Greenbaum; Photography, John Thomas; Music, Mark Suozzo, Tom Judson; Editor, Christopher Tellefsen; Costumes, Mary Jane Fort; Assistant Director, Larry Eudine; a Westerly Films presentation; Color; Rated PG-13; 98 minutes; August release

CAST

Audrey Rouget	Carolyn Farina
Tom Townsend	Edward Clements
Nick Smith	Christopher Eigeman
Charlie Black	Taylor Nichols
Jane Clarke	Allison Rutledge-Parisi
Sally Fowler	Dylan Hundley
Cynthia McLean	Isabel Gillies
Fred Neff	Bryan Leder
Rick Von Soneker	Will Kempe
Serena Slocum	Elizabeth Thompson
Victor Lemley	Stephen Uys
Man at bar	Roger W. Kirby
Mrs. Townsend	Alice Connorton
Mrs. Rouget	Linda Gillies
Allen Green	John Lynch
North Greenwich Preppie	Donal Lardner Ward
Cab Driver	Tom Voth
Sabina (Texas Deb)	Caroline Bennett
Cadet Frawley	Frank Creighton
A. T. Harris Salesman	Joel S. Schreiber
Catherine Atzen Clinician	Catherine Atzen
TV Voice of Debutante Ball	J. Harden Rose

and Victoria Chickering, Blayne Perry, Kevin Schack, Tina Thornton, Hank Foley, Andrew Lyle (SFRP Friends—Early Nighters)

Top: Isabel Gillies, Taylor Nichols, Dylan Hundley Left: Carolyn Farina, Edward Clements
© *Westerly Film-Video Inc.*

Bryan Leder, Edward Clements, Isabel Gillies, Taylor Nichols, Dylan Hundley, Carolyn Farina, Christopher Eigeman, Allison Rutledge-Parisi

Allison Rutledge-Parisi, Carolyn Farina, Christopher Eigeman, Edward Clements,
Dylan Hundley, Elizabeth Thompson, Will Kempe, Isabel Gillies, Taylor Nichols
Above: Brian Leder, Hundley, Nichols, Rutledge-Parisi, Eigeman

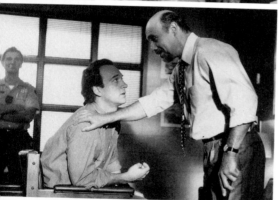

TAKING CARE OF BUSINESS

(HOLLYWOOD PICTURES/BUENA VISTA) Producer, Geoffrey Taylor; Executive Producer, Paul Mazursky; Director, Arthur Hiller; Screenplay, Jill Mazursky, Jeffrey Abrams; Photography, David M. Walsh; Music, Stewart Copeland; Designer, Jon Hutman; Co-Producer, Duncan Henderson; Editor, William Reynolds; Casting, Lynn Stalmaster; Associate Producer, Elizabeth Sayre; Assistant Director, Alan B. Curtiss; Presented in association with Silver Screen Partners IV; Dolby Stereo; Technicolor; Rated R; 108 minutes; August release

CAST

Jimmy Dworski	James Belushi
Spencer Barnes	Charles Grodin
Debbie	Anne DeSalvo
Jewel	Loryn Locklin
Walter Bentley	Stephen Elliott
The Warden	Hector Elizondo
Elizabeth	Veronica Hamel
Sakamoto	Mako
Diane	Gates McFadden
Ted	John de Lancie
Mike	Thom Sharp
J.B.	Ken Foree
LeBradford	J. J.
Heavy G	Andre Rosey Brown
Hamilton	Terrence E. McNally
Mediators	Lenny Hicks, Joe Bratcher
Prison Guards	Burke Byrnes, Tony Auer
Brenda	Marte Boyle Slout
Chauffeur	John P. Menese
Car Rental Man	Stanley DeSantis
Gang Members	Tommy Morgan, Buddy Daniels
Luggage Boy	Chris Barnes
Tennis Court Girl	Jill Johnson
Mr. Wright	Tom Nolan
Tennis Club Receptionist	Marjorie Bransfield
Woman in pro shop	Selma Archerd
Ira Breen	Joe Lerer
Sakamoto's Assistant	Howie Guma
Diane's Assistant	Elisabeth Barrett
Waiter	Tom Taglang
High Quality Receptionist	Michele Harrell
Radio Reporter	Stu Nahan
Prison Reporters	Andrew Amador, Sandra Eng
Guard	Louisa Abernathy
Main Gate Guard	Michael McNab
Malibu Jail Guard	Michael Kinney
Malibu Jail Woman	Leslie Suzan
Woman on plane	Janet Julian
Snooty Man	Dan Kern
Yuppie Dad	David Ruprecht
Yuppie Son	Whitby Hertford
National Anthem Singer	Baldo Dal Ponte
Themselves	Joe Torre, Mark Grace, Bert Blyleven
Stadium Guard	T. Rodgers
Umpire	Hank Robinson
Beach House Cops	Michael Blue, Ron Chenier
Jeep Driver	Darlene J. Hall
Twins	Jacqueline Alexandra Citron, Kristen Amber Citron

Top: Charles Grodin, James Belushi
Below: Loryn Locklin, Belushi
© *Hollywood Pictures*

Charles Grodin, Anne DeSalvo Above: James Belushi,
Hector Elizondo

Nicolas Cage, Willem Dafoe Top Left: Harry Dean Stanton,
Diane Ladd Left: Laura Dern, Cage
© Samuel Goldwyn Co.

WILD AT HEART

(SAMUEL GOLDWYN CO.) Producers, Monty Montgomery, Steve
Golin, Joni Sighvatsson; Director/Screenplay, David Lynch; Based on
the novel by Barry Gifford; Executive Producer, Michael Kuhn; Photography, Frederick Elmes; Editor, Duwayne Dunham; Designer, Patricia Norris; Music, Angelo Badalamenti; Songs performed by Nicolas
Cage: "Love Me" by Jerry Leiber and Mike Stoller, "Love Me Tender"
by Elvis Presley and Vera Matson; Casting, Johanna Ray; Assistant
Directors, Margaux Mackay, Charles Myers; a Polygram/Propaganda
Films production; Dolby Stereo; Panavision; Color; Rated R; 124
minutes; August release

CAST

Sailor Ripley	Nicolas Cage
Lula Pace Fortune	Laura Dern
Marietta Fortune	Diane Ladd
Bobby Peru	Willem Dafoe
Perdita Durango	Isabella Rossellini
Johnnie Farragut	Harry Dean Stanton
Dell	Crispin Glover
Juana	Grace Zabriskie
Marcello Santos	J. E. Freeman
Reginald Sula	Calvin Lockhart
Uncle Pooch	Marvin Kaplan
Mr. Reindeer	W. Morgan Sheppard
Dropshadow	David Patrick Kelly
George Kovich	Freddie Jones
Sparky	John Lurie
OO Spool	Jack Nance
Buddy	Pruitt Taylor Vince
Bob Ray Lemon	Gregg Dandridge
Girl in accident	Sherilyn Fenn
Pace Roscoe	Glenn Walker Harris, Jr.
Madam	Frances Bay
Hotel Custodian	Blair Bruce Bever
Aunt Rootie	Sally Boyle
Hotel Manager	Peter Bromilow
Reindeer Dancer	Lisa Ann Cabasa
Old Bum	Frank A. Caruso
Timmy Thompson	Frank Collison
Rex	Eddy Dixon
Idiot Punk	Brent Fraser
Man at Shell Station	Cage S. Johnson
Good Witch	Sheryl Lee

and Valli Leigh, Mia M. Ruiz (Mr. Reindeer's Resident Valets), Willy
Love (Man in wheelchair), Daniel Quinn (Young Cowboy), Charlie
Spradling (Irma), Billy Swann (Himself), Koko Taylor (Singer at
Zanzibar), Ed Wright (Desk Clerk), Darrell Zwerling (Singer's Manag-
er)

Laura Dern, Diane Ladd Above: Isabella Rossellini

Steven Martin Top Right: Leslie Cook, Rick Moranis, Martin,
Melissa Hurley Right: Carol Kane, Martin
© *Warner Bros.*

MY BLUE HEAVEN

(WARNER BROS.) Producers, Herbert Ross, Anthea Sylbert; Executive Producers, Goldie Hawn, Nora Ephron, Andrew Stone; Co-Producer, Joseph Caracciolo; Director, Herbert Ross; Screenplay, Nora Ephron; Photography, John Bailey; Designer, Charles Rosen; Music, Ira Newborn; Editors, Stephen A. Rotter, Robert Reitano; Costumes, Joseph G. Aulisi; Casting, Hank McCann; Title song, music by Walter Donaldson, lyrics by George Whiting/performed by Fats Domino; Choreographer, Lynne Taylor-Corbett; Assistant Director, Ariel Levy; a Hawn/Sylbert Production; Dolby Stereo; Technicolor; Rated PG-13; 95 minutes; August release

CAST

Vinnie Antonelli	Steve Martin
Barney Coopersmith	Rick Moranis
Hannah Stubbs	Joan Cusack
Crystal Rybak	Melanie Mayron
Kirby	William Irwin
Shaldeen	Carol Kane
Billy Sparrow	William Hickey
Linda	Deborah Rush
Will Stubbs	Daniel Stern
Jamie	Jesse Bradford
Tommie	Corey Carrier
Umberto Mello	Seth Jaffe
Lilo Mello	Robert Miranda
Underwood	Ed Lauter
Vinnie's Mother	Julie Bovasso
Margaret Snow	Colleen Camp
Wally Bunting	Gordon Currie
Dino	Raymond O'Connor
Nicky	Troy Evans
Rocco	Dick Boccelli
Richie	Ron Karabatsos
Benny	Tony Di Benedetto
Angela	Melissa Hurley
Marie	Leslie Cook
Supermarket Manager	Darren Chuckry
Supermarket Employee	Duke Stroud
Filomena	Carol Ann Susi
Gaetano	Frankie Gio
U.S. Attorney	Joel Polis
Defense Attorney	Larry Block

and Arthur Brauss (Judge), Greta Blackburn, Eva Charney (Stewardesses), Ellen Albertini Dow (Nun), David Knell (Checker), John Harnagel (Hotel Manager), La Wanda Page (Hotel Maid), Daniel Riordan (Removal Man), Thomas Wagner (Umpire), Jean Spray (Gazzo), James Emery, Matt Roe (FBI Men), John Rogers (Policeman at motel), Valerie Wildman (TV Reporter), Daniel Trent (Bailiff), Rudy E. Morrison (Maitre 'd), Frank Roach (Judge), Jeff Fredricks (Booking cop)

Steve Martin, Rick Moranis, Joan Cusack Above: Leslie Cook,
Moranis

PUMP UP THE VOLUME

(NEW LINE CINEMA) Producers, Rupert Harvey, Sandy Stern; Executive Producers, Sara Risher, Nicolas Stiliadis, Syd Cappe; Director/Screenplay, Allan Moyle; Photography, Walt Lloyd; Music, Cliff Martinez; Designer, Robb Wilson King; Editors, Janice Hampton, Larry Block; Casting, Judith Holstra; Song: *Everybody Knows* by Leonard Cohen, Sharon Robinson/performed by Concrete Blonde; presented in association with SC Entertainment International; Dolby Stereo; Color; Rated R; 100 minutes; August release

CAST

Mark Hunter ("Hard Harry")	Christian Slater
Jan Emerson	Ellen Greene
Loretta Creswood	Annie Ross
Nora DiNiro	Samantha Mathis
Brian Hunter	Scott Paulin
Janie	Lala
Paige	Cheryl Pollak
Marta Hunter	Mimi Kennedy
Joey	Seth Green
Jamie	Ahmet Zappa
Mazz Mazzilli	Billy Morrissette
Matt	Chris Jacobs
Malcolm	Anthony Lucero
Murdock	Andy Romano
Chris	Matt McGrath
Luis Chavez	Keith Stuart Thayer
Mr. Woodward	Jeff Chamberlain
Cheryl	Holly Sampson
Annie	Annie Rusoff
Jonathan	Jonathan Mazer
Alex	Alex Enberg
Doug	Robert Gavin
Donald	Dan Eisenstein
Eric	Mark Ballou
Cory	Daryl Sebert
Teacher Moore	Gregg Daniel
Teacher Stern	Marc Siegler
David Deaver	Robert Schenkkan
Alissa	Ariana Mohit
Mrs. Kaiser	Jill Jarres
Chip	Nolan Hemmings
Holden Chu	Justin Hessling
Gordon	Jay Lambert
Shep Sheppard	Clayton Landy
Detective Denny	Robert Harvey
Linda	Virginia Keehne
Marshall	Nigel Gibbs
Jack	David Glasser
Watts	James Hampton
Carlos Chavez	John Pinero
Joni	Juliet Landau
Gil	Ed Trotta
Mick	Kenneth McMurphy
Crispin	Roger Scott

and Allan Kolman (Postal Clerk), David McKnight (Detective #1), Tony Auer (Police Officer), Paulette Ballock (Police Dispatcher), Larry Clardy, John K. Shull, Lin Shaye, Michelle Bernath (PTA Parents), Stephen Duvall, Sherri Shaffner (Reporters), Steve Archer (Harry Video), Roger Scott, Gary Dubin (TV Announcers).

Top: Christian Slater Below: Lala, Samantha Mathis
© *New Line Cinema Corp.*

Ahmet Zappa, Lala

Samantha Mathis, Christian Slater Above: Slater, Mathis

81

Jason Patric, Rachel Ward (also top left) Top Right: Patric
© *Avenue Pictures*

AFTER DARK, MY SWEET

(AVENUE PICTURES) Producers, Robert Redlin, Ric Kidney; Executive Producer, Cary Brokaw; Director, James Foley; Screenplay, Robert Redlin, James Foley; Based on the novel by Jim Thompson; Photography, Mark Plummer; Designer, David Brisbin; Costumes, Hope Hanafin; Music, Maurice Jarre; Editor, Howard Smith; Casting, David Rubin; Assistant Director, David B. Householter; Dolby Stereo; Widescreen; Color; Rated R; 114 minutes; August release

CAST

Kevin "Collie" Collins	Jason Patric
Bert	Rocky Giordani
Fay Anderson	Rachel Ward
Uncle Bud	Bruce Dern
Counterman	Tom Wagner
Truck Driver	Michael G. Hagerty
Second Driver	James E. Bowen, Jr.
Doc Goldman	George Dickerson
Flashback Fighter	Vince Mazzella, Jr.
Boxing Referee	Napoleon Walls
Jack	Corey Carrier
Nanny	Jeanie Moore
Charlie	James Cotton
Cop	Burke Byrnes

Jason Patric, Rachel Ward Above: Bruce Dern

DARKMAN

(UNIVERSAL) Producer, Robert Tapert; Director/Story, Sam Raimi; Screenplay, Chuck Pfarrer, Sam Raimi, Ivan Raimi, Daniel Goldin, Joshua Goldin; Line Producer, Daryl Kass; Photography, Bill Pope; Designer, Randy Ser; Supervising Editors, Bud Smith, Scott Smith; Costumes, Grania Preston; Make-up Effects, Tony Gardner, Larry Hamlin; Music, Danny Elfman; Assistant Director, Scott Javine; Visual Effects, Introvision Systems International, Inc.; Stunts, Chris Doyle; Dolby Stereo; Deluxe color; Rated R; 95 minutes; August release

CAST

Peyton Westlake/Darkman	Liam Neeson
Julie Hastings	Frances McDormand
Louis Strack, Jr.	Colin Friels
Robert G. Durant	Larry Drake
Yakitito	Nelson Mashita
Eddie Black	Jesse Lawrence Ferguson
Rudy Guzman	Rafael H. Robledo
Skip	Danny Hicks
Rick	Theodore Raimi
Smiley	Dan Bell
Pauly	Nicholas Worth
Martin Katz	Aaron Lustig
Hung Fat	Arsenio "Sonny" Trinidad
Convenience Store Clerk	Said Faraj
Chinese Warriors	Nathan Jung, Prof. Toru Tanaka
Carnival Booth Attendant	John Lisbon Wood
Side Show Barker	Frank Noon
Limo Driver	William Dear
Gravedigger	Julius Harris
Doctor	Jenny Agutter
Computer Voice	Bridget Hoffman
Priest	Philip A. Gillis
Nurse	Maggie Moore
Policemen	Carl Bresk, Sean Daniel
Physician	John Landis
Screaming Woman	Carrie Hall
Bartender	John Cameron

and Craig Hosking (Helicopter Pilot), Karl Wickman, Cliff Fleming (Police Helicopter Pilots), Andy Bale, Neal McDonough, Stuart Cornfeld, William Lustig, Scott Spiegel, Cary Tyler (Dockworkers), Charles W. Young (Dockworker with bullet in forehead), Bruce Campbell (Final shemp)

Top: Liam Neeson Below: Larry Drake
Right: Frances McDormand, Neeson
© *Universal City Studios*

Nicholas Worth, Liam Neeson

Colin Friels, Frances McDormand

Diane Keaton, Kathryn Grody, Carol Kane Top Right: Ruben
Blades, Aidan Quinn Right: Grody, Keaton, Kane
© *Miramax Films*

THE LEMON SISTERS

(MIRAMAX) Producer, Joe Kelly; Executive Producers, Tom Kuhn,
Charles Mitchell, Arne Holland; Director, Joyce Chopra; Screenplay,
Jeremy Pikser; Co-Executive Producers, Harvey Weinstein, Robert
Weinstein; Associate Producer, Susan Slonaker; Photography, Bobby
Byrne; Designer, Patrizia Von Brandenstein; Editors, Joseph Wein-
traub, Michael R. Miller, Edward H. Glass; Musical Performances
Supervised and Arranged by Paul Shaffer; Music, Dick Hyman; Cos-
tumes, Susan Becker; Casting, Mary Colquhoun; Assistant Director,
Tony Lucibello; Choreographer, Anita Mann; Dolby Stereo; Color;
Rated PG-13; 93 minutes; August release

CAST

Eloise Hamer	Diane Keaton
Franki D'Angelo	Carol Kane
Nola Frank	Kathryn Grody
Fred Frank	Elliott Gould
C.W.	Rubén Blades
Frankie McGuinness	Aidan Quinn
Mrs. Kupchak	Estelle Parsons
Nicholas Panas	Richard Libertini
Baxter O'Neil	Sully Boyar
MC (TV Quiz Show)	Bill Boggs
Sadie Frank	Emily A. Rose
Sarah Frank	Ashley Peldon
Scotty Willard	Nicky Bronson
Charlene	Francine Fargo
Vinnie	Joe Milazzo
Stage Manager	Neil Miller
Charlie Sorrel	Nathan Lane
Real Estate Agent	Joanne Bradley
Man (Bacchanal Room)	Joel S. Fogel
Doorman	Julius Clifton Webb
Young Eloise	Kourtney Donohue
Young Nola	Rachel Hillman
Young Franki	Rachel Aviva
Hawker	Sal Domani
Teacher	Maggie Burke
Marilyn Fogelman	Tany Taylor Powers
Nola's Mother	Paulette Attie
Edward	Peter Costa
Bellhop	Ben Lin
Eloise's Father	Matthew Modine
Boardwalk Lady	Jessica James

and Tony Devon (Booker), Scheryll Anderson (Waitress), J. Mark
Danley, Nina Hodoruk .(Yuppie House Buyers), Nicole Weinstein
(Daddy's Girl Voice), Murray Weinstock (Piano Player), Monique
Nichole Alterman (Taffy Girl), Ashley Walls, Lauren Walls, Melissa
Walls (Baby)

Diane Keaton, Elliott Gould Above: Keaton, Kathryn Grody,
Carol Kane

Gary Oldman, Robin Wright, Sean Penn Top Right: Ed Harris,
R. D. Call Right: Penn, Oldman
© *Orion Pictures Corp.*

STATE OF GRACE

(ORION) Producers, Ned Dowd, Randy Ostrow, Ron Rotholz; Director, Phil Joanou; Screenplay, Dennis McIntyre; Photography, Jordan Cronenweth; Music, Ennio Morricone; Costumes, A.·de Bronson-Howard; Designers, Patrizia Von Brandenstein, Doug Kraner; Editor, Claire Simpson; Assistant Director, Thomas Mack; a Cinehaus Production; Dolby Stereo; Deluxe color; Rated R; 134 minutes; September release

CAST

Terry Noonan	Sean Penn
Frankie Flannery	Ed Harris
Jackie Flannery	Gary Oldman
Kathleen Flannery	Robin Wright
Nick	John Turturro
Stevie	John C. Reilly
Nicholson	R. D. Call
Borelli	Joe Viterelli
Finn	Burgess Meredith
Irene	Deirdre O'Connell
Cavello	Marco St. John
DeMarco	James Russo
Frankie's Men	Thomas G. Waites, Brian Burke, Michael Cumpsty, Michael Cunningham, Daniel O'Shea, Thomas F. Duffy
Alvarez	Jaime Tirelli
Stevie's Date	Sandra Beall
Borelli's Men	Vincent Guastaferro, John Anthony Williams, John Roselius, Louis Eppolito
Maureen	Mo Gaffney
Raferty	John MacKay
Raferty's Son	John Ottavino
Bar Customers	Tim Gallin, Timothy D. Klein
Matty's Bartender	Jack Wallace
Bartenders	Frank Girardeau, Michael P. Moran, Frank Coletta
Pool Hall Manager	Paul-Felix Montez
Waitress	Freddi Chandler
Police Detective	Tommy Sullivan
Hotel Doorman	Ben Fine
Frankie's Children	Saasha Costello, Catherine Stewart

Sean Penn, Gary Oldman, John C. Reilly Above: Penn,
John Turturro

85

POSTCARDS FROM THE EDGE

(COLUMBIA) Producers, Mike Nichols, John Calley; Director, Mike Nichols; Executive Producers, Neil Machlis, Robert Greenhut; Screenplay, Carrie Fisher, based on her novel; Photography, Michael Ballhaus; Designer, Patrizia Von Brandenstein; Music, Carly Simon; Editor, Sam O'Steen; Costumes, Ann Roth; Casting, Juliet Taylor, Ellen Lewis; Assistant Director, Michael Haley; Musical Numbers Supervisor, Howard Shore; *"I'm Checking Out"* by Shel Silverstein, *"You Don't Know Me"* by C. Walker and E. Arnold/performed by Meryl Streep; *"I'm Still Here"* by Stephen Sondheim/performed by Shirley MacLaine; Dolby Stereo; Technicolor; Rated R; 101 minutes; September release

CAST

Suzanne Vale	Meryl Streep
Doris Mann	Shirley MacLaine
Jack Falkner	Dennis Quaid
Lowell	Gene Hackman
Dr. Frankenthal	Richard Dreyfuss
Joe Pierce	Rob Reiner
Grandma	Mary Wickes
Grandpa	Conrad Bain
Evelyn Ames	Annette Bening
Simon Asquith	Simon Callow
Marty Wiener	Gary Morton
Julie Marsden	C. C. H. Pounder
Sid Roth	Sidney Armus
Aretha	Robin Bartlett
Carol	Barbara Garrick
George Lazan	Anthony Heald
Wardrobe Mistress	Dana Ivey
Neil Bleene	Oliver Platt
Robert Munch	Michael Ontkean
Raoul	Pepe Serna
Bart	Mark Lowenthal
Allen	Michael Byers
Ted	J. D. Souther
Carl	George Wallace
Cameraman	Peter Onorati
Make-up Man	Roy Helland
Soundman	Douglas Roberts
Assistant Director	R. M. Haley
Cindy	Kathleen Gray
Maid at party	Gloria Crayton
Sound Editors	Gary Matanky, Marc Tubert
Young Intern	John Verea
Passport Official	René Assa
Friends at airport	Natalia Nogulich, Susan Forristal
Airline Employee	Evelina Fernandez
Rob Sonnenfeld	Neil Machlis
Fan at party	Gary Jones
Nurse	Jane Galloway
Assistant Director	Steven Brill
Officer	Jason Tomlins
First Lady	Shelley Kirk
Script Supervisor	Jessica Z. Diamond
Pianist at party	Scott Frankel
Stand-in	Sheridan Leatherbury
Director of Photography	Ken Gutstein
Blue Rodeo Band	Jim Cuddy, Greg Keelor, Bazil Donovan, Mark French, Bob Weiseman

Top: Meryl Streep, Shirley MacLaine
Below: Gene Hackman, Streep
© *Columbia Pictures*

Mark Lowenthal, Michael Byers, Meryl Streep,
Shirley MacLaine

Meryl Streep, Shirley MacLaine, Gary Morton Top Left: Scott Frankel, MacLaine
Above Left: Streep, Dennis Quaid Top Right: Streep

WHITE HUNTER, BLACK HEART

(WARNER BROS.) Producer/Director, Clint Eastwood; Co-Producer, Stanley Rubin; Screenplay, Peter Viertel, James Bridges, Burt Kennedy; Based on the novel by Peter Viertel; Executive Producer, David Valdes; Photography, Jack N. Green; Designer, John Graysmark; Music, Lennie Niehaus; Costumes, John Mollo; Editor, Joel Cox; Casting, Mary Selway; Assistant Director, Patrick Clayton; Stunts, George Orrison; a Malpaso/Rastar production; Dolby Stereo; Technicolor; Rated PG; 112 minutes; September release

CAST

John Wilson	Clint Eastwood
Pete Verrill	Jeff Fahey
Miss Wilding	Charlotte Cornwell
Butler George	Norman Lumsden
Paul Landers	George Dzundza
Reissar	Edward Tudor Pole
Thompson	Roddy Maude-Roxby
Basil Fields	Richard Warwick
Gun Shop Salesman	John Rapley
Irene Saunders	Catherine Neilson
Kay Gibson	Marisa Berenson
Phil Duncan	Richard Vanstone
Mrs. Duncan	Jamie Koss
Scarf Girl	Anne Dunkley
Bongo Man	David Danns
Ape Man	Myles Freeman
Alec Laing	Geoffrey Hutchings
Tom Harrison	Christopher Fairbank
Ralph Lockhart	Alun Armstrong
Harry	Clive Mantle
Mrs. MacGregor	Mel Martin
Dickie Marlowe	Martin Jacobs
Desk Clerk	Norman Malunga
Hodkins	Timothy Spall
Zibelinsky	Alex Norton
Dorshka	Eleanor David
Kivu	Boy Mathias Chuma
Photographer	Andrew Whalley
Ogilvy	Conrad Asquith

Top: Clint Eastwood Below: Jeff Fahey, Conrad Asquith,
Eastwood Left: Boy Mathias Chuma, Eastwood
© *Warner Bros.*

Clint Eastwood, Jeff Fahey

Marisa Berenson, Richard Vanstone, Jamie Koss

Clint Eastwood

Clint Eastwood, Boy Mathias Chuma Above: George Dzundza,
Eastwood

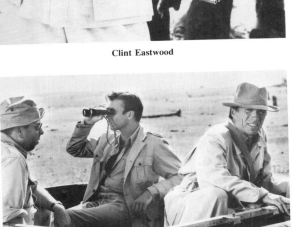

Clint Eastwood, Jeff Fahey Above Left: Timothy Spall, Fahey,
Eastwood

Martin Jacobs, Mel Martin, Clint Eastwood Above Right:
Martin, Eastwood

GOODFELLAS

(WARNER BROS.) Producer, Irwin Winkler; Director, Martin Scorsese; Screenplay, Nicholas Pileggi, Martin Scorsese; Based on the book *"Wiseguy"* by Nicholas Pileggi; Executive Producer, Barbara De Fina; Photography, Michael Ballhaus; Designer, Kristi Zea; Editor, Thelma Schoonmaker; Casting, Ellen Lewis; Associate Producer/Unit Production Manager, Bruce Pustin; Costumes, Richard Bruno; Assistant Director, Joseph Reidy; Dolby Stereo; Technicolor; Rated R; 146 minutes; September release

CAST

James Conway	Robert De Niro
Henry Hill	Ray Liotta
Tommy DeVito	Joe Pesci
Karen Hill	Lorraine Bracco
Paul Cicero	Paul Sorvino

and Frank Sivero (Frankie Carbone), Tony Darrow (Sonny Bunz), Mike Starr (Frenchy), Frank Vincent (Billy Batts), Chuck Low (Morris Kessler), Frank DiLeo (Tuddy Cicero), Henny Youngman (Himself), Gina Mastrogiacomo (Janice Rossi), Catherine Scorsese (Tommy's Mother), Charles Scorsese (Vinnie), Suzanne Shepherd (Karen's Mother), Debi Mazar (Sandy), Margo Winkler (Belle Kessler), Welker White (Lois Byrd), Jerry Vale (Himself), Julie Garfield (Mickey Conway), Christopher Serrone (Young Henry), Elaine Kagan (Henry's Mother), Beau Starr (Henry's Father), Kevin Corrigan (Michael Hill), Michael Imperioli (Spider), Robbie Vinton (Bobby Vinton), John Williams (Johnny Roastbeef), Daniel P. Conte (Dr. Dan), Tony Conforti (Tony), Frank Pellegrino (Johnny Dio), Ronald Maccone (Ronnie), Tony Sirico (Tony Stacks), Joseph D'Onofrio (Young Tommy), Steve Forleo, Richard Dioguardi (City Detectives), Frank Adonis (Anthony Stabile), John Manca (Nickey Eyes), Joseph Bono (Mikey Franzese), Katherine Wallach (Diane), Mark Evan Jacobs (Bruce), Angela Pietropinto (Cicero's Wife), Marianne Leone (Tuddy's Wife), Marie Michaels (Mrs. Carbone), Lo Nardo (Frenchy's Wife), Melissa Prophet (Angie), Illeana Douglas (Rosie), Susan Varon (Susan), Elizabeth Whitcraft (Tommy's Girlfriend at the Copa), Clem Caserta (Joe Buddha), Samuel L. Jackson (Stacks Edwards), Fran McGee (Johnny Roastbeef's Wife), Paul Herman (Dealer), Edward McDonald (Himself), Edward Hayes (Defense Attorney), Daniela Barbosa, Gina Mattia (Young Henry's Sisters), Joel Calendrillo (Young Henry's Brother), Anthony Valentin (Young Michael), Edward D. Murphy, Michael Citriniti (Liquor Cops), Peter Hock (Mailman), Erasmus C. Alfano (Barbeque Wiseguy), John DiBenedetto (Bleeding Man), Manny Alfaro (Gambling Doorman), Thomas Lowry (Hijacked Driver), Margaret Smith (School Guard), Richard Mullally (Cop #1), Frank Albanese (Mob Lawyer), Paul McIssac (Judge—1956), Bob Golub (Truck Driver at diner), Louis Eppolito (Fat Andy), Tony Lip (Frankie the Wop), Mikey Black (Freddy No Nose), Peter Cicale (Pete the Killer), Anthony Powers (Jimmy Two Times), Vinny Pastore (Man with coatrack), Anthony Alessandro, Victor Colicchio (Henry's 60's crew), Mike Contessa, Philip Suriano (Cicero's 60's crew), Paul Mougey (Terrorized Waiter), Norman Barbera (Bouncer), Anthony Polemeni (Copa Captain), James Quattrochi, Lawrence Sacco, Dino Laudicina (Henry Greeters), Thomas E. Camuti, Andrew Scudiero (Mr. Tony hoods), Irving Welzer (Copa Announcer), Jesse Kirtzman (Beach Club Waiter), Russell Halley, Spencer Bradley (Bruce's Brothers), Bob Altman (Karen's Dad), Joanna Bennett (Marie #1), Gayle Lewis (Marie #2), Gaetano Lisi (Paul #3), Luke Walter (Truck Driver), Ed Deacy (Det. Deacy), Larry Silvestri (Det. Silvestri), Johnny Cha Cha Ciarcia, Frank Aquilino (Batt's crew), Vito Picone (Vito), Janis Corsair (Vito's Girlfriend), Lisa Dapolito (Lisa), Michael Calandrino (Godfather at table), Vito Antuofermo (Prizefighter), Vito Balsamo, Peter Fain, Vinnie Gallo, Gaetano LoGiudice, Garry Blackwood (Henry's 70's crew), Nicole Burdette (Carbone's Girlfriend), Stella Kietel (Judy, Henry's older child), Dominique DeVito (Ruth, Henry's Baby), Michaelangelo Graziano (Bar Patron), Paula Gallo, Nadine Kay (Janice's Girlfriends), Tony Ellis (Bridal Shop Owner), Peter Onorati (Florida Bookie), Jamie DeRoy (Bookie's Sister), Joel Blake (Judge—1971), H. Clay Dear (Security Guard with lobsters), Thomas Hewson (Drug Buyer), Gene Canfield (Prison Guard in booth), Margaux Guerard (Judy Hill at 10 yrs.), Violet Gaynor (Ruth Hill at 8 years), Tobin Bell (Parole Officer), Berlinda Tolbert (Stacks' Girlfriend), Nancy Ellen Cassaro (Joe Buddha's Wife), Adam Wandt (Kid), Joseph P. Gioco (Garbage Man), Isiah Whitlock, Jr. (Doctor), Alyson Jones (Judy Hill at 13 yrs.), Ruby Gaynor (Ruth Hill at 11 yrs.), Richard "Bo" Dietl (Arresting Narc)

© *Warner Bros.*
Top: Ray Liotta, Robert De Niro, Mike Starr
Below: Lorraine Bracco, Liotta

Joe Pesci received the Academy Award for Best Supporting Actor of 1990

Christopher Serrone, Robert De Niro, Joseph D'Onofrio Above:
De Niro, Ray Liotta

Robert De Niro, Ray Liotta, Paul Sorvino Top Left: De Niro, Liotta Above Left: Liotta, Lorraine Bracco Top Right: Liotta, De Niro, Sorvino, Joe Pesci

FUNNY ABOUT LOVE

(PARAMOUNT) Producers, Jon Avnet, Jordan Kerner; Director, Leonard Nimoy; Screenplay, Norman Steinberg, David Frankel; Based upon the article "*Convention of the Love Goddesses*" by Bob Greene; Photography, Fred Murphy; Designer, Stephen Storer; Music, Miles Goodman; Editor, Peter E. Berger; Costumes, Albert Wolsky; Casting, Amanda Mackey; Assistant Director, Douglas E. Wise; Dolby Stereo; Technicolor; Rated PG-13; 101 minutes; September release

CAST

Duffy Bergman	Gene Wilder
Meg Lloyd	Christine Lahti
Daphne Delillo	Mary Stuart Masterson
Emil "E.T." Thomas Bergman	Robert Prosky
Dr. Hugo Blatt	Stephen Tobolowsky
Adele Bergman	Anne Jackson
Claire Raskin	Susan Ruttan
Vivian	Jean De Baer
Dr. Benjamin	David Margulies
Redhead	Tara Shannon
Nurse	Freda Foh Shen
Nurse Nancy	Wendie Malick
Roger	Robert Gorman
Jake	Scott Groff
Ellis Hayden	Ramy Zada
Sotto Voce Maitre d'	Lorenzo Caccialanza
Bill Hatcher	Paul Collins
Jerry	Andrew Hill Newman
Alexandra	Courtney Barilla
Waiters	Justin Ross, Kevin Shaw, Jeff Nimoy
Waitress	Sherlynn Hicks
Elevator Operators	Dave Nicolson, David Larson
Steve	Michael Bofshever
Avi	Lewis J. Stadlen
Bobbie	Anne Lange
Delta Gammas	Kathryn Miller, Celeste Yarnall, Jeannette Kerner, Kirstina Kochoff
Duffy's Doorman	R. J. Arterburn
Guest	Jonathan Tisch
Kathryn	Elizabeth Morehead
Themselves	Regis Philbin, Chantal Westerman, Patrick Ewing
Photographer	Tim Ottoman
Attendant	Dennison Samaroo

and Doug Sills (Italian Tenor), Michael Snyder (Video camera assistant), Paul J. Q. Lee (Moving Man), Joe Zaloom (Cappuccino Vendor).

Top: Christine Lahti, Gene Wilder Below: Wilder, Mary Stuart Masterson Right: Robert Prosky; Susan Ruttan
© *Paramount Pictures*

Christine Lahti, Gene Wilder

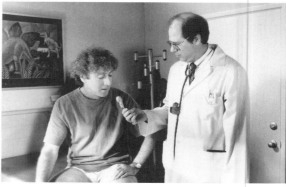

Gene Wilder, Stephen Tobolowsky

James B. Sikking, Gene Hackman Above: Hackman Top Right:
Anne Archer, Hackman

NARROW MARGIN

(TRI-STAR) Producer, Jonathan A. Zimbert; Director/Screenplay/
Photography, Peter Hyams; Executive Producers, Mario Kassar, An-
drew Vajna; Designer, Joel Schiller; Music, Bruce Broughton; Editor,
James Mitchell; Co-Producer, Jerry Offsay; Associate Producer, Mary
Eilts; Assistant Director, Jack Frost Sanders; Stunts, Glenn Wilder;
from Carolco Pictures; Dolby Stereo; Panavision; Technicolor; Rated
R; 97 minutes; September release

CAST

Robert Caulfield	Gene Hackman
Carol Hunnicut	Anne Archer
Nelson	James B. Sikking
Michael Tarlow	J. T. Walsh
Sgt. Dominick Benti	M. Emmet Walsh
Kathryn Weller	Susan Hogan
Jack Wootton	Nigel Bennett
Martin Larner	J. A. Preston
Keller	B. A. "Smitty" Smith
Nicholas	Codie Lucas Wilbee
Nicholas' Mother	Barbara E. Russell
Elderly Man	Antony Holland
Elderly Woman	Doreen Ramos
James Dahlbeck	Kevin McNulty
Nigro	Andrew Rhodes
Loughlin	Lon Katzman
Bellman with message	Dana Still
Larner's Secretary	Lesley Ewen
Ticket Agent	Barney O'Sullivan
Bartender	Natino Bellantoni
Conductors	Ted Stidder, Tom McBeath
Club Car Waiter	Lindsay Bourne
Dining Car Waiter	Robert Rozen
Hotel Valet	Ron Cummins
Leo Watts	Harris Yulin

M. Emmet Walsh, Gene Hackman, Anne Archer Above:
Hackman, Codie Lucas Wilbee

Albert Finney, Gabriel Byrne Top Left: Byrne, Jon Polito
Left: John Turturro
© 20th Century Fox

MILLER'S CROSSING

(20th CENTURY FOX) Producer, Ethan Coen; Director, Joel Coen; Screenplay, Joel Coen, Ethan Coen; Co-Producer, Mark Silverman; Line Producer, Graham Place; Executive Producer, Ben Barenholtz; Photography, Barry Sonnenfeld; Designer, Dennis Gassner; Costumes, Richard Hornung; Music, Carter Burwell; Editor, Michael Miller; Song: "Danny Boy" sung by Frank Patterson; Casting, Donna Isaacson, John Lyons; Assistant Director, Gary Marcus; Stunts, Jery Hewitt; a Ted and Jim Pedas/Ben Barenholtz/Bill Durkin Production presented by Circle Films; Dolby Stereo; Deluxe/DuArt color; Rated R; 114 minutes; September release

CAST

Tom Reagan	Gabriel Byrne
Verna	Marcia Gay Harden
Bernie Bernbaum	John Turturro
Johnny Caspar	Jon Polito
Eddie Dane	J. E. Freeman
Leo	Albert Finney
Frankie	Mike Starr
Tic-Tac	Al Mancini
Mayor Dale Levander	Richard Woods
O'Doole	Thomas Toner
Mink	Steve Buscemi
Clarence "Drop" Johnson	Mario Todisco
Tad	Olek Krupa
Adolph	Michael Jeter
Terry	Lanny Flaherty
Mrs. Caspar	Jeanette Kontomitras
Johnny Caspar, Jr.	Louis Charles Mounicou III
Cop (Brian)	John McConnell
Cop (Delahanty)	Danny Aiello III
Screaming Lady	Helen Jolly
Landlady	Hilda McLean
Gunmen in Leo's house	Monte Starr, Don Picard
Rug Daniels	Salvatore H. Tornaberie
Street Urchin	Kevin Dearie
Caspar's Driver	Michael Badalucco
Caspar's Butler	Charles Ferrara
Caspar's Cousins	Esteban Fernandez, George Fernandez
Hitman at Verna's	Charles Gunning
Hitman #2	Dave Drinkx
Lazarre's Messenger	David Darlow
Lazarre's Toughs	Robert LaBrosse, Carl Rooney
Man with pipe bomb	Jack David Harris
Son of Erin	Jery Hewitt
Snickering Gunman	Sam Raimi
Cop with bullhorn	John Schnauder, Jr.
Rabbi	Zolly Levin
Boxers	Joey Ancona, Bill Raye
Secretary	Frances McDormand

Jon Polito Above: Gabriel Byrne, Marcia Gay Harden

Gabriel Byrne, Albert Finney Top Left: J. E. Freeman Above Left: Byrne, Marcia
Gay Harden Top Right: John Turturro Above Right: Finney

Michael Keaton Top Left: Melanie Griffith,
Matthew Modine Left: Keaton, Griffith
© *Morgan Creek Film Partners*

PACIFIC HEIGHTS

(20th CENTURY FOX) Producers, Scott Rudin, William Sackheim; Director, John Schlesinger; Screenplay, Daniel Pyne; Executive Producers, James G. Robinson, Joe Roth; Co-Executive Producers, David Nicksay, Gary Barber; Co-Producer, Dennis E. Jones; Photography, Amir Mokri; Designer, Neil Spisak; Editor, Mark Warner; Music, Hans Zimmer; Costumes, Ann Roth, Bridget Kelly; Casting, Mali Finn; Assistant Director, Herb Gains; a Morgan Creek Production; Dolby Stereo; Deluxe color; Rated R; 103 minutes; September release

CAST

Patty Palmer	Melanie Griffith
Drake Goodman	Matthew Modine
Carter Hayes	Michael Keaton
Toshio Watanabe	Mako
Mira Watanabe	Nobu McCarthy
Stephanie MacDonald	Laurie Metcalf
Lou Baker	Carl Lumbly
Dennis Reed	Dorian Harewood
Greg	Luca Bercovici
Florence Peters	Tippi Hedren
Liz Hamilton	Sheila McCarthy
Warning Cop	Guy Boyd
Bennett Fidlow	Jerry Hardin
Anne	Beverly D'Angelo
Loan Officer	Dan Hedaya
District Attorney	James Staley
Realtor	Miriam Margolyes
Revilla	Luis Oropeza
Judge	F. William Parker
Hotel Manager	Nicholas Pryor
Desk Clerk	Tony Simotes
Hotel Maid	O-Lan Jones
Sergeant	Seth Isler
Mr. Thayer	Dabbs Greer
Mrs. Thayer	Florence Sundstrom
Mrs. Smith	Noel Evangelisti
Child	Nicolas Rutherford
Younger Man	Tim Pulice
Older Man	Ray Hanis
Bank Teller	Takayo Fischer
Al	Tom Nolan
George	Daniel MacDonald
Deputy Sheriffs	J. P. Bumstead, Hal Landon, Jr.
Locksmith	Hy Anzell
Exterminator	Tracey Walter
Mr. Hill	William Patterson
Bill	D. W. Moffett
Amy	Barbara Bush

and John Diaz (Shoe Shine), Roger Bearde (Arresting Cop), Ed Hodson (Other Cop), Frank Di Elsi (Precinct Cop), Michael J. Parker (Man at police station), Maggy Myers Davidson (Diamond Lady), Buddy Ekins, Danny Wynands (Thugs), David Lloyd Wilson (Television Host), Matthew Flint, Scott Freeman, Alice Barden, Danny Kovacs, Wat Takeshita, Frank Maruoka, Tohoru Masamune, Aida Anderson, Linda Austin (Neighbors), John Schlesinger (Man getting on elevator)

Matthew Modine, Melanie Griffith, Michael Keaton Above:
Modine

**Randy Quaid Top Left: Cybill Shepherd, Jeff Bridges
Left: Timothy Bottoms; William McNamara**
© *Columbia Pictures*

TEXASVILLE

(COLUMBIA) Producers, Barry Spikings, Peter Bogdanovich; Director/Screenplay, Peter Bogdanovich; Based on the novel by Larry McMurtry; Executive Producers, Jake Eberts, William Peiffer; Co-Producer, Al Ruban; Photography, Nicholas Von Sternberg; Designer, Phedon Papamichael; Editor, Richard Fields; Costumes, Rita Riggs; Casting, Gary Chason, Ross Brown; Assistant Director, John S. Curran; Key Makeup Artist, Zoltan; Songs by various artists; a Nelson Entertainment presentation; Deluxe color; Rated R; 123 minutes; September release

CAST

Duane Jackson	Jeff Bridges
Jacy Farrow	Cybill Shepherd
Karla Jackson	Annie Potts
Sonny Crawford	Timothy Bottoms
Ruth Popper	Cloris Leachman
Lester Marlow	Randy Quaid
Genevieve	Eileen Brennan
Dickie Jackson	William McNamara
Marylou Marlow	Angie Bolling
Suzie Nolan	Su Hyatt
Junior Nolan	Earl Poole Ball
Nellie	Katherine Bongfeldt
Billie Anne	Allison Marich
Lavelle Bates	Kay Pering
Julie	Romy Snyder
Jack	Jimmy Howell
Lee Roy	Loyd Catlett
Minerva	Pearl Jones
Old Man Balt	Harvey Christiansen
T.V. News Anchor	Meri Beth Moore
Shorty	Jake
Charlene Duggs	Sharon Ullrick
Ed Balt	Adam Englund
Dairy Queen Waitresses	Lou Toft, P. J. Johnson
Sheriff Burns	Gordon Hurst
Little Mike	Ty Chambers
Barbette	Leah Anne Worofka
Beulah Balt	Gena Sleete
Rev. G. G. Rawley	Leiland Jaynes
Joe Bob Blanton	Barclay Doyle

and Jim Bob Crowley (Ambulance Driver), James Harrell (Odessa Oil Man), Ella Marie Morris (Bus Depot waitress), Mikala Parrack (Girl with snow cone), Midwestern State Band (Pageant Band), Carlye Berre, Jolene Berre (Stauffer Girls), Leon Gibbs, Ryan Phillips (Fiddle Players), Charles Scribner (Egg Truck Driver), Race Rutledge, Jim Mortan, Tom Sokora, Mike Hukli, Jimmy Boggs, Paul Cass (Texas Knights Dance Band)

**Eileen Brennan, Cloris Leachman Above: Cybill Shepherd,
Annie Potts**

DESPERATE HOURS

(MGM) Producers, Dino De Laurentiis, Michael Cimino; Director, Michael Cimino; Screenplay, Lawrence Konner, Mark Rosenthal, Joseph Hayes; Based on the novel and play by Joseph Hayes; Executive Producer, Martha Schumacher; Photography, Doug Milsome; Designer, Victoria Paul; Music, David Mansfield; Supervising Editor, Peter Hunt; Costumes, Charles De Caro; Line Producer, Mel Dellar; Casting, Mary Colquhoun; Assistant Director, Brian Cook; from MGM/UA, a Dino De Laurentiis Communications production; Dolby Stereo; Deluxe color; Rated R; 105 minutes; October release

CAST

Michael Bosworth	Mickey Rourke
Tim Cornell	Anthony Hopkins
Nora Cornell	Mimi Rogers
Brenda Chandler	Lindsay Crouse
Nancy Breyers	Kelly Lynch
Wally Bosworth	Elias Koteas
Albert	David Morse
May Cornell	Shawnee Smith
Zack Cornell	Danny Gerard
Ed Tallent	Gerry Bamman
Kyle	Matt McGrath
Neff	John Christopher Jones
Maddox	Dean Norris
Lexington	John Finn
Chabon	Christopher Curry
Devereaux	Stanley White
Connelly	Peter Crombie
Kate	Ellen Parker
Judge	Elizabeth Ruscio
Repairman	Kenneth Bass
Mr. Nelson	Mike Nussbaum
Bank Teller	Ellen McElduff
College Girls	Brittney Lewis, Lise Wilburn
Prosecutor	James Rebhorn
Ornitz	Michael Flynn
Coogan	Jeff Olson
Trooper	Robert Condor
Police Detective	Bradley Leatham
Coroner	Brian James Anderson
Security Guard at bank	Matthew Rangi Brown

and Ron Bird, Alexis Fernandez, Bob Evans (Reporters), George Sullivan, Robert Rowe (Snipers), Daniel Cussiter, Gary Flener, Richard Hernandez, Gary Parker, James Thornton (SWAT Team)

Top: Kelly Lynch, Mickey Rourke Below: Danny Gerard, Mimi Rogers Left: Lindsay Crouse
© Metro-Goldwyn-Mayer

Mickey Rourke

Anthony Hopkins, Mimi Rogers, Shawnee Smith

Steven Seagal, Basil Wallace Top Left: Keith David Left: Seagal
© *20th Century Fox*

MARKED FOR DEATH

(20th CENTURY FOX) Producers, Michael Grais, Mark Victor, Steven Seagal; Director, Dwight H. Little; Screenplay, Michael Grais, Mark Victor; Co-Producer, Peter MacGregor-Scott; Photography, Ric Waite; Designer, Robb Wilson King; Editor, O. Nicholas Brown; Associate Producers, John Todgya, Julius R. Nasso; Music, James Newton Howard; Costumes, Isabella Van Soest Chubb; Casting, Fred Champion, Pamela Basker, Sue Swan; Assistant Director, Jerry Ziesmer; Produced in association with Steamroller Prods.; Dolby Stereo; Panavision; Deluxe color; Rated R; 96 minutes; October release

CAST

John Hatcher	Steven Seagal
Screwface	Basil Wallace
Max	Keith David
Charles	Tom Wright
Leslie	Joanna Pacula
Melissa	Elizabeth Gracen
Kate Hatcher	Bette Ford
Tracey	Danielle Harris
Tito	Al Israel
Duvall	Arlen Dean Snyder
Nesta	Victor Romero Evans
Monkey	Michael Ralph
Nago	Jeffrey Anderson-Gunter
Jimmy Fingers	Tony Di Benedetto
Roselli	Kevin Dunn
Pete Stone	Peter Jason
Hector	Danny Trejo
Chico	Richard Delmonte
Carmen	Elena Sahagun
Paco	Tom Dugan
Marta	Rita Verreos
Raoul	Joe Renteria
Little Richard	Carlos Cervantes
Mexican Bouncer	Wayne Montanio
Nicky	Nick Corello
Tommy	Grant Gelt
Freddy	Justin Murphy
Dr. Stein	Earl Boen
Sheriff O'Dwyer	Stanley White
Himself	Jimmy Cliff
Boys	Matt Levin, Philip Tanzini
Girls	Leslie Danon, Terri Ivens
News Reporter	Dale Harimoto
Sex Girls	Tracey Burch, Teri Weigel
Arms Dealer	Robert Ashiya Ganta Strickland

and Noel L. Walcott III (Posse Leader), Prince Ital Joe (Dread with Hostage), Andria Martel (Young Stripper), Nick Celozzi (Man in high hart bar), Debby Shively (Barmaid), Craig Pinkard (Bartender), Matt O'Toole (Yuppie Dealer), Linus Huffman (Dea Agent), Kerrie Cullen (Dept. Store Hostage)

Tom Wright, Joanna Pacula, Kevin Dunn Above: Basil Wallace

AVALON

(TRI-STAR) Producers, Mark Johnson, Barry Levinson; Director/Screenplay, Barry Levinson; Photography, Allen Daviau; Designer, Norman Reynolds; Music, Randy Newman; Editor, Stu Linder; Costumes, Gloria Gresham; Associate Producers, Marie Rowe, Charles J. Newirth; Casting, Ellen Chenoweth; Assistant Director, Peter Giuliano; a Baltimore Pictures production; Dolby Stereo; Technicolor; Rated PG; 126 minutes; October release

CAST

Hymie Krichinsky	Leo Fuchs
Dottie Kirk	Eve Gordon
Gabriel Krichinsky	Lou Jacobi
Sam Krichinsky	Armin Mueller-Stahl
Ann Kaye	Elizabeth Perkins
Eva Krichinsky	Joan Plowright
Izzy Kirk	Kevin Pollak
Jules Kaye	Aidan Quinn
Nathan Krichinsky	Israel Rubinek
Michael Kaye	Elijah Wood
Teddy Kirk	Grant Gelt
Mindy Kirk	Mindy Loren Isenstein
Nellie Krichinsky	Shifra Lerer
Alice Krichinsky	Mina Bern
Faye Krichinsky	Frania Rubinek
Herbie	Neil Kirk
Simka	Ronald Guttman
Elka	Rachel Aviva
Mrs. Parkes	Sylvia Weinberg
Principal Dunn	Ralph Tabakin
Moving Man	Steve Aronson
Gas Attendant	Miles A. Perman
Nursing Home Receptionist	Beatrice Yoffe
Country Club Page	Brian Sher
Mugger	Frank Tamburo
Fire Chief	Patrick Flynn
Rabbi at funeral	Herb Levinson
K&K Employee	Paul Quinn
Young Jules	Kevin Blum
The Father	Alvin Myerovich
William as a Young Man	Moishe Rosenfeld
Sam as a Young Man	Michael Krauss
Gabriel as a Young Man	Michael David Edelstein
Hymie as a Young Man	Bernard Hiller
Nathan as a Young Man	Brian Shait
Eva as a Young Woman	Dawne Hindle
Nellie as a Young Woman	Christine Mosere
Alice as a Young Woman	Anna Bergman
Faye as a Young Woman	Mary Lechter
Mollie as a Young Woman	Barbara Morris
Michael as an Adult	Tom Wood
Michael's Son Sam	Christopher James Lekas
David as a Baby	Ava Eileen Quinn
David at 8 months	David Thornhill
David at 10 years	Jordan Young
Camera Girl	Tammy Walker
TV Commercial Director	David Long
Night Club Singer	Brenda Alford
Country Club Singer	Thomas Joy
Supper Club Singer	James A. Zemarel

and Jesse Adelman, Judy Bach, Alisa Bernstein, Eva Cohen, Josh Lessner, Samantha Shenk, Patty Sherman, Irv Stein, Thelma Weiner, Robert Zalkind (Miscellaneous Family Members)

Top: Joan Plowright, Armin Mueller-Stahl, Aidan Quinn, Kevin Pollak Below: Aidan Quinn, Elizabeth Perkins
© *Tri-Star Pictures*

**Lou Jacobi, Leo Fuchs, Israel Rubinek, Armin Mueller-Stahl
Above: Mindy Loren Isenstein, Elijah Wood, Grant Gelt**

Armin Mueller-Stahl, Joan Plowright, Elizabeth Perkins, Elijah Wood, Aidan Quinn
Top Left: Perkins, Quinn, Plowright, Mueller-Stahl Above Left: Wood, Mueller-Stahl
Top Right: Wood, Quinn Above Right: Mina Bern, Plowright, Muller-Stahl,
Leo Fuchs

HENRY AND JUNE

(UNIVERSAL) Producer, Peter Kaufman; Director, Philip Kaufman; Screenplay, Philip Kaufman, Rose Kaufman; Based on the book by Anais Nin; Photography, Philippe Rousselot; Designer, Guy-Claude Francois; Editors, Vivien Hillgrove, William S. Scharf, Dede Allen; Costumes, Yvonne Sassinot De Nesle; Casting, Margot Capelier, Donna Isaacson, John Lyons; Associate Producer, Yannoulla Wakefield; Assistant Director, Eric Bartonio; a Walrus & Associates, Ltd. production; Dolby Stereo; Deluxe color; Rated NC-17; 136 minutes; October release

CAST

Henry Miller	Fred Ward
June Miller	Uma Thurman
Anais Nin	Maria De Medeiros
Hugo	Richard E. Grant
Osborn	Kevin Spacey
Eduardo	Jean-Philippe Ecoffey
Jack	Bruce Myers
Publisher/Editor	Jean-Louis Bunuel
Spanish Dance Instructor	Feodor Atkine
Emilia	Sylvie Huguel
Brassai	Artus De Penguern
Henry's Friend No. 1	Pierre Etaix
Henry's Friends (Magicians)	Pierre Edernac, Gaetan Bloom
Henry's Friend (Clown)	Alexandre De Gall
Osborn's Girlfriend	Karine Couvelard
Accordionist	Louis Bessieres
Contortionists	Erika Maury-Lascoux, Claire Joubert
Henry's Whore	Brigitte Lahaie
Frail Prostitute	Maite Maille
The Patronne	Annie Fratellini
Steamship Agent	Frank Heiler
Prostitute brushing long hair	Stephanie Leboulanger
Bal Negre Performer	Suzy Palatin
Black Musician (Quat'z Arts Ball)	Samuel Ateba
Man in silent film	Marc Maury
Fat Prostitute	Annie Vincent
Pop	Maurice Escargot
Jean	Liz Hasse

Top: Fred Ward, Uma Thurman Below: Richard E. Grant, Maria de Medeiros, Ward Right: de Medeiros, Thurman
© *Universal City Studios*

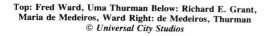

Richard E. Grant, Maria de Medeiros

Maria de Medeiros, Fred Ward, Uma Thurman

THE HOT SPOT

(ORION) Producer, Paul Lewis; Co-Producer, Deborah Capogrosso; Director, Dennis Hopper; Screenplay, Nona Tyson, Charles Williams; Based on the novel "Hell Hath No Fury" by Charles Williams; Executive Producers, Bill Gavin, Derek Power, Stephen Ujlaki; Photography, Ueli Steiger; Designer, Cary White; Music, Jack Nitzsche; Editor, Wende Phifer Mate; Costumes, Mary Kay Stolz; Casting, Lauren Lloyd, Gail Levin; Associate Producer, Valerie Tyson; Assistant Director, Frank Bueno; Stunts, Eddy Donno; Dolby Stereo; Deluxe color; Rated R; 129 minutes; October release

CAST

Harry Madox	Don Johnson
Dolly Harshaw	Virginia Madsen
Gloria Harper	Jennifer Connelly
Lon Gulik	Charles Martin Smith
Frank Sutton	William Sadler
George Harshaw	Jerry Hardin
Sheriff	Barry Corbin
Deputy Tate	Leon Rippy
Julian Ward	Jack Nance
Deputy Buck	Virgil Frye
Uncle Mort	John Hawker
Woman at gas station	Margaret Bowman
Irene Davey	Debra Cole
Cowgirl	Karen Culley
Cowboy	Cody Haynes
Mr. Haynes	George Haynes
Elderly Man	James Harrell
Elderly Woman	Edith Mills
Table Dancer	Shannon Quinlan
Grey Ghost	Roosevelt Williams

Top Right: Don Johnson, Virginia Madsen Right: Jennifer Connelly, Johnson © Orion Pictures

MISPLACED

(SUBWAY FILMS/ORIGINAL CINEMA) Producer, Lisa Zwerling; Director/Story, Louis Yansen; Screenplay, Louis Yansen, Thomas DeWolfe; Associate Producer, Ron Ellis; Photography, Igor Sunara; Designer, Beth Kuhn; Music, Michael Urbaniak; Editor, Michael Berenbaum; Casting, Robin Monroe; Assistant Director, Steve Apicella; Precision Film Lab color; Not rated; 98 minutes; October release

CAST

Jacek Nowak	John Cameron Mitchell
Zofia	Viveca Lindfors
Halina Nowak	Elzbieta Czyzewska
Bill	Drew Snyder
Ela	Deirdre O'Connell
David	John Christopher Jones
Mrs. Padway	Debralee Scott
Clayton	Tico Wells
Eric	Scott Tiler
Mary	Kellie Overbey
Moonshadow	Talia Paul
History Teacher	Irving Metzman
Roughnecks	Mark E. Patton, Thor Fields
Halina's Boss	Jacqueline Schultz
Beata	Liliana Komorowska
Jacek's Father	Olek Krupa

and Sylvia Kauders (Teacher), Colter Rule (Mr. Quakenbush), Henry Holden (Music Teacher), Sullivan Walker, Edouard Desoto (Interviewers), Paul Pliester (Voice of America Researcher), Paul Klementowicz (Polish Militia Man), Rev. Ferdinand Slejzer (Priest)

© Original Cinema

Viveca Lindfors, Elzbieta Czyzewska, John Christopher Jones Above: John Cameron Mitchell

WELCOME HOME ROXY CARMICHAEL

(PARAMOUNT) Producer, Penney Finkelman Cox; Director, Jim Abrahams; Executive Producer/Screenplay, Karen Leigh Hopkins; Photography, Paul Elliott; Editor, Bruce Green; Designer, Dena Roth; Music, Thomas Newman; Costumes, Betsy Heimann; Casting, Mali Finn; Assistant Director, John T. Kretchmer; Songs: "Don't Look at Me" and "In Roxy's Eyes (I Will Never Be the Same)" written and performed by Melissa Etheridge; an ITC Entertainment Group production; Dolby Stereo; Technicolor; Rated PG-13; 97 minutes; October release

CAST

Dinky Bossetti	Winona Ryder
Denton Webb	Jeff Daniels
Elizabeth Zaks	Laila Robins
Gerald Howells	Thomas Wilson Brown
Barbara Webb	Joan McMurtrey
Les Bossetti	Graham Beckel
Rochelle Bossetti	Frances Fisher
Beannie Billings	Robby Kiger
Evelyn Whittacher	Dinah Manoff
Libby Ohlemacher	Sachi Parker
Mayor Bill Klepler	Stephen Tobolowsky
Louise Garweski	Micole Mercurio
Ronald Reems	John Short
Scotty Sandholtzer	Robin Thomas
Miss Day Ashburn	Valerie Landsberg
Charmaine	Rhonda Aldrich
Roxy Carmichael	Ava Fabian
Young Roxy	Carla Gugino
Young Denton	Rob King
Denny, Jr.	Daniel Fekete
Lillian Logerfield	Beth Grant
Andrea Stein	Heidi Swedberg
Gloria Sikes	Angela Paton
David Skism	Patrick McCollough
Bill Crampton	Mark Arnott
Raymond Emirts	Hal Havins
Kathy Sherwin	Linda Cox
Gene Briskell	Kevin Skousen
Laurie Desmond	Nada Despotovich
Officer Tardo	John C. Moskoff
Wilt Groom	Ron Perkins
Eddie Wafers	Hank Underwood
1st Man at center	Raymond Hanis
Girls on bus	Tiffany Ashley, Amy Moore Davis
Red Haired Boy on bus	Ron Marlin, Jr.
Bus Driver	Gene Farrington
Jim Reese	Jim Pirri
Men at legion hall	Terrence Evans, Joe Nesnow
Second Fisherman	Peter Strong
Kids throwing buckeyes	Rocky Krakoff, Carl Steven
"Amen" Man	Frank Milewski
Baby Sarah Webb	Jennifer & Laura Loesch
Laura Collier	Meg Harrington
Woman on bench	Louise Yaffe
Woman's Friend on bench	Eleanor Schiff
Whipped Cream Boy	Damion Dietz
Linda Evans Look-alike	Judith Saunders
Sneeze Victim	Janet Graham
Libby's New Friend	Karen Mussette
Limo Driver at the ball	Richard Roylance

and Joseph Cocuzzo, Joanne Cocuzzo (Grandparents crossing street), Nancy Abrahams, Joseph Abrahams, Jamie Abrahams (Fishing Family)

Top: Jeff Daniels, Winona Ryder Below: Ryder
© *Paramount Pictures*

Jeff Daniels, Winona Ryder Above: Thomas Wilson Brown, Ryder

Mary Alice, Richard Brooks Left: Davis Roberts,
Paul Butler, Danny Glover
© *TSWA Inc.*

TO SLEEP WITH ANGER

(SAMUEL GOLDWYN CO.) Producers, Caldecot Chubb, Thomas
S. Byrnes, Darin Scott; Executive Producers, Edward R. Pressman,
Danny Glover, Harris E. Tulchin; Director/Screenplay, Charles
Burnett; Photography, Walt Lloyd; Designer, Penny Barrett; Music,
Stephen James Taylor; Editor, Nancy Richardson; Associate Produc-
ers, Michael Flynn, Linda Koulisis; Casting, Gail Levin, Lauren Lloyd;
Assistant Director, Johnathan Meizler; Presented in association with
SVS, Inc.; Ultra-Stereo; CFI color; Rated PG; 100 minutes; October
release

CAST

Gideon	Paul Butler
Sunny	Devaughn Walter Nixon
Suzie	Mary Alice
Rhonda	Reina King
Skip	Cory Curtis
Babe Brother	Richard Brooks
Linda	Sheryl Lee Ralph
Junior	Carl Lumbly
Pat	Vonetta McGee
Mrs. Baker	Paula Bellamy
Harry Mention	Danny Glover
Preacher	Wonderful Smith
Hattie	Ethel Ayler
Fred Jenkins	Deforest Coven
Marsh	Sy Richardson
Okra Tate	Davis Roberts
MC	John Hawker
Herman	Julius Harris
William Norwood	Irvin Mosley, Jr.
Loviray Norwood	Marguerite Ray
Phil	Rai Tasco
Cherry Bell	Lorrie Marlow
Percy	Jimmy Witherspoon
Woman in labor	Carnetta Jones
Nurse	Christina Harley
Man at hospital	James Grayer
E. R. Nurse	Robin Scholer
Paramedics	Mark Phelan, Robert Terry Lee
Virginia	Greta Brown
Neighbor	Sip Culler

Devaughn Walter Nixon, Paul Butler, Danny Glover Above:
Sheryl Lee Ralph

REVERSAL OF FORTUNE

(WARNER BROS.) Producers, Edward R. Pressman, Oliver Stone; Director, Barbet Schroeder; Screenplay, Nicholas Kazan; Based on the book by Alan Dershowitz; Executive Producer, Michael Rauch; Photography, Luciano Tovoli; Designer, Mel Bourne; Editor, Lee Percy; Music, Mark Isham; Co-Producers, Elon Dershowitz, Nicholas Kazan; Associate Producers, Michael Flynn, Diane Schneier; Assistant Director, Bobby Warren; Costumes, Judianna Makovsky; Casting, Howard Feuer; Presented in association with Shochiku Fuji Co. Ltd. and Sovereign Pictures; Dolby Stereo; Technicolor; Rated R; 110 minutes; October release

CAST

Sunny Von Bulow	Glenn Close
Claus Von Bulow	Jeremy Irons
Alan Dershowitz	Ron Silver
Carol	Annabella Sciorra
Maria	Uta Hagen
David Marriott	Fisher Stevens
Peter Macintosh	Jack Gilpin
Andrea Reynolds	Christine Baranski
Elon Dershowitz	Stephen Mailer
Alexandra	Julie Hagerty
Ellen	Christine Dunford
Minnie	Felicity Huffman
Raj	Mano Singh
Nancy	Johann Carlo
Dobbs	Keith Reddin
Chuck	Alan Pottinger
Curly	Mitchell Whitfield
Jack	Tom Wright
Tom Berman	Gordon Joseph Weiss
Ed	Michael Lord
Mary	Lisa Gay Hamilton
Bill	Bill Camp
John	John David Cullum
Alexander Von Auersberg	Jad Mager
Ala Von Auersberg	Sarah Fearon
Older Cosima	Kristi Hundt
Young Cosima	Kara Emerson
Steve Famiglietti	Michael Wikes
Brillhoffer	Thomas Dorff
Alfie Von Auersberg	Bruno Eierund
Alfie's Friend	Bernt Kuhlmann
Dr. Paultees	Redman Maxfield
Judge	Frederick Neumann
Sheriff	Conrad McLaren
Bailiff	Edwin McDonough
Jury Foreman	Brian Delate
Emergency Room Doctor	Dess Philpot
Maitre D'	Steven Black
Party Goers	Kender Jones, Haes Hill
Newscaster	Dan Rea
Englishmen	Leo Leyden, Malachy McCourt
Dinner Guests	Jessika Cardinahl, Erika Klein, Joko Zohrer

© *Warner Bros.*
Top: Glenn Close, Jeremy Irons
Jeremy Irons received the Academy Award for
Best Actor of 1990

Julie Hagerty, Uta Hagen, Sarah Fearon, Jad Mager Above: Ron Silver

Mano Singh, Felicity Huffman, Alan Pottinger, Annabella Sciorra, Ron Silver

Glenn Close, Jeremy Irons Top Left: Irons, Ron Silver Above Left: Irons, Christine
Baranski Top Right: Close, Irons

Alan Rickman Top Left: Tom Selleck, Rickman Left: Selleck
© Pathe Entertainment

QUIGLEY DOWN UNDER

(MGM) Producers, Stanley O'Toole, Alexandra Rose; Co-Producer, Megan Rose; Director, Simon Wincer; Screenplay, John Hill; Photography, David Eggby; Designer, Ross Major; Music, Basil Poledouris; Supervising Editor, Adrian Carr; Costumes, Wayne Finkelman; Assistant Director, Robert Donaldson; Casting, Michael Lynch, Rae Davidson; Stunts, Guy Norris; a Pathe Entertainment presentation from MGM/UA Distribution Co.; Dolby Stereo; Panavision; Colorfilm color; Rated PG-13; 120 minutes; October release

CAST

Matthew Quigley	Tom Selleck
Crazy Cora	Laura San Giacomo
Elliott Marston	Alan Rickman
Major Ashley Pitt	Chris Haywood
Grimmelman	Ron Haddrick
Dobkin	Tony Bonner
Coogan	Jerome Ehlers
Hobb	Conor McDermottroe
Brophy	Roger Ward
O'Flynn	Ben Mendelsohn
Kunkurra	Steve Dodd
Slatterns	Karen Davitt, Kylie Foster
Reilly	William Zappa
Sgt. Thomas	Jonathan Sweet
Tout	Jon Ewing
Miller	Tim Hughes
Mullion	David Slingsby
Mitchell	Danny Adcock
Cavanaugh	Maeliosa Stafford
Carver	Ollie Hall
Smythe	Danny Baldwin
Scotty	Jim Willoughby
Hayden	Spike Cherry
Whitey	Gerald Egan
Cliff	Guy Norris
Paddy	Mark Minchinton
Oliver	Brian Ellison
Bugler	Mark Pennell
Tribal Elders	Nosepeg O. B. E., Billy Stockman
Deserters	Michael Carmen, Greg Stuart
Mrs. Grimmelman	Evelyn Krape
Klaus Grimmelman	Eamon Kelly

and Graham Young, Allan "Happy" Bradford (Bullockys), Cory Tjapaltjarri (Little Bit), Don Bridges (Ticket Seller), David Le Page (French Canadian), Vic Gordon (Elderly Man), Joanie Thomas (Elderly Woman), Bruce Knappet, James Wright (Bushmen), Ian Lind, Fred Walsh (Startled Men)

Tom Selleck, Laura San Giacomo Above: San Giacomo

WHITE PALACE

(UNIVERSAL) Producers, Mark Rosenberg, Amy Robinson, Griffin Dunne; Executive Producer, Sydney Pollack; Director, Luis Mandoki; Screenplay, Ted Tally, Alvin Sargent; Based on the novel by Glenn Savan; Associate Producer, Robin Forman; Co-Producer, Bill Finnegan; Photography, Lajos Koltai; Designer, Jeannine C. Oppewall; Editor, Carol Littleton; Music, George Fenton; Costumes, Lisa Jensen; Casting, Nancy Naylor; Assistant Director, Chris J. Soldo; a Mirage/Double Play production; Dolby Stereo; Deluxe color; Rated R; 105 minutes; October release

CAST

Nora Baker	Susan Sarandon
Max Baron	James Spader
Neil	Jason Alexander
Rosemary	Kathy Bates
Judy	Eileen Brennan
Sol Horowitz	Steven Hill
Rachel	Rachel Levin
Larry Klugman	Corey Parker
Edith Baron	Renee Taylor
Marv Miller	Jonathan Penner
Sherri Klugman	Barbara Howard
Heidi Solomon	Kim Meyers
Ella Horowitz	Hildy Brooks
Sophie Rosen	Mitzi McCall
Stripper	K. C. Carr
White Palace Customer	Glenn Savan
Marcia	Fannie Bell Lebby
Jimmy the Bartender	Vernon Dudas
Reba Pasker	Maryann Kopperman
Janey	Maria Pitillo
Kahn	Jeremy Piven
Bachelor Party Men	Robert Bourgeois, Jordan Stone, Lantz Harshbarger
Eddie Lobodiak	William Oberbeck
Advertising Executive	John Flack
Helen	Wilma Myracle
Rabbi	Joseph Rosenbloom
Country Western Singer	Michael E. Arnett
Supermarket Checker	Janet Lofton
Mrs. Goodman	Sherry Grogan
Mr. Goodman	Patrick S. Harrigan
Brunch Guest	Adrienne Brett
Hostess	Toni Lynn
Waitress	Ellen Cantalupo
Restaurant Customer	Jonathan Ames
Elderly Man	Louis Brill
Elderly Woman	Blanche Brill

Top: James Spader, Susan Sarandon (also below and left)
© *Universal City Studios*

Eileen Brennan, James Spader

James Spader, Susan Sarandon

Kirstie Alley, Bill Pullman Top Right: Pullman
Right: Carrie Fisher; Sam Elliott
© *Castle Rock Entertainment*

SIBLING RIVALRY

(COLUMBIA) Producers, David Lester, Don Miller, Liz Glotzer; Director, Carl Reiner; Screenplay, Martha Goldhirsch; Executive Producers, George Shapiro, Howard West; Photography, Reynaldo Villalobos; Designer, Jeannine C. Oppewall; Music, Jack Elliott; Song: "*Just a Little Lovin'* " by Barry Mann and Cynthia Weill/sung by Estelle Reiner; Editor, Bud Molin; Costumes, Durinda Wood; Casting, Marci Liroff; Assistant Director, Marty Ewing; Presented by Castle Rock Entertainment in association with Nelson Entertainment; Dolby Stereo; Color; Rated PG-13; 88 minutes; October release

CAST

Marjorie Turner	Kirstie Alley
Nicholas Meany	Bill Pullman
Iris Turner-Hunter	Carrie Fisher
Jeanine	Jami Gertz
Harry Turner	Scott Bakula
Rose Turner	Frances Sternhagen
Charles Turner, Sr.	John Randolph
Charles Turner, Jr.	Sam Elliott
Wilbur Meany	Ed O'Neill
Dr. Plotner	Paul Benedict
Pat	Bill Macy
Dr. Casey Hunter	Matthew Laurance
Don, the Desk Clerk	Ron Orbach
911 Officer	Edward Escobar
Hotel Security Guard	Greg Collins
Gary Diamond	Patrick Cronin
Market Cashier	Dian Kobayashi
Roger, the Salesman	Teddy Haggarty
Mayor	Roy Van Swearingen
Minister	Ken Grantham
Doorman	Dan Sachoff
Delivery Man	Sean Ching
Priest	Bob Harks
Hostess	Adele Proom
Patient	Heather Marie Wierman
Aunt Rose	Maurine Houck
Young Marjorie	Crystan Leas
Young Jeanine	Yvonne De Barca

Jami Gertz, Ed O'Neill Above: Kirstie Alley, Scott Bakula

LISTEN UP:
The Lives of Quincy Jones

(WARNER BROS.) Producer, Courtney Sale Ross; Line Producer, Melissa Powell; Director, Ellen Weissbrod; Photography, Stephen Kazmierski; Music, Quincy Jones; Music Supervisor, Arthur Baker; Editors, Milton Moses Ginsberg, Pierre Kahn, Andrew Morreale, Laure Sullivan, Paul Zehrer; Dolby Stereo; Technicolor; Rated PG-13; 114 minutes; October release

WITH

Quincy Jones, Clarence Avant, George Benson, Richard Brooks, Tevin Campbell, Ray Charles, Miles Davis, El DeBarge, Kool Moe Dee, Sheila E., Billy Eckstine, Ahmet Ertegun, Ella Fitzgerald, Flavor Flav, Siedah Garrett, Dizzy Gillespie, Irvin Green, Alex Haley, Lionel Hampton, Herbie Hancock, Ice-T, James Ingram, Jesse Jackson, Lucy Jackson Rembert, Lloyd Jones, Jolie Jones, Big Daddy Kane, Michel Legrand, Morris Levy, Harry Lokofsky, Sidney Lumet, Bobby McFerrin, Benny Medina, Melle Mel, Chan Parker, Greg Philingaines, Ian Prince, Frank Sinatra, Steven Spielberg, Barbra Streisand, Al B. Sure!, Clark Terry, Bobby Tucker, Sarah Vaughan, Oprah Winfrey

Top Right: Quincy Jones, Ray Charles © Warner Bros.

Barbara Hershey, Keanu Reeves, Peter Falk Above: Falk

TUNE IN TOMORROW . . .

(CINECOM) formerly Aunt Julia and the Scriptwriter; Producers, John Fiedler, Mark Tarlov; Executive Producer, Joe Caracciolo, Jr.; Director, Jon Amiel; Screenplay, William Boyd; Based on the novel "Aunt Julia and the Scriptwriter" by Mario Vargas Llosa; Photography, Robert Stevens; Music, Wynton Marsalis; Editor, Peter Boyle; Casting, Billy Hopkins; Costumes, Betsy Heimann; Designer, Jim Clay; Assistant Director, Eric Heffron; Choreographer, Quinny Sacks; a Polar Entertainment production presented in association with Odyssey/Cinecom International; Dolby Stereo; Technicolor; Rated PG-13; 102 minutes; October release

CAST

Aunt Julia	Barbara Hershey
Martin Loader	Keanu Reeves
Pedro Carmichael	Peter Falk
Puddler	Bill McCutcheon
Aunt Olga	Patricia Clarkson
Uncle Luke	Richard Portnow
Sam & Sid	Jerome Dempsey
Leonard Pando	Richard B. Shull
Donald Loader	Paul Austin
Ted Orson	Joel Fabiani
Josephine Sanders	Crystal Field
Aunt Hortensia	Jayne Haynes
Frances Loader	Mary Joy
Jamie	Rob Kramer
Faith Hope	Anne Levine Thomson
Luther Aslinger	Peter Maloney
Producer—Detroit Radio	Irving Metzman
Duke Vermont	Bill Moor
Nellie	Dedee Pfeiffer
Brent Maconnochie	Jon Van Ness
Peter Loader	William Murray Weiss
Big John Coot	Henry Gibson
Richard Quince	Peter Gallagher
Robert Quince	Dan Hedaya
Father Serafim	Buck Henry
Margaret Quince	Hope Lange
Dr. Albert Quince	John Larroquette
Elena Quince	Elizabeth McGovern
Elmore Dubuque	Robert Sedgwick
Large Albanians	Danny Aiello III, Adam Lefevre, Chuck Margiotta
Albanian Protester	Paul Burke
Fireman	Jack Harvey
WXBU Engineer	Mert Hatfield
Jazz Singer	Shirley Horn
Waiter	Ishmond Jones, Jr.
News Man—Detroit	Howard Kingkade
Cub Reporter	Ray McKinnon
Secretary	Gladys Vega
Policeman	Jack Wallace
Themselves	The Wynton Marsalis Band, The Neville Brothers

Top Left: Keanu Reeves © Cinecom

JACOB'S LADDER

(TRI-STAR) Producer, Alan Marshall; Director, Adrian Lyne; Executive Producers, Mario Kassar, Andrew Vajna; Screenplay/Associate Producer, Bruce Joel Rubin; Photography, Jeffrey L. Kimball; Designer, Brian Morris; Editor, Tom Rolf; Music, Maurice Jarre; Costumes, Ellen Mirojnick; Casting, Risa Bramon, Billy Hopkins, Heidi Levitt; Assistant Director, Joseph Reidy; from Carolco Pictures; Dolby Stereo; Technicolor; Rated R; 115 minutes; November release

CAST

Jacob Singer	Tim Robbins
Jezzie	Elizabeth Peña
Louis	Danny Aiello
Michael	Matt Craven
Paul	Pruitt Taylor Vince
Geary	Jason Alexander
Sarah	Patricia Kalember
Frank	Eriq La Salle
George	Ving Rhames
Doug	Brian Tarantina
Rod	Anthony Alessandro
Jerry	Brent Hinkley
Elsa	S. Epatha Merkerson
Gabe Singer	Macaulay Culkin
Hospital Receptionist	Suzanne Shepherd
Group Leader	Doug Barron
Santa	Jan Saint
Street Singers	Kisha Skinner, Dion Simmons
Taxi Driver	Sam Coppola
Drunk	Patty Rosborough
Sam	Evan O'Meara
Tony	Kyle Gass
Mrs. Carmichael	Gloria Irizarry
Jacob's Doctor	Lewis Black
Policeman	Raymond Anthony Thomas
Field Medics	Christopher Fields, Jaime Perry
Field Doctors	Michael Tomlinson, A. M. Marxuach
Woman on subway	Antonia Rey
Army Officers	John Capodice, John Patrick McLaughlin
Emergency Ward Nurse	Bellina Logan
Resident Doctor	Scott Cohen

and David Thomson (Evil Doctor), Bryan Larkin (Jed), B. J. Donaldson (Eli), Thomas A. Carlin (Doorman), Carol Schneider, Becky Ann Baker, Diane Kagan (Nurses), Billie Neal (Della), Mike Stokie (Field Sergeant), James Ellis Reynolds (EMT Bearer), Dennis Green (Attendant), Brad Hamler, Byron Keith Minns (Orderlies), Reggie McFadden, Stephanie Berry, Chris Murphy, John-Martin Green (Partygoers), Arleigh Richards (Paul's Wife), Ann Pearl Gary, Barbara Gruen (Mourners), Joe Quintero (Street Kid), John Louis Fischer (Machine Gunner), Alva Williams (Masked Man), Elizabeth Abassi, Nora Burns, Alison Gordy, Jessica Roberts, Holly Kennedy, Blanche Irwin Stuart (Hospital Patients), Perry Lang (Jacob's Assailant)

**Top: Tim Robbins, Elizabeth Peña Below: Robbins
Right: Macaulay Culkin; Danny Aiello
© Tri-Star**

Tim Robbins

Tim Robbins, Matt Craven

WAITING FOR THE LIGHT

(TRIUMPH RELEASING) Producers, Caldecot Chubb, Ron Bozman; Director/Screenplay, Christopher Monger; Executive Producer, Edward R. Pressman; Photography, Gabriel Beristain; Designer, Phil Peters; Costumes, Isabella Van Soest Chubb; Editor, Eva Gardos; Music, Michael Storey; Song: "Jesus Hits Like an Atom Bomb" written by Lee V. McCullum/performed by The Blue Jay Singers; Associate Producers, Michael Flynn, Linda Koulisis; Casting, Pamela Rack; an Epic Productions and Sarlui/Diamant presentation; Ultra-Stereo; Deluxe color; Rated PG; 97 minutes; November release

CAST

Aunt Zena	Shirley MacLaine
Kay Harris	Teri Garr
Joe	Clancy Brown
Mullins	Vincent Schiavelli
Reverend Stevens	John Bedford Lloyd
Charlie	Jeff McCracken
Slim Slater	Jack McGee
Eddie Harris	Colin Baumgartner
Emily Harris	Hillary Wolf
Bob	Eric Helland
Iris	Peg Phillips
Miss Hicks/Miss Berg	Robin Ginsburg
Mr. Patterson	Arthur H. Cahn
Tommy	Matthew Magnano
Tommy's Dad	Michael Marinelli
Dr. Norman	Don Sinclair Davis
Waitress	Naomi Marquez
Judge Brown	Bob Henry
Preacher	Bob Nadir
Dr. Kelley	Robert Hardwick

and Mark Drusch (Mr. Trace), Kylee Martin (Bobby), Clara Boyce (Deaf Lady), Rob Keenan (Chuck), Angela DiMarco (Meg), Ron Lynch (Hot Dog), Barbara Benedetti (Nun), Jillayne Sorensen (Alice), Corey Gunnestad (Verne), Louis Guzzo (National Newscaster), Amanda Arguello, Michelle Wartman, Le Chelle Anne Goncalves (Screaming Girls), Lyn Tyrell (Woman in crowd), George Williams, Chester Bendt (Customers), Steve Henderson (Local Newscaster), John Boylan (Old Man at diner), Ken Davidson (Cop), Robert Peterson (Newspaper Vendor), James Cissel (TV Reporter), Rich Hawkins (German TV Reporter)

© Epic Productions

Hillary Wolf, Jack McGee, Colin Baumgartner Above: McGee, Teri Garr, Shirley MacLaine

GRAFFITI BRIDGE

(WARNER BROS.) Producers, Arnold Stiefel, Randy Phillips; Co-Producer, Craig Rice; Director/Screenplay/Music, Prince; Executive Producer, Peter MacDonald; Photography, Bill Butler; Designer, Vance Lorenzini; Editor, Rebecca Ross; Associate Producer, Simon Edery; Costumes, Helen Hiatt, Jim Shearon; Assistant Directors, Kelly Schroeder, Jack Gallagher; Casting, Lynn Blumenthal; Songs written by Prince, and others; Choreographer, Otis Sallid; a Paisley Park Film production; Dolby Stereo; Color; Rated PG-13; 95 minutes; November release

CAST

The Kid	Prince
Aura	Ingrid Chavez
Morris Day	Morris Day
Jerome	Jerome Benton
Kid's Band	Michael Bland, Phillip C, Rosie Gaines, Levi Seacer Jr., Damon Dickson, Kirk Johnson, Tony Mosley, Miko Weaver
The Time	Jellybean, Jesse Johnson, Jimmy Jam, Terry Lewis, Monte Moir
Melody Cool	Mavis Staples
George Clinton	George Clinton
Tevin	Tevin Campbell
T. C.	T. C. Ellis
Robin	Robin Power
Jill	Jill Jones

and Tracey M. Bass, Kimberly Dionne, Barbara Koval, Monique Mannen, David Robertson, Rocky Santo, Jonathan Webb (Glam Slam Dancers), Steeles Family (Melody Cool Choir), Patrick Adams, Stevo Armani, Atlanta Bliss, Morris Hayes, Eric Leeds, London, Scott March, Spark, Steve Star, Kenneth D. Towns, Chris "Doctor D." Worthy (George Clinton's Funkestra), Shari Bridell, David Earl Williams (On-lookers), Scott Parham (Clinton's House Bouncer), Todd Rask (Limo Driver)

© Warner Bros.

Jerome Benton, Morris Day Above: Ingrid Chavez, Prince

THE RESCUERS DOWN UNDER

(BUENA VISTA/WALT DISNEY PICTURES) Producer, Thomas Schumacher; Directors, Hendel Butoy, Mike Gabriel; Animation Screenplay, Jim Cox, Karey Kirkpatrick, Byron Simpson, Joe Ranft; Suggested by Characters Created by Margery Sharp; Associate Producer, Kathleen Gavin; Story Supervisor, Joe Ranft; Art Director, Maurice Hunt; Editor, Michael Kelly; Music, Bruce Broughton; Supervising Animators, Glen Keane, Mark Henn, Russ Edmonds, David Cutler, Ruben A. Aquino, Nik Ranieri, Ed Gombert, Anthony De Rosa, Kathy Zielinski, Duncan Marjoribanks; Produced in association with Silver Screen Partners IV; Dolby Stereo; Technicolor; Rated G; 74 minutes; November release

VOICE CAST

Bernard	Bob Newhart
Miss Bianca	Eva Gabor
Wilbur	John Candy
Jake	Tristan Rogers
Cody	Adam Ryen
McLeach	George C. Scott
Frank	Wayne Robson
Krebbs	Douglas Seale
Joanna/Additional Special Vocal Effects	Frank Welker
Chairmouse/Doctor	Bernard Fox
Red	Peter Firth
Baitmouse	Billy Barty
Francois	Ed Gilbert
Faloo/Mother	Carla Meyer
Nurse Mouse	Russi Taylor

and Charlie Adler, Jack Angel, Vanna Bonta, Peter Greenwood, Marii Mak, Mickie McGowan, Patrick Pinney, Phil Proctor (Additional Voices)

Top: Marahute, Cody Right: Bernard, Miss Bianca, Jake

Miss Bianca, Jake Above: Cody, Marahute

Wilbur, Bernard, Jake, Miss Bianca Above: Joanna, Frank

Sylvester Stallone, Talia Shire
Top Right: Tommy Morrison, Stallone
© *United Artists Pictures*

ROCKY V

(UNITED ARTISTS) Producers, Irwin Winkler, Robert Chartoff; Executive Producer, Michael S. Glick; Director, John G. Avildsen; Screenplay, Sylvester Stallone; Photography, Steven Poster; Designer, William J. Cassidy; Music, Bill Conti; Editors, John G. Avildsen, Michael N. Knue; Associate Producer, Tony Munafo; Casting, Caro Jones; Assistant Director, Clifford C. Coleman; from MGM/UA Distribution Co.; Dolby Stereo; Color; Rated PG-13; 103 minutes; November release

CAST

Rocky Balboa	Sylvester Stallone
Adrian Balboa	Talia Shire
Paulie	Burt Young
Rocky Balboa, Jr.	Sage Stallone
Mickey Goldmill	Burgess Meredith
Tommy "Machine" Gunn	Tommy Morrison
George Washington Duke	Richard Gant
Tony	Tony Burton
Jimmy	James Gambina
Karen	Delia Sheppard
Merlin Sheets	Michael Sheehan
Union Cane	Michael Williams
Chickie	Kevin Connolly
Jewel	Elisebeth Peters
Chickie's Pal	Hayes Swope
Fight Promoter	Nicky Blair
Marie	Jodi Letizia
Druggies	Chris Avildsen, Jonathan Avildsen
Andy	Don Sherman
Fight Commentators	Stu Nahan, Al Bernstein
James Binns	James Binns
Las Vegas Announcer	Meade Martin
Fight Announcer (3rd Fight)	Michael Buffer
Benson	Albert J. Myles
Gloria	Jane Marla Robbins
Cab Driver	Ben Geraci
Motorcycle Mechanic	Clifford C. Coleman
Referees	Lou Filippo, Frank Cappuccino
Contenders	Henry D. Tillman, Stan Ward
Dr. Rimlan	Patrick Cronin
Drinker	Helena Carroll
Fight Announcer	Leroy Neiman
Nicoli Koloff	Michael Pataki
Delivery Girls	Jennifer Flavin, Tricia Flavin, Julie Flavin
Timmy	Bob Giovane
Russian Woman	Carol A. Ready
Woman in Dressing Room	Katharine Margiotta

and Lauren K. Woods, Robert Seltzer, Albert S. Meltzer, John P. Clark, Stanley R. Hochman, Elmer Smith (Conference Reporters), Brian Phelps, Mark Thompson, Paul Cain, Kent H. Johnson, Cindy Roberts (Reporters), Tony Munafo, Bob Vazquez, Richard "Dub" Wright, Susan Persily, Lloyd Kaufman, Gary Compton, John J. Cahill (Drinkers)

Sylvester Stallone, Sage Stallone Above: Sylvester Stallone, Talia Shire

HOME ALONE

(20th CENTURY FOX) Producer/Screenplay, John Hughes; Executive Producers, Mark Levinson, Scott Rosenfelt, Tarquin Gotch; Director, Chris Columbus; Photography, Julio Macat; Designer, John Muto; Editor, Raja Gosnell; Costumes, Jay Hurley; Associate Producer/Assistant Director, Mark Radcliffe; Casting, Janet Hirshenson, Jane Jenkins; Music, John Williams; Song: *"Somewhere in My Memory"*, music by John Williams, lyrics by Leslie Bricusse. Dolby Stereo; Deluxe color; Rated PG; 102 minutes; November release

CAST

Kevin McCallister	Macaulay Culkin
Harry	Joe Pesci
Marv	Daniel Stern
Peter McCallister	John Heard
Marley	Roberts Blossom
Kate McCallister	Catherine O'Hara
Linnie McCallister	Angela Goethals
Buzz McCallister	Devin Ratray
Uncle Frank	Gerry Bamman
Megan McCallister	Hillary Wolf
Gus Polinski	John Candy
Officer Balzak	Larry Hankin
Jeff McCallister	Michael C. Maronna
Heather	Kristin Minter
Sondra	Daiana Campeanu
Rod	Jedidiah Cohen
Fuller	Kieran Culkin
Tracy	Senta Moses
Brook	Anna Slotky
Aunt Leslie	Terrie Snell
Mitch Murphy	Jeffrey Wiseman
Georgette	Virginia Smith
Steffan	Matt Doherty
Gangster #1 (Johnny)	Ralph Foody
Gangster #2 (Snakes)	Michael Guido
Uncle Rob	Ray Toler
Woman in airport	Billie Bird
Man in airport	Bill Erwin
Officers	Gerry Becker, Victor Cole
The Cousins	Porscha Radcliffe, Brittany Radcliffe
Officer Devereux	Clarke Devereux
Pizza Boy	Dan Charles Zulcoski
French Woman	Lynn Mansbach
Lineman	Peter Siragusa
Scranton Ticket Agent	Alan Wilder
French Ticket Agent	Hope Davis
Airline Counter Person	Dianne B. Shaw
Check Out Girl	Tracy Connor
Stock Boy	Jim Ryan
Santa	Kenneth Hudson Campbell
Santa's Elf	Sandra Macat
Stosh	Mark Beltzman
Drugstore Clerk	Ann Whitney
Store Manager	Richard J. Firfer
Herb, the Drugstore Clerk	Jim Ortlieb
Police Operator	Kate Johnson
Airport Drivers	Michael Hansen, Peter Pantaleo
French Gate Agent	Jean-Claude Sciore
Flight Attendant	Monica Devereux

and Edward Bruzan, Frank R. Cernugel, John Hardy, Eddie Korosa, Robert Okrzesik, Leo Perion, Vince Waidzulis (Polka Band)

Top: Macaulay Culkin (also below)
© *20th Century Fox*

Daniel Stern, Joe Pesci

Catherine O'Hara, Macaulay Culkin Top Right: Culkin (also top left)
Above Left: Culkin, Joe Pesci

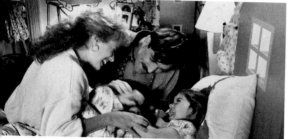

Nancy Travis, Tom Selleck, Robin Weisman
Top Left: Steve Guttenberg, Ted Danson, Selleck
Top Right: Selleck, Danson, Travis, Guttenberg
© Touchstone Pictures

THREE MEN AND A LITTLE LADY

(TOUCHSTONE) Producers, Ted Field, Robert W. Cort; Executive Producer, Jean Francois Lepetit; Co-Producer, Neil Machlis; Director, Emile Ardolino; Screenplay, Charlie Peters; Story, Sara Parriott, Josann McGibbon; Based on the film *Trois Hommes et un Couffin* written by Coline Serreau; Photography, Adam Greenberg; Designer, Stuart Wurtzel; Costumes, Louise Frogley; Music, James Newton Howard; *"The Three Men Rap"* by Charlie Peters and G. Love E.; Editor, Michael A. Stevenson; Casting, Ilene Starger, Mary Selway; Assistant Director, Yudi Bennett; an Interscope Communications Inc. co-production; Distributed by Buena Vista Pictures; Dolby Stereo; Technicolor; Rated PG; 100 minutes; November release

CAST

Peter Mitchell	Tom Selleck
Michael Kellam	Steve Guttenberg
Jack Holden	Ted Danson
Sylvia	Nancy Travis
Mary	Robin Weisman
Edward	Christopher Cazenove
Vera	Sheila Hancock
Miss Lomax	Fiona Shaw
Barrow	John Boswall
Vicar Hewitt	Jonathan Lynn
Laurie	Sydney Walsh
Morgan School Teacher	Lynne Marta
Boy #1	Everett Wong
Dr. Robinson	Edwina Moore
Mrs. Walker	Patricia Gaul
Mrs. Heard	Edith Fields
Waitress	Darcy Pulliam
Pretty Girl	Rosalind Allen
Party Lady	Lucia Neal
Old Englishman	Bryan Pringle
Wilfred Blair	Neil Hunt
English Farmer	Ian Redford
Stagehand	Charles David Richards
Usher	Steven L. Vaughn
Dancing Girl at party	Melissa Hurley

Nancy Travis, Christopher Cazenove, Ted Danson Above: Tom Selleck, Fiona Shaw

MR. & MRS. BRIDGE

(MIRAMAX) Producer, Ismail Merchant; Executive Producer, Robert Halmi; Director, James Ivory; Screenplay, Ruth Prawer Jhabvala; Based on the novels *"Mrs. Bridge"* and *"Mr. Bridge"* by Evan S. Connell, Jr.; Photography, Tony Pierce-Roberts; Designer, David Gropman; Costumes, Carol Ramsey; Music, Richard Robbins; Editor, Humphry Dixon; Assistant Director, David Sardi; a Merchant Ivory/Robert Halmi production; Dolby Stereo; Technicolor; Rated PG; 127 minutes; November release

CAST

Walter Bridge	Paul Newman
India Bridge	Joanne Woodward
Grace Barron	Blythe Danner
Dr. Alex Sauer	Simon Callow
Ruth Bridge	Kyra Sedgwick
Douglas Bridge (grown-up)	Robert Sean Leonard
Carolyn Bridge	Margaret Welsh
Harriet	Saundra McClain
Julia	Diane Kagan
Mr. Gadbury	Austin Pendleton
Dr. Forster	Malachy McCourt
Mabel Ong	Gale Garnett
Gil Davis	Marcus Giamatti
Virgil Barron	Remak Ramsay
Douglas Bridge (as a boy)	John Bell
Judge	Al Christy
Genevieve	Robyn Rosenfeld
Avrum Rhinegold	Robert Levine
Couperin	Spencer Keesee
Paquita	Kathy Quinn-Byrne
Rod	John Anthony
Rod's Girl	Jennifer Conforti
Ruth's Boyfriend	Robert Westenberg
Corporal Cipkowski	Lee Lambert
Plaintiff	Joe Tinoco
Law Clerk	Ben Stephenson
Band Vocalist	Alison Sneegas
Scoutmaster	Buck Baker
Bridal Gown Lady	Robin Humphrey
Prison Matron	Joanne Carr
The Barron's Maid	Florence Hall

and Addison Myers, Roger Burget (Men at Businessmen's table), Mark Yonally (Youth at high school dance), Danny Cox (Country Club Steward), Roch Leibovici (Watch Seller on the quai), Hubert Saint Macary (Copyist in the Louvre), Laurence Goua (Principal Can-Can Dancer), The Nicolodis (Moulin Rouge Tumblers), Judy Judd, Nora Denny (Bridge Players), Tom Hall (Aztec Room Waiter), Jocelyn Hamilton (Florist's Assistant), Andy Knoti (Flower Shop Owner), Melissa Newman (Young India at the pool), Charles Perkins, Allen Monroe, Richard Ross, Milton Abel (Jazz Musicians)

Top: Joanne Woodward, Paul Newman
Below: Kyra Sedgwick Right: Newman
© *Miramax Films*

Paul Newman, Margaret Welsh, Joanne Woodward

Paul Newman, Robert Sean Leonard

MISERY

(COLUMBIA) Producers, Andrew Scheinman, Rob Reiner; Director, Rob Reiner; Screenplay, William Goldman; Based on the novel by Stephen King; Co-Producers, Steve Nicolaides, Jeffrey Stott; Photography, Barry Sonnenfeld; Designer, Norman Garwood; Music, Marc Shaiman; Editor, Robert Leighton; Costumes, Gloria Gresham; Casting, Jane Jenkins, Janet Hirshenson; Assistant Director, Dennis Maguire; Presented by Castle Rock Entertainment in association with Nelson Entertainment; Dolby Stereo; CFI color; Rated R; 107 minutes; November release

CAST

Paul Sheldon	James Caan
Annie Wilkes	Kathy Bates
Buster	Richard Farnsworth
Virginia	Frances Sternhagen
Marcia Sindell	Lauren Bacall
Libby	Graham Jarvis
Pete	Jerry Potter
Anchorman	Tom Brunelle
Anchorwoman	June Christopher
Reporters	Julie Payne, Archie Hahn III, Gregory Snegoff
Waitress	Wendy Bowers
Herself	Misery, the Pig

Top: Kathy Bates, James Caan Left: Lauren Bacall, Caan
© Castle Rock Entertainment

Kathy Bates received the Academy Award for Best Actress of 1990

James Caan, Kathy Bates

Frances Sternhagen, Richard Farnsworth Above: Kathy Bates

Anjelica Huston, John Cusack, Annette Bening Top Left:
Cusack, Huston Below: Huston, Pat Hingle

THE GRIFTERS

(MIRAMAX) Producers, Martin Scorsese, Robert Harris, James Painten; Executive Producer, Barbara De Fina; Co-Producer, Peggy Rajski; Director, Stephen Frears; Screenplay, Donald Westlake; Based on the novel by Jim Thompson; Photography, Oliver Stapleton; Designer, Dennis Casner; Casting, Juliet Taylor, Vickie Thomas; Editor, Mike Audsley; Music, Elmer Bernstein; a Cineplex Odeon Films presentation; Dolby Stereo; Color; Rated R; 113 minutes; December release

CAST

Lilly Dillon	Anjelica Huston
Roy Dillon	John Cusack
Myra Langtry	Annette Bening
Guy at bar	Jan Munroe
Racetrack Announcer	Robert Weems
Jeweler	Stephen Tobolowsky
Bartender	Jimmy Noonan
Cop	Richard Holden
Simms	Henry Jones
Irv	Michael Laskin
Mintz	Eddie Jones
Doctor	Sandy Baron
Nurse	Lou Hancock
Joe	Gailard Sartain
Nurse Flynn	Noelle Harling
Maid	Ivette Soler
Bobo Justus	Pat Hingle
Sailor (Young Paul)	Paul Adelstein
Sailor (Freshman)	Jeremy Piven
Sailor (Spooney)	Gregory Sporleder
Sailor (Stinky)	David Sinaiko
Drunk	Jeff Perry
Drunk's Friend	Jonathan Gries
Waitress	Micole Mercurio
Hebbing	Charles Napier
Cole	J.T. Walsh
Receptionists	Teresa Gilmore Capps, Elizabeth Ann Feeley
FBI Man	Billy Ray Sharkey
Arizona Motel Clerk	Frances Bay
Lt. Pierson	Xander Berkeley

© *Miramax Films*

Annette Bening, John Cusack, Anjelica Huston
Above: Eddie Jones, Cusack

Vincent Price Top Left: Johnny Depp
Left: Depp, Winona Ryder
© *20th Century Fox*

EDWARD SCISSORHANDS

(20th CENTURY FOX) Producers, Denise Di Novi, Tim Burton; Director, Tim Burton; Screenplay, Caroline Thompson; Story, Tim Burton, Caroline Thompson; Executive Producer, Richard Hashimoto; Photography, Stefan Czapsky; Designer, Bo Welch; Editor, Richard Halsey; Costumes, Colleen Atwood; Music, Danny Elfman; Casting, Victoria Thomas; Special Makeup and Scissorhands Effects Producer, Stan Winston; Assistant Director, Jerry Fleck; Dolby Stereo; Deluxe color; Rated PG-13; 100 minutes; December release

CAST

Edward Scissorhands	Johnny Depp
Kim Boggs	Winona Ryder
Peg Boggs	Dianne Wiest
Jim	Anthony Michael Hall
Joyce Monroe	Kathy Baker
Kevin Boggs	Robert Oliveri
Helen	Conchata Ferrell
Marge	Caroline Aaron
Officer Allen	Dick Anthony Williams
Esmeralda	O-Lan Jones
The Inventor	Vincent Price
Bill Boggs	Alan Arkin
Tinka	Susan J. Blommaert
Cissy	Linda Perry
TV Host	John Davidson
George	Biff Yeager
Suzanne	Marti Greenberg
Max	Bryan Larkin
Denny	John McMahon
TV Newswoman	Victoria Price
Retired Man	Stuart Lancaster
Granddaughter	Gina Gallagher
Psychologist	Aaron Lustig
Loan Officer	Alan Fudge
Dishwasher Man	Steven Brill
Editor	Peter Palmer
Reporters	Marc Macaulay, Carmen J. Alexander, Brett Rice
Beefy Man	Andrew Clark
Pink Girl	Kelli Crofton
Older Woman—TV	Linda Jean Hess
Young Woman—TV	Rosalyn Thomson
Red-Haired Woman—TV	Lee Ralls
Teenage Girl—TV	Eileen Meurer
Rich Widow—TV	Bea Albano
Blonde—TV	Donna Pieroni
Policemen	Ken DeVaul, Michael Gaughan
Teenagers	Tricia Lloyd, Kathy Dombo
Police Sergeant	Rex Fox
Max's Mother	Sherry Ferguson
Little Girl on bike	Tabetha Thomas

Johnny Depp, Robert Oliveri

Dianne Wiest Top Left: Winona Ryder, Anthony Michael Hall Above Left: Alan
Arkin Top Right: Johnny Depp

Clint Eastwood, Raul Julia Top Left: Eastwood, Charlie Sheen
Left: Lara Flynn Boyle, Sheen
© *Warner Bros.*

THE ROOKIE

(WARNER BROS.) Producers, Howard Kazanjian, Steven Siebert, David Valdes; Director, Clint Eastwood; Screenplay, Boaz Yakin, Scott Spiegel; Photography, Jack N. Green; Designer, Judy Cammer; Editor, Joel Cox; Music, Lennie Niehaus; Assistant Director, Matt Earl Beesley; Casting, Phyllis Huffman; Special Effects, John Frazier; Stunts, Terry Leonard; a Malpaso production; Dolby Stereo; Panavision; Technicolor; Rated R; 121 minutes; December release

CAST

Nick Pulovski	Clint Eastwood
David Ackerman	Charlie Sheen
Strom	Raul Julia
Liesl	Sonia Braga
Eugene Ackerman	Tom Skerritt
Sarah	Lara Flynn Boyle
Lt. Ray Garcia	Pepe Serna
Loco	Marco Rodriguez
Cruz	Pete Randall
Laura Ackerman	Donna Mitchell
Blackwell	Xander Berkeley
Morales	Tony Plana
Max	David Sherrill
Powell	Hal Williams
Freeway Motorist	Lloyd Nelson
Interrogators	Pat Duval, Mara Corday, Jerry Schumacher
Wang	Matt McKenzie
Lance	Joel Polis
Maitre 'D	Roger LaRue
Waiter	Robert Dubac
Romano	Anthony Charnota
Bartender	Jordan Lund
Little Felix	Paul Ben-Victor
Connie Ling	Jeanne Mori
Alphonse	Anthony Alexander
Captain Hargate	Paul Butler
David as a child	Seth Allen
David's Brother	Coleby Lombardo
Heather Torres	Roberta Vasquez
Anchorman	Joe Farago
Whalen	Robert Harvey
Vito	Nick Ballo
Sal	Jay Boryea
Receptionist	Mary Lou Kenworthy
Det. Orrison	George Orrison

Sonia Braga, Clint Eastwood Above: Charlie Sheen

HAVANA

(UNIVERSAL) Producers, Sydney Pollack, Richard Roth; Director, Sydney Pollack; Screenplay, Judith Rascoe, David Rayfiel; Story, Judith Rascoe; Executive Producer, Ronald L. Schwary; Photography, Owen Roizman; Designer, Terence Marsh; Editors, Fredric Steinkamp, William Steinkamp; Costumes, Bernie Pollack; Music, Dave Grusin; Casting, Lynn Stalmaster; Assistant Director, David Tomblin; a Mirage production; Dolby Stereo; Deluxe color; Rated R; 140 minutes; December release

CAST

Jack Weil	Robert Redford
Bobby Duran	Lena Olin
Joe Volpi	Alan Arkin
Menocal	Tomas Milian
Marion Chigwell	Daniel Davis
Julio Ramos	Tony Plana
Arturo Duran	Raul Julia
Diane	Betsy Brantley
Patty	Lise Cutter
Professor	Richard Farnsworth
Meyer Lansky	Mark Rydell
Willy	Vasek Simek
Baby Hernandez	Fred Asparagus
Mike MacClaney	Richard Portnow
Roy Forbes	Dion Anderson
Captain Potts	Carmine Caridi
Corporal	James Medina
Cuban Businessman	Joe Lala
Menocal's Lieutenant	Salvadore Levy
Hotel Man	Bernie Pollack
Santos	Owen Roizman
Young Cubans	Victor Rivers, Alex Ganster
Sims	Rene Monclova, Miguel Angel Suarez
Ricardo	Segundo Tarrau
Tomas	Felix German
Monica	Giovanna Bonnelly
Bufano	David Jose Rodriguez
Jose	Franklin Rodriguez
Carlos	Hugh Kelly
Dancers	Terri Hendrickson, Karen Russell
Sailor	David Gibson
Rebel Captain	Adriano Gonzalez

and Raul Rosado (Roadblock Sergeant), Mildred I. Ventura (Woman at burning villa), Pepito Guerra (Floridita Manager), Anthony Bayarri (Modest Casino Cuban), Alfredo Vorshirm (Modest Casino Tuxedo), Bonita Marco, Sharon Velez, Darlene Wynn (Strippers), Miguel Bucarelly (Gomez), Carlos Miranda, Enrique Chao Barros (Inspectors), Daniel Vasquez (Kid at Finca), Carmen De Franco (Monica's Grandmother)

Top: Lena Olin, Raul Julia Below: Robert Redford, Olin
Left: Alan Arkin; Tony Plana
© Universal City Studios

James Medina, Lena Olin

Robert Redford, Tomas Milian

Bob Hoskins, Cher Top Right: Winona Ryder,
Michael Schoeffling Right: Cher, Hoskins
© *Orion Pictures Corp.*

MERMAIDS

(ORION) Producers, Lauren Lloyd, Wallis Nicita, Patrick Palmer; Director, Richard Benjamin; Screenplay, June Roberts; Based on the novel by Patty Dann; Photography, Howard Atherton; Designer, Stuart Wurtzel; Costumes, Marit Allen; Casting, Margery Simkin; Editor, Jacqueline Cambas; Associate Producer, Suzanne Rothbaum; Assistant Director, Jim Van Wyck; Song: *"The Shoop Shoop Song (It's in His Kiss)"* by Rudy Clark/performed by Cher; Dolby Stereo; Technicolor/Deluxe; Rated PG-13; 111 minutes; December release

CAST

Mrs. Flax	Cher
Lou Landsky	Bob Hoskins
Charlotte Flax	Winona Ryder
Joe	Michael Schoeffling
Kate Flax	Christina Ricci
Carrie	Caroline McWilliams
Mother Superior	Jan Miner
Mary O'Brien	Betsey Townsend
Mr. Crain	Richard McElvain
Mrs. Crain	Paula Plum
Coach Parker	Dossy Peabody
Boss in Oklahoma	William Paul Steele
Dr. Reynolds	Rex Trailer
Perfect Family Father	Pete Kovner
Perfect Family Mother	Patricia Madden
Perfect Family Boy	Justin Marchisio
Perfect Family Girl	Caitlin Marie Bottomley
Girls in bathroom	Amy Gollnick, Seacia Pavao
Nurse	Merle Perkins
Boss in Massachusetts	Baxter Harris
Boss' Fiancee	Carol Moss
Pretty Girl at shoe store	Denise Cormier
Crying Man on street	Al Hodgkins
Young Nun	Tamasin Scarlet Johnson
Crying Nun	Sandra Shipley
Judge at swim meet	Russell Jones
Charlotte—5 yrs. old	Shawna Sullivan
Charlotte's Dad	Bob Rogerson
Carrie's Husband	Tom Kemp
Policeman	Jerry Quinn

and Janice Janes, Bill McCann, Dotty Pagliaro (New Year's Partiers), Arnie Cox, Michelle Faith, Grace Costa, John McGee, Bill McDonald, Harry Cooper, Lynda Robinson (Kennedy Mourners)

Winona Ryder, Cher, Christina Ricci Above: Cher, Ricci,
Ryder

THE BONFIRE OF THE VANITIES

(WARNER BROS.) Producer/Director, Brian De Palma; Executive Producers, Peter Guber, Jon Peters; Screenplay, Michael Cristofer; Based on the novel by Tom Wolfe; Co-Producer, Fred Caruso; Photography, Vilmos Zsigmond; Designer, Richard Sylbert; Music, Dave Grusin; Editors, David Ray, Bill Pankow; Costumes, Ann Roth; Casting, Lynn Stalmaster; Associate Producer, Monica Goldstein; Assistant Director, Chris Soldo; Dolby Stereo; Technicolor; Rated R; 125 minutes; December release

CAST

Sherman McCoy	Tom Hanks
Peter Fallow	Bruce Willis
Maria Ruskin	Melanie Griffith
Judy McCoy	Kim Cattrall
Jed Kramer	Saul Rubinek
Judge White	Morgan Freeman
Abraham Weiss	F. Murray Abraham
Reverend Bacon	John Hancock
Tom Killian	Kevin Dunn
Albert Fox	Clifton James
Ray Andruitti	Louis Giambalvo
Det. Martin	Barton Heyman
Det. Goldberg	Norman Parker
Mr. McCoy	Donald Moffat
Arthur Ruskin	Alan King
Caroline Heftshank	Beth Broderick
Pollard Browning	Kurt Fuller
Rawlie Thorpe	Adam LeFevre
Ed Rifkin	Richard Libertini
Aubrey Buffing	Andre Gregory
Annie Lamb	Mary Alice
Sir Gerald Moore	Robert Stephens

and Marjorie Monaghan (Evelyn Moore), Rita Wilson (P.R. Woman), Kirsten Dunst (Campbell McCoy), Troy Windbush (Roland Auburn), Patrick Malone (Henry Lamb), Emmanuel Xuereb (Filippo Chirazzi), Scotty Bloch (Sally Rawthrote), Hansford Rowe (Leon Bavardage), Elizabeth Owens (Inez Bavardage), Malachy McCourt (Tony—Doorman), John Bentley (Bill—Doorman), William Clark (Eddie—Doorman), Jeff Brooks, T. J. Coan, Don McManus, James Lally, Marcia Mitzman (Bondsmen), William Woodson (Gene Lopwitz—V.O.), Nelson Vasquez (Pimp), Fanni Green (Prostitute), Roy Milton Davis (Latino), Shiek Mahmud-Bey (Lockwood), Stewart J. Zully (Court Clerk), Helen Stenborg (Mrs. McCoy), Timothy Jenkins (Billy Cortez), Sam Jenkins (Fox's Assist.), Vito D'Ambrosio (Intercom Man), Paul Bates (Buck), Camryn Manheim, J. D. Wyatt, Edye Byrde, David Lipman, George Merritt (Poe Picketers), Kirk Taylor (Aide), O. Laron Clark (Cecil Hayden), Louis P. Lebherz ("The Commandatori"), Walker Joyce (Bobby Shalfet/"Don Giovanni"), Anatoly Davydov (Boris Karlevskov), Nancy McDonald, Ray Iannicelli, Daniel Hagen, Kimberleigh Aarn, Walter Flanagan, Mike Hodge, Ernestine Jackson, Nicholas Levitin, Novella Nelson, Noble Lee Lester (Media Jackals), Adina Winston (Guest), Richard Belzer (TV Producer), Cynthia Mason (Maid), Ermal Williamson (Butler), W. M. Hunt (Nunnally Voyd), Gian-Carlo Scandiuzzi (Maitre D'), Jon Rashad Kamal (French Waiter), Channing Chase (Shocked Woman), Hal Englund, Joy Claussen, John Fink, Judith Burke (French Restaurant Patrons), Barry Michlin (Funeral Director), Connie Sawyer (Ruskin Family Member), Johnny Crear (Manny Leerman), Sherri Paysinger (Anchorwoman), Staci Francis, Barbara Gooding, Kathleen Murphy Palmer, Lorraine Moore, Doris Leggett (Gospel Singers), Kathryn Danielle (P.R. Assist.), Oliver Dixon (Diplomat), Jennifer Bassey (Diplomat's Wife), Katrina Braque (Diplomat's daughter), Richard Gilbert-Hill, Marie Chambers, Virginia Morris, Barry Neikrug (Weiss' Aides), George Plimpton, Susan Forristal (Well Wishers), Geraldo Rivera (Newsman)

Top: Tom Hanks, Bruce Willis Below: Hanks (C)
© Warner Bros.

Saul Rubinek, Tom Hanks, Kevin Dunn, Morgan Freeman
Above: Melanie Griffith, Bruce Willis

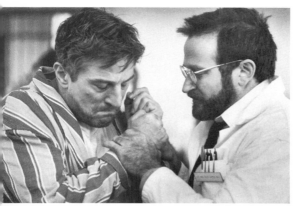

AWAKENINGS

(COLUMBIA) Producers, Walter F. Parkes, Lawrence Lasker; Executive Producers, Penny Marshall, Arne Schmidt, Elliot Abbott; Director, Penny Marshall; Screenplay, Steven Zaillian; Based on the book by Oliver Sacks, M.D.; Photography, Miroslav Ondricek; Designer, Anton Furst; Music, Randy Newman; Editors, Jerry Greenberg, Battle Davis; Costumes, Cynthia Flynt; Casting, Bonnie Timmermann; Associate Producer, Amy Lemisch; Assistant Director, Tony Gittelson; Dolby Stereo; Technicolor; Rated PG-13; 121 minutes; December release

CAST

Leonard Lowe	Robert De Niro
Dr. Malcolm Sayer	Robin Williams
Eleanor Costello	Julie Kavner
Mrs. Lowe	Ruth Nelson
Dr. Kaufman	John Heard
Paula	Penelope Ann Miller
Lucy	Alice Drummond
Rose	Judith Malina
Bert	Barton Heyman
Frank	George Martin
Miriam	Anne Meara
Sidney	Richard Libertini
Lolly	Laura Esterman
Rolando	Dexter Gordon
Frances	Jayne Haynes
Magda	le Clanche du Rand
Joseph	Yusef Bulos
Luis	Steve Randazzo
Dottie	Gloria Harper
Desmond	Gwyllum Evans
Nurse Beth	Mary Catherine Wright
Nurse Margaret	Mary Alice
Anthony	Keith Diamond
Ray	Steve Vinovich
Janitor	Tiger Haynes
Dr. Sullivan	John Christopher Jones
Dr. Tyler	Bradley Whitford
Dr. Peter Ingham	Max Von Sydow
Hospital Director	Harvey Miller
Psychiatrist	Tanya Berezin
Neurochemist	Peter Stormare
Man in hall	Shane Fistell
Hysterical Woman	Waheedah Ahmad
Mr. Kean	Charles Keating
Christina	Christina Huertes
Fishsticks	Linda Burns
Hospital Receptionist	Judy Jacksina
George, Security Guard	Gary Tacon
Orderly #1	Rico Elias
Nurse Sara	Mel Gorham
EEG Technician	Chris Carolan
Cafeteria Nurse	Debra Kovner-Zaks
Ward #5 Orderly	Max Rabinowitz
Ward #5 Patient	Gordon Joseph Weiss
Club Singer	Libby Titus
Bus Driver	Michael Hyde
Bartender	Tomislav Novakovic
Librarian	Adam Bryant
Young Leonard	Anthony J. Nici
Leonard's Friends	Oliver Block, Buck Smith
Teacher	Joan E. MacIntosh

and Gordon Joseph Weiss, Byron Utley, Anthony McGowen, Paul Montgomery, Leonard Tepper, Vinny Pastore, Howard Feller (Ward #5 Patients)

Top: Robert De Niro, Robin Williams
Below: De Niro, Penelope Ann Miller
© Columbia Pictures

Julie Kavner, Robin Williams Above: Williams

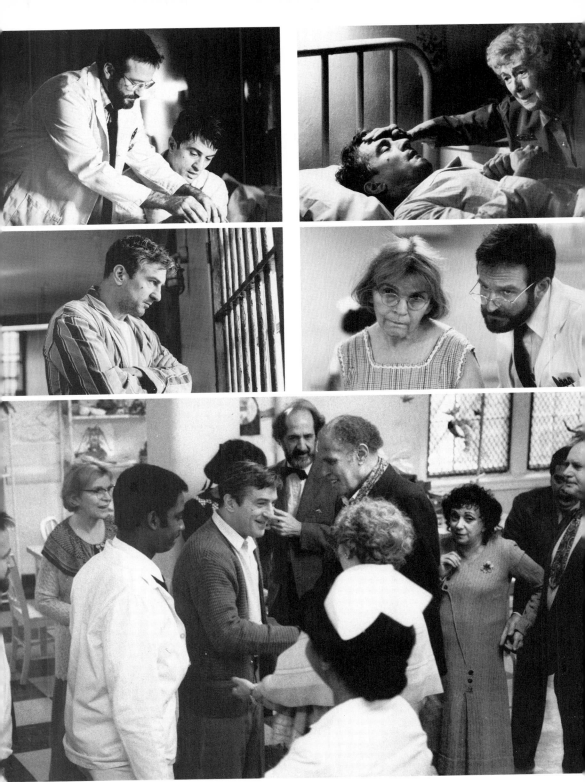

Alice Drummond, Keith Diamond, Robert De Niro, Richard Libertini, Dexter
Gordon, Judith Malina, Barton Heyman Top Left: Williams, De Niro
Above Left: De Niro Top Right: De Niro, Ruth Nelson Above Right: Drummond,
Williams

THE RUSSIA HOUSE

(MGM) Producers, Paul Maslansky, Fred Schepisi; Director, Fred Schepisi; Screenplay, Tom Stoppard; Based on the novel by John Le Carré; Photography, Ian Baker; Designer, Richard MacDonald; Music, Jerry Goldsmith, featuring Branford Marsalis; Editor, Peter Honess; Costumes, Ruth Myers; Casting, Mary Selway; Assistant Director, David Tringham; a Pathe Entertainment presentation from MGM/UA Distribution Co.; Dolby Stereo; Technovision; Technicolor; Rated R; 123 minutes; December release

CAST

Barley Blair	Sean Connery
Katya	Michelle Pfeiffer
Russell	Roy Scheider
Ned	James Fox
Brady	John Mahoney
Clive	Michael Kitchen
Quinn	J.T. Walsh
Walter	Ken Russell
Wicklow	David Threlfall
Dante	Klaus Maria Brandauer
Bob	Mac McDonald
Niki Landau	Nicholas Woodeson
Brock	Martin Clunes
Merrydew	Ian McNiece
Henziger	Colin Stinton
Paddy	Denys Hawthorne
Cy	George Roth
U.S. Scientist	Peter Mariner
Anna	Ellen Hurst
Sergey	Peter Knupffer
Uncle Matvey	Nikolai Pastukhov
Johnny	Jason Salkey
Nasayan	Eric Anzumonyin
Zapadny	Daniel Wozniak
Yuri	Georgi Andzhaparidze
Tout	Vladek Nikiforov
Larry	Christopher Lawford
Todd	Mark La Mura
Merv	Blu Mankuma
Stanley	Tuck Milligan
Spikey	Jay Benedict
George	David Timson
Anastasia	Elena Stroyeva

and Fyodor Smirnov, Pavel Sirotin (Watchers), Paul Jutkevitch (Misha), Margot Pinvidic (Interpreter), David Henry (Jr. Minister—Whitehall), Martin Wenner (Scientist—Whitehall), Paul Rattee (Army Officer—Whitehall), Simon Templeman (Psychoanalyst), Gina Nikiforov, Raisa Ryazanova (Russian Guests), Kate Lock (Jacky), Charlotte Cornwell (Charlotte), Craig Crosbie (Technician), Keith Edwards, Michael Fitzpatrick, Rob Freeman (Hoovers), Gennady Venov (Katya's Father), Vladimir Sidirov, Nikolai Nikitin (Leningrad Police), Sasha Yatsko (Russian Writer), Vladimir Zunetov (Dan), Jack Raymond (Lev), David Ryall (Colonial Type), Alexei Jawdokimov (Arkady), Constantine Gregory (KGB Interviewer), Sergei Reusenko (KGB Man), Yegueshe Tsturvan (Flute Player)

Top: Michelle Pfeiffer, Sean Connery
Below: Pfeiffer Right: Connery
© Pathe Entertainment

Sean Connery, Michelle Pfeiffer

Sean Connery, Klaus Maria Brandauer

KINDERGARTEN COP

(UNIVERSAL) Producers, Ivan Reitman, Brian Grazer; Executive Producers, Joe Medjuck, Michael C. Gross; Director, Ivan Reitman; Screenplay, Murray Salem, Herschel Weingrod, Timothy Harris; Story, Murray Salem; Photography, Michael Chapman; Designer, Bruno Rubeo; Editors, Sheldon Kahn, Wendy Greene Bricmont; Associate Producers, Sheldon Kahn, Gordon Webb; Costumes, Gloria Gresham; Music, Randy Edelman; Casting, Michael Chinich; Assistant Director, Peter Giuliano; Stunts, Joel Kramer; an Imagine Entertainment presentation; Dolby Stereo; Color; Rated PG-13; 111 minutes; December release

CAST

John Kimble	Arnold Schwarzenegger
Joyce Paulmarie	Penelope Ann Miller
Phoebe O'Hara	Pamela Reed
Miss Schlowski	Linda Hunt
Cullen Crisp	Richard Tyson
Eleanor Crisp	Carroll Baker
Dominic Paulmarie	Joseph Cousins, Christian Cousins
Sylvester's Mother	Cathy Moriarty
Samantha's Mother	Park Overall
Zach's Mother	Jayne Brook
Captain Salazar	Richard Portnow
Danny	Tom Kurlander
Cindy	Alix Koromzay

Kimble's Class:

Zach	Justin Page
Joshua	Peter Rakow
Emma	Sarah Rose Karr
Samantha	Marissa Rosen
Lowell	Ben McCreary
Joseph	Miko Hughes
John	Robert Cave
Sylvester	Ben Diskin
Keisha	Tameka Runnels
Latiana	Medha Garg
William	Brian Wagner
Kevin	John Christian Graas
Sedgewinn	Jim Jim Jackson
Sam	Ian Baumer
Sarah	Amy Wald
Tina	Tiffany Materas
Rina	Krystle Materas
Matthew	James Chance
Larry	Adam Wylie
Heather	Nicole Nagorsky
Harvey	Ross Malinger
Mary	Amber Reaves
Rosa	Odette Yustman
Dorothy	Tina Hart
Jennifer	Emily Ann Lloyd
Courtney	Haley Urman
Catherine	Bethany Jayne Allyn
Nick	Zachary Marsh
Tom	Anthony Wong
Erwin	Remone Bradley

and Betty Lou Henson (Keisha's Mother), Heidi Swedberg (Joshua's Mother), Stephen Root (Sheriff), Robert Nelson (Henry), Molly Cleator (Asst. to Schlowski), Gary Hollis (Superintendent Rice), Susan Burns (Waitress), Tom Dugan (Crisp's Lawyer), Roma (Manicurist), Jason Stuart (Hairstylist), Kim Delgado, Ray Glanzman, Ed Crick (Security Guards), Angela Bassett (Stewardess), Chi-Muoi Lo (Dope Dealer), John Hammil (Zach's Father), Steve Park (Asst. to Salazar), John Steinkamp (Toy Store Clerk), Charlie Holliday (Customer—Daryl), Lee Forest (Pharmacist), Judith Wix (Substitute Teacher), Galen Yulen, Frankie Avina, Terry Golden, Lee Dupree (Low Lifes), Teague O'Connor (Alex), Michael Chapman (Firefighter), Trevor Reed, Travis Reed, Jason Howard (Airplane Boys), Debra Casey (Punk Tramp), Peter Vasquez, Jacques Bolton, Leo Lee (Street Toughs), Evelyn Abrahams (Bus Driver), Kenneth Chapman (Fire Chief), Hanna J. Haynes (Drugstore Clerk), Rick Jones (Samantha's Father), Mimi J. Kauffman (Restaurant Hostess), Catherine Reitman (3rd Grade Student), Tiffany Reaves (Tiffany), Jason Reitman (Jason), Anne Merrem (Nurse), Arlene Phalon (Salon Receptionist)

Top: Pamela Reed, Arnold Schwarzenegger
Below: Schwarzenegger (C)
© *Universal City Studios*

Arnold Schwarzenegger Above: Richard Tyson, Carroll Baker

Whoopi Goldberg, Lexi Faith Randall
Top Right: Dwight Schultz, Sissy Spacek
Right: Goldberg, Ving Rhames
© *Miramax Films*

THE LONG WALK HOME

(**MIRAMAX**) Producers, Howard W. Koch, Jr., Dave Bell; Director, Richard Pearce; Screenplay, John Cork; Executive Producers, Taylor Hackford, Stuart Benjamin; Associate Producer, Edwin C. Atkins; Photography, Roger Deakins; Editor, Bill Yahraus; Music, George Fenton; Costumes, Shay Cunliffe; Designer, Blake Russell; Casting, Shari Rhodes, Jo Doster; Assistant Director, Victoria E. Rhodes; a New Vision Pictures presentation; Color; Rated PG; 97 minutes; December release

CAST

Miriam Thompson	Sissy Spacek
Odessa Cotter	Whoopi Goldberg
Norman Thompson	Dwight Schultz
Herbert Cotter	Ving Rhames
Tunker Thompson	Dylan Baker
Selma Cotter	Erika Alexander
Mary Catherine Thompson	Lexi Faith Randall
Theodore Cotter	Richard Habersham
Franklin Cotter	Jason Weaver
Sarah Thompson	Crystal Robbins
Claudia	Cherene Snow
Martin	Chelcie Ross
Charlie	Dan E. Butler
Winston	Phil Sterling
Judy (Girl at Oak Park)	Schuyler Elizabeth Fisk
Anne (Girl at Oak Park)	Nancy M. Atchison
Policeman at Oak Park	Haynes Brooke
Roger	Jim Aycock
Lucille	Rebecca Wackler
Mr. Cooper	Charles Hubbard
Mrs. Cooper	Harriet Sumner
Grandma Thompson	Gleaves Azar
Bus Driver	Jim Haffey
Tall Boy	Stacey Fleming
Boys	Jeff Taffet, Jay Reed
Taxi Driver	Afemo Omilami
Betsy	Debbie Hackett
Laura Ann	Lynne Pickering
Jeff Sewell	Fairley McDonald
Clyde Sellers	Graham Timbes
Preacher	Norman Matlock

and Dorrell Dorsey (Woman in church), Bobby Howard (Clipboard Man), Cynthia B. Williams (Housekeeper), Dan Jenkins (Auburn Fan #1), Katherine Conely (Mrs. Midgley), Sherwood "Ric" Pearson (George Millo), Kevin Thigpen (Worker #1), Everett McCorvey (Church Speaker), Dr. T. Clifford Bibb (Choir Leader), A. Bernard Sneed (Organist), David E. McCorvey (Older Black Man), Carl Stephens (Newscaster), Perry Carter (Sammy Chancelor), Henry Marcus, Jr. (Cliff), Troy La Don Pate (Party Guest), Michael Sansom (Angry Man—Eugene), Dorothy Love Coates (Lead Singer at car lot), Mary Steenburgen (Narrator)

Whoopi Goldberg, Lexi Faith Randall, Sissy Spacek, Haynes
Brooke Above: Spacek, Dylan Baker

COME SEE THE PARADISE

(20th CENTURY FOX) Producer, Robert F. Colesberry; Director/
Screenplay, Alan Parker; Photography, Michael Seresin; Designer,
Geoffrey Kirkland; Costumes, Molly Maginnis; Music, Randy
Edelman; Editor, Gerry Hambling; Casting, Lisa Clarkson; Associate
Producer, Nellie Nugiel; Assistant Director, Aldric La'Auli Porter;
"Jack's Theatre Song" by Alan Parker and Eddie Karam/performed by
Dennis Quaid; Dolby Stereo; Deluxe color; Rated R; 132 minutes;
December release

CAST

Jack McGurn	Dennis Quaid
Lily Kawamura	Tamlyn Tomita
Mr. Kawamura	Sab Shimono
Mrs. Kawamura	Shizuko Hoshi
Charlie Kawamura	Stan Egi
Harry Kawamura	Ronald Yamamoto
Dulcie Kawamura	Akemi Nishino
Joyce Kawamura	Naomi Nakano
Frankie Kawamura	Brady Tsurutani
Young Mini	Elizabeth Gilliam
Middle Mini	Shyree Mezick
Older Mini	Caroline Junko King
Augie Farrell	Pruitt Taylor Vince
Gerry McGurn	Colm Meaney
Marge McGurn	Becky Ann Baker
Brennan	John Finnegan
Mr. Fujioka	Takumaro Ikeguchi
Mr. Nishikawa	Danny Kamekona
Mr. Yamanaka	Yoshimi Imai
Japanese Actor	Lenny Imamura
Acting Troupe Manager	Goh Misawa
Social Club Singer	Sanae Hosaka
Reiko Sakoda	Shuko Akune
Master of Ceremonies	Keenan Shimizu
Mr. Ogata	Dale Ishimoto
Mrs. Ogata	Shinko Isobe
Fumiko	Mariko Fujinaka
Mr. Matsui	Fred Irinaga
Mr. Noji	Tad Horino
Theatre Men	George P. Wilbur, Allan Graf
McGurn Children	Frank Trocha, Tricia L. Campbell, Kelsy White
Japanese Girls	Cynthia Aso, Emi Endo
Fujioka's Mother	Marian Mukogawa
Dance Hall Singer	Fran Lucci
Wedding Singer	Mark Earley
Eddie	Paul DiCocco, Jr.
Detective	Joe Lisi
Santa	David MacIntyre
Store Manager	Doug MacHugh
Draft Clerk	Howard French
Kindergarten Teacher	Gigi Toya
Race Track Soldier	Don Alder
Camp Singers	Teri Eiko Koide, Jumi Emizawa, Cynthia Lauren
Basic Training Sergeant	Ian Woolf
Farmer	Ben Slack
Issei Gentleman	Bill M. Ryusaki
Kenji	Ken Katsumoto
Road Block Soldier	Kim Robillard
Administrators	George Buck, Kevin McDermott
Demonstration Leader	Harunobu Yoshida
Army Captain	David Carpenter
FBI Agent	Ben DiGregorio
Woman in uniform	Saachiko
Truck Driver	Robert Colesberry
Committee Chairman	Richard Iwamoto
Hecklers	Douglas Kato, Ken Y. Mayeno, Makio Sasaki
MP Soldiers	Tommy Allen, John McColpin
Dance Hall Band	John Jensen, John Mazzocco, Joe Heinemann, Michael York

**Top: Dennis Quaid, Caroline Junko King, Tamlyn Tomita
Below: Akemi Nishino, Ronald Yamamoto, Shizuko Hoshi,
Naomi Nakano, Elizabeth Gilliam, Tomita, Stan Egi, Brady
Tsurutani © 20th Century Fox**

Stan Egi, Tamlyn Tomita, Dennis Quaid, Elizabeth Gilliam

THE GODFATHER PART III

(PARAMOUNT) Producer/Director, Francis Ford Coppola; Executive Producers, Fred Fuchs, Nicholas Gage; Co-Producers, Fred Roos, Gray Frederickson, Charles Mulvehill; Screenplay, Mario Puzo, Francis Ford Coppola; Photography, Gordon Willis; Designer, Dean Tavoularis; Editors, Barry Malkin, Lisa Fruchtman, Walter Murch; Costumes, Milena Canonero; Music, Carmine Coppola, Nino Rota; Song: *"Promise Me You'll Remember (Love Theme from The Godfather Part III)"* performed by Harry Connick, Jr.; Associate Producer, Marina Gefter; Casting, Janet Hirshenson, Jane Jenkins, Roger Mussenden; Assistant Director, H. Gordon Boos; from Zoetrope Studios; Dolby Stereo; Technicolor; Rated R; 161 minutes; December release

CAST

Michael Corleone	Al Pacino
Kay Adams	Diane Keaton
Connie Corleone Rizzi	Talia Shire
Vincent Mancini	Andy Garcia
Don Altobello	Eli Wallach
Joey Zasa	Joe Mantegna
B.J. Harrison	George Hamilton
Grace Hamilton	Bridget Fonda
Mary Corleone	Sofia Coppola
Cardinal Lamberto	Raf Vallone
Anthony Corleone	Franc D'Ambrosio
Archbishop Gilday	Donal Donnelly
Al Neri	Richard Bright
Frederick Keinszig	Helmut Berger
Dominic Abbandando	Don Novello
Andrew Hagen	John Savage
Calo	Franco Citti
Mosca	Mario Donatone
Don Tommasino	Vittorio Duse
Licio Lucchesi	Enzo Robutti
Spara	Michele Russo
Johnny Fontane	Al Martino
Lou Pennino	Robert Cicchini
Twin Bodyguards: Armand	Rogerio Miranda
Francesco	Carlos Miranda
Anthony "The Ant" Squigliaro	Vito Antuofermo
Father John	Robert Vento
Party Politician	Willie Brown
Lucy Mancini	Jeannie Linero
Camerlengo Cardinal	Remo Remotti
Francesca Corleone	Jeanne Savarino Pesch
Kathryn Corleone	Janet Savarino Smith
Teresa Hagen	Tere L. Baker
Albert Volpe	Carmine Caridi
Frank Romano	Don Costello
Leo Cuneo	Al Ruscio
Matty Parisi	Mickey Knox
Masks	Rick Aviles, Michael Bowen
Douglas Michelson	Brett Halsey

and Gabriele Torrei (Enzo the Baker), John Abineri (Hamilton Banker), Brian Freilino (Stockholder), Gregory Corso (Unruly Stockholder), Marino Mase (Lupo), Dado Ruspoli (Vanni), Valeria Sabel (Sister Vincenza), Remo Remotti (Cardinal—Sistine), Luigi Laezza, Beppe Pianviti (Keinszig Killers), Santo Indelicato (Guardia del Corpo), Francesco Paolo Bellante (Autista di Don Tommasino), Paco Reconti (Gesu), Mimmo Cuticchio (Puppet Narrator), Richard Honigman (Party Reporter), Nicky Blair (Nicky, the Casino Host), Anthony Guidera (Anthony, the Bodyguard), Frank Tarsia (Frankie, the Bodyguard), Diane Agostini (Woman with child at street fair), Jessica Di Cicco (Child), Catherine Scorsese, Ida Bernardini (Women in cafe), Joseph Drago (Party Security), David Hume Kennerly (Party Photographer), James D. Damiano (Son playing soccer), Michael Boccio (Father of soccer player)

Top: Al Pacino, Richard Bright Below: Eli Wallach, Talia Shire
© *Paramount Pictures*

Al Pacino, Sofia Coppola, Andy Garcia **Above: Garcia (C)**

Donal Donnelly; Raf Vallone Top Left: Andy Garcia, Eli Wallach

Al Pacino, Andy Garcia Top Right: Bridget Fonda

Sofia Coppola, Diane Keaton, Al Pacino, George Hamilton, John Savage, Don Novello, Andy Garcia, Talia Shire

William Hurt; Cybill Shepherd Top Right: Joe Mantegna, Mia
Farrow Right: Blythe Danner; Alec Baldwin
© *Orion Pictures Corp.*

ALICE

(ORION) Producer, Robert Greenhut; Executive Producers, Jack Rollins, Charles H. Joffe; Co-Producers, Helen Robin, Joseph Hartwick; Director/Screenplay, Woody Allen; Photography, Carlo Di Palma; Designer, Santo Loquasto; Editor, Susan E. Morse; Costumes, Jeffrey Kurland; Casting, Juliet Taylor; Associate Producers, Thomas Reilly, Jane Read Martin; Assistant Director, Thomas Reilly; Deluxe color; Rated PG-13; 106 minutes; December release

CAST

Alice	Mia Farrow
Joe	Joe Mantegna
Doug	William Hurt
Dr. Yang	Keye Luke
Vicki	Judy Davis
Nancy Brill	Cybill Shepherd
Ed	Alec Baldwin
Dorothy	Blythe Danner
Alice's Mother	Gwen Verdon
Muse	Bernadette Peters
Hilda	June Squibb
Monica	Marceline Hugot
Kate	Dylan O'Sullivan Farrow
Dennis	Matt Williamson
Decorator	Julie Kavner
Trainer	Billy Taylor
Helen	Holland Taylor
Nina	Robin Bartlett
Penny	Linda Wallem
Joe's Daughter	Gina Gallagher
School Teacher	Patience Moore
Dr. Yang's Assistant	Diane Cheng
Alice's Father	Patrick O'Neal
Alice at 18 yrs	Kristy Graves
Young Dorothy	Laurie Nayber
Alice at 12 yrs	Rachel Miner
Mrs. Keyes	Amy Louise Barrett
Sue	Caroline Aaron
Kimberly	Alexi Henry
Professor	James Toback
Model	Elle MacPherson
Carol	Diane Salinger
Ken	David Spielberg
Sid Moscowitz	Bob Balaban

and Michael-Vaughn Sullivan (Hairstylist), Kim Chan (Dr. Yang's Patient), Lynda Bridges (Saleslady), Anthony Cortino (Dog Groomer), Katja Schumann (Circus Equestrian), Vanessa Thomas (Circus Aerialist), Ira Wheeler, Lisa Marie (Office Xmas party Guests), Alfred Cherry (Vicki's Analyst), Peggy Miley (Dorothy's Maid), George Manos, Kim Weston-Moran, Peter Tolan, Kenneth Edelson, Marvin Terban, James McDaniel, Roy Attaway (Dorothy's Xmas party Guests), Jodi Long, Suzann O'Neill, Don Snell, Robert Polenz (Park Avenue Couples), Judith Ivey

Gwen Verdon; Bernadette Peters Above: Mia Farrow,
Keye Luke

William Hickey in "Puppet Master" © *JGM Enterprises*

Doug Self, Joe Tolbe in "Men in Love"
© *Crystal Clear Communications*

PUPPET MASTER (JGM Enterprises) Producer, Hope Perello; Executive Producer, Charles Band; Director, David Schmoeller; Screenplay, Joseph G. Collodi; Story, Charles Band, Kenneth J. Hall; Photography, Sergio Salvati; Music, Richard Band; Editor, Tom Meshelski; Designer, John Myhre; Puppet Effects, David Allen Prods.; a Full Moon Production; Ultra-Stereo; Color; Rated R; 90 minutes; January release. CAST: Paul Le Mat (Alex), Irene Miracle (Dana Hadley), Matt Roe (Frank), Kathryn O'Reilly (Clarissa), Robin Frates (Megan Gallagher), Merrya Small (Theresa), Jimmie F. Scaggs (Neil), William Hickey (Andre Toulan), Barbara Crampton, David Boyd

SKI PATROL (Triumph Releasing) Producers, Phillip B. Goldfine, Donald L. West; Director, Richard Correll; Screenplay, Steven Long Mitchell, Craig W. Van Sickle; Story, Steven Long Mitchell, Craig W. Van Sickle, Wink Roberts; Executive Producer, Paul Maslansky; Music, Bruce Miller; Photography, John Stephens; Costumes, Angee Beckett; Editor, Scott Wallace; Casting, Fern Champion, Pamela Basker; an Epic Productions, Inc. and Sarlui/Diamant presentation; Ultra-Stereo; Deluxe color; Rated PG; 91 minutes; January release. CAST: Roger Rose (Jerry), Yvette Nipar (Ellen), T. K. Carter (Iceman), Leslie Jordan (Murray), Paul Feig (Stanley), Sean Gregory Sullivan (Suicide), Tess (Tiana), George Lopez (Eddie), Corby Timbrook (Lance), Stephen Hytner (Myron), Ray Walston (Pops), Martin Mull (Maris), Deborah Rose (Inspector Crabitz), Beirne Chisolm, Jim Allman (Lance's Thugs), Wink Roberts, Faith Minton (Skiing Couple), Lachlen French (Photographer), Margaret Aoki (Lady in car), Michelle Smoot-Hyde (Santa's Elf), James Alt (Young Father), John Garrison (Elder Skier), Kiyo Hamada (Japanese Lady), Nancy Ann Nahra

MEN IN LOVE (Crystal Clear Communications) Producer, Scott Catamas; Executive Producers, Richard Babson, David Charry; Director, Marc Huestis; Screenplay, Scott Catamas, Emerald Starr; Photography, Fawn Yacker, Marsha Kahm; Music, Donald James Regal; Editor, Frank Christopher; a Tantric Films production; Color; Not rated; 87 minutes; January release. CAST: Doug Self (Steven), Joe Tolbe (Peter), Emerald Starr (Robert), Kutira Decosterd (Christiana), Vincent Schwickert (B.S.), James A. Taylor (Jonathan), Carlo Incerto (Rocco), Jaiia (Jaiia), Scott Catamas (Victor), Renee De Palma (Laurel), Lulu, Steve Warren, Maura Nolan, Joe Capetta, Lily Gurk, Toni Maher

MORTAL PASSIONS (MGM) Producer, Gwen Field; Director, Andrew Lane; Screenplay, Alan Moskowitz; Executive Producers, Andrew Lane, Wayne Crawford, Joel Levine; Photography, Christian Sebaldt; Editor, Kimberly Ray; Designer, Robert Sissman; Casting, Maira Suro-Castles; Music, Parmer Fuller; from MGM/UA Distribution, in association with Gibraltar Releasing Organization; Foto-Kem color; Rated R; 98 minutes; January release. CAST: Zach Galligan (Todd Morrow), Michael Bowen (Berke Morrow), Krista Errickson (Emily Morrow), Luca Bercovici (Darcy), Sheila Kelley (Adele), David Warner (Dr. Powers), Cassandra Gava (Cinda), John Denos (Customer in bar), Alan Shearman (Pandarus), Ron Vernan (Paris), Kathleen Hart (Cafe Waitress)

THAT'S ADEQUATE (South Gate Entertainment) Producers, Irving Schwartz, Harry Hurwitz; Director/Screenplay, Harry Hurwitz; Executive Producer, John Manocherian; Photography, Joao Fernandes; Color/Black and white; Rated R; 80 minutes; January release. CAST: Tony Randall, James Coco, Jerry Stiller, Anne Meara, Ina Balin, Anne Bloom, Irwin Corey, Susan Dey, Robert Downey Jr., Richard Lewis, Chuck McCann, Stuart Pankin, Peter Riegert, Robert Staats, Brother Theodore, Robert Townsend, Robert Vaughn, Marshall Brickman, Martha Coolidge, Joe Franklin, Renee Taylor, Bruce Willis

SHADOWZONE (JGM Enterprises) Producer, Carol Kottenbrook; Director/Screenplay, J. S. Cardone; Photography, Karen Grossman; Executive Producer, Charles Band; Music, Richard Band; Editor, Tom Meshelski; Color; Rated R; 88 minutes; January release. CAST: Louise Fletcher, David Beecroft, James Hong, Shawn Weatherly, Miguel Nunez, Lu Leonard, Frederick Flynn, Maureen Flaherty, Robbie Rives

TRIPWIRE (New Line Cinema) Producer, Lisa M. Hansen; Co-Producer, Jefferson Richard; Executive Producer, Paul Hertzberg; Director, James Lemmo; Screenplay, B. J. Goldman; Story, William Lustig, Spiro Razatos; Photography, Igor Sunara; Editor, Christopher Cibelli; Music, Richard Stone; Designer, Bill Cornford; Casting, Susan Bluestein; a CineTel Films, Inc. presentation; Alpha Cine color; Rated R; 91 minutes; January release. CAST: Terence Knox (Jack DeForest), David Warner (Josef Szabo), Charlotte Lewis (Trudy), Isabella Hofmann (Annie Percy), Yaphet Kotto (Lee Pitt), Andras Jones (Ricky DeForest), Bobby Cummings (Moustaffa), Dean Tokuno (Mizoguchi), Marco Rodriguez (El Tigre), Jon Platten (Major Riley), Richard Stay (Jeff Szabo), Meg Foster (Julia), Lou Bonacki (Reese), Craig Clyde (Magruder), Tommy Chong (Merle Shine), Deano Herrera (Carlos), Frank Bare (Roamer), Sy Richardson (Turbo), Melinda Clarkson (Turbo's Girl), Antonio Martin (Hector), Corky Edgar, Jerry Ferguson

George Lopez, T. K. Carter in "Ski Patrol" © *Epic Prods.*

Zach Galligan, Krista Errickson, Luca Bercovici in "Mortal Passions" © *MGM/UA*

137

Ken Foree, Toni Hudson in "Leatherface" © *New Line Cinema*

Forest Whitaker, Anthony Edwards in "Downtown"
© *20th Century Fox*

LEATHERFACE: THE TEXAS CHAINSAW MASSACRE III (New Line Cinema) Producer, Robert Engelman; Associate Producer, Michael Deluca; Director, Jeff Burr; Screenplay, David J. Schow; Based on characters created by Kim Henkel and Tobe Hooper; Photography, James L. Carter; Stunts, Kane Hodder; Designer, Mick Strawn; Music, Jim Manzie, Pat Regan; Special Makeup Effects, Kurtzman Nicotero & Berger EFX Group; Dolby Stereo; Deluxe color; Rated R; 87 minutes; January release. CAST: Jennifer Banko (Little Girl), Ron Brooks (T.V. Newsman), William Butler (Ryan), Miriam Byrd-Nethery (Mama), David Cloud (Scott), Beth Depatie (Gina), Tom Everett (Alfredo), Ken Foree (Benny), Kate Hodge (Michelle), Toni Hudson (Sara), R. A. Mihailoff (Leatherface), Viggo Mortensen (Tex), Joe Unger (Tinker), Dwayne Whitaker (Kim), Michael Shamus Wiles (Checkpoint Officer)

LOVE OR MONEY (Hemdale) Producer, Elyse England; Executive Producer, Salah Hassanein; Director, Todd Hallowell; Screenplay, Elyse England, Michael Zausner, Bart Davis; Line Producer, Kathie Hersch; Associate Producers, Michael Zausner, Bart Davis; Photography, Igor Sunara; Designer, Robert P. Kracik; Editor, Ray Hubley; Music, Jim Lang; Costumes, Ileane Meltzer; Assistant Director, Kyle S. McCarthy; Color; Rated PG-13; 89 minutes; January release. CAST: Timothy Daly (Chris Murdoch), Michael Garin (Jeff Simon), Haviland Morris (Jennifer Reed), Kevin McCarthy (William Reed), Shelley Fabares (Lu Ann Reed), David Doyle (Arthur Reed), Allan Havey (Hank Peterson), Tisha Roth (Allison Simon), James Patrick Gillis (Dave Bradley), Katherine Cortez (Laura Baskin), Tom Signorelli (DeMartino), Rex Robbins (Al McDonough), Robert Stanton (Dudley), Geoffrey Nauffts (Clark), Ann Yen (Mollie), Lou Bedford (Jimmy Lorenz), Susan Blommaert (Midge Reed), Richard Gant (Zoo), Dena Dietrich (Receptionist), Antone Pagan (Messenger), Ron Yamamoto (Fish Store Manager), Sandy Richman, Stuart Burney (Customers), Jinsey Dauk, Kriss Ziemer (Girls), Ed Langsam (Referee)

BACK TO BACK (Concorde) Producers, Brad Krevoy, Steven Stabler; Executive Producer, Roger Corman; Director, John Kincade; Screenplay, George Francis Skrow; Photography, James L. Carter; Music, Rick Cox; Editors, Peter Maris, Kevin Michaels; Color; Rated R; 95 minutes; January release. CAST: Bill Paxton, Todd Field, Apollonia Kotero, Ben Johnson, Luke Askew, Susan Anspach, Sal Landi, David Michael Sterling, Roger Rook

DOWNTOWN (20th Century Fox) Producer, Charles H. Maguire; Director, Richard Benjamin; Screenplay, Nat Mauldin; Executive Producer, Gale Anne Hurd; Photography, Richard H. Kline; Designer, Charles Rosen; Costumes, Daniel Paredes; Casting, Reuben Cannon; Music, Alan Silvestri; Editors, Jacqueline Cambas, Brian Chambers; Dolby Stereo; Deluxe color; Rated R; 97 minutes; January release. CAST: Anthony Edwards (Alex Kearney), Forest Whitaker (Dennis Curren), Penelope Ann Miller (Lori Mitchell), David Clennon (Jerome Sweet), Art Evans (Henry Coleman), Rick Aiello (Mickey Witlin), Roger Aaron Brown (Lt. Sam Parral), Ron Canada (Lowell Harris), Wanda De Jesus (Luisa Diaz), Frank McCarthy (Inspector Ben Glass), Kimberly Scott (Christine Curren), Ryan McWhorter (Ephraim Can), Danuel Pipoly (Skip Markowitz), Catherine MacNeal (Mrs. Sweet), Stefanos Miltsakakis (Wayne), Russell Lunday (Sgt. Lehane), J. W. Smith (Sgt. Walter Hodo), James Craven (Man with uzi), Sonia Jackson (Female Detective), Vinnie Curto (Mr. Lopez), Angela Ruiz (Mrs. Lopez), Billy Kane (Ronnie), Glenn Plummer (Valentine), Kenneth J. McGregor (Gary Haber), Homeselle Joy (Minnie), Marc Robinson (Robert Curren), Tony T. Jackson (Adam Curren), Candace Mack (Amy Curren), Gwen E. Davis (Gloria Anderson), Ron Taylor (Bruce Tucker), Maurice Hill, Kathleen Jean Klein, Jeffrey P. Baggett, Robin D. Adler, Ella Mae Evans, Minnie Lindsey, Wren Brown, Michael Pniewski, Laura Williams, Michael Colyar, Robert Buckingham, Jerry Bossard, Burton Collins

STREETS (Concorde) Producer, Andy Ruben; Executive Producer, Roger Corman; Director, Katt Shea Ruben; Screenplay, Katt Shea Ruben, Andy Ruben; Photography, Phedon Papamichael; Music, Aaron Davis; Editor, Stephen Mark; Designer, Virginia Lee; Associate Producer, Rodman Flender; Foto-Kem color; Rated R; 83 minutes; January release. CAST: Christina Applegate (Dawn), David Mendenhall (Sy), Eb Lottimer (Lumley), Starr Andreef (Policewoman on horse), Jane Chung (Old Bag Woman), Alexander Folk (Bagley), David Lawrence (Plumber), Aron Eisenberg (Roach), Sheryl Bence (Punk Girl), Kady Tran (Dawn's blonde roommate), Julie Jay (Dawn's tattooed roommate), Mel Castelo (Elf), Jeni Anderson (Watch Girl), Alan Stock (Allen), Rhetta Green (Paramedic), Kay Lenz (Lieutenant), Jesse Ruben (Sergeant), Tom Williams, Alan Frazier, Pesha Rudnick, Nancy Tate (Troglodytes), Patty Peek (Mother with baby), Michael Vlastas (Man in bus station), Harri "Diana" James (Cigarette Girl), Bob Gray (Cowboy), Lisa Eye (Child with dog), J. Bartell, Paul Ben-Victor, Tom Ruben (Officers), Patrick Richwood (Bob), Sam Goffredo (Man in car)

Shelley Fabares, Kevin McCarthy, Timothy Daly, Michael Garin in "Love or Money" © *Hemdale Film Corp.*

Christina Applegate, David Mendenhall in "Streets"
© *Concorde*

Angela O'Neil, Vernon G. Wells in "Enemy Unseen" © *Triax*

Dean Cameron in "Rockula" © *Cannon Films*

ENEMY UNSEEN (Triax Entertainment) Producers, Elmo DeWitt, Desiree Markgraaff; Executive Producer, Barry Filby; Director, Elmo DeWitt; Story/Screenplay, Greg Latter; Photography, Hans Kuhle; an Ascension Releasing Corporation presentation; Color; Rated R; 90 minutes; January release. CAST: Vernon G. Wells (Steiger), Angela O'Neil (Roxanne Tangent), Stack Pierce (Stanley), Jeff Weston, Mel Noble

LOBSTER MAN FROM MARS (Electric Pictures) Producers, Eyal Rimmon, Steven S. Greene; Executive Producers, Nicole Seguin, Staffan Ahrenberg, Tom Eliasson; Director, Stanley Sheff; Screenplay, Bob Greenberg; Photography, Gerry Lively; Designer, Daniel White; Music, Sasha Matson; Editors, Stanley Sheff, Joan Peterson; a Filmrulen Production; Foto-Kem color; Rated R; 93 minutes; February release. CAST: Tony Curtis (J. P. Sheildrake), Deborah Foreman (Mary), Patrick Macnee (Prof. Piccostomos), Billy Barty (Throckmorton), Anthony Hickox (John), Tommy Sledge (Himself), Dean Jacobsen (Stevie Horowitz), Fred Holiday (Col. Ankrum), Bobby Pickett (King of Mars/The Astrologer), S. D. Nemeth (The Dreaded Lobster Man), Dr. Demento (Narrator)

LOOSE CANNONS (Tri-Star) Producers, Aaron Spelling, Alan Greisman; Director, Bob Clark; Screenplay, Richard Christian Matheson, Richard Matheson, Bob Clark; Executive Producer, René Dupont; Photography, Reginald H. Morris; Designer, Harry Pottle; Editor, Stan Cole; Music, Paul Zaza; Casting, Mike Fenton, Judy Taylor, Valorie Massalas; Assistant Director, Ken Goch; Stunts, Glenn Randall, Jr.; Title song by Peter Aykroyd, Ran Ballard/performed by Dan Aykroyd, Katey Sagal; Dolby Stereo; Panavision; Technicolor; Rated R; 94 minutes; February release. CAST: Gene Hackman (Mac Stern), Dan Aykroyd (Ellis Fielding), Dom DeLuise (Harry Gutterman), Ronny Cox (Bob Smiley), Nancy Travis (Riva), Robert Prosky (Curt Von Metz), Paul Koslo (Grimmer), Dick O'Neill (Capt. Doggett), Jan Triska (Steckler), Leon Rippy (Weskit), Robert Elliott (Monseigneur), Herb Armstrong (Chesire Cat), Robert Dickman (White Rabbit), David Alan Grier (Drummond), S. Epatha Merkerson (Rachel), Christopher Murney (Stan), Kay Joyner (Stan's Wife), Reg E. Cathey (Willie), Alex Hyde-White (Moderator), Tobin Bell (Gerber), Thomas Kopache (TV Station Man), Susan Peretz, Al Mancini (Tenants), Kevin McClarnon (Oaf), Debbee Hinchcliffe (Oaf's Sweetie), Jay Ingram (Patrolman), Arthur French (Bus Driver), Clem Moorman (Train Driver), Brad Greenquist (Embassy Officer), Ira Lewis (Hitler), Margaret Klenck (Eva Braun), John Bolger (Young Von Metz), Bill Fagerbakke (Giant), Robert Pentz (Guy at bar), Erik Cord, George P. Wilbur, Gene

LeBell, Danny Aiello III (Grimmer's Men), Billy Anagnos, Gary Tacon (Israeli Agents), Dean Mumford (Guy in baths), John J. Finn (Cop), Adrienne Hampton (Security Guard), Dutch Miller (Jacuzzi Guy), Gregory Goossen (Marsh Policeman), Chris S. MacGregor (Military Policeman), Ralph Redpath (Train Engineer), Nancy Parsons (Nurse), David Correia (Orderly), Jennifer Roach (Little Girl), Philip Shafran (Little Boy)

ROCKULA (Cannon) Producer, Jefery Levy; Executive Producers, Yoram Globus, Christopher Pearce; Director, Luca Bercovici; Screenplay, Luca Bercovici, Jefery Levy, Christopher Verwiel; Photography, John Schwartzman; Designer, Jane Ann Stewart; Editor, Maureen O'Connell; Music, Hilary Bercovici; Costumes, Pamela Sydney Skaist; Claire Louise Joseph; Color; Rated PG-13; 91 minutes; February release. CAST: Dean Cameron (Ralph), Toni Basil (Phoebe), Thomas Dolby (Stanley), Tawny Fere (Mona), Susan Tyrell (Chuck the Bartender), Bo Diddley (Axman), Kevin Hunter (Drunk), Nancye Ferguson (Robin), Rick Zumwalt (Boom Boom), Tamara DeTreaux (Bat Dork), Tony Cox (Big Al), Greg Rusin (Elmo), Joseph Bernard (Judge), William Brochtrup, Dean Minerd (Roadies), Mark McKerracher (Jury Foreman), Sloan Fischer (Cigar Man), Esther Richman (Socialite), Karen Bercovici (District Attorney), Sacred Johnson (Debutante), Adam Shankman (Driver), Rodney Bingenheimer (Himself), Zan Eisley, Cherra Savage (Vampire Groupies), Aries Hough, Luca Bercovici, Christopher Verwiel, Kenya Johnson, Allan Love, Shawn Klugman, Phillip "Fryer" Tuck, Maria Christina Urrea, Autumn Kimble, Alexandra Mothersbaugh, Scarlet Rouge Newton, Eddie Vail, Drew Steele

BASKET CASE 2 (Shapiro Glickenhaus) Producer, Edgar Ievins; Director/Screenplay, Frank Henenlotter; Executive Producer, James Glickenhaus; Photography, Robert M. Baldwin; Music, Joe Renzetti; Editor, Kevin Tent; Special Effects Make-up, Gabe Bartalos; Dolby Stereo; TVC color; Rated R; 89 minutes; February release. CAST: Kevin Van Hentenryck (Duane Bradley), Annie Ross (Granny Ruth), Kathryn Meisle (Marcie Elliott), Heather Rattray (Susan), Jason Evers (Editor Lou), Ted Sorel (Phil), Matt Mitler (Artie)

BOOK OF DAYS (Stutz Co.) Producers, Catherine Tatge, Dominique Lasseur; Director/Screenplay/Music, Meredith Monk; Photography, Jerry Pantzer; Editor, Girish Bhargava; Color/black and white; Not rated; 73 minutes; February release. CAST: Gerd Wameling, Lucas Hoving, Rob McBrien, Gail Turner, Gerger Hansen, Meredith Monk

Dom DeLuise, Dan Aykroyd, Gene Hackman in "Loose Cannons" © *Tri-Star Pictures*

"Basket Case 2" © *Shapiro Glickenhaus*

Joan Chen in "The Blood of Heroes" © *Kings Road Ent.*

Gary Kroeger, Gretchen German in "A Man Called Sarge"
© *Cannon*

BIG MAN ON CAMPUS (Vestron) Producer, Arnon Milchan; Executive Producers, Mitchell Cannold, Steven Reuther; Director, Jeremy Paul Kagan; Co-producers, Scott Rosenfelt, Mark Levinson; Screenplay, Allan Katz; Photography, Bojan Bazelli; Music, Joseph Vitarelli; Costumes, Lisa Jensen; Makeup, Ronnie Specter; Art Director, Michael Day; Deluxe color; Rated PG-13; 105 minutes; February release. CAST: Allan Katz (Bob), Corey Parker (Alex), Cindy Williams (Diane Girard), Melora Hardin (Cathy), Tom Skerritt (Dr. Webster), Jessica Harper (Dr. Fisk), Gerrit Graham (Stanley Hoyle), John Finnegan (Judge Ferguson)

DOG TAGS (Cinevest) Producers, Alain Adam, Dalu Jones; Director/Screenplay/Executive Producer, Romano Scavolini; Photography, John McCallum; Music, John Scott; Editor, Nicholas Pollock; a Daars production; Dolby Stereo; Panavision; Technicolor/Metrocolor; Rated R; 93 minutes; February release. CAST: Clive Wood (Cecil), Mike Monty (Capt. Newport), Baird Stafford, Robert Haufrecht, Peter Erlich, Chris Hilton, Gigi Doenas

THE BLOOD OF HEROES, aka The Salute of the Jugger (New Line Cinema) Producer, Charles Roven; Director/Screenplay, David Webb Peoples; Photography, David Eggby; Music, Todd Boekelhede; Designer, John Stoddart; Costumes, Terry Ryan; Editor, Richard Francis-Burke; 2nd Unit Director/Stunts, Guy Norris; Assistant Director, Keith Heygate; Special Makeup, Michael Westmore, Bob McCarron; a Kings Road Entertainment presentation; Dolby Stereo; Technicolor; Rated R; 90 minutes; February release. CAST: Rutger Hauer (Sallow), Joan Chen (Kidda), Vincent Phillip D'Onofrio (Young Gar), Delroy Lindo (Mbulu), Anna Katarina (Big Cimber), Gandhi Macintyre (Gandhi), Justin Monjo (Doy Boy), Max Fairchild (Gonzo), Hugh Keays-Byrne (Lord Vile), Lia Francisa (Maria), Aaron Martin (Samohin Boy), Steve Rackman (Feathers)

BIG BAD JOHN (Magnum Entertainment) Producer, Red Steagall; Director, Burt Kennedy; Screenplay, Joseph Berry, from an original screenplay by C. B. Wismar; Photography, Ken Lamkin; Music, Ken Sutherland; Editor, John W. Wheeler; Color; Rated PG-13; 92 minutes; February release. CAST: Jimmy Dean, Jack Elam, Ned Beatty, Romy Windsor, Bo Hopkins, Jeff Osterhage, Ned Vaughn, Buck Taylor, Jerry Potter, Amzie Strickland, Doug English, Red Steagall, Anne Lockhart

DAREDREAMER (Lensman Co.) Producer, Pat Royce; Executive Producers, Meier Mitchell & Co.; Director, Barry Caillier; Screenplay, Pat Royce, Barry Caillier; Story, Tim Noah, Pat Royce, Barry Caillier; Photography, Christopher G. Tufty; Music, Paul Speer, David Lanz; Editor, Karen Thorndike; Songs, Tim Noah; Choreographer, Wade Madsen; Dolby Stereo; Eastmancolor; Rated PG-13; 108 minutes; February release. CAST: Tim Noah (Winston), Alyce LaTourelle (Jennie), Adam Eastwood (Max), Michael A. Jackson (Zach), Jim Hechim, Billy Burke, Thomas Arthur, Whitey Shapiro, Renee Parent, Kirk Woller

THE GUMSHOE KID (Skouras) Producer/Director, Joseph Manduke; Executive Producer/Screenplay, Victor Bardack; Photography, Harvey Genkins; Music, Peter Matz; Editor, Richard G. Haines; Designer, Batia Grafka; Costumes, Ron Talsky; an Argus Entertainment production; Ultra-Stereo; Image Transform color; Rated R; 98 minutes; February release. CAST: Jay Underwood (Jeff Sherman), Tracy Scoggins (Rita Benson), Vince Edwards (Ben Sherman), Arlene Golonka (Gracie Sherman), Pamela Springsteen (Mona), Amy Lynne (Emily Sherman), Biff Yeager (Capt. Billings), Xander Berkeley (Monty), Gino Conforti (Meester), Miguel Sandoval, Tim Halderman, David Dunard, Michael Alaimo, Stephen Young

SPONTANEOUS COMBUSTION (Taurus Entertainment) Producer, Jim Rogers; Executive Producers, Henry Bushkin, Arthur Sarkissian; Director, Tobe Hooper; Screenplay, Tobe Hooper, Howard Goldberg; Photography, Levie Isaacks; Music, Graeme Revell; Editor, David Kern; Color; Rated R; 108 minutes; February release. CAST: Brad Dourif, Cynthia Bain, Jon Cypher, William Prince, Dey Young, Melinda Dillon, Tegan West, Michael Keys Hall, Dick Butkus, Dale Dye, Stacy Edwards, Brian Bremer, John Landis

THE SLEEPING CAR (Triax Entertainment) Producer/Director, Douglas Curtis; Executive Producer, Mark Amin; Associate Producer/Screenplay, Greg O'Neill; Photography, David Lewis; Music, Ray Colcord; Editors, Allan Holzman, Betty Cohen; Designer, Robert Benedict; Special Makeup Effects, John Carl Buechler; a Vidmark Entertainment presentation; CFI color; Rated R; 87 minutes; February release. CAST: David Naughton (Jason), Judie Aronson (Kim), Kevin McCarthy (Vincent Tuttle), Jeff Conaway (Bud Sorenson), Dani Minnick (Joanne), John Carl Buechler (Mr. Erickson), Ernestine Mercer (Mrs. Erickson), Steve Lundquist (Dwight), Bill Stevenson (Kerry), David Coburn (Harris), Nicole Hanson (Clarice), Sandra Margot (19-year old girl)

COURAGE MOUNTAIN (Triumph Releasing) Producer, Stephen Ujlaki; Executive Producer, Joel A. Douglas; Director, Christopher Leitch; Screenplay, Weaver Webb; Story, Fred Brogger, Mark Brogger; Editor, Martin Walsh; Photography, Jacques Steyn; Music, Sylvester Levay; Designer, Robb Wilson King; Costumes, Edith Poussou; Assistant Director, Peter Burrell; an Epic Productions, Inc. presentation of a Stone Group Ltd.—France Production; Ultra Stereo; CFI color; Rated PG; 98 minutes; February release. CAST: Juliette Caton (Heidi), Joanna Clarke (Ursula), Nicola Stapleton (Ilsa), Jade Magri (Clarissa), Kathryn Ludlow (Gudrun), Charlie Sheen (Peter), Jan Rubes (Grandfather), Leslie Caron (Jane Hillary), Yorgo Voyagis (Signor Bonelli), Laura Betti (Signora Bonelli), Marc Estrada (Aldolfo), Ruben Raiano (Giovanni), Urbano Barberini (Italian Captain), Massimo Sarchielli (Governor), Flora Alberti (Brookings Maid), David Ogilvie (Orphan Escape Witness)

A MAN CALLED SARGE (Cannon) Producer, Gene Corman; Director/Screenplay, Stuart Gillard; Executive Producers, Yoram Globus, Christopher Pearce; Photography, David Gurfinkel; Music, Chuck

Charlie Sheen, Juliette Caton in "Courage Mountain"
© *Epic Productions*

David Cronenberg, Craig Sheffer in "Nightbreed"
© *Morgan Creek Prods.*

Olivier Gruner, Theresa Saldana, Lupe Amador in "Angel Town" © *Rotecon B. V.*

Cirino; Assistant Director, Dov Maoz; Casting, Jeremy Zimmerman; Color; Rated PG-13; 88 minutes; February release. CAST: Gary Kroeger (Sarge), Marc Singer (Von Kraut), Jennifer Runyon (Fifi LaRue), Gretchen German (Sadie), Michael Mears (Chevalier), Andy Greenhalgh (Browning), Bobby Di Cicco (Anazalone), Travis McKenna (Billy Bob), Andrew Bumatai (Bearpaw), Howard Busgang (Steinmetz), Chris England (Fergus), Yehuda Efroni (Father Bruce), Aviva Marx (Sister Roxanne), Jeffrey Whickham (Fitzpatrick), Peter Dennis (Montgomery), Lior Hashin (Stewardess), Zafrir Kohanovsky (Oberlieutenant), Josef Bee (Von Kraut's Aide), Natasha Leon (Arab Girl), Tomer Yoseph (Arab Boy), Alexander Peleg (Gestapo Agent), Philip Zive (Conductor), David Turner (British Radio Operator), John Philips, Ralph Golomb (British Officers), Amikam Levi (Bartender), Ofer Shikazki (Waiter), Yuval Vill (Bellhop), Dudu Ben-Zeev (Von Kraut's Driver), Gabi Shushan (Murray, the Pumpman), Bruce Jenner.

NIGHTBREED (20th Century Fox) Producer, Gabriella Martinelli; Director/Screenplay, Clive Barker, based on his novel *"Cabal"* ; Executive Producers, James G. Robinson, Joe Roth; Music, Danny Elfman; Sound, Bruce Nyznik; Editors, Richard Marden, Mark Goldblatt; Photography, Robin Vidgeon; Designer, Steve Hardie; Special Make-up/Visual Effects, Image Animation; Assistant Director, Kieron Phipps; a Morgan Creek Production; Dolby Stereo; Deluxe color; Rated R; 101 minutes; February release. CAST: Craig Sheffer (Boone), Anne Bobby (Lori), David Cronenberg (Decker), Charles Haid (Capt. Eigerman), Hugh Quarshie (Det. Joyce), Hugh Ross (Narcisse), Doug Bradley (Lylesberg), Catherine Chevalier (Rachel), Malcolm Smith (Ashberry), Bob Sessions (Pettine), Oliver Parker (Peloquin), Debora Weston (Sheryl Ann), Nicholas Vince (Kinski), Simon Bamford (Ohnaka), Kim Robertson, Nina Robertson (Babette), Christine McCorkindale (Shuna Sassi), Tony Bluto (Leroy Gomm), Vincent Keene (Devil Lude), Bernard Henry (Baphomet), Richard Van Spall (Drummer), David Young (Otis and Clay), Valda Aviks (Melissa Rickman), Mac McDonald (Lou Rickman), Richard Bowman (Rickman Boy), McNally Segal, Daniel Kash, Bradley Lavelle, Stephen Hoye, Tom Hunsinger, George Roth, Peter Marinker, Lindsay Holiday, Kenneth Nelson, Carolyn Jones, Ted Maynard, Mitch Webb, Scott Gilmore, Eric Loren, John Agar

THE WHITE GIRL (Tony Brown Prods.) Producer, James Cannady; Director/Screenplay, Tony Brown; Executive Producer, Sheryl Cannady; Photography, Joseph M. Wilcots; Editors, Joseph M. Wilcots, Tony Vigna; Music, George Porter Martin, Jimmy Lee Brown; Designer, Bill Webb; Costumes, Paul Simmons; Associate Producers,

Joseph Ray, George Porter Martin; Ultra-Stereo; Precision Color; Rated PG-13; 88 minutes; February release. CAST: Troy Beyer (Kim Barnes), Taimak (Bob), Teresa Yvon Farley (Vanessa), O. L. Duke (Nick), DiAnne B. Shaw (Debbie), Petronia Paley (Dr. McCullough), Don Hannah (Karl), Donald Craig (Mr. W), Sherry Williams (Mrs. Barnes), Mike Deurloo (Charles), Twila Wolfe (Tracy), Kevin Campbell (Roger)

WELCOME TO OBLIVION (Concorde) Producer, Luis Llosa; Director, Augusto Tamayo; Screenplay, Len Jenken, Dan Kleinman; Co-Producer, Sally Mattison; Photography, Cursio Barrio; Editors, Dan Shalk, Craig Weller; Music, Kevin Klinger; Color; Rated R; 89 minutes; February release. CAST: Dack Rambo (Kenner), Claire Beresford (Grace), Meshach Taylor (Elijah), Mark Bringelson (Big), Charles Dougherty (Zig), Ramesy Ross (Lazarus/Sweethart), Diania Quijano (Radio), Orlando Sacha (Bishop), Emily Kreimer (Sheila), Ramon Garcia (Bad Guy), Tony Vasques (Yorrick), David Killerby (Buddy), Ian Igberg (Horst)

ANGEL TOWN (Taurus) Producers, Ash R. Shah, Eric Karson; Director, Eric Karson; Executive Producer, Sunil R. Shah; Screenplay, S. Warren; Photography, John LeBlanc; Art Director, Brian Densmore; Music, Terry Plumeri; Editor, Duane Hartzell; Stunts, Jeff Imada; Casting, Bob Morones; Color; Rated R; 106 minutes; February release. CAST: Olivier Gruner (Jacques), Theresa Saldana (Maria), Frank Aragon (Martin), Tony Valentino (Angel), Peter Kwong (Henry Lee), Mike Moroff (Frank), Daniel Villarreal (Jesus), Jim L. Jaimes (Chuey), Gregory Norman Cruz (Stoner), Robin Ann Harlin (Sara), Lupe Amador (Grandmother), Jeff Cadiente (Lookout), Linda Kurimoto (Sue Kim Lee), Claudine Penedo (Angel's Driver), Tom McGreevy (Dr. Rice), Bruce Locke (Mr. Park), Frankie Ayina, Lorenzo Gaspar, Fred Jin, Stephanie Sholtus, William Bassett, Nick Angotti

THE HAUNTING OF MORELLA (Concorde) Producer, Roger Corman; Director, Jim Wynorski; Screenplay, R. J. Robertson; Photography, Zoran Hochstatter; Music, Fredric Nesign Teetsel, Chuck Cirino; Editor, Diane Fingado; Associate Producers, Alida Camp, Rodman Flender; Color; Rated R; 87 minutes; February release. CAST: David McCallum (Gideon), Nicole Eggert (Morella/Lenora), Christopher Halsted (Guy), Lana Clarkson (Coed), Maria Ford (Diane), Jonathan Farwell (Dr. Gault), Brewster Gould (Miles Archer), Gail Harris (Ilsa), Clement Von Franckenstein (Judge), R. J. Robertson (Rev. Ward), Debbie Dutch (Serving girl)

Meshach Taylor in "Welcome to Oblivion" © *Concorde*

David McCallum in "The Haunting of Morella" © *Concorde*

141

Gail O'Grady, Chad Lowe in "Nobody's Perfect"
© *Moviestore Entertainment*

Brandon Call, Rutger Hauer in "Blind Fury"
© *Tri-Star Pictures*

NOBODY'S PERFECT (Moviestore Entertainment) Producer, Benni Korzen; Co-Producer, Just Betzer; Director, Robert Kaylor; Screenplay, Annie Korzen, Joel Block; Executive Producers, Steven Ader, Dennis Spiegelman; Associate Producer, Gary Adelman; Photography, Claus Loof; Music, Robert Randles; Editor, Robert Gordon; a Panorama Film International Production in association with Steve Ader Productions; Eastmancolor; Rated PG-13; 91 minutes; February release. CAST: Chad Lowe (Stephen/Stephanie), Gail O'Grady (Shelly), Patrick Breen (Andy), Kim Flowers (Jackie), Eric Bruskotter (Stanley), Carmen More (Carla), Todd Schaefer (Brad), Annie Korzen (Prof. Lucci), Mariann Aalda (Coach Harrison), Marcia Karr (Marge), Nomi Mitty (Mrs. Parker), Thomas R. Myers (Mr. Parker), Nicholas Frangakis (Dean Butler), Robert Hewes (Mysterious Man), Steven Ader (Tennis Umpire), Robert Vaughn (Dr. Duncan), Vitas Geruliatis (Men's Tennis Coach), Laura Summer, Barry Moren, Devon Kaylor, Themis Zambrzycki, Nikki Lusty.

HEART CONDITION (New Line Cinema) Producer, Steve Tisch; Director/Screenplay, James D. Parriott; Executive Producer, Robert Shaye; Co-Producers, Marie Cantin, Bernie Goldman; Photography, Arthur Albert; Designer, John Muto; Music, Patrick Leonard; Editor, David Finfer; Costumes, Louise Frogley; Casting, Karen Rea; Song: *"Have a Heart"* performed by Bonnie Raitt; Deluxe color; Rated R; 95 minutes; February release. CAST: Bob Hoskins (Jack Moony), Denzel Washington (Napoleon Stone), Chloe Webb (Crystal Gerrity), Roger E. Mosley (Capt. Wendt), Ja'Net Dubois (Mrs. Stone), Alan Rachins (Dr. Posner), Robert Apisa (Teller), Jeffrey Meek (Graham), Frank R. Roach (Senator Marquand), Kieran Mulroney (Dillnick), Lisa Stahl (Annie), Ray Baker (Harry Zara), Eva LaRue (Peisha), Clayton Landley (Posner's Assist.), Diane Civita (Terri), Monte Landis (Waiter), Ron Taylor (Bubba), Kendall McCarthy (Archimedes), Julie Silverman, Phyllis Hamlin, Jeff MacGregor, George Kyle, Bill Applebaum, Mary Catherine Wright, Kenneth J. Martinez, Johnny Walker, Anthony "Wink" Atkinson, Deidre Harris, Theresa Randle, Mark Lowenthal, Billy Oscar, Leontine Guilliard, Johnnie Johnson, Rick Marzan, Gary Sax, Dean Wein, Bobby Bass, Greg Barnett, Tom Huff.

BLIND FURY (Tri-Star) Producers, Daniel Grodnik, Tim Matheson; Executive Producers, Robert W. Cort, David Madden; Director, Phillip Noyce; Screenplay/Story, Charles Robert Carner; Based on a screenplay by Ryozo Kasahara; Associate Producers, Charles Robert Carner, Dennis Murphy; Photography, Don Burgess; Designer, Peter Murton; Editor, David Simmons; Music, J. Peter Robinson; Casting, June Lowry; Second Unit Director/Stunts, Max Kleven; an Interscope Communications Production; Dolby Stereo; Technicolor; Rated R; 86 minutes; March release. CAST: Rutger Hauer (Nick Parker), Terrance O'Quinn (Frank Devereaux), Brandon Call (Billy Devereaux), Noble Willingham (MacCready), Lisa Blount (Annie Winchester), Nick Cassavetes (Lyle Pike), Rick Overton (Tector Pike), Randall "Tex" Cobb (Slag), Charles Cooper (Cobb), Meg Foster (Lynn Devereaux), Sho Kosugi (The Assassin), Paul James Vasquez (Gang Leader), Julia Gonzalez (Latin Girl), Woody Watson, Alex Morris (Crooked Miami Cops), Mark Fickert (Bus Station Cop), Weasel Forshaw (Popcorn), Roy Morgan (Six Pack), Tim Mateer (Snow), C. K. McFarland (Female Biker), T. J. McFarland, Blue Deckert, Glenn Lampert, Red Mitchell (Cornfield Killers), Bonnie Suggs (Rockwell Mom), Harold Suggs (Rockwell Dad), Barbara Gulling-Goff, Dorothy Young (Freeway Ladies), Sharon Shackelford (Colleen), Debora Williams (Big Mama), Jay Pennison, Tiger Chung Lee, R. Nelson Brown, Lincoln Casey Jr., Gene Skillen, Kyle Thatcher, Patricia Mathews, Mitch Hrushowy, Ernest Mack, Linwood Walker, Robert Manning, Jeff Dashnaw, Glen Wilder, David Ellis, Mike Adams, David Bartholomew, Fred Lerner, Mike Shanks, Ray Colbert.

ACT OF PIRACY (Blossom Pictures) Producers, Igo Kantor, Hal Reed; Executive Producers, Edgar Bold, Franklin B. Lieberman; Director, John "Bud" Cardos; Screenplay, Hal Reed; Photography, Vincent G. Cox; Music, Morton Stevens; Editor, Ettie Feldman; a Marton Holdings presentation of a Major Arts production; Color; Rated R; 101 minutes; March release. CAST: Gary Busey (Ted Andrews), Belinda Bauer (Sandy Andrews), Ray Sharkey (Jack Wilcox), Nancy Mulford (Laura), Arnold Vosloo (Sean), Dennis Casey Park (Dennis), Ken Gampu (Herb), Anthony Fridjhon, Mathew Stewardson, Candice Hillebrand, Nadia Bilchik.

ELLIOT FAUMAN, PH.D (Taurus Entertainment) Producer/Director/Screenplay, Ric Klass; Photography, Erich Roland; Music, Roger Trefousse; Costumes, Sheri Dunn; Editor, Judy Herbert; Associate Producers, Robin Johnson, Richard Grodsky; Designer, Henry Shaffer; Color; Rated PG-13; 87 minutes; March release. CAST: Randy Dreyfuss (Elliot Fauman), Jean Kasem (Meredith Dashley), Tamara Williams (Stella), Shelley Berman (Stromboy/TV Cook Show Hostess), John Canada Terrell (Gene), Bryan Michael McGuire (Denton), Michael Willis (Sampson), Michael Fiske (Ben), Michael Gabel (Grub-

Denzel Washington, Ron Taylor, Bob Hoskins in "Heart Condition" © *New Line Cinema*

Jean Kasem, Randy Dreyfuss in "Elliot Fauman, Ph.D."
© *Taurus Entertainment*

Bill Nunn, Freddie Jackson, Robin Harmon in "Def By Temptation" © *Orpheus Pictures*

Lisa Pescia in "Body Chemistry" © *Concorde*

ber), Stan Brandorff (Morty), Jefferson Cronin (Dweezil), Timothy Abell, Randy Fink, Ira Smart (College Boys), Josh Billings (Ivan), Joni Injayin (Blanche), Carole Cianelli (Clio), Nancy Daly (Dafne), Hillary Rollins (Rhea), Amy Keys (Yvonne), Simon Carter (Stage Director), Chuck Lippman (Louie), G. Lee Fleming (Filch), Lynnie Raybuck ("Cross Me" Woman), Billie Schaeffer (Prof. Baker), Rick Foucheux (Prof. Goodluck), Jesse Foreman, Ann Amenta-Long, Ted Sutton, Sonya Ferguson, Yolanda Gaskins, Sabine Herts, Jose Rodriguez, Pamela Jackson, Mary Grace Schaeffer, Vivienne Shub, Lynn-Jane Foreman, Bradley Winston M.D.

DEF BY TEMPTATION (Troma) Producer/Director/Screenplay, James Bond III; Executive Producers, Charles Huggins, Kevin Harewood, Nelson George; Co-Producers, Kervin Simms, Hajna O. Moss; Photography, Ernest Dickerson; Music, Paul Laurence; Designer, David Carrington; Assistant Director, Marcus Turner; Editor, Li-Shin Yu; a Bonded Filmworks Prods. production; Technicolor; Rated R; 95 minutes; March release. CAST: James Bond III (Joel), Kadeem Hardison ("K"), Bill Nunn (Dougy), Samuel L. Jackson (Minister Garth), Minnie Gentry (Grandma), Rony Clanton (Married Man), Stephen Van Cleef (Jonathan), John Canada Terrell, Guy Davis (Bartenders), Cynthia Bond (Temptress), Freddie Jackson, Najee (Themselves), Melba Moore (Madam Sonya), Z Wright (Young Joel), Michael Rivera (Gay Guy), Sundra Jean Williams (Mrs. Garth), Beth Latty, Angela Stokes, Lahaina Kameha, Michael Michelle, Robin Harmon, Starlina Young (Ladies), Ellis Williams (Demon Limo Driver)

BODY CHEMISTRY (Concorde) Producer, Alida Camp; Executive Producer, Rodman Flender; Director, Kristine Peterson; Screenplay, Jackson Barr; Photography, Phedon Papamichael; Music, Terry Plumeri; Editor, Nina Gilberti; Stereo; Foto-Kem color; Rated R; 87 minutes; March release. CAST: Marc Singer (Tom Redding), Lisa Pescia (Claire Archer), Mary Crosby (Marlee Redding), David Kagen (Freddie), H. Bradley Barneson (Jason), Doreen Alderman (Kim), Lauren Tuerk (Wendy), Joseph Campanella (Dr. Pritchard), Rhonda Aldrich (Cindy), Elizabeth Harnett (Angie), John David Conti (Mr. Humphrey), Mercedes Brynton (Woman at party), Kevin Reidy (Fireman), Thom Babbes (Lab Asst.), David S. Rogers (Security Guard), Gray Daniels (Policeman), Steve Guri (Man in S&M Video), Stephanie Warner (Woman in S&M Video), Matthew Ray Cohen, Ray Leeper (Dancers)

CHOPPER CHICKS IN ZOMBIETOWN (Triax Entertainment) Producer, Maria Snyder; Director/Screenplay, Dan Hoskins; Photographer, Tom Fraser; Music, Daniel May; Editor, W. O. Garrett; Executive Producer, Arthur Sarkissian; a Chelsea Partners presentation; Color; Not rated; 89 minutes; March release. CAST: Jamie Ross (Dede), Catherine Carlen (Rox), Kristina Loggia (Jojo), Martha Quinn (Mae Clutter), Don Calfa (Ralph Willum), Whitney Reis

DEMONSTONE (Fries Entertainment) Producer, Antony I. Ginnane; Director, Andrew Prowse; Screenplay, John Trayne, David Phillips, Frederick Bailey; Executive Producer, Brian Trenchard-Smith; Line Producers, Clark Henderson, Isabel Sumayao; Editor, Michael Thibault; Music, Gary Stockdale; Photography, Kevan Lind; an International Film Entertainment Pty. Ltd. production; Color; Rated R; 92 minutes; March release. CAST: R. Lee Ermey (Maj. Joe Haines), Jan-Michael Vincent (Andrew Buck), Nancy Everhard (Sharon Gale), Pat Skipper (Tony McKee), Peter Brown (Admiral), Joonee Gamboa (Sen. Belfardo/Chief Pirate), Rolando Tinio (Prof. Olmeda), Noel Colet (Esteban Belfardo), Edgar Santiago (Nonoy Belfardo), Rey Malte-Cruz (Roberto Belfardo), Monsour Del Rosario (Pablo Belfardo), Jose Mari Avellana (Han Chin), Rina Reyes (Madeleine),

Marilyn Bautista (Julie), Crispin Medina (Gen. Santos), Fred Bailey (Navy Doctor), Symon Soler (R. J. Belfardo)

SIDE OUT (Tri-Star) Producer, Gary Foster; Director, Peter Israelson; Screenplay, David Thoreau; Executive Producer, Jay Weston; Associate Producer, Russ Krasnoff; Photography, Ron Garcia; Designer, Dan Lomino; Editor, Conrad Buff; Music, Jeff Lorber; Co-Producer, John Zane; Volleyball Technical Advisor, Jon Stevenson; Casting, Jane Jenkins, Janet Hirshenson, Robin Allan; presented in association with Aurora Prods. and Then Prods.; Dolby Stereo; Technicolor; Rated PG-13; 100 minutes; March release. CAST: C. Thomas Howell (Monroe Clark), Peter Horton (Zack Barnes), Courtney Thorne-Smith (Samantha), Harley Jane Kozak (Kate Jacobs), Christopher Rydell (Wiley Hunter), Terry Kiser (Uncle Max), Randy Stoklos (Rollo Vincent), Sinjin Smith (Billy), Tony Burton (Louie), Kathy Ireland (Marie), Martha Velez (Mrs. Salazar), Ben Rawnsley (Frank Clark), Jacquelyn Masche (Shirley Clark), Olivia Burnette (Jenny Clark), Jack Yates (Basketball Coach), Bebe Louie (Maid), Gianni Russo (Dick Sydney), Stanley Ralph Ross (Judge McKibbon), Chris Marlowe, Sam Lagana, Jim Arico, Scott Friederichsen, Andrew Smith (Themselves), Lynna Hopwood, Ollie Lake, Skip O'Brien, E. Lloyd Napier, Lance E. Nichols, Felicity Waterman, Gregory Littman, Jack Davis, Selma Archerd, Rachel Bailit, Greg Krause, Frank James Polito III, J. Robert Bailey, Hope Carlton, Dr. Michael Billauer

THE FORBIDDEN DANCE (Columbia) Producers, Marc S. Fischer, Richard L. Albert; Executive Producers, Menahem Golan, Ami Artzi; Director, Greydon Clark; Screenplay, Roy Langsdon, John Platt; Story, Joseph Goldman; Photography, R. Michael Stringer; Music, Vladimir Horunzhy; Choreographers, Miranda Garrison, Felix Chavez; Editors, Robert Edwards, Earl Watson; a 21st Century Corp. presentation; Ultra-Stereo; Panavision; Foto-Kem color; Rated PG-13; 97 minutes; March release. CAST: Laura Herring (Nisa), Jeff James (Jason), Barbara Brighton (Ashley), Miranda Garrison (Mickey), Sid Haig (Joa), Angela Moya (Carmen), Richard Lynch (Benjamin Maxwell), Shannon Farnon (Katherine Anderson), Linden Chiles (Bradley Anderson), Ruben Moreno (The King), Gene Mitchell (Cutter), Kenny Johnson (Dave), Connie Woods (Trish), Tom Alexander (Kurt), Steven Lloyd Williams (Weed), Sabrina Mance (Cami), Pilar Del Rey (The Queen), August Darnell (Kid Creole), Adriana Kaegi, Janique Svedberg, Taryn Hagey (Coconuts), Robert Apisa, Greg Niebel, Kenny Scott Carrie, Remy O'Neill, Charles Meshack, John Rice, Cory Daye

C. Thomas Howell, Peter Horton in "Side Out" © *Tri-Star Pictures*

Thomas McElroy, Dana Carvey in "Opportunity Knocks"
© Universal City Studios

Jurgen Prochnow, Brent Woolsey, Lara Harris, Roy Scheider in
"The Fourth War" © Kodiak Films

OPPORTUNITY KNOCKS (Universal) Producers, Mark R. Gordon, Christopher Meledandri; Executive Producer, Brad Grey; Director, Donald Petrie; Co-Producer, Raymond Hartwick; Photography, Steven Poster; Screenplay, Mitchel Katlin, Nat Bernstein; Editor, Marion Rothman; Designer, David Chapman; Costumes, Nan Cibula; Casting, Ilene Starger; Music, Miles Goodman; an Imagine Entertainment presentation; Dolby Stereo; Deluxe color; Rated PG-13; 105 minutes; March release. CAST: Dana Carvey (Eddie Farrell), Robert Loggia (Milt Malkin), Todd Graff (Lou Pasquino), Julia Campbell (Annie Malkin), Milo O'Shea (Max), James Tolkan (Sal Nichols), Doris Belack (Mona Malkin), Sally Gracie (Connie), Mike Bacarella (Pinkie), John M. Watson, Sr. (Harold Monroe), Beatrice Fredman (Bubbie), Thomas McElroy (Men's Room Attendant), Jack McLaughlin-Gray (Wine Steward), Gene Honda (Japanese Businessman), Del Close (Williamson), Michael Oppenheimer (Chase), Paul Greatbatch (Driver), Sarajane Avidon (Commissioner's Secretary), Mindy Suzanne Bell, Richard Steven Mann (Executives), Ron Max, Kent Logsdon (Sales Associates), Jed Mills (Club MC), Michelle Johnston (Club Singer), Bill Bradshaw (David), John Cothran, Jr. (Building Commissioner), Tal Galomb (Bar Mitzvah Boy), James Hassett (Vendor), Mark Hutter (Stan), Jill Shellabarger (Ginger), Joshua Livingstone (Nathan), Adam Jason Weiss (Myron), Lorna Raver Johnson (Eddie's Secretary), Michelle Quigley (Woman at accident), Judith Scott (Milt's Secretary), Mark Ross (Jonathan's voice)

OVEREXPOSED (Concorde) Producer, Roger Corman; Director, Larry Brand; Screenplay, Larry Brand, Rebecca Reynolds; Photography, David Sperling; Editor, Patrick Rand; Music, Mark Governor; Designer, Robert Franklin; ChaceSurround Stereo; Color; Rated R; 89 minutes; March release. CAST: Catherine Oxenberg (Kristen Halsy), David Naughton (Phillip Manzerack), Jennifer Edwards (Helen), William Bumiller (Hank), John Patrick Reger (Terrance), Gretchen Eickkolz (Trish), Karen Black (Mrs. Towbridge), Larry Brand (Morrison), Rebecca Reynolds (Pam), George Derby (Lt. Bryce), Ernst Alexander (Greg), Patrick McCord (Johnny), Joe Faust (Jordan), Reneta Scott (Sil), Bob Goldstein (Marvin), Tom Poster (Angie), Mellisa Young (Marla), Ken Kerman (Earl), Brewster Gould (Jensen), Charles Zucker (Jerome), Mark Governor (Lounge Singer), Aarika Wells (Kristin's Mother), Emily Rhodes (Young Kristin), Julie Asher (Young Helen)

WEDDING BAND (IRS Media) Producers, John Schouweiler, Tino Insana; Director, Daniel Raskov; Screenplay, Tino Insana; Photography, Christian Sebaldt; Editor, Jonas Thaler; Music, Steve Hunter; Designer, Tori Nourafchan; Executive Producers, Miles Copeland 3rd, Paul Colichman; Ultra-Stereo; Image Transform Color; Rated R; 82 minutes; March release. CAST: William Katt (Marshall Roman), Joyce Hyser (Karla Thompson), Tino Insana (Hugh Bowmont), Lance Kinsey (Ritchie), David Bowe (Max), Pauly Shore (Nicky), Fran Drescher (Veronica), David Rasche (Sloane Vaughn)

THE FOURTH WAR (Cannon/New Age) Producer, Wolf Schmidt; Director, John Frankenheimer; Screenplay, Stephen Peters, Kenneth Ross, based on the novel by Peters; Executive Producers, William Stuart, Sam Perlmutter; Line Producer, Robert L. Rosen; Photography, Gerry Fisher; Music, Bill Conti; Editor, Robert F. Shugrue; Designer, Alan Manzer; Costumes, Ray Summers; a Kodiak Films Presentation; Dolby Stereo; Deluxe color; Rated R; 95 minutes; March release. CAST: Roy Scheider (Col. Jack Knowles), Jürgen Prochnow (Col. N. A. Valachev), Tim Reid (Lt. Col. Timothy Clark), Lara Harris (Elena), Harry Dean Stanton (Gen. Hackworth), Dale Dye (Sgt. Maj.), Bill MacDonald (M. P. Corporal), David Palffy (Gawky Soldier), Neil Grahn (Needle-nose Soldier), Ernie Jackson (Knowles' Driver), Ron Campbell (Young U.S. Soldier), John Dodds (Defector), Harold Hecht Jr. (Dwayne), Alice Pesta (Hannelore), Gregory A. Gale (Communications Corporal), Henry Kope (Mayor), Richard Durven (Young Soldier), Garry Galinsky, Ed Soibelman, Gary Spivak, Yefim Korduner, Brent Woolsey, Kent McNeill, Brian Warren, Guy Buller, Roman Podhora, Joseph Vrba, George Scholl, Gordon Signer, Lilo Bahr, Claus Diedrich, Kyle Maschmeyer, Kurt Darmohray, Igor Burstyn, Matus Ginzberg, Boris Novogrudsky

RIVERBEND (Prism Entertainment) Producer/Screenplay, Sam Vance; Director, Sam Firstenberg; Executive Producers, Regina Dale, Troy Dale; Photography, Ken Lamkin; Music, Paul Loomis; Editor, Marcus Manton; a Vandale production; Ultra-Stereo; Allied Color; Rated R; 100 minutes; March release. CAST: Steve James (Maj. Quinton), Margaret Avery (Bell), Tony Frank (Sheriff Jake), Julius Tennon (Tony), Alex Morris (Butch), Vanessa Tate (Pauline), T. J. Kennedy (Capt. Monroe), Linwood Walker, Norm Colvin, Keith Kirk, John Norman, Al Evans

TWISTED JUSTICE (Seymour Borde & Associates) Producer/Director/Screenplay, David Heavener; Photography, David Hue; Editor, Gregory Schorer; Executive Producers, Gerald Milton, Arnie La-

David Naughton, Catherine Oxenberg in "Overexposed"
© Concorde

Margaret Avery in "Riverbend" © Prism Entertainment

Greta Cowan, Avi Hoffman in "The Imported Bridegroom"
© ASA Communications

Melora Hardin, J. Eddie Peck in "Lambada"
© Cannon Pictures

keyn, S. Leigh Savidge; a Hero Films production; Color; Rated R; 90 minutes; March release. CAST: David Heavener (James Tucker), Erik Estrada (Cmdr. Gage), Karen Black (Mrs. Granger), Shannon Tweed (Hinkle), Jim Brown (Morris), James Van Patten (Kelsey), Don Stroud (Luther Pantelli)

THE IMPORTED BRIDEGROOM (ASA Communications) Producer/Director/Screenplay, Pamela Berger; Story, Abraham Cahan; Executive Producer, Frank Moreno; Associate Producer, Chris Schmidt; Photography, Brian Heffron; Music, Bevan Manson, Rosalie Gerut; Editor, Amy Sumner; a Lara Classics, Inc. presentation; Color; Not rated; 93 minutes; March release. CAST: Eugene Troobnick (Asriel Stroon), Avi Hoffman (Shaya), Greta Cowan (Flora), Annette Miller (Mrs. Birnbaum), Miriam Varon (Tenant), Andreas Teuber (Mendele), Ted Jacobs (Matchmaker), Ira Solet (Mosheh), Ira Goldenberg (Sexton), Barry Karas (Reb Levy), Helene Lantry (Hannah), Moshe Waldoks (Reb Lippe), Seth Yorra (Tzalel)

KEATON'S COP (Cannon) Producer/Director, Bob Burge; Executive Producer, Maurice Duke; Screenplay, Michael B. Druxman; Photography, Ozzie Smith; Music, Kevin Barnes, David Connor; Editor, Terry Chambers; Designer, John Iacovelli; Stunts, Marvin Walters; Associate Producer, Peggy Slater; a Third Coast production; Ultra-Stereo; Film Service color; Rated R; 95 minutes; March release. CAST: Lee Majors (Mike Gable), Abe Vigoda (Louie Keaton), Tracy Brooks Swope (Susan Watson), Don Rickles (Jake Barber), June Wilkinson (Archie—"Big Mama"), Art LaFleur (Det. Hayes), Robert Hilliard (Lt. Spence), Clinton "Austin" Shirley (Jimmy Gable), Fredrika Duke (Marsha), Talbot Perry Simons (Al Sims), George A. Simonelli (Rick Dante), Louise Mililli (Receptionist), Richard Duran (Officer Diaz), Robert Anthony Foster (Woody Clark), Nick Gambella (Stan), Dominic Thomas Barto (Hotel Assassin), Peter Bryson (Fat Tony Monetti), Ed Geldart (Lenny Fontaine), Claire Applegate (Hooker on stand), Helen Ackerman (Agnes Marx), McCoy McLemore (Paramedic Doctor), Paul Bernstein (Killer), Blue, the Dog (Himself), David Born, Timothy C. Galvan, Mark Leon, Oscar Carles, Ronald Lee Jones, Jeff Jensen, Quenton Morgan, Sage N. Parker, Charlotte Stanton, Cathy A. O'Dell, Kimberly O'Quinn, Cathy Redmond, Kenneth Warren Thompson, Michelle Zevenbergen

LAMBADA (Warner Bros.) Producer, Peter Shepherd; Director/Story, Joel Silberg; Screenplay, Sheldon Renan, Joel Silberg; Designer, Bill Cornford; Photography, Roberto D'Ettorre Piazzoli; Editor, Marcus Manton; Music, Greg DeBelles; Choreographer, Shabba-

Doo; Casting, Ed Mitchell; Costumes, Hollywood Rags, Inc.; a Cannon Pictures production in association with Film and Television Co.; Dolby Stereo; Color; Rated PG; 98 minutes; March release. CAST: J. Eddie Peck (Kevin Laird/Blade), Melora Hardin (Sandy), Shabba-Doo (Ramone), Ricky Paull Goldin (Dean), Basil Hoffman (Superintendent Leland), Dennis Burkley (Uncle Big), Keene Curtis (Principal Singleton), Rita Bland (Leslie), Thalmus Rasulala (Wesley Wilson), Leticia Vasquez (Pink Toes), Jimmy Locust (Ricochet), Richard Giorla (Double J), Edgar Godineaux, Jr. (Tidal Wave), Elsie Sniffen (Bookworm), Gina Ravarra (Funk Queen), J. W. Fails (Fingers), Eddie Garcia (Chilli), Tony Burrer (Clay), Debra Spagnoli (Muriel), Vincent Tumeo (Eric), Geldie Burns (Monica), Eric Taslitz (Egghead), Tony Selznick (Rod Grieves), William Marquez (Trevino), Kristina Starman (Linda), Michael Gates (Collins), Geno Hart (Jose #1), Dash Hart (Jose #2), Tom Reda (Freeman), Olivia Villa Real (Maria), Ricki Maliwanag, Tony Cordell, Barry Bernal, Deborah Chesher, Shiela Roehm, Matt Feemster, Jennifer Mann, Smith Wordes, Lehua Reid, Lauren Gale, Dina Kay Bunn, Steve Cuevas

DANGEROUS OBSESSION (Panorama Entertainment) a.k.a. Mortal Sins; Producer/Screenplay, Allen Blumberg; Director, Yuri Silvo; Photography, Bobby Bukowski; Music, Simon Boswell; Editor, Dorian Harris; Designer, Ray Recht; a Silver Chariots production; Precision color; Rated R; 85 minutes; March release. CAST: Brian Benben (Nathan), Debrah Farentino (Laura Rollins), Anthony LaPaglia (Vito), James Harper (Malcolm Rollins), Brick Hartney (Billy Beau Backus), Maggie Jakobson (Marie), James Saito, Steven Marcus, Peter Onorati, Sully Boyar, Stephen Stout, William Cain, Tibor Feldman, Anna Berger, Michelle Kronin

THE LASERMAN (Original Cinema) Producer/Director/Screenplay, Peter Wang; Photography, Ernest Dickerson; Editor, Grahame Weinbren; Casting, MaryEllen Mulcahy; Music, Mason Daring; Executive Producers, Tsui Hark, Sophie Lo; Designer, Lester Cohen; an SJM Presentation; Color; Rated R; 93 minutes; March release. CAST: Marc Hayashi (Arthur Weiss), Tony Leung (Joey), Peter Wang (Lt. Lu), Joan Copeland (Ruth Weiss), Maryann Urbano (Janet Cosby), David Shoichi Chan (Jimmy Weiss), Sally Yeh (Susu), Leonard Thomas (Sgt. Williams), Christopher Curry (Oliver), George Bartenieff (Hanson), Neva Small (Martha), Natsuko Ohama (Mamasan), Willie Reale (Laboratory Technician), Alice Playten (Instructor), Carol-Jean Lewis, Ostaro, Lex Monson, Norman Matlock, Shirl Bernheim, Grey Kooritsky, Eric A. Payne, Steven Chen

Lee Majors in "Keaton's Cop" © Cannon Pictures

Joan Copeland, David Chan, Neva Small in "The Laserman"
© SJM

145

Jeff Fahey, Bill Paxton, Joe Pantoliano, Brian Dennehy in "The Last of the Finest" © Orion Pictures

Jim Varney in "Ernest Goes to Jail" © Buena Vista

THE LAST OF THE FINEST (Orion) Producer, John A. Davis; Director, John Mackenzie; Executive Producer/Story, Jere Cunningham; Screenplay, Jere Cunningham, Thomas Lee Wright, George Armitage; Music, Jack Nitzsche, Michael Hoenig; Photography, Juan Ruiz-Anchia; Designer, Laurence G. Paull; Co-Producer, Kurt Neumann; Editor, Graham Walker; Costumes, Marilyn Vance-Straker; Assistant Director, William P. Scott; Associate Producer, Darlene K. Chan; a Davis Entertainment Production; Dolby Stereo; Deluxe color; Rated R; 106 minutes; March release. CAST: Brian Dennehy (Frank Daly), Joe Pantoliano (Wayne Gross), Jeff Fahey (Ricky Rodriguez), Bill Paxton (Howard "Hojo" Jones), Michael C. Gwynne (Anthony Reece), Henry Stolow (Stant), Guy Boyd (R. J. Norringer), Henry Darrow (Capt. Joe Torres), J. Kenneth Campbell (Calvert), Deborra-Lee Furness (Linda Daly), Lisa Jane Persky (Hariett Gross), Patricia Clipper (Rose), Michelle Little (Anita), Susannah & Sheila Kelly (Daly Baby), Micah Rowe (Justin Daly), Joey Wright (Jimmy Gross), Georgie Paul (Myrna), John Finnegan (Tommy Grogan), Ron Canada (Cregan), Michael Strasser (McCade), Xander Berkeley (Fast Eddie), Pam Gidley (Haley), Burke Byrnes (Commander Orsini), Tom Nolan (Travers), Jason Ross (Braden), Kathleen Dennehy (Lab Technician), Patrick Stack (Press Officer), Larry Carroll (Newsman), Jeanne Mori (Female Journalist), Kimble Jemison (Scared Dealer), Michael Simpson (Disc Jockey), James Delesandro, Ray Vegas, Joe Minjares, Victor Contreras, Ramon Angeloni (Contras), David Allen Young, Chenoa Ellis, Frank V. Trevino, Charles Chiquette, Rudy F. Morrison, Robert Figg, John D. Johnston III, Robert Lee Jarvis, James W. Gavin

THINK BIG (Concorde) Producers, Brad Krevoy, Steven Stabler; Director, Jon Turteltaub; Screenplay, Edward Kovach, David Tausik, Jon Turteltaub; Story, R. J. Robertson, Jim Wynorski; Photography, Mark Morris; Music, Michael Sembello, Hilary Bercovici, Stephen Graziano; Editor, Jeff Reiner; Designer, Robert Schullenberg; Stunts, Gary Jensen; a Motion Picture Corp. of America presentation; Ultra-Stereo; Foto-Kem Color; Rated PG-13; 86 minutes; March release. CAST: Ari Meyers (Holly), Peter Paul (Rafe), David Paul (Victor), Martin Mull (Dr. Bruekner), David Carradine (Sweeney), Claudia Christian (Marsh), Richard Kiel (Irving), Richard Moll (Thornton), Peter Lupus, Sal Landi (Tough Guys), Michael Winslow (Hap), Thomas Gottschalk (Roberts), Jacob Kenner (Mitchell), Derek Rydell (Griffith), Judy Tolle (Giselle), Tony Alda (Sentry), David Bowe, Al Septien (Observers), Tony Longo (Supervisor), Cecil Krevoy (Blonde Babe), Darcy LaPier (Donna), Don Woodard (Ticket Agent)

ERNEST GOES TO JAIL (Touchstone) Producer, Stacy Williams; Director, John Cherry; Screenplay, Charlie Cohen; Executive Producer, Martin Erlichman; Photography, Peter Stein; Editor, Sharyn L. Ross; Costumes, Shawn Barry; Designer, Chris August; Co-Producer, Coke Sams; Music, Bruce Arntson, Kirby Shelstad; Casting, Ben Rubin; Visual Effects, Tim McHugh; Assistant Director, Patrice Leung; presented in association with Silver Screen Partners IV; Distributed by Buena Vista Pictures; Dolby Stereo; Technicolor; Rated PG; 81 minutes; April release. CAST: Jim Varney (Ernest P. Worrell/Mr. Nash/Auntie Nelda), Gailard Sartain (Chuck), Bill Byrge (Bobby), Barbara Bush (Charlotte Sparrow), Barry Scott (Rubin Bartlett), Randall "Tex" Cobb (Lyle), Dan Leegant (Oscar Pendlesmythe), Charles Napier (Warden), Jim Conrad (Eddie), Jackie Welch (Judge), Melanie Wheeler (Prosecutor), Buck Ford (Defense Attorney), Daniel Butler (Waiter), Charlie Lamb (Another Con), Mac Bennett (Con), Rick Schulman (Mean Guard), Bruce Arntson (Juror), Bob Babbitt (Washing Con), Myke Mueller (Vinnie), John Davis (Other Guard), Michael Montgomery (Warden's Assistant), Mike Hutchinson (Gate Guard), Barkley (Rimshot)

MR. HOOVER & I (Turin Film) Director/Screenplay, Emile DeAntonio; Photography, Morgan Wesson, Matthew Mindlin; Editor, George Spyros; produced in association with Channel 4 (U.K.); Duart color; Not rated; 85 minutes; April release. Documentary with Emile DeAntonio, John Cage

THROUGH THE WIRE (Original Cinema) Producer/Director, Nina Rosenblum; Co-Producer, Alexandra White; Screenplay, Nina Rosenblum, Carlos Norman; Music, Nona Hendryx; Editor, Angelo Corrao; Photography, Nancy Schreiber, Haskell Wexler; Narrator, Susan Sarandon; a Fox/Lorber presentation from Daedalus Productions, Inc.; Color; Not rated; 85 minutes; April release. A documentary featuring Silvia Baraldini, Susan Rosenberg and Alejandrina Torres

LISA (United Artists) Producer, Frank Yablans; Director, Gary Sherman; Screenplay, Gary Sherman, Karen Clark; Associate Producers, Lucas Foster, Ronald B. Colby; Photography, Alex Nepomniaschy; Designer, Patricia Van Ryker; Editor, Ross Albert; Music, Joe Renzetti; Assistant Director, Tom Davies; Casting, Michael Chinich; from MGM/UA Distribution Co.; Dolby Stereo; Deluxe color; Rated PG-13;

David Paul, Richard Moll, Peter Paul in "Think Big" © Motion Picture Corp. of America

Silvia Baraldini, Susan Rosenberg, Alejandrina Torres in "Through the Wire" © Daedalus Prods.

Cheryl Ladd, D. W. Moffett in "Lisa" © *United Artists*

Mickey Rourke, Carré Otis in "Wild Orchid" © *Vision p.d.g.*

PG-13; 93 minutes; April release. CAST: Staci Keanan (Lisa), Cheryl Ladd (Katherine), D. W. Moffett (Richard), Tanya Fenmore (Wendy), Jeffrey Tambor (Mr. Marks), Edan Gross (Ralph), Julie Cobb (Mrs. Marks), Michael Ayr (Scott), Lisa Moncure (Sarah), Tom Dugan (Mr. Adams), Frankie Thorn (Judy), John Hawker (Mr. Howard), Drew Pillsbury (Don), Elizabeth Gracen (Mary), Dennis Bowen (Alison's Boyfriend), Tom Burke (Maitre'D), Tom Nolan (Waiter), Hildy Brooks (Alison's Landlady), Bob Roitblat (Porsche Driver), Sharon Clark (Porsche Passenger), David Niven, Jr. (Flower Shop Patron)

MARTIANS GO HOME (Taurus Entertainment) Producer, Michael D. Pariser; Co-Producers, Ted Bafaloukos, Anthony Santa Croce; Executive Producer, Edward R. Pressman; Director, David Odell; Screenplay, Charlie Haas; Based on the novel by Fredric Brown; Executive in Charge of Production, Michael Flynn; Photography, Peter Deming; Designers, Catherine Hardwicke, Don Day; Editor, M. Kathryn Campbell; Music, Allan Zavod; Casting, April Webster; Assistant Director, Richard Strickland; Costumes, Robyn Reichek; Make-up, Leslie Lightfoot; Foto-Kem color; Rated PG-13; 87 minutes; April release. CAST: Randy Quaid (Mark Devereaux), Margaret Colin (Sara Brody), Anita Morris (Dr. Jane Buchanan), Barry Sobel, Vic Dunlop (Main Martians), John Philbin (Donny), Ronny Cox (The President), Timothy Stack (Seagrams), Bruce French (Elgins), Gerrit Graham (Stan Garrett), Dean Devlin (Joe Fledermaus), Roy Brocksmith (Mr. Kornheiser), Nick Katt (Hippie), Troy Evans (Cop), Steve Blacknell (Game Show Host), Allan Katz (Melvin Knudson), Cynthia Ettinger, Brent Hinkley, Steven Ruggles, James Terry (Dr. Jane's Patients), Dana James (Anchorwoman), Dennis Bowen (Tape Dealer), Larry Anderson (Newscaster), Harry Basil, Bobby Slayton, Lee Arenberg, Rob Schneider, Warren Thomas, Wally Ward, Bruce Baum, Gary Mule Deer, Keith Mackechnie, Mark Goldstein (Martians), Boyd Bodwell, Raye Birk, Laurelyn Scharkey, Nick Toth, Brian George, Mel Stewart, Kedric Robin Wolfe, Jeff Doucette, Doug Lee, Eugene B. Price, Mary Catherine Williford, Michelle Brite, Margie Balter, Jack Tate, Karen Lee Smith, The Rose Brothers, The Stupeds

WILD ORCHID (Triumph Releasing) Producers, Mark Damon, Tony Anthony; Co-Producer, Howard Worth; Director, Zalman King; Screenplay, Patricia Louisianna Knop, Zalman King; Executive Producers, David Saunders, James Dyer; Photography, Gale Tattersall; Editors, Marc Grossman, Glenn A. Morgan; Designer, Carlos Conti; Associate Producers, Robert H. Lemer; Music, Geoff MacCormack,

Simon Goldenberg; Costumes, Marlene Stewart, Ileane Meltzer; Choreographer, Morleigh Steinberg; a Vision p.d.g. presentation of a Damon/Saunders production; Dolby Stereo; Deluxe color; Rated R; 103 minutes; April release. CAST: Mickey Rourke (Wheeler), Jacqueline Bisset (Claudia), Carré Otis (Emily), Assumpta Serna (Hanna), Bruce Greenwood (Jerome), Oleg Vidov (Otto), Milton Goncalves (Flavio), Jens Peter (Volleyball Player), Antonio Mario Da Silva (Rambo), Paul Land (Big Sailor), Michael Villella (Elliot), Bernardo Jablonsky (Roberto), Luiz Lobo (Juan), Lester Berman, Steven Kaminsky (Interviewers), Hollister Whitworth, Franco Pisano (Bodyguards), Carlinhos Jesus (Conga Line Leader), Veluma (Manuella), David Rudder, Simone Moreno (Themselves), Kathleen Kaminsky (Emily's Mother), Anya Sartor, Joao Carlos Dos Santos, Mato Chi, Yomiko Ribeiro, Omi Raia, Daniel Anibal Blasco, Geronimo, Silvia Gomez Torres

MERIDIAN (KISS OF THE BEAST) (JGM Enterprises) Producers, Charles Band, Debra Dion; Director/Story, Charles Band; Screenplay, Dennis Paoli; Photography, Mac Ahlberg; Music, Pino Donaggio; Editor, Ted Nicolaou; Special Makeup Effects, Greg Cannom; a Full Moon production; Color; Rated R; 85 minutes; April release. CAST: Sherilynn Fenn (Catherine Bomarzini), Malcolm Jamieson (Oliver/Lawrence Fauvrey), Hilary Mason (Martha), Charlie (Gina), Alex Daniels (Beast), Phil Fondacaro (Dwarf), Vernon Dobtcheff (Priest), Vito Passeri (Adriano), Isabella Celani (Audrey)

THE GUARDIAN (Universal) Producer, Joe Wizan; Executive Producer, David Salven; Director, William Friedkin; Screenplay, Stephen Volk, Dan Greenburg, William Friedkin; Based on the novel "The Nanny" by Dan Greenburg; Photography, John A. Alonzo; Designer, Gregg Fonseca; Editor, Seth Flaum; Co-Producers, Todd Black, Mickey Borofsky, Dan Greenburg; Music, Jack Hues; Casting, Louis DiGiamimo; Assistant Director, Newton Dennis Arnold; Special Makeup Effects, Matthew W. Mungle; Stunts, Buddy Joe Hooker; Special Effects, Phil Cory; Dolby Stereo; Technicolor; Rated R; 98 minutes; April release. CAST: Jenny Seagrove (Camilla), Dwier Brown (Phil), Carey Lowell (Kate), Brad Hall (Ned Runcie), Miguel Ferrer (Ralph Hess), Natalia Nogulich (Molly Sheridan), Pamela Brull (Gail Krasno), Gary Swanson (Allan Sheridan), Jack David Walker, Willy Parsons, Frank Noon (Punks), Therese Randle (Arlene Russell), Xander Berkeley (Detective), Ray Reinhardt (Dr. Klein), Jacob Gelman (Scotty), Iris Bath (Mrs. Horniman), Rita Gomez (Rosaria), Dr. Barry Herman (Doctor at birth), Bonnie Snyder (Older Woman), Chris Nemeth, Craig Nemeth, Aaron Fischman, Josh Fischman (Baby Jake)

Margaret Colin, Randy Quaid, Vic Dunlop in "Martians Go Home" © *Taurus Entertainment*

Dwier Brown, Carey Lowell in "The Guardian" © *Universal City Studios*

Jeff Fahey, Theresa Russell in "Impulse" © *Warner Bros.*

Tyssen Butler, Robin Hurt in "In the Blood"
© *Endless Grass Sea*

THE GAME (Aquarius) Producer/Director/Story, Curtis Brown; Music/Executive Producer, Julia Wilson; Screenplay, Julia Wilson, Curtis Brown; Photography, Paul Gibson; Editor, Gloria Whittemore; a Visual Perspectives release of a Curtis Films Ltd. production; Duart Color; Not rated; 103 minutes; April release. CAST: Curtis Brown (Leon Hunter), Richard Lee Ross (Jason McNair), Vanessa Shaw (Silvia Yearwood), Billy Williams (Vail Yearwood), Charles Timm (Ben Egan), Michael P. Murphy (George Paturzo), Dick Biel (Carl Rydell), Carolina Beaumont (Gloria), Bruce Grossberg (Norman), Damon Clark (Arrington), Jerome King, Erick Shawn, Erick Coleman, Joanna Wahl, Rick Siler, Claire Waters

STREET ASYLUM (Original Cinema) Producer, Walter Gernert; Director, Gregory Brown; Screenplay, John Powers; Photography, Paul Desatoff; Music, Leonard Marcel; Editor, Kert Vander Meule; Color; Rated R; 89 minutes; April release. CAST: Wings Hauser, Alex Cord, G. Gordon Liddy, Roberta Vasquez, Sy Richardson, Brion James, Jesse Doran, Lisa Robins, Marie Chambers, Jose Aragon, Lisa Marlowe, Galen Yuen

IMPULSE (Warner Bros.) Producers, Albert S. Ruddy, Andre Morgan; Director, Sondra Locke; Screenplay, John De Marco, Leigh Chapman; Story, John De Marco; Executive Producer, Dan Kolsrud; Photography, Dean Semler; Designer, William A. Elliott; Editor, John W. Wheeler; Music, Michel Colombier; Casting, Glenn Daniels; Assistant Director, Doug Metzger; a Ruddy Morgan production; Dolby Stereo; Technicolor; Rated R; 108 minutes; April release. CAST: Theresa Russell (Lotte Mason), Jeff Fahey (Stan Harris), George Dzundza (Lt. Joe Morgan), Alan Rosenberg (Charley Katz), Nicholas Mele (Rossi), Eli Danker (Dimarjian), Charles McCaughan (Frank Munoff), Lynne Thigpen (Dr. Gardner), Shawn Elliott (Tony Peron), Angelo Tiffe (Luke), Christopher Lawford (Steve), Nick Savage (Edge), Dan Bell (Anson), Tom Dahlgren (District Attorney), Daniel Quinn (Ted Gates), David Crowley (Trick in car), Mark Rolston (Man in bar), Russell Curry (Bartender Mills), Pete Antico (Vice Cop in bar), Karl Anthony Smith (Gas Station Attendant), Paul Acerno (Junkie in apartment), Maria Rangel (Maria), Don Ruffin, Cliff McLaughlin (Munoff's Bodyguards), Paul A. Calabria (Man with dog), Valente Rodriguez (Doorman), Ronald L. Colby (Liquor Store Clerk), Robert Phalen (Coroner), Douglas Rowe (Criminologist), Wendy Gordon (TV Reporter), Jerry Dunphy (TV Anchorman), Jerry Martinez, Peder Melhuse (Vice Cops at motel), Sorin Serene Pricopie, Thomas Rosales, Jr. (Colombian Drug Dealers), Elaine Kagan (Stan's Receptionist),

Michael McCleery (Punk delivering flowers), James Edgcomb (Cop behind safe house)

BAIL JUMPER (Angelika) Producer, Josephine Wallace; Director, Christian Faber; Screenplay, Christian Faber, Josephine Wallace; Executive Producer, Jessica Saleh Hunt; Associate Producer, Michael Nossal; Photography, Tomasz Magierski; Editor, James Bruce; Music, Richard Robbins; Assistant Director, Gary Samuels; Color; 96 minutes; April release. CAST: Eszter Balint (Elaine), B. J. Spalding (Joe), Tony Askin (Dan), Bo Brinkman (Steve), Alexandra Auder (Bambi), Joie Lee (Athena), Ishmael Houston-Jones (Reed), Brad Warner (Reggie), Christine Vlasak (Cheryl)

IN THE BLOOD (White Mountain Films/Endless Grass Sea) Producer/Director, George Butler; Screenplay, George Butler, James Seay; Executive Producers, William E. Simon, Larry Wilson; Co-Producers, Deborah Boldt, Jacqueline Frank, John Leisenring; Photography, Dyanna Taylor; Editor, Janet Swanson; Color/Black and white; Rated PG; 90 minutes; April release. Documentary featuring Robin Hurt, Theodore Roosevelt, Tyssen Butler, Larry Wilson, Greg Martin, Harry Muller, Theodore Roosevelt IV, Theodore Roosevelt V, Webster Kalipswa, Makanyanga Mutio, Laboso Kipkenoi Sura

INSTANT KARMA (MGM) Producers, Dale Rosenbloom, Bruce A. Taylor, George Edwards; Executive Producers, Steven J. Bratter, Craig Sheffer; Director, Roderick Taylor; Screenplay, Bruce A. Taylor, Dale Rosenbloom; Photography, Thomas Jewett; Designers, George Edwards, Michele Seffman; Music, Joel Goldsmith; Editor, Frank Mazzola; Casting, Barbara Remsen, Ann Remsen Manners; a Rosenbloom Entertainment presentation of a Desert Wind Films Production from MGM/UA Communications; Ultra-Stereo; CFI color; Rated R; 95 minutes; April release. CAST: Craig Sheffer (Zane Smith), Chelsea Noble (Penelope Powell), David Cassidy (Reno), Orson Bean (Dr. Berlin), Marty Ingels (Jon Clark), Glenn Hirsch (David), William Smith (Pop), Alan Blumenfeld (Oscar Meyer), Annette Sinclair (Amy), Kristina Wotkyns (Cindy), Amy Lee Waddell (Julie), Ashley Quaine (Janet), James Gallery (Jerry), Tiffanie Poston (Laura), Brigitte Burdine (Susie), Rebekka Armstrong (Janie), Richard LePore (Radcliff), Blackie Dammett (Ed Polisky), Gino Conforti (Director), Gary Burden (Jesus Man), Catherine M. Cummings (Shakra Zula), Dan Clark (Steve Elias), Sarah G. Buxton (Cathy), John Lacy (Lucius), Larry B. Scott (Clapper Boy), Steve Fuji (Boom Man), Rick Diamond (1st A.D.), Doug Steindorff (Stoned Husband)

B. J. Spalding, Eszter Balint in "Bail Jumper"
© *Angelika Films*

David Cassidy, Craig Sheffer in "Instant Karma" © *MGM/UA*

Christopher Lloyd, Kim Greist, Christopher Lambert in "Why Me?" © Noval/International

Adrian Pasdar, Jack Gwaltney in "Vital Signs"
© 20th Century Fox

WHY ME? (Triumph Releasing) Producer, Marjorie Israel; Director, Gene Quintano; Executive Producer, Irwin Yablans; Screenplay, Donald E. Westlake, Leonard Maas, Jr.; Based on the book by Donald E. Westlake; Photography, Peter Deming; Editor, Alan Balsam; Music, Phil Marshall; Casting, Richard Pagano, Sharon Bialy, Ed Mitchell; Epic Productions, Inc. presents a Sarlui/Diamant presentation of a Carolina Production; Dolby Stereo; Consolidated Color; Rated R; 88 minutes; April release. CAST: Christopher Lambert (Gus Cardinale), Kim Greist (June Daley), Christopher Lloyd (Bruno Daley), J. T. Walsh (Francis Mahoney), Gregory Millar (Leon), Wendel Meldrum (Gatou Vardebedian), Michael J. Pollard (Ralph), John Hancock (Tiny), Tony Plana (Benjy Klopzik), Thomas Callaway (Zachary), Jack Kehler (Freedly), René Assa (Bob the Turk), Sebastian Massa (Tiny's Sidekick), Kate Benton (Spokeswoman), Jack Heller (Turk #2), Vachik Mangassarian (Mansourian), Lawrence Tierney, Mickey Yablans, Frank Collison (Armenian Robbers), Lance Kinsey (Phone Technician), Pete Chaconas, Maxwell Alexander (Security Guards), Rick Najera (Reporter), Zitto Kazann (Turkish Diplomat), Milton James (Armenian Diplomat), Jimmy Woodard, Hunter Person, Ralph Bruneau, Tino Insano, Emily Kuroda, John La Motta, John Volstad, Elena Stiteler, Jill Terashita, Shinko Isobe, Becky Herbst, Jacob Kenner, Douglas Roberts, Danny Wong, Cynthia Jay, Bart Lloyd, Michael La Violette, Debbie Evans

MODERN LOVE (SVS Films) Producer/Director/Screenplay, Robby Benson; Executive Producers, Michael S. Murphey, Joel Soisson; Photography, Christopher G. Tufty; Music, Don Peake; Song: *"Falling . . . in Love With You"* by Robby Benson/performed by Karla DeVito and Stan Brown; Editor, Gib Jaffe; Designer, Carl E. Copeland; Costumes, Robin Lewis; Associate Producers, Jane Rayleigh, Robert P. Cohen; presented in association with Michael Holzman and Jeffrey Ringler; a Lyric Films production; Dolby Stereo; CFI color; Panavision; Rated R; 109 minutes; April release. CAST: Robby Benson (Greg), Karla DeVito (Billie), Rue McClanahan (Evelyn), Burt Reynolds (Col. Frank Parker), Frankie Valli (Mr. Hoskins), Louise Lasser (Greg's Mom), Kaye Ballard (Receptionist), Lou Kaplan (Greg's Dad), Cliff Bemis (Dirk Martin), Lyric Benson (Chloe), Debra Port (Annabell), Stan Brown (Dr. Reed), Lori Tate (Delivery Nurse), Beth Meadows Calvert (Mary Miller), Sharyn Greene (Shayne), Dacey Parker (Chloe—3 yrs.), Jennifer Ray (Chloe—25 yrs.), Drucilla Brookshire (Real Estate Broker), Gene McKay (Award Presenter), Bert "Breeze" Timmons (Bouncer)

VITAL SIGNS (20th Century Fox) Producers, Laurie Perlman, Cathleen Summers; Director, Marisa Silver; Screenplay, Larry Ketron, Jeb Stuart; Story, Larry Ketron; Photography, John Lindley; Designer, Todd Hallowell; Editors, Robert Brown, Danford B. Greene; Music, Miles Goodman; Costumes, Deborah Everton; Casting, Margery Simkin; Unit Production Manager/Associate Producer, Tom Joyner; Assistant Director, Betsy Magruder; a Perlman Production; Dolby Stereo; Deluxe color; Rated R; 103 minutes; April release. CAST: Adrian Pasdar (Michael Chatham), Diane Lane (Gina Wyler), Jack Gwaltney (Kenny Rose), Laura San Giacomo (Lauren Rose), Jane Adams (Suzanne Maloney), Tim Ransom (Bobby Hayes), Bradley Whitford (Dr. Ballentine), Lisa Jane Persky (Bobby), William Devane (Dr. Chatham), Norma Aleandro (Henrietta), Jimmy Smits (Dr. David Redding), Wallace Langham (Gant), James Karen (Dean of Students), Leigh C. Kim (Dr. Chen), Enid Kent (Vivian), Telma Hopkins (Dr. Kennan), Daniel Ziskie (Dr. Kelly), Rob Neukirch (Rita's Resident), Grant Heslov (Rick), Karen Fineman (Julie), Laurie Souza (Mother), Stanley DeSantis (Loan Officer), Kenia (Rita), Steve Bean (OB/GYN Intern), Claudia Harrington (Pregnant Woman), Seth Isler (Male Resident), Jay Arlen Jones (Paramedic), Donna Lynn Leavy (Cynthia), Matt Thompson (Billy), Jeanne Mori (Billy's Nurse), Gigo Vorgan (Nell), Angelo Tiffe (George), Christine Avila, Mary Pat Gleason, Perla Walter, Paul Carlton Bryant, Ellaraino, Rose Weaver, Myra Turley, Lou Saint James, Joan Newlin, Vicki Winters, Doug Robinson, Charlie Hawke, Billy Bacon

JOURNEY TO SPIRIT ISLAND (Griffin Film Assoc.) Producer, Bruce Clark; Director, Laszlo Pal; Screenplay, Crane Webster; Executive Producers, Rodger Spero, Laszlo Pal, Bruce Clark; Photography, Vilmos Zsigmond; Music, Fred Myrow; Editor, Bonnie Koehler; a Pal Prods.-Seven Wonders Entertainment Film; Alpha Cine color; Rated PG; 93 minutes; May release. CAST: Bettina (Maria), Marie Antoinette Rodgers (Jimmy Jim), Brandon Douglas (Michael), Gabriel Damon (Willie), Tarek McCarthy (Klim), Tony Acierto (Hawk), Nick Ramus (Tom), Attila Gombacsi (Phil)

LETTER TO THE NEXT GENERATION (New Day Films/Heartland Prods.) Producer/Director, James Klein; Co-Producer, Susan Wehling; Photography, Don Lenzer; Editors, Jim Klein, Paul Barnes, Tony Heriza; Color; Not rated; 75 minutes; May release. A documentary look at Kent State 20 years later.

Robby Benson, Karla DeVito, Burt Reynolds in "Modern Love"
© SVS Inc.

"Letter to the Next Generation" © Heartland Prods.

Madeleine Reynal in "Dr. Caligari" © *Steiner Films*

Judge Reinhold, Beverly D'Angelo in "Daddy's Dyin' . . ."
© *MGM/UA*

DR. CALIGARI (Steiner Films) Producer, Joseph F. Robertson; Executive Producer, Gerald M. Steiner; Director/Designer, Stephen Sayadian; Screenplay, Stephen Sayadian, Jerry Stahl; Photography, Ladi von Jansky; Music, Mitchell Froom; Special Makeup Effects, Ken Diaz; Costumes, Belinda Williams-Sayadian; Color; Rated R; 80 minutes; May release. CAST: Madeleine Reynal (Dr. Caligari), Fox Harris (Dr. Avol), Laura Albert (Mrs. Van Houten), Jennifer Balgobin (Ramona Lodger), John Durbin (Gus Pratt), Gene Zerna (Mr. Van Houten), David Parry (Dr. Lodger), Barry Phillips (Cesare), Magie Song (Patient in strait-jacket), Jennifer Miro (Miss Koonce), Stephen Quadros (Scarecrow), Carol Albright (Screaming Patient), Catherine Case (Patient with extra hormones), Debra Deliso (Grace Butter), Lori Chacko, Marjean Holden (Patients in bed), Vera Butler (Human Lamp), Salvador R. Espinoza (Spanish Patient/Baby Man), Joseph Baratelli (Shoe Salesman on TV), April Hartz (Shoe Customer on TV), Anthony Robertson (Patient in doorway), Tequila Mockingbird (Door Tongue)

ANY MAN'S DEATH (INI Entertainment Group) Producers, John Karie, S. D. Nethersole; Director, Tom Clegg; Screenplay, Iain Roy, Chris Kelly; Executive Producers, Joseph Goldenberg, Sandi Conolly; Photography, Vincent G. Cox; Music, Jeremy Lubbock; Editor, Max Lemon; Designer, Robert van de Coolwijk; a Goldenberg Films presentation of an Intl. Entertainment Corp. production, in association with Independent Networks; Dolby Stereo; Technicolor; Rated R; 110 minutes; May release. CAST: John Savage (Leon Abrams), William Hickey (Schiller/Bauer), Mia Sara (Gerlind), Ernest Borgnine (Gantz), Michael Lerner (Harvey), James Ryan

CLASS OF 1999 (Taurus Entertainment) Producer/Director/Story, Mark L. Lester; Screenplay, C. Courtney Joyner; Executive Producers, Lawrence Kasanoff, Ellen Steloff; Co-Producer, Eugene Mazzola; Photography, Mark Irwin; Music, Michael Hoenig; Editor, Scott Conrad; Costumes, Leslie Ballard; Assistant Director, Richard Abramitis; Visual Effects Supervisor/2nd Unit Director, Eric Allard; Stunts, Paul Baxley; an Original Pictures Inc. Production, a Lightning Pictures presentation; CFI color; Rated R; 98 minutes; May release. CAST: Bradley Gregg (Cody Culp), Traci Lin (Christie Langford), Malcolm McDowell (Dr. Miles Langford), Stacy Keach (Dr. Bob Forrest), Patrick Kilpatrick (Mr. Bryles), Pam Grier (Ms. Connors), John P. Ryan (Mr. Hardin), Darren E. Burrows (Sonny), Joshua Miller (An-

gel), Sharon Wyatt (Janice Culp), Jimmy Medina Taggert (Hector), Jason Oliver (Curt), Brent Fraser (Flavio), Jill Gatsby (Dawn), Sean Haggerty (Reedy), Sean Gregory Sullivan (Mohawk), David Wasman (Guard), Landon Wine (Noser), Barbara Coffin (Matron), Linda Burden-Williams (Secretary), Lanny Rees (Desk Sergeant), Barry M. Press (Gould), James McIntie, Lee Arenberg (Technicians)

DADDY'S DYIN' . . . WHO'S GOT THE WILL? (MGM) Producers, Sigurjon Sighvatsson, Steve Golin, Monty Montgomery; Director, Jack Fisk; Executive Producers, Bobbie Edrick, Del Shores, Michael Kuhn, Nigel Sinclair; Screenplay, Del Shores, based on his play; Co-Producer, Jay Roewe; Photography, Paul Elliott; Designer, Michelle Minch; Costumes, Elizabeth Warner Nankin; Editor, Edward A. Warschilka, Jr.; Music, David McHugh; from MGM/UA Pictures, in association with Artist Circle Entertainment, a Propaganda Films Production; Ultra-Stereo; Deluxe color; Rated PG-13; 95 minutes; May release. CAST: Beau Bridges (Orville), Beverly D'Angelo (Evalita), Tess Harper (Sara Lee), Judge Reinhold (Harmony), Amy Wright (Lurlene), Patrika Darbo (Marlene), Bert Remsen (Daddy), Molly McClure (Mama Wheelis), Keith Carradine (Clarence), Newell Alexander (Sid), Emily Bridges (Little Evalita), Carolyn Brooks (Linnie Sue), Schuyler Fisk (Little Sara Lee), Justin Smith (Little Orville), Katherine A. Torn (Little Lurlene), Sandra Will (Jeannie)

THE FEUD (Castle Hill) Producers, Bill D'Elia, Carole Kivett; Director, Bill D'Elia; Screenplay, Bill D'Elia, Robert Uricola; Based on the novel by Thomas Berger; Photography, John Beymer; Editor, Bill Johnson; Associate Producers, Gary Nolin, Mike Listo; Designer, Charles Lagola; Costumes, Ron Leamon; Music, Brian Eddolls; Executive Producer, Frank Scaraggi; a Feud Co. production; Color; Rated R; 96 minutes; May release. CAST: Rene Auberjonois (Reverton), Ron McLarty (Dolf Beeler), Joe Grifasi (Bud Bullard), Scott Allegrucci (Tony Beeler), David Strathairn (The Stranger), Stanley Tucci (Harvey Yelton), Lynne Killmeyer (Eva Bullard), Kathleen Doyle (Frieda Bullard), Libby George (Bobby Beeler), Rob Vanderberry (Junior Bullard), Mert Hatfield (Clive Shell), James Eric (Walt Huff), Don Hartman (Ernie), Joshua Bo Lozoff (Dickie Herkimer), Rick Warner (Ray Dooley), John Bennes (Ivan), Kay Shrider (Ingrid), Michael Stanton Kennedy (Curly), Lynda Clark (Marie), Roger Black (Bartender), George Earl Lee (Doc Stevens), David Dwyer (Coach), Tom Davis (Teammate), Howard Kivett (Relative), Red Suydam (Red Sedan), Allen Kelman (Man at counter)

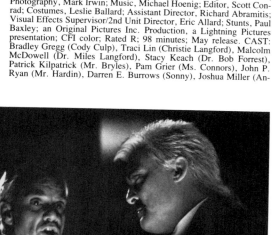

Malcolm McDowell, Stacy Keach in "Class of 1999"
© *Taurus Entertainment*

Rene Auberjonois in "The Feud" © *Castle Hill*

Tommy Lee Jones, Nicolas Cage in "Fire Birds"
© *Nova International Films*

Patty Mullen in "Frankenhooker" © *Shapiro Glickenhaus*

SPACE AVENGER (Manley Prods./New Wave) Producers, Ray Sundlin, Robert A. Harris, Richard W. Haines; Executive Producers, Timothy McGinn, David Smith; Director, Richard W. Haines; Screenplay, Richard W. Haines, Lynwood Sawyer; Photography, Mustupha Barat; Music, Richard Fiocca; Technicolor; Not rated; 88 minutes; May release. CAST: Robert Prichard, Mike McClerie, Charity Staley, Gina Mastrogiacomo, Kirk Fairbanks Fogg, Angela Nicholas

FIRE BIRDS (Touchstone) formerly *Wings of the Apache;* Producer, William Badalato; Director, David Green; Screenplay, Nick Thiel, Paul F. Edwards; Story, Step Tyner, John K. Swensson, Dale Dye; Co-Producers, John K. Swensson, Dale Dye; Executive Producers, Arnold Kopelson, Keith Barish; Photography, Tony Imi; Designer, Joseph T. Garrity; Editors, Jon Poll, Norman Buckley, Dennis O'Connor; Music, David Newman; Aerial Sequences Designed by Richard T. Stevens; Assistant Director, Matt Earl Beesley; Casting, Mike Fenton, Judy Taylor, Valorie Massalas; Costumes, Ellis Cohen; Aerial Photography, Peter McKernan; a Nova International Films release, distributed by Buena Vista Pictures; Dolby Stereo; Deluxe/Technicolor; Rated PG-13; 85 minutes; May release. CAST: Nicolas Cage (Jake Preston), Tommy Lee Jones (Brad Little), Sean Young (Billie Lee Guthrie), Bryan Kestner (Breaker), Dale Dye (A. K. McNeil), Mary Ellen Trainor (Janet Little), J. A. Preston (Gen. Olcott), Peter Onorati (Rice), Charles Lanyer (Darren Phillips), Illana Shoshan (Sharon Geller), Marshall Teague (Doug Daniels), Cylk Cozart (Dewar Proctor), Charles Kahlenberg (Oscar DeMarco), Gregory Vahanian (Tom Davis), Robert Lujan (Steward Rives), Scott Williamson (Scott Buzz), Mickey Yablans (Butch Tippet), Bert Rhine (Stoller), Peter Michaels (Lt. Steve Dobbs), Richard Soto (Capt. Tejada), Samuel Hernandez (Latino Pilot), Kristin Wynn (Jesse Little), Kristin Nicole Barnes (Sam Little), Phillip Troy (Dance Partner), Harrison Le Duke (Broker), Garth Le Master (Waiter), Judson Spence (Singer)

FAR OUT MAN (New Line Cinema) Producer, Lisa M. Hansen; Executive Producer, Paul Hertzberg; Co-Producer, Howard Brown; Director/Screenplay, Tommy Chong; Photography, Greg Gardiner, Eric Woster; Music, Jay Chattaway; Editors, Stephen Myers, Gilberto Costa Nunes; Associate Producer, Eric Woster; from CineTel Films; Dolby Stereo; Foto-Kem color; Rated R; 85 minutes; May release. CAST: Tommy Chong (Far Out Man), C. Thomas Howell (Himself), Rae Dawn Chong (Herself), Shelby Chong (Tree), Paris Chong (Kyle), Martin Mull (Psychiatrist), Bobby Taylor (Bobby), Reynaldo Rey (Lou), Peggy F. Sands (Misty), Al Mancini (Fresno Detective), Judd

Nelson (Himself), Cheech Marin (Himself), Michael Winslow (Airport Cop), Rae Allen (Holly), Paul Bartel (Weebee Cool), Mr. Bill (Mr. Bill the Dog), Patrick Campbell (Clerk), Alina Cenal (Maid), Carlos Cervantes (Mexican), Buddy Daniels (Gang Leader), Lewis Dix Jr. (Airport Guard), Tina Fava (Woman with Lou), Peter Ferrara (Rae Dawn's Director), Paul Hertzberg (Drunk Man with wine), K. Theodore Howard (Desk Sergeant), Myra J. (Young Lady), Henri Kingi (Mean Indian), Terence Kirkland (Hitchhiker), Paul Murray (Redneck in cafe), Robbi Chong (Dancer), Penelope Jane Reed, Lisa M. Hansen, Don Dokken, Paul Monroe, John Norum, Ronnie Tanksley, Patricia Van Santen, John Welsh, Glen Wilder, Guitar Shorty, Floyd Sneed

FRANKENHOOKER (Shapiro Glickenhaus) Producer, Edgar Ievins; Executive Producer, James Glickenhaus; Director, Frank Henenlotter; Screenplay, Robert Martin, Frank Henenlotter; Photography, Robert M. Baldwin; Music, Joe Renzetti; Editor, Kevin Tent; Special Makeup Effects, Gabe Bartalos; Color; Rated R; 90 minutes; May release. CAST: James Lorinz (Jeffrey Franken), Patty Mullen (Elizabeth), Charlotte Helmkamp (Honey), Shirley Stoler (Spike), Louise Lasser (Jeffrey's Mom), Joseph Gonzalez (Zorro), Lia Chang (Crystal), Jennifer Delora (Angel), Vicki Darnell (Sugar), Kimberly Taylor (Amber), Heather Hunter (Chartreuse), Sandy Colisimo (Monkey), Stephanie Ryan (Anise), Paul Felix Montez (Goldie)

FLEX (Triax Entertainment) Producer/Director/Screenplay, Harry Grant; Executive Producer, Jack Munari; Photography, Dan Swietlik; Music, Harry Manfredini; Editors, Skip Williams, Steve Denicola; Designer, Gary Randall; a North Star Entertainment Group production; Color; Rated R; 87 minutes; May release. CAST: Harry Grant (Vince DeCola), Lorin Jean Vail (Kim), Wendy Fraser (Gina Carlino), Ken Waller (Ken Waller), Tom Platz (Tom Steele), Dale Levine (Stevie)

PEACEMAKER (Paragon Arts/Fries Entertainment) Producers, Wayne Crawford, Andrew Lane; Co-Producer, Cary Glieberman; Director/Screenplay, Kevin S. Tenney; Photography, Thomas Jewett; Editor, Dan Duncin; Music, Dennis Michael Tenney; Stunts, B. J. Davis; Designer, Rob Sissman; Costumes, Lennie Barin; a Gibraltar Releasing Organization and Mentone Pictures production from Paragon Arts; Color; Rated R; 90 minutes; May release. CAST: Robert Forster (Yates), Lance Edwards (Townsend), Hilary Shepard (Dori Caisson), Robert Davi (Sgt. Frank Ramos), Bert Remsen (Doc), John Denos (Reeger), Wally Taylor (Moses), Kyra Stemple (Girl at beach), Garth LeMaster (Boy at beach)

Tommy Chong in "Far Out Man" © *CineTel Films*

Robert Forster in "Peacemaker" © *Fries Entertainment*

151

James Tobak, Joe Kanter in "The Big Bang" © *Triton Pictures*

Patrick Dempsey, Helen Slater in "Happy Together" © *IVE*

THE BIG BANG (Triton Pictures) Producer, Joseph H. Kanter; Director, James Toback; Photography, Barry Markowitz; Editor, Stephanie Kempf; Color; Rated R; 81 minutes; May release. Documentary featuring Emma Astner, Missy Boyd, Max Brockman, Darryl Dawkins, Eugene Fodor, Polly Frost, Veronica Geng, Julius Hemphill, Fred Hess, Elaine Kaufman, Sheila Kennedy, Anne Marie Keyes, Charles Lassiter, Marcia Oakley, Jack Richardson, Don Simpson, Tony Sirico, Jose Torres, Barbara Traub, Joseph H. Kanter, James Toback

WITHOUT YOU I'M NOTHING (M.C.E.G./New Line Cinema) Producer, Jonathan D. Krane; Executive Producer, Nicolas Roeg; Director, John Boskovich; Screenplay, Sandra Bernhard, John Boskovich; Photography, Joseph Yacoe; Designer, Kevin Rupnik; Editor, Pamela Malouf-Cundy; Music, Patrice Rushen; Choreographer, Karole Armitage; Costumes, Raymond Lee; Dolby Stereo; Foto-Kem color; Rated R; 95 minutes; May release. CAST: Sandra Bernhard (Herself), John Doe (Himself), Steve Antin (Himself), Lu Leonard (Sandra's Manager), Ken Foree (Emcee), Cynthia Bailey (Roxanne), Grace Broughton, Kimberli Williams, Axel Vera, Estuardo M. Volty ("Female" Backup Singers), Kevin Dorsey, Arnold McCuller, Oren Waters (Male Backup Singers), Vonté Sweet, Tonya Natalie Townsend, Jeff Wiener (Children Carolers), Stephanie Clark, Indrani DeSouza, Hardy Keith, Sebastian Russell, Ellen Sims, Carlton Wilborn (Ballet Dancers), Joe DiGiandomenico, Felix Montano, David Stuart Rodgers (Go Go Dancers), Paul Thorpe (Apollo), Denise Vlasis (Shoshanna), Djimon Hounson (Ex-Boyfriend), Roxanne Reese, Ludie C. Washington (Hecklers), Stephanie Albers, Robin Antin, Annie Livingstone (Hippie Girls)

HAPPY TOGETHER (Seymour Borde) Producer, Jere Henshaw; Director, Mel Damski; Screenplay, Craig J. Nevius; Associate Producer, Jeffrey Fleisig; Photography, Joe Pennella; Designer, Marcia Hinds; Music, Robert Folk; Editor, O. Nicholas Brown; Costumes, Dona Granata; Casting, Caro Jones; an Apollo Pictures presentation; Metrocolor; Rated PG-13; 96 minutes; May release. CAST: Patrick Dempsey (Christopher Wooden), Helen Slater (Alexandra Page), Dan Schneider (Gooseflesh), Kevin Hardesty (Slash), Marius Weyers (Denny Dollenbacker), Barbara Babcock (Ruth Carpenter), Gloria Hayes (Luisa Dellacova), Brad Pitt (Brian), Aaron Harnick (Wally), Ron Sterling (Trevor), Eric Lumbard (Gary), Michael D. Clarke (Steve), Wendy Lee Marconi (Dory), Yvette Rambo (Jill), Shawne Rowe (Geri), Kate Hall (Jo), Hugo Hulzar (Eddie), Aviva Skell (Mom), Joan

Kelly (Receptionist), Bryan J. Thompson (Waiter), Tom Tarpey (Bus Driver), James David Murphy (Bartender), Rocky Parker (Librarian/ Biker's Girlfriend)

HONEYMOON ACADEMY (Triumph Releasing) Producer, Tony Anthony; Executive Producers, Paul Maslansky, Eric Ellenbogen; Director/Story, Gene Quintano; Screenplay, Gene Quintano, Jerry Lazarus; Photography, John Cabrera; Music, Robert Folk; Editor, Hubert C. de la Bouillerie; Assistant Director, David Ian; a Sarlui/ Diamant presentation of a Fidelity Films/Paul Maslansky production from Trans World Entertainment; CFI color; Rated PG-13; 94 minutes; May release. CAST: Kim Cattrall (Chris Nelson), Robert Hays (Sean McDonald), Leigh Taylor-Young (Mrs. Kent), Jonathan Banks (Pitt), Christopher Lee (Lazos), Charles Rocket (Desbains), Jerry Lazarus (Marlis), Lance Kinsey (Lance), Max Alexander (Sack), Gordon Jump (Mr. Nelson), Doris Roberts (Mrs. Nelson), Judy Toll (Tina), Kate Benton (Tour Leader), Tino Insano (Friend at wedding), Jennifer Alin (Woman on bus), Isabel Mestres (Isabella), Laura Cepeda, Luis Lorenzo, Dennis Vaughan, Lorraine Clewes, Elmer Maudlin, Luis Bar Boo, Jose Carlos Ruiz, Chris Huertas, Richard Burr, Ballet Antonio Del Castillo

BLOOD SALVAGE (Paragon Arts) Producers, Martin J. Fischer, Ken Sanders; Executive Producers, Ken Sanders, Evander Holyfield; Director, Tucker Johnston; Screenplay, Tucker Johnston, Ken Sanders; Photography, Michael Karp; Designer, Robert Sissman; Music, Tim Temple; Editor, Jacquie Freeman Ross; Special Makeup Effects, Bill Johnson; presented in association with High Five Prods.; Ultra-Stereo; Color; Rated R; 98 minutes; May release. CAST: Danny Nelson (Jake Pruitt), Lori Birdsong (April Evans), John Saxon (Clifford Evans), Ray Walston (Mr. Stone), Christian Hesler (Hiram Pruitt), Ralph Pruitt Vaughn (Roy Pruitt), Laura Whyte (Pat Evans), Andy Greenway (Bobby Evans), Evander Holyfield (Boxer), Dan Albright (Sheriff Reynolds), Gil Ropert (Emcee), Lonnie Smith (Policeman), Byron Cherry, P. J. Shinall (Newlyweds), Lou Duva (Trainer), Ken Sanders (Boxing Spectator), Frank Kube (Sparring Partner), Suzanne Ventulett (Tina Matthews)

THE BIG DIS (Olympia Pictures) Producers/Directors/Screenplay/ Editors, Gordon Eriksen, John O'Brien; Photography, John O'Brien; Music, Kev Ses, Harry B., Dr. Cranium and the Big Dis Crew; Associate Producer, Heather Johnston; Black and white; Not rated; 84 minutes; June release. CAST: James Haig (J. D.), Kevin Haig, Monica

Sandra Bernhard in "Without You I'm Nothing" © *M.C.E.G.*

John Saxon in "Blood Salvage" © *Paragon Arts*

James Haig in "The Big Dis" © *Olympia Pictures*

Jared Rushton in "A Cry in the Wild" © *Concorde*

Sparrow, Lisa Rivers, Aratha Johnston, Allysunn Walker, Gordon Eriksen, Heather Johnston

FORCE OF CIRCUMSTANCE (AdHoc/Upfront Films) Producer/Director, Liza Bear; Editors, J-P Rolandlevy, Liza Bear; Photography, Zoran Hochstatter; Screenplay, Craig Gholson, Liza Bear; Music, M. Mader; from Ad Hoc Films; DuArt color; Not rated; 89 minutes; June release. CAST: Boris Major (Mouallem), Jessica Stutchbury (Katrina), Tom Wright (Hans), Eric Mitchell (The Envoy for a Foreign Despot), Glenn O'Brien (Charles Floris), Mark Boone, Jr. (Herman), Kathleen Anderson (Hortensia), Steve Buscemi (Virgil), Filip Pagowski (The Envoy's Bodyguard), Evan Lurie (Avian Hum), Rockets Redglare (The Factor), Pam Osowski (Maxine Lethford), Giuseppe Beaumont (Frank Davis), Anna Kohler (Sophia), Jane Lawrence Smith (Mildred), Steven Torton (Ahmed), Senor Banchs (Mohammed), Bob Salitt, Michael McClard, Karl Petrovich, James Chance (Intl. Organization of Experts), Josephine Byers, Alma Edwards, Margit Edwards, Annie Sandoval (Gossip Ladies)

A CRY IN THE WILD (Concorde) Producer, Julie Corman; Director, Mark Griffiths; Screenplay, Gary Paulsen, Catherine Cyran; Based on the novel "Hatchet" by Gary Paulsen; Photography, Gregg Heschong; Music, Arthur Kempel; Designer, Michael Clausen; Editor, Carol Oblath; a New Horizon Corp. co-release; Color; Rated PG; 81 minutes; June release. CAST: Jared Rushton (Brian Robeson), Pamela Sue Martin (Mom), Stephen Meadows (Dad), Ned Beatty (Pilot), Terrence H. Winkless (Boyfriend), Louise Baker (Woman at picnic), Deke Anderson (Store Clerk), John Jakes (Rescue plane Pilot), Lois Mallory (Grandma), Ollie Mann (Grandpa)

VIETNAM, TEXAS (Triumph Releasing) Producers, Robert Ginty, Ron Joy; Executive Producer, Mark Damon; Director, Robert Ginty; Screenplay, Tom Badal, C. Courtney Joyner; Photography, Robert M. Baldwin, Jr.; Music, Richard Stone; Editor, Jonathan P. Shaw; Designer, Phillip J. C. Duffin; from Epic Productions; Deluxe color; Rated R; 85 minutes; June release. CAST: Robert Ginty (Thomas McCain), Haing S. Ngor (Wong), Tim Thomerson (Max), Kieu Chinh (Mailan), Tomlyn Tomita (Lan), John Pleshette (Harold), David Chow (Minh), Burt Remsen (Msgr. Sheehan), Chi-Muoi Lo (Sammy), Michelle Chan (Tini)

GHOST DAD (Universal) Producer, Terry Nelson; Executive Producer, Stan Robertson; Director, Sidney Poitier; Screenplay, Chris Reese, Brent Maddock, S. S. Wilson; Story, Brent Maddock, S. S.

Wilson; Photography, Andrew Laszlo; Designer, Henry Bumstead; Editor, Pembroke Herring; Music, Henry Mancini; Associate Producer, David Wisnievitz; Stunts, Alan Oliney; Casting, Nancy Nayor; Assistant Director, Candace Allen; Visual Effects Supervisors, Richard Yuricich, Richard O. Helmer; Visual Effects, The Chandler Group, Apogee Productions, Inc.; Optical Effects, R/Greenburg Associates, Inc.; Song: "Strong as Steel" by Diane Warren/performed by Gladys Knight; a SAH Enterprises, Inc. production; Dolby Stereo; Deluxe color; Rated PG; 84 minutes; June release. CAST: Bill Cosby (Elliot Hopper), Kimberly Russell (Diane Hopper), Denise Nicholas (Joan), Ian Bannen (Sir Edith Moser), Christine Ebersole (Carol), Barry Corbin (Mr. Collins), Salim Grant (Danny Hopper), Brooke Fontaine (Amanda Hopper), Dakin Matthews (Mr. Seymour), Dana Ashbrook (Tony Ricker), Omar Gooding (Stuart), Raynor Scheine (Cabbie), Arnold Stang (Mr. Cohen), Brian Mitchell (Teacher), Lisa Mene Nemacheck (Jonelle), Donzaleigh Abernathy (E. R. Nurse), George Ganz (Mr. Nero), Cyndi James Gossett (E. R. Doctor), Joseph Hajduk, Kevin Lee, Becky Katzen, Bryant Edwards, Trenton Teigen (Students), Mary Munday, Norman Merrill, Ted Hayden, Raymond E. Foti, Frank Biro (Executives), Amy Hill, Patrika Darbo, Rita Vassallo, Jeanne Mori (Nurses), Kenny Ford, Jr., Adam Jeffries, Austin Garrett (Buddies), Douglas Johnson (Lab Technician), James McIntire (Sheriff), Eric Menyuk (Clinic Doctor), Jizelle Morris (Screaming Girl), Pamela Poitier (Nurse Satler), Robin Pearson Rose (Hospital Administrator), Becky Sweet (Classmate), Robert Covarrubias (Man in waiting room), Meredith Gordon (Woman in taxi), Cedric Scott (Announcer)

RED SURF (Arrowhead Entertainment) Producer, Richard C. Weinman; Executive Producer, Greg H. Sims; Director/Additional Written Material, H. Gordon Boos; Screenplay, Vincent Robert; Story, Brian Gamble, Jason Hoffs, Vincent Robert; Photography, John Schwartzmann; Music, Sasha Matson; Editor, Dennis Dolan; Co-Producer, Jason Hoffs; Ultra-Stereo; Color; Rated R; 105 minutes; June release. CAST: George Clooney (Remar), Doug Savant (Attila), Dedee Pfeiffer (Rebecca), Gene Simmons (Doc), Philip McKeon (True Blue), Rick Najera (Calvera), Vincent Klyn (Noga), Eddie Frias (Bullet)

FACE OF THE ENEMY (Tri-Culture Pictures) Producers, Behrouz Gueramian, Elizabeth Lynch Brown, Catherine Rocca; Director, Hassan Ildari; Screenplay, Philip Anderson; Photography, Peter Ingergand; Editor, Toby Brown; Music, Esfandiar Monfaredzadeh; CFI color; Rated R; 92 minutes; June release. CAST: Rosana DeSoto (Neiloufar), George DiCenzo (James Wald), Cindy Cryer (Darya)

Eric Mitchell in "Force of Circumstance" © *Ad Hoc Films*

Ian Bannen, Bill Cosby in "Ghost Dad" © *Universal City Studios*

153

Bretton Vail, Nicole Dillenberg, in "The Long Weekend" ©
Desperate Pictures

"Jetsons: "The Movie" © *Universal City Studios*

GHOSTS CAN'T DO IT (Triumph Releasing) Producer, Bo Derek; Director/Screenplay/Photography, John Derek; Music, Junior Homrich, Randy Tico; an Epic Prods. picture; Color; Rated R; 95 minutes; June release. CAST: Bo Derek (Kate), Anthony Quinn (Scott), Don Murray (Winston), Leo Damian (Fausto), Julie Newmar (Angel), Donald Trump (Himself)

THE LONG WEEKEND (O' DESPAIR) (Desperate Pictures) Producer/Director/Screenplay/Editor/Photography, Gregg Araki; Music, Steven Fields; Black and white; Not rated; 87 minutes; June release. CAST: Bretton Vail (Michael), Maureen Bondanville (Rachel), Andrea Beane (Leah), Nicole Dillenberg (Sara), Marcus D'Amico (Greg), Lance Woods (Alex)

FUN DOWN THERE (Bleecker St. Film) Producer/Director/Screenplay/Designer, Roger Stigliano; Photography, Peggy Ahwesh, Eric Saks; Music, James Baker, Wayne Hammond; Editors, Roger Stigliano, Keith Sanborn; an Angelina Production; Color; Not rated; 85 minutes; June release. CAST: Michael Waite (Buddy Fields), Nickolas B. Nagourney (Joseph), Martin Goldin (Angelo), Jeanne Smith (Judy Fields), Betty Waite (Mrs. Fields), Harold Waite (Mr. Fields), Yvonne Fisher (Sandy), Gretschen Somerville (Greta), Gary Onsum (Cary), Paul Saindon (Singer), Kenneth R. Clarke (Kent), Judy Joseph (Woman in red), Kayla Serotti (Kayla), Caroline Paddock (Catherine), Howard Roxs (Simon), Richard Hailey (Ricky)

FALSE IDENTITY (RKO Pictures) Producer, James Shavick; Executive Producers, Ted Hartley, Gerald Offsay, Daniel Sarnoff; Director, James Keach; Supervising Producer, Jason P. Clark; Screenplay/Associate Producer, Sandra Bailey; Photography, Bernard Auroux; Designer, Kevin Ryan; from the Image Organization; Color; Rated PG-13; 92 minutes; June release. CAST: Stacy Keach (Ben), Genevieve Bujold (Rachel), Tobin Bell (Marshall), Mike Champion (Luther), Veronica Cartwright (Vera), Mimi Maynard (Audrey), Todd Jeffries (Chad), Renee O'Connor (Angela), Granger Hines (Tommy Lawler), Anne Bloom (Elise), Tommy Calloway (Karl), Thom McFadden (Sheriff), Jack Murdock (Bill Hayes), Jan Merlin (Pete Potter), J. W. Smith, O-Lan Jones, William Lucking

JETSONS: THE MOVIE (Universal) Producers/Directors, William Hanna, Joseph Barbera; Screenplay, Dennis Marks; Additional Dialogue, Carl Sautter; Supervising Producer, Bruce David Johnson; Supervising Animation Director, David Michener; Supervising Director, Iwao Takamoto; Executive in Charge of Production, Jayne Barbera;

Michael Waite, Betty Waite, Harold Waite in "Fun Down There" © *Bleecker St. Film*

Music, John Debney; Songs by various artists/performed by Tiffany, and others; *"Jetsons Theme"* by William Hanna, Joseph Barbera, Hoyt Curtin; Supervising Editors, Pat Foley, Terry W. Moore, Larry C. Cowan; Production Designer, Al Gmuer; Computer Animation, deGraf/Wahrman, Inc.; Produced by Hanna-Barbera Studios, in association with Wang Film Productions Co., Inc., Cuckoos Nest Studios; Dolby Stereo; CFI color; Rated G; 82 minutes; July release. VOICE CAST: George O'Hanlon (George Jetson), Mel Blanc (Mr. Spacely), Penny Singleton (Jane Jetson), Tiffany (Judy Jetson), Patric Zimmerman (Elroy Jetson), Don Messick (Astro), Jean Vanderpyl (Rosie the Robot), Ronnie Schell (Rudy 2), Patti Deutsch (Lucy 2), Dana Hill (Teddy 2), Russi Taylor (Fergie Furbelow), Paul Kreppel (Apollo Blue), Rick Dees (Rocket Rick), Michael Bell, Jeff Bergman, Brian Cummings, Brad Garrett, Rob Paulsen, Susan Silo, Janet Waldo, B. J. Ward, Jim Ward, Frank Welker

CLOWNHOUSE (Triumph Releasing) Producers, Michael Danty, Robin Mortarotti, Victor Salva; Director/Screenplay, Victor Salva; Photography, Robin Mortarotti; Music, Michael Becker, Thomas Richardson; Editors, Roy Anthony Cox, Sabrina Plisco-Morris; a Commercial Pictures production; Deluxe color; Rated R; 84 minutes; July release. CAST: Nathan Forrest Winters (Casey), Brian McHugh (Geoffrey), Sam Rockwell (Randy), Tree (Cheezio), Byron Weible, David C. Reinecke

NO PICNIC (Great Jones Film Group) Producer, Doris Kornish; Director/Screenplay, Philip Hartman; Executive Producer, Chris Sievernich; Photography, Peter Hutton; Music, Ned Sublette, The Raunch Hands; Editor, Grace Tankersley; Black and white; Not rated; 88 minutes; July release. CAST: David Brisbin (Mac), Myoshin (Stripe), Anne D'Agnillo (Anne), Chandler (Rock 'n' Roll Porter), Clare Bauman (The Fan), Ryan Cutrona (Live Pimp), Lerode Tayken (Bobby Brusaloff), Lizzie Olesker (Polka Dot), David Jaffe (Big Pig Manager), Elaine Olesker (Mother), Craig Smith (86 Club Patron), Carl Fredericks (The Head Honcho), Richard Hell (Irate Neighbor), Catherine Jones (One Night Stand), Kevin O'Brien (Mac's Brother), Princess Pamela (Billy), Art Torres (Tour Guide), Margot Core (Amelia), Rafik (Belgian Expert), Keith Dunlap (Record Clerk), Al Batalla (Father), Steve Buscemi (Dead Pimp), Dudley Sabo (The Watcher), Milton Feuer (Landlord), Joseph "Slima" Williams (Poet)

THE ADVENTURES OF FORD FAIRLANE (20th Century Fox) Producers, Joel Silver, Steve Perry; Director, Renny Harlin; Screenplay, Daniel Waters, James Cappe, David Arnott; Story, James Cappe, David Arnott; Based on characters created by Rex Weiner; Photography, Oliver Wood; Designer, John Vallone; Executive Producer, Michael Levy; Editor, Michael Tronick; Costumes, Marilyn Vance-Straker; Music, Yello; Casting, Jackie Burch; Associate Producer, Suzanne Todd; Stunts/2nd Unit Director, Charles Picerni; a Silver Pictures production; Dolby Stereo; Panavision; Deluxe color; Rated R; 104 minutes; July release. CAST: Andrew Dice Clay (Ford Fairlane), Wayne Newton (Julian Grendel), Priscilla Presley (Colleen Sutton), Morris Day (Don Cleveland), Lauren Holly (Jazz), Maddie Corman (Zuzu Petals), Gilbert Gottfried (Johnny Crunch), David Patrick Kelly (Sam), Brandon Call (The Kid), Robert Englund (Smiley), Ed O'Neill (Lt. Amos), Vince Neil (Bobby Black), Sheila E. (Club Singer), David Arnott, Mark Goldstein (Club Guys), Cody Jarrett (Kyle Troy), William Shockley, Mark Zuelke (Punk Gunslingers), Steve White (Detective), Kari Wuhrer (Melodi), Delia Sheppard, Kimber Sissons, Monique Mannen, Pamela Segall (Pussycats), Hili Park, Gry Park (Twin Club Girls), Kurt Loder (MTV DJ), Cindy Lehre (Lydia), Tone Loc (Slam the Rapper), Phil Soussan, Carlos Cavazo, Randy Castillo, Kurt James Stefka, Jaz Kaner, David Bowe, Michael Alan Kahn, Willie

David Brisbin in "No Picnic" © *Great Jones*

Chuck Norris in "Delta Force 2" © *Cannon Entertainment*

Garson, Ladd Vance, Robert Mangiardi, Kristin Pearcey, Lori Pfeiffer, Diana Barrows, Lala, Lee Lawrence, Connie Johnson, Jordan Lund, Allan Wasserman, Charlie Hawke, Rita Bland, Kathleen Monica, Randy Crenshaw, John Hammond, Hot Tub Johnny West, Edward DiLorenzo, Sandra Sheeler, Edmund E. Villa, Consuela Nance, Diane Almeida, Aurorah Allain

DANGER ZONE III: STEEL HORSE WAR (Danger Zone Co.) Producer, Jason Williams; Director, Douglas Bronco; Executive Producer, Bernard Subkoski; Screenplay, Gregory Poirier, Jason Williams; Photography, Daniel Yarussi; Music, Robert Etoll; Editor, Bob Murawski; Crest color; Rated R; 91 minutes; August release. CAST: Jason Williams (Wade Olsen), Robert Random (Grim Reaper), Barne Subkoski (Rainmaker), Juanita Ranney (Skin), Rusty Cooper (Tester), Giles Ashford (Buford).

DELTA FORCE 2 (MGM) Producers, Yoram Globus, Christopher Pearce; Director, Aaron Norris; Screenplay, Lee Reynolds; Based on characters created by James Bruner and Menahem Golan; Photography, Joao Fernandes; Music, Frederic Talgorn; Editor, Michael J. Duthie; Associate Producers, Avi Kleinberger, Michael Hartman; Stunts, Dean Ferrandini; Aerial Coordinator, Jeff Habberstad; Fight Coordinator, Rick Prieto; from Cannon Entertainment, Inc.; Dolby Stereo; TVC Color; Rated R; 110 minutes; August release. CAST: Chuck Norris (Col. Scott McCoy), Billy Drago (Ramon Cota), John P. Ryan (Gen. Taylor), Richard Jaeckel (John Page), Begonia Plaza (Quinquina), Paul Perri (Maj. Bobby Chavez), Hector Mercado (Miguel), Mark Margolis (Gen. Olmedo), Mateo Gomez (Ernesto Flores), Ruth de Sosa (Rita Chavez), Gerald Castillo (DEA Director), Geof Brewer (Maj. Anderson), Rick Prieto (Rita's Killer), Sharlene Ross, Michael Heit, Richard Warlock (DEA Agents in van), Chris Castillejo (Alex), Dave Brodett (Mercenary Captain), Rina Reyes (Olmedo's Mistress), Subas Herrero (President Alcazar), Ronnie Lazaro (Quinquina's Husband), Miguel Faustmann (Host at Rio Ball), Kevin Kleppe (Wrong Ramon), Mimi Sananes Wilheim (Dancing Apple Girl), Jeff Hammett (Attorney), Kelly Wicker (Judge), Trevor Kunz (Stewardess), Ruel Vernal, Roland Dantes, Rolando Aquino, Kris Aguilar, Reynaldo Guiao, Jr., Alberto Dominguez (Ramon's Body Guards), Craig Judd, Michael Welborn, Roy Judd (Skinheads).

NEUROTIC CABARET (Kipp Prods.) Producers/Screenplay, John Woodward, Tammy Stones; Director/Editor, John Woodward; Photography, Danny Anaya; Executive Producer, Tammy Stones; Music,

John Mills; Designer, John Perdichi; Costumes, Angela Keen; Color; Not rated; 85 minutes; August release. CAST: Tammy Stones (Terri), Edwin Neal (Nolan), Dennis Worthington (Nick), Colleen Keegan (Annette), Pat Kelly (Pat), Paul Vasquez (Cheo)

THE EXORCIST III (20th Century Fox) Producer, Carter DeHaven; Executive Producers, James G. Robinson, Joe Roth; Director/Screenplay, William Peter Blatty, based on his novel *"Legion"*; Photography, Gerry Fisher; Designer, Leslie Dilley; Editors, Todd Ramsay, Peter Lee-Thompson; Music, Barry DeVorzon; Casting, Sally Dennison, Julie Selzer, Lou DiGaimo; Assistant Director, Richard Abramitis; a Morgan Creek Production; Dolby Stereo; Deluxe color; Rated R; 109 minutes; August release. CAST: George C. Scott (Lt. Kinderman), Ed Flanders (Father Dyer), Brad Dourif (The Gemini Killer), Jason Miller (Patient X), Nicol Williamson (Father Morning), Scott Wilson (Dr. Temple), Nancy Fish (Nurse Allerton), George DiCenzo (Stedman), Don Gordon (Ryan), Lee Richardson (University President), Grand L. Bush (Sgt. Atkins), Mary Jackson (Mrs. Clelia), Viveca Lindfors (Nurse X), Ken Lerner (Dr. Freedman), Tracy Thorne (Nurse Keating), Barbara Baxley (Shirley), Zohra Lampert (Mary Kinderman), Harry Carey Jr. (Father Kanavan), Sherrie Wills (Julie Kinderman), Edward Lynch (Patient A), Clifford David (Dr. Bruno), Alexander Zuckerman (Korner Boy), Lois Foraker (Nurse Merrin), Tyra Ferrell (Nurse Blaine), James Burgess (Thomas Kintry), Kevin Corrigan (Altar Boy), Peggy Alston (Mrs. Kintry), Father John Durkin, S. J. (Elderly Jesuit), Bobby Deren (Nurse Bierce), Jan Neuberger (Alice), Patrick Ewing (Angel of Death), Larry King, C. Everett Koop (Themselves), Alexis Chieffet, Debra Port, Walt MacPherson, David Dwyer, Daniel Epper, William Preston, Chuck Kinlaw, Demetrios Pappageorge, Nina Hansen, Shane Wexel, Ryan Paul Amick, John A. Coe, Jodi Long, Kathy Gerber, Samuel L. Jackson, Jan Smook, Amelia Campbell, Cherie Baron

HOLLYWOOD MAVERICKS (Roxie Releasing) Producer, Florence Dauman; Screenplay, Todd McCarthy, Michael Henry Wilson; Editor, Stacy Foiles; Produced by the American Film Institute and NHK Enterprises Inc.; Color; Not rated; 90 minutes; September release. A documentary featuring D. W. Griffith, Erich Von Stroheim, Josef Von Sternberg, King Vidor, John Ford, Orson Welles, Samuel Fuller, John Cassavetes, Dennis Hopper, Francis Coppola, Sam Peckinpah, Robert Altman, Alan Rudolph, David Lynch, Robert De Niro, Martin Scorsese, Paul Schrader, Peter Bogdanovich

Andrew Dice Clay, Wayne Newton, Lauren Holly in "The Adventures of Ford Fairlane" © *20th Century Fox*

Viveca Lindfors, George C. Scott in "The Exorcist III" © *Morgan Creek Films Partners*

Emilio Estevez, Charlie Sheen in "Men at Work" © *Epic Prods.*

Dennis Christopher in "Circuitry Man" © *Skouras*

MEN AT WORK (Triumph Releasing) Producer, Cassian Elwes; Co-Producer, Barbara Stordahl; Executive Producers, Irwin Yablans, Moshe Diamant; Director/Screenplay, Emilio Estevez; Photography, Tim Suhrstedt; Designer, Dins Danielsen; Music, Stewart Copeland; Editor, Craig Bassett; Costumes, Keith Lewis; Casting, Marci Liroff; Associate Producer, Frances Fleming; Assistant Director, Mark A. Radcliffe; an Epic Productions, Inc. presentation of an Epic/Elwes/Euphoria production; Dolby Stereo; Deluxe color; Rated PG-13; 99 minutes; August release. CAST: Charlie Sheen (Carl Taylor), Emilio Estevez (James St. James), Leslie Hope (Susan Wilkins), Keith David (Louis Fedders), Dean Cameron (Pizza Man), John Getz (Maxwell Potterdam III), Hawk Wolinski (Biff), John Lavachielli (Mario), Geoffrey Blake (Frost), Cameron Dye (Luzinski), John Putch (Mike), Tommy Hinckley (Jeff), Darrell Larson (Jack Berger), Sy Richardson (Walt Richardson), Kari Whitman (Judy), Troy Evans (Capt. Dalton), Brad Wyman, Matthew Robinson (Rent-a-Cops), Bob Brown, Erik Stabenau, Bobby Burns, Eddie Braun (Henchmen)

FULL FATHOM FIVE (Concorde) Producer, Luis Llosa; Executive Producer, Rodman Flender; Director, Carl Franklin; Screenplay, Bart Davis; Co-Producer, Beverly Gray; Photography, Pili Flores Guerra; Music, Allan Zavod; Editor, Karen Horn; Designer, Fernando Vasques de Velsaco; Foto-kem color; Rated PG; 80 minutes; August release. CAST: Michael Moriarty (MacKenzie), Maria Rangel (Justine), Diego Bertie (Miguel), German Gonzales (Sebastian), Daniel Faraldo (Santillo), John Lafayette (Lasovic), Brian Kally (Randall), Orlando Sacha (Barrista), Tono Vega (Torres), Ramsay Ross (Mishkin), Michael Cavanaugh (Garver), Carl Franklin (Fletcher), Roy Morris (Petrov), Todd Field (Johnson), Peter Sommers (Fire Control USA), Michael Lemoine (Helmsman USA), Philip Rebatta (Cuban Radio Man), Antonio Arrue (Cuban Cook), Carlos Victoria (Executive, Kirov), German Calderon (Torpedoman, Kirov), Gil Passos (Sonar Operator, Kirov), Peter Vennard (Ensign), Ernie Barret (Man in lab coat), Gus Chocly (Panamanian Colonel), Bill Ingini (Panamanian Soldier)

GRIM PRAIRIE TALES (Coe Hahn Inc.) Producer, Richard Hahn; Director/Screenplay, Wayne Coe; Executive Producers, Rick Blumenthal, Larry Haber; Co-Producer, Andrzej Kamrowski; Executive in Charge of Production, Shirley Honickman Hahn; Photography, Janusz Kaminski; Designer, Anthony Zierhut; Music, Steve Dancz; Editor, Earl Ghaffari; Casting, Herb Dufine; Assistant Director, Chris Bongirne; Color; Rated R; 90 minutes; August release. CAST: James Earl Jones (Morrison), Brad Dourif (Farley), Will Hare (Lee), Marc

McClure (Tom), Michelle Joyner (Jenny), William Atherton (Arthur), Lisa Eichhorn (Maureen), Wendy Cooke (Eva), Scott Paulin (Martin), Bruce Fischer (Colochez), Jennifer Barlow (Sarah), Tom Simcox (Horn), Dan Leegant (Dr. Lederman), William M. Brennan (Bluey), James Glick (Dying Chief), Hannah Fixico, Joan Lemmo (Old Indian Woman), Joel Shoptesse, Oscar Fragosa, Mony Bass (Indian Men), Darice Sampson, Jessica Vega Vasquez (Indian Women), Elena Lopez (Indian Girl), Eric Vega Vasquez (Indian Boy)

CIRCUITRY MAN (Skouras) Producers, Steven Reich, John Schouweiler; Director, Steven Lovy; Screenplay, Steven Lovy, Robert Lovy; Executive Producers, Miles A. Copeland III, Paul Colichman; Photography, Jamie Thompson; Music, Deborah Holland; Editor, Jonas Thaler; Designer, Robert Lovy; an IRS Media presentation; Ultra-Stereo; Foto-kem color; Rated R; 93 minutes; August release. CAST: Jim Metzler (Danner), Dana Wheeler-Nicholson (Lori), Lu Leonard (Juice), Vernon Wells (Plughead), Barbara Alyn Woods (Yoyo), Dennis Christopher (Leech), Paul Willson (Beany), Andy Goldberg (Squaid), Manu Tupou (Mahi), Gary Goodrow (Jugs), Jerry Tondo (Fatch), Darren A. Lott (Jackee), Barney Burman (Cheater), Steven Bottomley, Amy Hill (Bartenders), Andrew Steel (Trucker), Karen Maruyama (Biker Bandit), Steven Reich (Medic), Steve Hunter (Medic Assistant)

BACKSTREET DREAMS (Vidmark) Producers, Lance H. Robbins, Jason O'Malley; Director, Rupert Hitzig; Screenplay, Jason O'Malley; Photography, Stephen M. Katz; Designer, George Costello; Music, Bill Conti; Editor, Robert Gordon; Costumes, Elisabeth Scott; from O'Malley Film productions; Color; Rated R; 104 minutes; September release. CAST: Jason O'Malley (Dean Costello), Brooke Shields (Stevie Bloom), Sherilynn Fenn (Lucy Costello), Tony Fields (Manny Santana), Nick Cassavetes (Mikey Acosta), Ray Mancini (Aldo), Burt Young (Luca Garibaldi), Anthony Franciosa (Angelo Carnevale), John Vizzi, Joseph Vizzi (Shane Costello), Elias Koteas, Meg Register

LIVING TO DIE (PM Entertainment) Producers, Richard Pepin, Joseph Merhi; Director, Wings Hauser; Screenplay, Stephen Smoke; Photography, Richard Pepin; Music, John Gonzalez, Lon Price; Editor, Geraint Bell; Foto-Kem color; Rated R; 84 minutes; November release. CAST: Wings Hauser (Nick Carpenter), Darcy DeMoss (Maggie), Asher Brauner (Eddie), Arnold Vosloo (Jimmy), R. J. Walker (Lt. Howard), Minnie Madden (Jasmine), Wendy Mac Donald, Rebecca

Marc McClure, Michelle Joyner in "Grim Prairie Tales" © *East West Film Partner*

Brooke Shields, Jason O'Malley in "Backstreet Dreams" © *Vidmark Entertainment*

Steve Guttenberg, Jami Gertz in "Don't Tell Her It's Me"
© Hemdale Film Corp.

Katherine Borowitz, Jay O. Saunders in "Just Like in the Movies" © Cabriolet

Barrington, John Ross, Janice Carter, Raymond Martino, Carol Hooper, Cheryl Nishi, Denise Lash

DON'T TELL HER IT'S ME (Hemdale); formerly *The Boyfriend School;* Producers, George G. Braunstein, Ron Hamady; Executive Producers, John Daly, Derek Gibson; Director, Malcolm Mowbray; Screenplay, Sarah Bird, based on her novel *The Boyfriend School;* Photography, Reed Smoot; Designer, Linda Pearl; Music, Michael Gore; Editor, Marshall Harvey; Casting, Karen Rea; Associate Producer, Chris Coles; Costumes, Carol Wood; Assistant Director, Scott Easton; Ultra-Stereo; CFI color; Rated PG-13; 101 minutes; September release. CAST: Steve Guttenberg (Gus Kubicek), Jami Gertz (Emily Pear), Shelley Long (Lizzie Potts), Kyle MacLachlan (Trout), Kevin Scannell (Mitchell), Madchen Amick (Mandy), Beth Grant (Babette), Laura Alcade (Bartender), Perry Anzilotti (Hairdresser), Bill Applebaum (Man in bar), Stacy Areheart (Teenage Girl), O'Neil Compton (Gas Station Attendant), Nada Despotovich (Receptionist), Chris Ellis (Ugly Duckling voice over), Jeannie Epper, Tony Epper (Thugs), John "Speed" Finley (Biker), Kenneth Graham (Lawyer), Bert Hogue (Airport Security Guard), Francis "Jessie" Krosnick (Waiting Man), Caroline Lund (Annabelle), Sally Lund (Annabelle), Joe Mowbray (Boy on bike), Bonnie Terheggen (Woman in bar), William "Birdman" Thomas, Sam Youngblood (Men in line), William Torres (Ticket Agent)

BERKELEY IN THE SIXTIES (P.O.V. Theatrical Films/Tara Releasing) Producer/Director, Mark Kitchell; Photography, Stephen Lighthill; Editor, Veronica Selver; from Kitchell Films; Color/Black and white; Not rated; 117 minutes; September release. A documentary featuring Jack Weinberg, Jentri Anders, John Gage, Frank Bardacke, Jackie Goldberg, Michael Rossman, John Searle, Suzy Nelson, Ruth Rosen, Bobby Seale, David Hilliard, Hardy Frye, Barry Melton, Mike Miller, Susan Griffin, Mario Savio, Clark Kerr, Joan Baez, Allen Ginsberg, The Grateful Dead, and Huey Newton

MIRROR, MIRROR (Orphans Entertainment) Producer/Music, Jimmy Lifton; Director, Marina Sargenti; Screenplay, Yuri Zeltser, Marina Sargenti, Annette Cascone, Gina Cascone; Photography, Robert Brinkmann; Color; Rated R; 103 minutes; September release. CAST: Karen Black (Mrs. Gordon), Rainbow Harvest (Megan), Kristin Dattilo (Nikki), Ricky Paull Goldin (Ron), Yvonne De Carlo (Emelin), William Sanderson (Mr. Veze)

JUST LIKE IN THE MOVIES (Cabriolet Films) Producer, Alon Kasha; Director/Screenplay, Bram Towbin; Photography, Peter Fern-

berger; Music, John Hill; Editor, Jay Keuper; Designer, Marek Dobrowolski; Color; Rated R; 90 minutes; September release. CAST: Jay O. Saunders (Ryan Legrand), Alan Ruck (Dean), Katherine Borowitz (Tura), Michael Jeter (Vernon), Alex Vincent (Carter), Mark Margolis (John Zanasco), Lauren Thompson (Alice), Richard Council (Robert), Margaret Devine (Val), Martha Gehman (Leda), Joyce Reehling (Sara Zaloom), Larry Pine (Michael Stone), Fred Sanders (Astronomer), Francis Conroy (Simone Kassler), Kurt Peterson (Robert Kassler), Helen Hanft (Darcy Simons), Jon Sidel, Mark Lotito (Steve Rankin), Michael Jefferson, Tom Mandirosian, Ilene Kristen, Ralph Marrero, Silvio Luciano, Paul Bates, Frances Guinan, Steven Marcus, Reg E. Cathey, Sam Guncler, Marcella Lowrey, Judith Cohen, Dani Klein, Emma Terese, Nealla Spano, Joni Dee Bostwick

NIGHT ANGEL (Paragon Arts/Fries Entertainment) Producers, Joe Augustyn, Jeff Geoffray; Executive Producer, Walter Josten; Director, Dominique Othenin-Girard; Screenplay, Joe Augustyn, Walter Josten; Photography, David Lewis; Music, Cory Lerios; Editor, Jerry Brady; Costumes, Renee Johnston; Special Effects, Steve Johnson, XFX Group; Designer, Ken Aichele; a Paragon Arts Intl. production; Color; Rated R; 90 minutes; September release. CAST: Isa Anderson (Lilith), Karen Black (Rita), Linden Ashby (Craig), Debra Feuer (Kirstie), Helen Martin (Sadie), Doug Jones (Ken), Garry Hudson (Rod), Sam Hennings (Mr. Crenshaw), Tedra Gabriel (Mrs. Crenshaw), Ben Ganger (Tommy Crenshaw), Twink Caplan (Jenny), Celia Xavier (Koko)

OLD EXPLORERS (Taurus Entertainment) Producers, David Herbert, William Pohlad, Tom Jenz; Director/Screenplay, William Pohlad; Based on the play by James Cada, Mark Keller; Photography, Jeffrey Laszlo; Music, Billy Barber; Editor, Miroslav Janek; Designer, Peter Stolz; Costumes, Tessie Bundick; Casting, Riki Wuolle; Assistant Director, Eric Heffron; a River Road Prods. Films release; Dolby Stereo; Technicolor; Rated PG; 91 minutes; September release. CAST: Jose Ferrer (Warner Watney), James Whitmore (Leinen Roth), Jeffrey Gadbois (Alex Watney), Caroline Kaiser (Leslie Watney), William Warfield (Tugboat Captain), Christopher Pohlad (Billy Watney), Storm Richardson (Scott Watney), Dominique Berrand (Lafitte), Molly Atwood (Nurse), James Cada (Watch Commander), Marn Evan Jacobs (Waiter), Peter Stolz (Priest), Kristen Andersen (City Bartender), Peter Moore (Mongol Warrior), Mary Rehbein (Soho Harlot), Tessie Bundick (Woman with dog), Tom Jenz, David Herbert (Policemen), Clark Sanford (Sailor), Jeffrey Smalley, Patrick Stolz, Shawn Trusten (Soccer Team)

"Berkeley in the Sixties" © Jeffrey Blankfort

Isa Anderson, Karen Black in "Night Angel"
© Night Angel Partners

Ray Sharkey in "The Rain Killer" © *Califilm*

Anthony Starke, Leslie Nielsen, Linda Blair in "Repossessed"
© *Seven Arts*

PRESTON STURGES: THE RISE AND FALL OF AN AMER-ICAN DREAMER (Barking Dog Prods.) Producer/Director, Kenneth Bowser; Executive Producers, Susan Lacy, Marilyn Haft; Screenplay, Todd McCarthy; Narrator, Fritz Weaver; Photography, Dennis Maloney; Music, Michael Bacon; Editor, Ken Werner; an American Masters co-production; Color/black and white; Not rated; 75 minutes; September release. Documentary featuring Eddie Bracken, Thomas Quinn Curtiss, Edwin Gillette, Betty Hutton, A. C. Lyles, Joel McCrea, Frances Ramsden, Cesar Romero, Andrew Sarris, Paul Schrader, Sandy Sturges, Rudy Vallee, Priscilla Woolfan

THE RAIN KILLER (Concorde) Producer, Rodman Flender; Executive Producer/Director, Ken Stein; Screenplay, Ray Cunneff; Photography, Janusz Kaminski; Music, Terry Plumeri; Editor, Patrick Rand; a Califilm production; Ultra-Stereo; Fotokem color; Rated R; 93 minutes; September release. CAST: Ray Sharkey (Capra), David Beecroft (Dalton), Tania Coleridge (Adele), Michael Chiklis (Reese), Bill LaVallee (Hacket), Woody Brown (Rosewall), Mary Ingersol (Anchorwoman), Grey Daniels (Conductor), Kathleen Klein (Woman on train), Marlena Giovi (Woman in garage), Roger Michaelson (Passenger #1), Ellen Goffin (Maggie), Robert Miano (Allenby), Yvonne Winter (Sarah Keller), Herb Kay (Bartender), Maria Ford (Satin), Larry Manley (Angel), Channing Chase (Lawyer), Jane Ralston, John David Conti, David Giella, Mike Elliot, Michael Becker, Sharon Fine, Earl Finn

SLUMBER PARTY MASSACRE III (Concorde) Producer/Screenplay, Catherine Cyran; Director, Sally Mattison; Photography, Jügen Baum; Music, Jamie Sheriff; Editor, Tim Amyx; Special Makeup Effects, Dean Jones, Starr Jones; Designer, Stephanie Lytar; Ultra-Stereo; Foto-Kem color; Rated R; 77 minutes; September release. CAST: Keely Christian (Jackie), Brittain Frye (Ken), M. K. Harris (Morgan), David Greenlee (Duncan), Lulu Wilson (Juliette), Maria Ford (Maria), Brandi Burkett (Diane), Hope Marie Carlton (Janine), Maria Claire (Sonia), David Lawrence, Garon Grigsby, Devon Jenkin, Wayne Grace, Marta Kober

DIVING IN (Skouras) Producer, Martin Wiley; Executive Producers, Michael Maurer, Mark Shaw; Director, Strathford Hamilton; Screenplay, Eric Edson; Photography, Hanania Baer; Editor, Marcy Hamilton; Art Director, Marty Bercaw; Music, Paul Buckmaster, Guy Moon; a Creative Edge Films production; Color; Rated PG-13; 92 minutes; September release. CAST: Matt Adler (Wayne), Burt Young (Coach), Matt Lattanzi (Jerome), Kristy Swanson (Terry), Yolande Gilot (Amanda)

TOUCH OF A STRANGER (Raven-Star Pictures) Producers, Hakon Gundersen, Andre Stone Guttfreund; Director, Brad Gilbert; Screenplay, Joslyn Barnes, Brad Gilbert; Photography, Michael Negrin; Music, Jack Alan Goga; Editor, William Goldenberg; Color; Rated R; 87 minutes; September release. CAST: Shelley Winters (Lily), Anthony Nocerino (Jet), Danny Capri (Finny), Haley Taylor-Block (Grocery Girl)

REPOSSESSED (New Line Cinema) Producer, Steve Wizan; Director/Screenplay, Bob Logan; Co-Producer, Jean Higgins; Photography, Michael D. Margulies; Designer, Shay Austin; Editor, Jeff Freeman; Music, Charles Fox; Costumes, Timothy D'Arcy; a Seven Arts release; CFI color; Rated PG-13; 84 minutes; September release. CAST: Linda Blair (Nancy Aglet), Ned Beatty (Ernest Weller), Leslie Nielsen (Father Jedidiah Mayii), Anthony Starke (Father Luke Brophy), Thom J. Sharp (Braydon Aglet), Lana Schwab (Fanny Weller), Benj Thall (Ned Aglet), Dove Dellos (Frieda Aglet), Jacquelyn Masche (Nancy's Mother), Jake Steinfeld, Army Archerd, Jack LaLanne, Wally George, Jesse Ventura, Gene Okerlund (Themselves), Frazier Smith (Announcer)

PERMANENT VACATION (Anthology Film Archives/Indept.) Director/Screenplay/Editor, Jim Jarmusch; Photography, Thomas DiCillo; Music, Jim Jarmusch, John Lurie; 1980; Color; Not rated; 80 minutes; September release. CAST: Chris Parker (Allie), Leila Gastil (Leila), John Lurie (Sax Player), Richard Boes (Veteran), Lisa Rosen (Popcorn Girl), Ruth Bolton (Mother)

HOW TO BE LOUISE (Venus de Mylar Prods.) Producer/Director/Screenplay, Anne Flournoy; Photography, Vladimir Tukan; Music, Phillip Johnston; Editor, Kathleen Earle Killeen; Executive Producer, Mark M. Green; Black and white; Not rated; 82 minutes; September release. CAST: Lea Floden (Louise/Lola), Bruce McCarty (Stanley Fastwalker), Maggie Burke (Pinky), Mark Green (Dad), Lisa Emery (Nancy), Mary Carol Johnson (Sally), Mayda Sharrow (Rita), Michael Moneagle (Uncle Pete), William Zimmer (Uncle Ed), Wanda Pruska (Aunt Barbara), Phil Diaz (Mr. Mendez), Mark Serman (Cafe Waiter), Caroline McCarthy (Baby Louise), Larry Ungarten (Wiseguy), Paul Knox (Beer Thief), Eugene Corey (Lecher), Alice Spivak, Michael Patrick King, Stephen Payne, Dan Bonnell, Josh Pais, Steve Simpson, Steve Ahern

Matt Lattanzi, Burt Young in "Diving In" © *Skouras*

Lea Floden in "How to Be Louise" © *Venus de Mylar*

Robert Guillaume, Jean-Claude Van Damme in "Death Warrant" © *Pathe Entertainment*

Dolph Lundgren in "I Come in Peace" © *Vision p.d.g.*

DEATH WARRANT (MGM) Producer, Mark DiSalle; Director, Deran Sarafian; Screenplay, David S. Goyer; Photography, Russell Carpenter; Designer, Curtis Schnell; Music, Gary Chang; Editors, G. Gregg McLaughlin, John A. Barton; Associate Producer, Andrew G. La Marca; Costumes, Joseph Porro; Casting, Cathy Henderson, Michael Cutler; Stunts, Jeff Imada; from Pathe Entertainment Inc.; Dolby Stereo; Deluxe color; Rated R; 89 minutes; September release. CAST: Jean-Claude Van Damme (Louis Burke), Robert Guillaume (Hawkins), Cynthia Gibb (Amanda Beckett), George Dickerson (Tom Vogler), Art LaFleur (Sgt. DeGraf), Patrick Kilpatrick (Naylor, "The Sandman"), Joshua Miller (Douglas Tisdale), Hank Woessner (Romaker), George Jenesky (Konefke), Jack Bannon (Ben Keane), Abdul Salaam El Razzac (Priest), Armin Shimerman (Dr. Gottesman), John Lantz (Sam Walden), Hans Howes (Keller), Harry Waters, Jr. (Jersey), Dorothy Dells (Helen Vogler), Paulo Tocha (Perez), Carlease Burke (Sgt. Waters), Kamel Krifa (Keel), Al Leong (Bruce), David Erskine, Carlos Cervantes, C. E. Grimes (Inmates), Nick Gambella (Desk Guard), Robert Winley (Tall Convict), Danny Weselis (Scraggly Youth), Rick Allen, George Kmeck, James Hardie (Guards), John DeBello, Gerry Black (Officers), Mark DiSalle (Con Food Server), Richard Duran, Tommy Rosales (Punks)

I COME IN PEACE (Triumph Releasing) Producer, Jeff Young; Co-Producers, Jon Turtle, Rafael Eisenman; Director, Craig R. Baxley; Screenplay, Jonathan Tydor, Leonard Maas, Jr.; Executive Producers, Mark Damon, David Saunders; Photography, Mark Irwin; Designer, Phillip M. Leonard; Music, Jan Hammer; Editor, Mark Helfrich; Associate Producer, Ron Fury; Costumes, Joseph Porro; Casting, Karen Rea; Stunts, Paul Baxley; Makeup Effects, Tony Gardner, Larry Hamlin; a Vision p.d.g. presentation; Ultra-Stereo; Deluxe color; Rated R; 98 minutes; September release. CAST: Dolph Lundgren (Jack Caine), Brian Benben (Laurence Smith), Betsy Brantley (Diane Pallone), Matthias Hues (Bad Alien), Jay Bilas (Good Alien), Jim Haynie (Malone), David Ackroyd (Switzer), Sherman Howard (Victor Manning), Sam Anderson (Warren), Mark Lowenthal (Bruce, the Scientist), Michael J. Pollard (Boner), Jesse Vint (Man in Mercedes), Alex Morris (Ray Turner), Kevin Page, Robert Prentiss (White Boys), Nik Hagler (Bail Bondsman), Tony Brubaker (Garage Sweeper), Mimi Cochran (Mechanic), Matthew Posey, Alexander Johnston (Psychos), Jack Willis (Liquor store owner), Albert Leong (Luggage Salesman), Brandon Smith (Market Clerk), Wayne Dehart (Market Customer), Kevin Howard (Security Guard), Woody Watson (Federal Agent), Luis Lemus (Sgt. Hawkins), Chris Kinkade (Detective), Steve Chizmadia, Sebastian White, Dean Kinkel, David Poynter, Folkert Schmidt, Gary Baxley, Tom Campitelli, Kristin Baxley, Suzanne Savoy, Howard French, Willie Minor, Arienne Battiste, Jack Verbois, Stacey Cortez, Nino Candido

BLOODFIST II (Concorde) Producer, Roger Corman; Director, Andy Blumenthal; Screenplay, Catherine Cyran; Photography, Bruce Dorfman; Music, Nigel Holton; Editor, Karen Joseph; Color; Rated R; 88 minutes; October release. CAST: Don Wilson (Jake Raye), Rina Reyes (Mariella), Joe Mari Avellana (Su), Robert Marius (Dieter), Maurice Smith (Vinny), Tim Baker (Sai Taylor), James Warring (John Jones), Richard Hill (Bobby Rose), Steve Rogers (Ernest), Monsour del Rosario (Tobo Castenerra), Manny Samson (Manny Rivera), Jing Castaneda (Kat), Archie Ramirez (Ricco), Ned Hourani (Mickey Sheehan)

THE NATURAL HISTORY OF PARKING LOTS (Strand Releasing) Producer, Aziz Ghazal; Director/Screenplay/Editor, Everett Lewis; Photography, Hisham Abed; Music, John Hammer; a Little Deer production; Black and white; Not rated; 92 minutes; October release. CAST: Charlie Bean (Chris), B. Wyatt (Lance), Charles Taylor (Sam), Mark Williams (P.O.), Roy Heidicker (Neo-Nazi), Eli Guralnick (Mrs. Porter)

NIGHT OF THE LIVING DEAD (Columbia) Producers, John A. Russo, Russ Streiner; Executive Producers, Menahem Golan, George A. Romero; Co-Executive Producer, Ami Artzi; Director, Tom Savini; Screenplay, George A. Romero; Based on the original screenplay by John A. Russo and George A. Romero; Photography, Frank Prinzi; Designer, Cletus R. Anderson; Editor, Tom Dubensky; Music, Paul McCollough; Special Makeup Effects, John Vulich, Everett Burrell; Costumes, Barbara Anderson; from 21st Century Film Corp.; Ultra-Stereo; TVC color; Rated R; 96 minutes; October release. CAST: Tony Todd (Ben), Patricia Tallman (Barbara), Tom Towles (Harry), McKee Anderson (Helen), William Butler (Tom), Katie Finneran (Judy Rose), Bill Mosley (Johnnie), Heather Mazur (Sarah), David Butler (Hondo), Zachary Mott (Bulldog), Pat Reese (The Mourner), William Cameron (The Newsman), Pat Logan (Uncle Rege), Berle Ellis (The Flaming Zombie), Bill "Chilly Billy" Cardille (T.V. Interviewer), Greg Funk, Tim Carrier, John Hamilton, Dyrk Ashton, Jordan Berlant, Albert Shellhammer, Jay McDowell, Walter Berry, Kendal Kraft, David Grace, Stacie Foster, Charles Crawley

SHAKMA (Quest Entertainment) Producer/Director, Hugh Parks; Co-Director, Tom Logan; Screenplay, Roger Engle; Photography, Andrew Bieber; Music, David C. Williams; Editor, Mike Palma; Art Director, Edward Bennett; Special Makeup Effects, Rick Gonzales; Costumes, Leslie Gilbertson; Ultra-Stereo; TVC color; Rated R; 101 minutes; October release. CAST: Christopher Atkins (Sam), Amanda Wyss (Tracy), Ari Meyers (Kim), Roddy McDowall (Prof. Sorenson), Robb Morris (Gary), Greg Flowers (Richard), Tre Laughlin (Bradley), Ann Kymberlie (Laura), Donna Jarrett (Brenda), Typhoon (Shakma, the baboon)

SONNY BOY (Triumph Releasing) Producer, Ovidio G. Assonitis; Director, Robert Martin Carroll; Screenplay, Graeme Whifler; Photography, Robert D'Ettore Piazzoli; Editor, Claudio Cutry; Music, Carlo Mario Cordio; Theme song, David Carradine; Designer, Mario Molli; a Trans World Entertainment production; Dolby Stereo; Panavision; Color; Rated R; 98 minutes; October release. CAST: David Carradine (Pearl), Paul L. Smith (Slue), Brad Dourif (Weasel), Conrad Janis (Dr. Bender), Sydney Lassick (Charlie), Savina Gersak (Sandy), Alexandra Powers (Rose), Steve Carlisle (Sheriff), Michael Griffin (Sonny Boy)

Tom Towles, Patricia Tallman in "Night of the Living Dead" © *Columbia Pictures*

James Belushi, Michael Caine in "Mr. Destiny"
© *Buena Vista Pictures*

Jackson Sims, Andrew Lee Barrett in "The Kill-Off"
© *Cabriolet*

MR. DESTINY (Touchstone) Producers/Screenplay, James Orr, Jim Cruickshank; Director, James Orr; Executive Producer, Laurence Mark; Co-Producer, Susan B. Landau; Photography, Alex Thomson; Designer, Michael Seymour; Editor, Michael R. Miller; Casting, Risa Bramon, Billy Hopkins, Heidi Levitt; Music, David Newman; Visual Effects, Peter Donen; Costumes, Jane Greenwood; Assistant Director, Craig Huston; Presented in association with Silver Screen Partners IV; Distributed by Buena Vista Pictures; Dolby Stereo; Technicolor; Rated PG-13; 112 minutes; October release. CAST: James Belushi (Larry Burrows), Linda Hamilton (Ellen Burrows), Michael Caine (Mike), Jon Lovitz (Clip Metzler), Hart Bochner (Niles Pender), Bill McCutcheon (Leo Hansen), Rene Russo (Cindy Jo), Jay O. Sanders (Jackie Earle), Maury Chaykin (Guzelman), Pat Corley (Harry Burrows), Douglas Seale (Boswell), Courteney Cox (Jewel Jagger), Doug Barron (Lewis Flick), Jeff Weiss (Ludwig), Tony Longo (Huge Guy), Kathy Ireland (Gina), Andrew Stahl (Jerry Haskins), Bryan Buffinton (Boy), Sari Caine (Girl), Martin Thompson (Guest Stilton), Michael Genevie, Howard Kingkade (Guests), Osamu Sakabe (Nakamura), Eddita Hill (Juanita), Collin Bernsen (Tom Robertson), William Griffis (Maitre D'), John Garver (Waiter), Terry Loughlin (Wine Steward), Adam Eichhorst (Teenager), Jeffrey Pillars (Truck Driver), Richie Devaney (Young Larry), Bruce Evers (Team Coach), Whit Edwards (Young Jerry), Sky Berdahl (Young Clip), Raymond L. Anderson (Umpire), Heather Lynch (Young Ellen), James Douglas (Mr. Ripley), Chris Stacy (Teammate), Jesse J. Donnelly (The Cop)

COMEDY'S DIRTIEST DOZEN (Island) Producer/Creator, Stuart S. Shapiro; Director, Lenny Wong; Executive Producer, Martin Schwartz; Photography, Mark Benjamin; Music, Steve Treccase, Tommy Doucette; an International Harmony production; Color; Not rated; 88 minutes; October release. Documentary featuring Tim Allen, John Fox, Joey Gaynor, Bill Hicks, Stephanie Hodge, Monty Hoffman, Jackie "The Jokeman" Martling, Otto & George, Steven Pearl, Chris Rock, Larry Scarano, Thea Vidale; and Ben Creed (Host)

CORPORATE AFFAIRS (Concorde) Producer, Julie Corman; Director, Terence H. Winkless; Screenplay, Terence H. Winkless, Geoffrey Baere; Photography, Ricardo Jacques Gale; Costumes, Greg LaVoi; Designer, Adam Leventhal; Music, Jeff Winkless; Editor, Karen Horn; Ultra-Stereo; Fotokem color; Rated 85 minutes; October release. CAST: Peter Scolari (Simon Tanner), Mary Crosby (Jessica Pierce), Richard Herd (Cyrus Kindred), Ken Kercheval (Arthur Strickland), Chris Lemmon (Doug Franco), Lisa Moncure (Carolyn Bean),

Mary Crosby, Peter Scolari in "Corporate Affairs" © *Concorde*

Charlie Stratton (Peter McNally), Kim Gillingham (Ginny Malmquist), Frank Roman (Buster Santana), Sharon McNight (Astrid Hasselstein), Bryan Cranston (Darren), Jeanne Sal (Sandy), Shad Davis (Messenger), Ria Coyne (Mistress), Julie Glucksman (Miss Whitney), Jamie McNary (Impudent Co-ed), Lisa Gressett (Savvy Co-ed), Terence Henry (Party Hound), Steve Tannen (Security Guard), Elena Sahagun (Stacy), Devon Pierce (Lucy), Terri LeTenoux (Consuela), Chantal Marcks (Kimberly), Jeff Winkless (Businessman), Bill Frenzer, Stephen Davies, David Rich, Clay Frohman, Nicole Tocantins, Tony Snigoff, Patrick J. Statham, Peter Exline, Charles Z. Cohen, Christina Veronica

THE KILL-OFF (Cabriolet) Producer, Lydia Dean Pilcher; Executive Producers, Alexander W. Kogen, Jr., Barry Tucker; Director/Screenplay, Maggie Greenwald; Based on the novel by Jim Thompson; Photography, Declan Quinn; Music, Evan Lurie; Designer, Pamela Woodbridge; Editor, James Y. Kwei; Casting, Judy Claman; Costumes, Daryl Kerrigan; Technicolor; Rated R; 110 minutes; October release. CAST: Loretta Gross (Luane), Jackson Sims (Pete), Steve Monroe (Ralph), Cathy Haase (Danny Lee), Andrew Lee Barrett (Bobbie), Jordan Fox (Myra), William Russell (Rags), Sean O'Sullivan (Doctor), Ellen Kelly (Lily), Ralph Graff (Lily's Brother), Jim Woyt, Cesar Pares, Mike Towstik (Bar Regulars), Bill Busto (Policeman), Spencer Neyland (Dancing Drums)

THE MAN INSIDE (New Line Cinema) Producer, Philippe Diaz; Director/Screenplay/Executive Producer, Bobby Roth; Photography, Ricardo Aronovitch; Art Director, Didier Naert; Music, Tangerine Dream; Editor, Luce Grunewaldt; Color; Rated PG; 93 minutes; October release. CAST: Jurgen Prochnow (Gunter Wallraff), Peter Coyote (Henry Tobel), Nathalie Baye (Christine), Dieter Laser (Leonard Schroeter), Monique Van De Ven (Tina Wallraff), Philip Anglim (Rolf Gruel), Henry G. Sanders (Evans), James Laurenson (Mueller), Sylvie Granotier (Kathy Heller), Hippolyte Girardot (Rudolph Schick), Joseph Sheridan (Karl), Philippe Leroy-Beaulieu (Borges), Christine Murillo (Angela), Barbara Williams (Julie Brandt), Florence Pernel (Angel), Sophie Sperlich (Esher Wallraff), Dieter Prochnow (Franz Messer), Jean-Michel Dagory (Eduardo), Nicole Casey (Rose Wallraff), Rene Bazinet (Herbert Stroh), Gert Haucke (Heinz Herbert Schultz), Marion Stalens (Sarah), Manfred Andrae (Hermes Brauner), Gunter Meisner (Judge), Alfred Urankar (Foreman), Nils Tavernier (Klamph), Jochen Kolenda, Laszlio I. Kish (State Security Men), Bruno Tendera (Light Haired Man in car), Nanouk Broche (Optometrist), Andre Lacombe (Fritz Hegenberg), Oliver Loisdeau (Schick's Assassin), Philippe Mercier (Torture Victim), Horst Scheel, Jacques Alric, Necati Sahin, Fernand Guiot, Mark Zak, Ivan Kharitonoff, Walter Gontermann, Pierre-Alain Chapuis, Geoffrey Lawrence Carey, Pascal Aron, Ernst Petry

ETERNITY (Paul Entertainment) Executive Producers, Hank Paul, Dorothy Koster Paul; Director, Steven Paul; Screenplay, Jon Voight, Steven Paul, Dorothy Koster Paul; Photography, John Lambert; Music, Michel Legrand; Editors, Christopher Greenbury, Peter Zinner, Michael Sheridan; Designer, Martin Zboril; Ultra-Stereo; Crest color; Rated R; 125 minutes; October release. CAST: Jon Voight (James/Edward), Armand Assante (Sean/Roni), Eileen Davidson (Valerie/Dahlia), Wilford Brimley (Eric/King), Kaye Ballard (Selma/Sabrina), Joey Villa (Spinelli/Jester), Steven Keats (Harold/Tax Collector), Lainie Kazan (Bernice/Mother), Eugene Roche (Governor/Ridley), Robert Carricart (Domingo/Grandpa), Charles Knapp (Judge/Tax Collector), Frankie Valli (Guido/Taxpayer), John P. Ryan (Prosecutor/Thomas), Charles Dierkop (Video Editor), Steven Paul (Stage Manager), Perri Lister, Jilly Rizzo

Peter Coyote, Jurgen Prochnow in "The Man Inside"
© *New Line Cinema*

Moon Zappa, David Cassidy in "The Spirit of 76"
© *Black Diamond Prods.*

STEPHEN KING'S GRAVEYARD SHIFT (Paramount) Producers, William J. Dunn, Ralph S. Singleton; Executive Producers, Bonnie Sugar, Larry Sugar; Director, Ralph S. Singleton; Screenplay, John Esposito, based on the short story by Stephen King; Photography, Peter Stein; Designer, Gary Wissner; Visual Consultant, Harold Michelson; Costumes, Sarah Lemire; Editors, Jim Gross, Randy Jon Morgan; Associate Producers, Joan V. Singleton, Anthony Labonte; Music, Anthony Marinelli, Brian Banks; Dolby Stereo; Color; Rated R; 87 minutes; October release. CAST: David Andrews (John Hall), Kelly Wolf (Jane Wisconsky), Stephen Macht (Warwick), Brad Dourif (Tucker Cleveland), Andrew Divoff (Danson), Vic Polizos (Brogan), Robert Alan Beuth (Ippeston), Ilona Margolis (Nardello), Jimmy Woodard (Carmichael), Jonathan Emerson (Jason Reed), Minor Rootes (Stevenson), Kelly L. Goodman (Mill Secretary)

SOULTAKER (Action Intl. Pictures) Producers, Eric Parkinson, Connie Kingrey; Director, Michael Rissi; Screenplay, Vivian Schilling; Story, Vivian Schilling, Eric Parkinson; Photography, James A. Rosenthal; Music, Jon McCallum; Editor, Jason Coleman, Michael Rissi; a Pacific West Entertainment Group production in association with Victory Pictures; Image Transform & Crest color; Rated R; 95 minutes; October release. CAST: Joe Estevez (Soultaker), Vivian Schilling (Natalie), Gregg Thomsen (Zach Taylor), Robert Z'dar (Angel of Death), David Shark (Brad), Chuck Williams (Tommy), Jean Reiner, David Fawcett, Gary Kohler, Dave Scott

THE SPIRIT OF 76 (Columbia) Producers, Susie Landau, Simon Edery; Director/Screenplay, Lucas Reiner; Story, Roman Coppola, Lucas Reiner; Executive Producers, Roman Coppola, Fred Fuchs; Photography, Stephen Lighthill; Designer, Daniel Talpers; Music, David Nichtern; Costumes, Sofia Coppola; Editor, Glen Scantlebury; Visual Effects, Dan Kohne; Casting, Susie Landau; a Black Diamond production, a Commercial Pictures production; Dolby Stereo; Deluxe color; Rated PG-13; 82 minutes; October release. CAST: David Cassidy (Adam-11), Olivia D'Abo (Chanel-6), Geoff Hoyle (Heinz-57), Leif Garrett (Eddie Trojan), Jeff McDonald (Chris), Steve McDonald (Tommy), Martin Von Haselberg, Brian Routh (Agents 1 & 2), Liam O'Brien (Rodney Snodgrass), Barbara Bain (Hipster), Julie Brown (Ms. Liberty), Tommy Chong (Stoner), DEVO (Ministers of Knowledge), Don Novello (Translator), Carl Reiner (Dr. Von Mobil), Rob Reiner (Dr. Cash), Moon Zappa (Cheryl Dickman), Iron Eyes Cody (Himself), Nancye Ferguson (Nurse), Ann Block (Chris' Mom), Charles Dean (Chris' Dad), Maud Winchester (Cyndi the Waitress),

Lorri Holt (Cop #1), Jerry Carlton (Streaker), Shelby Chong (Cashier), Todd A. Rolle (Clovis), Tree (Guard), Lucas Reiner (Fireworks Barker), Michael McShane (Angry Driver), Morgan Upton (Teacher), Ryan Wallace (Chester), Lisa Houston (Heckler), Leigh French (Voice of the Future)

ALLIGATOR EYES (Castle Hill) Producer, John Feldman, Ken Schwenker; Director/Screenplay, John Feldman; Photography, Todd Crockett; Executive Producer, David Marlow; Co-Executive Producer, Jo Manuel; Music, Sheila Silver; Editors, John Feldman, Cynthia Rogers, Mike Frisino; a Laughing Man Partnership presentation; Color; Rated R; 95 minutes; November release. CAST: Annabelle Larsen (Pauline), Roger Kabler (Robbie), Mary McLain (Marjorie), Allen McCullough (Lance), John MacKay (Dr. Peterson), Cyrece Dyonn (Pauline's Mother), Theodora "Teddi" Tarnoff (Pauline as a child), Terri Chale (Woman with dog), Cindi Wyatt, Donna Cannon (Chickenettes), John Lawrence (Man with dog at motel), John Patrick Rice (Man in bed), Alan Spaulding (Assailant), Diane DiBernardo (Nurse), Julia Eller (Motel Clerk), David McLawhorn (Captain Mack), John Feldman (Ted Bradford), Scotty Elliott (Randy), John B. Berry (Tractor Driver), Sheila Silver, Mike Frisino (Passengers on ferry)

STAGES (Paul-Thompson Films) Producer/Director/Music, Randy Thompson; Screenplay, Randy Thompson, Ron Reid, Dan Lishner; Photography, William Brooks Baum; Color; Not rated; 114 minutes; November release. CAST: Ron Reid (Doug Atkin), Dan Lishner (Brock Mason), Randy Thompson (Andy Miller), Mayme Paul-Thompson (Charlie McKnight)

MUHAMMAD ALI, THE GREATEST (Films Paris) Director/Photography, William Klein; Presented by the Walker Art Center; 1974; Color/black and white; Not rated; 120 minutes; November release. Documentary

OTHELLO (Rockbottom/Uptown Films) Producer, Katherine A. Kaspar; Executive Producer/Director/Adaptation, Ted Lange; Based on the play by William Shakespeare; Photography/Supervising Producer, James M. Swain; Music, Domenick Allen, Tom Borten; Editor, Tim Tobin; Designer, Christine Remsen; CFI color; Not rated; 123 minutes; November release. CAST: Ted Lange (Othello), Hawthorne James (Iago), Mary Otis (Desdemona), Domenick Allen (Cassio), Dawn Comer (Emilia), Marina Palmier (Bianca), Stuart Rogers (Roderigo), David Kozubel, Ben Schick, John Serembe, Nelson Handel, Darryl Wright, Christa Marcione

David Andrews in "Graveyard Shift" © *Graveyard Inc.*

Annabelle Larsen in "Alligator Eyes" © *Castle Hill Prods.*

Ruben Blades, Maria Conchita Alonso, Danny Glover in
"Predator 2" © *20th Century Fox*

Erik Estrada, Dona Speir in "Guns" © *Andy Sidaris*

ROUTE ONE/USA (Interama) Director/Photography, Robert Kramer; Music, Barre Phillips; Editors, Guy Lecorne, Robert Kramer, Pierre Choukroun, Claire Laville, Keja Kramer; Produced by Les Films d'Ici/LA SEPT/Channel Four/RAI 3; Color; Not rated; 255 minutes; November release. Documentary

PREDATOR 2 (20th Century Fox) Producers, Lawrence Gordon, Joel Silver, John Davis; Director, Stephen Hopkins; Screenplay, Jim Thomas, John Thomas; Photography, Peter Levy; Designer, Lawrence G. Paull; Executive Producers, Michael Levy, Lloyd Levin; Editor, Mark Goldblatt; Music, Alan Silvestri; Costumes, Marilyn Vance-Straker; Casting, Jackie Burch, Ferne Cassel; Co-Producers, Tom Joyner, Terry Carr; Associate Producer, Suzanne Todd; Assistant Director, Josh McLaglen; Dolby Stereo; Deluxe color; Rated R; 108 minutes; December release. CAST: Danny Glover (Harrigan), Gary Busey (Keyes), Rubén Blades (Danny), Maria Conchita Alonso (Leona), Bill Paxton (Jerry), Robert Davi (Heinemann), Adam Baldwin (Garber), Kent McCord (Capt. Pilgrim), Kevin Peter Hall (The Predator), Morton Downey, Jr. (Pope), Calvin Lockhart (King Willie), Steve Kahan (Sgt.), Henry Kingi (El Scorpio), Elpidia Carrillo (Anna), Corey Rand (Ramon Vega), Lilyan Chauvin (Irene Edwards), Michael Mark Edmondson (Gold Tooth), Teri Weigel (Columbian Girl), William R. Perry (Subway Gang Leader), Alex Chapman, Gerard G. Williams, John Cann, Michael Papajohn (Subway Gang), Lou Eppolito (Patrolman), Charlie Haugk (Charlie), Sylvia Kauders (Ruth), Charles David Richards (Commuter), Julian Reyes (Juan Beltran), Casey Sander, Pat Skipper, Carmine Zozzora (Federal Team), Valerie Karasek, Chuck Boyd, David Starwalt, Abraham Alvarez, Jim Ishida, George Christy, Lucinda Weist (Reporters), Richard Anthony Crenna, Billy "Sly" Williams (Paramedics), Paulo Tocha, Nick Corri (Detectives), DeLynn Binzel (Hooker), Tom Finnegan, Patience Moore (Officers), Kashka, Jeffrey Reed (Jamaicans), Carl Pistilli (Cop on phone), Vonte Sweet (Sweet), Ron Moss (Jerome), Brian Levinson (Anthony), Diana James (Leona's Friend), Beth Kanar (Officer), Paul Abascal, Michael Wiseman (Cops)

EATING (International Rainbow Pictures) Producer, Judith Wolinsky; Director/Screenplay, Henry Jaglom; Photography, Hanania Baer; Editors, Michelle Hart, Mary Pritchard; a Jagfilm; Deluxe color; Not rated; 110 minutes; November release. CAST: Nelly Alard (Martine), Frances Bergen (Mrs. Williams), Mary Crosby (Kate), Marlena Giovi (Sadie), Marina Gregory (Lydia), Daphna Kastner (Jennifer), Elizabeth Kemp (Nancy), Lisa Richards (Helene), Gwen Welles (Sophie), Toni Basil (Jackie), Savannah Smith Bouchér (Eloise),

Claudia Brown (Gabby), Rachelle Carson (Cathy), Anne E. Curry (Cory), Donna Germain (Gerri), Beth Grant (Bea), Aloma Ichinose (Maria), Taryn Power (Anita), Jacquelin Woolsey (Milly)

GUNS (Malibu Bay Films) Producer, Arlene Sidaris; Director/ Screenplay, Andy Sidaris; Photography, Howard Wexler; Designer, Cherie Day Ledwith; Music, Richard Lyons; Editor, Michael Haight; Costumes, Rina Eliashiv; Stunts, James Lew; Ultra-Stereo; Filmservice color; Rated R; 95 minutes; November release. CAST: Erik Estrada (Jack of Diamonds), Dona Speir (Donna Hamilton), Roberta Vasquez (Nicole Justin), Bruce Penhall (Bruce Christian), Cynthia Brimhall (Edy Stark), William Bumiller (Lucas), Devin Devasquez (Cash), Michael Shane (Shane Abilene), Phyllis Davis (Kathryn Hamilton), Chuck McCann (Abe), Chu Chu Malave (Cubby), Richard Cansino (Tito), George Kee Cheung (Sifu), Danny Trejo (Tong), Rodrigo Obregon (Large Marge), John Brown (Brown), Kym Malin (Kym), Liv Lindeland (Ace), Lisa London (Rocky), Donna Spangler (Hugs Huggins), Allegra Curtis (Robyn), Rustam Branaman (Rustam), Jeff Silverman (Ramon), Drew Sidaris (The California Kid), James Lew, Eric Chen (Ninjas), Cynthia Bardi (Joan), Caron Leslie, Kelley Menighan, Paul Matthews, Todd Dos Reis, Diane K. Shah, Ans Scott, Thad Camara, Dave Hadder, David Grossman

LITTLE VEGAS (I.R.S. Releasing) Producer, Peter MacGregor-Scott; Director/Screenplay, Perry Lang; Photography, King Baggot; Executive Producer, Harold Welb; Designer, Michael Hartog; Costumes, Cynthia Flint; Editor, John Tintori; Casting, Junie Lowry; Music, Mason Daring; Assistant Director, Kelly Schroeder; a MacLang Film; Deluxe color; Rated R; 90 minutes; November release. CAST: Anthony John Denison (Carmine), Catherine O'Hara (Lexie), Anne Francis (Martha), Michael Nouri (Frank), Perry Lang (Steve), P. J. Ochlan (Max), John Sayles (Mike), Bruce McGill (Harvey), Jay Thomas (Bobby), Sam McMurray (Kreimach), Michael Talbott (Linus), Ronald G. Joseph (Cecil), Jerry Stiller (Sam), Kamaron Harper (Phyllis), Jessica James (Grace), Laurie Thompson (Bethanne), A. J. Pirri (Pancho), Marit Fotland (Cecil's Girl), Carmine Zozzora (Geno), M. Jennifer Evans (Charity), Max Vogler (Waiter), Dante DiLoreto (Doctor), Linus Huffman (Burly Man)

ANTIGONE/RITES FOR THE DEAD (ASA Communications) Producer/Director/Screenplay/Choreographer, Amy Greenfield; Based on the plays *Antigone* and *Oedipus at Colonus* by Sophocles; Photography, Hilary Harris, Judy Irola; Editors, Amy Greenfield, Bernard

Frances Bergen, Nelly Alard in "Eating"
© *International Rainbow*

Perry Lang, Catherine O'Hara in "Little Vegas" © *I.R.S.*

162

Steve James in "Street Hunter" © *21st Century Prods.*

James Shigeta, France Nuyen in "China Cry"
© *TBN Films*

Hajdenberg; Music, Glenn Branca, Diamanda Galas, Paul Lemos, Elliott Sharp, David Van Tieghem; Costumes, Betty Howard, Jane Townsend; an Eclipse production; Duart/TVC color; Not rated; 85 minutes; November release. CAST: Amy Greenfield (Antigone), Bertram Ross (Oedipus/Creon), Janet Eilber (Ismene), Sean McElory (Haemon), Henry Montes (Polynices), Silvio Facchin (Eteocles)

STREET HUNTER (DGP/21st Century Films) Producer, David Gil; Director, John A. Gallagher; Screenplay, John A. Gallagher, Steve James; Photography, Phil Parmet; Music, Dana Walden, Barry Fasman; Editor, Mary Hickey; Casting, Judy Henderson, Alycia Aumuller; Designer, John Paino; Stunts, Phil Neilson; TVC color; Rated R; 93 minutes; November release. CAST: Steve James (Logan Blade), Reb Brown (Col. Walsh), John Leguizamo (Angel), Valarie Pettiford (Denise), Frank Vincent (Don Mario Romano), Tom Wright (Rilely), Richie Havens (Daze), Richard Panebianco (Louis Romano), Sam Coppola (Jannelli), Thom Christopher (Wellman), Emilio Del Pozo (Rivera), Victor Colicchio (Mustache Diablo), Nelson Vasquez (Vasquez), Anthony Powers (Benny), Ralph Marrero (Eddie), Carlos Laucho (Hector), Tony V (Jamie), K. Todd Freeman (Pretzel), Michael Jefferson (Wilson), Peter Buccosi (Armando), Jay Hargrove (Veteran Cop), Chloe Amateau (Rookie Cop), Tracy Jabara (Girl at bar), Garry Blackwood, Ron Castellano (Don Mario's Bodyguards), Adriana Dasby, Stephanie Ryan (Eddie's Girls), Paul Buccosi, Angel Elon, Joe Fitos, Lance Guecia, Jeffrey Iorio, Anthony McGowan, Gary Tacon, Norman Douglass, George E. Sanchez, Edgard Mourino, Maxamillion Olivas, Terry Golden, David Lomax, Bernard Lunon, Dominic Marcus, Andy Nichols, Elliot Santiago, Manny Siverio, Jeff Ward, Andy Duppin (Diablos)

CHILD'S PLAY 2 (Universal) Producer/Chucky Doll Creator, David Kirschner; Director, John Lafia; Screenplay, Don Mancini; Co-Producer, Laura Moskowitz; Executive Producer, Robert Latham Brown; Photography, Stefan Czapsky; Designer, Ivo Cristante; Editor, Edward Warschilka; Music, Graeme Revell; Chucky Designed and Engineered by Kevin Yagher; Costumes, Pamela Skaist; Casting, Karen Rea; Dolby Stereo; Deluxe color; Rated R; 95 minutes; November release. CAST: Alex Vincent (Andy Barclay), Jenny Agutter (Joanne Simpson), Gerrit Graham (Phil Simpson), Christine Elise (Kyle), Brad Dourif (Voice of Chucky), Grace Zabriskie (Grace Poole), Peter Haskell (Sullivan), Beth Grant (Miss Kettlewell), Greg Germann (Mattson), Raymond Singer (Social Worker), Charles C. Meshack (Van Driver), Stuart Mabray (Homicide Investigator), Matt Roe

(Policeman in car), Herb Braha (Liquor Store Clerk), Don Pugsley, Ed Krieger, Vince Melocchi (Technicians), Edan Gross (Voice of Tommy doll), Adam Ryen (Rick Spires), Adam Wylie (Sammy), Bill Stevenson (Adam)

CHINA CRY (Penland) Producer, Don LeRoy Parker; Director/Screenplay, James F. Collier; Based on the book by Nora Lam and Matt Crouch; Photography, David Worth; Music, Al Kasha, Joel Hirschhorn; Editor, Duane Hartzell; Designer, Norman Baron; Executive Producer, Paul F. Crouch; Costumes, Gigi Choa; Line Producer, Robert Smawley; a TBN Films presentation of a Parakletos production; CFI color; Rated PG-13; 107 minutes; November release. CAST: Julia Nickson-Soul (Sung Neng Yee), Russell Wong (Lam Cheng Shen), James Shigeta (Dr. Sung), France Nuyen (Mrs. Sung), Philip Tan (Col. Cheng), Elizabeth Sung (The Interrogator), Bennett Ohta (Labor Camp Doctor), Lloyd Kino (Police Captain), Lau Lee Foon (Young Neng Yee), Chau Fung Bing (Governess), Daphne Cheung (Chung Sing), Catherine Dao (Ling Mei), Jane Chung (Fortune Teller), Dennis Chan (University Professor), Ernest Kwan (Yau Lit Bing), Angelina Law (Eric Yuen), Angela Yu (Chan Lap Run), James Lew (Kickboxer Instructor), Bill Lee (Police Clerk), Alice Lo (Chemistry Teacher), John Hugh (Eldest Lam Brother), Lily Leung (Mrs. Lam), Leung Wai Lin (Maid), Sandie Yeung (Tutor), Ho Pak Kwong (Gardener), Lee Hung (Chauffeur), Chak Wan Keung (Motorcycle Soldier), David Ho (Pastor), Michael Lee, Ralph Ahn, Masami Saito, Tad Horino

AMERICAN BLUE NOTE (Panorama Entertainment) Producer/Director, Ralph Toporoff; Screenplay, Gilbert Girion; Story, Ralph Toporoff, Gilbert Girion; Photography, Joey Forsyte; Music, Larry Schanker; Editor, Jack Haigis; Technicolor; Rated PG-13; 97 minutes; November release. CAST: Peter MacNicol (Jack), Carl Capotorto (Jerry), Tim Guinee (Bobby), Bill Christopher-Myers (Lee), Jonathan Walker (Tommy), Charlotte d'Amboise (Benita), Trini Alvarado (Lorraine), Louis Guss, Zohra Lampert, Eddie Jones, Sam Behrens

COMPLEX WORLD (Heartbreak Hits) Producers, Geoff Adams, Rich Lupo, Dennis Maloney; Executive Producer, Rich Lupo; Director/Screenplay, James Wolpaw; Photography, Dennis Maloney; Music, Stephen Snyder; Editor, Steven Gentile; Color/black and white; Not rated; 81 minutes; November release. CAST: Stanley Matis (Morris Brock), Dan Welch (Jeff Burgess), Margot Dionne (Gilda), Daniel von Bargen (Malcolm), Bob Owczarek (Robert Burgess), Captain Lou Albano (Boris Lee), Andrew Mutnick, The Young Adults, NRBQ, Roomful of Blues

Christine Elise, Grace Zabriskie in "Child's Play 2"
© *Universal City Studios*

Peter MacNicol, Charlotte d'Ambroise in "American Blue Note"
© *Fakebook Prods.*

163

Nathan Purdee in "Return of Superfly" © *Triton Pictures*

John Hurt, Raul Julia in "Frankenstein Unbound"
© *20th Century Fox*

DISTURBED (Live Entertainment/Odyssey Distributors) Producer, Brad Wyman; Director, Charles Winkler; Screenplay, Emerson Bixby, Charles Winkler; Photography, Bernd Heinl; Music, Steven Scott Smalley; Editor, David Handman; Designer, Marek Dobrowolski; Costumes, Pia Dominiquez; Casting, Tony Markes; Color; Rated R; 96 minutes; November release. CAST: Malcolm McDowell (Dr. Russell), Geoffrey Lewis (Michael), Priscilla Pointer (Nurse Francine), Pamela Gidley (Sandy Ramirez), Irwin Keyes (Pat Tuel), Clint Howard (Brian)

THE RETURN OF SUPERFLY (Triton Pictures) Producers, Sig Shore, Anthony Wisdom; Executive Producers, Rudy Cohen, Jon Goldwater; Director, Sig Shore; Screenplay, Anthony Wisdom; Photography, Anghel Decca; Music, Curtis Mayfield; Editor, John Mullen; Designer, Jeremie Frank; a Crash Pictures production; Precision Film Lab color; Rated R; 95 minutes; November release. CAST: Nathan Purdee (Priest), Margaret Avery (Francine), Leonard Thomas (Joey), Christopher Curry (Tom Perkins), Carlos Carrasco (Hector), Sam Jackson (Nate Cabot), Luis Ramos (Manuel), Kirk Taylor (Renaldo), David Groh (Inspector Wolinski), John Gabriel (Sarge Joyner), Tico Wells (Willy), Patrice Ablack (Irene), Arnold Mazer (Marty Ryan), Eric Payne (Security Guard), Ruthanna Graves (Jasmine Jackson), David Weinberg (DEA Officer), John Patrick Hayden (Ike—Cop #1), Joe Spataro (Mike—Cop #2), Timothy Stickney (Rasta Cab Driver), Eric Griffin, Stanley Mathis, Angel Ramirez (Dealers), Bill Corsair (Lt. Kinsella), John Canada Terrell (Det. Loomey), Hollis Granville, Charles Padem, Merrault Almoner (Policemen), Douglas Wade (Bartender—Mr. Bee's), Gregory Cook, Tye Pierson, Sonia Hensley, Randy Frazier, Ronny Clanton, Lisa Jolliff, Oscar Colon, Rynel Johnson, Maxine Harrison, Sixto Sanchez

H-2 WORKER (First Run Features) Producer/Director, Stephanie Black; Photography, Maryse Alberti; Editor, John Mullen; presented in association with Valley Filmworks; Duart color; Not rated; November release. Documentary.

ROBOT JOX (Triumph Releasing) Producer, Albert Band; Director/Story, Stuart Gordon; Screenplay, Joe Haldeman; Executive Producer, Charles Band; Photography, Mac Ahlberg; Designer, Giovanni Natalucci; Editor, Ted Nicolaou, Lori Scott Ball; Music, Frederic Talgorn; Visual Effects, David Allen; Associate Producer, Frank Hildebrand; an Empire Pictures presentation; Ultra-Stereo; Color; Rated PG; 85

minutes; November release. CAST: Gary Graham (Achilles), Anne-Marie Johnson (Athena), Paul Koslo (Alexander), Robert Sampson (Commissioner Jameson), Danny Kamekona (Dr. Matsumoto), Hilary Mason (Prof. Laplace), Michael Alldredge (Tex Conway), Jeffrey Combs, Michael Saad (Proles), Ian Patrick Williams (Phillip), Jason Marsden (Tommy), Carolyn Purdy-Gordon (Kate), Thyme Lewis (Sargon), Gary Houston (Sportscaster), Russel Case (Hercules), Geoffrey Coplestone (Confederation Commissioner), Jacob Wheeler, Del Russel (Technicians), Larry Dolgin (Head Referee), David Cameron (Ajax), Hal Yomanouchi, Alex Vitale, Luca Amitrano (Tubies), Jenai Ricci, Matteo Barzini, Jillian Gordon, Suzanna Gordon, Wayne Brewer, John Shannon, James Sampson, Steve Pelot, Bruce McGuire, Mark D'Auria, Claire Hardwick, Marisa Menkins, Michael Vermaaten, Sung Yee Tchao

ROGER CORMAN'S FRANKENSTEIN UNBOUND (20th Century Fox) Producers, Roger Corman, Thom Mount, Kabi Jaeger; Director, Roger Corman; Screenplay, Roger Corman, F. X. Feeney, based on the novel by Brian W. Aldiss; Photography, Armando Nannuzzi, Michael Scott; Designer, Enrico Tovaglieri; Costumes, Franca Zuchelli; Music, Carl Davis; Editors, Jay Cassidy, Mary Bauer; Special Visual Effects, Illusion Arts, Syd Dutton, Bill Taylor; Special Makeup Effects/Monster Design, Nick Dudman; Casting, Caro Jones; Associate Producers, Laura Medina, Jay Cassidy; a Mount Co. production; Ultra-Stereo; Deluxe color; Rated R; 85 minutes; November release. CAST: John Hurt (Dr. Joe Buchanan), Raul Julia (Dr. Frankenstein), Bridget Fonda (Mary Godwin), Nick Brimble (Frankenstein Monster), Catherine Rabett (Elizabeth), Jason Patric (Lord Byron), Michael Hutchence (Percy Shelley), Catherine Corman (Justine), Mickey Knox (General), Terri Treas (Voice of car)

STEEL & LACE (Fries/Paragon Arts) Producers, John Schouweiler, David DeCoteau; Director, Ernest Farino; Screenplay, Joseph Dougherty, Dave Edison; Photography, Thomas L. Callaway; Music, John Massari; Editor, Chris Roth; Designer, Blair Martin; a Cinema Home Video production; Foto-Kem color; Rated R; 90 minutes; November release. CAST: Clare Wren (Gaily), Bruce Davison (Albert), Stacy Haiduk (Alison), David Naughton (Det. Dunn), Michael Cerveris (Daniel), Scott Burkholder (Tobby), Paul Lieber (Oscar), Brian Backer (Norman), John J. York (Craig), Nick Tate (Duncan), David L. Lander (Schumann), John DeMita, Brenda Swanson, Cindy Brooks, Hank Garrett, Beverly Mickins, William Prince, Mary Boucher, Dave Edison

Paul Koslo, Gary Graham in "Robot Jox" © *Empire Ent.*

Michael Cerveris, Brian Backer in "Steel & Lace"
© *Paragon Arts/Fries*

Megan Milner, John Travolta, Lorne Sussman in "Look Who's Talking Too" © Tri-Star Pictures

Peter Berg, Michelle Johnson, Terence Stamp in "Genuine Risk" © I.R.S.

LOOK WHO'S TALKING TOO (Tri-Star) Producer, Jonathan D. Krane; Director, Amy Heckerling; Screenplay, Amy Heckerling, Neal Israel; Co-Producer, Bob Gray; Photography, Thomas Del Ruth; Designer, Reuben Freed; Editor, Debra Chiate; Costumes, Molly Maginnis; Music, David Kitay; Casting, Stuart Aikins; Assistant Director, Bill Mizel; Dolby Stereo; Technicolor; Rated PG-13; 81 minutes; December release. CAST: John Travolta (James), Kirstie Alley (Mollie), Olympia Dukakis (Rosie), Elias Koteas (Stuart), Twink Caplan (Rona), Bruce Willis (Voice of Mikey), Roseanne Barr (Voice of Julie), Damon Wayans (Voice of Eddie), Gilbert Gottfried (Joey), Mel Brooks (Voice of Mr. Toilet Man), Lorne Sussman (Mikey), Megan Milner (Julie—1 yr.), Georgia Keithley (Julie—4 months), Nikki Graham (Julie—newborn), Danny Pringle (Eddie), Louis Heckerling (Lou), Neal Israel (Mr. Ross), Lesley Ewen (Debbie), Noëlle Parker, Douglas Warhit (Clients), Terry David Mulligan (IRS Inspector), Paul Shaffer (Taxi Businessman), Don S. Davis (Dr. Fleischer), Morris Panych (Arrogant Businessman), Alex Bruhanski (Needle Doctor), Dorothy Fehr (Blonde), Heather Lea Gerdes (Hot Babe on fire escape), Robin Trapp (Cool Chick), Rick Avery (Burglar), Steven Dimopoulos (Fire Chief), James Galeota (Punk Baby), Frank Totino (Candy Man), Coleman Lumley (Blonde Baby), Constance Barnes McCansh (Sexy Dancer), Janet Munro (Businessman's Babe), Mollie Israel (Mikey's Dream Friend), Alicia Mizel (Slob Child)

THE END OF INNOCENCE (Skouras) Producers, Thom Tyson, Vince Cannon; Director/Screenplay, Dyan Cannon; Executive Producer, Leonard Rabinowitz; Co-Executive Producer, Stanley Fimberg; Photography, Alex Nepomniaschy; Designer, Paul Eads; Costumes, Carole Little; Editor, Bruce Cannon; Music, Michael Convertino; Song: "Everlasting Joy" by Sandra & Andre Crouch; an O.P.V. Productions presentation; Color; Rated R; 102 minutes; December release. CAST: Dyan Cannon (Stephanie Lewis), John Heard (Dean), George Coe (Dad), Lola Mason (Mom), Rebecca Schaeffer (Stephanie—18 yrs.), Steve Meadows (Michael), Billie Bird (Mrs. Yabledablov), Dennis Burkley (Tiny), Viveka Davis (Honey), Eric Harrison (Sister), Stoney Jackson (Leroy), Paul Lieber (Rabbi), Michael Madsen (Earl), Madge Sinclair (Nurse Bowlin), Renee Taylor (Angel)

GENUINE RISK (I.R.S. Releasing) Producers, Larry J. Rattner, Guy J. Louthan, William Ewart; Executive Producers, Miles A. Copeland III, Paul Colichman; Director/Screenplay, Kurt Voss; Story, Larry Rattner, Kurt Voss; Photography, Dean Lent; Designer, Elisabeth A. Scott; Costumes, Angela Balogh-Calin; Editor, Christopher Koefoed; Casting, Don Pemrick, Jeff Gerrard; Music, Deborah Holland; Ultra-Stereo; Color; Rated R; 89 minutes; December release. CAST: Terence Stamp (Paul Hellwart), Peter Berg (Henry), Michelle Johnson (Girl), M. K. Harris (Cowboy Jack), Teddy Wilson (Billy), Sid Haig (Curly), Max Perlich (Chris Woodbury), Hal Shafer (Loren), Joe Shea (Lyman), Jeffrey Arbaugh (J. J. Birke), John Lavachielli (Tall Thug), George Fisher, Tony Cecere (Thugs), Steven Brill (Jimmy), Michael Deluna (Restaurant Assassin), Richard Haje (Pool Player), Ellen Albertini Dow (Receptionist)

ALMOST AN ANGEL (Paramount) Producer/Director, John Cornell; Screenplay/Executive Producer, Paul Hogan; Photography, Russell Boyd; Designer, Henry Bumstead; Editor, David Stiven; Costumes, April Ferry; Music, Maurice Jarre; Song: "Some Wings" by Maurice Jarre (music) and Ray Underwood (lyrics)/performed by Vanessa Williams; Associate Producer/Assistant Director, Mark Turnbull; Casting, Dianne Crittenden; an Ironbark Films production; Dolby Stereo; Technicolor; Rated PG; 96 minutes; December release. CAST: Paul Hogan (Terry Dean), Elias Koteas (Steve), Linda Kozlowski (Rose Garner), Doreen Lang (Mrs. Garner), Robert Sutton (Guido), Travis Venable (Bubba), Douglas Seale (Father), Ruth Warshawsky (Irene Bealeman), Parley Baer (George Bealeman), Ben Slack (Rev. Barton), Troy Curvey, Jr. (Tom the Guard), Charlton Heston ("Probation Officer"), Eddie Frias (Young Guard Trainee), Peter Mark Vasquez (Thug), Lyle J. Omori (Thug's Crony), Joseph Walton (Prisoner #1), Michael Alldredge (Sgt. Freebody), David Alan Grier (Det. Bill), Larry Miller, Steven Brill (Tellers), Richard Grove (Uniformed Cop), Susie Duff (Mother), Justin Murphy (Small Boy), Greg Barnett (Van Driver), Ray Reinhardt (Doctor), Laurie Souza (Young Nurse), Hank Worden (Pop), Vickilyn Reynolds, Shawn Schepps (Bank Customers), Candi Milo (Bank Teller), Randy Vasquez (Hood Nervo at bank), Mike Runyard (Hood Driver at bank), Joe Dallesandro (Bank Hood Leader), Tony Veneto (Wino in lane), Doug Ford (Man with "T" shirt), Charles David Richards (Homeless Man), Linda Kurimoto (TV Reporter), Stephanie Hodge (Diner Waitress), Bob Minor, Leslie Morris, Don G. Ross, Hal Landon, Jr., Steph Duvall, William DeAcutis, Sean Faro, Christian Benz Belnavis, Jeri Windom, E'Lon Jason Marsden, Bert David DeFrancis, Anthony Trujillo, Peter Stader, Joey LeMond

Dyan Cannon, John Heard in "End of Innocence" © Skouras

Paul Hogan in "Almost an Angel" © Paramount Pictures

Joan Fontaine

Joel Grey

Kim Hunter

Sidney Poitier

Marlee Matlin

Peter Ustinov

PREVIOUS ACADEMY AWARD WINNERS

(1) Best Picture, (2) Actor, (3) Actress, (4) Supporting Actor, (5) Supporting Actress, (6) Director, (7) Special Award, (8) Best Foreign Language Film, (9) Best Feature Documentary

1927–28: (1) "Wings," (2) Emil Jannings in "The Way of All Flesh," (3) Janet Gaynor in "Seventh Heaven," (6) Frank Borzage for "Seventh Heaven," (7) Charles Chaplin.

1928–29: (1) "Broadway Melody," (2) Warner Baxter in "Old Arizona," (3) Mary Pickford in "Coquette," (6) Frank Lloyd for "The Divine Lady."

1929–30: (1) "All Quiet on the Western Front," (2) George Arliss in "Disraeli," (3) Norma Shearer in "The Divorcee," (6) Lewis Milestone for "All Quiet on the Western Front."

1930–31: (1) "Cimarron," (2) Lionel Barrymore in "A Free Soul," (3) Marie Dressler in "Min and Bill," (6) Norman Taurog for "Skippy."

1931–32: (1) "Grand Hotel," (2) Fredric March in "Dr. Jekyll and Mr. Hyde" tied with Wallace Beery in "The Champ," (3) Helen Hayes in "The Sin of Madelon Claudet," (6) Frank Borzage for "Bad Girl."

1932–33: (1) "Cavalcade," (2) Charles Laughton in "The Private Life of Henry VIII," (3) Katharine Hepburn in "Morning Glory," (6) Frank Lloyd for "Cavalcade."

1934: (1) "It Happened One Night," (2) Clark Gable in "It Happened One Night," (3) Claudette Colbert in "It Happened One Night," (6) Frank Capra for "It Happened One Night," (7) Shirley Temple.

1935: (1) "Mutiny on the Bounty," (2) Victor McLaglen in "The Informer," (3) Bette Davis in "Dangerous," (6) John Ford for "The Informer," (7) D. W. Griffith.

1936: (1) "The Great Ziegfeld," (2) Paul Muni in "The Story of Louis Pasteur," (3) Luise Rainer in "The Great Ziegfeld," (4) Walter Brennan in "Come and Get It," (5) Gale Sondergaard in "Anthony Adverse," (6) Frank Capra for "Mr. Deeds Goes to Town."

1937: (1) "The Life of Emile Zola," (2) Spencer Tracy in "Captains Courageous," (3) Luise Rainer in "The Good Earth," (4) Joseph Schildkraut in "The Life of Emile Zola," (5) Alice Brady in "In Old Chicago," (6) Leo McCarey for "The Awful Truth," (7) Mack Sennett, Edgar Bergen.

1938: (1) "You Can't Take It with You," (2) Spencer Tracy in "Boys' Town," (3) Bette Davis in "Jezebel," (4) Walter Brennan in "Kentucky," (5) Fay Bainter in "Jezebel," (6) Frank Capra for "You Can't Take It with You," (7) Deanna Durbin, Mickey Rooney, Harry M. Warner, Walt Disney.

1939: (1) "Gone with the Wind," (2) Robert Donat in "Goodbye, Mr. Chips," (3) Vivien Leigh in "Gone with the Wind," (4) Thomas Mitchell in "Stagecoach," (5) Hattie McDaniel in "Gone with the Wind," (6) Victor Fleming for "Gone with the Wind," (7) Douglas Fairbanks, Judy Garland.

1940: (1) "Rebecca," (2) James Stewart in "The Philadelphia Story," (3) Ginger Rogers in "Kitty Foyle," (4) Walter Brennan in "The Westerner," (5) Jane Darwell in "The Grapes of Wrath," (6) John Ford for "The Grapes of Wrath," (7) Bob Hope.

1941: (1) "How Green Was My Valley," (2) Gary Cooper in "Sergeant York," (3) Joan Fontaine in "Suspicion," (4) Donald Crisp in "How Green Was My Valley," (5) Mary Astor in "The Great Lie," (6) John Ford for "How Green Was My Valley," (7) Leopold Stokowski, Walt Disney.

1942: (1) "Mrs. Miniver," (2) James Cagney in "Yankee Doodle Dandy," (3) Greer Garson in "Mrs. Miniver," (4) Van Heflin in "Johnny Eager," (5) Teresa Wright in "Mrs. Miniver," (6) William Wyler for "Mrs. Miniver," (7) Charles Boyer, Noel Coward.

1943: (1) "Casablanca," (2) Paul Lukas in "Watch on the Rhine," (3) Jennifer Jones in "The Song of Bernadette," (4) Charles Coburn in "The More the Merrier," (5) Katina Paxinou in "For Whom the Bell Tolls," (6) Michael Curtiz for "Casablanca."

1944: (1) "Going My Way," (2) Bing Crosby in "Going My Way," (3) Ingrid Bergman in "Gaslight," (4) Barry Fitzgerald in "Going My Way," (5) Ethel Barrymore in "None but the Lonely Heart," (6) Leo McCarey for "Going My Way," (7) Margaret O'Brien, Bob Hope.

1945: (1) "The Lost Weekend," (2) Ray Milland in "The Lost Weekend," (3) Joan Crawford in "Mildred Pierce," (4) James Dunn in "A Tree Grows in Brooklyn," (5) Anne Revere in "National Velvet," (6) Billy Wilder for "The Lost Weekend," (7) Walter Wanger, Peggy Ann Garner.

1946: (1) "The Best Years of Our Lives," (2) Fredric March in "The Best Years of Our Lives," (3) Olivia de Havilland in "To Each His Own," (4) Harold Russell in "The Best Years of Our Lives," (5) Anne Baxter in "The Razor's Edge," (6) William Wyler for "The Best Years of Our Lives," (7) Laurence Olivier, Harold Russell, Ernst Lubitsch, Claude Jarman, Jr.

1947: (1) "Gentleman's Agreement," (2) Ronald Colman in "A Double Life," (3) Loretta Young in "The Farmer's Daughter," (4) Edmund Gwenn in "Miracle On 34th Street," (5) Celeste Holm in "Gentleman's Agreement," (6) Elia Kazan for "Gentleman's Agreement," (7) James Baskette, (8) "Shoe Shine," (Italy).

1948: (1) "Hamlet," (2) Laurence Olivier in "Hamlet," (3) Jane Wyman in "Johnny Belinda," (4) Walter Huston in "The Treasure of the Sierra Madre," (5) Claire Trevor in "Key Largo," (6) John Huston for "The Treasure of the Sierra Madre," (7) Ivan Jandl, Sid Grauman, Adolph Zukor, Walter Wanger, (8) "Monsieur Vincent," (France).

1949: (1) "All the King's Men," (2) Broderick Crawford in "All the King's Men," (3) Olivia de Havilland in "The Heiress," (4) Dean Jagger in "Twelve O'Clock High," (5) Mercedes McCambridge in "All the King's Men," (6) Joseph L. Mankiewicz for "A Letter to Three Wives," (7) Bobby Driscoll, Fred Astaire, Cecil B. DeMille, Jean Hersholt, (8) "The Bicycle Thief," (Italy).

1950: (1) "All about Eve," (2) Jose Ferrer in "Cyrano de Bergerac," (3) Judy Holliday in "Born Yesterday," (4) George Sanders in "All about Eve," (5) Josephine Hull in "Harvey," (6) Joseph L. Mankiewicz for "All about Eve," (7) George Murphy, Louis B. Mayer, (8) "The Walls of Malapaga," (France/Italy).

1951: (1) "An American in Paris," (2) Humphrey Bogart in "The African Queen," (3) Vivien Leigh in "A Streetcar Named Desire," (4) Karl Malden in "A Streetcar Named Desire," (5) Kim Hunter in "A Streetcar Named Desire," (6) George Stevens for "A Place in the Sun," (7) Gene Kelly, (8) "Rashomon," (Japan).

1952: (1) "The Greatest Show on Earth," (2) Gary Cooper in "High Noon," (3) Shirley Booth in "Come Back, Little Sheba," (4) Anthony Quinn in "Viva Zapata," (5) Gloria Grahame in "The Bad and the Beautiful," (6) John Ford for "The Quiet Man," (7) Joseph M. Schenck, Merian C. Cooper, Harold Lloyd, Bob Hope, George Alfred Mitchell, (8) "Forbidden Games," (France).

1953: (1) "From Here to Eternity," (2) William Holden in "Stalag 17," (3) Audrey Hepburn in "Roman Holiday," (4) Frank Sinatra in "From Here to Eternity," (5) Donna Reed in "From Here to Eternity," (6) Fred Zinnemann for "From Here to Eternity," (7) Pete Smith, Joseph Breen, (8) no award.

1954: (1) "On the Waterfront," (2) Marlon Brando in "On the Waterfront," (3) Grace Kelly in "The Country Girl," (4) Edmond O'Brien in "The Barefoot Contessa," (5) Eva Marie Saint in "On the Waterfront," (6) Elia Kazan for "On the Waterfront," (7) Greta Garbo, Danny Kaye, Jon Whitely, Vincent Winter, (8) "Gate of Hell," (Japan).

1955: (1) "Marty," (2) Ernest Borgnine in "Marty," (3) Anna Magnani in "The Rose Tattoo," (4) Jack Lemmon in "Mister Roberts," (5) Jo Van Fleet in "East of Eden," (6) Delbert Mann for "Marty," (8) "Samurai," (Japan).

1956: (1) "Around the World in 80 Days," (2) Yul Brynner in "The King and I," (3) Ingrid Bergman in "Anastasia," (4) Anthony Quinn in "Lust for Life," (5) Dorothy Malone in "Written on the Wind," (6) George Stevens for "Giant," (7) Eddie Cantor, (8) "La Strada," (Italy).

1957: (1) "The Bridge on the River Kwai," (2) Alec Guinness in "The Bridge on the River Kwai," (3) Joanne Woodward in "The Three Faces of Eve," (4) Red Buttons in "Sayonara," (5) Miyoshi Umeki in "Sayonara," (6) David Lean for "The Bridge on the River Kwai," (7) Charles Brackett, B. B. Kahane, Gilbert M. (Bronco Billy) Anderson, (8) "The Nights of Cabiria," (Italy).

1958: (1) "Gigi," (2) David Niven in "Separate Tables," (3) Susan Hayward in "I Want to Live," (4) Burl Ives in "The Big Country," (5) Wendy Hiller in "Separate Tables," (6) Vincente Minnelli for "Gigi," (7) Maurice Chevalier, (8) "My Uncle," (France).

1959: (1) "Ben-Hur," (2) Charlton Heston in "Ben-Hur," (3) Simone Signoret in "Room at the Top," (4) Hugh Griffith in "Ben-Hur," (5) Shelley Winters in "The Diary of Anne Frank," (6) William Wyler for "Ben-Hur," (7) Lee de Forest, Buster Keaton, (8) "Black Orpheus," (Brazil).

1960: (1) "The Apartment," (2) Burt Lancaster in "Elmer Gantry," (3) Elizabeth Taylor in "Butterfield 8," (4) Peter Ustinov in "Spartacus," (5) Shirley Jones in "Elmer Gantry," (6) Billy Wilder for "The Apartment," (7) Gary Cooper, Stan Laurel, Hayley Mills, (8) "The Virgin Spring," (Sweden).

1961: (1) "West Side Story," (2) Maximilian Schell in "Judgment at Nuremberg," (3) Sophia Loren in "Two Women," (4) George Chakiris in "West Side Story," (5) Rita Moreno in "West Side Story," (6) Robert Wise for "West Side Story," (7) Jerome Robbins, Fred L. Metzler, (8) "Through a Glass Darkly," (Sweden).

1962: (1) "Lawrence of Arabia," (2) Gregory Peck in "To Kill a Mockingbird," (3) Anne Bancroft in "The Miracle Worker," (4) Ed Begley in "Sweet Bird of Youth," (5) Patty Duke in "The Miracle Worker," (6) David Lean for "Lawrence of Arabia," (8) "Sundays and Cybele," (France).

1963: (1) "Tom Jones," (2) Sidney Poitier in "Lilies of the Field," (3) Patricia Neal in "Hud," (4) Melvyn Douglas in "Hud," (5) Margaret Rutherford in "The V.I.P.'s," (6) Tony Richardson for "Tom Jones," (8) "8½," (Italy).

1964: (1) "My Fair Lady," (2) Rex Harrison in "My Fair Lady," (3) Julie Andrews in "Mary Poppins," (4) Peter Ustinov in "Topkapi," (5) Lila Kedrova in "Zorba the Greek," (6) George Cukor for "My Fair Lady," (7) William Tuttle, (8) "Yesterday, Today and Tomorrow," (Italy).

1965: (1) "The Sound of Music," (2) Lee Marvin in "Cat Ballou," (3) Julie Christie in "Darling," (4) Martin Balsam in "A Thousand Clowns," (5) Shelley Winters in "A Patch of Blue," (6) Robert Wise for "The Sound of Music," (7) Bob Hope, (8) "The Shop on Main Street," (Czech).

1966: (1) "A Man for All Seasons," (2) Paul Scofield in "A Man for All Seasons," (3) Elizabeth Taylor in "Who's Afraid of Virginia Woolf?," (4) Walter Matthau in "The Fortune Cookie," (5) Sandy Dennis in "Who's Afraid of Virginia Woolf?," (6) Fred Zinnemann for "A Man for All Seasons," (8) "A Man and A Woman," (France).

1967: (1) "In the Heat of the Night," (2) Rod Steiger in "In the Heat of the Night," (3) Katharine Hepburn in "Guess Who's Coming to Dinner," (4) George Kennedy in "Cool Hand Luke," (5) Estelle Parsons in "Bonnie and Clyde," (6) Mike Nichols for "The Graduate," (8) "Closely Watched Trains," (Czech).

1968: (1) "Oliver!," (2) Cliff Robertson in "Charly," (3) Katharine Hepburn in "The Lion in Winter" tied with Barbra Streisand in "Funny Girl," (4) Jack Albertson in "The Subject Was Roses," (5) Ruth Gordon in "Rosemary's Baby," (6) Carol Reed for "Oliver!," (7) Onna White for "Oliver!" choreography, John Chambers for "Planet of the Apes" make-up, (8) "War and Peace," (USSR).

1969: (1) "Midnight Cowboy," (2) John Wayne in "True Grit," (3) Maggie Smith in "The Prime of Miss Jean Brodie," (4) Gig Young in "They Shoot Horses, Don't They?," (5) Goldie Hawn in "Cactus Flower," (6) John Schlesinger for "Midnight Cowboy," (8) "Z," (Algeria).

1970: (1) "Patton," (2) George C. Scott in "Patton," (3) Glenda Jackson in "Women in Love," (4) John Mills in "Ryan's Daughter," (5) Helen Hayes in "Airport," (6) Franklin J. Schaffner for "Patton," (7) Lillian Gish, Orson Welles, (8) "Investigation of a Citizen above Suspicion," (Italy).

1971: (1) "The French Connection," (2) Gene Hackman in "The French Connection," (3) Jane Fonda in "Klute," (4) Ben Johnson in "The Last Picture Show," (5) Cloris Leachman in "The Last Picture Show," (6) William Friedkin for "The French Connection," (7) Charles Chaplin, (8) "The Garden of the Finzi-Continis," (Italy).

1972: (1) "The Godfather," (2) Marlon Brando in "The Godfather," (3) Liza Minnelli in "Cabaret," (4) Joel Grey in "Cabaret," (5) Eileen Heckart in "Butterflies Are Free," (6) Bob Fosse for "Cabaret," (7) Edward G. Robinson, (8) "The Discreet Charm of the Bourgeoisie," (France).

1973: (1) "The Sting," (2) Jack Lemmon in "Save the Tiger," (3) Glenda Jackson in "A Touch of Class," (4) John Houseman in "The Paper Chase," (5) Tatum O'Neal in "Paper Moon," (6) George Roy Hill for "The Sting," (8) "Day for Night," (France).

1974: (1) "The Godfather Part II," (2) Art Carney in "Harry and Tonto," (3) Ellen Burstyn in "Alice Doesn't Live Here Anymore," (4) Robert DeNiro in "The Godfather Part II," (5) Ingrid Bergman in "Murder on the Orient Express," (6) Francis Ford Coppola for "The Godfather Part II," (7) Howard Hawks, Jean Renoir, (8) "Amarcord," (Italy).

1975: (1) "One Flew over the Cuckoo's Nest," (2) Jack Nicholson in "One Flew over the Cuckoo's Nest," (3) Louise Fletcher in "One Flew over the Cuckoo's Nest," (4) George Burns in "The Sunshine Boys," (5) Lee Grant in "Shampoo," (6) Milos Forman for "One Flew over the Cuckoo's Nest," (7) Mary Pickford, (8) "Dersu Uzala," (U.S.S.R.), (9) "The Man Who Skied Down Everest."

1976: (1) "Rocky," (2) Peter Finch in "Network," (3) Faye Dunaway in "Network," (4) Jason Robards in "All the President's Men," (5) Beatrice Straight in "Network," (6) John G. Avildsen for "Rocky," (8) "Black and White in Color" (Ivory Coast), (9) "Harlan County U.S.A."

1977: (1) "Annie Hall," (2) Richard Dreyfuss in "The Goodbye Girl," (3) Diane Keaton in "Annie Hall," (4) Jason Robards in "Julia," (5) Vanessa Redgrave in "Julia," (6) Woody Allen for "Annie Hall," (7) Maggie Booth (film editor), (8) "Madame Rosa" (France), (9) "Who Are the DeBolts?"

1978: (1) "The Deer Hunter," (2) Jon Voight in "Coming Home," (3) Jane Fonda in "Coming Home," (4) Christopher Walken in "The Deer Hunter," (5) Maggie Smith in "California Suite," (6) Michael Cimino for "The Deer Hunter," (7) Laurence Olivier, King Vidor, (8) "Get Out Your Handkerchiefs" (France), (9) "Sacred Straight."

1979: (1) "Kramer vs. Kramer," (2) Dustin Hoffman in "Kramer vs. Kramer," (3) Sally Field in "Norma Rae," (4) Melvyn Douglas in "Being There," (5) Meryl Streep in "Kramer vs. Kramer," (6) Robert Benton for "Kramer vs. Kramer," (7) Robert S. Benjamin, Hal Elias, Alec Guinness, (8) "The Tin Drum" (Germany), (9) "Best Boy."

1980: (1) "Ordinary People," (2) Robert DeNiro in "Raging Bull," (3) Sissy Spacek in "Coal Miner's Daughter," (4) Timothy Hutton in "Ordinary People," (5) Mary Steenburgen in "Melvin and Howard," (6) Robert Redford for "Ordinary People," (7) Henry Fonda, (8) "Moscow Does Not Believe in Tears" (Russia), (9) "From Mao to Mozart: Isaac Stern in China."

1981: (1) "Chariots of Fire," (2) Henry Fonda in "On Golden Pond," (3) Katharine Hepburn in "On Golden Pond," (4) John Gielgud in "Arthur," (5) Maureen Stapleton in "Reds," (6) Warren Beatty for "Reds," (7) Fuji Photo Film Co., Barbara Stanwyck, (8) "Mephisto" (Germany/Hungary), (9) "Genocide."

1982: (1) "Gandhi," (2) Ben Kingsley in "Gandhi," (3) Meryl Streep in "Sophie's Choice," (4) Louis Gossett, Jr. in "An Officer and a Gentleman," (5) Jessica Lange in "Tootsie," (6) Richard Attenborough for "Gandhi," (7) Mickey Rooney, (8) "Volver a Empezar" (To Begin Again) (Spain), (9) "Just Another Missing Kid."

1983: (1) "Terms of Endearment," (2) Robert Duvall in "Tender Mercies," (3) Shirley MacLaine in "Terms of Endearment," (4) Jack Nicholson in "Terms of Endearment," (5) Linda Hunt in "The Year of Living Dangerously," (6) James L. Brooks for "Terms of Endearment," (7) Hal Roach, (8) "Fanny and Alexander" (Sweden), (9) "He Makes Me Feel Like Dancin'."

1984: (1) "Amadeus," (2) F. Murray Abraham in "Amadeus," (3) Sally Field in "Places in the Heart," (4) Haing S. Ngor in "The Killing Fields," (5) Peggy Ashcroft in "A Passage to India," (6) Milos Forman for "Amadeus," (7) James Stewart, (8) "Dangerous Moves" (Switzerland), (9) "The Times of Harvey Milk."

1985: (1) "Out of Africa," (2) William Hurt in "Kiss of the Spider Woman," (3) Geraldine Page in "The Trip to Bountiful," (4) Don Ameche in "Cocoon," (5) Anjelica Huston in "Prizzi's Honor," (6) Sydney Pollack for "Out of Africa," (7) Paul Newman, Alex North, (8) "The Official Story" (Argentina), (9) "Broken Rainbow."

1986: (1) "Platoon," (2) Paul Newman in "The Color of Money," (3) Marlee Matlin for "Children of a Lesser God," (4) Michael Caine for "Hannah and Her Sisters," (5) Dianne Wiest for "Hannah and Her Sisters," (6) Oliver Stone for "Platoon," (7) Ralph Bellamy, (8) "The Assault" (Netherlands), (9) "Artie Shaw: Time Is All You've Got" tied with "Down and Out in America"

1987: (1) "The Last Emperor," (2) Michael Douglas in "Wall Street," (3) Cher in "Moonstruck," (4) Sean Connery in "The Untouchables," (5) Olympia Dukakis in "Moonstruck," (6) Bernardo Bertolucci for "The Last Emperor," (8) "Babette's Feast" (Denmark), (9) "The Ten-Year Lunch: The Wit and Legend of the Algonquin Round Table"

1988: (1) "Rain Man," (2) Dustin Hoffman in "Rain Man," (3) Jodie Foster in "The Accused," (4) Kevin Kline in "A Fish Called Wanda," (5) Geena Davis in "The Accidental Tourist," (6) Barry Levinson for "Rain Man," (8) "Pelle the Conqueror," (9) "Hotel Terminus: the Life and Times of Klaus Barbie."

1989: (1) "Driving Miss Daisy," (2) Daniel Day Lewis in "My Left Foot," (3) Jessica Tandy in "Driving Miss Daisy," (4) Denzel Washington in "Glory," (5) Brenda Fricker in "My Left Foot," (6) Oliver Stone for "Born on the Fourth of July," (7) Akira Kurosawa, (8) "Cinema Paradiso," (9) "Common Threads"

1990 ACADEMY AWARDS

(presented Monday, March 25, 1991)

DANCES WITH WOLVES

(ORION) Producers, Jim Wilson, Kevin Costner; Executive Producer, Jake Eberts; Director, Kevin Costner; Screenplay, Michael Blake, based on his novel; Photography, Dean Semler; Designer, Jeffrey Beecroft; Costumes, Elsa Zamparelli; Music, John Barry; Editor, Neil Travis; Associate Producer, Bonnie Arnold; Unit Production Manager/Line Producer, Derek Kavanagh; Assistant Director, Douglas C. Metzger; Stunts, Norman L. Howell; a Tig Productions presentation; Dolby Stereo; Panavision; Deluxe color; Rated PG-13; 181 minutes; November release

CAST

Lt. John J. Dunbar	Kevin Costner
Stands With A Fist	Mary McDonnell
Kicking Bird	Graham Greene
Wind In His Hair	Rodney A. Grant
Ten Bears	Floyd Red Crow Westerman
Black Shawl	Tantoo Cardinal
Timmons	Robert Pastorelli
Lt. Elgin	Charles Rocket
Major Fambrough	Maury Chaykin
Stone Calf	Jimmy Herman
Smiles A Lot	Nathan Lee Chasing His Horse
Otter	Michael Spears
Worm	Jason R. Lone Hill
Spivey	Tony Pierce
Pretty Shield	Doris Leader Charge
Sgt. Pepper	Tom Everett
Sgt. Bauer	Larry Joshua
Edwards	Kirk Baltz
Major	Wayne Grace
General Tide	Donald Hotton
Christine	Annie Costner
Willie	Conor Duffy
Christine's Mother	Elisa Daniel
Big Warrior	Percy White Plume
Escort Warrior	John Tail
Sioux #1/Warrior #1	Steve Reevis
Sioux #2/Warrior #2	Sheldon Wolfchild
Toughest Pawnee	Wes Studi
Pawnees	Buffalo Child, Clayton Big Eagle, Richard Leader Charge
Sioux Warriors	Redwing Ted Nez, Marvin Holy
Sioux Courier	Raymond Newholy
Kicking Bird's Son	David J. Fuller
Kicking Bird's Eldest Son	Ryan White Bull
Kicking Bird's Daughter	Otakuye Conroy
Village Mother	Maretta Big Crow
Guard	Steve Chambers
General's Aide	William H. Burton
Confederate Cavalryman	Bill W. Curry
Confederate Soldiers	Nick Thompson, Carter Hanner
Wagon Driver	Kent Hays
Union Soldier	Robert Goldman
Tucker	Frank P. Costanza
Ray	James A. Mitchell
Ambush Wagon Driver	R. L. Curtin
Cisco	Justin
Two Socks	Teddy & Buck

Top: Kevin Costner © *Orion Pictures Corp.*

1990 Academy Awards for Best Picture, Director, Screenplay Adaptation, Cinematography, Film Editing, Original Score, and Sound

Nathan Lee Chasing His Horse, Jason Lone Hill, Michael Spears Above: Kevin Costner, Mary McDonnell

Kevin Costner

Floyd Red Crow Westerman; Robert Pastorelli Top Right:
Mary McDonnell, Kevin Costner

Kevin Costner, Two Socks Above Left: Rodney A. Grant;
Graham Greene

Kevin Costner, Rodney A. Grant Above Right: Costner,
Graham Greene (C)

169

JEREMY IRONS
in "Reversal of Fortune"
© *Warner Bros.*
ACADEMY AWARD FOR BEST ACTOR
OF 1990

KATHY BATES
in "Misery"
© *Castle Rock Entertainment*
**ACADEMY AWARD FOR BEST ACTRESS
OF 1990**

JOE PESCI
in "GoodFellas"
© *Warner Bros.*
ACADEMY AWARD FOR BEST
SUPPORTING ACTOR OF 1990

WHOOPI GOLDBERG
in "Ghost"
© *Paramount Pictures*
**ACADEMY AWARD FOR BEST
SUPPORTING ACTRESS OF 1990**

JOURNEY OF HOPE

(MIRAMAX) Producers, Alfi Sinniger (Catpics), Peter Fueter (Condor Prods.); Director, Xavier Koller; Screenplay, Xavier Koller, Feride Cicekoglu; Photography, Elemer Ragalyi; Editor, Galip Iyitanir; Music Producer, Manfred Eicher; from Catpics and Condor Productions; Swiss; Color; Not rated; 110 minutes; April 1991 release

CAST

Haydar	Necmettin Cobanoglu
Meryem	Nur Surer
Mehmet Ali	Emin Sivas
Turkmen	Yaman Okay
Truckdriver Ramser	Mathias Gnadinger
Massimo	Dietmar Schonherr

Top: Necmettin Cobanoglu, Emin Sivas, Nur Surer
Left: Cobanoglu
© *Condor Productions*

ACADEMY AWARD FOR BEST FOREIGN-LANGUAGE FILM OF 1990

Nur Surer, Necmettin Cobanoglu, Mathias Gnadinger, Emin Sivas

PROMISING NEW ACTORS
OF 1990

ANNETTE BENING

EDWARD CLEMENTS

HARRY CONNICK, JR.

MARCIA GAY HARDEN

TONY GOLDWYN

HARLEY JANE KOZAK

MARY McDONNELL

STEPHEN MAILER

MARY-LOUISE PARKER

CAMPBELL SCOTT

ANNABELLA SCIORRA

WESLEY SNIPES

FOREIGN FILMS RELEASED IN THE U.S.

SWEETIE

(AVENUE) Producer, John Maynard; Co-Producer, William MacKinnon; Director, Jane Campion; Screenplay, Gerard Lee, Jane Campion; Photography, Sally Bongers; Editor, Veronika Haussler; Music, Martin Armiger; Art Director, Peter Harris; Costumes, Amanda Lovejoy; Assistant Director, John Fretz; Australian; Color; Rated R; 100 minutes; January release

CAST

Sweetie	Genevieve Lemon
Kay	Karen Colston
Louis	Tom Lycos
Gordon	Jon Darling
Flo	Dorothy Barry
Bob	Michael Lake
Clayton	Andre Pataczek
Mrs. Schneller	Jean Hadgraft
Teddy Schneller	Paul Livingston
Cheryl	Louise Fox
Paula	Ann Merchant
Ruth	Robyn Frank
Sue	Bronwyn Morgan
Boy Clerk	Sean Fennell
Simboo	Sean Callinan
Notary	Norm Galton
Man Handshakes	Warren Hensley
Meditation Teacher	Charles Abbott
Melony	Diana Armer
Clayton's Mum	Barbara Middleton
Little Sweetie	Emma Fowler
Mandy	Irene Curtis
Lead Jakaroo	Ken Porter
Nosey Neighbors	Norman Phillips, Shirley Sheppard
Boys in tree	Ben Cochrane, Kristoffer Pershouse
Man with saw	Bruce Currie

Top: Genevieve Lemon, Karen Colston Right: Lemon, Michael Lake © *Avenue Pictures*

Cecilia Roth, Imanol Arias

LABYRINTH OF PASSION

(CINEVISTA) Director/Screenplay/Designer, Pedro Almodovar; Photography, Angel L. Fernandez; Editor, Jose Salcedo; Assistant Director, Miguel Angel Perez Campos; an Alphaville Production; Spanish, 1982; Color; Not rated; 100 minutes; January release

CAST

Sexilia	Cecilia Roth
Riza Niro	Imanol Arias
Toraya	Helga Line
Queti	Marta Fernandez-Muro
Eusebio	Angel Alcazar
Sadeq	Antonio Banderas
Hassan	Agustin Almodovar

© *Cinevista, Inc.*

STRIKE IT RICH

(MILLIMETER) Producers, Christine Oestreicher, Graham Easton; Director/Screenplay, James Scott; Based on the novel "Loser Takes All" by Graham Greene; Associate Producer, Susan Slonaker; Editor, Thomas Schwalm; Photography, Robert Paynter; Designer, Christopher Hobbs; Costumes, Tom Rand; Assistant Director, Guy Travers; British; Color; Rated PG; 87 minutes; January release

CAST

Ian Bertram	Robert Lindsay
Cary Porter	Molly Ringwald
Herbert Dreuther	Sir John Gielgud
Bowles	Max Wall
Philippe	Simon de la Brosse
Bowles' Nurse	Margi Clarke
Kinski	Vladek Sheybal
Hotel Manager	Michel Blanc
Mrs. De Vere	Frances De La Tour
Henri	Gerard Dimiglio
Head Waiter	Stephen Marlowe
Wine Waiter	Nadio Fortune
A Waiter	Yves Aubert
Croupier	Terence Beesley
Fat Man	John C. P. Mattocks
Receptionist	Lawrence Davidson
Chinese Woman	Su Yong
Man with chips	Claude LeSache
Man with wink	Patrick Holt
Casino Attendant	Stephen Gressieux
Old Lady	Margaret Clifton
Cashier at casino	Jack Raymond
Blixon	Narius Goring
Miss Bullen	Richenda Carey
Naismith	Godfrey Talbot

and Tim Seely (Arnold), Victoria Wicks (Jane Truefitt), John Otway (Harry Truefitt), Nicolas Mead (Barman in hotel), Jeffrey Robert, Marianne Price (Bus Conductors), Willie Ross (Man at theatre), David Marrick (Waiter), Al Fiorenti (Little Man at hotel)

Top: Molly Ringwald, Robert Lindsay Right: Ringwald, John Gielgud © Millimeter Films

ROSALIE GOES SHOPPING

(FOUR SEASONS ENTERTAINMENT) Producers/Screenplay, Percy Adlon, Elenore Adlon; Director, Percy Adlon; Line Producer, Jill Griffith; Co-Screenplay, Christopher Doherty; Photography, Bernd Heinl; Music, Bob Telson; Designer, Stephen Lineweaver; Casting, Rody Kent; Editor, Jean-Claude Piroue; Costumes, Elizabeth Warner Nankin; a Pelemele Film Production; West German; Dolby Stereo; Color; Rated PG; 94 minutes; February release

CAST

Rosalie Greenspace	Marianne Sägebrecht
Ray Greenspace	Brad Davis
Priest	Judge Reinhold
Rosalie's Parents	Erika Blumberger, Willy Harlander
Schatzi	Alex Winter
Barbara	Patricia Zehentmayr
Schnucki	John Hawkes
Kindi	David Denney
April	Courtney Kraus
Herzi	Dina Chandel
Twins	Lisa Fitzhugh, Lori Fitzhugh
Chris	Bill Butler
Burt	Ed Geldart
Linda	Bonnie Pemberton
Receptionist	Jane Hutchison
Museum Guide	Helen Boyd
Meg	Sara Van Horn
Ellen	Betty King
Bank President	John William Galt
Bank Manager	Phyllis A. Kirklin
Saleswoman	Maria Roth
Bank Clerk	Todd Tongen

Lisa Fitzhugh, John Hawkes, Lori Fitzhugh Above: Brad Davis, Marianne Sagebrecht © Four Seasons Ent. Inc.

BLACK RAIN

(ANGELIKA) Producer, Hisa Iino; Director, Shohei Imamura; Screenplay, Toshiro Ishido, Shohei Imamura; Based on the novel by Masuji Ibuse; Photography, Takashi Kawamata; Music, Toru Takemitsu; Editor, Hajime Okayasu; Art Director, Hisao Inagaki; Japanese; Black and white; 123 minutes; February release

CAST

Yasuko .... Yoshiko Tanaka
Shigematsu .... Kazuo Kitamura
Shigeko .... Etsuko Ichihara
Shokichi .... Shoichi Ozawa
Kotaro .... Norihei Miki
Yuichi .... Keisuke Ishida

© *Angelika Films*

Etsuko Ichihara, Yoshiko Tanaka, Katzuo Kitamura

Nastassja Kinski, William Forsythe

TORRENTS OF SPRING

(MILLIMETER FILMS) Producer, Angello Rizzoli; Executive Producer, Mario Cotone; Director, Jerzy Skolimowski; Screenplay, Jerzy Skolimowski, Arcangelo Bonaccorso; Based on the novel by Ivan Turgenev; Music, Stanley Myers; Photography, Dante Spinotti, Witold Sobocinski; Designer, Francesco Bronzi; Costumes, Theodor Pistek, Sibylle Ulsamer; Editors, Cesare D'Amico, Andrzej Kostenko; Erre Produzioni S.r.l.—Reteitalia S.p.a.—Rome—Les Films Ariane Films A2—Paris—in association with Curzon Films Distributors Ltd—London; Italian-French; Technicolor; Not rated; 93 minutes; February release

CAST

Dimitri Sanin .... Timothy Hutton
Maria Polozov .... Nastassja Kinski
Gemma Rosselli .... Valeria Golino
Polozov .... William Forsythe
Von Doenhof .... Urbano Barberini
Signora Rosselli .... Francesca De Sapio
Pantaleone .... Jacques Herlin
Richter .... Antonio Cantafora
Kluber .... Christopher Janczar
Emilio .... Christian Dottorini
Frau Stoltz .... Alexia Korda
Luisa .... Marinella Anaclerio
Man with glasses .... Pietro Bontempo
The Moon .... Thierry Langerak
Pulcinella .... Xavier Maly
and Anna Piccioni, Massimo Sarchielli (Gypsies), Serge Spira (Doctor), Elena Schaprova, Antonella Ponziani (Maids), Jerzy Skolimowski (Victor Victorovich)

© *Millimeter Films*
Top left: Nastassja Kinski, William Forsythe, Timothy Hutton, Valeria Golino

TIME OF THE GYPSIES

ʹ(COLUMBIA) Producer, Mirza Pasic; Co-Producer, Harry Saltzman; Director, Emir Kusturica; Photography, Vilko Filac; Screenplay, Emir Kusturica, Gordan Mihic; Editor, Andrija Zafranovic; Music, Goran Bregovic; Costumes, Mirjana Ostojic; a Forum Film/Sarajevo Production; Yugoslavian; Color; Rated R; 142 minutes; February release

CAST

Perhan .... Davor Dujmovic
Ahmed .... Bora Todorovic
Perhan's Grandmother .... Ljubica Adzovic
Azra .... Sinolicka Trpkova
Uncle Merdzan .... Husnija Hasimovic
Zabit .... Zabit Memedov
Danira .... Elvira Sali
Zef .... Mirsad Zulic
and Suada Karisik, Predrag Lakovic, Ajnur Redzepi, Bedrije Halim, Branko Duric, Marijeta Gregorac

© *Columbia Pictures*

Zabit Memedov, Husnija Hasimovic, Elvira Sali, Ljubica Adzovic, Davor Dujmovic

Gerard Depardieu, Josiane Balasko Center Right: Depardieu, Carole Bouquet

LONELY WOMAN SEEKS LIFE COMPANION

(INTERNATIONAL FILM EXCHANGE) Director, Viacheslav Krishtofovich; Screenplay, Viktor Merezhko; Photography, Vasily Trutkovsky; Music, Vadim Khrapachev; Art Director, Alexei Levchenko; Soviet; Color; Not rated; 91 minutes; March release

CAST

Klavida	Irina Kupchenko
Valentin	Alexander Zbruyev
Neighbor	Elena Solovei
Anya	Marianna Vertinskaya
Kasianov	Valery Sheptekita

© IFEX

TOO BEAUTIFUL FOR YOU

(ORION CLASSICS) Director/Screenplay, Bertrand Blier; Editor, Claudine Merlin; Photography, Philippe Rousselot; Set Decoration, Theobald Meurisse; Assistant Director, Luc Goldenberg; Costumes, Michele Marmande-Cerf; Cine Valse—D.D. Productions—Orly Films—S.E.D.I.F.—T.F.1—Films Productions; French; Dolby Stereo; Panavision; Color; Rated R; 91 minutes; March release

CAST

Bernard	Gérard Depardieu
Colette	Josiane Balasko
Florence	Carole Bouquet
Marcello	Roland Blanche
Pascal	Francois Cluzet
Leonce	Didier Benureau
Tanguy	Philippe Loffredo
Marie-Catherine	Sylvie Orcier
Genevieve	Myriam Boyer
The Son	Flavien Lebarbe
The Daughter	Juana Marques
Colette's Neighbor	Carole Bouquet
Lorene	Denise Chalem
Gaby	Jean-Louis Cordina
Paula	Stephane Auberghen
Colette's Husband	Philippe Faure
The Pianist	Jean-Paul Farre
The Man on the tram	Richard Martin
The Receptionist	Sylvie Simon

© *Orion Pictures Corp.*
Top: Josiane Balasko, Gérard Depardieu Left: Depardieu, Carole Bouquet

Irina Kupchenko, Alexander Zbruyev

NUNS ON THE RUN

(20th CENTURY FOX) Producer, Michael White; Executive Producers, George Harrison, Denis O'Brien; Director/Screenplay, Jonathan Lynn; Co-Producer, Simon Bosanquet; Photography, Michael Garfath; Music, Yello, Hidden Faces; Designer, Simon Holland; Editor, David Martin; Costumes, Susan Yelland; Casting, Mary Selway; Assistant Director, David Brown; a Handmade Films presentation; British; Dolby Stereo; Technicolor; Rated PG-13; 94 minutes; March release

CAST

Brian Hope ("Sister Euphemia")	Eric Idle
Charlie McManus ("Sister Inviolata")	Robbie Coltrane
Faith	Camille Coduri
Sister Superior	Janet Suzman
Sister Mary of the Sacred Heart	Doris Hare
Sister Mary of the Annunciation	Lila Kaye
"Case" Casey	Robert Patterson
Abbott	Robert Morgan
Morley	Winston Dennis
Father Seamus	Tom Hickey
Norm	Colin Campbell
Mr. Norris	Richard Simpson
Louis	Nicholas Hewetson
Ronnie Chang	Gary Tang
Henry Ho	David Forman
Dwayne Lee	Nigel Fan
Ernie Wong	Ozzie Yue
Michelle	Tatiana Strauss
Julie	Wabei Siyolwe
Tracey	Helen Fitzgerald
Faith's Father	Stewart Harwood
Faith's Brother	Peter Geeves
Hysterical Bank Manageress	Irene Marot
Bank Security Guard	Louis Mellis
Policeman in Car Park	Craig Crosbie
Gate Keeper	Fred Haggerty
Bewildered Policeman	Michael Beint
Taxi Driver	Tex Fuller

and Lee Simpson (Policeman with radio), Oliver Parker (Doctor), Julie Graham (Casino Waitress), Dan Hildebrand (Casino Manager), Joanne Campbell (Ward Nurse), Gedren Heller (Chemist Shop Assistant), Britt Morrow (Hospital Receptionist), David Becalick (Police Sergeant), Aran Bell (Police Constable), Francine Walker, Shirley Anne Selby (Tied-up Nurses), Jennifer Hall (Airport Ticket Girl), John Pythian (Airport Policeman)

© *HandMade Films*

Camille Coduri, Eric Idle Above: Idle, Robbie Coltrane

THE PERFECT MURDER

(MERCHANT IVORY PRODS.) Executive Producer, Ismail Merchant; Producer, Wahid Chowhan; Director, Zafar Hai; Screenplay, H.R.F. Keating, Zafar Hai, based on the novel by Keating; Photography, Walter Lassally; Music, Richard Robbins; Editor, Charles Rees; Costumes, Sally Turner; Designers, Kiran Patki, Sartaj Noorani; presented in association with Perfect Movie Productions; Indian-British; Color; Not rated; 90 minutes; March release

CAST

Inspector Ghote	Naseeruddin Shah
Axel Svenssen	Stellan Skarsgard
Mrs. Lal	Madhur Jaffrey
Neena Lal	Sakina Jaffrey
Lala Heera Lal	Amjad Khan
Pratima Ghote	Ratna Pathak Shah
Dilap Lal	Dalip Tahil
Minister	Vinod Nagpal
Mr. Perfect	Dinshaw Daji
Miss Twinkle	Archana Puran Singh
Prem Lal	Nayeem Hafizka
Zero Police	Rajesh Vivek
Jeweller	Baba Majgaokar
Tiny Man	Anu Kapoor
Head Constable	Vijoo Khote
A.C.P. Samant	Mohan Agashe
Jain	Johnny Walker
Felix Sousa	Sameer Kakkad
Ved Ghote	Imaaduddin Shah

and Gopi Krishna (Dance Master), Ashley D'Silva (Photographer), Pearl Padamsee (Nurse), Liliput (Black Shirt), P. M. Maniar (Drunken Guest), Aida Noorani (Student), Salim Ghouse (Caste-Marks Goonda), Bomi Kapadia (Sgt. Moos)

Stellen Skarsgard, Naseeruddin Shah

© *Merchant Ivory Prods.*

MONSIEUR HIRE

(ORION CLASSICS) Producers, Philippe Carcassonne, Rene Cleitman; Director, Patrice Leconte; Screenplay Adaptation, Patrice Leconte, Patrick DeWolf; Based on the novel *"Les Fiancailles de Monsieur Hire"* by Georges Simenon; Photography, Denis Lenoir; Music, Michael Nyman; Editor, Joëlle Hache; Costumes, Elizabeth Tavernier; a co-production of Cinea—Hachette Premiere et Compagnie Europe 1 Communication—F.R. 3 Films Productions with the participation of Sofica: Sofinergie—Sofimage Creations and Centre National de la Cinematographie; French; Color; Rated PG-13; 88 minutes; April release

CAST

Monsieur Hire	Michel Blanc
Alice	Sandrine Bonnaire
Emile	Luc Thuillier
Police Inspector	Andre Wilms

© *Orion Pictures Corp.*
Below: Michel Blanc, Sandrine Bonnaire

Luc Thuillier, Sandrine Bonnaire Above: Bonnaire, Michel Blanc

BYE BYE BLUES

(CIRCLE RELEASING) Producers, Anne Wheeler, Arvi Liimatainen; Director/Screenplay, Anne Wheeler; Executive Producer, Tony Allard; Photography, Vic Sarin; Designer, John Blackie; Music, George Blondheim; Editor, Christopher Tate; Costumes, Maureen Hiscox; Song: *"When I Sing"* by Bill Henderson/performed by Rebecca Jenkins; an Allarcom-True Blue Films production, produced with the participation of Telefilm Canada/Alberta Motion Picture Development Corporation/National Film Board of Canada/CFCN TV/CITV TV; Canadian; Color; Rated PG; 110 minutes; April release

CAST

Daisy Cooper	Rebecca Jenkins
Max Gramley	Luke Reilly
Slim Godfrey	Stuart Margolin
Pete	Wayne Robson
Frances Cooper	Robyn Stevan
Teddy Cooper	Michael Ontkean
Mary Wright	Kate Reid
Richard Cooper (5 yrs.)	Chad Krowchuk
Richard Cooper (9 yrs.)	Kirk Duffee
Will Wright	Vincent Gale
Arthur Wright	Leslie Yeo
Doreen Cooper	Sheila Moore
Emma Cooper	Aline Levasseur
Iyah (Nancy)	Jyoti Dhembre
Gilbert Wilson	Tom Alter
Lady Wilson	Susan Wooldridge
Joyce Kuchern	Susan Sneath
Ivan	Francis Damberger
Bernie Blitzer	Leon Pownell
Billy	Aaron Goettel
Rosie	Beverly Elliot
Duncan	John Ferguson
Brad	Frank Mandreli

and Dr. Wohanagashe (Rug Merchant), Ron Carothers (Porter), Kaye Grieve (Drunk Woman), Laurie Bardsley (Clarinet Player), Gary Koliger (Guitar Player), Margaret Bard (Woman in Ladies Room), Rose Campbell (Saxophone Player), Murray McCune (Returning POW)

© *Circle Releasing Corp.*

Rebecca Jenkins, Kate Reid, Vincent Gale Above: Luke Reilly, Jenkins

MAMA, THERE'S A MAN IN YOUR BED

(MIRAMAX) Producers, Jean-Louis Piel, Philippe Carcassonne; Director/Screenplay, Coline Serreau; Photography, Jean-Noel Ferragut; Designer, Jean-Marc Stehle; Associate Producer, Elizabeth Parniere; Editor, Catherine Renault; Costumes, Monique Perrot, Dominique Morlotti; Casting, Evy Figliolini; French; Color; Not rated; 108 minutes; April release

CAST

Romuald	Daniel Auteuil
Juliette	Firmine Richard
Blache	Pierre Vernier
Cloquet	Maxime Leroux
Paulin	Gilles Privat
Nicole	Muriel Combeau
Francoise	Catherine Salviat
Benjamin	Alexandre Basse
Felicite	Aissatou Bah
Desire	Mamadou Bah
Claire	Marina M'Boa Ngong
Aime	Sambou Tati
Valerie	Isabelle Carre
Patrick	Jean-Christophe Itier
Housing Dept. Deputy	Nicolas Serreau
Vidal	Alain Tretout
Marton	Alain Fromager
Civil Servant	Jacques Poitrenaud
New Secretary	Caroline Jaquin
Driver	Gilles Cohen

Top: Firmine Richard, Daniel Auteuil Left: Auteuil, Alexandre Basse © *Miramax Films*

THE MAHABHARATA

(MK2) Producer, Michel Propper; Co-Producers, Ed Myerson, Rachel Tabori, Micheline Rozan, William Wilkinson; Executive Producers, Michael Birkett, Michael Kustow, Harvey Lichtenstein; Director, Peter Brook; Screenplay, Jean-Claude Carriere, Peter Brook, Marie-Helene Estienne; Photography, William Lubtchansky; Designer/Costumes, Chloe Obolensky; Music, Toshi Tsuchitori, Djamchid Chemirani, Kudsi Erguner, Kim Menzer, Mahmond Tabrizi-Zadeh; Editor, Nicolas Gaster; a Reiner Moritz presentation; British-French; Color; Not rated; 171 minutes; April release

CAST

Vyasa	Robert Langdon-Lloyd
The Boy	Antonin Stahly-Vishwanadan
Ganesha/Krishna	Bruce Myers
Arjuna	Vittorio Mezzogiorno
Yudhishthira	Andrzej Seweryn
Bhima	Mamadou Dioume
Nakula	Jean-Paul Denizon
Sahadeva	Mahmoud Tabrizi-Zadeh
Draupadi	Mallika Sarabhai
Kunti	Miriam Goldschmidt
Madri/Hidimbi	Erika Alexander
Dhritharashtra	Ryszard Cieslak
Gandhari	Helen Patarot
Duryodhana	George Corraface
Dushassana	Urs Bihler
Karna	Jeffrey Kissoon
Drona	Yoshi Oida
Bhishma/Parashurama	Sotigui Kouyate
Shiva/Pandu	Tapa Sudana
Shakuni	Tuncel Kurtiz
Ghatotkatcha/The Sun	Bakary Sangare
Amba/Sikandin	Corinne Jaber
The Gazelle	Clement Masdongar
Gandhari's Servant	Myriam Tadesse

© *MK2*

Mallika Sarabhai

Alan Howard, Richard Bohringer, Helen Mirren,
Michael Gambon, Tim Roth Right: Mirren
© *Miramax Films*

THE COOK, THE THIEF, HIS WIFE AND HER LOVER

(MIRAMAX) Producer, Kees Kasander; Co-Producers, Denis Wigman, Pascal Dauman, Daniel Toscan du Plantier; Director/Screenplay, Peter Greenaway; Photography, Sacha Vierny; Casting, Sharon Howard Field; Assistant Director, Gerrit Martijn; Designers, Ben Van Os, Jan Roelfs; Costumes, Jean Paul Gaultier; Editor, John Wilson; Music, Michael Nyman; an Allarts Cook Ltd/Erato Films Inc. co-production; British-French; Rank color; Not rated; 123 minutes; April release

CAST

Richard	Richard Bohringer
Albert Spica	Michael Gambon
Georgina	Helen Mirren
Michael	Alan Howard
Mitchel	Tim Roth
Cory	Ciaran Hinds
Spangler	Gary Olsen
Harris	Ewan Stewart
Turpin	Roger Ashton Griffiths
Mews	Ron Cook
Grace	Liz Smith
Patricia	Emer Gillespie
Alice	Janet Henfrey
Eden	Arnie Breevelt
Troy	Tony Alleff
Pup	Paul Russell
Adele	Alex Kingston
Phillipe	Ian Sears
Roy	Willie Ross
Terry Fitch	Ian Dury
May Fitch	Diane Langton
Corelle Fitch	Prudence Oliver
Geoff	Roger Lloyd Pack
Starkie	Bob Goody
Melter	Peter Rush
Fish Girl	Pauline Mayer
Meat Boy	Ben Stoneham
Diners	Andy Wilson, John Mullis
Cabaret Singer	Flavia Brilli
Dancers	Brenda Edwards, Sophie Goodchild

and Nick Brozovic, Michael Clark, Hywel Williams Ellis, Alex Fraser, Tim Geary, Gary Logan, Michael Maguire, Sue Maund, Karrie Pagano, Saffron Rainey, Patricia Walters (Waiters and kitchen staff)

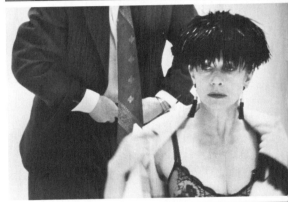

Tim Roth (2nd L), Michael Gambon (C) Roger Ashton Griffiths (R)
Above: Helen Mirren

185

Rémy Girard, Robert Lepage Top Left: Lothaire Bluteau
Top Right: Catherine Wilkening, Johanne-Marie Tremblay
Right: Bluteau, Wilkening
© *Orion Pictures Corp.*

JESUS OF MONTREAL

(ORION CLASSICS) Producers, Roger Frappier, Roger Gendron; Director/Screenplay, Denys Arcand; Photography, Guy Dufaux; Editor, Isabelle Dedieu; Art Director, François Séguin; Music, Yves Laferriére; Costumes, Louise Jobin; Casting, Lucie Robitaille; Produced by Max Films Productions Inc. and Gerard Mital Productions in association with The National Film Board of Canada; French-Canadian; Dolby Stereo; Color; Rated R; 119 minutes; May release

CAST

Daniel Coulombe	Lothaire Bluteau
Mireille	Catherine Wilkening
Constance	Johanne-Marie Tremblay
Martin	Rémy Girard
René	Robert Lepage
Father Leclerc	Gilles Pelletier
Richard Cardinal	Yves Jacques
Judge	Denys Arcand
Yvan Karamazov	Michael Barnard
Shirley Spivak	Maria Bircher
François Bastien	Claude Blanchard
Neal Sherman	James Bradford
Tony Griffith	Alexander Chapman
Paul Bigras	Robert-Pierre Coté
Linda Morrisson	Lois Dellar
Pierre Bouchard	Bob Della Serra
Rosalie Lazure	Andréanne Deneault
Marcel Brochu	Roy Dupuis
Fabienne	Sylvie Drapeau
Claudine Bouchard	Lisette Guertin
James Rigby	Dean Hagopian
Director	Jacques Lavallée
Sam Rosen	Ron Lea
Régine Malouin	Véronique Le Flaguais
Bob Chalifoux	Gaston Lepage
France Garibaldi	Pauline Martin
Alain Sénécal	Hrothgar Mathews
John Lambert	Marc Messier
Pascale Berger	Cédric Noel
Zabou Johnson	Isabelle Truchon

Lothaire Bluteau Above: Bluteau, Gilles Pelletier

TIE ME UP! TIE ME DOWN!

(MIRAMAX) Producer, El Deseo, S. A.; Director/Screenplay, Pedro Almodovar; Executive Producer, Augustin Almodovar; Photography, Jose Luis Alcaine; Set Director, Ferran Sanchez; Costumes, Jose Maria de Cossio; Editor, Jose Salcedo; Assistant Director, Jose Luis Escolar; Spanish; Eastmancolor; Not rated; 105 minutes; May release

CAST

Marina	Victoria Abril
Ricky	Antonio Banderas
Maximo Espejo	Francisco Rabal
Lola	Loles Leon
Alma	Julieta Serrano
Berta	Maria Barranco
Girl with moped	Rossy De Palma
Director of Psychiatric Center	Lola Cardona
Decorator	Emiliano Redondo
Journalist	Montse G. Romeu
Pharmacist	Concha Rabal
Elderly Psychiatric Patient	Jose Maria Tasso
Lola's Brothers	Victor Aparicio, Carlos G. Cambero
Phantom	Oswaldo Delgado
Editor	Angelina Llongueras
Producer	Alberto Fernandez
Marina's Mother	Francisca Caballero
Lola's Daughter	Francisca Pajuelo
Black Man	Alito Rodgers
Tango Dancers	Virginia Diez, Manuel Bandera
Candy Store Sales Clerk	Juana Cordero
Camel	Jose Miguel, Illera Tamaki
Nurse	Almudena Gracia

Top: Victoria Abril Right: Abril, Antonio Banderas
© Miramax Films

Blair Brown, Bridget Fonda Above: Brown, Bruno Ganz

STRAPLESS

(MIRAMAX) Producer, Rick McCallum; Director/Screenplay, David Hare; Photography, Andrew Dunn; Music, Nick Bicat; Editor, Edward Marnier; Co-Producer, Patsy Pollock; Casting, Mary Selway; Designer, Roger Hall; a Granada Film Productions presentation in association with Film Four International; British; Technicolor; Rated R; 103 minutes; May release

CAST

Lillian Hempel	Blair Brown
Raymond Forbes	Bruno Ganz
Colin	Hugh Laurie
Gerry	Billy Roch
Mrs. Clark	Camille Coduri
Mr. Clark	Gary O'Brien
Amy Hempel	Bridget Fonda
Hus	Spencer Leigh
Mr. Cooper	Alan Howard
Romaine Salmon	Suzanne Burden
Nurse	Julie Foy
Staff Nurse	Jacqui Gordon-Lawrence
Harold Sabola	Cyril Niu
Carlos	Julian Bunster
Madeleine	Gedren Heller
Imogen	Imogen Annesley
Imre Kovago	Constantin Alexandrov
Julie Kovago	Dana Gillespie
Prisoner	Stephen Holland
Prisoner's Bride	Giselle Glasman
Registrar	Edward Lyon
Croupier	Derek Webster
Faulkner	Jeremy Gagan
Peverill	Clive Shilson
Secretary	Francesca Longrigg
Helen	Alexandra Pigg

and Helen Lindsay (Neighbour), Michael Gough (Douglas Brodie), Ann Firbank (Daphne Brodie), Rohan McCullough (Annie Rice), Joe Hare (Richard Forbes), Liam De Staic (Phil), Kirsty Buckland (Mary Hempel), Natasha Brice (Natasha), Andrea Linz (Andrea), Saira Whisker (Saira), Melanie Roe (Girl at station)

© Miramax Films

LAST EXIT TO BROOKLYN

(CINECOM) Producer, Bernd Eichinger; Director, Uli Edel; Screenplay, Desmond Nakano; Based on the book by Hubert Selby, Jr.; Photography, Stefan Czapsky; Designer, David Chapman; Editor, Peter Przygodda; Costumes, Carol Oditz; Music, Mark Knopfler; Co-Producer, Herman Weigel; Casting, Deborah Aquila, Jeffrey Passero; Line Producers, Dieter Meyer, G. Mac Brown; Associate Producers, Anna Gross, Jake Eberts; Assistant Directors, Don French, Carla Corwin; Stunts, Jery Hewitt; a Neue Constantin Film production, in collaboration with Bavaria Film and Allied Filmmakers; West German; DuArt color; Rated R; 102 minutes; May release

CAST

Harry Black	Stephen Lang
Tralala	Jennifer Jason Leigh
Big Joe	Burt Young
Vinnie	Peter Dobson
Boyce	Jerry Orbach
Sal	Stephen Baldwin
Tony	Jason Andrews
Freddy	James Lorinz
Al	Sam Rockwell
Mary Black	Maia Danziger
Ella	Camille Saviola
Donna	Ricki Lake
Spook	Cameron Johann
Tommy	John Costelloe
Paulie	Christopher Murney
Eddie	Frank Acciarito
Teresa	Lisa Passero
Brickowski	Mike Cicchetti
Stump	Nick Giangiulio
Georgette	Alexis Arquette
Regina	Zette
Goldie	Robi Martin
Rosie	Sarah Rose
Camille	Julian Alexon
Alex	Robert Weil
Willie	Mark Boone Junior
Submarine Annie	Sylvie Spector
Ruthie	Colleen Flynn
Steve	Frank Military
Mike	David Warshofsky
Bill	Daniel O'Shea
Tral's Trick	Daniel Beer
Georgette's Mother	Rutanya Alda
Arthur	Al Shannon

and Bruce Smolanoff, James McDonald, Andrew Van Dusen (Lost Soldiers), James Harper (Cop), Ray Gill (Dowland), Mike Starr (Security Guard), Christopher Curry, Michael O'Hare (Riot Police), Bob Martana (Truck Driver), Joseph Carberry (Uptown Bartender), John Michael Bennet, Bill Mondy (Uptown Doggies), Frank Vincent (Priest), Brent Katz (Bobby), Marc Ryan (Jack), Robert Kramer (Fred), Hubert Selby, Jr. (Cab Driver)

Top: Jennifer Jason Leigh Below: Burt Young, Ricki Lake, Camille Saviola
© *Cinecom*

Stephen Lang Above: Peter Dobson, Alexis Arquette

Frank Military, Jennifer Jason Leigh

MAY FOOLS

(ORION CLASSICS) Executive Producer, Vincent Malle; Director, Louis Malle; Screenplay, Louis Malle, Jean-Claude Carrière; Photography, Renato Berta; Music, Stéphane Grappelli; Editor, Emmanuelle Castro; a Nouvelles Editions de Films/TFi Films/Ellepi Films production; French; Color; Rated R; 105 minutes; June release

CAST

Milou	Michel Piccoli
Camille	Miou-Miou
Georges	Michel Duchaussoy
Claire	Dominique Blanc
Lily	Harriet Walter
Grimaldi	Bruno Carette
Daniel	François Berleand
Adele	Martine Gautier
Madame Vieuzac	Paulette Dubost
Marie-Laure	Rozenn Le Tallec
Pierre-Alain	Renaud Danner
Françoise	Jeanne Herry-Leclerc
The Twins	Benjamin Prieur, Nicolas Prieur
Leonce	Marcel Bories
Mr. Boutelleau	Etienne Draber
Mrs. Boutelleau	Valérie Lemercier
Paul	Hubert Saint-Macary
The Priest	Bernard Brocas
Delmas	Georges Vaur
Neighbors	Jacqueline Staup, Anne-Marie Bonange
Madame Abel	Denise Juskiewenski
Young Man	Stéphane Broquedis
Adele's Fiancé	Serge Angeloff

Top: Valérie Lemercier, Miou-Miou, Michel Piccoli
Left: Michel Duchaussoy, Martin Gautier
Below Right: Gautier, Harriet Walter, Piccoli

Rozenn Le Tallec, Renaud Danner

HOW TO MAKE LOVE TO A NEGRO WITHOUT GETTING TIRED

(ANGELIKA) Producers, Richard Sadler, Ann Burke, Henry Lange; Director, Jacques W. Benoit; Screenplay, Dany LaFerrière, Richard Sadler; Based on the novel by Dany LaFerrière; Photography, John Berrie; Music, Manu DiBango; Editor, Dominique Roy; French; Color; Not rated; 98 minutes; June release

CAST

Man	Isaach De Bankolé
Bouba	Maka Kotto
Francois	Antoine Durand
Miz Literature	Roberta Bizeau
Miz Suicide	Miriam Cyr

Isaach De Bankole, Roberta Bizeau

THE MISADVENTURES OF MR. WILT

(SAMUEL GOLDWYN CO.) Producer, Brian Eastman; Director, Michael Tuchner; Screenplay, Andrew Marshall, David Renwick; Based on the novel *"Wilt"* by Tom Sharpe; Photography, Norman Langley; Designer, Leo Austin; Music, Anne Dudley; Editor, Chris Blunden; Costumes, Liz Waller; Casting, Rebecca Howard; Associate Producer, Donna Grey; Song: *"Love Hurts"* written by Bordleaux Bryant/performed by Leo Sayer; British; Color; Rated R; 92 minutes; June release

CAST

Henry Wilt	Griff Rhys Jones
Inspector Russell Flint	Mel Smith
Eva Wilt	Alison Steadman
Sally	Diana Quick
Hugh	Jeremy Clyde
Dave	Roger Allam
Rev. Froude	David Ryall
Dr. Pittman	Roger Lloyd Pack
Braintree	Dermot Crowley
Treadaway	John Normington
Gladden	Tony Mathews
Cranham	Charles Lawson
Mrs. Bulstrode	Gabrielle Blunt
Mossop	Edward Clayton
Macari	Geoffrey Chiswick
Mrs. McClaren	Julia McCarthy
Mr. Yeo	Geoffrey McGivern
Manageress	Ling Tai
Vice Principal	Christopher Saul
Ms. Clinch	Barbara Hicks
Board	Adam Bareham
Science Teacher	Ian Barritt
Japanese Visitor	Togo Igawa
Jessell	Fergus McLarnon
Figgis	Mark Monero
Gilmore	Sam Smart
Student	Christopher Priest
Miss Leuchers	Josephine Tewson
Familoe	Ken Drury
Boffin	David Quilter

and Debra Hearst (WPC Longman), Beccy Wright (WPC Duncan), Dan Hildebrand (Constable), Don Williams (Adam), Billy Geraghty (Dee-Jay), Imogen Claire, Peter Gluckstein, Gina McKee, Neville Phillips, Ann Queensbury (Party Guests), Jim Dunn (Urwin), Sidney Livingstone (Barney), Stewart Harwood (Driver), John Melainey (Reporter)

Top: Griff Rhys Jones, Mel Smith Below: Diana Quick, Alison Steadman, Jones © *Samuel Goldwyn Co.*

Catherine Hiegel, Daniel Gelin

LIFE IS A LONG QUIET RIVER

(MK2) Producer, Charles Gassot; Executive Producer, Florence Quentin; Director, Etienne Chatiliez; Screenplay, Florence Quentin, Etienne Chatiliez; Photography, Pascal Lebegue; Designer, Geoffroy Larcher; Editor, Chantal Delattre; Music, Gerard Kawczynski; Costumes, Elisabeth Tavernier; from MK2 Productions/FR3 Films Production in association with Sofica Investimage with the participation of the National Center of Cinematography; French; Color; Not rated; 95 minutes; July release

CAST

Momo	Benoit Magimel
Bernadette	Valerie Lalande
Million	Tara Romer
Toc-Toc	Jerome Floc'h
Ghislaine	Sylvie Cubertafon
Pierre	Emmanuel Cendrier
Paul	Guillaume Hacquebart
Mathieu	Jean-Brice Van Keer
Emmanuelle	Praline La Moult
Franck	Axel Vicart
Roselyne	Claire Prevost
Madame Le Quesnoy	Helen Vincent
Monsieur Le Quesnoy	Andre Wilms
Madame Groseille	Christine Pignet
Monsieur Groseille	Maurice Mons
Doctor Mavial	Daniel Gelin
Josette	Catherine Hiegel
Marie-Therese	Catherine Jacob
Father Auberge	Patrick Bouchitey
Hamed	Abbes Zahmani
Latifa	Khadou Fghoul
Rachid	Israel Bourabaa
Grandmother	Louise Comte
Madame Mavial	Liliane Ledun

and Gilles Defacque (Taxi Driver), Luc Samaille (Delivery Man), Philippe Peltier (School Teacher), Pierre Rougier (English Professor), Marc Spillman, Louis-Marie Taillefer (Policemen), Philippe Vacher (Doctor), Roger Dancoine (Brigadier), Jean-Pierre Fouillet (E.D.F. Agents), Denis Barbier (S.N.C.F. Controler), Elisabeth Tavernier, Frederique Moino (Nurses), Marie-Luce Delesalle, Rina Garfneur (Speakers), Francois Paoli (Television reporter)

© *MK2 Prods.*

ARIEL

(KINO INTERNATIONAL) Producer/Director/Screenplay, Aki Kaurismäki; Photography, Timo Salminen; Designer, Risto Karhula; Costumes, Tuula Hilkamo; Editor, Raija Talvio; Produced by Villeafla Film productions with assistance from the Finnish Film Foundation; Finnish; Color; Not rated; 74 minutes; August release

CAST

Taisto Kasurinen	Turo Pajala
Irmeli	Susanna Haavisto
Mikkonen	Matti Pellonpää
Riku	Eetu Hilkamo
Miner	Erkki Pajala
Mugger	Matti Jaaranen
Accomplice	Hannu Viholainen
Tallyman	Jorma Markkula
Woman in the harbor	Tarja Keinänen
Man on the beach	Eino Kuusela
Flophouse Nightman	Kauko Laalo
Man in the flophouse	Jyrki Olsonen
Car Dealer	Eskko Nikkari
Judge	Marja Packalen
Prison Doctor	Mikko Remes
Mayor	Veikko Uusimäki
Crook	Esko Salminen
Doorman	Hannu Kivasalo
Skipper	Pekka Wilen
Guards	Tomi Salmela, Reijo Marin, Heiki Salomaa

© *Kino International*

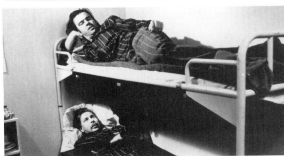

Maurizio Nichetti, Mattio Auguardi, Heidi Komarek

THE ICICLE THIEF

(ARIES FILMS) Producer, Ernesto di Sarro; Director, Maurizio Nichetti; Screenplay, Maurizio Nichetti, Mauro Monti; Photography, Mario Battistoni; Designer, Ada Legori; Costumes, Maria Pia Angelini; Music, Manuel De Sica; Editor, Rita Olivati; Assistant Director, Laura Zagordi; Bambu Productions; Italian; Color/Black and white; Not rated; 90 minutes; August release

CAST

The Television Studio:

The TV Producer	Lella Costa
The Film Critic	Claudio G. Fava
The Director of the film	Maurizio Nichetti

The Piermattei Family:

Antonio, the father	Maurizio Nichetti
Maria, the mother	Caterina Sylos Labini
Bruno, the son	Federico Rizzo
Paolo, the baby boy	Mattio Auguardi
Don Italo, the priest	Renato Scarpa
The Model	Heidi Komarek

The Television-viewing Family:

The Mother	Carlina Torta
The Father	Massimo Sacilotto

Heidi Komarek, Federico Rizzo Above Left: Maurizio Nichetti

© *Aries Films*

191

Akira Terao (R) Top Left: Mieko Harada Top Right: Terao, Martin Scorsese Right: Terao, Chosuke Ikariya
© *Warner Bros.*

AKIRA KUROSAWA'S DREAMS

(WARNER BROS.) Producers, Hisao Kurosawa, Mike Y. Inoue; Director/Screenplay, Akira Kurosawa; Associate Producers, Allan H. Liebert, Seikichi Iizumi; Photography, Takao Saito, Masaharu Ueda; Costumes, Emi Wada; Music, Shinichiro Ikebe; Art Directors, Yoshiro Muraki, Akira Sakuragi; Visual Effects, Industrial Light & Magic; Editor, Tome Minami; Assistant Director, Takashi Koizumi; an Akira Kurosawa USA Inc. production; Japanese; Dolby Stereo; Color; Rated PG; 120 minutes; August release

CAST

I	Akira Terao
Vincent Van Gogh	Martin Scorsese
The Old Man	Chishu Ryu
Snow Fairy	Mieko Harada
Mother of I	Mitsuko Baisho
The Weeping Demon	Chosuke Ikariya
Power Station Worker	Hisashi Igawa
Private Noguchi	Yoshitaka Zushi
Child-carrying Mother	Toshie Negishi
I as a boy	Mitsunori Isaki
I as a young child	Toshihiko Nakano
Young I's Sister	Mie Suzuki

Chishu Ryu

BAXTER

(EXPANDED ENTERTAINMENT) Producers, Ariel Zeitoun, Patrick Godeau; Director, Jerome Boivin; Screenplay, Jacques Audiard, Jerome Boivin; Adapted from the novel "*Hell Hound*" by Ken Greenhall; Photography, Yves Angélo; Music, Marc Hillman, Patrick Roffé; Editor, Marie-Jo Audiard; Designer, Marc Brunin Jardin; Costumes, Anne David, Claudine Lachaud; Trainer, Jacana; a coproduction of Partner's Production—P.C.C. Productions—Christian Bourgois Productions—Gerard Mital Productions—Issa & Alicelleo with the participation of Centre National de la Cinématographie in association with Sofimage—Sofica Investimage—Sofinergie; a Backstreet Film; French; Color; Not rated; 82 minutes; August release

CAST

Madame Deville	Lise Delamare
Monsieur Cuzzo	Jean Mercure
Michel Ferrer	Jacques Spiesser
Florence Morel	Catherine Ferran
Joseph Barsky	Jean-Paul Roussillon
Noëlle	Sabrina Leurquin
Jean	Daniel Rialet
Marie Cuzzo	Evelyn Didi
Roger Morel	Rémy Carpentier
Anne Ferrer	Jany Gastaldi
Charles	François Driancourt
Veronique	Eve Ziberlin
Jean-Jean	Malcolm Scrannage
Eva Braun	Léa Gabrièle

Top: Baxter, Francois Driancourt Right: Jean Mercure, Lise Delamare © *Back Street Films*

FOOLS OF FORTUNE

(NEW LINE CINEMA) Producer, Sarah Radclyffe; Executive Producers, Tim Bevan, Graham Bradstreet; Director, Pat O'Connor; Screenplay, Michael Hirst; Based on the novel by William Trevor; Photography, Jerzy Zielinski; Associate Producer, Caroline Hewitt; Editor, Michael Bradsell; Music, Hans Zimmer; Designer, Jamie Leonard; Costumes, Judy Moorcroft; Casting, Debbie McWilliams; Assistant Director, Bill Craske; Presented by Polygram and Working Title in association with Film Four International; British; Dolby Stereo; Color; Rated PG-13; 109 minutes; September release

CAST

Marianne	Mary Elizabeth Mastrantonio
Willie	Iain Glen
Mrs. Quinton	Julie Christie
Mr. Quinton	Michael Kitchen
Young Willie	Sean McClory
Tim Paddy	Frankie McCafferty
Mrs. Flynn	Ronnie Masterson
Father Kilgarriff	Tom Hickey
Geraldine	Hazel Flanagan
Deirdre	Amy Hastings
Mr. Derenzy	Mick Lally
Johnny Lacy	John Kavanagh
O'Neill	Jimmy Keogh
Josephine	Niamh Cusack
Aunt Fitzeustace	Rosaleen Linehan
Aunt Pansy	Anita Reeves
Doyle	Sean McGinley
Sgt. Rudkin	Neil Dudgeon
Lanigan	Niall Toibin
Mrs. Woodcombe	Eileen Colgan
Imelda	Catherine McFadden
Stranger	Ian McElhinney
Bridie Sweeney	Sighle Toibin
O'Dwyer	Seamus Forde
Mr. Sweeney	Johnny Murphy
Mrs. Sweeney	Pat Leavy
Theresa Shea	Joanne Foley

© *New Line Cinema*

Iain Glen; Mary Elizabeth Mastrantonio Above: Julie Christie

KING OF NEW YORK

(NEW LINE CINEMA) Producer, Mary Kane; Executive Producers, Jay Julien, Vittorio Squillante; Director, Abel Ferrara; Screenplay, Nicholas St. John; Photography, Bojan Bazelli; Associate Producer/ Casting, Randy Sabusawa; Designer, Alex Tavoularis; Music, Joe Delia; Editor, Anthony Redman; Costumes, Carol Ramsey; Assistant Director, David Sardi; a Reteitalia S.p.a. and Scena International S.r.l. presentation from Seven Arts; Italian; Dolby Stereo; Color; Rated R; 103 minutes; September release

CAST

Frank White	Christopher Walken
Dennis Gilley	David Caruso
Jimmy Jump	Larry Fishburne
Roy Bishop	Victor Argo
Thomas Flannigan	Wesley Snipes
Jennifer Poe	Janet Julian
Larry Wong	Joey Chin
Lance	Giancarlo Esposito
Joey Dalesio	Paul Calderon
Moses	Steve Buscemi
Raye	Theresa Randle
Blood	Leonard Lee Thomas
Edmund Tanner	Roger Smith
Melanie	Carrie Nygren
King Tito	Ernest Abuba
Paul Calgari	Frank Adonis
British Female	Vanessa Angel
Waiter (Chicken Hut)	David Batiste
Taxi Driver	Michael Battin
Johnny Chick	Frankie Cee
Gangmember	Kim Lia Chang
Dr. Shute	Erica Gimpel
Artie Clay	Frank Gio
Musta	Lance Guecia
Carter	Michael Guess
Emilio El Zapa	Freddy Howard
Millie	Nancy Hunter
Abraham Cott	Jay Julien

and Jack Goode, Jr., Susannah Julien, Marty Pesci (Palladium Patrons), Robert LaSardo (Italian Guard), Phoebe Legere (Bordello Woman), James Lorinz (Tip Connolly), Gary Landon Mills (Chilly), Gerald Murphy (Mulligan), Harold Perrineau (Thug Leader), George Lawrence Perry (Cop), Peter Richardson (Emperor Jones), Lonnie Shaw (Kathleen Mulligan), Wendell Sweda (Man at breakfast table), Freddy Jackson, Ariane Koizumi, Pete Hamill, Sari Chang

Top: Janet Julian, Christopher Walken Below: David Caruso,
Larry Fishburne, Wesley Snipes, David Batiste
© *New Line Cinema*

Frank Gio, Larry Fishburne, Frankie Cee, Christopher Walken

INTERROGATION

(CIRCLE RELEASING) Producer, Tadeusz Drewno; Director/ Screenplay, Richard Bagajski; Executive Producer, Andrzej Wajda; Photography, Jacek Petrycki; Editor, Katarzyna Maciejko; Designer, Janusz Sosnowski; Assistant Director, Hanna Hartowicz; a Unit X. Zespoly Filmowe production; Polish; Color; Not rated; 118 minutes; September release

CAST

Tonia Dziwisz	Krystyna Janda
Major	Janusz Gajos
Lt. Morawski	Adam Ferency
The Communist Woman	Agnieszka Holland
Mira	Anna Romantowska
Kostek, Tonia's Husband	Olgierd Lukaszewicz
The Peasant Woman	Bozena Dykiel
Chief Warden	Jan Jurewicz

© *Circle Releasing Corp.*

Krystyna Janda

(NEW YORKER FILMS) Producers, Mamadou Mbengue, Mustapha Ben Jemia, Ouzid Dahmane; Directors/Screenplay, Ousmane Sembene, Thierno Faty Sow; Photography, Ismail Lakhdar Hamina; Editor, Kahena Attia-Riveill; Music, Ismaila Lo; Costumes, Deba Ndiaye; Produced by SNPC (Dakar)/ENAPROC (Algiers)/SATPEC (Tunis), with the participation of Filmi Dooni Reew (Dakar), and Film Kajoor (Thies); Senegal-Tunisia-Algeria/French, 1988; Color; Not rated; 157 minutes; September release

CAST

Sergeant-Major Diatta .... Ibrahima Sane and Sigiri Bakara, Hamed Camara, Ismaila Cissé, Ababacar Sy Cissé, Moussa Cissoko, Eloi Coly, Ismaila Lo, Pierre Londiche, Camara Med Dansogho, Elhadg Ndiaye, Thierno Ndiaye, Oumarou Neino, Pierre Orma, Daniel Odimbossoukou, Jean Daniel Simon, Gustave Sorgho, Gabriel Zahon, Koffi Saturnin Zinga, Casimir Zoba dit Zao

© *New Yorker Films*

"Elephant!" Dancers Top Right: Jeff Goldblum
© *Miramax Films*

THE TALL GUY

(MIRAMAX) Producer, Paul Webster; Director, Mel Smith; Screenplay, Richard Curtis; Executive Producer, Tim Bevan; Photography, Adrian Biddle; Designer, Grant Hicks; Costumes, Denise Simmons; Editor, Dan Rae; Assistant Director, Waldo Roeg; Casting, Sheila Trezise; Prosthetic Make-up Effects, Daniel Parker, Animated Extras; Choreographer, Charles Augins; Music, Peter Brewis; a Working Title production; British; Dolby Stereo; Color; Rated R; 90 minutes; September release

CAST

Dexter King	Jeff Goldblum
Kate Lemon	Emma Thompson
Ron Anderson	Rowan Atkinson
Cyprus Charlie	Emil Wolk
Carmen	Geraldine James
Cheryl	Kim Thomson
Tamara	Joanna Kanska
Dr. Karabekian	Hugh Thomas
Dr. Freud	Susan Field
Mary	Anna Massey
Gavin	Peter Kelly
Mr. Morrow	Timothy Barlowe
Timothy	Harold Innocent
Disgustingly Drunk Man at party	Mel Smith

Jeff Goldblum, Emma Thompson Above: Goldblum, Rowan Atkinson

LIFE AND NOTHING BUT
(La Vie et Rien D'Autre)

(ORION CLASSICS) Executive Producers, Frederic Bourboulon, Albert Prevost; Director, Bertrand Tavernier; Screenplay and Adaptation, Jean Cosmos, Bertrand Tavernier; Dialogue, Jean Cosmos; Photography, Bruno De Keyzer; Sets, Guy-Claude Francois; Costumes, Jacqueline Moreau; Associate Producer, Rene Cleitman; Music, Oswald d'Andrea; Songs, Jean Cosmos, Oswald d'Andrea; a co-production of Hachette Premiere/A.B. Films/Little Bear/Films A2 with the participation of Soficas Sofinergie and Investimage and the National Center of Cinematography; French; Panavision; Color; Rated PG; 135 minutes; September release

CAST

Major Dellaplane	Philippe Noiret
Irene	Sabine Azema
Alice	Pascale Vignal
Marcadot	Maurice Barrier
Perrin	Francois Perrot
Andre	Jean-Paul Dubois
Lt. Trevise	Daniel Russo
Gen. Villerieux	Michel Duchaussoy
Valentine	Arlette Gilbert
Valentin	Louis Lyonnet
Cora Mabel	Charlotte Maury
Julien	Francois Caron
Engineer Corps Adjutant	Thierry Gimenez
Madame Lebegue	Frederique Meninger
Eugene Dilatoire	Pierre Trabaud
Monsieur Lebegue	Jean-Roger Milo
Nun on horseback	Catherine Verlor
The Amnesiac	Jean-Christophe Lebert
Rougeaud	Bruno Therasse
Man without legs	Philippe Uchan
Solange de Boissancourt	Marion Loran
Nun in hospital	Charlotte Kadi
Professor Mortier	Gabriel Cattand
Poirleau	Christophe Odent
Lagrange	Jean Champion
Lecordier	Philippe Deplanche
Abel Mascle	Michel Cassagne
Marcel	Frederic Pierrot
Georges	Francois Domange
Fagot	Jean-Paul Comart

and Patrick Massieu (Cemetery Guard), Dider Harlmann (One-armed Man), Pascal Elso (Blind Man), Odile Cointepas (Madame Hannesson), Louba Guertchikoff (Blue-eyed Lady), Jean-Claude Calon (Zealous Sergeant), Jean-Yves Gauthier (Corporal), Gilles Janeyrand (Sous-officer), Nicolas Trone (Pvt. Lefebvre), Jerome Frossard (Soldat Commissar), Michele Gleizer (Farm Woman), Daniel Langlet (Monsieur Ichac), Marcel Zanini (Leo), Marc Perrone (Pochin), Georges Staquet (Parish Priest), Alain Frerot (Pelat), Francois Dyrek (Vergnes), Mike Zwerin (Jennings), Bruno Raffaelli (Maginot), Eric Dufay (Cpl. Thain)

© *Orion Pictures Corp.*
Top: Philippe Noiret, Maurice Barrier Below: Sabine Azema, Pascale Vignal Right: Noiret, Azema

Tania Palaiologou, Michalis Zeke

LANDSCAPE IN THE MIST

(NEW YORKER FILMS) Producer/Director/Story, Theo Angelopoulos; Screenplay, Theo Angelopoulos, Tonino Guerra, Thanassis Valtinos; Photography, Giorgos Arvanitis; Art Director, Mikes Karapiperis; Costumes, Anastasia Arseni; Music, Eleni Karaindrou; Editor, Yannis Tsitsopoulos; a co-production of Paradis Films (Paris), Greek Film Centre, Greek Television ET-1 (Athens), Basicinematografica (Rome); Greek, 1988; Color; Not rated; 126 minutes; September release

CAST

Alexander	Michalis Zeke
Voula	Tania Palaiologou
Orestes	Stratos Tzortzoglou

and Eva Kotamanidou, Aliki Georgouli, Vassilis Kolovos, Vassilis Bouyouklakis, Ilias Logothetis, Vangelis Kazan, Stratos Pachis, Michalis Yannatos

© *New Yorker Films*

THE NASTY GIRL

(MIRAMAX) Director/Screenplay, Michael Verhoeven; Photography, Axel de Roche; Music, Mike Herting, Elmar Schloter; Editor, Barbara Hennings; Costumes, Ute Truthmann; Designer, Hubert Popp; Assistant Director, Brigitte Liphardt; a Sentana Film production; West German; Color; Rated PG-13; 94 minutes; October release

CAST

Sonja	Lena Stolze
Mother (Maria)	Monika Baumgartner
Father (Paul)	Michael Gahr
Uncle	Fred Stillkrauth
Grandmother	Elisabeth Bertram
Martin	Robert Giggenbach
Robert	Michael Guillaume
Nina	Karin Thaler
Dr. Juckenack	Hans-Richard Müller
Fraülein Juckenack	Barbara Gallauner
Father Brummel	Willi Schultes
Burgomaster	Richard Süsmeier
Schulz	Udo Thomer
Merganthaler	Ludwig Wühr
Dr. Fasching	Herbert Lehnert
Frau Stangl	Irmgard Henning-Bayrhammer
Abtretter	Ossi Eckmüller
Roeder	Hermann Hummel

Top: Lena Stolze (C) **Right:** Stolze, Ottfried **Below Left:** Stolze, Robert Giggenbach **Below Right:** Giggenbach, Stolze
© *Miramax Films*

Johanna Ter Steege, Gene Bervoets

THE VANISHING

(TARA RELEASING) Producers, George Sluizer, Anne Lordon; Director/Editor, George Sluizer; Screenplay, Tim Krabbe, George Sluizer; Based on the novel *"The Golden Egg"* by Tim Krabbe; Photography, Toni Kuhn; A Golden Egg Films/MGS Film Production in co-production with Ingrid Production Paris presentation from Movie Visions; Dutch, 1988; Color; Not rated; 107 minutes; October release

CAST

Raymond Lemorne	Bernard-Pierre Donnadieu
Rex	Gene Bervoets
Saskia	Johanna Ter Steege

and Gwen Eckhaus

© *Tara Releasing*

MEMPHIS BELLE

(WARNER BROS.) Producers, David Puttnam, Catherine Wyler; Director, Michael Caton-Jones; Screenplay, Monte Merrick; Photography, David Watkin; Designer, Stuart Craig; Music, George Fenton; Song: *"Danny Boy"* performed by Harry Connick, Jr.; Associate Producer, Eric Rattray; Editor, Jim Clark; Casting, Marion Dougherty, Juliet Taylor; Costumes, Jane Robinson; Supervising Special Effects and Model Unit Director, Richard Conway; Assistant Director, Bill Westley; Aerial Unit Director/Cameraman, James Devis; an Enigma Production presented in association with Fujisankei Communications Group, British Satellite Broadcasting and County Natwest Ventures; British; Dolby Stereo; Color; Rated PG-13; 106 minutes; October release

CAST

Dennis Dearborn	Matthew Modine
Danny Daly	Eric Stoltz
Luke Sinclair	Tate Donovan
Phil Rosenthal	D. B. Sweeney
Val Kozlowski	Billy Zane
Richard "Rascal" Moore	Sean Astin
Clay Busby	Harry Connick, Jr.
Virgil	Reed Edward Diamond
Eugene McVey	Courtney Gains
Jack Bocci	Neil Giuntoli
The Commanding Officer	David Strathairn
Col. Bruce Derringer	John Lithgow
Faith	Jane Horrocks
Les	Mac MacDonald
Singer	Jodie Wilson
"S-2"	Keith Edwards
Stan the Rookie	Steven Mackintosh
Adjutant	Greg Charles
Sergeant	Bradley Lavell
Rookie Captain	Ben Browder
Group Navigator	Mitch Webb
Lieutenant	Paul Birchard
Farmer	Bill Cullum
Cook	Eric Loren
Jitterbuggers	Cathy Murphy, Morag Siller
Footballers	Steve Elm, Jason Salkey, Martin McDougal

Top: Matthew Modine Below: Tate Donovan, Reed Edward Diamond, Modine Left: Diamond, Neil Giuntoli, Sean Astin, Billy Zane © *Warner Bros.*

Harry Connick, Jr.

D. B. Sweeney, Tate Donovan, Matthew Modine, Billy Zane

Courtney Gains, Sean Astin, Reed Edward Diamond, Tate Donovan, Neil Giuntoli, Harry Connick, Jr., D. B. Sweeney (in jeep), Eric Stoltz, Billy Zane, Matthew Modine

Eric Stoltz

David Strathairn, John Lithgow

MY TWENTIETH CENTURY

(ARIES FILMS) Producers, Gabor Hanak, Norbert Friedlander; Director/Screenplay, Ildiko Enyedi; Photography, Tibor Mathe; Designer, Zoltan Labas; Costumes, Agnes Gyarmathy; Music, Laszlo Vidovszky; Editor, Maria Rigo; a Budapest Film-Studio/Mafilm (Hungary), Friedlander Filmproduktion/Hamburger Film Buro (West Germany), I.C.A.I.C. (Cuba); Hungarian-West German-Cuban; Black and white; Not rated; 104 minutes; November release

CAST

Dora/Lili/Their Mother	Dorotha Segda
Z	Oleg Jankowski
Thomas Edison	Peter Andorai
X	Gabor Mate

and Paulus Manker, Gyula Keri, Andrej Schwartz, Sandor Teri, Sandor Czvetko, Endre Koronczi, Agnes Kovacs, Eszter Kovacs

Top: Dorotha Segda Right: Oleg Jankowski © *Aries Films*

Wladimir Yordanoff, Paul Rhys Above: Tim Roth

VINCENT & THEO

(HEMDALE) Producer, Ludi Boeken; Director, Robert Altman; Executive Producer, David Conroy; Screenplay, Julian Mitchell; Photography, Jean Lepine; Designer, Stephen Altman; Music, Gabriel Yared; Editors, Francoise Coispeau, Geraldine Peroni; Costumes, Scott Bushnell; Associate Producers, Harry Prins, Jacques Fansten; a Belbo Films—Central Films—La SEPT—Telepool—RAI Uno—Vara—Sofica Valor coproduction; French-British; Color; Rated PG-13; 138 minutes; November release

CAST

Vincent Van Gogh	Tim Roth
Theo Van Gogh	Paul Rhys
Uncle Cent	Andrian Brine
Léon Boussod	Jean-François Perrier
René Valadon	Vincent Vallier
Andries Bonger	Hans Kesting
Anton Mauve	Peter Tuinman
Jet Mauve	Marie-Louise Stheins
Ida	Oda Spelbos
Sien Hoornik	Jip Wijngaarden
Marie	Anne Canovas
Marie Hoornik	Sarah Bentham
Emile Bernard	Jean-Denis Monory
Jo Bonger	Johanna Ter Steege
"Pere" Tanguy	Jean-Pierre Castaldi
Painters	Anne Chaplin, Humbert Camerlo
Paul Gauguin	Wladimir Yordanoff
Mme Ginoux	Louise Boisvert
Paul Millet	Vincent Souliac
Zouave	Klaus Stoeber
Rachel	Florence Muller
Mme Viviane	Viviane Fauny Camerlo
Dr. Rey	Alain Vergne
Dr. Peyron	Feodor Atkine
Trabuc	Jean-Pierre Gos
Dr. Paul Gachet	Jean-Pierre Cassel
Marguerite Gachet	Bernadette Giraud
Mr. Ravoux	Mogan Mehlem
Mme Ravoux	Therese Cremieux

© *Hemdale Film Corp.*

HIDDEN AGENDA

(HEMDALE) Producer, Eric Fellner; Co-Producer, Rebecca O'Brien; Executive Producers, John Daly, Derek Gibson; Director, Ken Loach; Screenplay, Jim Allen; Photography, Clive Tickner; Designer, Martin Johnson; Costumes, Daphne Dare; Music, Stewart Copeland; Editor, Jonathan Morris; British; Dolby Stereo; Eastmancolor; Rated R; 107 minutes; November release

CAST

Ingrid	Frances McDormand
Kerrigan	Brian Cox
Paul	Brad Dourif
Moa	Mai Zetterling
Sir Robert Neil	Bernard Archard
Maxwell	John Benfield
Henri	Bernard Bloch
Teresa Doyle	Michelle Fairley
Alec Nevin	Patrick Kavanagh
Sgt. Kennedy	Des McAleer
Jack Cunningham	Ian McElhinney
Brodie	Jim Norton
Harris	Maurice Roëves
Ian Logan	Robert Patterson
Molloy	Brian McCann
Det. Sgt. Hughes	John Keegan
Mrs. Molloy	Maureen Bell
Carol	Kym Dyson
Superintendent Fraser	Oliver Maguire
Tall Man	George Staines
RUC Policewoman	Mandy McIlwaine
TV Reporter	Ivan Little

and Llew Gardner (TV Announcer), John McDonnell (Labour MP), Kate Smith (News Reporter), Victoria D'Angelo (Journalist), Stephen Brigden (Army Major), Ron Kavana, Terry Woods (Musicians), Gerry Fearon (Taxi Driver)

Top: Brian Cox, Frances McDormand Right: McDormand, Brad Dourif © *Hemdale Film Corp.*

Gary Kemp, Martin Kemp (C) Above: Martin Kemp, Billie Whitelaw, Gary Kemp

THE KRAYS

(MIRAMAX) Producers, Dominic Anciano, Ray Burdis; Executive Producers, Jim Beach, Michele Kimche; Director, Peter Medak; Screenplay, Philip Ridley; Photography, Alex Thomson; Designer, Michael Pickwoad; Costumes, Lindy Hemming; Music, Michael Kamen; Editor, Martin Walsh; Assistant Director, Michael Zimbrich; British; Dolby Stereo; Color; Rated R; 119 minutes; November release

CAST

Violet Kray	Billie Whitelaw
Ronald Kray	Gary Kemp
Reginald Kray	Martin Kemp
Rose	Susan Fleetwood
May	Charlotte Cornwell
Cannonball Lee	Jimmy Jewel
Helen	Avis Bunnage
Frances	Kate Hardie
Charlie Kray, Sr.	Alfred Lynch
Jack "The Hat" McVitie	Tom Bell
George Cornell	Steven Berkoff
Steve	Gary Love
Mr. Lawson	Victor Spinetti
Mrs. Lawson	Barbara Ferris
Judy Garland	Julia Migenes
Charlie Kray, Jr.	Roger Monk
Ron & Reg (age 3)	John-Paul & Michael White
Ron & Reg (age 8)	Harlon & Sam Haveland
Ron & Reg (age 10)	Jason & Jamie Bennett
Charlie Pelham	John McEnery
Iris	Patti Love

and Murray Melvin, Norman Rossington

Miramax Films

CYRANO DE BERGERAC

(ORION CLASSICS) Producers, Rene Cleitman, Michel Seydoux; Director, Jean-Paul Rappeneau; Screenplay/Adaptation, Jean-Paul Rappeneau, Jean-Claude Carriere; Based on the play by Edmond Rostand; English Subtitles, Anthony Burgess; Photography, Pierre Lhomme; Designer, Franca Squarciapino; Design for Cyrano's Nose, Michele Burke; Music, Jean-Claude Petit; Casting, Romain Bremond; Editor, Noelle Boisson; French; Dolby Stereo; Color; Rated PG; 138 minutes; November release

CAST

Cyrano de Bergerac	Gerard Depardieu
Roxane	Anne Brochet
Christian de Neuvillette	Vincent Perez
Comte De Guiche	Jacques Weber
Ragueneau	Roland Bertin
Le Bret	Philippe Morier-Genoud
Carbon de Castel-Jaloux	Pierre Maguelon
Roxane's Handmaid	Josiane Stoleru
The Child	Anatole Delalande
The Little Sister	Ludivine Sagnier
The Father	Alain Rimoux
Vicomte de Valvert	Philippe Volter
Ligniere	Jean-Marie Winling
Le Facheux	Louis Navarre
Montfleury	Gabriel Monnet
Bellerose	Francois Marie
Jodelet	Pierre Triboulet
Military Officers	Baptiste Roussillon, Christian Roy
Le Tire-laine	Jacques Pater
Marquis	Pierre Aussedat, Yves Aubert
The Academy Member	Lucien Pascal
The Young Snob	Jean-Damien Barbin
The Matron	Nicole Felix
The Cadets	Christian Loustau, Alain Perez, Franck Jazede, Eric Bernard, Franck Ramon, Alain Dumas, Herve Pauchon
Officer De Guiche	Philippe Girard
The Cook	Quentin Ogier
Lise Ragueneau	Catherine Ferran
Ragueneau Poets	Vincent Nemeth, Michel Fau
Uranie	Christiane Culerier
Gremoine	Cecile Camp
Lysimon	Benoit Vergne
Poets	Eric Fry, Eric Picou
The Mother Superior	Madeleine Marion
Sister Marthe	Amelie Gonin
Sister Colette	Sandrine Kiberlain
Sister Claire	Isabelle Gruault
The Naughty Sister	Claudine Gabay

© Orion Pictures Corp.
Top: Gerard Depardieu, Anne Brochet Below: Depardieu, Vincent Perez Left: Philippe Volter, Depardieu
1990 Academy Award for Best Costume Design

Anne Brochet, Josiane Stoleru

Gerard Depardieu, Philippe Morier-Genoud

Gerard Depardieu, Anne Brochet Above Left: Vincent Perez, Depardieu Top Left:
Brochet, Perez, Depardieu Above Right: Depardieu, Jacques Weber Top Right:
Depardieu

LENINGRAD COWBOYS GO AMERICA

(ORION CLASSICS) Producers, Aki Kaurismäki, Klas Olofsson, Katinka Farago; Director/Screenplay, Aki Kaurismäki; Story, Sakke Järvenpää, Aki Kaurismäki, Mato Valtonen; Music, Mauri Sumén; Editor, Raija Talvio; a Villealfa Filmproductions/The Swedish Film Institute production, in association with Finnkino Oy, Megamania Ky, Esselte Video AB; Finnish; Color; Rated PG-13; 80 minutes; November release

CAST

Vladimir (Manager)	Matti Pellonpää
Igor (Village Idiot)	Kari Väänänen
The Leningrad Cowboys	Sakke Järvenpää, Heikki Keskinen, Sakari Kuosmanen, Puka Oinonen, Silu Sepälä, Mauri Sumén, Mato Valtonen, Pekka Virtanen
Lost Cousin	Nicky Tesco
Siberian Svengali	Olli Tuominen
Father of the Cowboys	Jatimatic Ohlström
Rock Promoter	Richard Boes
Car Dealer	Jim Jarmusch
Barber	William W. Robertson
Nightclub Owner	Duke Robillard
Mexican Singer	Jose G. Salas

Top: The Sleepy Sleepers Right: William W. Robertson, Kari Vaananen © Orion Pictures Corp.

C'EST LA VIE

(SAMUEL GOLDWYN CO.) Producer, Alexandre Arcady; Executive Producer, Robert Benmussa; Director, Diane Kurys; Screenplay, Diane Kurys, Alain Le Henry; Photography, Giuseppe Lanci; Music, Philippe Sarde; Editor, Raymonde Guyot; Costumes, Caroline De Vivaise; French; Color; Not rated; 97 minutes; November release

CAST

Lena	Nathalie Baye
Michel	Richard Berry
Bella	Zabou
Leon	Jean-Pierre Bacri
Jean-Claude	Vincent London
Odette	Valeria Bruni-Tedeschi
Ruffier	Didier Benureau
Frederique	Julie Bataille
Sophie	Candice Lefranc
Daniel	Alexis Derlon
Suzanne	Emmanuelle Boidron
Rene	Maxime Boidron
Titi	Benjamin Sacks

© Samuel Goldwyn Co.

Nathalie Baye, Jean-Pierre Bacri, Zabou, Vincent Lindon
Above: Julie Bataille, Baye, Candice Lefranc

TILAï

(NEW YORKER FILMS) Producer/Director/Screenplay, Idrissa Ouedraogo; Executive Producer, Beatrice Korc; Photography, Jean Monsigny, Pierre Laurent Chenieux; Music, Abdullah Ibrahim; Editor, Luc Barnier; Mooré; Color; Not rated; 81 minutes; November release

CAST

Saga	Rasmane Ouedraogo
Nogma	Ina Cisse
Kuilga	Roukietou Barry
Kougri	Assane Ouedraogo
Poko	Sibidou Sidibe
Tenga	Moumouni Ouedraogo
Bore	Mariam Barry
Nomenaba	Seydou Ouedraogo
Koudpoko	Mariam Ouedraogo
Porgo	Daouda Porgo
Maiga	Kogre Warma
Ganame	Mamdou Ganame

Top: Rasmane Ouedraogo, Mariam Barry © *New Yorker Films*

Sean Bean, Richard Harris Top Left: Harris
© *Avenue Pictures*

THE FIELD

(AVENUE PICTURES) Producer, Noel Pearson; Director/Screenplay, Jim Sheridan; Based on the play by John B. Keane; Executive Producer, Steve Morrison; Line Producer, Arthur Lappin; Photography, Jack Conroy; Designer, Frank Conway; Costumes, Joan Bergin; Editor, J. Patrick Duffner; Music, Elmer Bernstein; Casting, Nuala Moiselle; a Granada Film; Irish; Dolby Stereo; Technicolor; Rated PG-13; 107 minutes; December release

CAST

"Bull" McCabe	Richard Harris
Tadgh McCabe	Sean Bean
Widow	Frances Tomelty
Maggie McCabe	Brenda Fricker
"Bird" O'Donnell	John Hurt
Tinker Woman	Ruth McCabe
Tinker Girl's Father	Jer O'Leary
Tomas	Noel O'Donovan
Flanagan	John Cowley
Tinker	Ronan Wilmot
Tinker Girl	Jenny Conroy
Tinker Woman #2	Joan Sheehy
Father Doran	Sean McGinley
Sergeant	Malachy McCourt
Quarrymen	Frank McDonald, Brendan Gleeson
The American	Tom Berenger
Dan Paddy Andy	Eamon Keane
McRoarty Girl	Sara Jane Scaife
Boy at dance	David Wilmot
Girls at dance	Sarah Cronin, Rachel Dowling
Paddy Joe O'Reilly	Peadar Lamb
Priest's Housekeeper	Aine Ni Mhuire

John Hurt, Richard Harris Above: Tom Berenger; Brenda Fricker

Mel Gibson Top Right: Alan Bates, Gibson, Glenn Close
Top Left: Gibson Below: Gibson, Paul Scofield
© *Icon Distrib.*

HAMLET

(WARNER BROS.) Producer, Dyson Lovell; Director, Franco Zef-
firelli; Screenplay, Christopher De Vore, Franco Zeffirelli; Based on
the play by William Shakespeare; Executive Producer, Bruce Davey;
Photography, David Watkin; Designer, Dante Ferretti; Costumes,
Maurizio Millenotti; Music, Ennio Morricone; Editor, Richard
Marden; Casting, Joyce Nettles; Assistant Director, Michael Murray;
an Icon Production presented by Nelson Entertainment; British; Dolby
Stereo; Rank color; Rated PG; 135 minutes; December release

CAST

Hamlet	Mel Gibson
Gertrude	Glenn Close
Claudius	Alan Bates
The Ghost	Paul Scofield
Polonius	Ian Holm
Ophelia	Helena Bonham-Carter
Horatio	Stephen Dillane
Laertes	Nathaniel Parker
Guildenstern	Sean Murray
Rosencrantz	Michael Maloney
The Gravedigger	Trevor Peacock
Osric	John McEnery
Bernardo	Richard Warwick
Marcellus	Christien Anholt
Francisco	Dave Duffy
Reynaldo	Vernon Dobtcheff
Player King	Pete Postlethwaite
Player Queen	Christopher Fairbank

and Sarah Phillips, Ned Mendez, Roy York, Marjorie Bell, Justin Case,
Roger Low, Pamela Sinclair, Baby Simon Sinclair, Roy Evans (The
Players)

Glenn Close, Alan Bates, Ian Holm Above: Helena
Bonham-Carter, Holm

Mel Gibson, Glenn Close Above Left: Helena Bonham-Carter (C) Top Left: Gibson

Glenn Close, Alan Bates Above Right: John McEnery, Nathaniel Parker, Mel Gibson Top Right: Close, Gibson

THE SHELTERING SKY

(WARNER BROS.) Producer, Jeremy Thomas; Director, Bernardo Bertolucci; Screenplay, Mark Peploe, Bernardo Bertolucci; Based on the novel by Paul Bowles; Executive Producer, William Aldrich; Photography, Vittorio Storaro; Designer, Gianni Silvestri; Music, Ryuichi Sakamoto, Richard Horowitz; Editor, Gabriella Cristiani; Costumes, James Acheson; Assistant Director, Serena Canevari; Casting, Juliet Taylor; British-Italian; Dolby Stereo; Color; Rated R; 137 minutes; December release

CAST

Kit Moresby	Debra Winger
Port Moresby	John Malkovich
George Tunner	Campbell Scott
Mrs. Lyle	Jill Bennett
Eric Lyle	Timothy Spall
Balqassim	Eric Vu-An
Narrator	Paul Bowles

Top: Debra Winger, John Malkovich Left: Campbell Scott, Winger, Malkovich Below Left: Winger Below Right: Eric Vu-An, Winger © *Warner Bros.*

FREEZE—DIE—COME TO LIFE

(INTERNATIONAL FILM EXCHANGE) Producers, Vitaly Kanevski, Valentna Tarasova; Director/Screenplay, Vitaly Kanevski; Photography, Vladimir Brylyakov; Music, Sergei Banevich; Editor, Galina Kornilova; Costumes, Tatyana Kochergina, Natalya Milliant; a Lenfilm Studios production; Soviet; Black and white; Not rated; 105 minutes; December release

CAST

Valerka	Pavel Nazarov
Galiya	Dinara Drukarova
Valerka's Mother	Yelena Popova
Vitka	Vyacheslav Bambushek
School Principal	Vadim Ermolayev

© *IFEX Ltd.*

Dinara Drukarova, Pavel Nazarov

Gérard Depardieu, Andie MacDowell Top Right: Gregg
Edelman, MacDowell Top Left: MacDowell, Depardieu
Below: Bebe Neuwirth, MacDowell
© *Lam Ping Ltd.*

GREEN CARD

(TOUCHSTONE) Producer/Director/Screenplay, Peter Weir; Executive Producer, Edward S. Feldman; Photography, Geoffrey Simpson; Co-Producers, Jean Gontier, Duncan Henderson; Designer, Wendy Stites; Music, Hans Zimmer; Editor, William Anderson; Casting, Dianne Crittenden; Associate Producer, Ira Halberstadt; Assistant Director, Alan B. Curtiss; Distributed by Buena Vista Pictures; Australian-French; Dolby Stereo; Technicolor; Rated PG-13; 108 minutes; December release

CAST

George Faure	Gérard Depardieu
Brontë Parrish	Andie MacDowell
Lauren	Bebe Neuwirth
Phil	Gregg Edelman
Bronte's Lawyer	Robert Prosky
Mrs. Bird	Jessie Keosian
Gorsky	Ethan Phillips
Mrs. Sheehan	Mary Louise Wilson
Bronte's Parents	Lois Smith, Conrad McLaren
Anton	Ronald Guttman
Oscar	Danny Dennis
Mr. Adler	Stephen Pearlman
Mrs. Adler	Victoria Boothby
Party Guests	Ann Wedgeworth, Stefan Schnabel, Anne Shropshire, Simon Jones, Malachy McCourt, Emily Cho
Harry	John Spencer
Peggy	Ann Dowd
Marriage Celebrant	Novella Nelson
House Committee	John Scanlan, Arthur Anderson
Maitre D'	Vasek Simek
Waiters	Christian Mulot, Francis Dumaurier
Butler	Ernesto Gasco
Oscar's Children	Jeb Handwerger, Michael David Tanney
Taxi Drivers	Conrad Roberts, Ed Feldman
Immigration Supervisor	Chris Odo
Immigration Clerk	Michele Nevirs
Vincent	Rick Aviles
Street Beggar	Abdoulaye N'Gom
Flower Seller	Clint Chin
Drummer	Larry Wright

Gerard Depardieu, Andie MacDowell Above: MacDowell,
Depardieu

209

Sharon Corder, Noam Zylberman, Aaron Schwartz in "The
Outside Chance of Maximilian Glick" © *South Gate Ent.*

Joi Wong in "Reincarnation of Golden Lotus"
© *East-West Classics*

LETTERS FROM THE PARK (Fox/Lorber) Producer, Santiago
Liapur; Director, Tomás Gutiérrez Alea; Screenplay, Eliseo Alberto
Diego, Tomás Gutiérrez Alea, Gabriel García Márquez; Story, Gabriel
García Márquez; Photography, Mario Garcia Joya; Music, Gonzalo
Rubaicaba; Editor, Miriam Talavera; a production of International
Network Group S.A. and Television Espanola S.A., in association with
ICAID: Spanish; Color; Not rated; 85 minutes; January release. CAST:
Victor Laplace (Pedro), Ivonne Lopez (Maria), Miguel Paneque (Juan),
Mirta Ibarra (Milagros), Adolfo Llaurado (René Simón), Elio Mesa
(Manuel), Paula Ali (Madrina), Amelita Pita (Consuelo), Dagoberto
Gainza (Cartero), José Pelayo (Marcia)

**THE OUTSIDE CHANCE OF MAXIMILIAN GLICK (South
Gate Entertainment)** Producers, Stephen Foster, Richard Davis; Director, Allan A. Goldstein; Screenplay, Phil Savath, based on the novel
by Morley Torgov; Photography, Ian Elkin; Designer, Kim Steer;
Editor, Richard Martin; Music, Graeme Coleman; A Northern Lights
Media Corp. in association with The National Film Board of Canada
and the Canadian Broadcasting Corp. presentation, produced by Out-
side Chance Prods. Inc., with the participation of Telefilm Canada,
British Columbia Film Development Society, Canada-Manitoba Cultu-
ral Industries Development Org., Beacon Group Ltd. and B.C.T.V.;
Canadian; Color; Rated G; 96 minutes; January release. CAST: Jan
Rubes (Augustus Glick), Aaron Schwartz (Henry Glick), Sharon Cord-
er (Sarah Glick), Susan Douglas Rubes (Bryna Glick), Ken Zelig
(Morris Moskover), Howard Jerome (Zelig Peikes), Noam Zylberman
(Maximilian Glick), Alec McClure (Sandy Lubchuk), Matthew Ball
(Sarge Sargent), Nigel Bennett (Derek Blackthorn), Joan Nakamoto
(Shizuko Blackthorn), William Marantz (Rabbi Kaminsky), Casey
Chisick (Bobby Rosenberg), Allan Stratton (Prof. LaCoste), Rosalie
Rudelier (Mrs. Rosenberg), Stan Lesk (Dr. Rosenberg), Fairuza Balk
(Celia Brzjinski), Cathryn Balk (Mrs. Brzjinski), Wayne Nicklas (Con-
stable Brzjinski), Saul Rubinek (Rabbi Teitelman), Nancy Drake (Mrs.
MacWatters), Dennis Persowitch (Mr. Lubchuk), Debbi Kremski
(Mrs. Lubchuk), Bagriel Hall (Donnie Brzjinski), William Krawetz
(Mayor Burns), Evan Stillwater (Ruben Calish), Shayla Fink (Woman
in band), Jon Ted Wynne (Talent Host), Ernest Slutchuk (Rabbi Rosen-
thal)

Celine Griffin, Steven Vidler in "Encounter at Raven's Gate"
© *Hemdale*

ENCOUNTER AT RAVEN'S GATE (Hemdale) Producers/
Screenplay, Rolf de Heer, Marc Rosenberg; Executive Producer, An-
tony I. Ginnae; Director, Rolf de Heer; Adapted from an original
screenplay by James Michael Vernon; Music, Graham Tardif, Roman
Kronen; Photography, Richard Michalak; Designer, Judith Russell;
Costumes, Clarissa Patterson; Editor, Suresh Ayyar; Special Effects,
Jon Armstrong, Sue Richter; an FGH presentation for International
Film Management Ltd., distributed by FILMPAC; Australian; Color;
Rated R; 89 minutes; January release. CAST: Steven Vidler (Eddie
Cleary), Celine Griffin (Rachel Cleary), Ritchie Singer (Richard Cle-
ary), Vince Gil (Skinner), Saturday Rosenberg (Annie), Max Cullen
(Taylor), Terry Camilleri (Hemmings), Kevin Thiele (Bill McCullum),
Sylvia Thiele (Kate), Peter Douglas (Bruce), Paul Philpott (Pinhead),
Ernie Ellison (George), Max Lorenzin (Weasel)

L'ETAT SAUVAGE *(The Savage State)* **(Interama)** Executive Producer, Louis Wipf; Director, Francis Girod; Screenplay, George Con-
chon, Francis Girod; Photography, Pierre Lhomme; Editor, Genevieve
Winding; Produced by Films 66—Gaumont S.A.; French, 1978; Color;
Not rated; 111 minutes; January release. CAST: Marie-Christine Barrault (Laurence), Claude Brasseur (Gravenoire), Jaques Dutronc
(Avit), Doura Mane (Doumbe), Michel Piccoli (Orlaville), Baaron
(Modimbo), Umban U'kset (Kotoko), Jean-Baptiste Tiemele (Gohan-
da), Rudiger Vogler (Tristan), Peter Bachelier (Renard), Philippe Bri-
zard (Paul), Pierre Walker (Swiss Minister), Marblum Jequier (Minist-
er's Wife), Celia (Irene), Sidiki Bakaba (Cornac), Akonio Dolo (Boy
Elie), Joseph Mono (Boy Raoul), Jaques Sereys (Prime Minister),
Assane Falle, Cheik Doukoure, Alphonse Beni, Lazare Kenmegne

VERONICO CRUZ (Cinevista) Producers, Julio Lencina, Sasha
Menocki; Director/Original Script, Miguel Pereira; Photography/
Editor, Gerry Feeny; Screenplay, Eduardo Leiva Muller, Miguel Pe-
reira; Based on the experiences of Fortunato Ramos; Assistant Director,
Ariel Piluso; a Yacoraite Film Limitada and Mainframe Films Produc-
tion in association with the British Film Institute and Channel Four
Television; British-Spanish; Color; Not rated; 106 minutes; January
release. CAST: Juan José Carnero (The Teacher), Gonzalo Morales
(Veronico Cruz), René Olaguivel (The Commissioner), Guillermo
Delgado (The Policeman), Don Leopoldo Abán (Don Domingo), Ana
Maria Gonzales (The Grandmother), Fortunato Ramos (Cástulo Cruz),
Juana Daniela Cáceres (Juanita), Titina Gaspar (Veronico's Mother),
Raul Calles, Leo Salgado (Officers), Luis Uceda, Juan Carlos Ocampo
(Soldiers), Adolfo Blois (Post Office Clerk)

**THE REINCARNATION OF GOLDEN LOTUS (East-West
Classics)** Producer/Music, Teddy Robin; Executive Producer,
Raymond Chow; Director, Clara Law; Screenplay, Lee Pik Wah;
Photography, Ma Chor Shing; Editor, Hamilton Yu; produced by
Friend Cheers Ltd./Golden Harvest Group; Chinese; Color; Not rated;
99 minutes; February release. CAST: Joi Wong (Lotus), Eric Tsang
(Wu-dai), Lam Chun Yen (Wu-long/Wu-song), Sin Lap Man (Simon
Hsiu/Dada)

THE RAGGEDY RAWNEY (L.W. Blair Films) Producer, Bob
Weis; Executive Producers, George Harrison, Denis O'Brien; Director,
Bob Hoskins; Screenplay, Bob Hoskins, Nicole De Wilde; Editor, Alan
Jones; Photography, Frank Tidy; Music, Michael Kamen; Designer,
Jiri Matolin; Costumes, Theodor Pistek; Assistant Director, Luciano
Sacripanti; Associate Producer, Garth Thomas; a Handmade Films
production; British; Color; Rated R; 102 minutes; February release.
CAST: Bob Hoskins (Darky), Dexter Fletcher (Tom), Zoe Nathenson
(Jessie), Dave Hill (Lamb), Ian Dury (Weasel), Zoe Wanamaker (Elle).

Bob Hoskins (L) in "The Raggedy Rawney" © *L. W. Blair*

Guy Stockwell, Blancha Guerra in "Santa Sangre"
© *Expanded Entertainment*

J. G. Devlin (Jake), Perry Fenwick (Victor), Timothy Lang (Simon), Veronica Quilligan (Lou), Jane Wood (Vie), John Tams (Blakey), Rosemary Martin (Becky), Ian McNeice (Stanley), Veronica Clifford (Mildred), Gawn Grainger (Officer Sc. 1), Emma D'Inverno (Carla), Melissa Wilks (Lilly), Sheila Reid (Doris), Graham Fletcher-Cook (Stanwich), Steve Fletcher (Clancy), Alan Talbot (Wag), Jennifer Platt, Sammy Pasha, Jan Badurora, Tomas Badura, Ladislav Cinlar, Robert Cureja, Renata Curejora

SPEAKING PARTS (Zeitgeist) Executive Co-Producer, Don Ranvaud; Director/Screenplay, Atom Egoyan; Photography, Paul Sarossy; Music, Mychael Danna; Editor, Bruce McDonald; Art Director, Linda Del Rosario; an Ego Film Arts Production; Produced with the participation of Telefilm Canada, The Ontario Film Development Corp., Academy Pictures (Rome), Film Four Intl. (London); Canadian; Color; Not rated; 93 minutes; February release. CAST: Michael McManus (Lance), Arsinée Khanjian (Lisa), Gabrielle Rose (Clara), Tony Nardi (Eddy), David Hemblen (Producer), Patricia Collins (Housekeeper), Gerard Parkes (The Father), Jackie Samuda (The Bride), Peter Krantz (The Groom), Frank Tata (Clara's Brother), Patrick Tierney (Clerk), Robert Dodds (Doctor), Leszek Lis (Housekeeper's Pet), David Mackay (Man)

THE TENANTS (International Home Cinema) Executive Producer, Mohammad-Ali Aligholi; Director/Screenplay, Darioush Mehrjui; Photography, Hassan Gholizadeh; Music, Nasser Cheshm-Azar, Resa Remin; Editors, Hassan Hassan-Doost, Darioush Mehejui; Iranian; Color; Not rated; 110 minutes; March release. CAST: Ezatolah Entezami (Mr. Abbas Derakhshesh), Hamideh Khier-Abadi (Mother), Hossein Sarshar (Saady—Opera Singer), Akbar Abdi (Qandy), Akbar Hassan-Rad (Mr. Jaavad Tavassoli), Reza Rayegari (Mr. Engineer), Ferdos Kaviani (Mash Mehdi—Foreman), Mannijeh Salimi (Mrs. Tavassoli), Farimah Farjami (Lady Engineer), Nasrin Ghasemzadeh (The Engineer's Wife), Reza Hamedi (Mr. Baagery), Hassan Tohmoores (Mr. Qolaam), Shapour Shahidi (Asgar), Ali Alinaghikani (Akbar), Golamreza Banafshehkhah, Mohamad Alinaghkani, Ali Reza Asadian

DRIVING ME CRAZY (First Run Features) Producer, Andrew Braunsberg; Director/Screenplay, Nick Broomfield; Photography, Robert Levi; Editor, John Mister; a Virgin Vision/VCL Communications/Telemunchen Production; British; Color; Not rated; 85 minutes; March release. CAST: Andre Heller (Impresario), Mercedes Ellington, George Faison, Graciela Daniele (Choreographers), Howard Porter (Assistant Director), Andrew Braunsberg (Producer), Nick Broomfield (Director/Writer)

SANTA SANGRE (Expanded Entertainment) Producer, Claudio Argento; Director, Alejandro Jodorowsky; Executive Producers, Rene Cardona Jr., Angelo Iacono; Photography, Daniele Nannuzi; Screenplay, Alejandro Jodorowsky, Roberto Leoni, Claudio Argento; Music, Simon Boswell; Designer, Alejandro Luna; Editor, Mauro Bonanni; Italian-Mexican; Dolby Stereo; Color; Not rated; 120 minutes; March release. CAST: Axel Jodorowsky (Fenix), Blanca Guerra (Concha), Guy Stockwell (Orgo), Thelma Tixou (The Tattooed Woman), Sabrina Dennison (Alma), Adan Jodorowsky (Young Fenix), Faviola Elenka Tapia (Young Alma), Jesus Juarez (Aladin), Sergio Bustamante (Monsignor)

MR. UNIVERSE (Zeitgeist Films) Producers, Andras Ozorai, Gabe Von Dettre, Kathi Gati; Director, Gyorgy Szomjas; Screenplay, Ibolya Fekete, Ferenc Grunwalsky, Gyorgy Szomjas; Photography, Ferenc Grunwalsky; Editor, Anna Korniss; a Cine-Universe Corp. pre-

sentation; Hungarian; Color/black and white; Not rated; 94 minutes; March release. CAST: Laszlo Szabo (Laszlo), George Pinter (Lord), Mickey Hargitay (Himself)

SUMMER VACATION: 1999 (New Yorker) Producers, Naoya Narita, Mitsuhisa Hida; Director, Shusuke Kaneko; Screenplay, Rio Kishida; Photography, Kenji Takama; Music, Yuriko Nakamura; Editor, Isao Tomita; a New Century Producers & CBS/Sony Group production; Japanese; Color; Not rated; 90 minutes; March release. CAST: Eri Miyajima (Yu-Kaoru), Tomoko Otakara (Kazuhiko), Miyuki Nakano (Naoto), Rie Mizuhara (Norio)

THE GODS MUST BE CRAZY II (Columbia) Producer, Boet Troskie; Director/Screenplay, Jamie Uys; Photography, Buster Reynolds; Music, Charles Fox; Editors, Renee Engelbrecht, Ivan Hall; presented in association with Weintraub Entertainment Group; Botswana; Dolby Stereo; Color; Rated PG; 97 minutes; April release. CAST: N!Xau (Xixo), Lena Farugia (Dr. Ann Taylor), Hans Strydom (Dr. Stephen Marshall), Eiros (Xiri), Nadies (Xisa), Erick Bowen (Mateo), Treasure Tshabalala (Timi), Pierre Van Pletzen (George), Lourens Swanepoel (Brenner), Richard Loring (Jack), Lesley Fox (Ann's Secretary), Simon Sabela (General), Ken Marshall (Convener), Peter Tunstall (Chief Game Warden), Andrew Dibb (Computer Operator), Shimane Mpepela (Man on bike), Paddy O'Byrne (Narrator)

A UN (Buddies) (Toho Pictures) Director, Yasuo Furuhata; Screenplay, Tutoma Nakamura; Photography, Daisaku Kimura; Art Director, Shinobu Muraki; a Film Face production; Japanese; Color; Not rated; 114 minutes; April release. CAST: Shuzo Kadokura, Ken Takadura Kimiko, Nobuko Miyamoto, Senichi Mizuta, Eiji Bando Tami, Samuko Tuji Satoko, Yasuko Tomita

DETAILS OF A DUEL (First Run Features) Director, Sergio Cabrera; Screenplay, Humberto Dorado; Photography, Jose Madeiros; Music, Juan Marquez; Editor, Justo Vega; a Focine-Fotograma-Icaic production; Colombian-Cuban; Color; Not rated; 97 minutes; April release. CAST: Frank Ramirez (Prof. Albarracin), Humberto Dorado (Carnicero Oquendo), Florina Lemaitre (Miriam), Vicky Hernandez (Encarnacion), Edgardo Roman (Sargento), Fausto Cabrera (Padre Troncoso), Manuel Pachon (Alcalde)

Nadies, N!Xau, Eiros in "The Gods Must Be Crazy II"
© *Columbia Pictures*

211

Chloe Webb, Brian Dennehy, Lambert Wilson, Stefania Casini
in "Belly of an Architect" © *Hemdale*

Alma Prica, Davor Janjic in "My Uncle's Legacy" © *IFEX*

THE BELLY OF AN ARCHITECT (Hemdale) Producers, Colin Callender, Walter Donohue; Director/Screenplay, Peter Greenaway; Photography, Sacha Vierny; Music, Wim Mertens, Glenn Branca; Editor, John Wilson; Associate Producers, Conchita Airoldi, Dino Di Dionisio; Costumes, Maurizio Millenotti; Art Director, Luciana Vedovelli; a Callender Company Production from Film Four International and British Screen in association with Hemdale and Sacis; British-Italian; Technicolor; Not rated; 118 minutes; May release. CAST: Brian Dennehy (Stourley Kracklite), Chloe Webb (Louisa Kracklite), Lambert Wilson (Caspasian Speckler), Sergio Fantoni (Io Speckler), Stephania Cassini (Flavia Speckler), Vanni Corbellini (Frederico), Alfredo Varelli (Julio), Geoffrey Coppleston (Caspetti), Geoffrey Carnelutti (Pastarri), Claudio Spadaro (Mori), Riccardo Ussani (Boy), Enrica Scrivano (Mother), Julian Jenkins (1st Doctor), Marino Mase (Trettorio), Andrea Prodan (Young Doctor), Marne Maitland (Battistino), Fabio Sartor (Policeman), Stephano Gragnani (Nose Man), Rate Furlan (Violinist)

POSITIVE (First Run Features) Producer/Director/Screenplay, Rosa von Praunheim; Photography, Mike Kuchar, Evan Estern; Editors, Mike Shepard, Rosa von Praunheim; West German; Color; Not rated; 80 minutes; May release. Documentary featuring Larry Kramer, Phil Zwickler, Michael Callen, Peter Staley, Gary Eller, Diamanda Gallas, Jay Corocoram, John Finch, Sarah Schulman, Larry Mass, and others

DANGEROUS GAME (Four Seasons Entertainment) Producers, Judith Kennedy, Basil Appleby; Executive Producer, Robert Mercieca; Director, Stephen Hopkins; Screenplay, Peter West; Photography, Peter Levy; Designer, Igor Nay; Music, Les Gock; a Quantum Films presentation of a Virgo Productions Picture; Australian; Dolby Stereo; Color; Rated R; 102 minutes; May release. CAST: Miles Buchanan (David Forrest), Marcus Graham (Jack Hayward), Steven Grives (Murphy), Kathryn Walker (Kathryn), Sandie Lillingston (Ziggy), John Polson (Tony), Max Meldrum (History Tutor), Raquel Suarstzman (Girl #1), Kerry McKay (Student), Robbie McGregor (Police Superintendent), Christopher Dibb (Senior Officer), Susan Stenmark (TV Weather Girl), Peter West, Jim Richards (Cops), Terry Flanagan (Detective #1), Robin Menzies (Prostitute), Paris Jefferson (TV Movie Girl)

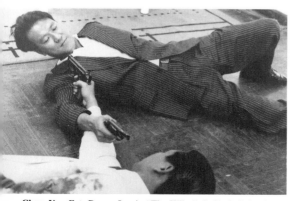

Chow Yun Fat, Danny Lee in "The Killer" © *Circle Releasing*

A RUSTLING OF LEAVES (Empowerment Project) Producer/Director/Screenplay, Nettie Wild; Photography, Kirk Tougas; Music, Joey Ayala, Salvador Terreras, Rob Porter, David Byrne, The Talking Heads; Editor, Peter Wintonick; a Kalasikas Prod./Channel Four production; Canadian-British; Color; Not rated; 110 minutes; May release. Documentary with Father Frank Navaro, Bernabe Buscayno, Jun Pala, Father Ed de la Torre, Members of the Alsa Masa

SILENCE = DEATH (First Run Features) Producer/Director/Screenplay, Rosa von Praunheim; Photography, Mike Kuchar, Evan Estern; Music, Diamanda Gallas; Editors, Mike Shepard, Rosa von Praunheim; West German; Color; Not rated; 60 minutes; May release. Documentary featuring David Wojnarowicz, Keith Haring, Allen Ginsberg, Peter Kunz, Paul Smith, Emilio Cubiero, Rafael Gamba, Don Moffet, Bern Boyle, and others

THE KILLER (Circle Releasing) Producer, Tsui Hark; Director/Screenplay, John Woo; Photography, Wong Wing Hang, Peter Pao; Music, Lowell Lowe; Editor, Fan Kung Ming; Art Director, Luk Man Wah; A Film Workshop production; Hong Kong; Color; Not rated; 110 minutes; June release. CAST: Chow Yun-Fat (Jeffrey Chow), Danny Lee (Inspector Lee), Sally Yeh (Jennie), Chu Kong (Sydney Fung), Kenneth Tsang (Sgt. Randy Chang), Shing Fui-On (Johnny Weng), Ip Wing-Cho (Tony Weng), Yee Fan-Wai (Frank), Wong Kwong-Leung (Wong Tong), Barry Wong (Chief Inspector Tu), Parkman Wong (Inspector Chan), Ng Siu-Hung (A Killer), Yeung Sing, Ngan Siu-Hung (Bodyguards)

SHADOW OF THE RAVEN (L. W. Blair Films) Producer, Christer Abrahamsen; Director/Screenplay, Hrafn Gunnlaugsson; Photography, Esa Vuorinen; Music, Hans-Erik Philip; Editor, Edda Kristjansdottir; Icelandic-Swedish; Fujicolor; Not rated; 108 minutes; June release. CAST: Reine Brynolfsson (Trausti), Tinna Gunnlaugsdottir (Isold), Egil Olafsson (Hjörleif), Sune Mangs (The Bishop), Kristbjörg Kjeld (Sigrid), Klara Iris Vigfusdottir (Sol), Helgi Skulason (Grim), Johann Neumann (Leonardo), Helga Backman (Edda), Sigurdur Sigurjonsson (Egil)

MY UNCLE'S LEGACY (International Film Exchange) Producer, Ben Stassen; Executive Producers, Tomica Milanovski, Ben Stassen; Director, Krsto Papic; Screenplay, Ivan Aralica, Krsto Papic; Based on the novel "*Framework for Hatred*" by Ivan Aralica; Photography, Boris Turkovic; Music, Branislav Zivkovic; Editor, Robert Lisjak; Costumes, Jasna Novak; Uraniafilm/Stassen Productions; Yugoslav; Color; Not rated; 105 minutes; June release. CAST: Davor Janjic (Martin), Alma Prica (Martha), Anica Dobra (Korina), Miodrag Krivokapic (Uncle Stephen), Fabijan Sovagovic (Grandfather), Filip Sovagovic (Martin's Friend, Baba), Branislav Lecic (Prof. Maglica), Ivo Gregurevic (Police Inspector Rado), Radko Polic (Martin as an adult)

DESIRE: SEXUALITY IN GERMANY 1910–1945 (Mayavision) Producer, Rebecca Dobbs; Director, Stuart Marshall; Photography, Anne Cottringer; Editor, Joy Chamberlain; for Channel Four Television; British; Color/black & white; Not rated; 87 minutes; June release. Documentary.

FULL MOON IN NEW YORK (Grand Essex Enterprises) Producer, Henry Fong; Director, Stanley Kwan; Screenplay, Zhong Acheng, Yan Tai On Ping; Photography, Bill Wong; Editors, Steve Wong, Chow Cheung Kan; Music, Chang-Hung Yi; a Shiobu Film Co. production; Hong Kong; Color; Not rated; 88 minutes; June release. CAST: Sylvia Chang (Wang Hsiung Ping), Maggie Cheung (Li Feng Jiao), Sichingowa (Chao Hong)

Joe Mantegna, Faye Dunaway in "Wait Until Spring Bandini"
© *Orion Pictures Corp.*

Kiefer Sutherland, Keith Allen, Emily Lloyd in "Chicago Joe
and the Showgirl" © *New Line Cinema*

BASHU, THE LITTLE STRANGER (International Home Cinema) Producer, Ali Reza Zarrin; Director/Screenplay/Editor, Bahram Beizai; Photography, Firooz Malekzadeh; Produced by the Institute for the Intellectual Development of Children and Young Adults; Iranian; Color; Not rated; 120 minutes; June release. CAST: Susan Taslimi (Nai), Adnan Afravian (Bashu), Parviz Pourhosseini (Nai's Husband)

WAIT UNTIL SPRING, BANDINI (Orion Classics) Producers, Erwin Provoost, Tom Luddy, Fred Roos; Executive Producers, Christian Charret, Giorgio Silvagni, Amadeo Pagani; Director/Screenplay, Dominique Deruddere; Based on a novel by John Fante; Photography, Jean-François Robin; Music, Angelo Badalamenti; Editor, Ludo Troch; Designer, Bob Ziembicki; Costumes, Shay Cunliffe; a Dusk-CFC-Zoetrope Studios production, in collaboration with Intermedias/Basic Cinematografica and Dusk Partners in Belgium; French-Italian-Belgian-U.S.; Eastmancolor; Rated PG; 100 minutes; June release. CAST: Faye Dunaway (Mrs. Effie Hildegarde), Joe Mantegna (Svevo Bandini), Ornella Muti (Maria Bandini), Michael Bacall (Arturo Bandini), Daniel Wilson (August Bandini), Alex Vincent (Federico Bandini), Burt Young (Rocco Saccone), Sean Baca (Wally), Nathalie Gregory (Rose Helmer), Renata Vanni (Donna Toscana), Tanya Lopert (Sister Celia), Francois Beukelaers (Mr. Helmer), Karston Carr (Boy in class), Aaron Carr (Bologna Boy), Donna Todd (Mrs. Johnson), Rebecca Clarck (Gertie), Florence Healy French (Sister Superior), Josse De Pauw (Mr. Craik), Debra MacFarlane (Mrs. Helmer), Corrine Troester (Servant)

THE CASSANDRA CAT (Ceskoslovensky Filmexport) Director, Vojtěch Jasný; Screenplay, Jiří Brdečka, Vojtěch Jasný; Photography, Jaroslav Kučera; Music, Svatopluk Havelka; Czechoslovak, 1963; Color; Not rated; 87 minutes; July release. CAST: Jan Werich, Emilie Vašáryová, Jiří Sovak, Vladimir Brodsky

CHICAGO JOE AND THE SHOWGIRL (New Line Cinema) Producer, Tim Bevan; Director, Bernard Rose; Screenplay, David Yallop; Photography, Mike Southon; Associate Producer, Jane Frazer; Designer, Gemma Jackson; Music, Hans Zimmer, Shirley Walker; Editor, Dan Rae; Costumes, Bob Ringwood; a Polygram and Working Title Films in association with B.S.B. presentation; British; Dolby Stereo; Color; Rated R; 103 minutes; July release. CAST: Kiefer Sutherland (Ricky Allen), Emily Lloyd (Georgina Grayson), Patsy Kensit (Joyce Cook), Keith Allen (Lenny Bexley), Liz Fraser (Mrs. Evans), Alexandra Pigg (Violet), Ralph Nossek (Inspector Tonsill), Colin Bruce (Robert De Mott), Roger Ashton-Griffiths (Inspector Tarr), Harry Fowler (Morry), Janet Dale (Mrs. Cook), John Surman (Mr. Cook), John Junkin (George Heath), John Dair (John), Hugh Millais (U.S. Colonel), Stephen Hancock (Doctor), Gerard Horan (John Wilkins), Angela Morant (Customer), Richard Ireson, Malcolm Terris, Gary Parker, Karen Gledhill, Niven Boyd (Reporters), John Lahr (Commentator), Harry Jones (Taxi Driver)

CALAMARI UNION (World Sales) Director/Screenplay, Aki Kaurismaki; Photography, Timo Salminen; Music, Casablanca Vox; Editors, Aki Kaurismaki, Raija Talvio; Finnish; Black and white; Not rated; 89 minutes; August release. CAST: Markku Toikka, Kari Vaananen, Osmo Hurula, Matti Pellonpaa, Mato Valtonen, Saku Kuosmanen

SHADOWS IN PARADISE (World Sales) Director/Screenplay, Aki Kaurismaki; Photography, Timo Salminen; Editor, Raija Talvio; Finnish; Eastmancolor; Not rated; 73 minutes; August release. CAST:

Matti Pellonpaa (Nikander), Kati Outinen (Ilona), Kylli Kongas (Nikander's Friend), Esko Nikkari, Jukka-Pekka Palo

SILENCE LIKE GLASS (Moviestore Entertainment) Producers, Michael Rohrig, Carl Schenkel; Executive Producers, Gunter Rohrbach, Karl Spiehs, Luggi Waldleitner; Director, Carl Schenkel; Screenplay, Bea Hellman, Carl Schenkel; Associate Producer, Goetz George; Photography, Dietrich Lohmann; Music, Anne Dudley; Editor, Norbert Herzner; a Bavaria Film/Lisa Film/Roxy Film production; West German; Color; Rated R; 105 minutes; August release. CAST: Jami Gertz (Eva Martin), Martha Plimpton (Claudia Jacoby), George Peppard (Mr. Martin), Bruce Payne (Dr. Burton), Rip Torn (Dr. Markowitz), Gayle Hunnicutt (Mrs. Martin), Dayle Haddon (Darlene), James Remar (Charley), John Farren (Ivanov), Madeleine Sherwood (Eva's Grandmother), Yeardley Smith (Karin), Kathleen Doyle (Mrs. Jacoby), Theresa Merritt (Nurse Wilson), Carin C. Tietze (Nurse Flannery), Jessica Kosmalla (Alison), Gedeon Burkhard (Bud)

QUEEN OF TEMPLE STREET (Grand Essex Enterprises) Producers, William Tam, Wong Yat-ping; Director, Lawrence Ah Mon; Screenplay, Chan Mankeung; Photography, Chan Yingkit; a Filmways Production; Hong Kong; Color; Not rated; 110 minutes; August release. CAST: Sylvia Chang (Big Sis Wah), Rain Lau (Yan), Alice Lau (Connie), Lo Lieh (Elvis), Ha Ping (Mabel), Wang Wai-tak (Simon), Sandy Chan (Octopussy), Yuen King (Candy), Lo Koon Lan (Ku Swallow), Lee Ming (Mandy)

CRIME AND PUNISHMENT (World Sales) Producer, Mika Kaurismaki; Director/Screenplay, Aki Kaurismaki; Based on the novel by F. M. Dostoevsky; Photography, Timo Salinen; Editor, Veiko Aaltonen; Finnish; Color; Not rated; 91 minutes; August release. CAST: Markku Toikka (Rahikainen), Aino Seppo (Eeva), Esko Nikkari (Inspector)

LENSMAN (Streamline Pictures) Executive Producer, Hiroshi Suto; Producers, Akihito Ito, Mitsuru Kaneko, Michihiro Tomii, Tadami Watanabe; Directors, Yoshiaki Kawajiri, Kazuyuki Hirokawa; Animation Directors, Kazuo Tomizawa, Kobuyuki Kitajaima; English Adaptation/Producer, Carl Macek; English Adaptation Dialogue/Director, Steve Kramer; Japanese; Color; Not rated; 107 minutes; August release. Animated

Jami Gertz in "Silence Like Glass" © *Moviestore Entertainment*

213

Spencer Nakasako, Cora Miao in "Life is Cheap . . ."
© *Silverlight Entertainment*

Jeff Goldblum in "Twisted Obsession" © *IVE*

LIFE IS CHEAP . . . BUT TOILET PAPER IS EXPENSIVE (Silverlight Entertainment) Producer, Winnie Fredriksz; Executive Producers, John Koon-chung Chan, Wayne Wang; Directors, Wayne Wang, Spencer Nakasako; Screenplay, Spencer Nakasako; Story, Amir M. Mokri, Spencer Nakasako, Wayne Wang; Chinese Dialogue, John Koon-chung Chan; Photography, Amir M. Mokri; Music, Mark Adler; Editors, Chris Sanderson, Sandy Nervig; Art Director, Collette Koo; a Forever Profits Investments film; Hong Kong-U.S.; Color; Not rated; 89 minutes; August release. CAST: Chan Kim Wan (The Duck Killer), Spencer Nakasako (The-Man-with-No-Name), Victor Wong (The Blind Man), Cheng Kwan Min (Uncle Cheng), Cora Miao (Money), Lam Chung (The Red Guard), Allen Fong (The Taxi Driver), John K. Chan (The Anthropologist), Bonnie Ngai (The Daughter), Lo Wai (The Big Boss), Cinda Hui (Kitty), Gary Kong, Rocky Ho (Punks), Yu Chien (Blue Velvet), Wu Kin Man (The Spiritualist), Lo Lieh (The Pianist), Dennis Dun (Narrator)

THE SHRIMP ON THE BARBIE (Unity Pictures) Producer, R. Ben Efraim; Executive Producer, Jerry Offsay; Director, Alan Smithee; Screenplay, Grant Morris, Ron House, Alan Shearman; Editor, Fred Chulack; Australian; Color; Rated PG-13; 86 minutes; August release. CAST: Cheech Marin (Carlos Munoz), Emma Samms (Alex Hobart), Vernon Wells (Bruce Woodley), Terence Cooper (Ian Hobart), Jeanette Cronin (Maggie), Carole Davis (Dominique), Bruce Spence (Wayne), Jonathan Coleman (Postman)

LA MAISON ASSASSINÉE (Morris Projects/Cine Qua Non) Producer, Alain Poire; Director, Georges Lautner; Screenplay, Georges Lautner, Jacky Cukier, Didier Cauwelaert; Based on the novel by Pierre Magnan; Photography, Yves Rodallec; Music, Philippe Sarde; Editor, Michelle David; a Gaumont production; French; Color; Not rated; 110 minutes; August release. CAST: Patrick Bruel (Seraphin Monge), Sophie Brochet (Marie Dormeur), Agnes Blanchot (Rose Pujol), Ingrid Held (Charmaine Dupin), Yann Collette (Patrice Dupin), Jean-Pierre Sentier (Celstat Dormeur), Roger Zendly (Zorme)

THE TERRITORY (International Film Circuit) Producers, Pierre Cottrell, V.O. Filmes, Roger Corman, The Portugese Film Institute; Director, Raul Ruiz; Screenplay, Raul Ruiz, Gilbert Adair; Editor,

Jose Nascimento in "The Territory" © *Intl. Film Circuit*

Valeria Armiento; Photography, Henri Alekan; Music, Jorge Arriagada; Portugese; Color; Not rated; 104 minutes; August release. CAST: Isabelle Weingarten (Francoise), Rebecca Pauly (Barbara), Jeoffrey Carey (Peter), Jeffrey Kime (Jim), Paul Getty, Jr. (Gilbert), Ethan Stone (Ron), Camila Mora (Annie), Jose Nascimento (Joe)

TWISTED OBSESSION (Avenue/IVE), formerly *The Mad Monkey*; Producer, Andres Vicente Gomez; Director, Fernando Trueba; Screenplay, Fernando Trueba, Manolo Matji; Based on the novel *The Mad Monkey* by Christopher Frank; Associate Producer, Emmanuel Schlumberger; Photography, Jose Luis Alcaine; Music, Antoine Duhamel; Editor, Carmen Frias; French-Spanish; Color; Rated R; 103 minutes; August release. CAST: Jeff Goldblum (Dan Gillis), Miranda Richardson (Marilyn), Anemone (Marianne), Dexter Fletcher (Malcolm), Daniel Ceccaldi (Legrand), Liza Walker (Jenny), Jerome Natali (Danny), Arielle Dombasle (Marion Derain), Asuncion Blaguer (Juana), Catherine Hamilton (Legrand's Secretary), Nathalie Gaches (Marilyn's Secretary), Eric Picou (Claude Besson), Laurent Moussard, Raul Lopez Cabello, Xavier Maly (Students), Jaime Alberto Zamora, Nadine Sapena Negel (Rockers)

HARDWARE (Millimeter) Producers, Joanne Sellar, Paul Trybits; Director/Screenplay, Richard Stanley; Executive Producers, Nik Powell, Stephen Woolley, Trix Worrell; Co-Executive Producers, Harvey Weinstein, Bob Weinstein; Photography, Steve Chivers; Designer, Joseph Bennett; Music, Simon Boswell; Editor, Derek Trigg; Costumes, Michael Baldwin; Special Effects, Barney Jeffrey; Special Make-up Effects/Robotics Creators, Image Animation; British; presented by Palace Pictures and Millimeter Films in association with British Screen and BSB, a Wicked Films production; Dolby Stereo; Color; Rated R; 91 minutes; September release. CAST: Dylan McDermott (Mo), Stacey Travis (Jill), John Lynch (Shades), Iggy Pop (Voice of Angry Bob), William Hootkins (Lincoln), Mark Northover (Alvy), Oscar James (Chief), Paul McKenzie (Vernon), Carl McCoy (Nomad), Lemmy (Taxi Driver)

STRAIGHT FOR THE HEART (L.W. Blair Films) Producers, Denise Robert, Robin Spry, Ruth Waldburger; Director, Léa Pool; Screenplay, Léa Pool, Marcel Beaulieu, based on the novel *"Kurwenal"* by Yves Navarre; Photography, Pierre Mignot; Music, Osvaldo Montes; Editor, Michel Arcand; Canadian-Swiss; Color/black and white; Not rated; 92 minutes; September release. CAST: Matthias Habich (Pierre Kurwenal), Johanne-Marie Tremblay (Sarah), Michel Voita (David), Jean François Pichette (Quentin), Kim Yaroshevskaya (Noémie), Jacqueline Bertrand (Mother)

SALUT VICTOR! (Frameline) Producer, Monique Létourneau; Director, Anne Claire Poirier; Screenplay, Marthe Blackburn, based on the book *"Matthew and Chauncy"* by Edward O. Phillips; Photography, Michel Brault; Music, Joël Vincent Bienvenue; Editor, Suzanne Allard; a National Film Board of Canada-Les Producteurs TV Films Associes production, with Telefilm Canada; Canadian; Eastmancolor; Not rated; 84 minutes; October release. CAST: Jean-Louis Roux (Philippe Lanctot), Jacques Godin (Victor Laprade)

BEIJING WATERMELON (New Yorker) Producer, Michio Morioka; Director/Editor, Nobuhiko Obayashi; Screenplay, Yoshihiro Ishimatsu; Story, Lin Xiao-Li, Toru Kugayama; Photography, Shigekazu Nagano; Music, Tetsuo Konda; from Shochiku; Japanese; Color; Not rated; 135 minutes; October release. CAST: Bengal (Shunzo), Masako Motai (Michi), Toru Minegishi (Dr. Muraki), Takashi Sasano (Yamada), Akira Emoto (Teramoto), Haruhiko Saito (Ioka), Wu Yue (Li), Fang Qing-Lin (Chen), Li Juan (Zhu), Li Han (Zhang)

Stacey Travis. Dylan McDermott in "Hardware"
© *Millimeter Films*

Katja Teichmann in "Prisoner of St. Petersburg"
© *Kim Lewis Marketing*

WAIT FOR ME IN HEAVEN (MD Wax/Courier Films) Executive Producer, José Maria Calleja; Director, Antonio Mercero; Screenplay, Antonio Mercero, Horacio Valcárcel, Román Gubern; Photography, Manuel Rojas; Music, Carmelo Bernaola; a BMG production in collaboration with Televisión Española; Color; Not rated; 106 minutes; October release. CAST: Pepe Soriano, José Sazatornil, Chus Lampreave, Manolo Codeso, Amparo Valle, J. Luis Barceló, Federico Cambres, Francisco Javier

THE FIFTH MONKEY (Columbia) Producer, Menahem Golan; Director/Screenplay, Eric Rochat; Based on the novel *Le Cinquieme Singe* by Jacques Zibi; Photography, Gideon Porath; Art Director, Pedro Nanni; Line Producers, Fabio Barreto, Carlos Da Silva; Editors, Alain Jakubowicz, Fabien D. Tordjmann; Music, Robert O. Ragland; Associate Producer, Avram Berman; from 21st Century Film Corp.; French-Brazilian-U.S.; Ultra-Stereo; Rank color; Rated PG-13; 93 minutes; October release. CAST: Ben Kingsley (Cunda), Mika Lins (Octavia), Vera Fischer (Mrs. Watts), Silvia De Carvalho (Maria), Carlos Kroeber (Mr. Garcia), Milton Gonzalves (Judge), Julio Levy (Lawyer), Rinaldo Rinaldi (Mr. Watts), Paulo Vinicius (Mario), Henrique Cuckerman (Store Owner), Rui Polanah (Marcos), Ariel Coelho (Pastor), Paulo Gorgulho (Commander), Brooks Williams (Dr. Howard), Breno Moroni (Bartender), Antonio Ameijeiras, Tonico Pereira (Men), Nei Leonntsinis (Drunk), Chico Expedito, Enrique Diaz (Miners), Messias Santos (Guard at Miner's), Procopio Mariano (Butler), Thiago Justino (Chauffeur), Katia Bronstein (Mrs. Tramp), Bety Shumacher (Mrs. Doodle), Victor Villair (Mr. Wood), A. J., Bubbles, Land Rover, Boma, Reggie (The Chimpanzees), Sammy Muradye Founth, Aloisio Flores, Sandro Solviatti (Prisoners), Gilson Moura (Guard at Jail), Catalina Bonakie, Juliana Teixeira, Leonor Gottlieb, Tania Boscoli, Antonio Pitanga, Nadinho Da Ilha, Lourival Felix, Luiz Octavio De Moraes, Andre Barros, Romeu Evaristo, Alexandre Zachia, Christovao Costa Garcia

THE PRISONER OF ST. PETERSBURG (Kim Lewis Marketing) Producers, Daniel Scharf, Klaus Sungen; Director, Ian Pringle; Screenplay, Michael Wren; Photography, Ray Argall; Designer, Peta Lawson; Music, Paul Schutze; from Seon Films/Panorama Films; Australian-German; Black and white; Not rated; 82 minutes; October release. CAST: Noah Taylor (Jack), Katja Teichmann (Johanna), Solveig Dommartin (Elena), René Schönenberger (Businessman), Dennis Staunton (Irishman), Johanna Karl-Lory (Old Woman), Olivier Picot (Stefan), Christian Zertz (Lorenzo), Hans-Martin Stier (Truckdriver), Wieland Speck (Youth in bar), Pat O'Connell (Singing Irishman), Ralph Wittgrebe (German drunk)

TONG TANA: A JOURNEY TO THE HEART OF BORNEO (First Run Features) Directors, Jan Roed, Fredrik von Krusenstjerna, Bjorn Cederberg, Kristian Petri; Journal Texts/Interviews, Bjorn Cederberg; Photography, Jan Roed; Music, Harold Budd, Brian Eno; Editor, Michal Leszezylowski; a Swedish Film Institute presentation; Swedish; Dolby Stereo; Eastmancolor; Not rated; 88 minutes; October release. Documentary featuring Bruno Manser

THE NUTCRACKER PRINCE (Warner Bros.) Producer, Kevin Gillis; Director, Paul Schibli; Screenplay, Patricia Watson; Based on the story "The Nutcracker and the Mouseking" by E. T. A. Hoffman; Executive Producer, Sheldon S. Wiseman; Music, Peter Ilyich Tchaikovsky; Songs by Kevin Gillis and Jack Lenz: "Always Come Back to You (Love Theme from 'The Nutcracker Prince')"/performed by Natasha's Brother and Rachele Cappelli; "Save This Dance" performed by Megan Follows; Editor, Sue Robertson; Layout Director, Sue Butterworth; Background Director, Michel Guerin; Animation Producer, Hinton Animation Studios, Inc.; a Lacewood Production; Canadian; Dolby Stereo; Technicolor; Rated G; 74 minutes; November release. VOICE CAST: Kiefer Sutherland (Nutcracker Prince), Megan Follows (Clara), Mike MacDonald (Mouseking), Peter O'Toole (Pantaloon), Phyllis Diller (Mousequeen), Peter Boretski (Uncle Drosselmeier), Len Carlson (King/Mouse/Court Attendant/Band Member #2/Spectator/Soldier), Marvin Goldhar (Mr. Schaeffer/Mouse/Guest #3/First Guard/Soldier/Band Member #1/Contestant/Spectator), Lynne Gorman (Trudy), Keith Hampshire (Mouse/Guest/Second Guard/Contestant/Spectator/Soldier), Liz Hanna (Marie/Mrs. Schaeffer/Doll/Guest #4/Spectator), George Merner (Dr. Stahlbaum), Stephanie Morgenstern (Louise), Christopher Owens (Erik), Susan Roman (Mouse/Mrs. Miller/Guest #1/Doll/Spectator), Theresa Sears (Queen/Mouse/Guest #2/Doll/Spectator), Diane Stapley (Mrs. Ingrid Stahlbaum), Mona Waserman (Princess Perlipat), Noam Zylberman (Fritz)

Ben Kingsley in "The Fifth Monkey" © *Columbia Pictures*

Clara, Uncle Drosselmeier in "The Nutcracker Prince"
© *Warner Bros.*

215

Colin Dale in "Diamond's Edge" © *JGM Enterprises*

Kathy Baker, Jeff Goldblum in "Mr. Frost" © *SVS*

DIAMOND'S EDGE (Castle Hill/JGM Enterprises) formerly *Just Ask for Diamond;* Producer, Linda James; Director, Stephen Bayly; Screenplay, Anthony Horowitz, based on his book *"The Falcon's Malteser"*; Photography, Billy Williams; Designer, Peter Murton; Editor, Scott Thomas; Music, Trevor Jones; Costumes, Maria Price; a Coverstop Film Finances Ltd./The Children's Film & Television Foundation/British Screen presentation of a Red Rooster Films production, released by Kings Road Entertainment; British; Dolby Stereo; Eastmancolor; Rated PG; 94 minutes; November release. CAST: Dursley McLinden (Tim Diamond), Colin Dale (Nick Diamond), Susannah York (Lauren Bacardi), Patricia Hodge (Brenda von Falkenberg), Roy Kinnear (Jack Splendide), Michael Medwin (The Professor), Peter Eyre (Gott), Nickolas Grace (Himmell), Bill Paterson (Chief Inspector Snape), Jimmy Nail (Boyle), Saeed Jaffrey (Mr. Patel), Rene Ruiz (Johnny Naples), Michael Robbins (The Fat Man), Donald Standen (Lawrence), Jim McManus (Hammett), Jonathan Linsley, "RJ" Bell, Robert Bathurst, Jenny Tomasin, Joanna Dickens, Christina Avery, Charles Simon, Geraldine Muir, Gerald Campion, Ricky Diamond, Mammoth

THE MODEL COUPLE (Films Paris) Director/Photography/Screenplay/Designer, William Klein; French, 1976; Color; Not rated; 100 minutes; November release. CAST: André Dussollier (Jean-Michel), Anémone (Claudine), Eddie Constantine, Zouc, Jacques Boudet

MR. FROST (Triumph/SVS) Producer, Xavier Gelin; Executive Producers, Stephane Marsil, Claude Ravier, Michael Holzman; Director, Philippe Setbon; Screenplay, Philippe Setbon, Brad Lynch; Photography, Dominique Brenguier; Art Director, Max Berto; Costumes, Judy Schrewsbury, Steve Levine; a Hugo Films/AAA/OMM co-production; French-British; Color; Rated R; 95 minutes; November release. CAST: Jeff Goldblum (Mr. Frost), Alan Bates (Felix Detweiller), Kathy Baker (Sarah Day), Roland Giraud (Dr. Reynhardt), Jean-Pierre Cassel (Inspector Corelli), Daniel Gélin (Simon Scolari), Maxime Leroux (Frank Larcher), François Negret (Christopher Kovac), Charlie Boorman (Thief)

A VERY OLD MAN WITH ENORMOUS WINGS (Original Cinema) Executive Producers, Camilo Vives, Settimio Presutto, Luis Reneses; Director, Fernando Birri; Screenplay, Fernando Birri, Gabriel García Márquez; Photography, Raul Perez Ureta; Music, José Maria Vitier, Gianni Nocenzi; Set Designer, Raul Oliva; Cuban-Italian-Spanish; Color; Not rated; 90 minutes; December release. CAST: Fernando Birri (Old Man), Asdrubal Melendez (Pelayo), Daisy Granados (Elisenda), Silvia Planas (Doña Eulalia), Maria Luisa Mayor (Myrurgia), Luis Alberto Ramirez (Padre Gonzaga), Parmenia Silva (Pia), Adolfo Llaurado (Lucky o'Capitone), Marcia Barreto, Rene Martinez, Marabu, Rodrigo Utria

L'EAU À LA BOUCHE (A Game for Six Lovers) (Interama) Producer, Pierre Braunberger; Director/Screenplay, Jacques Doniol-Valcroze; Inspired by Ingmar Bergman's *"Smiles of a Summer Night"*; Photography, Roger Fellous; Music, Serge Gainsbourg; French, 1960; Not rated; 86 minutes; December release. CAST: Bernadette Lafont (Prudence), Françoise Brion (Miléna), Alexandra Stewart (Fifine), Michel Galabru (César), Jacques Riberolies (Robert), Gérard Barray (Miguel)

FROM RUSSIA WITH ROCK (International Film Circuit) Producer, Pauli Pentti; Executive Producer, Aki Kaurismaki; Director, Marjaana Mykkänen; Photography, Heikki Ortamo, Christian Valdes, Olli Varja; Finnish-Soviet; Color; Not rated; 108 minutes; December release. Documentary featuring Nautilus Pompilius, Brigada S, Billy Bragg and Aquarium, Boris Grebentsykov, Mister Twister, Avia, Nuance, Va Bank, Cruise, Uriah Heep, Televizor

JOURNEY OF LOVE (Centaur Releasing) Producer/Director, Ottavio Fabbri; Screenplay, Tonino Guerra; Photography, Mauro Marchetti; Designer, Tommaso Bordone; Music, Andrea Guerra; Editor, Mauro Bonanni; a Paravalley production in association with Reteitalia; Italian; Dolby Stereo; Color; Not rated; 98 minutes; December release. CAST: Omar Sharif (Rico), Lea Massari (Zaira), Florence Guerin, Stephane Bonnet, Leopoldo Trieste, Ciccio Ingrassia

THE LITTLE RICHARD STORY (OKO Productions) Director/Screenplay, William Klein; German, 1980; Color; Not rated; 90 minutes; December release. Documentary featuring Little Richard

SHE'S BEEN AWAY (BBC/The Sales Co.) Producer, Kenith Trodd; Director, Peter Hall; Screenplay, Stephen Poliakoff; Photography, Philip Bonham-Carter; Designer, Gary Williamson; Music, Stephen Edwards; Editor, Ardan Fisher; British; Color; Not rated; 103 minutes; December release. CAST: Peggy Ashcroft (Lillian Huckle), Geraldine James (Harriet Ambrose), James Fox (Hugh Ambrose), Jackson Kyle (Dominic Ambrose), Rosalie Crutchley (Gladys), Rachel Kempson (Matilda), Rebecca Pidgeon (Young Lillian), Cryss Jean Healey (Young Margaret), Leslie and Edgar Goodall (Old Cousin Edward and Thomas), Rene Zagger (Young Thomas), Barnaby Holm (Young Edward), Donald Douglas (Lillian's Father), Hugh Lloyd (George), Brid Brennan (Lillian's Nurse), David Hargreaves (Lillian's Doctor), Hugh Ross (1920's Doctor), Carrie Thomas (1920's Nurse), Sally Ann Goodworth (Hotel Pianist), Robyn Moore (Louisa), Pamela Dale (Theresa), Jon Strickland, Michael Carter, Nick Kemp, The Harry Tait Trio, Claire Williamson, Graham Callan, James Griffiths, Francesca Buller, Maureen Nelson, Richard Haddon Haines, David Timson, Richard Huw, Malcolm Mudie, Anne Haydn, Doyle Richmond

STEP ACROSS THE BORDER (Cine Nomades Filmproduction) Directors/Screenplay, Nicolas Humbert, Werner Penzel; Photography, Oscar Saigodo; Music, Fred Frith, Joey Baron, Ciro Batista, Iva Bitova; Editor, Gisela Castronari; a Res Balzli & Cie co-production; German-Swiss; Black and white; Not rated; 90 minutes; December release. A documentary with Robert Frank, Jolia Judge, Jonas Mekas, Ted Milton

Geraldine James in "She's Been Away" © *The Sales Co.*

Danny
Aiello

Anouk
Aimee

John
Amos

Joan
Allen

Armand
Assante

Ann-
Margret

BIOGRAPHICAL DATA

(Name, real name, place and date of birth, school attended)

AAMES, WILLIE (William Upton): CA, July 15, 1960.

AARON, CAROLINE: Richmond, VA, Aug. 7, 1954, CatholicU.

ABBOTT, DIAHNNE: NYC, 1945.

ABBOTT, JOHN: London, June 5, 1905.

ABRAHAM, F. MURRAY: Pittsburgh, PA, Oct. 24, 1939. UTx.

ADAMS, BROOKE: NYC, Feb. 8, 1949. Dalton.

ADAMS, DON: NYC, Apr. 13, 1926.

ADAMS, EDIE (Elizabeth Edith Enke): Kingston, PA, Apr. 16, 1929. Juilliard, Columbia.

ADAMS, JULIE (Betty May): Waterloo, Iowa, Oct. 17, 1928. Little Rock Jr. College.

ADAMS, MAUD (Maud Wikstrom): Lulea, Sweden, Feb. 12, 1945.

ADDY, WESLEY: Omaha, NE, Aug. 4, 1913. UCLA.

ADJANI, ISABELLE: Germany, June 27, 1955.

ADRIAN, IRIS (Iris Adrian Hostetter): Los Angeles, May 29, 1913.

AGAR, JOHN: Chicago, Jan. 31, 1921.

AGUTTER, JENNY: Taunton, Eng, Dec. 20, 1952.

AIELLO, DANNY: NYC. June 20, 1935.

AIMEE, ANOUK (Dreyfus): Paris, Apr. 27, 1934. Bauer-Therond.

AKERS, KAREN: NYC, Oct. 13, 1945, Hunter Col.

AKINS, CLAUDE: Nelson, GA, May 25, 1936. Northwestern U.

ALBERGHETTI, ANNA MARIA: Pesaro, Italy, May 15, 1936.

ALBERT, EDDIE (Eddie Albert Heimberger): Rock Island, IL, Apr. 22, 1908. U. of Minn.

ALBERT, EDWARD: Los Angeles, Feb. 20, 1951. UCLA.

ALBRIGHT, LOLA: Akron, OH, July 20, 1925.

ALDA, ALAN: NYC, Jan. 28, 1936. Fordham.

ALEJANDRO, MIGUEL: NYC, Feb. 21, 1958.

ALEXANDER, ERIKA: Philadelphia, PA, 1970.

ALEXANDER, JANE (Quigley): Boston, MA, Oct. 28, 1939. Sarah Lawrence.

ALEXANDER, JASON: Irvington, NJ, Sept. 23, 1959. Boston U.

ALICE, MARY: Indianola, MS, Dec. 3, 1941.

ALLEN, DEBBIE: (Deborah) Houston, TX, Jan. 16, 1950, HowardU.

ALLEN, JOAN: Rochelle, IL, Aug. 20, 1956, EastIllU.

ALLEN, KAREN: Carrollton, IL. Oct. 5, 1951. UMd.

ALLEN, NANCY: NYC June 24, 1950.

ALLEN, REX: Wilcox, AZ, Dec. 31, 1922.

ALLEN, STEVE: New York City, Dec. 26, 1921.

ALLEN, WOODY (Allen Stewart Konigsberg): Brooklyn, Dec. 1, 1935.

ALLEY, KIRSTIE: Wichita, KS, Jan. 12, 1955.

ALLYSON, JUNE (Ella Geisman): Westchester, NY, Oct. 7, 1917.

ALONSO, MARIA CONCHITA: Cuba 1957.

ALT, CAROL: Queens, NY. Dec. 1, 1960. HofstraU.

ALVARADO, TRINI: NYC, 1967.

AMECHE, DON (Dominic Amichi): Kenosha, WI, May 31, 1908.

AMES, LEON (Leon Wycoff): Portland, IN, Jan. 20, 1903.

AMIS, SUZY: Oklahoma City, OK, Jan. 5, 1958. Actors Studio.

AMOS, JOHN: Newark, NJ, Dec. 27, 1940. Colo. U.

ANDERSON, JUDITH: Adelaide, Australia, Feb. 10, 1898.

ANDERSON, KEVIN: Illinois, Jan. 13, 1960.

ANDERSON, LONI: St. Paul, MN, Aug. 5, 1946.

ANDERSON, MELODY: Edmonton, Canada 1955, Carlton U.

ANDERSON, MICHAEL, JR.: London, Eng., 1943.

ANDERSON, RICHARD DEAN: Minneapolis, MN, Jan. 23, 1953.

ANDERSSON, BIBI: Stockholm, Nov. 11, 1935. Royal Dramatic Sch.

ANDES, KEITH: Ocean City, NJ, July 12, 1920. Temple U., Oxford.

ANDRESS, URSULA: Berne, Switz., Mar. 19, 1936.

ANDREWS, ANTHONY: London, 1948.

ANDREWS, DANA: Collins, MS, Jan. 1, 1909. Sam Houston Col.

ANDREWS, JULIE (Julia Elizabeth Wells): Surrey, Eng., Oct. 1, 1935.

ANGLIM, PHILIP: San Francisco, CA, Feb. 11, 1953.

ANNABELLA (Suzanne Georgette Charpentier): Paris, France, July 14, 1912/1909.

ANN-MARGRET (Olsson): Valsjobyn, Sweden, Apr. 28, 1941. Northwestern U.

ANSARA, MICHAEL: Lowell, MA, Apr. 15, 1922. Pasadena Playhouse.

ANSPACH, SUSAN: NYC, Nov. 23, 1945.

ANTHONY, LYSETTE: London, 1963.

ANTHONY, TONY: Clarksburg, WV, Oct. 16, 1937. Carnegie Tech.

ANTON, SUSAN: Yucaipa, CA. Oct. 12, 1950. Bernardino Col.

ANTONELLI, LAURA: Pola, Italy.

ARANHA, RAY: Miami, FL, May 1, 1939. FlaA&M, AADA.

ARCHER, ANNE: Los Angeles, Aug. 25, 1947.

ARCHER, JOHN (Ralph Bowman): Osceola, NB, May 8, 1915. USC.

ARKIN, ALAN: NYC, Mar. 26, 1934. LACC.

ARMSTRONG, BESS: Baltimore, MD, Dec. 11, 1953.

ARNAZ, DESI, JR.: Los Angeles, Jan. 19, 1953.

ARNAZ, LUCIE: Hollywood, July 17, 1951.

ARNESS, JAMES (Aurness): Minneapolis, MN, May 26, 1923. Beloit College.

ARQUETTE, ROSANNA: NYC, Aug. 10, 1959.

ARTHUR, BEATRICE (Frankel): NYC, May 13, 1924. New School.

ARTHUR, JEAN: NYC, Oct. 17, 1905.

ASHCROFT, PEGGY: London, Eng., Dec. 22, 1907.

ASHLEY, ELIZABETH (Elizabeth Ann Cole): Ocala, FL, Aug. 30, 1939.

ASNER, EDWARD: Kansas City, KS, Nov. 15, 1929.

ASSANTE, ARMAND: NYC, Oct. 4, 1949. AADA.

ASTIN, JOHN: Baltimore, MD, Mar. 30, 1930. U. Minn.

ASTIN, MacKENZIE: Los Angeles, 1973.

ASTIN, SEAN: Santa Monica, Feb. 25, 1971.

ATHERTON, WILLIAM: Orange, CT, July 30, 1947. Carnegie Tech.

ATKINS, CHRISTOPHER: Rye, NY, Feb. 21, 1961.

ATTENBOROUGH, RICHARD: Cambridge, Eng., Aug. 29, 1923. RADA.

AUBERJONOIS, RENE: NYC, June 1, 1940. Carnegie Tech.

AUDRAN, STEPHANE: Versailles, Fr., 1933.

AUGER, CLAUDINE: Paris, Apr. 26, 1942. Dramatic Cons.

AULIN, EWA: Stockholm, Sweden, Feb. 14, 1950.

AUMONT, JEAN PIERRE: Paris, Jan. 5, 1909. French Nat'l School of Drama.

AUTRY, GENE: Tioga, TX, Sept. 29, 1907.

AVALON, FRANKIE (Francis Thomas Avallone): Philadelphia, Sept. 18, 1940.

AYKROYD, DAN: Ottawa, Can., July 1, 1952.

AYRES, LEW: Minneapolis, MN, Dec. 28, 1908.

AZNAVOUR, CHARLES (Varenagh Aznourian): Paris, May 22, 1924.

AZZARA, CANDICE: Brooklyn, NY, May 18, 1947.

BACALL, LAUREN (Betty Perske): NYC, Sept. 16, 1924. AADA.

BACH, BARBARA: Queens, NY, Aug. 27, 1946.

BACKER, BRIAN: NYC, Dec. 5, 1956. Neighborhood Playhouse.

BACON, KEVIN: Philadelphia, PA., July 8, 1958.

BAIN, BARBARA: Chicago, Sept. 13, 1934. U. ILL.

BAIO, SCOTT: Brooklyn, NY, Sept. 22, 1961.

BAKER, BLANCHE: NYC, Dec. 20, 1956.

BAKER, CARROLL: Johnstown, PA, May 28, 1931. St. Petersburg Jr. College.

BAKER, DIANE: Hollywood, CA, Feb. 25, 1938. USC.

BAKER, JOE DON: Groesbeck, TX, Feb. 12, 1936.

BAKER, KATHY: Midland, TX., June 8, 1950. UCBerkley.

BALABAN, BOB: Chicago, Aug. 16, 1945. Colgate.

BALDWIN, ADAM: Chicago, Feb. 27, 1962.

BALDWIN, ALEC: Massapequa, NY, Apr. 3, 1958. NYU.

BALE, CHRISTIAN: Pembrokeshire, West Wales, Jan. 30, 1974.

BALLARD, KAYE: Cleveland, OH, Nov. 20, 1926.

BALSAM, MARTIN: NYC, Nov. 4, 1919. Actors Studio.

BANCROFT, ANNE (Anna Maria Italiano): Bronx, NY, Sept. 17, 1931. AADA.

BANES, LISA: Chagrin Falls, OH, July 9, 1955. Juilliard.

BANNEN, IAN: Airdrie, Scot., June 29, 1928.

BARANSKI, CHRISTINE: Buffalo, NY, May 2, 1952, Juilliard.

BARBEAU, ADRIENNE: Sacramento, CA. June 11, 1945. Foothill Col.

BARDOT, BRIGITTE: Paris, Sept. 28, 1934.

BARKIN, ELLEN: Bronx, NY, Apr. 16, 1954. Hunter Col.

BARNES, BINNIE (Gitelle Enoyce Barnes): London, Mar. 25, 1906

BARNES, C. B. (Christopher): Portland, ME, 1973.

BARR, JEAN-MARC: San Diego, CA, Sept. 1960.

BARR, ROSEANNE: Salt Lake City, UT, Nov. 3, 1953.

BARRAULT, JEAN-LOUIS: Vesinet, France, Sept. 8, 1910.

BARRAULT, MARIE-CHRISTINE: Paris, Mar. 21, 1946.

BARRETT, MAJEL (Hudec): Columbus, OH, Feb. 23. Western Reserve U.

BARRIE, BARBARA: Chicago, IL, May 23, 1931.

BARRON, KEITH: Mexborough, Eng., Aug. 8, 1936. Sheffield Playhouse.

BARRY, GENE (Eugene Klass): NYC, June 14, 1921.

BARRY, NEILL: NYC, Nov. 29, 1965.

BARRYMORE, DEBORAH: London, London Acad.

BARRYMORE, DREW: Los Angeles, Feb. 22, 1975.

BARRYMORE, JOHN BLYTH: Beverly Hills, CA, June 4, 1932. St. John's Military Academy.

BARTEL, PAUL: NYC, Aug. 6, 1938. UCLA.

BARTHOLOMEW, FREDDIE: London, Mar. 28, 1924.

BARTY, BILLY: Millsboro, PA, Oct. 25, 1924.

BARYSHNIKOV, MIKHAIL: Riga, Latvia, Jan. 27, 1948.

BASINGER, KIM: Athens, GA., Dec. 8, 1953. Neighborhood Playhouse.

BATEMAN, JUSTINE: Rye, NY, Feb. 19, 1966.

BATES, ALAN: Allestree, Derbyshire, Eng., Feb. 17, 1934. RADA.

BATES, JEANNE: San Francisco, CA., May 21. RADA.

BATES, KATHY: Memphis, TN, June 18, 1948. S. Methodist U.

BAUER, STEVEN: (Steven Rocky Echevarria): Havana, Cuba, Dec. 2, 1956. UMiami.

BAXTER, KEITH: South Wales, Apr. 29, 1933. RADA.

BEACHAM, STEPHANIE: England, 1946.

BEAL, JOHN (J. Alexander Bliedung): Joplin, MO, Aug. 13, 1909. PA. U.

BEART, EMMANUELLE: Gassin, France, 1965.

BEATTY, NED: Louisville, KY. July 6, 1937.

BEATTY, ROBERT: Hamilton, Ont., Can., Oct. 19, 1909. U. of Toronto.

BEATTY, WARREN: Richmond, VA, March 30, 1937.

BECK, JOHN: Chicago, IL, Jan. 28, 1943.

BECK, MICHAEL: Memphis, TN, Feb. 4, 1949. Millsap Col.

BEDELIA, BONNIE: NYC, Mar. 25, 1946. Hunter Col.

BEDI, KABIR: India, 1945.

BEERY, NOAH, JR.: NYC, Aug. 10, 1916. Harvard Military Academy.

BEGLEY, ED, JR.: NYC, Sept. 16, 1949.

BELAFONTE, HARRY: NYC, Mar. 1, 1927.

BELASCO, LEON: Odessa, Russia, Oct. 11, 1902.

BEL GEDDES, BARBARA: NYC, Oct. 31, 1922.

BELL, TOM: Liverpool, Eng., 1932.

BELLAMY, RALPH: Chicago, June 17, 1904.

BELLER, KATHLEEN: NYC, Feb. 10, 1957.

BELLWOOD, PAMELA (King): Scarsdale, NY June 26.

BELMONDO, JEAN PAUL: Paris, Apr. 9, 1933.

BELUSHI, JAMES: Chicago, May 15, 1954.

BENEDICT, DIRK (Niewoehner): White Sulphur Springs, MT. March 1, 1945. Whitman Col.

BENEDICT, PAUL: Silver City, NM, Sept. 17, 1938.

BENING, ANNETTE: Topeka, KS, May 29, 1958. SFSt.U.

BENJAMIN, RICHARD: NYC, May 22, 1938. Northwestern U.

BENNENT, DAVID: Lausanne, Sept. 9, 1966.

BENNETT, BRUCE (Herman Brix): Tacoma, WA, May 19, 1909. U. Wash.

BENSON, ROBBY: Dallas, TX, Jan 21, 1957.

BERENGER, TOM: Chicago, May 31, 1950, UMo.

BERENSON, MARISA: NYC, Feb. 15, 1947.

BERGEN, CANDICE: Los Angeles, May 9, 1946. U. PA.

BERGEN, POLLY: Knoxville, TN, July 14, 1930. Compton Jr. College.

BERGER, HELMUT: Salzburg, Aus., 1942.

BERGER, SENTA: Vienna, May 13, 1941. Vienna Sch. of Acting.

BERGER, WILLIAM: Austria, Jan. 20, 1928. Columbia.

BERGERAC, JACQUES: Biarritz, France, May 26, 1927. Paris U.

BERLE, MILTON (Berlinger): NYC, July 12, 1908.

BERLIN, JEANNIE: Los Angeles, Nov. 1, 1949.

BERLINGER, WARREN: Brooklyn, Aug. 31, 1937. Columbia.

BERNHARD, SANDRA: Flint, MI, June 6, 1955.

BERNSEN, CORBIN: Los Angeles, Sept. 7, 1954, UCLA.

BERRI, CLAUDE (Langmann): Paris, July 1, 1934.

BERRIDGE, ELIZABETH: Westchester, NY, May 2, 1962. Strasberg Inst.

BERTINELLI, VALERIE: Wilmington, DE, Apr. 23, 1960.

BERTO, JULIET: Grenoble, France, Jan. 1947.

BEST, JAMES: Corydon, IN, July 26, 1926.

BETTGER, LYLE: Philadelphia, Feb. 13, 1915. AADA.

BEYMER, RICHARD: Avoca, IA, Feb. 21, 1939.

BIEHN, MICHAEL: Anniston, AL, 1957.

BIKEL, THEODORE: Vienna, May 2, 1924. RADA.

BILLINGSLEY, PETER: NYC, 1972.

BIRNEY, DAVID: Washington, DC, Apr. 23, 1939. Dartmouth, UCLA.

BIRNEY, REED: Alexandria, VA., Sept. 11, 1954. Boston U.

BISHOP, JOEY (Joseph Abraham Gottlieb): Bronx, NY, Feb. 3, 1918.

BISHOP, JULIE (formerly Jacqueline Wells): Denver, CO, Aug. 30, 1917. Westlake School.

BISSET, JACQUELINE: Waybridge, Eng., Sept. 13, 1944.

BIXBY, BILL: San Francisco, Jan. 22, 1934. U. CAL.

BLACK, KAREN (Ziegler): Park Ridge, IL, July 1, 1942. Northwestern.

BLADES, RUBEN: Panama, July 16, 1948, Harvard.

BLAINE, VIVIAN (Vivian Stapleton): Newark, NJ, Nov. 21, 1921.

BLAIR, BETSY (Betsy Boger): NYC, Dec. 11, 1923.

BLAIR, JANET (Martha Jane Lafferty): Blair, PA, Apr. 23, 1921.

BLAIR, LINDA: Westport, CT, Jan. 22, 1959.

BLAKE, ROBERT (Michael Gubitosi): Nutley, NJ, Sept. 18, 1933.

BLAKELY, SUSAN: Frankfurt, Germany, Sept. 7, 1950. U. TEX.

BLAKLEY, RONEE: Stanley, ID, 1946. Stanford U.

BLOOM, CLAIRE: London, Feb. 15, 1931. Badminton School.

BLOOM, VERNA: Lynn, MA, Aug. 7, 1939. Boston U.

BLUM, MARK: Newark, NJ, May 14, 1950. UMinn.

| Ellen Barkin | Richard Benjamin | Betty Buckley | Pierce Brosnan | Irene Cara | Dennis Christopher |

BLYTH, ANN: Mt. Kisco, NY, Aug. 16, 1928. New Wayburn Dramatic School.
BOCHNER, HART: Toronto, Oct. 3, 1956. U. San Diego.
BOGARDE, DIRK: London, Mar. 28, 1918. Glasgow & Univ. College.
BOGOSIAN, ERIC: Woburn, MA, Apr. 24, 1953. Oberlin Col.
BOHRINGER, RICHARD: 1942 Paris
BOLKAN, FLORINDA (Florinda Soares Bulcao): Ceara, Brazil, Feb. 15, 1941.
BOND, DEREK: Glasgow, Scot., Jan. 26, 1920. Askes School.
BONET, LISA: San Francisco, Nov. 16, 1967.
BONHAM-CARTER, HELENA: England, May 26, 1966.
BONO, SONNY (Salvatore): Detroit, MI, Feb. 16, 1935.
BOONE, PAT: Jacksonville, FL, June 1, 1934. Columbia U.
BOOTH, SHIRLEY (Thelma Ford): NYC, Aug. 30, 1907.
BOOTHE, POWERS: Snyder, TX, 1949. So. Methodist U.
BORGNINE, ERNEST (Borgnino): Hamden, CT, Jan. 24, 1918. Randall School.
BOSCO, PHILIP: Jersey City, NJ, Sept. 26, 1930. CatholicU.
BOSTWICK, BARRY: San Mateo, CA., Feb. 24, 1945. NYU.
BOTTOMS, JOSEPH: Santa Barbara, CA, Aug. 30, 1954.
BOTTOMS, SAM: Santa Barbara, CA, Oct. 17, 1955.
BOTTOMS, TIMOTHY: Santa Barbara, CA, Aug. 30, 1951.
BOULTING, INGRID: Transvaal, So. Africa, 1947.
BOUTSIKARIS, DENNIS: Newark, NJ, Dec. 21, 1952. CatholicU.
BOVEE, LESLIE: Bend, OR, 1952.
BOWIE, DAVID: (David Robert Jones) Brixton, South London, Eng. Jan. 8, 1947.
BOWKER, JUDI: Shawford, Eng., Apr. 6, 1954.
BOXLEITNER, BRUCE: Elgin, IL., May 12, 1950.
BOYLE, PETER: Philadelphia, PA, Oct. 18, 1933. LaSalle Col.
BRACCO, LORRAINE: Brooklyn, NY, 1955.
BRACKEN, EDDIE: NYC, Feb. 7, 1920. Professional Children's School.
BRAEDEN, ERIC: (Hans Gudegast): Braeden, Germany.
BRAGA, SONIA: Maringa, Brazil, 1951.
BRANAGH, KENNETH: Belfast, No. Ire., Dec. 10, 1960.
BRAND, NEVILLE: Kewanee, IL, Aug. 13, 1920.
BRANDAUER, KLAUS MARIA: Altaussee, Austria, June 22, 1944.
BRANDO, JOCELYN: San Francisco,

Nov. 18, 1919. Lake Forest College, AADA.
BRANDO, MARLON: Omaha, NB, Apr. 3, 1924. New School.
BRANDON, CLARK: NYC 1959.
BRANDON, MICHAEL (Feldman): Brooklyn, NY.
BRANTLEY, BETSY: Rutherfordton, NC, 1955. London Central Sch. of Drama.
BRAZZI, ROSSANO: Bologna, Italy, Sept. 18, 1916. U. Florence.
BRENNAN, EILEEN: Los Angeles, CA., Sept. 3, 1935. AADA.
BRIALY, JEAN-CLAUDE: Aumale, Algeria, 1933. Strasbourg Cons.
BRIAN, DAVID: NYC, Aug. 5, 1914. CCNY.
BRIDGES, BEAU: Los Angeles, Dec. 9, 1941. UCLA.
BRIDGES, JEFF: Los Angeles, Dec. 4, 1949.
BRIDGES, LLOYD: San Leandro, CA, Jan. 15, 1913.
BRIMLEY, WILFORD: Salt Lake City, UT, Sept. 27, 1934.
BRINKLEY, CHRISTIE: Malibu, CA., Feb. 2, 1954.
BRISEBOIS, DANIELLE: Brooklyn, June 28, 1969.
BRITT, MAY (Maybritt Wilkins): Sweden, Mar. 22, 1936.
BRITTANY, MORGAN: (Suzanne Caputo): Los Angeles, 1950.
BRITTON, TONY: Birmingham, Eng., June 9, 1924.
BRODERICK, MATTHEW: NYC, Mar. 21, 1962.
BRODIE, STEVE (Johnny Stevens): Eldorado, KS, Nov. 25, 1919.
BROLIN, JAMES: Los Angeles, July 18, 1940. UCLA.
BROMFIELD, JOHN (Farron Bromfield): South Bend, IN, June 11, 1922. St. Mary's College.
BRONSON, CHARLES (Buchinsky): Ehrenfield, PA, Nov. 3, 1920.
BROOKES, JACQUELINE: Montclair, NJ, July 24, 1930, RADA.
BROOKS, ALBERT (Einstein): Los Angeles, July 22, 1947.
BROOKS, MEL (Melvyn Kaminski): Brooklyn, June 28, 1926.
BROSNAN, PIERCE: County Meath, Ireland, May 16, 1952.
BROWN, BLAIR: Washington, DC, 1948; Pine Manor.
BROWN, BRYAN: Panania, Australia, June 23, 1947.
BROWN, GARY (Christian Brando): Hollywood, CA, 1958.
BROWN, GEORG STANFORD: Havana, Cuba, June 24, 1943. AMDA.
BROWN, JAMES: Desdemona, TX, Mar. 22, 1920. Baylor U.
BROWN, JIM: St. Simons Island, NY, Feb. 17, 1935. Syracuse U.

BROWNE, CORAL: Melbourne, Aust., July 23, 1913.
BROWNE, LESLIE: NYC, 1958.
BROWNE, ROSCOE LEE: Woodbury, NJ, May 2, 1925.
BUCHHOLZ, HORST: Berlin, Ger., Dec. 4, 1933. Ludwig Dramatic School.
BUCKLEY, BETTY: Big Spring, TX, July 3, 1947. TxCU.
BUJOLD, GENEVIEVE: Montreal, Can., July 1, 1942.
BURGHOFF, GARY: Bristol, Ct., May 24, 1943.
BURGI, RICHARD: July 30, 1958, Montclair, NJ
BURKE, DELTA: Orlando, FL, July 30, 1956, LAMDA.
BURKE, PAUL: New Orleans, July 21, 1926. Pasadena Playhouse.
BURNETT, CAROL: San Antonio, TX, Apr. 26, 1933. UCLA.
BURNS, CATHERINE: NYC, Sept. 25, 1945. AADA.
BURNS, GEORGE (Nathan Birnbaum): NYC, Jan. 20, 1896.
BURR, RAYMOND: New Westminster, B.C., Can., May 21, 1917. Stanford, U. CAL., Columbia.
BURSTYN, ELLEN (Edna Rae Gillooly): Detroit, MI, Dec. 7, 1932.
BURTON, LeVAR: Los Angeles, CA. Feb. 16, 1958. UCLA.
BUSEY, GARY: Goose Creek, TX, June 29, 1944.
BUSKER, RICKY: Rockford, IL., 1974
BUTTONS, RED (Aaron Chwatt): NYC, Feb. 5, 1919.
BUZZI, RUTH: Wequetequock, RI, July 24, 1936. Pasadena Playhouse.
BYGRAVES, MAX: London, Oct. 16, 1922. St. Joseph's School.
BYRNE, GABRIEL: Dublin, Ireland, 1950.
BYRNES, EDD: NYC, July 30, 1933. Haaren High.
CAAN, JAMES: Bronx, NY, Mar. 26, 1939.
CAESAR, SID: Yonkers, NY, Sept. 8, 1922.
CAGE, NICOLAS: Long Beach, CA. Jan. 7, 1964.
CAINE, MICHAEL (Maurice Micklewhite): London, Mar. 14, 1933.
CAINE, SHAKIRA (Baksh): Guyana, Feb. 23, 1947. Indian Trust Col.
CALHOUN, RORY (Francis Timothy Durgin): Los Angeles, Aug. 8, 1922.
CALLAN, MICHAEL (Martin Calinieff): Philadelphia, Nov. 22, 1935.
CALLOW, SIMON: London, June 15, 1949. Queens U.
CALVERT, PHYLLIS: London, Feb. 18, 1917. Margaret Morris School.
CALVET, CORRINE (Corrine Dibos): Paris, Apr. 30, 1925. U. Paris.

CAMERON, KIRK: Panorama City, CA, Oct. 12, 1970.

CAMP, COLLEEN: San Francisco, 1953.

CAMPBELL, BILL: Chicago 1960.

CAMPBELL, GLEN: Delight, AR, Apr. 22, 1935.

CAMPBELL, TISHA: Newark, NJ, 1969.

CANALE, GIANNA MARIA: Reggio Calabria, Italy, Sept. 12.

CANDY, JOHN: Toronto, Can., Oct. 31, 1950.

CANNON, DYAN (Samille Diane Friesen): Tacoma, WA, Jan. 4, 1937.

CANTU, DOLORES: San Antonio, TX., 1957.

CAPERS, VIRGINIA: Sumter, SC, 1925. Juilliard.

CAPSHAW, KATE: Ft. Worth, TX, 1953. UMo.

CARA, IRENE: NYC, Mar. 18, 1958.

CARDINALE, CLAUDIA: Tunis, N. Africa, Apr. 15, 1939. College Paul Cambon.

CAREY, HARRY, JR.: Saugus, CA, May 16, 1921. Black Fox Military Academy.

CAREY, MACDONALD: Sioux City, IA, Mar. 15, 1913. U. of Wisc., U. Iowa.

CAREY, PHILIP: Hackensack, NJ, July 15, 1925. U. Miami.

CARIOU, LEN: Winnipeg, Can., Sept. 30, 1939.

CARLIN, GEORGE: NYC, May 12, 1938.

CARMEN, JULIE: Mt. Vernon, NY, Apr. 4, 1954.

CARMICHAEL, IAN: Hull, Eng., June 18, 1920. Scarborough Col.

CARNE, JUDY (Joyce Botterill): Northampton, Eng., 1939. Bush-Davis Theatre School.

CARNEY, ART: Mt. Vernon, NY, Nov. 4, 1918.

CARON, LESLIE: Paris, July 1, 1931. Nat'l Conservatory, Paris.

CARPENTER, CARLETON: Bennington, VT, July 10, 1926. Northwestern.

CARRADINE, DAVID: Hollywood, Dec. 8, 1936. San Francisco State.

CARRADINE, KEITH: San Mateo, CA, Aug. 8, 1950. Colo. State U.

CARRADINE, ROBERT: San Mateo, CA, Mar. 24, 1954.

CARREL, DANY: Tourane, Indochina, Sept. 20, 1936. Marseilles Cons.

CARRERA, BARBARA: Managua, Nicaragua, Dec. 31, 1945.

CARREY, JIM: Jacksons Point, Ontario, Can., Jan. 17, 1962.

CARRIERE, MATHIEU: West Germany 1950.

CARROLL, DIAHANN (Johnson): NYC, July 17, 1935. NYU.

CARROLL, PAT: Shreveport, LA, May 5, 1927. Catholic U.

CARSON, JOHN DAVID: 1951, Calif. Valley Col.

CARSON, JOHNNY: Corning, IA, Oct. 23, 1925. U. of Neb.

CARSTEN, PETER (Ransenthaler): Weissenberg, Bavaria, Apr. 30, 1929. Munich Akademie.

CARTER, NELL: Birmingham, AL., Sept. 13, 1948.

CARTWRIGHT, VERONICA: Bristol, Eng., 1949.

CARVEY, DANA: Missoula, MT, Apr. 2, 1955. SFST.Col.

CASEY, BERNIE: Wyco, WV, June 8, 1939.

CASH, ROSALIND: Atlantic City, NJ, Dec. 31, 1938. CCNY.

CASS, PEGGY (Mary Margaret): Boston, May 21, 1925.

CASSAVETES, NICK: NYC 1959, Syracuse U, AADA.

CASSEL, JEAN-PIERRE: Paris, Oct. 27, 1932.

CASSIDY, DAVID: NYC, Apr. 12, 1950.

CASSIDY, JOANNA: Camden, NJ, Aug. 2, 1944. Syracuse U.

CASSIDY, PATRICK: Los Angeles, CA, Jan. 4, 1961.

CATES, PHOEBE: NYC, 1963.

CATTRALL, KIM: Liverpool, Eng. Aug. 21, 1956, AADA.

CAULFIELD, JOAN: Orange, NJ, June 1, 1922. Columbia U.

CAULFIELD, MAXWELL: Glasgow, Scot., Nov. 23, 1959.

CAVANI, LILIANA: Bologna, Italy, Jan. 12, 1937. U. Bologna.

CAVETT, DICK: Gibbon, NE, Nov. 19, 1936.

CHAKIRIS, GEORGE: Norwood, OH, Sept. 16, 1933.

CHAMBERLAIN, RICHARD: Beverly Hills, CA, March 31, 1935. Pomona.

CHAMPION, MARGE: Los Angeles, Sept. 2, 1923.

CHANNING, CAROL: Seattle, WA, Jan. 31, 1921. Bennington.

CHANNING, STOCKARD (Susan Stockard): NYC, Feb. 13, 1944. Radcliffe.

CHAPIN, MILES: NYC, Dec. 6, 1954. HB Studio.

CHAPLIN, GERALDINE: Santa Monica, CA, July 31, 1944. Royal Ballet.

CHAPLIN, SYDNEY: Los Angeles, Mar. 31, 1926. Lawrenceville.

CHARISSE, CYD (Tula Ellice Finklea): Amarillo, TX, Mar. 3, 1922. Hollywood Professional School.

CHARLES, WALTER: Apr. 4, 1945, East Strousburg, PA. Boston U.

CHASE, CHEVY (Cornelius Crane Chase): NYC, Oct. 8, 1943.

CHAVES, RICHARD: Jacksonville, FL, Oct. 9, 1951, Occidental Col.

CHEN, JOAN: Shanghai, 1961. CalState.

CHER (Cherilyn Sarkisian) May 20, 1946, El Centro, CA.

CHIARI, WALTER: Verona, Italy, 1930.

CHILES, LOIS: Alice, TX, 1950.

CHONG, RAE DAWN: Vancouver, Can., 1961.

CHONG, THOMAS: Edmonton, Alberta, Can., May 24, 1938.

CHRISTIAN, LINDA (Blanca Rosa Welter): Tampico, Mex., Nov. 13, 1923.

CHRISTIE, JULIE: Chukua, Assam, India, Apr. 14, 1941.

CHRISTOPHER, DENNIS (Carrelli): Philadelphia, PA, Dec. 2, 1955. Temple U.

CHRISTOPHER, JORDAN: Youngstown, OH, Oct. 23, 1940. Kent State.

CILENTO, DIANE: Queensland, Australia, Oct. 5, 1933. AADA.

CLAPTON, ERIC: London, Mar. 30, 1945.

CLARK, CANDY: Norman, OK, June 20, 1947.

CLARK, DANE: NYC, Feb. 18, 1915. Cornell, Johns Hopkins U.

CLARK, DICK: Mt. Vernon, NY, Nov. 30, 1929. Syracuse U.

CLARK, MAE: Philadelphia, Aug. 16, 1910.

CLARK, PETULA: Epsom, England, Nov. 15, 1932.

CLARK, SUSAN: Sarnid, Ont., Can., Mar. 8, 1940. RADA.

CLAY, ANDREW DICE: Brooklyn, 1958, Kingsborough Col.

CLAYBURGH, JILL: NYC, Apr. 30, 1944. Sarah Lawrence.

CLEESE, JOHN: Weston-Super-Mare, Eng., Oct. 27, 1939, Cambridge.

CLERY, CORRINNE: Italy, 1950.

CLOONEY, ROSEMARY: Maysville, KY, May 23, 1928.

CLOSE, GLENN: Greenwich, CT., Mar. 19, 1947. William & Mary Col.

COBURN, JAMES: Laurel, NB, Aug. 31, 1928. LACC.

COCA, IMOGENE: Philadelphia, Nov. 18, 1908.

CODY, KATHLEEN: Bronx, NY, Oct. 30, 1953.

COFFEY, SCOTT: HI, 1967.

COLBERT, CLAUDETTE (Lily Chauchoin): Paris, Sept. 15, 1903. Art Students League.

COLE, GEORGE: London, Apr. 22, 1925.

COLEMAN, GARY: Zion, IL., Feb. 8, 1968.

COLEMAN, DABNEY: Austin, TX, Jan. 3, 1932.

COLIN, MARGARET: NYC, 1957.

COLEMAN, JACK: 1958. Easton, PA., Duke U.

COLLET, CHRISTOPHER: NYC, Mar. 13, 1968. Strasberg Inst.

COLLINS, JOAN: London, May 21, 1933. Francis Holland School.

COLLINS, PAULINE: Devon, Eng., Sept. 3, 1940.

COLLINS, STEPHEN: Des Moines, IA, Oct. 1, 1947. Amherst.

COLON, MIRIAM: Ponce, PR., 1945. UPR.

COLTRANE, ROBBIE: Ruthergien, Scot., 1950.

COMER, ANJANETTE: Dawson, TX, Aug. 7, 1942. Baylor, Tex. U.

CONANT, OLIVER: NYC, Nov. 15, 1955. Dalton.

CONAWAY, JEFF: NYC, Oct. 5, 1950. NYC.

CONNERY, SEAN: Edinburgh, Scot., Aug. 25, 1930.

CONNERY, JASON: London 1962.

CONNICK, HARRY, JR.: New Orleans, LA, 1967.

CONNORS, CHUCK (Kevin Joseph Connors): Brooklyn, Apr. 10, 1921. Seton Hall College.

CONNORS, MIKE (Krekor Ohanian): Fresno, CA, Aug. 15, 1925. UCLA.

CONRAD, WILLIAM: Louisville, KY, Sept. 27, 1920.

CONROY, KEVIN: Westport, CT, 1956. Juilliard.

CONSTANTINE, MICHAEL: Reading, PA, May 22, 1927.

CONTI, TOM: Paisley, Scotland, Nov. 22, 1941.

CONVERSE, FRANK: St. Louis, MO, May 22, 1938. Carnegie Tech.

CONVY, BERT: St. Louis, MO, July 23, 1935. UCLA.

CONWAY, KEVIN: NYC, May 29, 1942.

CONWAY, TIM (Thomas Daniel): Willoughby, OH, Dec. 15, 1933. Bowling Green State.

COOGAN, KEITH (Keith Mitchell Franklin): Palm Springs, CA, Jan. 13, 1970.

COOK, ELISHA, JR.: San Francisco, Dec. 26, 1907. St. Albans.

COOK, PETER: Torquay, Eng., Nov. 17, 1937.

COOPER, BEN: Hartford, CT, Sept. 30, 1932. Columbia U.

COOPER, CHRISTOPHER: July 9, 1951, Kansas City, MO, UMo.

COOPER, JACKIE: Los Angeles, Sept. 15, 1921.

COPELAND, JOAN: NYC, June 1, 1922. Brooklyn Col. RADA.

CORBETT, GRETCHEN: Portland, OR, Aug. 13, 1947. Carnegie Tech.

CORBY, ELLEN (Hansen): Racine, WI, June 13, 1913.

CORCORAN, DONNA: Quincy, MA, Sept. 29, 1942.

CORD, ALEX (Viespi): Floral Park, NY, Aug. 3, 1931. NYU, Actors Studio.

CORDAY, MARA (Marilyn Watts): Santa Monica, CA, Jan. 3, 1932.

COREY, JEFF: NYC, Aug. 10, 1914. Fagin School.

CORLAN, ANTHONY: Cork City, Ire., May 9, 1947. Birmingham School of Dramatic Arts.

CORLEY, AL: Missouri, 1956. Actors Studio.

CORNTHWAITE, ROBERT: St. Helens, OR. Apr. 28, 1917. USC.

CORRI, ADRIENNE: Glasgow, Scot., Nov. 13, 1933. RADA.

CORT, BUD (Walter Edward Cox): New Rochelle, NY, Mar. 29, 1950. NYU.

CORTESE, VALENTINA: Milan, Italy, Jan. 1, 1925.

COSBY, BILL: Philadelphia, July 12, 1937. Temple U.

COSTER, NICOLAS: London, Dec. 3, 1934. Neighborhood Playhouse.

COSTNER, KEVIN: Compton, CA, Jan. 18, 1955. CalStaU.

COTTEN, JOSEPH: Petersburg, VA, May 13, 1905.

COURTENAY, TOM: Hull, Eng., Feb. 25, 1937. RADA.

COURTLAND, JEROME: Knoxville, TN, Dec. 27, 1926.

COYOTE, PETER (Cohon): NYC, 1942.

COX, COURTNEY: Birmingham, AL, June 15, 1964.

COX, RONNY: Cloudcroft, NM, Aug. 23, 1938.

CRAIG, MICHAEL: India, Jan. 27, 1929.

CRAIN, JEANNE: Barstow, CA, May 25, 1925.

CRAWFORD, MICHAEL (Dumbel-Smith): Salisbury, Eng., Jan. 19, 1942.

CREMER, BRUNO: Paris, 1929.

CRENNA, RICHARD: Los Angeles, Nov. 30, 1926. USC.

CRISTAL, LINDA (Victoria Moya): Buenos Aires, Feb. 25, 1934.

CRONYN, HUME (Blake): Ontario, Can, July 18, 1911.

CROSBY, DENISE: Hollywood, CA, 1958.

CROSBY, HARRY: Los Angeles, CA, Aug. 8, 1958.

CROSBY, MARY FRANCES: Calif., Sept. 14, 1959.

CROSS, BEN: London, Dec. 16, 1948. RADA.

CROSS, MURPHY (Mary Jane): Laurelton, MD, June 22, 1950.

CROUSE, LINDSAY: NYC, May 12, 1948. Radcliffe.

CROWLEY, PAT: Olyphant, PA, Sept. 17, 1932.

CRUISE, TOM (T. C. Mapother IV): July 3, 1962, Syracuse, NY.

CRYER, JON: NYC, Apr. 16, 1965, RADA.

CRYSTAL, BILLY: Long Beach, NY, Mar. 14, 1947, Marshall U.

CULKIN, MACAULAY: NYC, Aug. 26, 1980.

CULLUM, JOHN: Knoxville, TN, Mar. 2, 1930. U. Tenn.

CULLUM, JOHN DAVID: NYC, Mar. 1, 1966.

CULP, ROBERT: Oakland, CA., Aug. 16, 1930. U. Wash.

CUMMINGS, CONSTANCE: Seattle, WA, May 15, 1910.

CUMMINGS, QUINN: Hollywood, Aug. 13, 1967.

CUMMINS, PEGGY: Prestatyn, N. Wales, Dec. 18, 1926. Alexandra School.

CURRY, TIM: England, 1946.

CURTIN, JANE: Cambridge, MA; Sept. 6, 1947.

CURTIS, JAMIE LEE: Los Angeles, CA., Nov. 22, 1958.

CURTIS, KEENE: Salt Lake City, UT, Feb. 15, 1925. U. Utah.

CURTIS, TONY (Bernard Schwartz): NYC, June 3, 1924.

CUSACK, CYRIL: Durban, S. Africa, Nov. 26, 1910. Univ. Col.

CUSACK, JOAN: Evanston, IL, Oct. 11, 1962.

CUSACK, JOHN: Chicago, IL, June 28, 1966.

CUSHING, PETER: Kenley, Surrey, Eng., May 26, 1913.

DAFOE, WILLEM: Appleton, WI. July 22, 1955.

DAHL, ARLENE: Minneapolis, Aug. 11, 1928. U. Minn.

DALE, JIM: Rothwell, Eng., Aug. 15, 1935.

DALLESANDRO, JOE: Pensacola, FL, Dec. 31, 1948.

DALTON, TIMOTHY: Colwyn Bay, Wales, Mar. 21, 1946, RADA.

DALTREY, ROGER: London, Mar. 1, 1945.

DALY, TIMOTHY: NYC, Mar. 1, 1956. Bennington Col.

DALY, TYNE: Madison, WI, Feb. 21, 1947. AMDA.

DAMONE, VIC (Vito Farinola): Brooklyn, June 12, 1928.

DANCE, CHARLES: Plymouth, Eng., Oct. 10, 1946.

D'ANGELO, BEVERLY: Columbus, OH., Nov. 15, 1953.

DANGERFIELD, RODNEY (Jacob Cohen): Babylon, NY, Nov. 22, 1921.

DANIELS, JEFF: Georgia, Feb. 19, 1955. EastMichState.

DANIELS, WILLIAM: Bklyn, Mar. 31, 1927. Northwestern.

DANNER, BLYTHE: Philadelphia, PA. Feb. 3, 1944, Bard Col.

DANO, ROYAL: NYC, Nov. 16, 1922. NYU.

DANSON, TED: San Diego, CA, Dec. 29, 1947. Stanford, Carnegie Tech.

DANTE, MICHAEL (Ralph Vitti): Stamford, CT, 1935. U. Miami.

DANTON, RAY: NYC, Sept. 19, 1931. Carnegie Tech.

DANZA, TONY: Brooklyn, NY., Apr. 21, 1951. UDubuque.

DARBY, KIM: (Deborah Zerby): North Hollywood, CA, July 8, 1948.

DARCEL, DENISE (Denise Billecard): Paris, Sept. 8, 1925. U. Dijon.

DARREN, JAMES: Philadelphia, June 8, 1936. Stella Adler School.

DARRIEUX, DANIELLE: Bordeaux, France, May 1, 1917. Lycee LaTour.

DAVID, KEITH: NYC, May 8, 1954. Juilliard.

DAVIDSON, JOHN: Pittsburgh, Dec. 13, 1941. Denison U.

DAVIES, JOHN RHYS: Salisbury, Eng., May 5, 1944.

DAVIS, BRAD: Tallahassee, FL, Nov. 6, 1949. AADA.

DAVIS, CLIFTON: Chicago, Oakwood-Col., Oct. 4, 1945.

DAVIS, GEENA: Wareham, MA, Jan. 21, 1957.

DAVIS, MAC: Lubbock, TX, Jan. 21, 1942.

DAVIS, NANCY (Anne Frances Robbins): NYC July 6, 1921, Smith Col.

DAVIS, OSSIE: Cogdell, GA, Dec. 18, 1917. Howard U.

DAVIS, SAMMI: Kidderminster, Worcestershire, Eng., 1965.

DAVIS, SKEETER (Mary Frances Penick): Dry Ridge, KY. Dec. 30, 1931.

DAVISON, BRUCE: Philadelphia, PA, June 28, 1946.

DAY, DORIS (Doris Kappelhoff); Cincinnati, Apr. 3, 1924.

DAY, LARAINE (Johnson): Roosevelt, UT, Oct. 13, 1917.

DAY-LEWIS, DANIEL: London, 1957, Bristol Old Vic.

DAYAN, ASSEF: Israel, 1945. U. Jerusalem.

DEAKINS, LUCY: NYC 1971.

DEAN, JIMMY: Plainview, TX, Aug. 10, 1928.

DeCAMP, ROSEMARY: Prescott, AZ, Nov. 14, 1913.

DeCARLO, YVONNE (Peggy Yvonne Middleton): Vancouver, B.C., Can., Sept. 1, 1922. Vancouver School of Drama.

DEE, FRANCES: Los Angeles, Nov. 26, 1907. Chicago U.

DEE, JOEY (Joseph Di Nicola): Passaic, NJ, June 11, 1940. Patterson State College.

DEE, RUBY: Cleveland, OH, Oct. 27, 1924. Hunter Col.

DEE, SANDRA (Alexandra Zuck): Bayonne, NJ, Apr. 23, 1942.

DeFORE, DON: Cedar Rapids, IA, Aug. 25, 1917. U. Iowa.

DeHAVEN, GLORIA: Los Angeles, July 23, 1923.

DeHAVILLAND, OLIVIA: Tokyo, Japan, July 1, 1916. Notre Dame Convent School.

DELAIR, SUZY: Paris, Dec. 31, 1916.

DELANY, DANA: NYC, March 13, 1956. Wesleyan U.

DELPY, JULIE: Paris, 1970.

DELON, ALAIN: Sceaux, Fr., Nov. 8, 1935.

DELORME, DANIELE: Paris, Oct. 9, 1927. Sorbonne.

DeLUISE, DOM: Brooklyn, Aug. 1, 1933. Tufts Col.

DeLUISE, PETER: Hollywood, Ca., 1967.

DEMONGEOT, MYLENE: Nice, France, Sept. 29, 1938.

DeMORNAY, REBECCA: Los Angeles, 1962. Strasberg Inst.

DEMPSEY, PATRICK: Lewiston, ME, 1966.

DeMUNN, JEFFREY: Buffalo, NY, Apr. 25, 1947. Union Col.

DENEUVE, CATHERINE: Paris, Oct. 22, 1943.

DE NIRO, ROBERT: NYC, Aug. 17, 1943, Stella Adler.

DENISON, MICHAEL: Doncaster, York, Eng., Nov. 1, 1915. Oxford.

DENNEHY, BRIAN: Bridgeport, CT, Jul. 9, 1938. Columbia.

DENNER, CHARLES: Tarnow, Poland, May 29, 1926.

DENNIS, SANDY: Hastings, NB, Apr. 27, 1937. Actors Studio.

DENVER, BOB: New Rochelle, NY, Jan. 9, 1935.

DEPARDIEU, GERARD: Chateauroux, France, Dec. 27, 1948.

DEPP, JOHNNY: Owensboro, KY, June 9, 1963.

DEREK, BO (Mary Cathleen Collins): Long Beach, CA, Nov. 20, 1956.

DEREK, JOHN: Hollywood, Aug. 12, 1926.

DERN, BRUCE: Chicago, June 4, 1936. U PA.

DERN, LAURA: Los Angeles, 1966.

DeSALVO, ANNE: Philadelphia, Apr. 3.

DEVANE, WILLIAM: Albany, NY, Sept. 5, 1939.

DEVINE, COLLEEN: San Gabriel, CA, June 22, 1960.

DeVITO, DANNY: Asbury Park, NJ., Nov. 17, 1944.

DEWHURST, COLLEEN: Montreal, June 3, 1926. Lawrence U.

| Kirk Douglas | Shelley Duvall | Stephen Geoffreys | Betty Garrett | Peter Frechette | Estelle Getty |

DEXTER, ANTHONY (Walter Reinhold Alfred Fleischmann): Talmadge, NB, Jan. 19, 1919. U. Iowa.

DEY, SUSAN: Pekin, IL, Dec. 10, 1953.

DeYOUNG, CLIFF: Los Angeles, CA, Feb. 12, 1945. Cal State.

DHIEGH, KHIGH: New Jersey, 1910.

DIAMOND, NEIL: NYC, Jan. 24, 1941. NYU.

DICKINSON, ANGIE: Kulm, ND, Sept. 30, 1932. Glendale College.

DIETRICH, MARLENE (Maria Magdalene von Losch): Berlin, Ger., Dec. 27, 1901. Berlin Music Academy.

DILLER, PHYLLIS (Driver): Lima, OH, July 17, 1917. Bluffton College.

DILLMAN, BRADFORD: San Francisco, Apr. 14, 1930. Yale.

DILLON, KEVIN: Mamaroneck, NY, Aug. 19, 1965.

DILLON, MATT: Larchmont, NY., Feb. 18, 1964. AADA.

DILLON, MELINDA: Hope, AR, Oct. 13, 1939. Goodman Theatre School.

DIXON, DONNA: Alexandria, VA, July 20, 1957.

DOBSON, KEVIN: NYC, Mar. 18, 1944.

DOBSON, TAMARA: Baltimore, MD, 1947. MD. Inst. of Art.

DOLAN, MICHAEL: Oklahoma City, OK, June 21, 1965.

DOMERGUE, FAITH: New Orleans, June 16, 1925.

DONAHUE, TROY (Merle Johnson): NYC, Jan. 27, 1937. Columbia U.

DONAT, PETER: Nova Scotia, Jan. 20, 1928. Yale.

DONNELLY, DONAL: Bradford, Eng., July 6, 1931.

D'ONOFRIO, VINCENT: Brooklyn, 1960.

DOOHAN, JAMES: Vancouver, BC, Mar. 3, 1920. Neighborhood Playhouse.

DOOLEY, PAUL: Parkersburg, WV, Feb. 22, 1928. U. WV.

DOUGLAS, DONNA (Dorothy Bourgeois): Baywood, LA, Sept. 26, 1935.

DOUGLAS, KIRK (Issur Danielovitch): Amsterdam, NY, Dec. 9, 1916. St. Lawrence U.

DOUGLAS, MICHAEL: New Brunswick, NJ, Sept. 25, 1944. U. Cal.

DOUGLASS, ROBYN: Sendai, Japan; June 21, 1953. UCDavis.

DOURIF, BRAD: Huntington, WV, Mar. 18, 1950. Marshall U.

DOVE, BILLIE: NYC, May 14, 1904.

DOWN, LESLEY-ANN: London, Mar. 17, 1954.

DOWNEY, ROBERT, JR.: NYC, Apr. 4, 1965.

DRAKE, BETSY: Paris, Sept. 11, 1923.

DRAKE, CHARLES (Charles Rupert): NYC, Oct. 2, 1914. Nichols College.

DREW, ELLEN (formerly Terry Ray): Kansas City, MO, Nov. 23, 1915.

DREYFUSS, RICHARD: Brooklyn, NY, Oct. 19, 1947.

DRILLINGER, BRIAN: Brooklyn, NY, June 27, 1960. SUNY/Purchase.

DRU, JOANNE (Joanne LaCock): Logan, WV, Jan. 31, 1923. John Robert Powers School.

DRYER, JOHN: Hawthorne, CA, July 6, 1946.

DUBBINS, DON: Brooklyn, NY, June 28.

DUDIKOFF, MICHAEL: Redondo Beach, CA, Oct. 8.

DUFFY, PATRICK: Townsend, MT, Mar. 17, 1949. U. Wash.

DUGAN, DENNIS: Wheaton, IL, Sept. 5, 1946.

DUKAKIS, OLYMPIA: Lowell, MA, June 20, 1931.

DUKE, PATTY (Anna Marie): NYC, Dec. 14, 1946.

DUKES, DAVID: San Francisco, June 6, 1945.

DULLEA, KEIR: Cleveland, NJ, May 30, 1936. SF State Col.

DUNAWAY, FAYE: Bascom, FL, Jan. 14, 1941. Fla. U.

DUNCAN, SANDY: Henderson, TX, Feb. 20, 1946. Len Morris Col.

DUNNE, GRIFFIN: NYC June 8, 1955, Neighborhood Playhouse.

DUNNOCK, MILDRED: Baltimore, Jan. 25, 1900. Johns Hopkins and Columbia U.

DUPEREY, ANNY: Paris, 1947.

DURBIN, DEANNA (Edna): Winnipeg, Can., Dec. 4, 1921.

DURNING, CHARLES: Highland Falls, NY, Feb. 28, 1933. NYU.

DUSSOLLIER, ANDRE: Annecy, France, Feb. 17, 1946.

DUTTON, CHARLES: Baltimore, MD, Jan. 30, 1951. Yale.

DUVALL, ROBERT: San Diego, CA, Jan 5, 1930. Principia Col.

DUVALL, SHELLEY: Houston, TX, July 7, 1949.

DYSART, RICHARD: Brighton, ME, Mar. 30, 1929.

EASTON, ROBERT: Milwaukee, WI, Nov. 23, 1930. U. Texas.

EASTWOOD, CLINT: San Francisco, May 31, 1931. LACC.

EATON, SHIRLEY: London, 1937. Aida Foster School.

EBSEN, BUDDY (Christian, Jr.): Belleville, IL, Apr. 2, 1910. U. Fla.

ECKEMYR, AGNETA: Karlsborg, Swed., July 2. Actors Studio.

EDELMAN, GREGG: Chicago, IL, Sept. 12, 1958. Northwestern U.

EDEN, BARBARA (Moorhead): Tucson, AZ, Aug. 23, 1934.

EDWARDS, ANTHONY: Santa Barbara, CA. July 19, 1962. RADA

EDWARDS, VINCE: NYC, July 9, 1928. AADA.

EGGAR, SAMANTHA: London, Mar. 5, 1939.

EICHHORN, LISA: Reading, PA, Feb. 4, 1952. Queens Ont. U. RADA.

EIKENBERRY, JILL: New Haven, CT, Jan. 21, 1947.

EILBER, JANET: Detroit, MI, July 27, 1951. Juilliard.

EKBERG, ANITA: Malmo, Sweden, Sept. 29, 1931.

EKLAND, BRITT: Stockholm, Swed. Oct. 6, 1942.

ELDARD, RON: NYC 1964.

ELIZONDO, HECTOR: NYC, Dec. 22, 1936.

ELLIOTT, CHRIS: NYC 1960.

ELLIOTT, DENHOLM: London, May 31, 1922. Malvern College.

ELLIOTT, PATRICIA: Gunnison, CO, July 21, 1942, UCol.

ELLIOTT, SAM: Sacramento, CA, Aug. 9, 1944. U. Ore.

ELWES, CARY: London, Oct. 26, 1962.

ELY, RON (Ronald Pierce): Hereford, TX, June 21, 1938.

ENGLISH, ALEX: USCar, 1954.

ENGLUND, ROBERT: Hollywood, CA, June 6, 1949.

ERDMAN, RICHARD: Enid, OK, June 1, 1925.

ERICSON, JOHN: Dusseldorf, Ger., Sept. 25, 1926. AADA.

ESMOND, CARL: Vienna, June 14, 1906. U. Vienna.

ESTEVEZ, EMILIO: NYC, May 12, 1962.

ESPOSITO, GIANCARLO: Copenhagen, Den., Apr. 26, 1958.

ESTRADA, ERIK: NYC, Mar. 16, 1949.

EVANS, DALE (Francis Smith): Uvalde, TX, Oct. 31, 1912.

EVANS, GENE: Holbrook, AZ, July 11, 1922.

EVANS, LINDA (Evanstad): Hartford, CT., Nov. 18, 1942.

EVERETT, CHAD (Ray Cramton): South Bend, IN, June 11, 1936.

EVERETT, RUPERT: Norfolk, Eng., 1959.

EVIGAN, GREG: South Amboy, NJ, 1954.

EWELL, TOM (Yewell Tompkins): Owensboro, KY, Apr. 29, 1909. U. Wisc.

FABARES, SHELLEY: Los Angeles, Jan. 19, 1944.

FABIAN (Fabian Forte): Philadelphia, Feb. 6, 1943.

FABRAY, NANETTE (Ruby Nanette Fabares): San Diego, Oct. 27, 1920.

FAIRBANKS, DOUGLAS JR.: NYC, Dec. 9, 1907. Collegiate School.

FAIRCHILD, MORGAN: (Patsy McClenny) Dallas, TX., Feb. 3, 1950. UCLA.
FALK, PETER: NYC, Sept. 16, 1927. New School.
FARENTINO, JAMES: Brooklyn, Feb. 24, 1938. AADA.
FARINA, DENNIS: Chicago, IL, 1944.
FARINA, SANDY (Sandra Feldman): Newark, NJ, 1955.
FARR, FELICIA: Westchester, NY, Oct. 4, 1932. Penn State Col.
FARROW, MIA (Maria): Los Angeles, Feb. 9, 1945.
FAULKNER, GRAHAM: London, Sept. 26, 1947. Webber-Douglas.
FAWCETT, FARRAH: Corpus Christie, TX. Feb. 2, 1947. TexU.
FAYE, ALICE (Ann Leppert): NYC, May 5, 1912.
FEINSTEIN, ALAN: NYC, Sept. 8, 1941.
FELDMAN, COREY: Encino, CA, July 16, 1971.
FELDON, BARBARA (Hall): Pittsburgh, Mar. 12, 1941. Carnegie Tech.
FELDSHUH, TOVAH: NYC, Dec. 27, 1953, Sarah Lawrence Col.
FELLOWS, EDITH: Boston, May 20, 1923.
FERRELL, CONCHATA: Charleston, WV, Mar. 28, 1943. Marshall U.
FERRER, JOSE: Santurce, P.R., Jan. 8, 1912. Princeton U.
FERRER, MEL: Elberon, NJ, Aug. 25, 1912. Princeton U.
FERRER, MIGUEL: Santa Monica, CA, Feb. 7, 1954.
FERRIS, BARBARA: London, 1943.
FERZETTI, GABRIELE: Italy, 1927. Rome Acad. of Drama.
FIEDLER, JOHN: Plateville, Wi, Feb. 3, 1925.
FIELD, SALLY: Pasadena, CA, Nov. 6, 1946.
FIERSTEIN, HARVEY: Brooklyn, NY, June 6, 1954. Pratt Inst.
FIGUEROA, RUBEN: NYC 1958.
FINNEY, ALBERT: Salford, Lancashire, Eng., May 9, 1936. RADA.
FIORENTINO, LINDA: Philadelphia, PA.
FIRESTONE, ROCHELLE: Kansas City, MO., June 14, 1949. NYU.
FIRTH, COLIN: Grayshott, Hampshire, Eng., Sept. 10, 1960.
FIRTH, PETER: Bradford, Eng., Oct. 27, 1953.
FISHER, CARRIE: Los Angeles, CA, Oct. 21, 1956. London Central School of Drama.
FISHER, EDDIE: Philadelphia, PA, Aug. 10, 1928.
FITZGERALD, BRIAN: Philadelphia, PA, 1960, West Chester U.
FITZGERALD, GERALDINE: Dublin, Ire., Nov. 24, 1914. Dublin Art School.
FLANNERY, SUSAN: Jersey City, NJ, July 31, 1943.
FLEMING, RHONDA (Marilyn Louis): Los Angeles, Aug. 10, 1922.
FLEMYNG, ROBERT: Liverpool, Eng., Jan. 3, 1912. Haileybury Col.
FLETCHER, LOUISE: Birmingham, AL, July 1934.
FOCH, NINA: Leyden, Holland, Apr. 20, 1924.
FOLDI, ERZSEBET: Queens, NY, 1967.
FOLLOWS, MEGAN: Toronto, CA., 1967.
FONDA, JANE: NYC, Dec. 21, 1937. Vassar.
FONDA, PETER: NYC, Feb. 23, 1939. U. Omaha.
FONTAINE, JOAN: Tokyo, Japan, Oct. 22, 1917.
FOOTE, HALLIE: NYC 1953. UNH.

FORD, GLENN (Gwyllyn Samuel Newton Ford): Quebec, Can., May 1, 1916.
FORD, HARRISON: Chicago, IL, July 13, 1942. Ripon Col.
FOREST, MARK (Lou Degni): Brooklyn, Jan. 1933.
FORREST, FREDERIC: Waxahachie, TX, Dec. 23, 1936.
FORREST, STEVE: Huntsville, TX, Sept. 29, 1924. UCLA.
FORSLUND, CONNIE: San Diego, CA, June 19, 1950, NYU.
FORSTER, ROBERT (Foster, Jr.): Rochester, NY, July 13, 1941. Rochester U.
FORSYTHE, JOHN (Freund): Penn's Grove, NJ, Jan. 29, 1918.
FOSTER, MEG: May 10, 1948.
FOSTER, JODIE (Ariane Munker): Bronx, NY, Nov. 19, 1962. Yale.
FOX, EDWARD: London, Apr. 13, 1937, RADA.
FOX, JAMES: London, May 19, 1939.
FOX, MICHAEL J.: Vancouver, BC, June 9, 1961.
FOXWORTH, ROBERT: Houston, TX, Nov. 1, 1941. Carnegie Tech.
FOXX, REDD (John Elroy Sanford): St. Louis, MO, Dec. 9, 1922.
FRAKES, JOHNATHAN: Bethlehem, PA., 1952. Harvard.
FRANCIOSA, ANTHONY (Papaleo): NYC, Oct. 25, 1928.
FRANCIS, ANNE: Ossining, NY, Sept. 16, 1932.
FRANCIS, ARLENE (Arlene Kazanjian): Boston, Oct. 20, 1908. Finch School.
FRANCIS, CONNIE (Constance Franconero): Newark, NJ, Dec. 12, 1938.
FRANCISCUS, JAMES: Clayton, MO, Jan. 31, 1934. Yale.
FRANCKS, DON: Vancouver, Can., Feb. 28, 1932.
FRANK, JEFFREY: Jackson Heights, NY, 1965.
FRANKLIN, PAMELA: Tokyo, Feb. 4, 1950.
FRANZ, ARTHUR: Perth Amboy, NJ, Feb. 29, 1920. Blue Ridge College.
FRANZ, DENNIS: Chicago, IL, Oct. 28, 1944.
FRAZIER, SHEILA: NYC, Nov. 13, 1948.
FRECHETTE, PETER: Warwick, RI, Oct. 3, 1956. URI.
FREEMAN, AL, JR.: San Antonio, TX, Mar. 21, 1934. CCLA.
FREEMAN, MONA: Baltimore, MD, June 9, 1926.
FREEMAN, MORGAN: Memphis, TN, June 1, 1937, LACC.
FREWER, MATT: Washington, DC, Jan. 4, 1958, Old Vic.
FULLER, PENNY: Durham, NC, 1940. Northwestern U.
FURNEAUX, YVONNE: Lille, France, 1928. Oxford U.
FYODOROVA, VICTORIA: Russia 1946.
GABLE, JOHN CLARK: Mar. 20, 1961, Los Angeles. Santa Monica Col.
GABOR, EVA: Budapest, Hungary, Feb. 11, 1920.
GABOR, ZSA ZSA (Sari Gabor): Budapest, Hungary, Feb. 6, 1918.
GAIL, MAX: Detroit, MI, Apr. 5, 1943.
GAINES, BOYD: Atlanta, GA., May 11, 1953. Juilliard.
GALLAGHER, PETER: Armonk, NY, Aug. 19, 1955, Tufts U.
GALLIGAN, ZACH: NYC, Feb. 14, 1963. ColumbiaU.
GAM, RITA: Pittsburgh, PA, Apr. 2, 1928.
GAMBON, MICHAEL: Dublin, Ire., Oct. 19, 1940.
GARBER, VICTOR: Montreal, Can., Mar. 16, 1949.

GARCIA, ANDY: Havana, Cuba. 1956. FlaInt1U.
GARDENIA, VINCENT: Naples, Italy, Jan. 7, 1922.
GARFIELD, ALLEN (Allen Goorwitz): Newark, NJ, Nov. 22, 1939. Actors Studio.
GARFUNKEL, ART: NYC, Nov. 5, 1941.
GARLAND, BEVERLY: Santa Cruz, CA, Oct. 17, 1930. Glendale Col.
GARNER, JAMES (James Baumgarner): Norman, OK, Apr. 7, 1928. Okla U.
GARR, TERI: Lakewood, OH, Dec. 11, 1949.
GARRETT, BETTY: St. Joseph, MO, May 23, 1919. Annie Wright Seminary.
GARRISON, SEAN: NYC, Oct. 19, 1937.
GARSON, GREER: Ireland, Sept. 29, 1908.
GARY, LORRAINE: NYC, Aug. 16, 1937.
GASSMAN, VITTORIO: Genoa, Italy, Sept. 1, 1922. Rome Academy of Dramatic Art.
GAVIN, JOHN: Los Angeles, Apr. 8, 1935. Stanford U.
GAYLORD, MITCH: Van Nuys, CA, 1961, UCLA.
GAYNOR, MITZI (Francesca Marlene Von Gerber): Chicago, Sept. 4, 1930.
GAZZARA, BEN: NYC, Aug. 28, 1930. Actors Studio.
GEARY, ANTHONY: Coalsville, UT, May 29, 1947. UUt.
GEDRICK, JASON: Chicago, 1965, Drake U.
GEESON, JUDY: Arundel, Eng., Sept. 10, 1948. Corona.
GEOFFREYS, STEPHEN: Cincinnati, OH, Nov. 22, 1964. NYU.
GEORGE, SUSAN: West London, Eng. July 26, 1950.
GERARD, GIL: Little Rock, AR, Jan. 23, 1940.
GERE, RICHARD: Philadelphia, PA, Aug. 29, 1947. U. Mass.
GERROLL, DANIEL: London, Oct. 16, 1951. Central.
GERTZ, JAMI: Chicago, IL, Oct. 28, 1965.
GETTY, BALTHAZAR: Jan. 22, 1975.
GETTY, ESTELLE: NYC, July 25, 1923, New School.
GHOLSON, JULIE: Birmingham, AL, June 4, 1958.
GHOSTLEY, ALICE: Eve, MO, Aug. 14, 1926. Okla U.
GIAN, JOE: North Miami Beach, FL, 1962.
GIANNINI, CHERYL: Monessen, PA., June 15.
GIANNINI, GIANCARLO: Spezia, Italy, Aug. 1, 1942. Rome Acad. of Drama.
GIBB, CYNTHIA: Bennington, VT, Dec. 14, 1963.
GIBSON, HENRY: Germantown, PA, Sept. 21, 1935.
GIBSON, MEL: Peekskill, NY., Jan. 3, 1956. NIDA.
GIELGUD, JOHN: London, Apr. 14, 1904. RADA.
GILBERT, MELISSA: Los Angeles, CA, May 8, 1964.
GILES, NANCY: NYC, July 17, 1960, Oberlin Col.
GILLETTE, ANITA: Baltimore, MD, Aug. 16, 1938.
GILLIAM, TERRY: Minneapolis, MN, Nov. 22, 1940.
GILLIS, ANNE (Alma O'Connor): Little Rock, AR, Feb. 12, 1927.
GINTY, ROBERT: NYC, Nov. 14, 1948, Yale.
GIRARDOT, ANNIE: Paris, Oct. 25, 1931.
GIROLAMI, STEFANIA: Rome, 1963.

GISH, LILLIAN: Springfield, OH, Oct. 14, 1896.

GLASER, PAUL MICHAEL: Boston, MA, Mar. 25, 1943. Boston U.

GLASS, RON: Evansville, IN, July 10, 1945.

GLEASON, JOANNA: Winnipeg, Can, June 2, 1950, UCLA.

GLEASON, PAUL: Jersey City, NJ, May 4, 1944.

GLENN, SCOTT: Pittsburgh, PA, Jan. 26, 1942; William and Mary Col.

GLOVER, CRISPIN: NYC, 1964.

GLOVER, DANNY: San Francisco, CA, July 22, 1947, SFStateCol.

GLOVER, JOHN: Kingston, NY, Aug. 7, 1944.

GLYNN,CARLIN: Cleveland, Oh, Feb. 19, 1940, Actors Studio.

GODUNOV, ALEXANDER (Aleksandr): Sakhalin, USSR, Nov. 28, 1949.

GOLDBERG, WHOOPI (Caryn Johnson): NYC, Nov. 13, 1949.

GOLDBLUM, JEFF: Pittsburgh, PA, Oct. 22, 1952. Neighborhood Playhouse.

GOLDEN, ANNIE: Brooklyn, NY, Oct. 19, 1951.

GOLDSTEIN, JENETTE: Beverley Hills, CA, 1960.

GOLDTHWAIT, BOB: Syracuse, NY, 1962.

GONZALEZ, CORDELIA: Aug. 11, 1958, San Juan, PR. UPR.

GONZALES-GONZALEZ, PEDRO: Aguilares, TX, Dec. 21, 1926.

GOODMAN, DODY: Columbus, OH, Oct. 28, 1915.

GOODMAN, JOHN: St. Louis, MO, June 20, 1952.

GORDON, GALE (Aldrich): NYC, Feb. 2, 1906.

GORDON, KEITH: NYC, Feb. 3, 1961.

GORING, MARIUS: Newport Isle of Wight, 1912. Cambridge, Old Vic.

GORMAN, CLIFF: Jamaica, NY, Oct. 13, 1936. NYU.

GORSHIN, FRANK: Pittsburgh, PA, Apr. 5, 1933.

GORTNER, MARJOE: Long Beach, CA, Jan. 14, 1944.

GOSSETT, LOUIS: Brooklyn, May 27, 1936. NYU.

GOULD, ELLIOTT (Goldstein): Brooklyn, Aug. 29, 1938. Columbia U.

GOULD, HAROLD: Schenectady, NY, Dec. 10, 1923. Cornell.

GOULET, ROBERT: Lawrence, MA, Nov. 26, 1933. Edmonton.

GRAF, DAVID: Lancaster, OH, Apr. 16, 1950. OhStateU.

GRAF, TODD: NYC, Oct. 22, 1959, SUNY/Purchase.

GRANGER, FARLEY: San Jose, CA, July 1, 1925.

GRANGER, STEWART (James Stewart): London, May 6, 1913. Webber-Douglas School of Acting.

GRANT, DAVID MARSHALL: Westport, CT, June 21, 1955. Yale.

GRANT, KATHRYN (Olive Grandstaff): Houston, TX, Nov. 25, 1933. UCLA.

GRANT, LEE: NYC, Oct. 31, 1930. Juilliard.

GRANT, RICHARD E: Mbabane, Swaziland, May 5, 1957. Cape Town U.

GRAVES, PETER (Aurness): Minneapolis, Mar. 18, 1926. U. Minn.

GRAVES, RUPERT: Weston-Super-Mare, Eng., June 30, 1963.

GRAY, CHARLES: Bournemouth, Eng., 1928.

GRAY, COLEEN (Doris Jensen): Staplehurst, NB, Oct. 23, 1922. Hamline U.

GRAY, LINDA: Santa Monica, CA; Sept. 12, 1940.

GRAY, SPALDING: Barrington, RI, 1941.

GRAYSON, KATHRYN (Zelma Hedrick): Winston-Salem, NC, Feb. 9, 1922.

GREEN, KERRI: Fort Lee, NJ, 1967. Vassar.

GREENE, ELLEN: NYC, Feb. 22, 1950. Ryder Col.

GREER, JANE: Washington, DC, Sept. 9, 1924.

GREER, MICHAEL: Galesburg, IL, Apr. 20, 1943.

GREGORY, MARK: Rome, Italy. 1965.

GREIST, KIM: Stamford, CT, May 12, 1958.

GREY, JENNIFER: NYC, Mar. 26, 1960.

GREY, JOEL (Katz): Cleveland, OH, Apr. 11, 1932.

GREY, VIRGINIA: Los Angeles, Mar. 22, 1917.

GRIEM, HELMUT: Hamburg, Ger. U. Hamburg.

GRIFFITH, ANDY: Mt. Airy, NC, June 1, 1926. UNC.

GRIFFITH, MELANIE: NYC, Aug. 9, 1957 Pierce Col.

GRIMES, GARY: San Francisco, June 2, 1955.

GRIMES, SCOTT: Lowell, MA, July 9, 1971.

GRIMES, TAMMY: Lynn, MA, Jan. 30, 1934. Stephens Col.

GRIZZARD, GEORGE: Roanoke Rapids, NC, Apr. 1, 1928. UNC.

GRODIN, CHARLES: Pittsburgh, PA, Apr. 21, 1935.

GROH, DAVID: NYC, May 21, 1939. Brown U., LAMDA.

GROSS, MARY: Chicago, IL, Mar. 25, 1953.

GROSS, MICHAEL: Chicago, June 21, 1947.

GUARDINO, HARRY: Brooklyn, Dec. 23, 1925. Haaren High.

GUEST, CHRISTOPHER: NYC, Feb. 5, 1948.

GUEST, LANCE: Saratoga, CA, July 21, 1960. UCLA.

GUILLAUME, ROBERT (Williams): St. Louis, MO, Nov. 30, 1937.

GUINNESS, ALEC: London, Apr. 2, 1914. Pembroke Lodge School.

GUNN, MOSES: St. Louis, MO, Oct. 2, 1929. Tenn. State U.

GUTTENBERG, STEVE: Massapequa, NY, Aug. 24, 1958. UCLA.

GWILLIM, DAVID: Plymouth, Eng., Dec. 15, 1948. RADA.

GWYNNE, FRED: NYC, July 10, 1926.

HAAS, LUKAS: West Hollywood, CA, Apr. 16, 1976.

HACKETT, BUDDY (Leonard Hacker): Brooklyn, Aug. 31, 1924.

HACKMAN, GENE: San Bernardino, CA, Jan. 30, 1931.

HADDON, DALE: Montreal, Can., May 26, 1949. Neighborhood Playhouse.

HAGERTY, JULIE: Cincinnati, OH, June 15, 1955. Juilliard.

HAGMAN, LARRY: (Hageman): Weatherford, TX., Sept. 21, 1931. Bard.

HAIM, COREY: Toronto, Can, Dec. 23, 1972.

HALE, BARBARA: DeKalb, IL, Apr. 18, 1922. Chicago Academy of Fine Arts.

HALEY, JACKIE EARLE: Northridge, CA, July 14, 1961.

HALL, ALBERT: Boothton, AL, Nov. 10, 1937. Columbia.

HALL, ANTHONY MICHAEL: Boston, MA, Apr. 14, 1968.

HALL, ARSENIO: Cleveland, OH, Feb. 12, 1959.

HALL, KEVIN PETER: Pittsburgh, PA, 1955. GeoWashU.

HAMEL, VERONICA: Philadelphia, PA, Nov. 20, 1943.

HAMILL, MARK: Oakland, CA, Sept. 25, 1952. LACC.

HAMILTON, CARRIE: NYC, Dec. 5, 1963.

HAMILTON, GEORGE: Memphis, TN, Aug. 12, 1939. Hackley.

HAMILTON, LINDA: Salisbury, MD, Sept. 26.

HAMLIN, HARRY: Pasadena, CA, Oct. 30, 1951. Yale.

HAMPSHIRE, SUSAN: London, May 12, 1941.

HAN, MAGGIE: Providence, RI, 1959.

HANKS, TOM: Concord, CA., Jul. 9, 1956. CalStateU.

HANNAH, DARYL: Chicago, IL., 1960, UCLA.

HANNAH, PAGE: Chicago, IL., Apr. 13, 1964.

HARDIN, TY (Orison Whipple Hungerford II): NYC, June 1, 1930.

HAREWOOD, DORIAN: Dayton, OH, Aug. 6, 1950. U. Cinn.

HARMON, MARK: Los Angeles, CA, Sept. 2, 1951; UCLA.

HARPER, JESSICA: Chicago, IL, Oct. 10, 1949.

HARPER, TESS: Mammoth Spring, AK, 1952. SWMoState.

HARPER, VALERIE: Suffern, NY, Aug. 22, 1940.

HARRELSON, WOODY: Lebanon, OH, 1962.

HARRINGTON, PAT: NYC, Aug. 13, 1929. Fordham U.

HARRIS, BARBARA (Sandra Markowitz): Evanston, IL, July 25, 1935.

HARRIS, ED: Tenafly, NJ, Nov. 28, 1950. Columbia.

HARRIS, JULIE: Grosse Point, MI, Dec. 2, 1925. Yale Drama School.

HARRIS, MEL (Mary Ellen): Bethlehem, PA, 1957. Columbia.

HARRIS, RICHARD: Limerick, Ire., Oct. 1, 1930. London Acad.

HARRIS, ROSEMARY: Ashby, Eng., Sept. 19, 1930. RADA.

HARRISON, GEORGE: Liverpool, Eng., Feb. 25, 1943.

HARRISON, GREGORY: Catalina Island, CA, May 31, 1950; Actors Studio.

HARRISON, NOEL: London, Jan. 29, 1936.

HARROLD, KATHRYN: Tazewell, VA, Aug. 2, 1950. Mills Col.

HARRY, DEBORAH: Miami, FL, July 1, 1945.

HART, ROXANNE: Trenton, NJ, 1952, Princeton.

HARTLEY, MARIETTE: NYC, June 21, 1941.

HARTMAN, DAVID: Pawtucket, RI, May 19, 1935. Duke U.

HASSETT, MARILYN: Los Angeles, CA, Dec. 17, 1947.

HAUER, RUTGER: Amsterdam, Hol. Jan. 23, 1944.

HAVER, JUNE: Rock Island, IL, June 10, 1926.

HAVOC, JUNE (Hovick): Nov. 8, 1916, Seattle, WA.

HAWKE, ETHAN: Austin, TX, Nov. 6, 1970.

HAWN, GOLDIE: Washington, DC, Nov. 21, 1945.

HAYES, HELEN: (Helen Brown): Washington, DC, Oct. 10, 1900. Sacred Heart Convent.

HAYS, ROBERT: Bethesda, MD, July 24, 1947, SD State Col.

HEADLY, GLENNE: New London, CT, Mar. 13, 1955. AmCol.

HEALD, ANTHONY: New Rochelle, NY, Aug. 25, 1944, MiStateU.

HEARD, JOHN: Washington, DC, Mar. 7, 1946. Clark U.

HEATHERTON, JOEY: NYC, Sept. 14, 1944.

HECKART, EILEEN: Columbus, OH, Mar. 29, 1919. Ohio State U.

HEDISON, DAVID: Providence, RI, May 20, 1929. Brown U.

HEGYES, ROBERT: NJ, May 7, 1951.

HELMOND, KATHERINE: Galveston, TX, July 5, 1934.

HEMINGWAY, MARIEL: Ketchum, ID, Nov. 22, 1961.

HEMMINGS, DAVID: Guilford, Eng. Nov. 18, 1938.

HENDERSON, FLORENCE: Dale, IN, Feb. 14, 1934.

HENDERSON, MARCIA: Andover, MA, July 22, 1932. AADA.

HENDRY, GLORIA: Jacksonville, FL. 1949.

HENNER, MARILU: Chicago, IL. Apr. 6, 1952.

HENREID, PAUL: Trieste, Jan. 10, 1908.

HENRY, BUCK (Henry Zuckerman): NYC, 1931. Dartmouth.

HENRY, JUSTIN: Rye, NY, May 25, 1971.

HEPBURN, AUDREY: Brussels, Belgium, May 4, 1929.

HEPBURN, KATHARINE: Hartford, CT, Nov. 8, 1907. Bryn Mawr.

HERMAN, PEE-WEE (Paul Reubenfeld): Peekskill, NY, July, 1952.

HERRMANN, EDWARD: Washington, DC, July 21, 1943. Bucknell, LAMDA.

HERSHEY, BARBARA (Herzstein): Hollywood, CA, Feb. 5, 1948.

HESSEMAN, HOWARD: Lebanon, OR, Feb. 27, 1940.

HESTON, CHARLTON: Evanston, IL, Oct. 4, 1922. Northwestern U.

HEWITT, MARTIN: Claremont, CA, 1960; AADA.

HEYWOOD, ANNE (Violet Pretty): Birmingham, Eng., Dec. 11, 1932.

HICKEY, WILLIAM: Brooklyn, NY, 1928.

HICKMAN, DARRYL: Hollywood, CA, July 28, 1933. Loyola U.

HICKMAN, DWAYNE: Los Angeles, May 18, 1934. Loyola U.

HICKS, CATHERINE: NYC, Aug. 6, 1951. Notre Dame.

HIGGINS, MICHAEL: Brooklyn, NY, Jan. 20, 1926, AmThWing.

HILL, ARTHUR: Saskatchewan, Can., Aug. 1, 1922. U. Brit. Col.

HILL, BENNY: Southampton, Eng., Jan. 21, 1925.

HILL, STEVEN: Seattle, WA, Feb. 24, 1922. U. Wash.

HILL, TERENCE (Mario Girotti): Venice, Italy, Mar. 29, 1941. U. Rome.

HILLER, WENDY: Bramhall, Cheshire, Eng., Aug. 15, 1912. Winceby House School.

HILLERMAN, JOHN: Denison, TX, Dec. 20, 1932.

HINGLE, PAT: Denver, CO, July 19, 1923. Tex. U.

HIRSCH, JUDD: NYC, Mar. 15, 1935. AADA.

HOBEL, MARA: NYC, June 18, 1971.

HODGE, PATRICIA: Lincolnshire, Eng., 1946. LAMDA.

HOFFMAN, DUSTIN: Los Angeles, Aug. 8, 1937. Pasadena Playhouse.

HOGAN, JONATHAN: Chicago, IL, June 13, 1951.

HOGAN, PAUL: Lightning Ridge, Australia, Oct. 8, 1939.

HOLBROOK, HAL (Harold): Cleveland, OH, Feb. 17, 1925. Denison.

HOLLIMAN, EARL: Tennessee Swamp, Delhi, LA, Sept. 11, 1928. UCLA.

HOLM, CELESTE: NYC, Apr. 29, 1919.

HOLM, IAN: Ilford, Essex, Eng., Sept. 12, 1931. RADA.

HOMEIER, SKIP (George Vincent Homeier): Chicago, Oct. 5, 1930. UCLA.

HOOKS, ROBERT: Washington, DC, Apr. 18, 1937. Temple.

HOPE, BOB (Leslie Townes Hope): London, May 26, 1903.

HOPKINS, ANTHONY: Port Talbot, So. Wales, Dec. 31, 1937, RADA.

HOPPER, DENNIS: Dodge City, KS, May 17, 1936.

HORNE, LENA: Brooklyn, June 30, 1917.

HORSLEY, LEE: Muleshoe, TX, May 15, 1955.

HORTON, ROBERT: Los Angeles, July 29, 1924. UCLA.

HOSKINS, BOB: Bury St. Edmunds, Eng., Oct. 26, 1942.

HOUGHTON, KATHARINE: Hartford, CT, Mar. 10, 1945. Sarah Lawrence.

HOUSER, JERRY: Los Angeles, July 14, 1952. Valley Jr. Col.

HOUSTON, DONALD: Tonypandy, Wales, 1924.

HOWARD, ARLISS: Independence, MO, 1955. Columbia Col.

HOWARD, KEN: El Centro, CA, Mar. 28, 1944. Yale.

HOWARD, RON: Duncan, OK, Mar. 1, 1954. USC.

HOWARD, RONALD: Norwood, Eng., Apr. 7, 1918. Jesus College.

HOWELL, C. THOMAS: Los Angeles, Dec. 7, 1966.

HOWELLS, URSULA: London, Sept. 17, 1922.

HOWES, SALLY ANN: London, July 20, 1930.

HOWLAND, BETH: Boston, MA., May 28, 1941.

HUBLEY, SEASON: NYC, May 14, 1951.

HUDDLESSON, DAVID: Vinton, VA, Sept. 17, 1930.

HUDDLESTON, MICHAEL: Roanoke, VA., AADA.

HUGHES, BARNARD: Bedford Hills, NY, July 16, 1915. Manhattan Col.

HUGHES, KATHLEEN (Betty von Gerkan): Hollywood, CA, Nov. 14, 1928. UCLA.

HULCE, TOM: Plymouth, MI, Dec. 6, 1953. N.C.Sch. of Arts.

HUNNICUT, GAYLE: Ft. Worth, TX, Feb. 6, 1943. UCLA.

HUNT, HELEN: Los Angeles, June 15, 1963.

HUNT, LINDA: Morristown, NJ, Apr. 2, 1945. Goodman Theatre.

HUNT, MARSHA: Chicago, Oct. 17, 1917.

HUNTER, HOLLY: Atlanta, GA, Mar. 20, 1958, Carnegie-Mellon.

HUNTER, KIM (Janet Cole): Detroit, Nov. 12, 1922.

HUNTER, TAB (Arthur Gelien) NYC, July 11, 1931.

HUPPERT, ISABELLE: Paris, Fr., Mar. 16, 1955.

HURT, JOHN: Lincolnshire, Eng., Jan. 22, 1940.

HURT, MARY BETH (Supinger): Marshalltown, IA, Sept. 26, 1948. NYU.

HURT, WILLIAM: Washington, D.C., Mar. 20, 1950. Tufts, Juilliard.

HUSSEY, RUTH: Providence, RI, Oct. 30, 1917. U. Mich.

HUTTON, BETTY (Betty Thornberg): Battle Creek, MI, Feb. 26, 1921.

HUTTON, LAUREN (Mary): Charleston,

SC, Nov. 17, 1943. Newcomb Col.

HUTTON, ROBERT (Winne): Kingston, NY, June 11, 1920. Blair Academy.

HUTTON, TIMOTHY: Malibu, CA, Aug. 16, 1960.

HYDE-WHITE, WILFRID: Gloucestershire, Eng., May 13, 1903. RADA.

HYER, MARTHA: Fort Worth, TX, Aug. 10, 1924. Northwestern U.

IDLE, ERIC: South Shields, Durham, Eng., Mar. 29, 1943. Cambridge.

INGELS, MARTY: Brooklyn, NY, Mar. 9, 1936.

IRELAND, JOHN: Vancouver, B.C., Can., Jan. 30, 1914.

IRONS, JEREMY: Cowes, Eng. Sept. 19, 1948. Old Vic.

IRVING, AMY: Palo Alto, CA, Sept. 10, 1953. LADA.

IRWIN, BILL: Santa Monica, CA, Apr. 11, 1950.

IVANEK, ZELJKO: Lujubljana, Yugo., Aug. 15, 1957. Yale, LAMDA.

IVES, BURL: Hunt Township, IL, June 14, 1909. Charleston IL. Teachers College.

IVEY, JUDITH: El Paso, TX, Sept. 4, 1951.

JACKSON, ANNE: Alleghany, PA, Sept. 3, 1926. Neighborhood Playhouse.

JACKSON, GLENDA: Hoylake, Cheshire, Eng., May 9, 1936. RADA.

JACKSON, KATE: Birmingham, AL. Oct. 29, 1948. AADA.

JACKSON, MICHAEL: Gary, IN, Aug. 29, 1958.

JACKSON, VICTORIA: Miami, FL, Aug. 2, 1958.

JACOBI, DEREK: Leytonstone, London, Eng. Oct. 22, 1938. Cambridge.

JACOBI, LOU: Toronto, Can., Dec. 28, 1913.

JACOBS, LAWRENCE-HILTON: Virgin Islands, 1954.

JACOBY, SCOTT: Chicago, Nov. 19, 1956.

JAECKEL, RICHARD: Long Beach, NY, Oct. 10, 1926.

JAGGER, DEAN: Lima, OH, Nov. 7, 1903. Wabash College.

JAGGER, MICK: Dartford, Kent, Eng. July 26, 1943.

JAMES, CLIFTON: NYC, May 29, 1921. Ore. U.

JAMES, JOHN (Anderson): Apr. 18, 1956, New Canaan, CT, AADA.

JARMAN, CLAUDE, JR.: Nashville, TN, Sept. 27, 1934.

JASON, RICK: NYC, May 21, 1926. AADA.

JEAN, GLORIA (Gloria Jean Schoonover): Buffalo, NY, Apr. 14, 1927.

JEFFREYS, ANNE (Carmichael): Goldsboro, NC, Jan. 26, 1923. Anderson College.

JEFFRIES, LIONEL: London, 1927, RADA.

JERGENS, ADELE: Brooklyn, Nov. 26, 1922.

JETER, MICHAEL: Lawrenceburg, TN, Aug. 26, 1952. Memphis St.U.

JETT, ROGER (Baker): Cumberland, MD, Oct. 2, 1946. AADA.

JILLIAN, ANN (Nauseda): Cambridge, MA, Jan. 29, 1951.

JOHANSEN, DAVID: Staten Island, NY, Jan. 9, 1950.

JOHN, ELTON: (Reginald Dwight) Middlesex, Eng., Mar. 25, 1947. RAM.

JOHNS, GLYNIS: Durban, S. Africa, Oct. 5, 1923.

JOHNSON, BEN: Pawhuska, OK, June 13, 1918.

JOHNSON, DON: Galena, MO, Dec. 15, 1950. UKan.

JOHNSON, PAGE: Welch, WV, Aug. 25, 1930. Ithaca.

JOHNSON, RAFER: Hillsboro, TX, Aug. 18, 1935. UCLA.

JOHNSON, RICHARD: Essex, Eng., July 30, 1927. RADA.

JOHNSON, ROBIN: Brooklyn, NY: May 29, 1964.

JOHNSON, VAN: Newport, RI, Aug. 28, 1916.

JONES, CHRISTOPHER: Jackson, TN, Aug. 18, 1941. Actors Studio.

JONES, DEAN: Morgan County, AL, Jan. 25, 1936. Actors Studio.

JONES, GRACE: Spanishtown, Jamaica, May 19, 1952.

JONES, JACK: Bel-Air, CA, Jan. 14, 1938.

JONES, JAMES EARL: Arkabutla, MS, Jan. 17, 1931. U. Mich.

JONES, JEFFREY: Buffalo, NY, Sept. 28, 1947, LAMDA.

JONES, JENNIFER (Phyllis Isley): Tulsa, OK, Mar. 2, 1919. AADA.

JONES, SAM J.: Chicago, IL, Aug. 12, 1954.

JONES, SHIRLEY: Smithton, PA, March 31, 1934.

JONES, TERRY: Wales, Feb. 1, 1942.

JONES, TOMMY LEE: San Saba, TX, Sept. 15, 1946. Harvard.

JORDAN, RICHARD: NYC, July 19, 1938. Harvard.

JOURDAN, LOUIS: Marseilles, France, June 18, 1920.

JOY, ROBERT: Montreal, Can, Aug. 17, 1951, Oxford.

JULIA, RAUL: San Juan, PR, Mar. 9, 1940. U PR.

JURADO, KATY (Maria Christina Jurado Garcia): Guadalajara, Mex., Jan. 16, 1927.

KACZMAREK, JANE: Milwaukee, WI, Dec. 21.

KAHN, MADELINE: Boston, MA, Sept. 29, 1942. Hofstra U.

KANE, CAROL: Cleveland, OH, June 18, 1952.

KAPLAN, MARVIN: Brooklyn, Jan. 24, 1924.

KAPOOR, SHASHI: Bombay 1940.

KAPRISKY, VALERIE: Paris, 1963.

KARRAS, ALEX: Gary, IN, July 15, 1935.

KATT, WILLIAM: Los Angeles, CA, Feb. 16, 1955.

KAUFMANN, CHRISTINE: Lansdorf, Graz, Austria, Jan. 11, 1945.

KAVNER, JULIE: Burbank, CA, Sept. 7, 1951, UCLA.

KAYE, STUBBY: NYC, Nov. 11, 1918.

KAZAN, LAINIE (Levine): Brooklyn, NY, May 15, 1942.

KEACH, STACY: Savannah, GA, June 2, 1941. U. Cal., Yale.

KEATON, DIANE (Hall): Los Angeles, CA, Jan. 5, 1946. Neighborhood Playhouse.

KEATON, MICHAEL: Coraopolis, PA., Sept. 9, 1951. KentStateU.

KEATS, STEVEN: Bronx, NY, 1945.

KEDROVA, LILA: Leningrad, 1918.

KEEL, HOWARD (Harold Leek): Gillespie, IL, Apr. 13, 1919.

KEELER, RUBY (Ethel): Halifax, N.S., Aug. 25, 1909.

KEITEL, HARVEY: Brooklyn, NY, May 13, 1941.

KEITH, BRIAN: Bayonne, NJ, Nov. 15, 1921.

KEITH, DAVID: Knoxville, TN, May 8, 1954. UTN.

KELLER, MARTHE: Basel, Switz., 1945. Munich Stanislavsky Sch.

KELLERMAN, SALLY: Long Beach, CA, June 2, 1938. Actors Studio West.

KELLEY, DeFOREST: Atlanta, GA, Jan. 20, 1920.

KELLY, GENE: Pittsburgh, Aug. 23, 1912. U. Pittsburgh.

KELLY, JACK: Astoria, NY, Sept. 16, 1927. UCLA.

KELLY, NANCY: Lowell, MA, Mar. 25, 1921. Bentley School.

KEMP, JEREMY: (Wacker) Chesterfield, Eng., Feb. 3, 1935, Central Sch.

KENNEDY, ARTHUR: Worcester, MA, Feb. 17, 1914. Carnegie Tech.

KENNEDY, GEORGE: NYC, Feb. 18, 1925.

KENNEDY, LEON ISAAC: Cleveland, OH, 1949.

KERR, DEBORAH: Helensburg, Scot., Sept. 30, 1921. Smale Ballet School.

KERR, JOHN: NYC, Nov. 15, 1931. Harvard, Columbia.

KERWIN, BRIAN: Chicago, IL, Oct. 25, 1949.

KEYES, EVELYN: Port Arthur, TX., Nov. 20, 1919.

KHAMBATTA, PERSIS: Bombay, Oct. 2, 1950.

KIDDER, MARGOT: Yellow Knife, Can., Oct. 17, 1948. UBC.

KIEL, RICHARD: Detroit, MI, Sept. 13, 1939.

KIER, UDO: Germany, Oct. 14, 1944.

KILEY, RICHARD: Chicago, Mar. 31, 1922. Loyola.

KILMER, VAL: Los Angeles, Dec. 31, 1959. Juilliard.

KINCAID, ARON (Norman Neale Williams III): Los Angeles, June 15, 1943. UCLA.

KING, ALAN (Irwin Kniberg): Brooklyn, Dec. 26, 1927.

KING, PERRY: Alliance, OH, Apr. 30, 1948. Yale.

KINGSLEY, BEN (Krishna Bhanji): Snaiton, Yorkshire, Eng., Dec. 31, 1943.

KINSKI, KLAUS: (Claus Gunther Nakszynski) Sopot, Poland, 1926.

KINSKI, NASTASSJA: Berlin, Germany, Jan. 24, 1960.

KIRKLAND, SALLY: NYC, Oct. 31, 1944. Actors Studio

KITT, EARTHA: North, SC, Jan. 26, 1928.

KLEIN, ROBERT: NYC, Feb. 8, 1942. Alfred U.

KLEMPERER, WERNER: Cologne, Mar. 22, 1920.

KLINE, KEVIN: St. Louis, MO, Oct. 24, 1947, Juilliard.

KLUGMAN, JACK: Philadelphia, PA, Apr. 27, 1925. Carnegie Tech.

KNIGHT, MICHAEL: Princeton, NJ, 1959.

KNIGHT, SHIRLEY: Goessel, KS, July 5, 1937. Wichita U.

KNOWLES, PATRIC (Reginald Lawrence Knowles): Horsforth, Eng., Nov. 11, 1911.

KNOX, ALEXANDER: Strathroy, Ont., Can., Jan. 16, 1907.

KNOX, ELYSE: Hartford, CT, Dec. 14, 1917. Traphagen School.

KOENIG, WALTER: Chicago, IL, Sept. 14. UCLA.

KOHNER, SUSAN: Los Angeles, Nov. 11, 1936. U. Calif.

KORMAN, HARVEY: Chicago, IL, Feb. 15, 1927. Goodman.

KORSMO, CHARLIE: Minneapolis, MN, 1978.

KORVIN, CHARLES (Geza Korvin Karpathi): Czechoslovakia, Nov. 21. Sorbonne.

KOSLECK, MARTIN: Barkotzen, Ger., Mar. 24, 1907. Max Reinhardt School.

KOTEAS, ELIAS: Montreal, Quebec, Canada, 1961. AADA.

KOTTO, YAPHET: NYC, Nov. 15, 1937.

KRABBE, JEROEN: Amsterdam, The Netherlands, Dec. 5, 1944.

KREUGER, KURT: St. Moritz, Switz., July 23, 1917. U. London.

KRIGE, ALICE: Upington, So. Africa, June 28, 1955.

KRISTEL, SYLVIA: Amsterdam, Hol., Sept. 28, 1952.

KRISTOFFERSON, KRIS: Brownsville, TX, June 22, 1936, Pomona Col.

KRUGER, HARDY: Berlin Ger., April 12, 1928.

KULP, NANCY: Harrisburg, PA, Aug. 28, 1921.

KUNTSMANN, DORIS: Hamburg, 1944.

KURTZ, SWOOSIE: Omaha, NE, Sept. 6, 1944.

KWAN, NANCY: Hong Kong, May 19, 1939. Royal Ballet.

LaBELLE, PATTI: Philadelphia, PA, May 24, 1944.

LACY, JERRY: Sioux City, IA, Mar. 27, 1936. LACC.

LADD, CHERYL: (Stoppelmoor): Huron, SD, July 12, 1951.

LADD, DIANE: (Ladnier): Meridian, MS, Nov. 29, 1932. Tulane U.

LaGRECA, PAUL: Bronx, NY, June 23, 1962. AADA.

LAHTI, CHRISTINE: Detroit, MI, Apr. 4, 1950; U. Mich.

LAKE, RICKI: NYC, 1967.

LAMARR, HEDY (Hedwig Kiesler): Vienna, Sept. 11, 1913.

LAMAS, LORENZO: Los Angeles, Jan. 28, 1958.

LAMB, GIL: Minneapolis, June 14, 1906. U. Minn.

LAMBERT, CHRISTOPHER: NYC, 1958.

LAMOUR, DOROTHY (Mary Dorothy Slaton): New Orleans, LA.; Dec. 10, 1914. Spence School.

LANCASTER, BURT: NYC, Nov. 2, 1913. NYU.

LANDAU, MARTIN: Brooklyn, NY, June 20, 1931. Actors Studio.

LANDON, MICHAEL (Eugene Orowitz): Collingswood, NJ, Oct. 31, 1936. USC.

LANDRUM, TERI: Enid, OK., 1960.

LANE, ABBE: Brooklyn, Dec. 14, 1935.

LANE, DIANE: NYC, Jan. 22, 1963.

LANG, STEPHEN: NYC, July 11, 1952. Swarthmore Col.

LANGAN, GLENN: Denver, CO, July 8, 1917.

LANGE, HOPE: Redding Ridge, CT, Nov. 28, 1931. Reed Col.

LANGE, JESSICA: Cloquet, MN, Apr. 20, 1949. U. Minn.

LANGELLA, FRANK: Bayonne, NJ, Jan. 1, 1940, SyracuseU.

LANSBURY, ANGELA: London, Oct. 16, 1925. London Academy of Music.

LANSING, ROBERT (Brown): San Diego, CA, June 5, 1929.

LaPLANTE, LAURA: St. Louis, MO, Nov. 1, 1904.

LARROQUETTE, JOHN: New Orleans, LA, Nov. 25, 1947.

LASSER, LOUISE: NYC. Apr. 11, 1939. Brandeis U.

LAUGHLIN, JOHN: Memphis, TN, Apr. 3.

LAUGHLIN, TOM: Minneapolis, MN, 1938.

LAUPER, CYNDI: Astoria, Queens, NYC. June 20, 1953.

LAURE, CAROLE: Montreal, Can., 1951.

LAURIE, PIPER (Rosetta Jacobs): Detroit, MI, Jan. 22, 1932.

LAUTER, ED: Long Beach, NY, Oct. 30, 1940.

LAW, JOHN PHILLIP: Hollywood, Sept. 7, 1937. Neighborhood Playhouse, U. Hawaii.

| Page Johnson | Ricki Lake | Yaphet Kotto | Diane Lane | Brian Kerwin | Angela Lansbury |

LAWRENCE, BARBARA: Carnegie, OK, Feb. 24, 1930. UCLA.

LAWRENCE, CAROL (Laraia): Melrose Park, IL, Sept. 5, 1935.

LAWRENCE, VICKI: Inglewood, CA, Mar. 26, 1949.

LAWSON, LEIGH: Atherston, Eng., July 21, 1945. RADA.

LEACHMAN, CLORIS: Des Moines, IA, Apr. 30, 1930. Northwestern U.

LEAUD, JEAN-PIERRE: Paris, 1944.

LEDERER, FRANCIS: Karlin, Prague, Czech., Nov. 6, 1906.

LEE, BRANDON: Feb. 1, 1965. EmersonCol.

LEE, CHRISTOPHER: London, May 27, 1922. Wellington College.

LEE, MARK: Australia, 1958.

LEE, MICHELE (Dusiak): Los Angeles, June 24, 1942. LACC.

LEE, PEGGY (Norma Delores Egstrom): Jamestown, ND, May 26, 1920.

LEE, SPIKE (Shelton Lee): Atlanta, GA, Mar. 20, 1957.

LEIBMAN, RON: NYC, Oct. 11, 1937. Ohio Wesleyan.

LEIGH, JANET (Jeanette Helen Morrison): Merced, CA, July 6, 1926. College of Pacific.

LEIGH, JENNIFER JASON: Los Angeles, 1958.

LEMMON, CHRIS: Los Angeles, Jan. 22, 1954.

LEMMON, JACK: Boston, Feb. 8, 1925. Harvard.

LENO, JAY: New Rochelle, NY, Apr. 28, 1950. Emerson Col.

LENZ, KAY: Los Angeles, Mar. 4, 1953.

LENZ, RICK: Springfield, IL, Nov. 21, 1939. U. Mich.

LEONARD, ROBERT SEAN: Westwood, NJ, Feb. 28, 1969.

LEONARD, SHELDON (Bershad): NYC, Feb. 22, 1907, Syracuse U.

LEROY, PHILIPPE: Paris, Oct. 15, 1930. U. Paris.

LESLIE, BETHEL: NYC, Aug. 3, 1929. Brearley School.

LESLIE, JOAN (Joan Brodell): Detroit, Jan. 26, 1925. St. Benedict's.

LESTER, MARK: Oxford, Eng., July 11, 1958.

LEVELS, CALVIN: Cleveland, OH., Sept. 30, 1954. CCC.

LEVIN, RACHEL: NYC, 1954. Goddard Col.

LEVINE, JERRY: New Brunswick, NJ, Mar. 12, 1957, Boston U.

LEVY, EUGENE: Hamilton, Can., Dec. 17, 1946. McMasterU.

LEWIS, CHARLOTTE: London, 1968.

LEWIS, JERRY (Joseph Levitch): Newark, NJ, Mar. 16, 1926.

LIGON, TOM: New Orleans, LA, Sept. 10, 1945.

LINCOLN, ABBEY (Anna Marie Woolridge): Chicago, Aug. 6, 1930.

LINDEN, HAL: Bronx, NY, Mar. 20, 1931. City Col. of NY.

LINDFORS, VIVECA: Uppsala, Sweden, Dec. 29, 1920. Stockholm Royal Dramatic School.

LINDSAY, ROBERT: Ilketson, Derbyshire, Eng., Dec. 13, 1951, RADA.

LINN-BAKER, MARK: St. Louis, MO, June 17, 1954, Yale.

LIOTTA, RAY: Newark, NJ, Dec. 18, 1955. UMiami.

LISI, VIRNA: Rome, Nov. 8, 1937.

LITHGOW, JOHN: Rochester, NY, Oct. 19, 1945. Harvard.

LITTLE, CLEAVON: Chickasha, OK, June 1, 1939. San Diego State.

LLOYD, CHRISTOPHER: Stamford, CT, Oct. 22, 1938.

LLOYD, EMILY: London, Sept. 29, 1970.

LOCKE, SONDRA: Shelbyville, TN, May, 28, 1947.

LOCKHART, JUNE: NYC, June 25, 1925. Westlake School.

LOCKWOOD, GARY: Van Nuys, CA, Feb. 21, 1937.

LOGGIA, ROBERT: Staten Island, NY., Jan. 3, 1930. UMo.

LOLLOBRIGIDA, GINA: Subiaco, Italy, July 4, 1927. Rome Academy of Fine Arts.

LOM, HERBERT: Prague, Czechoslovakia, Jan 9, 1917. Prague U.

LOMEZ, CELINE: Montreal, Can., 1953.

LONDON, JULIE (Julie Peck): Santa Rosa, CA, Sept. 26, 1926.

LONE, JOHN: Hong Kong, 1952. AADA

LONG, SHELLEY: Ft. Wayne, IN, Aug. 23, 1949. Northwestern U.

LOPEZ, PERRY: NYC, July 22, 1931. NYU.

LORD, JACK (John Joseph Ryan): NYC, Dec. 30, 1928. NYU.

LOREN, SOPHIA (Sofia Scicolone): Rome, Italy, Sept. 20, 1934.

LOUISE, TINA (Blacker): NYC, Feb. 11, 1934, Miami U.

LOVTIZ, JON: Tarzana, CA, July 21, 1957.

LOWE, CHAD: Dayton, OH, Jan, 15, 1968.

LOWE, ROB: Charlottesville, VA, Mar. 17, 1964.

LOWITSCH, KLAUS: Berlin, Apr. 8, 1936. Vienna Academy.

LOY, MYRNA (Myrna Williams): Helena, MT, Aug. 2, 1905. Westlake School.

LUCAS, LISA: Arizona, 1961.

LUCKINBILL, LAURENCE: Fort Smith, AK, Nov. 21, 1934.

LUFT, LORNA: Los Angeles, Nov. 21, 1952.

LULU: Glasglow, Scot., 1948.

LUNA, BARBARA: NYC, Mar. 2, 1939.

LUND, JOHN: Rochester, NY, Feb. 6, 1913.

LUNDGREN, DOLPH: Stockholm, Sw., 1959. Royal Inst.

LUPINO, IDA: London, Feb. 4, 1916. RADA.

LuPONE, PATTI: Northport, NY, Apr. 21, 1949, Juilliard.

LYDON, JAMES: Harrington Park, NJ, May 30, 1923.

LYNCH, KELLY: Minneapolis, MN, 1959.

LYNLEY, CAROL (Jones): NYC, Feb. 13, 1942.

LYNN, JEFFREY: Auburn, MA, Feb. 16, 1909. Bates College.

LYON, SUE: Davenport, IA, July 10, 1946.

LYONS, ROBERT F.: Albany, NY. AADA.

MacARTHUR, JAMES: Los Angeles, Dec. 8, 1937. Harvard.

MACCHIO, RALPH: Huntington, NY., Nov. 4, 1961.

MacCORKINDALE, SIMON: Cambridge, Eng., Feb. 12, 1953.

MacGINNIS, NIALL: Dublin, Ire., Mar. 29, 1913. Dublin U.

MacGRAW, ALI: NYC, Apr. 1, 1938. Wellesley.

MacLAINE, SHIRLEY (Beaty): Richmond, VA, Apr. 24, 1934.

MacLEOD, GAVIN: Mt. Kisco, NY, Feb. 28, 1931.

MacMAHON, ALINE: McKeesport, PA, May 3, 1899. Barnard College.

MacMURRAY, FRED: Kankakee, IL, Aug. 30, 1908. Carroll Col.

MACNAUGHTON, ROBERT: NYC, Dec. 19, 1966.

MACNEE, PATRICK: London, Feb. 1922.

MacNICOL, PETER: Dallas, TX, Apr. 10, 1954. UMN.

MADIGAN, AMY: Chicago, IL, Sept. 11, 1950. Marquette U.

MADISON, GUY (Robert Moseley): Bakersfield, CA, Jan. 19, 1922. Bakersfield Jr. College.

MADONNA (Madonna Louise Veronica Cicone): Bay City, MI, Aug. 16, 1958. UMi.

MADSEN, VIRGINIA: Winnetka, IL, 1963.

MAGNUSON, ANN: Charleston, WV, 1956.

MAHARIS, GEORGE: Astoria, NY, Sept. 1, 1928. Actors Studio.

MAHONEY, JOHN: Manchester, Eng., June 20, 1940, WUIll.

MAILER, KATE: NYC, 1962.

MAILER, STEPHEN: NYC, Mar. 10, 1966. NYU.

MAJORS, LEE: Wyandotte, MI, Apr. 23, 1940. E. Ky. State Col.

MAKEPEACE, CHRIS: Toronto, Can., Apr. 22, 1964.

MAKO: Kobe, Japan, 1934. Pratt Inst.

MALDEN, KARL. (Malden Sekulovich): Gary, IN, Mar. 22, 1914.

MALET, PIERRE: St. Tropez, Fr., 1955.

MALKOVICH, JOHN: Christopher, IL, Dec. 9, 1953, IllStateU.

MALONE, DOROTHY: Chicago, Jan. 30, 1925. S. Methodist U.

MANN, KURT: Roslyn, NY, July 18, 1947.

MANOFF, DINAH: NYC, Jan. 25, 1958. CalArts.

MANTEGNA, JOE: Chicago, IL, Nov. 13, 1947, Goodman Theatre.

MANZ, LINDA: NYC, 1961.

MARAIS, JEAN: Cherbourg, France, Dec. 11, 1913. St. Germain.

MARCHAND, NANCY: Buffalo, NY, June 19, 1928.

MARCOVICCI, ANDREA: NYC, Nov. 18, 1948.

MARGOLIN, JANET: NYC, July 25, 1943. Walden School.

MARIN, CHEECH (Richard): Los Angeles, July 13, 1946.

MARIN, JACQUES: Paris, Sept. 9, 1919. Conservatoire National.

MARINARO, ED: NYC, 1951. Cornell.

MARS, KENNETH: Chicago, IL, 1936.

MARSH, JEAN: London, Eng., July 1, 1934.

MARSHALL, BRENDA (Ardis Anderson Gaines): Isle of Negros, P.I., Sept. 29, 1915. Texas State College.

MARSHALL, E. G.: Owatonna, MN, June 18, 1910. U. Minn.

MARSHALL, KEN: NYC, 1953. Juilliard.

MARSHALL, PENNY: Bronx, NY, Oct. 15, 1942. U. N. Mex.

MARSHALL, WILLIAM: Gary, IN, Aug. 19, 1924. NYU.

MARTIN, ANDREA: Portland, ME, Jan. 15, 1947.

MARTIN, DEAN (Dino Crocetti): Steubenville, OH, June 17, 1917.

MARTIN, GEORGE N.: NYC, Aug. 15, 1929.

MARTIN, MARY: Weatherford, TX, Dec. 1, 1914. Ward-Belmont School.

MARTIN, MILLICENT: Romford, Eng., June 8, 1934.

MARTIN, PAMELA SUE: Westport, CT, Jan. 15, 1953.

MARTIN, STEVE: Waco, TX, Aug. 14, 1945. UCLA.

MARTIN, TONY (Alfred Norris): Oakland, CA, Dec. 25, 1913. St. Mary's College.

MASINA, GIULIETTA: Giorgio di Piano, Italy, Feb. 22, 1921.

MASON, MARSHA: St. Louis, MO, Apr. 3, 1942. Webster Col.

MASON, PAMELA (Pamela Kellino): Westgate, Eng., Mar. 10, 1918.

MASSEN, OSA: Copenhagen, Den., Jan. 13, 1916.

MASSEY, DANIEL: London, Oct. 10, 1933. Eton and King's Col.

MASTERS, BEN: Corvallis, OR, May 6, 1947, UOr.

MASTERSON, MARY STUART: NYC, 1967, NYU.

MASTERSON, PETER: Angleton, TX, June 1, 1934. Rice U.

MASTRANTONIO, MARY ELIZABETH: Chicago, IL, Nov. 17, 1958. UIll.

MASTROIANNI, MARCELLO: Fontana Liri, Italy, Sept. 28, 1924.

MASUR, RICHARD: NYC, Nov. 20, 1948.

MATHESON, TIM: Glendale, CA, Dec. 31, 1947. CalState.

MATLIN, MARLEE: Morton Grove, IL., Aug. 24, 1965.

MATTHAU, WALTER (Matuschanskayasky): NYC, Oct. 1, 1920.

MATTHEWS, BRIAN: Philadelphia, Jan. 24, 1953. St. Olaf.

MATURE, VICTOR: Louisville, KY, Jan. 29, 1915.

MAY, ELAINE (Berlin): Philadelphia, Apr. 21, 1932.

MAYEHOFF, EDDIE: Baltimore, July 7, 1914. Yale.

MAYO, VIRGINIA (Virginia Clara Jones): St. Louis, MO, Nov. 30, 1920.

MAYRON, MELANIE: Philadelphia, PA, Oct. 20, 1952. AADA.

MAZURSKY, PAUL: Brooklyn, NY, Apr. 25, 1930. Bklyn Col.

McCALLUM, DAVID: Scotland, Sept. 19, 1933. Chapman Col.

McCAMBRIDGE, MERCEDES: Jolliet, IL, Mar. 17, 1918. Mundelein College.

McCARTHY, ANDREW: NYC, 1963, NYU.

McCARTHY, KEVIN: Seattle, WA, Feb. 15, 1914. Minn. U.

McCARTNEY, PAUL: Liverpool, England, June 18,1942.

McCLANAHAN, RUE: Healdton, OK, Feb. 21, 1934.

McCLORY, SEAN: Dublin, Ire., Mar. 8, 1924. U. Galway.

McCLURE, DOUG: Glendale, CA, May 11, 1935. UCLA.

McCLURE, MARC: San Mateo, CA, Mar. 31, 1957.

McCLURG, EDIE: Kansas City, MO, July 23, 1950.

McCOWEN, ALEC: Tunbridge Wells, Eng., May 26, 1925. RADA.

McCRANE, PAUL: Philadelphia, PA, Jan. 19, 1961.

McCRARY, DARIUS: Walnut, CA, 1976.

McDERMOTT, DYLAN: Waterbury, CT, Oct. 26, 1962. Neighborhood Playhouse.

McDONNELL, MARY: Wilkes-Barre, PA, 1952.

McDORMAND, FRANCES: Illinois, 1958.

McDOWALL, RODDY: London, Sept. 17, 1928. St. Joseph's.

McDOWELL, MALCOLM (Taylor): Leeds, Eng., June 19, 1943. LAMDA.

McENERY, PETER: Walsall, Eng., Feb. 21, 1940.

McFARLAND, SPANKY: Dallas, TX, Oct. 2, 1926.

McGAVIN, DARREN: Spokane, WA, May 7, 1922. College of Pacific.

McGILL, EVERETT: Miami Beach, FL, Oct. 21, 1945.

McGILLIS, KELLY: Newport Beach, CA, July 9, 1957. Juilliard.

McGOVERN, ELIZABETH: Evanston, IL, July 18, 1961. Juilliard.

McGOVERN, MAUREEN: Youngstown, OH, July 27, 1949.

McGREGOR, JEFF: Chicago, 1957. UMn.

McGUIRE, BIFF: New Haven, CT, Oct. 25, 1926. Mass. State Col.

McGUIRE, DOROTHY: Omaha, NE, June 14, 1918.

McHATTIE, STEPHEN: Antigonish, NS, Feb. 3. AcadiaU, AADA.

McKAY, GARDNER: NYC, June 10, 1932. Cornell.

McKEAN, MICHAEL: NYC, Oct. 17, 1947.

McKEE, LONETTE: Detroit, MI, 1954.

McKELLEN, IAN: Burnley, Eng., May 25, 1939.

McKENNA, VIRGINIA: London, June 7, 1931.

McKEON, DOUG: Pompton Plains, NJ, June 10, 1966.

McKUEN, ROD: Oakland, CA, Apr. 29, 1933.

McLERIE, ALLYN ANN: Grand Mere, Can., Dec. 1, 1926.

McNAIR, BARBARA: Chicago, Mar. 4, 1939. UCLA.

McNALLY, STEPHEN (Horace McNally): NYC, July 29, 1913. Fordham U.

McNAMARA, WILLIAM: Dallas, TX, 1965.

McNICHOL, KRISTY: Los Angeles, CA, Sept. 11, 1962.

McQUEEN, ARMELIA: North Carolina, Jan. 6, 1952. Bklyn Consv.

McQUEEN, BUTTERFLY: Tampa, FL, Jan. 8, 1911. UCLA.

McQUEEN, CHAD: Los Angeles, CA, Dec. 28, 1960. Actors Studio.

McRANEY, GERALD: Collins, MS, Aug. 19, 1948.

McSHANE, IAN: Blackburn, Eng., Sept. 29, 1942. RADA.

MEADOWS, AUDREY: Wuchang, China, 1924. St. Margaret's.

MEADOWS, JAYNE (formerly, Jayne Cotter): Wuchang, China, Sept. 27, 1920. St. Margaret's.

MEARA, ANNE: Brooklyn, NY, Sept. 20, 1929.

MEDWIN, MICHAEL: London, 1925. Instut Fischer.

MEISNER, GUNTER: Bremen, Ger., Apr. 18, 1926. Municipal Drama School.

MEKKA, EDDIE: Worcester, MA, 1932. Boston Cons.

MELATO, MARIANGELA: Milan, Italy, 1941. Milan Theatre Acad.

MELL, MARISA: Vienna, Austria, Feb. 25, 1939.

MERCADO, HECTOR JAIME: NYC, 1949. HB Studio.

MERCOURI, MELINA: Athens, Greece, Oct. 18, 1925.

MEREDITH, BURGESS: Cleveland, OH, Nov. 16, 1908. Amherst.

MEREDITH, LEE (Judi Lee Sauls): Oct., 1947. AADA.

MERRILL, DINA (Nedinia Hutton): NYC, Dec. 9, 1925. AADA.

METCALF, LAURIE: Edwardsville, IL, June 16, 1955. IllStU.

METZLER, JIM: Oneonda, NY, June 23. Dartmouth Col.

MICHELL, KEITH: Adelaide, Aus., Dec. 1, 1926.

MIDLER, BETTE: Honolulu, HI., Dec. 1, 1945.

MIFUNE, TOSHIRO: Tsingtao, China, Apr. 1, 1920.

MILANO, ALYSSA: Brooklyn, NY, 1975.

MILES, JOANNA: Nice, France, Mar. 6, 1940.

MILES, SARAH: Ingatestone, Eng., Dec. 31, 1941. RADA.

MILES, SYLVIA: NYC, Sept. 9, 1932. Actors Studio.

MILES, VERA (Ralston): Boise City, OK, Aug. 23, 1929. UCLA.

MILLER, ANN (Lucille Ann Collier): Chireno, TX, Apr. 12, 1919. Lawler Professional School.

MILLER, PENELOPE ANN: Santa Monica, CA, Jan. 13, 1964.

MILLER, BARRY: Los Angeles, CA, Feb. 6, 1958

MILLER, JASON: Long Island City, NY, Apr. 22, 1939. Catholic U.

MILLER, LINDA: NYC, Sept. 16, 1942. Catholic U.

MILLER, REBECCA: Roxbury, CT, 1962. Yale.

MILLS, HAYLEY: London, Apr. 18, 1946. Elmhurst School.

MILLS, JOHN: Suffolk, Eng., Feb. 22, 1908.

MILNER, MARTIN: Detroit, MI, Dec. 28, 1931.

MIMIEUX, YVETTE: Los Angeles, Jan. 8, 1941. Hollywood High.

MINNELLI, LIZA: Los Angeles, Mar. 12, 1946.

MIOU-MIOU: Paris, Feb. 22, 1950.

MIRREN, HELEN: England, 1946.

MITCHELL, CAMERON (Mizell): Dallastown, PA, Nov. 4, 1918. N.Y. Theatre School.

MITCHELL, JAMES: Sacramento, CA, Feb. 29, 1920. LACC.

MITCHUM, JAMES: Los Angeles, CA, May 8, 1941.

MITCHUM, ROBERT: Bridgeport, CT, Aug. 6, 1917.

MODINE, MATTHEW: Loma Linda, CA, Mar. 22, 1959.

MOKAE, ZAKES: Johannesburg, So. Africa, Aug. 5, 1935. RADA.

MOLINA, ALFRED: London, May 24, 1953. Guildhall

MONTALBAN, RICARDO: Mexico City, Nov. 25, 1920.

MONTAND, YVES (Yves Montand Livi): Mansummano, Tuscany, Oct. 13, 1921.

MONTGOMERY, BELINDA: Winnipeg, Can., July 23, 1950.

MONTGOMERY, ELIZABETH: Los Angeles, Apr. 15, 1933. AADA.

MONTGOMERY, GEORGE (George Letz): Brady, MT, Aug. 29, 1916. U. Mont.

MOOR, BILL: Toledo, OH, July 13, 1931. Northwestern.

MOORE, CONSTANCE: Sioux City, IA, Jan. 18, 1919.

MOORE, DEMI (Guines): Roswell, NMx, Nov. 11, 1962.

MOORE, DICK: Los Angeles, Sept. 12, 1925.

MOORE, DUDLEY: Dagenham, Essex, Eng. Apr. 19, 1935.

MOORE, FRANK: Bay-de-Verde, Newfoundland, 1946.

MOORE, KIERON: County Cork, Ire., 1925. St. Mary's College.

MOORE, MARY TYLER: Brooklyn, Dec. 29, 1936.

MOORE, ROGER: London, Oct. 14, 1927. RADA.

MOORE, TERRY (Helen Koford): Los Angeles, Jan. 1, 1929.

MORALES, ESAI: Brooklyn, 1963.

MORANIS, RICK: Toronto, Can., Apr. 18.

MOREAU, JEANNE: Paris, Jan. 23, 1928.

MORENO, RITA (Rosita Alverio): Humacao, P.R., Dec. 11, 1931.

MORGAN, DENNIS (Stanley Morner): Prentice, WI, Dec. 10, 1910. Carroll College.

MORGAN, HARRY (HENRY) (Harry Bratsburg): Detroit, Apr. 10, 1915. U. Chicago.

MORGAN, MICHELE (Simone Roussel): Paris, Feb. 29, 1920. Paris Dramatic School.

MORIARTY, CATHY: Bronx, NY, Nov. 29, 1960.

MORIARTY, MICHAEL: Detroit, MI, Apr. 5, 1941. Dartmouth.

MORISON, PATRICIA: NYC, 1915.

MORITA, NORIYUKI "PAT": Isleton, CA, June 28, 1933.

MORLEY, ROBERT: Wiltshire, Eng., May 26, 1908. RADA.

MORRIS, ANITA: Durham, NC, 1932.

MORRIS, GREG: Cleveland, OH, Sept. 27, 1934. Ohio State.

MORRIS, HOWARD: NYC, Sept. 4, 1919. NYU.

MORSE, DAVID: Hamilton, MA, 1953.

MORSE, ROBERT: Newton, MA, May 18, 1931.

MORTON, JOE: NYC, Oct. 18, 1947, HofstraU.

MOSES, WILLIAM: Los Angeles, Nov. 17, 1959.

MOSTEL, JOSH: NYC, Dec. 21, 1946. Brandeis U.

MOUCHET, CATHERINE: Paris, 1959, Ntl. Consv.

MOYA, EDDY: El Paso, TX, Apr. 11, 1963. LACC.

MULGREW, KATE: Dubuque, IA, Apr. 29, 1955. NYU.

MULHERN, MATT: Philadelphia, PA, July 21, 1960. Rutgers Univ.

MULL, MARTIN: N. Ridgefield, OH, Aug. 18, 1941. RISch. of Design.

MULLIGAN, RICHARD: NYC, Nov. 13, 1932.

MUMY, BILL (Charles William Mumy Jr.): San Gabriel, CA, Feb. 1, 1954.

MURPHY, EDDIE: Brooklyn, NY, Apr. 3, 1961.

MURPHY, GEORGE: New Haven, CT, July 4, 1902. Yale.

MURPHY, MICHAEL: Los Angeles, CA, May 5, 1938, UAz.

MURRAY, BILL: Evanston, IL, Sept. 21, 1950. Regis Col.

MURRAY, DON: Hollywood, July 31, 1929. AADA.

MUSANTE, TONY: Bridgeport, CT, June 30, 1936. Oberlin Col.

NABORS, JIM: Sylacauga, GA, June 12, 1932.

NADER, GEORGE: Pasadena, CA, Oct. 19, 1921. Occidental College.

NADER, MICHAEL: Los Angeles, CA, 1945.

NAMATH, JOE: Beaver Falls, PA, May 31, 1943. UAla.

NATWICK, MILDRED: Baltimore, June 19, 1908. Bryn Mawr.

NAUGHTON, DAVID: Hartford, CT, Feb. 13, 1951.

NAUGHTON, JAMES: Middletown, CT, Dec. 6, 1945. Yale.

NAVIN, JOHN P., JR.: Philadelphia, PA, 1968.

NEAL, PATRICIA: Packard, KY, Jan. 20, 1926. Northwestern U.

NEESON, LIAM: Ballymena, Northern Ireland, June 7, 1952.

NEFF, HILDEGARDE (Hildegard Knef): Ulm, Ger., Dec. 28, 1925. Berlin Art Academy.

NEILL, SAM: No. Ireland, 1948. U Canterbury.

NELL, NATHALIE: Paris, Oct. 1950.

NELLIGAN, KATE: London, Ont., Can., Mar. 16, 1951. U Toronto.

NELSON, BARRY (Robert Nielsen): Oakland, CA, Apr. 16, 1920.

NELSON, CRAIG T.: Spokane, WA, Apr. 4, 1946.

NELSON, DAVID: NYC, Oct. 24, 1936. USC.

NELSON, GENE (Gene Berg): Seattle, WA, Mar. 24, 1920.

NELSON, HARRIET HILLIARD (Peggy Lou Snyder): Des Moines, IA, July 18, 1914.

NELSON, JUDD: Portland, ME, Nov. 28, 1959. Haverford Col.

NELSON, LORI (Dixie Kay Nelson): Santa Fe, NM, Aug. 15, 1933.

NELSON, TRACY: Santa Monica, CA, Oct. 25, 1963.

NELSON, WILLIE: Abbott, TX, Apr. 30, 1933.

NEMEC, CORIN: Little Rock, AK, Nov. 5, 1971.

NETTLETON, LOIS: Oak Park, IL. Actors Studio.

NEWHART, BOB: Chicago, IL, Sept. 5, 1929. Loyola U.

NEWLEY, ANTHONY: Hackney, London, Sept. 24, 1931.

NEWMAN, BARRY: Boston, MA, Mar. 26, 1938. Brandeis U.

NEWMAN, PAUL: Cleveland, OH, Jan. 26, 1925. Yale.

NEWMAR, JULIE (Newmeyer): Los Angeles, Aug. 16, 1935.

NEWTON-JOHN, OLIVIA: Cambridge, Eng., Sept. 26, 1948.

NGUYEN, DUSTIN: Saigon, 1962.

NICHOLAS, PAUL: London, 1945.

NICHOLSON, JACK: Neptune, NJ, Apr. 22, 1937.

NICKERSON, DENISE: NYC, 1959.

NICOL, ALEX: Ossining, NY, Jan. 20, 1919. Actors Studio.

NIELSEN, BRIGITTE: Denmark, 1963.

NIELSEN, LESLIE: Regina, Saskatchewan, Can., Feb. 11, 1926. Neighborhood Playhouse.

NIMOY, LEONARD: Boston, MA, Mar. 26, 1931. Boston Col., Antioch Col.

NIXON, CYNTHIA: NYC, Apr. 9, 1966. Columbia U.

NOBLE, JAMES: Dallas, TX, Mar. 5, 1922, SMU.

NOLAN, KATHLEEN: St. Louis, MO, Sept. 27, 1933. Neighborhood Playhouse.

NOLTE, NICK: Omaha, NE, Feb. 8, 1940. Pasadena City Col.

NORRIS, CHRISTOPHER: NYC, Oct. 7, 1943. Lincoln Square Acad.

NORRIS, CHUCK (Carlos Ray): Ryan, OK, Mar. 10, 1940.

NORTH, HEATHER: Pasadena, CA, Dec. 13, 1950. Actors Workshop.

NORTH, SHEREE (Dawn Bethel): Los Angeles, Jan. 17, 1933. Hollywood High.

NORTON, KEN: Aug. 9, 1945.

NOURI, MICHAEL: Washington, DC, Dec. 9, 1945.

NOVAK, KIM (Marilyn Novak): Chicago, Feb. 13, 1933. LACC.

NUREYEV, RUDOLF: Russia, Mar. 17, 1938.

NUTE, DON: Connellsville, PA, Mar. 13, Denver U.

NUYEN, FRANCE (Vannga): Marseilles, France, July 31, 1939. Beaux Arts School.

O'BRIAN, HUGH (Hugh J. Krampe): Rochester, NY, Apr. 19, 1928. Cincinnati U.

O'BRIEN, CLAY: Ray, AZ, May 6, 1961.

O'BRIEN, MARGARET (Angela Maxine O'Brien): Los Angeles, Jan. 15, 1937.

O'CONNOR, CARROLL: Bronx, NY, Aug. 2, 1924. Dublin National Univ.

O'CONNOR, DONALD: Chicago, Aug. 28, 1925.

O'CONNOR, GLYNNIS: NYC, Nov. 19, 1956. NYSU.

O'CONNOR, KEVIN: Honolulu, HI, May 7, 1938, U. Hi.

O'HANLON, GEORGE: Brooklyn, NY, Nov. 23, 1917.

O'HARA, CATHERINE: Toronto, Can., Mar. 4, 1954.

O'HARA, MAUREEN (Maureen Fitz-Simons): Dublin, Ire., Aug. 17, 1920. Abbey School.

O'HERLIHY, DAN: Wexford, Ire., May 1, 1919. National U.

O'KEEFE, MICHAEL: Paulland, NJ, Apr. 24, 1955, NYU, AADA.

OLDMAN, GARY: New Cross, South London, Eng., Mar. 21, 1958.

OLIN, LENA: Stockholm, Sweden, 1955.

OLMOS, EDWARD JAMES: Los Angeles, Feb. 24, 1947. CSLA.

O'LOUGHLIN, GERALD S.: NYC, Dec. 23, 1921. U. Rochester.

| Michael Ontkean | Diana Rigg | Michael Palin | Katharine Ross | Howard E. Rollins Jr. | Janice Rule |

OLSON, JAMES: Evanston, IL, Oct. 8, 1930.
OLSON, NANCY: Milwaukee, WI, July 14, 1928. UCLA.
O'NEAL, GRIFFIN: Los Angeles, 1965.
O'NEAL, PATRICK: Ocala, FL, Sept. 26, 1927. U. Fla.
O'NEAL, RON: Utica, NY, Sept. 1, 1937. Ohio State.
O'NEAL, RYAN: Los Angeles, Apr. 20, 1941.
O'NEAL, TATUM: Los Angeles, Nov. 5, 1963.
O'NEIL, TRICIA: Shreveport, LA, Mar. 11, 1945. Baylor U.
O'NEILL, ED: Youngstown, OH, 1946.
O'NEILL, JENNIFER: Rio de Janeiro, Feb. 20, 1949. Neighborhood Playhouse.
ONTKEAN, MICHAEL: Vancouver, B.C., Can., Jan. 24, 1946.
ORBACH, JERRY: Bronx, NY, Oct. 20, 1935.
O'SHEA, MILO: Dublin, Ire., June 2, 1926.
O'SULLIVAN, MAUREEN: Byle, Ire., May 17, 1911. Sacred Heart Convent.
O'TOOLE, ANNETTE (Toole): Houston, TX, Apr. 1, 1952. UCLA.
O'TOOLE, PETER: Connemara, Ire., Aug. 2, 1932. RADA.
OVERALL, PARK: Nashville, TN, Mar. 15, 1957. Tusculum Col.
PACINO, AL: NYC, Apr. 25, 1940.
PACULA, JOANNA: Tamaszow Lubelski, Poland, Jan. 2, 1957. Polish Natl. Theatre Sch.
PAGE, TONY (Anthony Vitiello): Bronx, NY, 1940.
PAGET, DEBRA (Debralee Griffin): Denver, Aug. 19, 1933.
PAIGE, JANIS (Donna Mae Jaden): Tacoma, WA, Sept. 16, 1922.
PALANCE, JACK (Walter Palanuik): Lattimer, PA, Feb. 18, 1920. UNC.
PALIN, MICHAEL: Sheffield, Yorkshire, Eng., May 5, 1943. Oxford.
PALMER, BETSY: East Chicago, IN, Nov. 1, 1926. DePaul U.
PALMER, GREGG (Palmer Lee): San Francisco, Jan. 25, 1927. U. Utah.
PAMPANINI, SILVANA: Rome, Sept. 25, 1925.
PANEBIANCO, RICHARD: NYC, 1971.
PANTALIANO, JOE: Jersey City, NJ, Sept. 12, 1954.
PAPAS, IRENE: Chiliomodion, Greece, Mar. 9, 1929.
PARE, MICHAEL: Brooklyn, NY, Oct. 9, 1959.
PARKER, COREY: NYC, July 8, 1965. NYU.
PARKER, ELEANOR: Cedarville, OH, June 26, 1922. Pasadena Playhouse.
PARKER, FESS: Fort Worth, TX, Aug. 16, 1925. USC.

PARKER, JAMESON: Baltimore, MD, Nov. 18, 1947. Beloit Col.
PARKER, JEAN (Mae Green): Deer Lodge, MT, Aug. 11, 1912.
PARKER, NATHANIEL: 1963 London.
PARKER, SUZY (Cecelia Parker): San Antonio, TX, Oct. 28, 1933.
PARKER, WILLARD (Worster Van Eps): NYC, Feb. 5, 1912.
PARKINS, BARBARA: Vancouver, Can., May 22, 1943.
PARKS, MICHAEL: Corona, CA, Apr. 4, 1938.
PARSONS, ESTELLE: Lynn, MA, Nov. 20, 1927. Boston U.
PARTON, DOLLY: Sevierville, TN, Jan. 19, 1946.
PATINKIN, MANDY: Chicago, IL, Nov. 30, 1952. Juilliard.
PATRIC, JASON: NYC, 1966.
PATRICK, DENNIS: Philadelphia, Mar. 14, 1918.
PATTERSON, LEE: Vancouver, Can., Mar. 31, 1929. Ontario Col.
PATTON, WILL: Charleston, SC, June 14, 1954.
PAVAN, MARISA (Marisa Pierangeli): Cagliari, Sardinia, June 19, 1932. Torquado Tasso College.
PAYS, AMANDA: Berkshire, Eng., June 6, 1959.
PEACH, MARY: Durban, S. Africa, 1934.
PEARL, MINNIE (Sarah Cannon): Centerville, TN, Oct. 25, 1912.
PEARSON, BEATRICE: Denison, TX, July 27, 1920.
PECK, GREGORY: La Jolla, CA, Apr. 5, 1916. U. Calif.
PELIKAN, LISA: Paris, July 12. Juilliard.
PENDLETON, AUSTIN: Warren, OH, Mar. 27, 1940. Yale U.
PENHALL, BRUCE: Balboa, CA, 1958.
PENN, SEAN: Burbank, CA, Aug. 17, 1960.
PEPPARD, GEORGE: Detroit, Oct. 1, 1928. Carnegie Tech.
PEREZ, JOSE: NYC, 1940.
PERKINS, ANTHONY: NYC, Apr. 14, 1932. Rollins College.
PERKINS, ELIZABETH: Queens, NY, Nov. 18, 1960. Goodman School.
PERLMAN, RON: NYC, Apr. 13, 1950. UMn.
PERREAU, GIGI (Ghislaine): Los Angeles, Feb. 6, 1941.
PERRINE, VALERIE: Galveston, TX, Sept. 3, 1944. U. Ariz.
PESCI, JOE: Newark, NJ, Feb. 9, 1943.
PESCOW, DONNA: Brooklyn, NY, Mar. 24, 1954.
PETERS, BERNADETTE (Lazzara): Jamaica, NY, Feb. 28, 1948.
PETERS, BROCK: NYC, July 2, 1927. CCNY.

PETERS, JEAN (Elizabeth): Canton, OH, Oct. 15, 1926. Ohio State U.
PETERS, MICHAEL: Brooklyn, NY, 1948.
PETERSEN, WILLIAM: Chicago, IL, 1953.
PETERSON, CASSANDRA: Colorado Springs, CO, Sept. 17, 1951.
PETTET, JOANNA: London, Nov. 16, 1944. Neighborhood Playhouse.
PFEIFFER, MICHELLE: Santa Ana, CA, Apr. 29, 1958.
PHILLIPS, LOU DIAMOND: Phillipines, 1962. UTx.
PHILLIPS, MacKENZIE: Alexandria, VA, Nov. 10, 1959.
PHILLIPS, MICHELLE (Holly Gilliam): Long Beach, CA, June 4, 1944.
PHOENIX, RIVER: Madras, OR, Aug. 24, 1970.
PICARDO, ROBERT: Philadelphia, PA, Oct. 27, 1953. Yale.
PICERNI, PAUL: NYC, Dec. 1, 1922. Loyola U.
PINCHOT, BRONSON: NYC, May 20, 1959, Yale.
PINE, PHILLIP: Hanford, CA, July 16, 1925. Actors' Lab.
PISCOPO, JOE: Passaic, NJ. June 17, 1951.
PISIER, MARIE-FRANCE: Vietnam, May 10, 1944. U. Paris.
PITILLO, MARIA: Mahwah, NJ, 1965.
PLACE, MARY KAY: Port Arthur, TX, Sept. 23, 1947. U. Tulsa.
PLAYTEN, ALICE: NYC, Aug. 28, 1947. NYU.
PLEASENCE, DONALD: Workshop, Eng., Oct. 5, 1919. Sheffield School.
PLESHETTE, SUZANNE: NYC, Jan. 31, 1937. Syracuse U.
PLOWRIGHT, JOAN: Scunthorpe, Brigg, Lincolnshire, Eng., Oct. 28, 1929. Old Vic.
PLUMB, EVE: Burbank, CA, Apr. 29, 1958.
PLUMMER, AMANDA: NYC, Mar. 23, 1957. Middlebury Col.
PLUMMER, CHRISTOPHER: Toronto, Can., Dec. 13, 1927.
PODESTA, ROSSANA: Tripoli, June 20, 1934.
POITIER, SIDNEY: Miami, FL, Feb. 27, 1924.
POLITO, LINA: Naples, Italy, Aug. 11, 1954.
POLLAN, TRACY: NYC, 1962.
POLLARD, MICHAEL J.: Pacific, NJ, May 30, 1939.
PORTER, ERIC: London, Apr. 8, 1928. Wimbledon Col.
POTTS, ANNIE: Nashville, TN, Oct. 28, 1952. Stephens Col.
POWELL, JANE (Suzanne Burce): Port-

land, OR, Apr. 1, 1928.
POWELL, ROBERT: Salford, Eng., June 1, 1944. Manchester U.
POWER, TARYN: Los Angeles, CA, 1954.
POWER, TYRONE IV: Los Angeles, CA, Jan. 1959.
POWERS, MALA (Mary Ellen): San Francisco, Dec. 29, 1921. UCLA.
POWERS, STEFANIE (Federkiewicz): Hollywood, CA, Oct. 12, 1942.
PRENTISS, PAULA (Paula Ragusa): San Antonio, TX, Mar. 4, 1939. Northwestern U.
PRESLE, MICHELINE (Micheline Chassagne): Paris, Aug. 22, 1922. Rouleau Drama School.
PRESNELL, HARVE: Modesto, CA, Sept. 14, 1933. USC.
PRESTON, WILLIAM: Columbia, PA, Aug. 26, 1921. PaStateU.
PRICE, LONNY: NYC, Mar. 9, 1959, Juilliard.
PRICE, VINCENT: St. Louis, May 27, 1911. Yale.
PRIMUS, BARRY: NYC, Feb. 16, 1938. CCNY.
PRINCE (P. Rogers Nelson): Minneapolis, MN, June 7, 1958.
PRINCE, WILLIAM: Nicholas, NY, Jan. 26, 1913. Cornell U.
PRINCIPAL, VICTORIA: Fukuoka, Japan, Jan. 3, 1945. Dade Jr. Col.
PROCHNOW, JURGEN: Germany, 1941.
PROSKY, ROBERT: Philadelphia, PA, Dec. 13, 1930.
PROVAL, DAVID: Brooklyn, NY, 1943.
PROVINE, DOROTHY: Deadwood, SD, Jan. 20, 1937. U. Wash.
PROWSE, JULIET: Bombay, India, Sept. 25, 1936.
PRYCE, JONATHAN: Wales, UK, June 1, 1947, RADA.
PRYOR, RICHARD: Peoria, IL, Dec. 1, 1940.
PULLMAN, BILL: Delhi, NY, 1954, SUNY/Oneonta, UMass.
PURCELL, LEE: Cherry Point, NC, June 15, 1947. Stephens.
PURDOM, EDMUND: Welwyn Garden City, Eng., Dec. 19, 1924. St. Ignatius College.
PYLE, DENVER: Bethune, CO, May 11, 1920.
QUAID, DENNIS: Houston, TX, Apr. 9, 1954.
QUAID, RANDY: Houston, TX, 1950, UHouston.
QUINLAN, KATHLEEN: Mill Valley, CA, Nov. 19, 1954.
QUINN, AIDAN: Chicago, IL, Mar. 8, 1959.
QUINN, ANTHONY: Chihuahua, Mex., Apr. 21, 1915.
RAFFERTY, FRANCES: Sioux City, IA, June 16, 1922. UCLA.
RAFFIN, DEBORAH: Los Angeles, Mar. 13, 1953. Valley Col.
RAGSDALE, WILLIAM: El Dorado, AK, Jan. 19, 1961. Hendrix Col.
RAINER, LUISE: Vienna, Aust., Jan. 12, 1910.
RALSTON, VERA: (Vera Helena Hruba) Prague, Czech., July 12, 1919.
RAMPLING, CHARLOTTE: Surmer, Eng., Feb. 5, 1946. U. Madrid.
RAMSEY, LOGAN: Long Beach, CA, Mar. 21, 1921. St. Joseph.
RANDALL, TONY (Leonard Rosenberg): Tulsa, OK, Feb. 26, 1920. Northwestern U.
RANDELL, RON: Sydney, Australia, Oct. 8, 1920. St. Mary's Col.
RASCHE, DAVID: St. Louis, MO, Aug. 7, 1944.

RASULALA, THALMUS (Jack Crowder): Miami, FL, Nov. 15, 1939. U. Redlands.
RAY, ALDO (Aldo DeRe): Pen Argyl, PA, Sept. 25, 1926. UCLA.
RAYE, MARTHA (Margie Yvonne Reed): Butte, MT, Aug. 27, 1916.
RAYMOND, GENE (Raymond Guion): NYC, Aug. 13, 1908.
REAGAN, RONALD: Tampico, IL, Feb. 6, 1911. Eureka College.
REASON, REX: Berlin, Ger., Nov. 30, 1928. Pasadena Playhouse.
REDDY, HELEN: Australia, Oct. 25, 1942.
REDFORD, ROBERT: Santa Monica, CA, Aug. 18, 1937. AADA.
REDGRAVE, CORIN: London, July 16, 1939.
REDGRAVE, LYNN: London, Mar. 8, 1943.
REDGRAVE, VANESSA: London, Jan. 30, 1937.
REDMAN, JOYCE: County Mayo, Ire., 1919. RADA.
REED, OLIVER: Wimbledon, Eng., Feb. 13, 1938.
REED, PAMELA: Tacoma, WA, Apr. 2, 1949.
REEMS, HARRY (Herbert Streicher): Bronx, NY, 1947. U. Pittsburgh.
REEVE, CHRISTOPHER: NYC, Sept. 25, 1952. Cornell, Juilliard.
REEVES, KEANU: Beiruit, Lebanon, Sept. 2, 1964.
REEVES, STEVE: Glasgow, MT, Jan. 21, 1926.
REGEHR, DUNCAN: Lethbridge, Can., 1954.
REID, ELLIOTT: NYC, Jan. 16, 1920.
REID, KATE: London, Nov. 4, 1930.
REINER, CARL: NYC, Mar. 20, 1922. Georgetown.
REINER, ROB: NYC, Mar. 6, 1945. UCLA.
REINHOLD, JUDGE (Edward Ernest, Jr.): Wilmington, DE, 1956. NCSchool of Arts.
REINKING, ANN: Seattle, WA, Nov. 10, 1949.
REISER, PAUL: NYC, Mar. 30, 1957.
REMAR, JAMES: Boston, Ma., Dec. 31, 1953. Neighborhood Playhouse.
REMICK, LEE: Quincy, MA. Dec. 14, 1935. Barnard College.
RETTIG, TOMMY: Jackson Heights, NY, Dec. 10, 1941.
REVILL, CLIVE: Wellington, NZ, Apr. 18, 1930.
REY, ANTONIA: Havana, Cuba, Oct. 12, 1927.
REY, FERNANDO: La Coruna, Spain, Sept. 20, 1917.
REYNOLDS, BURT: Waycross, GA, Feb. 11, 1935. Fla. State U.
REYNOLDS, DEBBIE (Mary Frances Reynolds): El Paso, TX, Apr. 1, 1932.
REYNOLDS, MARJORIE: Buhl, ID, Aug. 12, 1921.
RHOADES, BARBARA: Poughkeepsie, NY, 1947.
RICHARDS, JEFF (Richard Mansfield Taylor): Portland, OR, Nov. 1. USC.
RICHARDSON, LEE: Chicago, Sept. 11, 1926.
RICHARDSON, NATASHA: London, May 11, 1963.
RICKLES, DON: NYC, May 8, 1926. AADA.
RIEGERT, PETER: NYC, Apr. 11, 1947. U Buffalo.
RIGG, DIANA: Doncaster, Eng., July 20, 1938. RADA.
RINGWALD, MOLLY: Rosewood, CA, Feb. 14, 1968.

RITTER, JOHN: Burbank, CA, Sept. 17, 1948. U.S. Cal.
RIVERS, JOAN (Molinsky): Brooklyn, NY, June 8, 1933.
ROBARDS, JASON: Chicago, July 26, 1922. AADA.
ROBBINS, TIM: NYC, Oct. 16, 1958. UCLA.
ROBERTS, ERIC: Biloxi, MS, Apr. 18, 1956. RADA.
ROBERTS, JULIA: Atlanta, GA, Oct. 28, 1967.
ROBERTS, RALPH: Salisbury, NC, Aug. 17, 1922. UNC.
ROBERTS, TANYA (Leigh): NYC, 1955.
ROBERTS, TONY: NYC, Oct. 22, 1939. Northwestern U.
ROBERTSON, CLIFF: La Jolla, CA, Sept. 9, 1925. Antioch Col.
ROBERTSON, DALE: Oklahoma City, July 14, 1923.
ROBINSON, CHRIS: West Palm Beach, FL, Nov. 5, 1938. LACC.
ROBINSON, JAY: NYC, Apr. 14, 1930.
ROBINSON, ROGER: Seattle, WA, May 2, 1941. USC.
ROCHEFORT, JEAN: Paris, 1930.
ROCK-SAVAGE, STEVEN: Melville, LA, Dec. 14, 1958. LSU.
ROGERS, CHARLES "BUDDY": Olathe, KS, Aug. 13, 1904. U. Kan.
ROGERS, GINGER (Virginia Katherine McMath): Independence, MO, July 16, 1911.
ROGERS, MIMI: Coral Gables, FL, Jan. 27, 1956.
ROGERS, ROY (Leonard Slye): Cincinnati, Nov. 5, 1912.
ROGERS, WAYNE: Birmingham, AL, Apr. 7, 1933. Princeton.
ROLAND, GILBERT (Luis Antonio Damaso De Alonso): Juarez, Mex., Dec. 11, 1905.
ROLLINS, HOWARD E., JR.: Baltimore, MD, Oct. 17, 1950.
ROMAN, RUTH: Boston, Dec. 23, 1922. Bishop Lee Dramatic School.
ROMANCE, VIVIANE (Pauline Ronacher Ortmanns): Vienna, Aust. 1912.
ROMERO, CESAR: NYC, Feb. 15, 1907. Collegiate School.
RONSTADT, LINDA: Tucson, AZ, July 15, 1946.
ROONEY, MICKEY (Joe Yule, Jr.): Brooklyn, Sept. 23, 1920.
ROSE, REVA: Chicago, IL, July 30, 1940. Goodman.
ROSS, DIANA: Detroit, MI, Mar. 26, 1944.
ROSS, JUSTIN: Brooklyn, NY, Dec. 15, 1954.
ROSS, KATHARINE: Hollywood, Jan. 29, 1943. Santa Rosa Col.
ROSSELLINI, ISABELLA: Rome, June 18, 1952.
ROSSOVICH, RICK: Palo Alto, CA, Aug. 28, 1957.
ROUNDTREE, RICHARD: New Rochelle, NY, Sept. 7, 1942. Southern Ill.
ROURKE, MICKEY: Schenectady, NY, 1950.
ROWE, NICHOLAS: London, Nov. 22, 1966. Eton.
ROWLANDS, GENA: Cambria, WI, June 19, 1934.
RUBIN, ANDREW: New Bedford, MA, June 22, 1946. AADA.
RUBINSTEIN, JOHN: Los Angeles, CA, Dec. 8, 1946, UCLA.
RUBINSTEIN, ZELDA: Pittsburg, PA.
RUCKER, BO: Tampa, Fl, Aug. 17, 1948.
RUDD, PAUL: Boston, MA, May 15, 1940.
RULE, JANICE: Cincinnati, OH, Aug. 15, 1931.

RUPERT, MICHAEL: Denver, CO, Oct. 23, 1951. Pasadena Playhouse.

RUSH, BARBARA: Denver, CO, Jan. 4, 1929. U. Calif.

RUSSELL, JANE: Bemidji, MI, June 21, 1921. Max Reinhardt School.

RUSSELL, JOHN: Los Angeles, Jan. 3, 1921. U. Calif.

RUSSELL, KURT: Springfield, MA, Mar. 17, 1951.

RUSSELL, THERESA: San Diego, CA, Mar. 20, 1957.

RUSSO, JAMES: NYC, Apr. 23, 1953.

RUTHERFORD, ANN: Toronto, Can., Nov. 2, 1920.

RUYMEN, AYN: Brooklyn, July 18, 1947. HB Studio.

RYAN, MEG: Faifield, CT, Nov. 19, 1961. NYU.

RYAN, TIM (Meineslschmidt): Staten Island, NY. 1958. Rutgers U.

RYDER, WINONA: Winona, MN, Oct. 1971.

SACCHI, ROBERT: Bronx, NY, 1941. NYU.

SÄGEBRECHT, MARIANNE: Starnberg, Bavaria, 1945.

SAINT, EVA MARIE: Newark, NJ, July 4, 1924. Bowling Green State U.

ST. JAMES, SUSAN (Suzie Jane Miller): Los Angeles, Aug. 14, 1946. Conn. Col.

ST. JOHN, BETTA: Hawthorne, CA, Nov. 26, 1929.

ST. JOHN, JILL (Jill Oppenheim): Los Angeles, Aug. 19, 1940.

SALA, JOHN: Los Angeles, CA., Oct. 5, 1962.

SALDANA, THERESA: Brooklyn, NY, 1955.

SALINGER, MATT: New Hampshire, 1960. Princeton, Columbia.

SALT, JENNIFER: Los Angeles, Sept. 4, 1944. Sarah Lawrence Col.

SAN GIACOMO, LAURA: NJ, 1962.

SANDS, JULIAN: Yorkshire, Eng., 1958.

SANDS, TOMMY: Chicago, Aug. 27, 1937.

SAN JUAN, OLGA: NYC, Mar. 16, 1927.

SARA, MIA: Brooklyn, NY, 1968.

SARANDON, CHRIS: Beckley, WV, July 24, 1942. U. WVa., Catholic U.

SARANDON, SUSAN (Tomalin): NYC, Oct. 4, 1946. Catholic U.

SARGENT, DICK (Richard Cox): Carmel, CA, 1933. Stanford.

SARRAZIN, MICHAEL: Quebec City, Can., May 22, 1940.

SAVAGE, FRED: Highland Park, IL, July 9, 1976.

SAVAGE, JOHN (Youngs): Long Island, NY, Aug. 25, 1949. AADA.

SAVALAS, TELLY (Aristotle): Garden City, NY, Jan. 21, 1925. Columbia.

SAVIOLA, CAMILLE: Bronx, NY, July 16, 1950.

SAVOY, TERESA ANN: London, July 18, 1955.

SAXON, JOHN (Carmen Orrico): Brooklyn, Aug. 5, 1935.

SBARGE, RAPHAEL: NYC, Feb. 12, 1964.

SCALIA, JACK: Brooklyn, NY, 1951.

SCARPELLI, GLEN: Staten Island, NY, July 1966.

SCARWID, DIANA: Savannah, GA. AADA, Pace U.

SCHEIDER, ROY: Orange, NJ, Nov. 10, 1932. Franklin-Marshall.

SCHEINE, RAYNOR: Emporia, VA, Nov. 10. VaCommonwealthU.

SCHELL, MARIA: Vienna, Jan. 15, 1926.

SCHELL, MAXIMILIAN: Vienna, Dec. 8, 1930.

SCHLATTER, CHARLIE: NYC, 1967. Ithaca Col.

SCHNEIDER, MARIA: Paris, Mar. 27, 1952.

SCHRODER, RICK: Staten Island, NY, Apr. 13, 1970.

SCHUCK, JOHN: Boston, MA, Feb. 4, 1940.

SCHWARZENEGGER, ARNOLD: Austria, July 30, 1947.

SCHYGULLA, HANNA: Katlowitz, Poland. 1943.

SCIORRA, ANNABELLA: NYC, 1964.

SCOFIELD, PAUL: Hurstpierpoint, Eng., Jan. 21, 1922. London Mask Theatre School.

SCOLARI, PETER: Scarsdale, NY, Sept. 12, 1956. NYCC.

SCOTT, DEBRALEE: Elizabeth, NJ, Apr. 2.

SCOTT, GEORGE C.: Wise, VA, Oct. 18, 1927. U. Mo.

SCOTT, GORDON (Gordon M. Werschkul): Portland, OR, Aug. 3, 1927. Oregon U.

SCOTT, LIZABETH (Emma Matso): Scranton, PA, Sept. 29, 1922.

SCOTT, MARTHA: Jamesport, MO, Sept. 22, 1914. U. Mich.

SCOTT-TAYLOR, JONATHAN: Brazil, 1962.

SEAGAL, STEVEN: Detroit, MI, 1951.

SEARS, HEATHER: London, Sept. 28, 1935.

SECOMBE, HARRY: Swansea, Wales, Sept. 8, 1921.

SEGAL, GEORGE: NYC, Feb. 13, 1934. Columbia.

SELBY, DAVID: Morganstown, WV, Feb. 5, 1941. UWV.

SELLARS, ELIZABETH: Glasgow, Scot., May 6, 1923.

SELLECK, TOM: Detroit, MI, Jan. 29, 1945. USCal.

SELWART, TONIO: Watenberg, Ger., June 9, 1906. Munich U.

SERNAS, JACQUES: Lithuania, July 30, 1925.

SERRAULT, MICHEL: Brunoy, France, 1928, Paris Consv.

SETH, ROSHAN: New Delhi, India, 1942.

SEYLER, ATHENE (Athene Hannen): London, May 31, 1889.

SEYMOUR, JANE (Joyce Frankenberg): Hillingdon, Eng., Feb. 15, 1951.

SHARIF, OMAR (Michel Shalhoub): Alexandria, Egypt, Apr. 10, 1932. Victoria Col.

SHARKEY, RAY: Brooklyn, NY, 1952. HB Studio.

SHATNER, WILLIAM: Montreal, Can., Mar. 22, 1931. McGill U.

SHAVER, HELEN: St. Thomas, Ontario, Can., 1951.

SHAW, SEBASTIAN: Holt, Eng., May 29, 1905. Gresham School.

SHAW, STAN: Chicago, IL, 1952.

SHAWN, WALLACE: NYC, Nov. 12, 1943. Harvard.

SHEA, JOHN: North Conway, NH, Apr. 14, 1949. Bates, Yale.

SHEARER, HARRY: Los Angeles, Dec. 23, 1943. UCLA.

SHEARER, MOIRA: Dunfermline, Scot., Jan. 17, 1926. London Theatre School.

SHEEDY, ALLY: NYC, June 13, 1962. USC.

SHEEN, CHARLIE (Carlos Irwin Estevez): Santa Monica, CA, Sept. 3, 1965.

SHEEN, MARTIN (Ramon Estevez): Dayton, OH, Aug. 3, 1940.

SHEFFIELD, JOHN: Pasadena, CA, Apr. 11, 1931. UCLA.

SHEPARD, SAM (Rogers): Ft. Sheridan, IL, Nov. 5, 1943.

SHEPHERD, CYBILL: Memphis, TN, Feb. 18, 1950. Hunter, NYU.

SHIELDS, BROOKE: NYC, May 31, 1965.

SHIRE, TALIA: Lake Success, NY, Apr. 25, 1946, Yale.

SHIRLEY, ANNE (Dawn Evelyn Paris): NYC, Apr. 17, 1918.

SHORE, DINAH (Frances Rose Shore): Winchester, TN, Mar. 1, 1917. Vanderbilt U.

SHORT, MARTIN: Toronto, Can, Mar. 26, 1950, McMasterU.

SHOWALTER, MAX (formerly Casey Adams): Caldwell, KS, June 2, 1917. Pasadena Playhouse.

SHULL, RICHARD B.: Evanston, IL, Feb. 24, 1929.

SIDNEY, SYLVIA: NYC, Aug. 8, 1910. Theatre Guild School.

SIEMASZKO, CASEY: Chicago, IL, March 17.

SIKKING, JAMES B.: Los Angeles, Mar. 5, 1934.

SILVER, RON: NYC, July 2, 1946. SUNY.

SILVERMAN, JONATHAN: Los Angeles, CA, Aug. 5, 1966, USCal.

SIMMONS, JEAN: London, Jan. 31, 1929. Aida Foster School.

SIMON, PAUL: Newark, NJ, Nov. 5, 1942.

SIMON, SIMONE: Marseilles, France, Apr. 23, 1910.

SIMPSON, O. J. (Orenthal James): San Francisco, CA, July 9, 1947. UCLA.

SINATRA, FRANK: Hoboken, NJ, Dec. 12, 1915.

SINCLAIR, JOHN (Gianluigi Loffredo): Rome, Italy, 1946.

SINDEN, DONALD: Plymouth, Eng., Oct. 9, 1923. Webber-Douglas.

SINGER, LORI: Corpus Christi, TX, May 6, 1962. Juilliard.

SKALA, LILIA: Vienna. U. Dresden.

SKELTON, RED (Richard): Vincennes, IN, July 18, 1910.

SKERRITT, TOM: Detroit, MI, Aug. 25, 1933. Wayne State U.

SKYE, IONE (Leitch): London, Eng. 1971.

SLATER, CHRISTIAN: NYC, Aug. 18, 1969.

SLATER, HELEN: NYC, Dec. 15, 1965.

SMIRNOFF, YAKOV (Yakov Pokhis): Odessa, USSR. Jan. 24, 1951.

SMITH, ALEXIS: Penticton, Can., June 8, 1921. LACC.

SMITH, CHARLES MARTIN: Los Angeles, CA, Oct. 30, 1953. CalState U.

SMITH, JACLYN: Houston, TX, Oct. 26, 1947.

SMITH, JOHN (Robert E. Van Orden): Los Angeles, Mar. 6, 1931. UCLA.

SMITH, KURTWOOD: New Lisbon, WI, Jul. 3, 1942.

SMITH, LEWIS: Chattanooga, TN, 1958. Actors Studio.

SMITH, LOIS: Topeka, KS, Nov. 3, 1930. U. Wash.

SMITH, MAGGIE: Ilford, Eng., Dec. 28, 1934.

SMITH, ROGER: South Gate, CA, Dec. 18, 1932. U. Ariz.

SMITHERS, WILLIAM: Richmond, VA, July 10, 1927. Catholic U.

SMITS, JIMMY: Brooklyn, NY, July 9, 1955. Cornell U.

SNODGRESS, CARRIE: Chicago, Oct. 27, 1946. UNI.

SOLOMON, BRUCE: NYC, 1944. U. Miami, Wayne State U.

SOMERS, SUZANNE (Mahoney): San Bruno, CA, Oct. 16, 1946. Lone Mt. Col.

SOMMER, ELKE (Schletz): Berlin, Nov. 5, 1940.

SOMMER, JOSEF: Greifswald, Germany, June 26, 1934.

SORDI, ALBERTO: Rome, Italy, June 15, 1919.

SORVINO, PAUL: NYC, 1939. AMDA.

SOTHERN, ANN (Harriet Lake): Valley City, ND, Jan. 22, 1907. Washington U.

SOTO, TALISA: Brooklyn, NY, 1968.

SOUL, DAVID: Chicago, IL, Aug. 28, 1943.

SPACEK, SISSY: Quitman, TX, Dec. 25, 1949. Actors Studio.

SPACEY, KEVIN: So. Orange, NJ, July 26, 1959. Juilliard.

SPADER, JAMES: MA, Feb. 7, 1960.

SPANO, VINCENT: Brooklyn, NY, Oct. 18, 1962.

SPENSER, JEREMY: Ceylon, 1937.

SPRINGFIELD, RICK (Richard Springthorpe): Sydney, Aust. Aug. 23, 1949.

STACK, ROBERT: Los Angeles, Jan. 13, 1919. USC.

STADLEN, LEWIS J.: Brooklyn, Mar. 7, 1947. Neighborhood Playhouse.

STALLONE, FRANK: NYC, July 30, 1950.

STALLONE, SYLVESTER: NYC, July 6, 1946. U. Miami.

STAMP, TERENCE: London, July 23, 1939.

STANDER, LIONEL: NYC, Jan. 11, 1908. UNC.

STANG, ARNOLD: Chelsea, MA, Sept. 28, 1925.

STANLEY, KIM (Patricia Reid): Tularosa, NM, Feb. 11, 1925. U. Tex.

STANTON, HARRY DEAN: Lexington, KY, July 14, 1926.

STAPLETON, JEAN: NYC, Jan. 19, 1923.

STAPLETON, MAUREEN: Troy, NY, June 21, 1925.

STARR, RINGO (Richard Starkey): Liverpool, England, July 7, 1940.

STEEL, ANTHONY: London, May 21, 1920. Cambridge.

STEELE, TOMMY: London, Dec. 17, 1936.

STEENBURGEN, MARY: Newport, AR, 1953. Neighborhood Playhouse.

STEIGER, ROD: Westhampton, NY, Apr. 14, 1925.

STERLING, JAN (Jane Sterling Adriance): NYC, Apr. 3, 1923. Fay Compton School.

STERLING, ROBERT (William Sterling Hart): Newcastle, PA, Nov. 13, 1917. U. Pittsburgh.

STERN, DANIEL: Bethesda, MD, Aug. 28, 1957.

STERNHAGEN, FRANCES: Washington, DC, Jan. 13, 1932.

STEVENS, ANDREW: Memphis, TN, June 10, 1955.

STEVENS, CONNIE (Concetta Ann Ingolia): Brooklyn, Aug. 8, 1938. Hollywood Professional School.

STEVENS, FISHER (Steven Fisher): Chicago, IL, Nov. 27, 1963. NYU.

STEVENS, KAYE (Catherine): Pittsburgh, July 21, 1933.

STEVENS, MARK (Richard): Cleveland, OH, Dec. 13, 1920.

STEVENS, STELLA (Estelle Eggleston): Hot Coffee, MS, Oct. 1, 1936.

STEVENSON, PARKER: CT, June 4, 1953. Princeton.

STEWART, ALEXANDRA: Montreal, Can., June 10, 1939. Louvre.

STEWART, ELAINE: Montclair, NJ, May 31, 1929.

STEWART, JAMES: Indiana, PA, May 20, 1908. Princeton.

STEWART, MARTHA (Martha Haworth): Bardwell, KY, Oct. 7, 1922.

STIERS, DAVID OGDEN: Peoria, IL, Oct. 31, 1942.

STILLER, JERRY: NYC, June 8, 1931.

STIMSON, SARA: Helotes, TX, 1973.

STING (Gordon Matthew Sumner): Wallsend, Eng., Oct. 2, 1951.

STOCKWELL, DEAN: Hollywood, Mar. 5, 1935.

STOCKWELL, JOHN (John Samuels IV): Galveston, Texas, March 25, 1961. Harvard.

STOLER, SHIRLEY: Brooklyn, NY, Mar. 30, 1929.

STOLTZ, ERIC: California, 1961, USC.

STONE, DEE WALLACE (Deanna Bowers): Kansas City, MO, Dec. 14. ULks.

STORM, GALE (Josephine Cottle): Bloomington, TX, Apr. 5, 1922.

STRAIGHT, BEATRICE: Old Westbury, NY, Aug. 2, 1916. Dartington Hall.

STRASBERG, SUSAN: NYC, May 22, 1938.

STRASSMAN, MARCIA: New Jersey, Apr. 28, 1948.

STRAUSS, PETER: NYC, Feb. 20, 1947.

STREEP, MERYL (Mary Louise): Summit, NJ, June 22, 1949., Vassar, Yale.

STREISAND, BARBRA: Brooklyn, Apr. 24, 1942.

STRITCH, ELAINE: Detroit, MI, Feb. 2, 1925. Drama Workshop.

STRODE, WOODY: Los Angeles, 1914.

STROUD, DON: Honolulu, HI, Sept. 1, 1937.

STRUTHERS, SALLY: Portland, OR, July 28, 1948. Pasadena Playhouse.

SULLIVAN, BARRY (Patrick Barry): NYC, Aug. 29, 1912. NYU.

SUMMER, DONNA (LaDonna Gaines): Boston, MA, Dec. 31, 1948.

SUTHERLAND, DONALD: St. John, New Brunswick, Can., July 17, 1935. U. Toronto.

SUTHERLAND, KIEFER: Los Angeles, CA, Dec. 18, 1966.

SVENSON, BO: Goteborg, Swed., Feb. 13, 1941. UCLA.

SWAYZE, PATRICK: Houston, TX, Aug. 18, 1952.

SWEENEY, D. B. (Daniel Bernard): Shoreham, NY, 1961.

SWINBURNE, NORA: Bath, Eng., July 24, 1902. RADA.

SWIT, LORETTA: Passaic, NJ, Nov. 4. 1937. AADA.

SYLVESTER, WILLIAM: Oakland, CA, Jan. 31, 1922. RADA.

SYMONDS, ROBERT: Bistow, AK, Dec. 1, 1926, TexU.

SYMS, SYLVIA: London, June 1, 1934. Convent School.

SZARABAJKA, KEITH: Oak Park, IL, Dec. 2, 1952, UChicago.

T, MR. (Lawrence Tero): Chicago, May 21, 1952.

TABORI, KRISTOFFER (Siegel): Los Angeles, Aug. 4, 1952.

TAKEI, GEORGE: Los Angeles, CA, Apr. 20. UCLA.

TALBOT, LYLE (Lysle Hollywood): Pittsburgh, Feb. 8, 1904.

TALBOT, NITA: NYC, Aug. 8, 1930. Irvine Studio School.

TAMBLYN, RUSS: Los Angeles, Dec. 30, 1934.

TANDY, JESSICA: London, June 7, 1909. Dame Owens' School.

TAYLOR, DON: Freeport, PA, Dec. 13, 1920. Penn State U.

TAYLOR, ELIZABETH: London, Feb. 27, 1932. Byron House School.

TAYLOR, ROD (Robert): Sydney, Aust., Jan. 11, 1929.

TAYLOR-YOUNG, LEIGH: Wash., DC, Jan. 25, 1945. Northwestern.

TEAGUE, ANTHONY SKOOTER: Jacksboro, TX, Jan. 4, 1940.

TEAGUE, MARSHALL: Newport, TN.

TEEFY, MAUREEN: Minneapolis, MN, 1954; Juilliard.

TEMPLE, SHIRLEY: Santa Monica, CA, Apr. 23, 1927.

TENNANT, VICTORIA: London, Eng., Sept. 30, 1950.

TERZIEFF, LAURENT: Paris, June 25, 1935.

TEWES, LAUREN: 1954, Pennsylvania

THACKER, RUSS: Washington, DC, June 23, 1946, Montgomery Col.

THAXTER, PHYLLIS: Portland, ME, Nov. 20, 1921. St. Genevieve.

THELEN, JODI: St. Cloud, MN, 1963.

THOMAS, DANNY (Amos Jacobs): Deerfield, MI, Jan. 6, 1914.

THOMAS, HENRY: San Antonio, TX, 1971.

THOMAS, MARLO (Margaret): Detroit, Nov. 21, 1938. USC.

THOMAS, PHILIP MICHAEL: Columbus, OH, May 26, 1949. Oakwood Col.

THOMAS, RICHARD: NYC, June 13, 1951. Columbia.

THOMPSON, JACK (John Payne): Sydney, Aus., 1940. U. Brisbane.

THOMPSON, LEA: Rochester, MN, May 31, 1961.

THOMPSON, MARSHALL: Peoria, IL, Nov. 27, 1925. Occidental.

THOMPSON, REX: NYC, Dec. 14, 1942.

THOMPSON, SADA: Des Moines, IA, Sept. 27, 1929. Carnegie Tech.

THOMSON, GORDON: Ottawa, Can., 1945.

THORSON, LINDA: June 18, 1947, Toronto, Can. RADA

THULIN, INGRID: Solleftea, Sweden, Jan. 27, 1929. Royal Drama Theatre.

TICOTIN, RACHEL: Bronx, NY, Nov. 1, 1958.

TIERNEY, GENE: Brooklyn, Nov. 20, 1920. Miss Farmer's School.

TIERNEY, LAWRENCE: Brooklyn, Mar. 15, 1919. Manhattan College.

TIFFIN, PAMELA (Wonso): Oklahoma City, Oct. 13, 1942.

TIGHE, KEVIN: Los Angeles, Aug. 13, 1944.

TILLY, MEG: Texada, Can., 1960.

TODD, ANN: Hartford, Eng., Jan. 24, 1909.

TODD, BEVERLY: Chicago, IL, July 11, 1946.

TODD, RICHARD: Dublin, Ire., June 11, 1919. Shrewsbury School.

TOLKAN, JAMES: Calumet, MI, 1931.

TOLO, MARILU: Rome, Italy, 1944.

TOMEI, MARISA: Brooklyn, NY, Dec. 4, 1964, NYU.

TOMLIN, LILY: Detroit, MI, Sept. 1, 1939. Wayne State U.

TOOMEY, REGIS: Pittsburgh, PA, Aug. 13, 1902.

TOPOL (Chaim Topol): Tel-Aviv, Israel, Sept. 9, 1935.

TORN, RIP: Temple, TX, Feb. 6, 1931. U. Tex.

TORRES, LIZ: NYC, 1947. NYU.

TOTTER, AUDREY: Joliet, IL, Dec. 20, 1918.

TOWSEND, ROBERT: Chicago, Feb. 6, 1957.

TRAVANTI, DANIEL J.: Kenosha, WI, Mar. 7, 1940.

TRAVERS, BILL: Newcastle-on-Tyne, Engl., Jan. 3, 1922.

| Kathleen Turner | Jan-Michael Vincent | Rita Tushingham | Robert Vaughn | Twiggy | Max Von Sydow |

TRAVIS, RICHARD (William Justice): Carlsbad, NM, Apr. 17, 1913.

TRAVOLTA, JOEY: Englewood, NJ, 1952.

TRAVOLTA, JOHN: Englewood, NJ, Feb. 18, 1954.

TREMAYNE, LES: London, Apr. 16, 1913. Northwestern, Columbia, UCLA.

TREVOR, CLAIRE (Wemlinger): NYC, March 8, 1909.

TRINTIGNANT, JEAN-LOUIS: Pont-St. Esprit, France, Dec. 11, 1930. Dullin-Balachova Drama School.

TRYON, TOM: Hartford, CT, Jan. 14, 1926. Yale.

TSOPEI, CORINNA: Athens, Greece, June 21, 1944.

TUBB, BARRY: 1963, Snyder, TX, AmConsv.Th.

TUCKER, MICHAEL: Baltimore, MD, Feb. 6, 1944.

TUNE, TOMMY: Wichita Falls, TX, Feb. 28, 1939.

TURNER, KATHLEEN: Springfield, MO, June 19, 1954. UMd.

TURNER, LANA (Julia Jean Mildred Frances Turner): Wallace, ID, Feb. 8, 1921.

TURNER, TINA: (Anna Mae Bullock) Nutbush, TN, Nov. 26, 1938.

TURTURRO, JOHN: Brooklyn, NY, Feb. 28, 1957. Yale.

TUSHINGHAM, RITA: Liverpool, Eng., Mar. 14, 1940.

TUTIN, DOROTHY: London, Apr. 8, 1930.

TWIGGY (Lesley Hornby): London, Sept. 19, 1949.

TWOMEY, ANNE: Boston, MA, June 7, 1951, Temple U.

TYLER, BEVERLY (Beverly Jean Saul): Scranton, PA, July 5, 1928.

TYRRELL, SUSAN: San Francisco, 1946.

TYSON, CATHY: Liverpool, Eng., 1966, RoyalShakeCo.

TYSON, CICELY: NYC, Dec. 19, 1933, NYU.

UGGAMS, LESLIE: NYC, May 25, 1943, Juilliard.

ULLMAN, TRACEY: Slough, Eng., 1960.

ULLMANN, LIV: Tokyo, Dec. 10, 1938. Webber-Douglas Acad.

UMEKI, MIYOSHI: Otaru, Hokaido, Japan, 1929.

UNDERWOOD, BLAIR: 1964, Tacoma, Wa. Carnegie-MellonU.

URICH, ROBERT: Toronto, Can., Dec. 19, 1946.

USTINOV, PETER: London, Apr. 16, 1921. Westminster School.

VACCARO, BRENDA: Brooklyn, Nov. 18, 1939. Neighborhood Playhouse.

VALANDREY, CHARLOTTE: (Anne-Charlotte Pascal) Paris, 1968.

VALLI, ALIDA: Pola, Italy, May 31, 1921. Rome Academy of Drama.

VALLONE, RAF: Riogio, Italy, Feb. 17, 1916. Turin U.

VAN ARK, JOAN: NYC, June 16, 1943, Yale.

VAN DE VEN, MONIQUE: Holland, 1957.

VAN DEVERE, TRISH (Patricia Dressel): Englewood Cliffs, NJ, Mar. 9, 1945. Ohio Wesleyan.

VAN DOREN, MAMIE (Joan Lucile Olander): Rowena, SD, Feb. 6, 1933.

VAN DYKE, DICK: West Plains, MO, Dec. 13, 1925.

VAN FLEET, JO: Oakland, CA, Dec. 30, 1919.

VAN DAMME, JEAN CLAUDE: Brussels, Belgium, 1961.

VANITY (Denise Mathews): 1963, Niagra, Ont., Can.

VAN PALLANDT, NINA: Copenhagen, Denmark, July 15, 1932.

VAN PATTEN, DICK: NYC, Dec. 9, 1928.

VAN PATTEN, JOYCE: NYC, Mar. 9, 1934.

VAN PEEBLES, MARIO: NYC, 1958, ColumbiaU.

VANCE, COURTNEY B.: Detroit, MI, Mar. 12, 1960.

VARNEY, JIM: Lexington, KY, June 15, 1950.

VARSI, DIANE: San Francisco, CA, Feb. 23, 1938.

VAUGHN, ROBERT: NYC, Nov. 22, 1932. USC.

VEGA, ISELA: Mexico, 1940.

VENNERA, CHICK: Herkimer, NY, Mar. 27, 1952. Pasadena Playhouse.

VENORA, DIANE: Hartford, CT, 1952. Juilliard.

VENUTA, BENAY: San Francisco, Jan. 27, 1911.

VERDON, GWEN: Culver City, CA, Jan. 13, 1925.

VEREEN, BEN: Miami, FL, Oct. 10, 1946.

VERNON, JOHN: Canada, 1936.

VICTOR, JAMES (Lincoln Rafael Peralta Diaz): Santiago, D.R., July 27, 1939. Haaren HS/NYC.

VILLECHAIZE, HERVE: Paris, Apr. 23, 1943.

VINCENT, JAN-MICHAEL: Denver, CO, July 15, 1944. Ventura.

VIOLET, ULTRA (Isabelle Collin-Dufresne): Grenoble, France.

VITALE, MILLY: Rome, Italy, July 16, 1938. Lycee Chateaubriand.

VOHS, JOAN: St. Albans, NY, July 30, 1931.

VOIGHT, JON: Yonkers, NY, Dec. 29, 1938. Catholic U.

VOLONTE, GIAN MARIA: Milan, Italy, Apr. 9, 1933.

VON DOHLEN, LENNY: Augusta, GA, Dec. 22, 1958. UTex.

VON SYDOW, MAX: Lund, Swed., July 10, 1929. Royal Drama Theatre.

WAGNER, LINDSAY: Los Angeles, June 22, 1949.

WAGNER, ROBERT: Detroit, Feb. 10, 1930.

WAHL, KEN: Chicago, IL, Feb. 14, 1956.

WAITE, GENEVIEVE: South Africa, 1949.

WAITS, TOM: Pomona, CA, Dec. 7, 1949.

WALKEN, CHRISTOPHER: Astoria, NY, Mar. 31, 1943. Hofstra.

WALKER, CLINT: Hartfold, IL, May 30, 1927. USC.

WALKER, NANCY (Ann Myrtle Swoyer): Philadelphia, May 10, 1921.

WALLACH, ELI: Brooklyn, Dec. 7, 1915. CCNY, U. Tex.

WALLACH, ROBERTA: NYC, Aug. 2, 1955.

WALLIS, SHANI: London, Apr. 5, 1941.

WALSH, M. EMMET: Ogdensburg, NY, Mar. 22, 1935, Clarkson Col., AADA.

WALSTON, RAY: New Orleans, Nov. 22, 1917. Cleveland Playhouse.

WALTER, JESSICA: Brooklyn, NY, Jan. 31, 1940. Neighborhood Playhouse.

WALTER, TRACEY: Jersey City, NJ, Nov. 25.

WALTERS, JULIE: London, Feb. 22, 1950.

WALTON, EMMA: London, Nov. 1962, Brown U.

WANAMAKER, SAM: Chicago, June 14, 1919. Drake.

WARD, BURT (Gervis): Los Angeles, July 6, 1945.

WARD, FRED: San Diego, Ca., 1943.

WARD, RACHEL: London, 1957.

WARD, SIMON: London, Oct. 19, 1941.

WARDEN, JACK: Newark, NJ, Sept. 18, 1920.

WARNER, DAVID: Manchester, Eng., July 29, 1941. RADA.

WARREN, JENNIFER: NYC, Aug. 12, 1941. U. Wisc.

WARREN, LESLEY ANN: NYC, Aug. 16, 1946.

WARREN, MICHAEL: South Bend, IN, Mar. 5, 1946. UCLA.

WARRICK, RUTH: St. Joseph, MO, June 29, 1915. U. Mo.

WASHINGTON, DENZEL: Mt. Vernon, NY, Dec. 28, 1954. Fordham.

WASSON, CRAIG: Ontario, OR, Mar. 15, 1954. UOre.

WATERSTON, SAM: Cambridge, MA, Nov. 15, 1940. Yale.

WATLING, JACK: London, Jan. 13, 1923. Italia Conti School.

WATSON, DOUGLASS: Jackson, GA, Feb. 24, 1921. UNC.

WAYANS, KEENEN IVORY: NYC, 1958. Tuskegee Inst.

WAYNE, DAVID (Wayne McKeehan): Travers City, MI, Jan. 30, 1914. Western Michigan State U.

| Cathy
Tyson | Ray
Walston | Lesley Ann
Warren | Fred
Williamson | Mare
Winningham | Paul
Winfield |

WAYNE, PATRICK: Los Angeles, July 15, 1939. Loyola.
WEATHERS, CARL: New Orleans, LA, Jan. 14, 1948. Long Beach CC.
WEAVER, DENNIS: Joplin, MO, June 4, 1924. U. Okla.
WEAVER, FRITZ: Pittsburgh, PA, Jan. 19, 1926.
WEAVER, MARJORIE: Crossville, TN, Mar. 2, 1913. Indiana U.
WEAVER, SIGOURNEY (Susan): NYC, Oct. 8, 1949. Stanford, Yale.
WEDGEWORTH, ANN: Abilene, TX, Jan. 21, 1935. U. Tex.
WELCH, RAQUEL (Tejada): Chicago, Sept. 5, 1940.
WELD, TUESDAY (Susan): NYC, Aug. 27, 1943. Hollywood Professional School.
WELDON, JOAN: San Francisco, Aug. 5, 1933. San Francisco Conservatory.
WELLER, PETER: Stevens Point, WI, June 24, 1947. AmThWing.
WELLES, GWEN: NYC, Mar. 4.
WENDT, GEORGE: Chicago, IL, Oct. 17, 1948.
WESLEY, BILLY: NYC, July 1966.
WEST, ADAM (William Anderson): Walla Walla, WA., Sept. 19, 1929.
WESTON, JACK (Morris Weinstein): Cleveland, OH, Aug. 21, 1924.
WHALLEY-KILMER, JOANNE: Manchester, Eng., Aug. 25, 1964.
WHEATON, WIL: Burbank, CA, Jul. 29, 1972.
WHITAKER, FOREST: Longview, TX, July 15, 1961.
WHITAKER, JOHNNY: Van Nuys, CA, Dec. 13, 1959.
WHITE, BETTY: Oak Park, IL, Jan. 17, 1922.
WHITE, CAROL: London, Apr. 1, 1944.
WHITE, CHARLES: Perth Amboy, NJ, Aug. 29, 1920. Rutgers U.
WHITE, JESSE: Buffalo, NY, Jan. 3, 1919.
WHITMAN, STUART: San Francisco, Feb. 1, 1929. CCLA.
WHITMORE, JAMES: White Plains, NY, Oct. 1, 1921. Yale.
WHITNEY, GRACE LEE: Detroit, MI, Apr. 1, 1930.
WHITTON, MARGARET: Philadelphia, PA., Nov. 30.
WIDDOES, KATHLEEN: Wilmington, DE, Mar. 21, 1939.
WIDMARK, RICHARD: Sunrise, MN, Dec. 26, 1914. Lake Forest.
WIEST, DIANNE: Kansas City, MO, Mar. 28, 1948, UMd.
WILBY, JAMES: Burma, 1958.
WILCOX, COLIN: Highlands, NC, Feb. 4, 1937. U. Tenn.
WILDER, GENE (Jerome Silberman): Milwaukee, WI, June 11, 1935. UIowa.
WILLIAMS, BILLY DEE: NYC, Apr. 6, 1937.

WILLIAMS, CINDY: Van Nuys, CA, Aug. 22, 1947. LACC.
WILLIAMS, CLARENCE III: NYC, Aug. 21, 1939.
WILLIAMS, DICK A.: Chicago, IL, Aug. 9, 1938.
WILLIAMS, ESTHER: Los Angeles, Aug. 8, 1921.
WILLIAMS, JOBETH: Houston, TX, 1953. BrownU.
WILLIAMS, PAUL: Omaha, NE, Sept. 19, 1940.
WILLIAMS, ROBIN: Chicago, IL, July 21, 1952. Juilliard.
WILLIAMS, TREAT (Richard): Rowayton, CT. Dec. 1, 1951.
WILLIAMSON, FRED: Gary, IN, Mar. 5, 1938. Northwestern.
WILLIAMSON, NICOL: Hamilton, Scot; Sept. 14, 1938.
WILLIS, BRUCE: Penns Grove, NJ, Mar. 19, 1955.
WILLISON, WALTER: Monterey Park, CA., June 24, 1947.
WILSON, DEMOND: NYC, Oct. 13, 1946. Hunter Col.
WILSON, ELIZABETH: Grand Rapids, Apr. 4, 1925.
WILSON, FLIP (Clerow Wilson): Jersey City, NJ, Dec. 8, 1933.
WILSON, LAMBERT: Paris, 1959.
WILSON, NANCY: Chillicothe, OH, Feb. 20, 1937.
WILSON, SCOTT: Atlanta, GA, 1942.
WINCOTT, JEFF: 1957; Toronto, Canada.
WINDE, BEATRICE: Chicago, Jan. 6.
WINDOM, WILLIAM: NYC, Sept. 28, 1923. Williams Col.
WINDSOR, MARIE (Emily Marie Bertelson): Marysvale, UT, Dec. 11, 1924. Brigham Young U.
WINFIELD, PAUL: Los Angeles, May 22, 1940. UCLA.
WINFREY, OPRAH: Kosciusko, MS, Jan. 29, 1954. TnStateU.
WINGER, DEBRA: Cleveland, OH, May 17, 1955. Cal State.
WINKLER, HENRY: NYC, Oct. 30, 1945. Yale.
WINN, KITTY: Wash., D.C., 1944. Boston U.
WINNINGHAM, MARE: Phoenix, AZ, May 6, 1959.
WINSLOW, MICHAEL: Spokane, WA, Sept. 6, 1960
WINTER, ALEX: London, July 17, 1965, NYU.
WINTERS, JONATHAN: Dayton, OH, Nov. 11, 1925. Kenyon Col.
WINTERS, SHELLEY (Shirley Schrift): St. Louis, Aug. 18, 1922. Wayne U.
WITHERS, GOOGIE: Karachi, India, Mar. 12, 1917. Italia Conti.
WITHERS, JANE: Atlanta, GA, Apr. 12, 1926.

WONG, B. D.: San Francisco, Oct. 24, 1962.
WONG, RUSSELL: Troy, NY, 1963, Santa Monica Col.
WOODARD, ALFRE: Tulsa, OK. Nov. 2, 1953, Boston U.
WOODLAWN, HOLLY (Harold Ajzenberg): Juana Diaz, PR, 1947.
WOODS, JAMES: Vernal, UT, Apr. 18, 1947. MIT.
WOODWARD, EDWARD: Croyden, Surrey, Eng., June 1, 1930.
WOODWARD, JOANNE: Thomasville, GA, Feb. 27, 1930. Neighborhood Playhouse.
WORONOV, MARY: Brooklyn, Dec. 8, 1946. Cornell.
WORTH, IRENE (Hattie Abrams): Nebraska, June 23, 1916, UCLA.
WRAY, FAY: Alberta, Can., Sept. 15, 1907.
WRIGHT, AMY: Chicago, Apr. 15, 1950.
WRIGHT, MAX: Detroit, MI, Aug. 2, 1943, WayneStateU.
WRIGHT, ROBIN: Texas, 1966.
WRIGHT, TERESA: NYC, Oct. 27, 1918.
WUHL, ROBERT: Union City, NJ, Oct. 9, 1951. UHouston.
WYATT, JANE: NYC, Aug. 10, 1910. Barnard College.
WYMAN, JANE (Sarah Jane Fulks): St. Joseph, MO, Jan. 4, 1914.
WYMORE, PATRICE: Miltonvale, KS, Dec. 17, 1926.
WYNN, MAY (Donna Lee Hickey): NYC, Jan. 8, 1930.
WYNTER, DANA (Dagmar): London, June 8, 1927. Rhodes U.
YORK, DICK: Fort Wayne, IN, Sept. 4, 1928. De Paul U.
YORK, MICHAEL: Fulmer, Eng., Mar. 27, 1942. Oxford.
YORK, SUSANNAH: London, Jan. 9, 1941. RADA.
YOUNG, ALAN (Angus): North Shield, Eng., Nov. 19, 1919.
YOUNG, BURT: Queens, NY, Apr. 30, 1940.
YOUNG, LORETTA (Gretchen): Salt Lake City, Jan. 6, 1912. Immaculate Heart College.
YOUNG, ROBERT: Chicago, Feb. 22, 1907.
YOUNG, SEAN: Louisville, KY, Nov. 20, 1959. Interlochen.
ZACHARIAS, ANN: Stockholm, Sw., 1956.
ZADORA, PIA: Hoboken, NJ. 1954.
ZAPPA, DWEEZIL: Hollywood, CA, 1970.
ZETTERLING, MAI: Sweden, May 27, 1925. Ordtuery Theatre School.
ZIMBALIST, EFREM, JR.: NYC, Nov. 30, 1918. Yale.
ZUNIGA, DAPHNE: 1963, Berkeley, CA. UCLA.

| Eve Arden | Pearl Bailey | Ina Balin | Joan Bennett | Capucine | Ian Charleson |

OBITUARIES

EVE ARDEN (Eunice Quedens), 82, California-born screen, stage, TV and radio actress died on Nov. 12, 1990 in Los Angeles of heart failure. One of the movies' most welcome and adept supporting players, she specialized in wisecracking sidekicks, receiving an Academy Award nomination for her role in *Mildred Pierce* in 1945. Following her 1929 debut in *Song of Love* she appeared in such films as *Dancing Lady, Oh Doctor, Stage Door, Having Wonderful Time, At the Circus, Comrade X, Ziegfeld Girl, That Uncertain Feeling, Whistling in the Dark, Let's Face It, Cover Girl, The Doughgirls, Night and Day, My Reputation, The Voice of the Turtle, One Touch of Venus, The Lady Takes a Sailor, Paid in Full, Curtain Call at Cactus Creek, Tea for Two, Three Husbands, We're Not Married, The Lady Wants Mink, Our Miss Brooks, Anatomy of a Murder, The Dark at the Top of the Stairs, Sergeant Deadhead, Grease, Under the Rainbow,* and *Grease 2.* She had a tremendous success starring in radio and on television in the long running series *Our Miss Brooks* for which she won an Emmy. She is survived by 2 sons and 2 daughters.

CHARLES ARNT, 83, Indiana-born screen, stage and TV character actor died on Aug. 6, 1990 of pancreatic and liver cancer at his home on Orcas Island, WA. His numerous films include *Ladies Should Listen, Remember the Night, Blossoms in the Dust, My Gal Sal, Up in Arms, Take a Letter Darling, Miss Susie Slagle's, Dangerous Intruder, My Favorite Brunette, Sitting Pretty* (1948), *Wabash Avenue, Miracle of the Hills, Wild in the Country,* and *Sweet Bird of Youth.* He is survived by his wife, two sons, and a daughter.

PEARL BAILEY, 72, Virginia-born screen, stage, and TV singer-actress, whose unique casual singing style made her one of America's most beloved entertainers, died on Aug. 17, 1990 in Philadelphia after collapsing at a local hotel. She had a long history of heart ailments. After her 1947 film debut in *Variety Girl,* she subsequently appeared in *Isn't It Romantic?, Carmen Jones, That Certain Feeling, St. Louis Blues, Porgy and Bess, All the Fine Young Cannibals, The Landlord, Norman . . . Is That You?,* and *The Fox and the Hound* (as the voice of the Owl, Big Mama). She is survived by her husband, drummer Louis Bellson Jr., two children, and two sisters.

KATHARINE BALFOUR, 69, New York City-born screen, stage, radio, and TV actress and writer, died on Apr. 3, 1990 of amyotrophic lateral sclerosis at her Manhattan home. She appeared in such films as *America America, The Adventurers, Love Story* (as Ryan O'Neal's mother), and *Teachers.* She is survived by a daughter and a brother.

INA BALIN, 52, Brooklyn-born screen, stage and TV actress, who helped evacuate hundreds of Vietnamese orphans at the end of the Vietnam War, died on June 20, 1990 in New Haven, CT, of pulmonary hypertension. Her films include *The Black Orchid* (debut, 1959), *From the Terrace, The Comancheros, The Young Doctors, The Patsy, Act of Reprisal, The Greatest Story Ever Told, The Desperate Mission, Charro!, The Don Is Dead,* and *The Projectionist.* She is survived by her father, three daughters, and a brother.

BARBARA BAXLEY, 63, California-born screen, stage and TV actress was found dead in her New York apartment on June 7, 1990 of an apparent heart attack. Her movies include *East of Eden, The Savage Eye, All Fall Down, Countdown, No Way to Treat a Lady, Nashville,* and *Norma Rae.* No reported survivors.

MADGE BELLAMY, 92, Texas-born silent screen actress died on Jan. 24, 1990 in Upland, CA, of heart failure. Her many films include *The Cup of Life, Hail the Woman, The Call of the North, Love Never Dies, The Hottentot, Lorna Doone, Garrison's Finish, His Forgotten Wife, The Iron Horse, Love and Glory, A Fool and His Money, The Man in Blue, The Telephone Girl, Thunder Mountain, Lazybones, Black Paradise, Colleen, The Play Girl, Mother Knows Best, Fugitives,* and such talking pictures as *Tonight at Twelve, White Zombie,* and *The Daring Young Man.* No survivors.

JILL BENNETT, 59, British screen, stage and TV actress died on Oct. 4, 1990 in London of undisclosed causes. Her movies include *Moulin Rouge, Hell Below Zero, Lust for Life, The Skull, The Nanny, Inadmissible Evidence, The Charge of the Light Brigade* (1968), *Julius Caesar* (1971), *I Want What I Want, Mr. Quilp, For Your Eyes Only, Britannia Hospital, Lady Jane, Hawks,* and her last, *The Sheltering Sky,* in 1990. No reported survivors.

JOAN BENNETT, 80, New Jersey-born screen, stage and TV actress, a popular star during the 1930s and 40s who appeared in over 70 films, died on December 7, 1990 of cardiac arrest at her home in Scarsdale, NY. Her movies include *Bulldog Drummond, Three Live Ghosts, Disraeli, Puttin' on the Ritz, Little Women* (1933), *The Pursuit of Happiness, Private Worlds, Mississippi, Two for Tonight, The Man Who Broke the Bank at Monte Carlo, 13 Hours by Air, Big Brown Eyes, Wedding Present, The Texans, Trade Winds, The House across the Bay, The Man I Married, Man Hunt, The Wife Takes a Flyer, Margin for Error, Woman in the Window, Nob Hill, Scarlet Street, The Macomber Affair, Woman on the Beach, The Reckless Moment, Father of the Bride, For Heaven's Sake, Father's Little Dividend, We're No Angels* (1955), *There's Always Tomorrow,* and *House of Dark Shadows.* She was the sister of actresses Barbara (who died in 1958) and Constance Bennett (who died in 1965). She is survived by her fourth husband, David Wilde, four daughters from previous marriages, and 13 grandchildren.

HERBERT BERGHOF, 81, actor, teacher, and co-founder with his wife Uta Hagen, of HB Studio in New York, died on Nov. 5, 1990 in New York of heart failure. He acted in such films as *Five Fingers, Cleopatra, Harry and Tonto, Those Lips Those Eyes, Times Square,* and *Target.* He is survived by his wife and stepdaughter.

LEONARD BERNSTEIN, 72, Massachusetts-born musician, conductor, and composer, one of the great artists of the music world, died on Oct. 14, 1990 at his Manhattan home of a heart attack caused by progressive lung failure. He received an Academy Award nomination for scoring the 1954 film *On the Waterfront,* while two of his Broadway musicals *On the Town* and *West Side Story,* were successfully adapted into motion pictures. He is survived by two daughters, a son, his mother, a sister, and a brother.

EDWARD BINNS, 74, Philadelphia-born screen, stage and TV character actor, died December 4, 1990 of a heart attack in Brewster, NY, while enroute to his Connecticut home. His films include *Teresa, 12 Angry Men, Compulsion, North by Northwest, Judgment at Nuremberg, The Americanization of Emily, Fail Safe, Patton, Lovin' Molly, Night Moves, Oliver's Story,* and *The Verdict.* He is survived by his wife, actress Elizabeth Franz, three daughters, and a brother.

HENRY BRANDON (Henry Kleinbach), 77, Berlin-born screen, stage and TV actor, perhaps best known for playing the villainous Silas Barnaby in Laurel & Hardy's *Babes in Toyland,* died on Feb. 15, 1990 in Los Angeles of an apparent heart attack. His more than 75 films include *The Garden of Allah, Black Legion, If I Were King, Three Comrades, Spawn of the North, Beau Geste* (1939), *The Paleface, Joan* of Arc, Wake of the Red Witch, The War of the Worlds, The Caddy, The Ten Commandments (1956), The Searchers, Auntie Mame, Two Rode Together, Assault on Precinct 13 and To Be Or Not To Be (1983). He is survived by a brother and a sister.

KARL BROWN, 93, Pennsylvania-born cinematographer, writer and director, died on Mar. 25, 1990 in Woodland Hills, CA, of kidney failure. He served as a cameraman on The Birth of a Nation, photographed such features as The Fourteenth Man, The Covered Wagon, Merton of the Movies (1924), Pony Express (1925), and Ruggles of Red Gap (1923), directed Stark Love and Prince of Diamonds among others. His writing credits include The Mississippi Gambler, Military Academy, One in a Million, Tarzan Escapes, and The Man With Nine Lives. No survivors.

TOM BROWN, 77, screen and TV actor died on June 3, 1990 of cancer in Woodland Hills, CA. He appeared on the long-running TV series Gunsmoke, and his film career, which began in the silent era, included appearances in The Hoosier Schoolmaster, Queen High, Tom Brown of Culver, Three Cornered Moon, Judge Priest, Anne of Green Gables, Freckles, Maytime, In Old Chicago, Navy Blue & Gold, House on 92nd Street, Buck Privates Come Home, and The Quiet Gun. He is survived by two sons, a daughter, and five grandchildren.

CAPUCINE (Germaine Lefebvre), 57, France-born international film actress of the 1960's, died on March 17, 1990 in Lausanne, Switzerland after jumping from the window of her eighth-floor apartment. Her movies include Song without End, North to Alaska, Walk on the Wild Side, The Lion, The Pink Panther, The Seventh Dawn, What's New Pussycat?, The Honey Pot, The Queens, Fraulein Doktor, Fellini Satyricon, Red Sun, Trail of the Pink Panther, and Curse of the Pink Panther. No reported survivors.

BARBARA CASON, 61, Memphis-born screen, stage and TV actress died on June 18, 1990 of a heart attack at her home in the Hollywood Hills area of Los Angeles. She appeared in such movies as The Honeymoon Killers, Cold Turkey, and Exorcist II: The Heretic, and was a regular on such TV series as Carter Country, New Temperature's Rising, and It's Garry Shandling's Show. She is survived by her husband, actor Dennis Patrick.

IAN CHARLESON, 40, British screen, stage and TV actor, best known for his role as the Scottish Olympic runner, Eric Liddell, in the Oscar winning film Chariots of Fire, died on Jan. 6, 1990 of AIDS at his home in London. His other movies are Gandhi, Greystoke: The Legend of Tarzan Lord of the Apes, Car Trouble, and Opera. He is survived by his parents, two brothers, and a sister.

RODERICK COOK, 58, British screen, stage and TV actor, died on Aug. 17, 1990 in Los Angeles of an apparent heart attack. He was perhaps best known for his stage revue Oh Coward!, and had small roles in such films as The Great Waldo Pepper, Girlfriends, Garbo Talks, Amadeus, and 9½ Weeks. He is survived by his stepfather.

AARON COPLAND, 90, noted American composer died on Dec. 2, 1990 in North Tarrytown, NY, of complications from strokes and respiratory problems. In addition to his compositions for ballet and opera he wrote the scores to such films as Of Mice and Men, Our Town, The North Star, The Red Pony, and The Heiress, for which he received an Academy Award in 1949. No reported survivors.

XAVIER CUGAT, 90, Spanish bandleader who helped to popularize the rumba in America, died on Oct. 27, 1990 in Barcelona of heart failure. He appeared in such movies as You Were Never Lovelier, Two Girls and a Sailor, Stage Door Canteen, Weekend at the Waldorf, Holiday in Mexico, This Time for Keeps, A Date with Judy, Neptune's Daughter, Chicago Syndicate, and The Phynx. He is survived by a brother.

ROBERT CUMMINGS, 82, Missouri-born screen, stage and TV actor, a major film star of the 1930s and 40s who later had a successful career as the star of various television sitcoms, died on Dec. 2, 1990 of kidney failure and complications from pneumonia at the Motion Picture and Television Hospital in Woodland Hills, CA. He had suffered from Parkinson's disease. His many movies include So Red the Rose, Border Flight, Hollywood Boulevard, The Accusing Finger, Last Train from Madrid, Souls at Sea, Wells Fargo, College Swing, You and Me, The Texan, Three Smart Girls Grow Up, The Under-Pup, Everthing Happens at Night, Private Affairs, One Night in the Tropics, Moon over Miami, The Devil and Miss Jones, It Started with Eve, Kings Row, Saboteur, Forever and a Day, Princess O'Rourke, Flesh and Fantasy, You Came Along, The Bride Wore Boots, The Lost Moment, Sleep My Love, The Accused (1949), Reign of Terror, Paid in Full, For Heaven's Sake, Marry Me Again, Lucky Me, Dial M for Murder, How to Be Very Very Popular, My Geisha, Beach Party, What a Way to Go!, The Carpetbaggers, Promise Her Anything, Stagecoach, and Five Golden

Dragons. He is survived by his fifth wife, seven children, and nine grandchildren.

SAMMY DAVIS, JR., 64, New York City-born screen, stage and TV actor, dancer and singer, one of America's most versatile and best loved entertainers, died on May 16, 1990 at his home in Beverly Hills of throat cancer. He began in vaudeville as a child performer and by the 1950's became one of the first black entertainers to break down racial barriers and obtain wide acceptance in show business. His film appearances include The Benny Goodman Story, Anna Lucasta (1958), Porgy and Bess, Ocean's 11, Pepe, Sergeants 3, Convicts 4, Johnny Cool, Threepenny Opera (1963), Robin and the 7 Hoods, Nightmare in the Sun, A Man Called Adam, Salt and Pepper, Sweet Charity, One More Time, The Cannonball Run, Moon over Parador, and Tap. He is survived by his wife, his mother, a sister, a daughter, two sons, and two grandchildren.

JOSE DE VEGA, JR., 56, San Diego-born screen, stage and TV actor and dancer, who played Chino in the Broadway and 1961 film versions of West Side Story, died on April 8, 1990, in Westwood, CA, of AIDS. His other films include Blue Hawaii, The Spiral Road, A Covenant with Death, and Ash Wednesday. He is survived by his mother and a sister.

JACQUES DEMY, 59, French film director, best known for his 1963 musical The Umbrellas of Cherbourg, died on Oct. 27, 1990 in Paris of a brain hemorrhage brought on by leukemia. His other movies include Lola, La Baie Des Anges, The Young Girls of Rochefort, The Model Shop, The Pied Piper, The Slightly Pregnant Man, and A Room in Town. He is survived by his wife, director Agnes Varda, a son, Mathieu, who is an actor, and a daughter.

FABIA DRAKE, 86, British screen, stage and TV actress died on Feb. 28, 1990 in London. Her film credits include Meet Mr. Penny, All over the Town, Young Wives' Tale, Fast and Loose, The Good Companions, and Valmont. No reported survivors.

HOWARD DUFF, 76, Washington-born screen, stage, TV and radio character actor, died on July 8, 1990 in Santa Barbara, CA, of a heart attack. His films include Brute Force, The Naked City, All My Sons, Woman in Hiding, Shakedown (1950), The Lady from Texas, Roar of the Crowd, The Yellow Mountain, Tanganyika, Flame of the Islands, Women's Prison, While the City Sleeps, Boys' Night Out, The Late Show, A Wedding, Kramer vs. Kramer, Oh God! Book II, No Way Out (1987), and Too Much Sun. He is survived by his wife, brother, and a daughter by his marriage to actress Ida Lupino.

IRENE DUNNE (Irene Marie Dunn), 91, Kentucky-born screen and stage actress, one of the top stars of the 1930s and '40s, equally adept at comedy, drama and music, died on September 4, 1990 of heart failure at her home in the Holmby Hills section of Los Angeles. She received Academy Award nominations for her performances in Cimarron, Theodora Goes Wild, The Awful Truth, Love Affair, and I Remember Mama. Her many other films include Leathernecking (her debut in 1930), Symphony of Six Million, Back Street (1932), No Other Woman, Ann Vickers, If I Were Free, Stingaree, Age of Innocence, Roberta, Magnificent Obsession (1935), Show Boat (1936), High Wide and Handsome, Joy of Living, Invitation to Happiness, When Tomorrow Comes, My Favorite Wife, Penny Serenade, A Guy Named Joe, The White Cliffs of Dover, Over 21, Anna and the King of Siam, Life With Father, Never a Dull Moment (1950), The Mudlark, and her last, It Grows on Trees, in 1952. She was later named alternate delegate to the United Nations 12th General Assembly and was awarded the Kennedy Center Honor for the Performing Arts in 1985. She is survived by her daughter and two grandchildren.

HELEN JEROME EDDY, 92, silent screen actress who began her career in 1915 died on Jan. 27, 1990 in Alhambra, CA. Her many silent movie appearances include Rebecca of Sunnybrook Farm, The First Born, The Flirt, To the Ladies, The Dark Angel (1925), Quality Street (1927), and 13 Washington Square. She had many small parts in such talking pictures as The Divine Lady, The Bitter Tea of General Yen, Mr. Deeds Goes to Town, Winterset, and Strike Up the Band, her last film, in 1940. No reported survivors.

RENE ENRIQUEZ, 58, San Francisco-born screen, stage and television character actor, who appeared on the TV series Hill Street Blues, died on March 23, 1990 in Tarzana, CA of pancreatic cancer. His films include Bananas, Serpico, Harry and Tonto, and Under Fire. He is survived by two sisters and a brother.

JILL ESMOND, 82, British screen, and stage actress, died on July 28, 1990 in Wimbledon, England. Her films include No Funny Business, Once a Lady, Ladies of the Jury, The Bandit of Sherwood Forest, This Above All, Journey for Margaret, Casanova Brown, Escape, Night People, and A Man Called Peter. She is survived by a son from her marriage to Laurence Olivier, which lasted from 1930 to 1940.

| Robert Cummings | Sammy Davis, Jr. | Howard Duff | Irene Dunne | Charles Farrell | Greta Garbo |

ALDO FABRIZI, 85, Italian screen and stage comedian, actor and director died on April 2, 1990 in Rome of heart failure. He was best known to foreign audiences for his role in Roberto Rossellini's *Open City*. His other films include *Avanti C'e Posto, To Live in Peace, The Flowers of St. Francis, I Vitelloni, Three Steps North, Cops and Thieves, Emigrants, The Passaguai Family,* and *We All Loved Each Other So Much.* He is survived by his son and daughter.

CHARLES FARRELL, 89, Massachusetts-born screen and TV actor, best known for his many roles opposite Janet Gaynor, died on May 6, 1990 in Palm Springs, CA, of cardiac arrest. With Gaynor he appeared in the movies *Seventh Heaven, Street Angel, Lucky Star, Sunny Side Up, Happy Days, High Society Blues, The Man Who Came Back, Tess of the Storm Country, Merely Mary Ann, Delicious, The First Year,* and *Change of Heart;* other films include *Wings of Youth, Liliom,* and *Fighting Youth.* In the 1950's he co-starred in the television series *My Little Margie.* No reported survivors.

JACK FLETCHER, 68, screen, stage and TV character actor, died on Feb 15, 1990 of heart failure while auditioning for a commercial in Los Angeles. His films include *Any Wednesday, The Tiger Makes Out, Rabbit Test,* and *Pennies From Heaven* (1981). No reported survivors.

JOEL FLUELLEN, 82, Louisiana-born screen and TV character actor, who, in the 1940's, fought for better treatment of blacks in Hollywood, was found dead on Feb. 2, 1990 in his Los Angeles home of an apparent self-inflicted gunshot wound. His films include *The Jackie Robinson Story, Friendly Persuasion, Run Silent Run Deep, The Chase* and *The Learning Tree.* No reported survivors.

VALERIE FRENCH, 59, London-born screen, stage and TV actress died on Nov. 3, 1990 in New York of leukemia. Her films include *The Constant Husband, Jubal, The Garment Jungle, Decision at Sundown, The Four Skulls of Jonathan Drake,* and *Shalako.* No reported survivors.

GRETA GARBO (Greta Louisa Gustafsson), 84, Stockholm-born screen actress, the epitome of the glamorous Hollywood star of the 1930's, died on April 15, 1990 in New York City of cardiac arrest. Her early retirement at the height of her career in 1941, along with her reclusive nature, only added to her legendary stature. She received Academy Award nominations for her performances in *Anna Christie, Romance, Camille,* and *Ninotchka,* and was awarded a special "Oscar" in 1955. Her other films include *Peter the Tramp, The Story of Gosta Berling, The Street of Sorrow, The Torrent, The Temptress, Flesh and the Devil, Love, The Divine Woman, The Mysterious Lady, A Woman of Affairs, Wild Orchids, The Single Standard, The Kiss, A Man's Man, Inspiration, Susan Lenox—Her Fall and Rise, Mata Hari, Grand Hotel, As You Desire Me, Queen Christina, The Painted Veil, Anna Karenina, Conquest,* and *Two-Faced Woman.* A niece survives.

AVA GARDNER, 67, North Carolina-born screen and TV actress who became one of Hollywood's most popular stars of the 1940's and '50's died on Jan. 25, 1990 of pneumonia at her home in London. Known at first for her great beauty and sex appeal she later widened her range as an actress, winning an Academy Award nomination for her role in *Mogambo.* Her many other films include *We Were Dancing* (her debut in 1942), *Du Barry Was a Lady, The Killers* (1946), *The Hucksters, One Touch of Venus, The Great Sinner, The Bribe, Show Boat* (1951), *Pandora and the Flying Dutchman, Lone Star, The Snows of Kilimanjaro, Knights of the Round Table, The Barefoot Contessa, Bhowani Junction, The Little Hut, The Sun Also Rises, On the Beach, 55 Days at Peking, Seven Days in May, The Night of the Iguana, The Bible, The Life and Times of Judge Roy Bean,* and *The Cassandra Crossing.* She is survived by two sisters.

JACK GILFORD (Jacob Gellman), 81, New York City-born screen, stage and TV actor, one of the most recognizable character players, died on June 4, 1990 of stomach cancer in New York. His films include *Hey Rookie, Mister Buddwing, A Funny Thing Happened on the Way to the Forum* (repeating his stage role), *Enter Laughing, Who's Minding the*

Mint?, The Incident, Catch-22, They Might Be Giants, Save the Tiger (for which he received an Academy Award nomination), *Harry and Walter Go to New York, Wholly Moses!, Caveman,* and *Cocoon.* He is survived by his wife, a daughter, and two sons.

PAULETTE GODDARD, 84, New York-born screen, stage and TV actress, a top female star of the 1940's, died on April 23, 1990 at her villa in Ronco, Switzerland of heart failure. She began by playing small parts in such features as *The Kid from Spain, City Streets,* and *Roman Scandals,* before coming to prominence in *Modern Times,* and *The Great Dictator,* co-starring with her then-husband, Charlie Chaplin. Her many other films include *The Women, The Cat and the Canary, The Ghost Breakers, Northwest Mounted Police, Second Chorus, Pot o' Gold, Nothing But the Truth, Hold Back the Dawn, Reap the Wild Wind, The Forest Rangers, So Proudly We Hail!* (for which she received an Academy Award nomination), *Standing Room Only, I Love a Soldier, Kitty, Diary of a Chambermaid, Suddenly It's Spring, Unconquered, On Our Merry Way, Bride of Vengeance, Babes in Bagdad, Paris Model,* and *Time of Indifference.* No reported survivors.

DEXTER GORDON, 67, noted jazz saxophonist who received an Academy Award nomination for his starring role in the 1986 film *'Round Midnight,* died on April 25, 1990 in Philadelphia of kidney failure. His only other movie appearances were in *Unchained* and *Awakenings.* He is survived by his wife, two daughters and three sons.

ALAN HALE JR., 71, Los Angeles-born screen and TV actor, who played the Skipper on the television series *Gilligan's Island,* died on Jan. 2, 1990 in Los Angeles of cancer of the thymus. Son of the popular 40's character actor, he appeared in such films as *I Wanted Wings, Dive Bomber!, Wake Island, To the Shores of Tripoli, Eagle Squadron, Watch on the Rhine, The Gunfighter, Young at Heart, The Indian Fighter, Many Rivers to Cross, The Sea Chase, Hang 'Em High, There Was a Crooked Man, The North Avenue Irregulars,* and *Johnny Dangerously.* He is survived by his wife, three sons, a daughter, and a sister.

ROBIN HARRIS, 36, Chicago-born stand-up comic-turned-film actor, died in his sleep on March 18, 1990 in Chicago where he had been performing at the Regal Theatre. He appeared in the movies *I'm Gonna Git You Sucka, Do the Right Thing, Harlem Nights, House Party,* and *Mo' Better Blues.* He is survived by his wife, son, parents, a brother and a sister.

SIR REX HARRISON (Reginald Carey Harrison), 82, British screen, stage and TV actor, whose urbane wit and style made him one of the screen's great sophisticated performers, died on June 2, 1990 of pancreatic cancer at his Manhattan home. He is best known for playing Prof. Henry Higgins in the classic Broadway musical *My Fair Lady.* He won an Academy Award for Best Actor for repeating the role in the 1964 Oscar-winning film version of the show. His other movies include *School for Scandal, Storm in a Teacup, St. Martin's Lane (Sidewalks of London), The Citadel, Night Train to Munich, Major Barbara, Blithe Spirit, The Notorious Gentleman (The Rake's Progress), Anna and the King of Siam, The Ghost and Mrs. Muir, The Foxes of Harrow, Unfaithfully Yours, The Fourposter, King Richard and the Crusaders, The Constant Husband, The Reluctant Debutante, Midnight Lace, The Happy Thieves, Cleopatra* (Academy Award nomination), *The Yellow Rolls Royce, The Agony and the Ecstasy, The Honey Pot, Doctor Dolittle, A Flea in Her Ear, Staircase,* and *Crossed Swords.* He is survived by his sixth wife, and two sons, one of whom, Noel, is an actor.

JIM HENSON, 53, Mississippi-born puppeteer, producer, director, and performer, whose Muppet characters delighted TV and movie audiences, died on May 16, 1990 at New York Hospital in Manhattan from streptococcus pneumonia. For the television shows *Sesame Street* and *The Muppet Show* he created such memorable puppet characters as Miss Piggy, Big Bird, Fozzie, the Cookie Monster, and most im-

Ava
Gardner

Jack
Gilford

Paulette
Goddard

Dexter
Gordon

Rex
Harrison

Jim
Henson

portantly, Kermit the Frog, for whom he supplied the voice. In 1965 he received an Academy Award nomination for the short subject *Timepiece*. His feature film credits are: *The Muppet Movie* (producer and character performer), *The Great Muppet Caper* (director and character performer), *The Dark Crystal* (co-director, story, and character performer), *The Muppets Take Manhattan* (executive producer and character performer), *Into the Night* (cameo), *Sesame Street Presents Follow That Bird* (character performer), *Labyrinth* (director and story), and *The Witches* (executive producer). His Creature Workshop supplied characters for the films *Dream Child, The Bear,* and *Teenage Mutant Ninja Turtles.* He is survived by his wife, three daughters and two sons.

TIM HOVEY, 44, former screen and TV child actor, died on Sept. 9, 1989 at his home in Watsonville, CA, of a drug overdose. He appeared in such movies as *The Private War of Major Benson; Toy Tiger; Everything But the Truth; Man Afraid;* and *Money, Women and Guns.* He is survived by his wife, parents and a brother.

JILL IRELAND, 54, British screen and TV actress, died on May 18, 1990 at her home in Malibu, CA, after a long battle with cancer. She appeared opposite husband Charles Bronson in 15 movies including *Someone behind the Door, The Valachi Papers, Hard Times, Breakout, From Noon Till Three, Breakheart Pass, Love and Bullets,* and *Assassination.* Other films include *Oh Rosalinda!, Three Men in a Boat, Hell Drivers,* and *So Evil So Young.* She is survived by Bronson, her parents, and six children.

GORDON JACKSON, 66, Scotland-born screen, stage and TV actor, died on Jan. 14, 1990 in London after a short illness. Best known for his continuing role in the TV series *Upstairs Downstairs,* he appeared in some 60 films including *Whisky Galore (Tight Little Island), Tunes of Glory, The Great Escape, The Ipcress File, Cast a Giant Shadow, The Prime of Miss Jean Brodie, Run Wild Run Free,* and *The Whistle Blower.* He is survived by his wife and two sons.

JESSICA JAMES, 60, Los Angeles-born screen, stage and TV actress, best known for her long-running appearance in the Broadway hit *Gemini,* died on May 7, 1990 at her Los Angeles home of breast cancer. She appeared in such films as *Hook Line and Sinker, So Fine, Soup for One, Diner, I the Jury, Spring Break, Easy Money, Power, Alien Nation, Illegally Yours, Immediate Family,* and *The Lemon Sisters.* She is survived by a daughter, a son, and two grandchildren.

GABRIEL KATZKA, 58, screen, stage and TV producer died on Feb. 19, 1990 in Los Angeles of a heart attack. His movie credits include *Marlowe, Kelly's Heroes, The Parallax View, The Heartbreak Kid, The Taking of Pelham 1-2-3, Sleuth, A Bridge Too Far, The Falcon and the Snowman,* and *The Lords of Discipline.* He is survived by his wife, son and sister.

ARTHUR KENNEDY, 75, Massachusetts-born screen, stage and TV actor, who starred in over 70 films in a career spanning nearly fifty years, died on Jan. 5, 1990 in Branford, CT, of a brain tumor. He received Academy Award nominations for his work in *Champion, Bright Victory, Trial, Peyton Place,* and *Some Came Running.* His other films include *City for Conquest* (debut, 1940), *High Sierra, They Died with Their Boots On, Air Force, Boomerang!, The Window, Chicago Deadline, Rancho Notorious, The Glass Menagerie* (1950), *The Man From Laramie, The Desperate Hours, Bend of the River, Twilight for the Gods, A Summer Place, Murder She Said, Barabbas, Lawrence of Arabia, Cheyenne Autumn, Nevada Smith, Hail Hero, The Sentinel,* and *Signs of Life.* He is survived by his daughter Laurie, an actress.

MARGARET LOCKWOOD (Margaret Day), 73, Pakistan-born British screen, stage and TV actress who was one of Great Britain's leading stars during the 1930s and 40s, died on July 15, 1990 in London of undisclosed causes. She is probably best remembered by American audiences for her leading role in Alfred Hitchcock's *The Lady Vanishes.*

Her many other films include *Lorna Doone, The Amateur Gentleman, The Beloved Vagabond, Dr. Syn, The Stars Look Down, Susannah of the Mounties, Rulers of the Sea, Night Train to Munich, Quiet Wedding, Alibi, The Man in Grey, Dear Octopus, Love Story* (1944), *A Place of One's Own, I'll Be Your Sweetheart, The Wicked Lady* (1945), *Hungry Hill, The White Unicorn, Cardboard Cavalier, Highly Dangerous, Trent's Last Case, Trouble in the Glen, Cast a Dark Shadow,* and *The Slipper and the Rose.* She is survived by her daughter, Julia, also an actress.

KEN LYNCH, 79, screen, TV and radio character actor, died on Feb. 13, 1990 in Burbank, CA, of a virus. His many films include *Anatomy of a Murder, The Honeymoon Machine, Days of Wine and Roses, Walk on the Wild Side, Dead Ringer, Dear Heart, Mister Buddwing, Hotel,* and *P.J.* He is survived by two daughters and a son.

DOROTHY MACKAILL, 87, England-born screen, stage and TV actress, died on Aug. 12, 1990 of kidney failure in Honolulu, HI. She made her film debut in *The Face at the Window* in 1920, followed by such films as *The Lotus Eater, The Streets of New York, The Bridge of Sighs, Joanna, Lady Be Good, The Man Who Came Back, The Barker, Bright Lights, The Love Racket, Curtain at Eight, Cheaters,* and her last, *Bulldog Drummond at Bay,* in 1937. No reported survivors.

MARY MARTIN, 76, Texas-born screen, stage and TV actress, one of the leading stars of the Broadway theatre, died of cancer on Nov. 4, 1990 in Rancho Mirage, CA. Her New York stage successes include such musicals as *South Pacific, Peter Pan,* and *The Sound of Music.* She also appeared in the movies *The Great Victor Herbert, Rhythm on the River, Love Thy Neighbor, Kiss the Boys Goodbye, New York Town, Birth of the Blues, Star Spangled Rhythm, Happy Go Lucky, True to Life, Night and Day,* and *Main Street to Broadway.* She is survived by a son from her first marriage, actor Larry Hagman, and a daughter.

MIKE MAZURKI (Michail Mazuruski), 82, Austria-born wrestler-turned-actor who appeared in tough-guy roles in over 100 films died on Dec. 9, 1990 in Glendale, CA, of undisclosed causes, following years of failing health. His movies include *Black Fury, Mission to Moscow, Behind the Rising Sun, Murder My Sweet, The Canterville Ghost, Abbott & Costello in Hollywood, Dick Tracy* (1945), *The Horn Blows at Midnight, The Spanish Main, Mysterious Intruder, Sinbad the Sailor, I Walk Alone, Nightmare Alley, Unconquered, Come to the Stable, Neptune's Daughter, Rope of Sand, Samson and Delilah, The Egyptian, Blood Alley, Kismet* (1955), *Around the World in 80 Days, The Buccaneer* (1958), *Alias Jesse James, Some Like It Hot, Pocketful of Miracles, Five Weeks in a Balloon, Four for Texas, It's a Mad Mad Mad Mad World, Cheyenne Autumn, Won Ton Ton the Dog Who Saved Hollywood, Amazon Women on the Moon,* and *Dick Tracy* (1990). He is survived by his wife and 2 daughters.

JOEL McCREA, 84, South Pasadena-born screen and TV actor, a leading actor of the 1930's and 40's who later specialized in Western roles, died on Oct. 20, 1990 of pulmonary complications in Woodland Hills, CA. Following early work as an extra, stunt man and bit player he appeared in such movies as *The Silver Horde, Lightnin', Girls about Town, Bird of Paradise, The Most Dangerous Game, Rockabye, One Man's Journey, Half a Sinner, Private Worlds, Our Little Girl, Barbary Coast, These Three, Adventure in Manhattan, Come and Get It, Interns Can't Take Money, Wells Fargo, Dead End, Three Blind Mice, Union Pacific, They Shall Have Music, He Married His Wife, The Primrose Path, Foreign Correspondent, Reaching for the Sun, Sullivan's Travels, The Great Man's Lady, The Palm Beach Story, The More the Merrier, Buffalo Bill, The Great Moment, The Unseen, The Virginian* (1946), *Ramrod, South of St. Louis, Colorado Territory, Stars in My Crown, Frenchie, Cattle Drive, Stranger on Horseback, Wichita, Trooper Hook, Gunfight at Dodge City, Ride the High Country,* and *Mustang Country.* He is survived by his wife of 57 years, actress Frances Dee, and three sons, one of whom, Jody, had also been an actor.

| Jill Ireland | Arthur Kennedy | Margaret Lockwood | Mary Martin | Joel McCrea | Gary Merrill |

GARY MERRILL, 74, Hartford, CT.-born screen, stage, radio and TV actor died on March 5, 1990 of lung cancer at his home in Falmouth, ME. His most notable film appearance was in *All About Eve* opposite Bette Davis, to whom he was married for ten years. His other movies include *Winged Victor, Slattery's Hurricane, Twelve O'Clock High, Decision Before Dawn, Another Man's Poison, Phone Call from a Stranger, Night without Sleep, The Human Jungle, The Wonderful Country, The Great Imposter, The Pleasure of His Company, Mysterious Island, A Girl Named Tamiko, Cast a Giant Shadow, Around the World under the Sea, The Incident, Clambake, The Last Challenge, Huckleberry Finn,* and *Thieves.* He is survived by a son, a daughter, a brother, and two grandchildren.

JACKIE MORAN (John E. Moran), 65, Chicago-born child actor who played Huckleberry Finn in the 1938 version of *The Adventures of Tom Sawyer,* died on Sept. 20, 1990 in Greenfield, MA, of cancer. His many other films include *Valiant Is the Word for Carrie, Mad about Music, And So They Were Married, Gone with the Wind, Meet Mr. Christian, Song of the Open Road, Since You Went Away,* and his last, *Betty Co-Ed,* in 1947. No reported survivors.

LOIS MORAN (Young), 81, Pittsburgh-born screen, stage and TV actress, died on July 13, 1990 in Sedona, AZ, of cancer. Her most notable role was in the silent version of *Stella Dallas.* Other films include *The Reckless Lady, The Road to Mandalay, God Gave Me Twenty Cents, The Music Master, The Irresistible Lover,* and *Transatlantic.* She had not appeared in a film since the 1930's. Her son survives.

JANE NOVAK, 94, St. Louis-born silent screen actress, who made her first film in 1913, died on Feb. 6, 1990 in Woodland Hills, CA of complications caused by a stroke. Her movies include *The Scarlet Sin, The Tiger Man, Behind the Door, The Nine O'Clock Town, Road of Destiny, The Blackguard,* and such sound features as *Hollywood Boulevard, Desert Fury* and *The File on Thelma Jordan.* She is survived by her daughter.

SUSAN OLIVER, 61, New York City-born screen, stage and TV actress, died of cancer on May 10, 1990 in Woodland Hills, CA. Her films include *The Green-Eyed Blonde, Up Periscope, Butterfield 8, The Gene Krupa Story, The Disorderly Orderly, Your Cheatin' Heart, A Man Called Gannon, Looking for Love,* and *Change of Mind.* She is survived by three half-brothers.

HERMES PAN (Panagiotopolous), 80, Memphis-born dancer and choreographer, best known for his many collaborations with Fred Astaire, died on Sept. 19, 1990 at his home in Beverly Hills, CA, of an apparent stroke. He staged dances for all ten of the Astaire-Ginger Rogers films, from *Flying Down to Rio* through *The Barkleys of Broadway,* and other Astaire musicals such as *A Damsel in Distress* (for which he received an Academy Award), *Blue Skies,* and *Silk Stockings.* In addition to his many other choreographic credits he appeared in *Moon over Miami, My Gal Sal, Sweet Rosie O'Grady,* and *Pin Up Girl* among others. In 1980 he received the National Film Award for achievement in cinema. He is survived by a sister, four nieces, and a nephew.

MICHAEL POWELL, 84, British film director, producer and writer whose collaboration with Emeric Pressburger created some of Great Britain's most notable and influential movies of the 1940's, died on Feb. 19, 1990 of cancer in Avening, Gloucestershire, England. His credits include *The Thief of Bagdad* (1940), *The 49th Parallel (The Invaders), One of Our Aircraft Is Missing, The Life and Death of Colonel Blimp, A Canterbury Tale, I Know Where I'm Going, A Matter of Life and Death (Stairway to Heaven), Black Narcissus, The Red Shoes, The Small Back Room (Hour of Glory), The Elusive Pimpernel, Tales of Hoffman, Oh Rosalinda,* and *Peeping Tom.* He is survived by his wife, film editor Thelma Schoonmaker, and two sons by a previous marriage.

EDDIE QUILLAN, 83, Philadelphia-born screen, stage and TV actor, died on July 19, 1990 in Burbank, CA, of cancer. His many films include *Big Money, Mutiny on the Bounty* (1935), *Young Mr. Lincoln, The Grapes of Wrath, Flying Blind, The Big City, Brigadoon, The Ghost and Mr. Chicken,* and *Angel in My Pocket.* He is survived by five sisters.

DAVID RAPPAPORT, 39, British screen and TV actor was found dead on May 2, 1990 in a San Fernando Valley park with a gunshot wound in his chest, an apparent suicide. The dwarf actor had appeared in such films as *Cuba, Time Bandits, Sword of the Valiant,* and *The Bride.* No reported survivors.

ANNE REVERE, 87, New York City-born screen, stage and TV actress, who won an Academy Award for her role in *National Velvet,* died on Dec. 18, 1990 in Locust Valley, NY, of pneumonia. Following her film debut in *Double Door* in 1934 she appeared in such movies as *The Howards of Virginia; Men of Boys Town; H. M. Pulham Esq.; Remember the Day; The Gay Sisters; Star Spangled Rhythm; Old Acquaintance; Standing Room Only; Rainbow Island; The Thin Man Goes Home; Fallen Angel; Dragonwyck; Keys of the Kingdom; The Shocking Miss Pilgrim; Body and Soul; Forever Amber; Scudda Hoo! Scudda Hay!; Deep Waters; You're My Everything; A Place in the Sun; Tell Me That You Love Me, Junie Moon;* and *Birch Interval.* She received additional Oscar nominations for *The Song of Bernadette* and *Gentleman's Agreement.* She is survived by her husband and a sister.

ERIK RHODES (Earnest Sharpe), 84, Oklahoma-born screen, stage and TV actor, best remembered for his Continental gigolo roles in the Fred Astaire-Ginger Rogers musicals *The Gay Divorcee* and *Top Hat,* died on Feb. 17, 1990 in Oklahoma City of pneumonia. His other films include *Charlie Chan in Paris, The Nitwits, One Rainy Afternoon, Criminal Lawyer, Woman Chases Man, Dramatic School, Say It in French,* and *On Your Toes.* No reported survivors.

MARTIN RITT, 76, New York City-born director responsible for some of Hollywood's finest dramatic films, died on Dec. 8, 1990 in Santa Monica, CA, of cardiac disease. Following a short period as an actor and director on TV, he was a victim of the Hollywood blacklist. His credits include *Edge of the City, The Long Hot Summer, Black Orchid, Paris Blues, Hud* (Academy Award nomination), *The Outrage, The Spy who Came in from the Cold, Hombre, The Molly Maguires, The Great White Hope, Sounder, Pete 'n Tillie, Conrack, The Front, Norma Rae, Cross Creek, Murphy's Romance, Nuts,* and his last, *Stanley & Iris,* in 1990. He acted in such movies as *Winged Victory, End of the Game,* and *The Slugger's Wife.* He is survived by his wife, a daughter and a son.

FRANK ROSS, 85, motion picture producer died on Feb. 18, 1990 in Los Angeles following brain surgery. His credits include *The Devil and Miss Jones, A Lady Takes a Chance, The Flame and the Arrow, The Robe, Demetrius and the Gladiators, The Rains of Ranchipur,* and *Kings Go Forth.* He received a special "Oscar" for the short film *The House I Live In.* He is survived by his son and a brother.

CRAIG RUSSELL, 42, Toronto-born actor and female impersonator died on Oct. 30, 1990 in Toronto of a stroke resulting from AIDS. He appeared in the 1977 film *Outrageous!* and its sequel *Too Outrageous!* He is survived by his wife.

RAYMOND ST. JACQUES, 60, Connecticut-born screen, stage and TV actor, died on August 27, 1990 in Los Angeles of cancer of the lymph glands. His films include *Black Like Me, The Pawnbroker, Mister Moses, The Comedians, The Green Berets, Madigan, If He Hollers Let Him Go!, Uptight, Change of Mind, Cotton Comes to Harlem, Come Back Charleston Blue, Cool Breeze, Book of Numbers* (which he also produced and directed), *Lost in the Stars, Eyes of Laura Mars, The Evil That Men Do, They Live,* and *Glory.* He is survived by his mother.

| Anne Revere | Erik Rhodes | Raymond St. Jacques | Albert Salmi | Barbara Stanwyck | Terry-Thomas |

ALBERT SALMI, 62, Brooklyn-born screen, stage and TV character actor, was found dead on April 23, 1990 at his home in Spokane, WA. He had shot himself after killing his terminally ill wife. His many films include *The Brothers Karamazov, The Bravados, The Unforgiven, Wild River, The Ambushers, The Flim Flam Man, The Big Bounce, Lawman, The Deserter, Something Big, Escape from the Planet of the Apes, Brubaker, Caddyshack, Dragonslayer, I'm Dancing As Fast As I Can, Love Child, Hard to Hold,* and *Breaking In.*

FRANKLYN SEALES, 37, Caribbean-born screen, stage and TV actor, who played criminal Jimmy Smith in the 1979 movie *The Onion Field,* died on May 21, 1990 in Brooklyn of AIDS. He also appeared in the film *Southern Comfort* and as a regular on the television series *Silver Spoons.* He is survived by his mother, three sisters and three brothers.

DELPHINE SEYRIG, 58, Beirut-born French screen and stage actress, best known to American audiences for her leading role in the 1961 film *Last Year at Marienbad,* died on Oct. 15, 1990 in Paris of lung disease. Her other movies include *Muriel, La Musica, Mister Freedom, Accident, Stolen Kisses, Donkey Skin, Daughters of Darkness, The Discreet Charm of the Bourgeoise, The Day of the Jackal, The Black Windmill, A Doll's House, Cry of the Heart, Jeanne Dielman,* and *I Sent a Letter to My Love.* She is survived by a son.

STANLEY SHAPIRO, 65, Brooklyn-born screenwriter, who won an Academy Award for Best Original Screenplay for the 1959 comedy *Pillow Talk,* died on July 21, 1990 in Los Angeles of leukemia. His credits include *The Perfect Furlough, Operation Petticoat, Come September, That Touch of Mink, Bedtime Story, How to Save a Marriage—And Ruin Your Life, For Pete's Sake,* and *Dirty Rotten Scoundrels.* He is survived by a daughter.

BILL SHERWOOD, 37, American filmmaker, who directed and wrote the acclaimed 1986 feature *Parting Glances,* died on Feb. 10, 1990 of AIDS in New York City. His parents survive.

BARBARA STANWYCK, 82, Brooklyn-born screen, stage and TV actress, whose versatility in both comedy and drama made her one of Hollywood's greatest stars, died on Jan. 20, 1990 of congestive heart failure at St. John's Hospital and Health Center in Santa Monica, CA. She was nominated for four Best Actress Oscars, for her performances in *Stella Dallas, Ball of Fire, Double Indemnity,* and *Sorry Wrong Number.* Her many other films include *Ladies of Leisure, Miracle Woman, Night Nurse, So Big* (1932), *The Bitter Tea of General Yen, Gambling Lady, The Woman in Red, Annie Oakley, A Message to Garcia, The Plough and the Stars, Interns Can't Take Money, The Mad Miss Manton, Union Pacific, Golden Boy, Remember the Night, The Lady Eve, Meet John Doe, You Belong to Me, The Great Man's Lady, Lady of Burlesque, Hollywood Canteen, Christmas in Connecticut, My Reputation, The Bride Wore Boots, The Strange Love of Martha Ivers, California, The File on Thelma Jordan, The Furies, Clash by Night, Titanic, Executive Suite, Cattle Queen of Montana, These Wilder Years, Walk on the Wild Side, Roustabout,* and *The Night Walker.* Survivors include a nephew.

VIC TAYBACK, 60, Brooklyn-born screen, stage and TV actor, died on May 25, 1990 in Glendale, CA, of a heart attack. He was best known for his role as Mel in the television series *Alice,* a part he had played in the 1974 movie, *Alice Doesn't Live Here Anymore.* His other films include *Five Minutes to Live, Love with the Proper Stranger, Bullitt, Papillon, The Gambler, Report to the Commissioner, The Big Bus, Special Delivery, The Shaggy D.A., The Choirboys, The Cheap Detective,* and *Loverboy.* He is survived by his wife, a son, his mother, a sister and a brother.

TERRY-THOMAS (Thomas Terry Hoar Stevens), 78, British screen, stage, and TV character actor and comedian, died on Jan. 8, 1990 of Parkinson's disease at a nursing home in Godalming, Surrey, England. The popular gap-toothed star appeared in such films as *Pri-*

vate's Progress, Brothers in Law, Lucky Jim, Blue Murder at St. Trinian's, tom thumb, Too Many Crooks, Carlton-Browne of the F.O. (The Man in the Cocked Hat), I'm All Right Jack, School for Scoundrels, Make Mine Mink, Bachelor Flat, Operation Snatch, The Mouse on the Moon, The Wonderful World of the Brothers Grimm, It's a Mad Mad Mad Mad World, Those Magnificent Men in Their Flying Machines, How to Murder Your Wife, Munster Go Home!, Those Fantastic Flying Fools (Blast Off), Where Were You When the Lights Went Out?, A Guide for the Married Man, Those Daring Young Men in Their Jaunty Jalopies (Monte Carlo or Bust), The Abominable Dr. Phibes, and *The Last Remake of Beau Geste.* His second wife and two sons survive.

UGO TOGNAZZI, 68, Italian screen, stage and TV actor and director, best known to American audiences for his role as the homosexual cabaret owner, Georges, in the 1979 French film *La Cage aux Folles,* died on Oct. 27, 1990 in Rome of a cerebral hemorrhage. His many other films include *The Fascist, Crazy Desire, The Conjugal Bed, The Ape Woman, Pigsty, The Man with the Balloons, Wedding March, The Papal Audience, La Grande Bouffe, Barbarella, The Magnificent Cuckold, Run for Your Wife, Come and Have Coffee with Us, La Califfa, All My Friends, Tragedy of a Ridiculous Man, La Cage aux Folles II & III, The Terrace,* and *Sunday Lovers.* Survivors include his wife, Franca Bettoja, an actress.

JIMMY VAN HEUSEN (Edward Chester Babcock), 77, Syracuse-born songwriter whose collaborations with lyricists Johnny Burke and Sammy Cahn earned him four Best Song Oscars, died on Feb. 6, 1990 in Rancho Mirage, CA., after a long illness. With Burke he wrote songs for 16 Bing Crosby musicals including *Road to Zanzibar, Road to Morocco, Going My Way, The Bells of St. Mary's, Road to Utopia, Road to Rio, The Emperor Waltz, A Connecticut Yankee in King Arthur's Court,* and *Riding High,* and his work with Cahn appeared in such films as *The Tender Trap, High Time, Come Blow Your Horn,* and *Robin and the 7 Hoods.* He received his Academy Awards for *"Swinging on a Star"* (from *Going My Way*), *"All the Way"* (from *The Joker is Wild*), *"High Hopes"* (from *A Hole in the Head*), and *"Call Me Irresponsible"* (from *Papa's Delicate Condition*). His widow survives.

IRVING WALLACE, 74, Chicago-born screenwriter and best-selling author, died on June 29, 1990 of pancreatic cancer in Los Angeles. His screenplays include *The West Point Story, Meet Me at the Fair, Bad for Each Other, Sincerely Yours, The Burning Hills,* and *The Big Circus.* His novels *The Chapman Report, The Prize, The Man,* and *The Seven Minutes* were adapted for films. He is survived by his wife, a daughter, a son, and a sister.

JEAN WALLACE (Walasek), 66, Chicago-born screen actress died on Feb. 14, 1990 in Beverly Hills, CA, of a gastrointestinal hemorrhage. Her films include *Blaze of Noon, Jigsaw, The Man on the Eiffel Tower, The Good Humor Man, Sudden Fear,* and several appearances with her former husband, Cornel Wilde: *The Big Combo, Maracaibo, Lancelot and Guinevere, Beach Red,* and *No Blade of Grass.* She is survived by three sons, two by her marriage to actor Franchot Tone, and one by Wilde.

LYLE WHEELER, 84, Massachusetts-born art director who became one of Hollywood's leading production designers, died on Jan. 10, 1990 of pneumonia in Woodland Hills, CA. He was honored with five Academy Awards for his work on *Gone with the Wind, Anna and the King of Siam, The Robe, The King and I,* and *The Diary of Anne Frank.* He is survived by three sons and three daughters.

DAVID WHITE, 74, screen, stage and TV character actor, best known for his role on the hit television show *Bewitched,* died on Nov. 26, 1990 in Hollywood, CA, of a heart attack. He appeared in such movies as *Sweet Smell of Success, The Apartment, Sunrise at Campobello, The Great Impostor,* and *Madison Avenue.* He is survived by a daughter.

INDEX

242

247

255

258